This book is published in eight languages (English, Dutch, Polish, Korean, Chinese, Turkish, Indonesian, and Rumanian).

Puts the psyche of advertising on the analyst's couch to reveal the sometimes surprising mind of commercial persuasion.

Jim Spaeth, Former President, Advertising Research Foundation

This is a well-informed and engagingly written description of the processes involved in the communication of advertising. It does not share the problems of advertising text books, which are generally superficial as well as being invariably out-of-date. Nor is it one of those populist works that receive a wide sale by propagating over-simple theories.

John Philip Jones, author of *When Ads Work* and
Professor of Marketing, Syracuse University

I learned a lot from the book, while thoroughly enjoying it. It has much to offer for both the novice and the experienced advertising person. Insights about the advertising process are backed up with many examples of real advertising, research monitoring hundreds of advertising campaigns around the world, and a wide variety of academic research. Amazingly, all this is combined in a delightful writing style that entertains while it teaches.

Alan Sawyer, Professor of Marketing, University of Florida

A thought-provoking and practical book on how ads work and how advertising campaigns can be most effectively managed that also contains many useful ideas for achieving more effective advertising campaigns.

Professor John Rossiter, University of Wollongong, co-author of
Marketing Communications: Theory and applications

Breakthroug'   'siness and
have taugh   ve never
found a bo   ssociated
with effecti'

                                                              Iniversity

Finally, a k   psychological fac   way you
advertise a

                                                              idea.org

A very stir   tical and
memorabl

                                                              Iniversity

ADVERTISING
AND THE MIND OF
THE CONSUMER

What works, what doesn't, and why

REVISED 3rd INTERNATIONAL EDITION

MAX SUTHERLAND

ALLEN&UNWIN

This edition published in 2008
First published in 1993

Allen & Unwin
83 Alexander Street
Crows Nest NSW 2065
Australia
Phone: (61 2) 8425 0100
Fax: (61 2) 9906 2218
Email: info@allenandunwin.com
Web: www.allenandunwin.com

National Library of Australia
Cataloguing-in-Publication entry:

Sutherland, Max.

Advertising and the mind of the consumer: what works,
what doesn't and why/Max Sutherland, Alice K. Sylvester.

3rd ed.

9781741755992 (pbk.)

Advertising – Psychological aspects.

Consumer behaviour.

659.1019

Set in 10/14pt Utopia by Midland Typesetters, Australia
Printed and bound in Australia by Griffin Press

10 9 8 7 6 5 4 3 2 1

CONTENTS

FIGURES AND TABLES

Figures

Tables

ACKNOWLEDGMENTS

So many people have contributed to this book that it is impossible to cite everyone by name. In this third edition, I particularly want to thank readers of earlier editions as well as regular readers of my monthly column (posted at www.sutherlandsurvey.com) for their feedback comments and suggestions.

The opportunity to work with the many valued MarketMind clients, to track their and their competitors' advertising over time, provided much raw material from which to discover how advertising really does work as opposed to how folklore or pure theory says it works. I thank them sincerely and the co-founder of MarketMind, Bruce Smith, for his constant support and encouragement in the writing of this book.

It is through the communicating and sharing of ideas and case-study observations over many years that a body of knowledge such as this emerges. Therefore many of the MarketMind staff contributed either directly or indirectly to this book. My thanks also to Alice Sylvester, my former co-author for her efforts on the second edition and for her contribution of some of the case examples retained in this third edition.

Special thanks for the contribution made to the revised editions goes to Stephen Holden of Bond University, who provided international ad examples, as well as Professor Andy Gross for his continued assistance throughout the process. Thanks also to John Wigzell (consultant) for his advice on European case examples and Malcolm Stewart (CUSTOMeDIA) and Pat Williams for their media advice.

My wife, Mel Sutherland, suffered through many iterations of the proofreading of each edition as well as a somewhat impoverished social and family life when the book was first written. My now adult son, Kent, and daughters Keli and Julia still envy their friends whose households chatted during ad breaks whereas in ours, they now tell me, they felt they had to keep quiet 'because Dad was watching the ads'. And whereas these other households recorded TV programs and fast forwarded the ads, their dad had to record and fast-forward through the programs to *watch* the ads. Thanks to all of them for their understanding and the time to make the book happen.

Many valued academic colleagues and friends have influenced my thinking over the years. In particular I want to mention Professor John Rossiter (Wollongong University), Dr John Galloway (NetMap), Larry Percy (consultant), Professors Joe Danks and David Riccio (Kent State University), Dr Rob Donovan (University of Western Australia), Geoff Alford (Alford Research), Shelby McIntyre (Santa Clara University), and from the 'earlier years', Drs Bob March, Stan Glaser and Graham Pont. All of these and many others have influenced the direction and content of this book. Of course that does not imply that they will all agree with everything that is written here. The ultimate responsibility for the content, together with any omissions or errors, must remain mine.

To Karen Gee, my thanks for a great job in editing this third edition.

Lastly, I am indebted to the three people who constantly urged the writing of the original book until it finally happened: Malcolm Cameron, Mike Hanlon and Tom Valenta.

ABOUT THE AUTHOR

Dr Max Sutherland is an author, columnist and marketing psychologist who works as an independent consultant in Australia and the USA. An expert in the psychology of communication, his monthly column is posted on the web at www.sutherlandsurvey.com. He is Adjunct Professor of Marketing at Bond University and Honorary Principal Research Fellow at Wollongong University.

The highly successful company he founded in 1989, MarketMind,[1] specialized in tracking the effects of advertising communication for many of the leading global advertisers including Gillette, Merck, Kodak, McDonald's, Miller, Qantas, Nestlé and Pfizer. MarketMind was ultimately acquired by a US conglomerate.

His early career included retail sales as well as positions in market research with the Coca-Cola Export Corporation and the Overseas Tele-communications Commission.

With degrees in marketing and psychology, Dr Sutherland has held senior academic positions at a number of universities in the USA and Australia. He has held full-time lectureships in market research and consumer behavior at the University of New South Wales and the David Syme Business School (now Monash University) as well as Visiting Professor at Kent State University and Santa Clara University in the USA. He has published numerous papers in American, European and Australasian journals and currently serves on the editorial board of the International Journal of Brand Management and the International Journal of Advertising.

He is a former editor of the *Australian Marketing Researcher*, a Fellow and former Chairman of the Australian Market & Social Research Society and a Fellow of the Australian Marketing Institute.

He can be contacted at msutherland@adandmind.com.

WHY ADVERTISING HAS REMAINED A MYSTERY FOR SO LONG

INTRODUCTION

The subject of advertising seems to be riddled with mystique and apparent contradictions. This book resolves some of those contradictions. It had its beginnings in regular columns for various trade publications and journals; Part B brings together some of those articles and subsequent articles and more material can be found at www.adandmind.com.

This book is not just aimed at advertisers and their ad agencies but also at the people to whom they advertise. As David Ogilvy, a leading advertising expert, said (in the chauvinistic 1960s): 'The consumer is not a moron. She is your wife!'[1] Our wives, our husbands, our partners, our children are all consumers. The consumer is not an idiot. The consumer is you and me.

Many years ago the advertiser's dilemma was expressed in this way: 'I know that half my advertising is wasted—but I don't know which half.'[2] But developments in market research are beginning to change all that by better enabling advertisers to identify what works and what doesn't.[3] This book draws on the experience of tracking week by week the effects of hundreds of advertising campaigns over a period of more than fifteen years.

Almost everybody is interested in advertising. The average consumer is exposed to hundreds of ads every day. By the time we die we will have spent an estimated one and a half years watching TV commercials.[4] Yet advertising continues to be something of a mystery.

The response 'Gee, I didn't know that' to an advertisement tends to be the exception. A round trip special price to New York for $400 is news. Ads that announce the release of new products like iPhone, the Segway, self cleaning windows or voice-operated computers are news. And if we are someone who is compulsive about germs maybe Mr Clean with a new disinfectant that kills germs 50 per cent better than the old Mr Clean might also be news. With news advertising we can easily recognize the potential of the advertising to affect us.

But most advertising is not 'news' advertising. Much of the advertising we encounter doesn't impart news and it is difficult for us to see how it works on us. As consumers we generally believe it does not really affect us personally. Despite this, advertisers keep on advertising. So something must be working—but on whom, and exactly how?

This book demystifies the effects of advertising and describes some of the psychological mechanisms underlying them. It is written primarily for those who foot the bill for advertising and those who produce advertising. In other words, for those many organizations involved with advertising—the marketing directors, marketing managers, product managers, advertising managers, account execs, media people and creatives. However, in the various editions it has also been read by many interested consumers who wonder how advertising works and why advertisers keep on advertising. Understanding the mechanisms and their limitations tends to lessen the anxieties we may have about wholesale, unconscious manipulation by advertising.

It may come as a surprise to many consumers that those who foot the bill for advertising are often frustrated by knowing little more than the consumers themselves about how, why or when their advertising works. Advertising agencies, the makers of advertising, also know less about these things than we might think. They are seen as wizards at selling, but an agency's most important pitch is to organizations that *want* to advertise—companies that will engage the agency's services to design their advertising on an ongoing basis. To keep clients coming back, advertising agencies need to sell the effectiveness of their advertising to those clients and to the world. Inevitably, some agencies become much more accomplished at selling their clients and the world on the great job the advertising is doing than they do at creating advertising that is truly effective.

Like the skills of tribal healers, ad agencies' powers and methods are seen to be all the greater because of the mystery that surrounds advertising. Books like Vance Packard's *The Hidden Persuaders*[5] enhance this image of the power of advertising agencies because they portray them as having witch-doctor-like powers. So in a way the mystique and aura of advertising works in favor of its makers—the advertising agencies—by boosting their image, status and perceived power.

Way back in 1978 Alec Benn, an advertising agency principal in the United States, claimed in his book *The 27 Most Common Mistakes in Advertising*: 'There is a great conspiracy participated in by advertising agencies, radio and television stations and networks, advertising consultants, newspapers, magazines and others to mislead corporate management about the effectiveness of advertising.'[6] Benn was pointing out that advertising failed more often than it succeeded, usually because its effects 'are not measured objectively'.

Since then, advertising has begun to be measured more objectively and more often (indeed continuously) and this has highlighted the hard fact that many ads still fail. Part of the reason is that advertising agencies get too little in the way of 'news' to work with—there aren't the breakthrough things to say about existing brands to cause immediate impacts. But the other part of it is a historical overreliance on intuition and introspection.[7] When these qualities are used instead of objective measurement as the basis for deciding what works and what doesn't, there are more ads that fail than ads that are outstandingly successful. Sustained effects occur less than half the time.[8] Until recently these failures stood a good chance of going unrecognized because the majority of campaigns were not tracked in a formal way.[9]

In the general population there are those who believe that advertising is all powerful and that the mechanism of advertising must be unconscious and subliminal, because its effects do not seem open to introspection. Such views are associated with the 'dark and manipulative' view of advertising. This book reveals a much more benign interpretation of advertising's so-called 'unconscious' effects. In elaborating on some of the subtler mechanisms of advertising, it dispels many myths and exaggerated claims. At the same time it reveals just how subtle advertising's influence can be and how much of an impact it can have on the success or failure of one brand over another.

This book will help advertising agencies to diagnose the *why* of what works, and what doesn't. It shows advertisers how to get better results from their advertising budget and their agency. And it reveals to consumers how advertising works to influence which brands we choose—especially if the choice doesn't matter to us personally—and why it is that we find it difficult to introspect on advertising's effect.

1 INFLUENCING PEOPLE: MYTHS AND MECHANISMS

- Why do people buy bottled water that is available free from the tap?
- Why does advertising work on everybody else but not on us?
- Why do advertisers keep repeating an ad that we have already seen?

All these questions reflect the general belief that advertising works by persuading us, yet we don't feel personally that we are at all persuaded by it.

Why is it so difficult for us to introspect on advertising and how it influences us? Because we look for major effects, that's why! Too often, we look for the ability of a single ad to persuade us rather than for more subtle, minor effects. Big and immediate effects of advertising do occur when the advertiser has something new to say. Then it is easy for us to introspect on its effect.

But most effects of advertising fall well short of persuasion. These minor effects are not obvious but they are more characteristic of the way advertising works. To understand advertising we have to understand and measure these effects. When our kids are growing up we don't notice their physical growth each day but from time to time we become aware that they have grown. Determining how much a child has grown in the last 24 hours is like evaluating the effect of being exposed to a single commercial. In both cases, the changes are too small for us to notice. But even small effects of advertising can influence which brand we choose, especially when all other factors are equal and when alternative brands are much the same.

Weighing the alternatives: evaluation

It is easiest to understand this with low-involvement buying situations. The situation is like a 'beam balance' in which each brand weighs the same. With one brand on each side, the scale is balanced. However, it takes only a feather added to one side of the balance to tip us in favor of the brand on that side. The brands consumers have to choose from are often very similar. Which one will the buying balance tip towards? When we look for advertising effects we are looking for feathers rather than heavy weights.[1]

The buying of cars, appliances, vacations and other high-priced items are examples of high-involvement decision-making. This high level of involvement contrasts with the low level brought to bear on the purchase of products like shampoo or soft drink or margarine. For most of us, the buying of these smaller items is no big deal. We have better things to do with our time than agonize over which brand to choose every time we buy something.

Figure 1.1: Low-involvement decision: deciding between two virtually identical alternatives.

The fact is that in many low-involvement product categories, the alternative brands are extremely similar and in some cases almost identical. Most consumers don't really care which one they buy and could substitute easily if their brand ceased to exist. It is in these low-involvement categories that the effects of advertising can be greatest and yet hardest to introspect upon.

Even with high-involvement products the beam balance analogy is relevant because very different alternatives can have equal weight. We often have to weigh up complex things like 'average quality at a moderate price' against 'premium quality at a higher price'. Often we find ourselves in a state of indecision between the alternatives. When the choices weigh equally in our mind, whether they be low-involvement products or high-involvement products, it can take just a feather to swing that balance.[2]

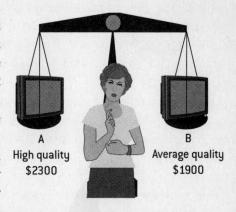

Figure 1.2: High-involvement decision: very different alternatives can have equal weight.

With high-involvement decisions we are more concerned about the outcome of the weighing-up process, so we think more about how much weight to give to each feature (quality, size or power). How many extra dollars is it worth paying for a feature? Automotive writers for example can reach very different opinions. The more complex a product's features the more complex this assessment because there are usually both positive and negative perspectives. For example, a compact car is positive in regard to both fuel economy and maneuverability but negative in regard to leg room and comfort.

So which way should we see it? What weight *should* we give to a particular feature in our minds? When advertising emphasizes points that favor a brand, it doesn't have to *persuade* us—merely raise our awareness of the positive perspectives. Chances are we will notice *confirmatory* evidence more easily as a result. When we subsequently read a newspaper or consumer report or talk with friends, research shows that we are prone to interpret such information slightly more favorably.[3] This effect is a long way from heavyweight persuasion. Rather it is a gentle, mental biasing of our subsequent perceptions, and we will see in Chapter 2 how perspective can influence our interpretation. It is not so much persuasion as a shifting of the mental spotlight . . . playing the focal beam of attention on one perspective rather than another.

Repetition

As with the amount by which our kids grow in a day, we are just not aware of the small differences advertising can make. Even though these imperceptibly small changes in time add up to significant effects, individual increments are too small for us to notice. They are just below what is known as the just noticeable difference (JND).

Through the process of repetition these small increments can produce major perceived differences between brands, but we are rarely aware of the process taking place.

The cumulative effects of changes in brand image become starkly noticeable only in rare cases:

Figure 1.3: Small cumulative increments. We don't notice a child's growth in 24 hours.

for instance, when we return home after a long absence and find that an old brand is now seen by people in a different light—that in the intervening period the brand has acquired a different image.

Registering a claim in our minds (e.g. 'Taste the difference' or 'Good to the last drop') does not necessarily mean we believe it. However, it makes us aware that there *are* claimed differences between brands. This is a proposition (a 'feather', if you will) that, when everything else is equal, may tip the balance of brand selection, even if only to prompt us to find out if it is true.

Repetition increases our familiarity with a claim. In the absence of evidence to the contrary, a feeling of greater likelihood that the claim *is* true begins to accompany the growing familiarity. This effect of repetition is known as 'the truth effect'.[4]

We tend to think that if something is not true it would somehow be challenged. If it is repeated constantly and not challenged, our minds seem to regard this as *prima facie* evidence that perhaps it is true. The effect of repetition is to produce small but cumulative increments in this 'truth' inference.[5] It is hardly rational but we don't really think about it. We don't go out of our way to think about it because low involvement, by definition, means we don't care much either way. Such claims are 'feathers'.

In summary, the reasons we are unable to introspect on advertising's effects—especially in low-involvement situations—are:

- the effect of each single ad exposure is small;[6]
- with repetition, even imperceptibly small effects can build into larger perceived differences between brands;[7]
- if something is repeated constantly without challenge, our minds seem to regard this as *prima facie* evidence that maybe, just maybe, it *is* true (the 'truth' effect);
- often it is no big deal to us which of the alternative brands we choose, anyway.

If you have ever wondered why advertisers seem to persist in repeating the same ad—if you have ever wondered why they think this could possibly influence sane people like us—then here is the answer. Much of advertising creates only marginal differences, but small differences can build into larger differences. Even small differences can tip the balance in favor of the advertised brand. This is especially true of 'image advertising'.

Image advertising

The effect of image advertising is easier to see in relation to high-involvement products, so let us start with a high-involvement example—Volvo cars.

Volvo traditionally focused its image advertising on safety. Through repetition, it built up a strong image of the Volvo as a safe car. Other brands have caught up a lot in recent years but on a scale of 1 to 10 for safety, most people would still rate Volvo higher than almost any other car. Safety is now an integral part of our perception of this brand. (The fact that the car actually delivers on this promise has of course been a very important ingredient in the success of the safety campaign—but that is another story.)

One effect of image advertising, then, is to produce gradual shifts in our perceptions of a brand with regard to a particular attribute—in Volvo's case, safety (in other words, to effect marginal changes in our mental rating of the brand on that attribute). This is often not perceptible after just one exposure because the change, if it occurs, is too small for us to notice.

Now let's take a low-involvement product in the very late stages of its product life cycle—hair spray—and tease out some insights from its history of brand image advertising.

The first brands of hair spray originally fought for market share on the basis of the attribute of 'hair holding'. That is, each brand claimed to hold hair. To the extent that they all claimed the same thing, they were what are called 'me-too' brands.

To break out of this, one brand began to claim that it 'holds hair longer'. Just as Volvo claimed that it was safer, and thereby moved Volvo higher up the perceived safety scale, so this brand of hair spray made people aware that some brands of hair spray might hold hair longer than others. It then attempted to shift perception of itself on this attribute and marginally increase the mental rating consumers would give it on 'length of hold'.

The next brand of hair spray to enter the market, instead of tackling that brand head-on, cleverly avoided doing battle on 'length of hold'. The new brand claimed that it was 'long holding', but also that it 'brushes out easier'—a dual benefit. In doing so it successfully capitalized on the fact that hair sprays that hold longer were harder to brush out (or were until then). Many years later came the attribute of 'flexible hold'.

These examples of image advertising for hair spray and cars illustrate how one effect of advertising is to alter our perceptions of a brand. Advertising can marginally change our image of a brand by leading us to associate it with a particular attribute (like 'longer holding' or 'brushes out easily'), and to associate in our minds that attribute with the brand more than we associate it with any other competitive brand.

Gauging the effects image advertising has on us is made even more complex because these effects may not operate directly on the image of the brand itself. Image advertising may produce small, incremental differences in the image of a brand, as in the case of Volvo—but sometimes it is aimed at changing not so much the image of the brand itself but who we see in our mind's eye as the typical user of that brand.

User image

In advertising for Levis, Revlon, Guess, Louis Vuitton, or Dolce & Gabbana, the focus is often on people who use the brand. What changes is not so much our perception, or image, of the product as our perception of the user-stereotype—the kind of person who typically uses the brand, or the situation in which the brand is typically used.

When these brands are advertised, the focus is very much on image but often with this important, subtle difference. The advertising aims to change not how we see the brand itself—the brand image—but how we see:

- the stereotypical user of the brand—the user image;
- the stereotypical situation in which the brand is used.

Figure 1.4: Jim Beam ad reinforcing the stereotypical user image—young, single males.

If the user image of a brand resembles us, or the type of person we aspire to be, what happens when we come to buy that product category? The user image acts as a feather on one side of the beam balance. If everything else is equal it can tip the scale (but note, only if everything else is equal).

User, or situational, image changes usually fall short of the kinds of rational, heavyweight reasons that make perfect sense of any choice.

But they can nevertheless tilt the balance in favor of one brand. Minor effects such as these constitute much of the impact of advertising. Yet they are usually much more difficult for us as consumers to analyze introspectively, and we tend to discount them because they clearly fall well short of persuasion.

Product image: bottled water

Advertising can marginally change our image not just of a brand but also of a product. When we associate a product in our minds with a desirable attribute, it can influence our behavior. Let's examine the question posed earlier. Why do people purchase so much bottled water when perfectly good water is available almost free from the tap?

The question is, are we in fact drinking bottled water as a substitute for tap water? It may seem that way . . . but is it? Certainly that is not the way it started. In the USA particularly, bottled water's success can be traced to its original positioning as a substitute not for water but for cocktails and non-alcoholic soda/soft drinks. The image appeal and usage evolved from there.

Let me explain.[8] In 1977, an American, Bruce Nevin, brought Perrier bottled water to the USA and launched it as a pure and healthier alternative for when you were having a cocktail or some non-alcoholic soda.[9] Consistent with the new emphasis on a healthy lifestyle, it was positioned as an accepted, healthier alternative, especially (though not exclusively) when consumed in social situations. The brand name 'Perrier' helped this social acceptance, giving it an up-market 'designer' connotation consistent with France's fashion and wine image. In addition, the Perrier launch commercials starred Orson Welles, thereby blending celebrity associations with this product. Its appeal as a healthier substitute was buttressed by purity and celebrity and this worked to make Perrier a huge success. With the media constantly urging us to eat more healthily and drink less alcohol, the brand took off. Perrier bottled water became a socially acceptable alternative to drinking alcohol and drinking soda/soft drinks that were not so healthy. Perrier sold US$20 million of bottled water in its first year in the US and tripled its sales to US$60 million the next year. This ultimately attracted other 'me-too' entrants.

The next major entrant in the USA was Evian, coming seven years later in 1984. Evian did a 'me-too' with pure and healthy while at the same time playing the spotlight of attention on difference in taste. Reportedly, research showed that Americans preferred a still taste to a sparkling taste and Perrier was a *sparkling* water. So Evian offered a still taste and avoided claiming that it was healthier, but instead cleverly associated the brand with a different aspect of health i.e. active lifestyles and the gymnasium—images associated with young, healthy, toned bodies. Consistent with this active lifestyles image, Evian matched Perrier on celebrity associations by using cool, young celebrities like Madonna (who would drink it on stage).

Such positioning was reinforced even further by Evian being the first to offer a lightweight plastic bottle nationwide. Evian's lighter, unbreakable bottle was easier to carry and more suitable for on-the-go lifestyles than Perrier's signature glass bottle. In other words, Evian not only matched Perrier on purity, health, French name connotation and celebrity endorsement but it also projected a user image appeal of toned, active, good looking bodies. If that was not enough of a feather to tip the balance, then being more convenient to carry meant that it was not only 'cool' but functional. This paid double dividends for Evian; it extended the way bottled water was consumed and broadened the market to 'active lifestyle', socially visible situations.

As new, lower cost entrants like Dusani (from Coca-Cola) and Aquafina (from Pepsi) came in, the usage of bottled water evolved and extended, further becoming somewhat more commodified. Nevertheless the basic heritage of health and purity is intact and bottled water remains better for us than either soda/soft drink or alcohol. As Charles Fishman noted in his article 'Message in a Bottle', '. . . today, water has come to signify how we think of ourselves. We want to brand ourselves—as Madonna did—even with something as ordinary as a drink of water . . . We imagine there is a difference between showing up at the weekly staff meeting with Aquafina, or Fiji, or a small glass bottle of Pellegrino.'[10]

The reason we drink bottled water today is partly self branding and partly self statement about healthier lifestyle choices. Did advertising persuade us to use bottled water instead of tap water? No. Did it persuade us to use bottled water instead of less healthy alcohol and sodas? Perhaps that's closer to the mark, but did anyone feel any persuasion? No. It was not persuasion so much as a series of image influences where virtue, convenience, self branding and self statement were aligned.

Persuasion is the exception

We have been told so often that the role of advertising is to persuade, that we seem to have come to believe it.

How often do we hear the comment, 'It wouldn't make me run out and buy it?' This is common in market research when participants are asked to analyze introspectively how they react to an ad—especially if it is an image ad. It demonstrates the myth of how advertising is supposed to influence. No one really believes that any ad will make them run out and buy the advertised product. Nothing has that kind of persuasive or coercive power. So why do people say, 'It wouldn't make me run out and buy it'? Because they can't think of any other way the ad could work. The effect of advertising is not to make us 'run out and buy'. This is especially true with low-involvement products and especially true with image advertising. Rather, it is beam balance stuff.

High involvement

High-involvement buying contrasts with low-involvement, low cost purchases. When people are parting with substantial sums of money to buy a TV, a car or a vacation, they do not take the decision lightly. These are high-involvement decisions for most consumers. Before making them, we actively hunt down information, talk with friends and generally find out all we can about our prospective purchase.

Furthermore, the alternative brands available will usually have many more differences. They are unlikely to be almost identical, as is the case with many low-involvement products.

Advertising is one influence in high-involvement buying decisions, but it is only one among many. Often it is a relatively weak influence, especially in comparison with other influences like word of mouth, previous experience and recommendations by 'experts'. In the case of high-involvement products, much of advertising's effect is not so much on the final decision as on whether a brand gets considered—whether we include it in the set of alternatives that we are prepared to spend time weighing up. This is one of the ways that advertising influences our thinking indirectly. For example, there are hundreds of brands and types of cars, far too many for us to consider individually in the same detail. We seriously consider only those that make it onto our short list. But what determines which cars make it onto our short list? This is where advertising comes into play.[11]

If we are unlikely to be in the market for a new car, television or wall unit for several years, the advertising we see and hear for these products falls on low-involved ears. However, if our old car or appliance unexpectedly breaks down today, we may find ourselves propelled into the market for a new one. Suddenly, the ads we saw yesterday or last week or last month under low-involvement conditions become more relevant. One test of their effectiveness will be whether they have left enough impact to get their brand onto our short list.

A lot of advertising, even for high-priced items, thus has its effect in a low-involvement way. Again we see that, in looking for the effects of advertising, we need to look for subtle effects. It is a case of 'feathers' rather than persuasion—'feathers' that influence what alternatives get weighed up as well as 'feathers' that add their weight to one side of the weighing-up process.

Two mental processes in decision-making

There are two fundamentally different mental processes at work in choice decisions. We have already considered the most obvious one, the weighing up of alternatives. But there is another process that consumers and advertisers tend to be less conscious of. *Weighing up the alternatives is one thing. Which alternatives get weighed up is another!*

Which alternatives get weighed up?

What determines the alternatives that are actually considered?

Think about a consumer decision that you probably make every day. It's getting on for noon, you are feeling hungry and you ask yourself, 'What am I going to have for lunch today?' Your mind starts to generate alternatives and evaluate each alternative as you think of it. The process goes something like this:

- 'Will I have a salad? No, I had a salad yesterday.'
- 'A sandwich? No, the sandwich store is too far away and besides, it's raining.'
- 'I could drive to McDonald's. Yes . . . I'll do that.'

There are two things to note here. First, what the mind does is produce alternatives, one at a time. This 'mental agenda' of alternatives is ordered like this:

What's the choice for lunch?
1. Salad
2. Sandwich
3. McDonald's
4. TGI Friday's
5. Subway

Second, the order in which the alternatives are arranged is the order in which they are elicited by the mind. This order can influence your final choice. You may enjoy Subway more than McDonald's. But in the example, you didn't go to Subway, you went to McDonald's.

Had you continued your thought process instead of stopping at the third alternative (McDonald's), you would probably have gone to Subway. But if Subway is only fifth on your mental agenda of lunch alternatives, it is unlikely to get much of your business. You didn't get to Subway because you didn't think of it before you hit on a satisfactory solution—McDonald's. You didn't get there *physically* because you never got there *mentally*. Even if we like or prefer something, if it is not reasonably high on our mental agenda it is likely to miss out.

How many times have you found yourself doing something and realized too late that there was something else you would rather have been doing but hadn't thought about in time? The most preferred alternatives are not necessarily the ones you think of first. (Anyone who has ever left an important person off an invitation list will appreciate this.) Next time you go out for dinner and are trying to decide which restaurant to go to, observe your thought pattern. There are two separate processes at work. One is generation of alternatives; the other is evaluation of those alternatives.

To affect the outcome of buying decisions, advertisers can try to influence:

- the order in which the alternatives are evoked;
- the evaluation of a particular alternative; or
- both.

When we think of advertising's effects we almost invariably think of how advertising influences our evaluation of a brand. Yet much of advertising's influence is not on our evaluations of a brand but on the order in which alternative brands are evoked.

Agenda-setting effect

Influencing the order of alternatives has its basis in what is known as the agenda-setting theory of mass communications. This says: the mass media don't tell us what to think. But they do tell us what to think about! They set the mental agenda.

The agenda-setting theory was originally developed to explain the influence of the mass media in determining which political issues become important in elections. Adroit committee members and politicians claim that if you can control the agenda you can control the meeting. The relevance of this to advertising was recognized over a quarter of a century ago.[12] We can produce mental agendas for lots of things.

Table 1.1 Mental agendas for lots of things

What's news?	What's the choice for lunch?
1. Presidential election	1. Salad
2. The stock market	2. Sandwich
3. Youth suicide rate	3. McDonald's
4. A child abducted	4. TGI Friday's
5. The Olympics	5. Subway

We can discover our mental agenda by pulling out what is in our minds under a particular category and examining the order (in which it emerges). The category may be 'What's the choice for lunch?', 'What's news?', or 'What brand of soft drink should I buy?'

When we reach into our minds to generate any of these agendas, the items do not all come to mind at once. They are elicited one at a time and in an order. The items on top of the mental agenda are the most salient and the ones we are most likely to remember first. It's the same with choosing which restaurant to go to or which department store to visit or which supermarket to shop at this week. It is the same with the decision about which cars or televisions to short-list and which dealers to visit. The order in which we retrieve the items from our memories seems almost inconsequential to us but may be critically important in determining the chances of our going to McDonald's rather than Subway.

This effect also occurs if we have a list of the alternatives or a display of them such as in the supermarket. Even here, where the brands are all set out in front of us, all of them do not get noticed simultaneously. In fact, they do not all get noticed.

Think about the process. We stand there at the display. We notice first one brand, then another and then another. It happens rapidly, but in sequence. So despite the fact that the brands are all displayed, they are not necessarily all equal in terms of the probability that they will come to mind or be noticed. For the last decade, supermarkets have carried more than 30,000 items, up from 17,500 a decade before.[13] This raises a question. At supermarket displays, what makes a brand stand out? To use the marketing term, what makes it 'break through the clutter' of all the alternative packs and get noticed? What makes one brand get noticed more quickly than others at the supermarket display?

This introduces the concept of *salience*, which is formally defined in the next section. In this context we ask how a brand can be moved up from fifth, to fourth, to third, to second, to become the first one noticed. The higher up it is in this order, the better the chance it has of being considered and, consequently, the better the chance of being purchased.

The brand's physical prominence, the amount of shelf space it occupies and its position in the display are very important. But advertising can influence choice when other factors (like shelf space or position) are otherwise equal. Advertising can help tip the balance.

Asking what makes one brand more salient—more likely to come to mind or get noticed—than another is like asking what influences Subway's position on our mental lunch agenda. In the supermarket, instead of having to recall all the alternatives by ourselves, we are prompted by the display. However, the brands we notice and the order in which we notice them can be influenced by more than just the display.

Salience

We think much more often about people and things that are important to us than about those that are not. The psychological term for this prominence in our thoughts is *salience*. Advertisers would like us to think of their brands as 'more important' but they will settle for 'more often'.[14] In other words, they would like their brands to be more salient for us.

My definition of salience is the probability that something will be in the conscious mind at any given moment. One way advertising can increase this probability is through repetition. We have all had the experience of being unable to rid our minds of a song we have heard a lot. The repetition of the song has increased its salience; it has increased its probability of being in the conscious mind at any moment. Repetition of an advertisement, especially a jingle, can have a similar effect. Through repetition of the ad, the salience of the brand—the star of the ad—is increased in our minds.

Another way that advertising influences what we think about and notice is through 'cueing'. To explain this, answer a few questions:

- What's the first thing you think of when you see: *'Just Do It'*?
- What's the first thing you think of when someone says: *'Don't leave home without it'*?
- What comes to mind if you hear the remark: *'I'm lovin' it'*?
- What's the first thing you think of when someone says: *'Can you hear me now'*?
- What's the first thing you think of when someone asks *'Where's the beef?'* in America or *'Which bank?'* in Australia?

Words or expressions such as these come up naturally in everyday conversation. When a brand is linked to them through repetition, they become cues that help increase the salience of the brand.

An actor in a play takes his cue from a line or some other happening or event. The human mind takes its cue from its intentions and its immediate environment. Such cues can influence what we think about next.[15] That's how we go to sleep at night. We turn off the cues. We turn off the light and the radio. We try to reduce distractions or cues so that things won't keep popping into our minds.

One way advertising can use cues is by tying a brand to something that frequently recurs in the ordinary environment. There are many common words, expressions, symbols or tunes that can be developed by means of repetition into mnemonic devices that trigger recollection of the brand.

Table 1.2 Common brand cues

Cue (mnemonic)	Brand/product	Country
I'm lovin' it	McDonald's	Global
You're in good hands	Allstate Insurance	USA
Take care	Garnier	Global
Can you hear me now?	Verizon	USA
Gimme a break	Have a Kit Kat	USA
Have a break . . .	Have a Kit Kat	UK, Australia
Mmmmmmmm . . .	Big M flavored milk	Australia
MmmmmMmmmmm Good	Campbell's Soup	USA
Don't leave home without it . . .	American Express	Global
Do you know me?	American Express	Global
Just do it.	Nike	Global
Where do you want to go today?	Microsoft	Global
The real thing . . .	Coca-Cola	Global
Always . . .	Coca-Cola	Global
Think different.	Apple	Global
Because you're worth it . . .	L'Oreal	Global
Reach out and touch someone	AT&T	USA
Thanks! I needed that!	Mennen Skin Bracer	USA
Have a good weekend . . .	*(& don't forget the Aeroguard)* insect repellant	Australia
Good weekend . . . good VSD	VSD Magazine	France
Which bank?	Commonwealth Bank	Australia
Wednesday . . .	*is Prince Spaghetti night*	USA
Good on you mum . . .	*Tip Top's the one.* Bread	Australia
Where's the beef?	Wendys Restaurants	USA

Cue (mnemonic)	Brand/product	Country
The car in front is . . .	(*a Toyota*)	UK
Oh what a feeling . . .	(*Toyota*)	USA, Australia
Ring around the collar	Wisk detergent	USA
Anyhow* . . .	*Have a Winfield* Cigarettes	Australia
I feel like . . .	*. . . a Tooheys* Tooheys beer	Australia
Who cares?	Boots pharmacies	UK
You deserve a break today	McDonald's	USA, UK, Australia
Thank you for your support	Bartles and Jaymes wine	USA
All because . . .	*the lady loves . . . Milk Tray*	UK
Cross your heart	Playtex bras	UK, Australia

If the cue recurs in the circumstances under which the product is likely to be consumed, such as at lunch time, all the better. The ideal mnemonic cue is not just frequently recurring but occurs *at these strategic times*.

This cueing effect is so much a part of the way we respond to our environment that we are largely oblivious to it. As someone once said, fish are probably unaware of water because it is all round them. However, most people are aware of cueing to some degree. Almost everybody has had the experience of a particular smell evoking special memories. Cigars perhaps remind you of your grandfather; the smell of new carpet may trigger a vivid memory of the first day you moved into your new house. When these memories pop into our mind we are then prone to reminisce on those past days.

If you have ever had trouble getting to sleep at night because your mind can't switch off, you can relate to how involuntary this process usually is. In other words, what pops into our minds at any point in time is not totally under our control.

When you hear the words 'Don't leave home without . . .', the speaker may be referring to your keys or your coat or whatever . . . but your mind is involuntarily reminded of American Express. When a driver assures you 'You're in good hands', can your mind help but be reminded of Allstate Insurance? When someone says 'Just do it', can you help but think of Nike?

Celebrities, expressions and music extracts can come to be so 'owned' by a brand that they automatically prompt our thoughts in that direction. In the USA, Paul Hogan (Crocodile Dundee) was linked to the Subaru brand. In Australia he was traditionally linked to Winfield cigarettes. The word 'Anyhow*' still makes older Australians think of Paul Hogan and Winfield cigarettes because it was uttered by Hogan as part of the commercial ('Anyhow* . . . Have a Winfield'). Like Joe Camel in the USA, Hogan and the expression 'Anyhow*' came to stand for the brand and automatically trigger it in people's minds. Even the classical theme music behind the

Winfield campaign came to be thought of as 'the Winfield music' and would recall the brand in people's memories. The Marlboro brand did the same thing globally with the theme music from *The Magnificent Seven*, which came to be thought of as 'the Marlboro music'.

Our minds are in a sense a 'stream of consciousness'—an inexorable flow that is frequently diverted, sometimes paused but never stopped. Environmental cues can influence what enters the flow and what direction it takes. One type of advertising focuses on tying a brand to one or more such cues, so that whenever we hear, see or think

Figure 1.5: In Australia, Paul Hogan triggered instant recall of the brand Winfield.

of the cue there is a high probability that we will think of the brand or notice its presence. It pulls it into our 'slipstream of thought'.[16]

The product category as a cue

Advertisers want us to think of their brand, but they particularly want us to think of their brand when we are making a decision involving the product category. One important cue is therefore the category itself. When I say 'soft drink', what do you think of? When I say 'lunch', what do you think of? If our conscious mind is in the process of being cued by a product category (e.g. it is noon and we are thinking 'lunch'), then what is likely to flit into our head is not a brand of hair gel or a car—we are much more likely to see in our mind's eye the first item on the mental agenda we have for the category 'lunch'.

When our mind is cued in to a particular product category, we almost automatically begin to think of the 'top-of-mind' members of that category. In the case of the category 'lunch', we will think of McDonald's or Subway or some other food alternative rather than hair gel or cars or anything else.

The technical term for this is *category-cued salience*, or the probability that the brand will come to mind whenever its product category does.

It is possible to measure category-cued salience and assess the influence of advertising on it. This is done by asking people what is the first brand that comes to mind when they hear or see the product category name, and then the next brand and the next.[17] In this way the agenda of brands can be elicited. The rank of a given brand in the product category agenda indicates its category-cued salience. It is a rough index of the probability that it will come to our mind when in the normal course of events we are prompted by the product category name.

If this questioning procedure is carried out periodically with a different random sample of consumers, the agenda and the salience of each brand can be tracked, over time. Market research can detect any improvements resulting from advertising by the order in which the advertised brand is elicited. Advertising a brand generally improves its salience.

Point-of-sale advertising: how to upset the agenda

Many people wonder why Coca-Cola, which is so well known, needs to advertise so much and why it needs to 'waste all that money' on signage. The answer is that if it did not have its signs in these places, Pepsi or some other competitor certainly would. These other brands would try to upset consumers' mental agendas by 'jumping the queue'—by inducing us, at the point of sale, to consider them as well as Coke.

Both point-of-sale, reminder advertising and our own mental agenda of brands can prompt us with alternatives to consider, before we ask for what we want. Advertisers therefore try to influence a brand's salience at the point of sale by not leaving it to our mental agendas alone. They erect signs in an attempt to visually cue us into their brand.

When we walk into a convenience store to buy a soft drink, we are already in a category-cued state. We are already thinking about soft drink and which one we will have. If Coke is not already top of our mind when we enter, it almost inescapably will be once we have been inside for a moment, because Coke as a brand is likely to be prompted in our minds by a) the product category cue and b) the Coca-Cola signs in the store.

Coke may be on top of most people's minds but if they are confronted with a Pepsi sign they may consider both brands. So Coke tries to dominate the clutter of mental alternatives as well as the clutter of point-of-sale advertising and point-of-sale display. This makes it difficult for other brands to cut through into people's minds at the point of sale.[18] It protects Coke's category salience—something that it has invested a lot of money in building up through years of advertising.

Supermarket shopping: mental agendas vs brand displays
In the supermarket it may be thought that, because the brands are all displayed, they are all equally likely to be noticed—and considered. If this were so, then our mental agenda of brands would be irrelevant to super-market shopping. However, this is not the case.

On average, people take no more than 12 seconds to select a brand and in 85 per cent of purchases only the chosen brand is handled.[19] Observation studies of supermarket shoppers indicate that more than half of all buying is just 'simple locating behavior'.[20] That is, most people are simply locating the brand they bought last time, or the one that they came in to buy. They put it into their shopping cart with little or no attention to evaluating the alternatives.

For an alternative brand or pack to be noticed, let alone considered, it would have to cut through the display clutter and stand out in some way. In order to be considered it first has to cut through into conscious attention.

In low-involvement situations many people tend to do what they did last time unless there is something to interrupt the routine. Thus a brand or pack has to cut through the display clutter just as an ad has to cut through the clutter of other ads. And the two, the pack and the advertising, can work together.

The importance of being noticed shows up when regular buyers of a product category are shown color photographs of any new brand. Without advertising and promotional support, the percentage saying that they have seen it on the supermarket shelves will likely remain very low. Of course supermarkets know this and that's why they insist on a new brand being backed by advertising and promotional support if they agree to stock it.

Just because something is present does not mean we will necessarily notice it or consider it. The more cluttered the environment, the more alternatives there are in the product category, the greater this problem is for the advertiser. Advertising signs at the point of purchase can help considerably here, especially when they tie in with advertising that we have already seen. They are then more likely to 'connect' with us and get us to notice the brand.

In the supermarket, it is not signs but usually the brands themselves that are displayed. Potentially we are able to be reminded of every brand in the display by its physical presence. So is our mental agenda of brands still relevant? Yes, though it is now one influence among several. In particular, it orients us by determining which brands we notice in the display.

To illustrate this, imagine you are in a supermarket doing the shopping. As you approach the detergent section, what is in your mind? The category 'detergents'. Why? Because the layout of the supermarket is familiar to you, or because when you approach that section the category is prompted by the display in front of you.

Even in the supermarket, then, the product category as a cue is likely to be triggered in our minds at a particular point and to trigger in turn expectations of the brands we are likely to see in that category. What we see first in the display is likely to be influenced not only by a brand's position and shelf space but also by our expectations of seeing the brand there. All other things being equal, we tend to notice first the brands we are familiar with. Of course, this is especially true when our mind set is that of looking to locate the one that we bought last time.

When something is heavily advertised, it is more likely to come to mind and, other things being equal, to be noticed faster in a display. We know from the psychological literature that people recognize the familiar more quickly, so it will come as no surprise that familiar brands will be very salient and be noticed more quickly.[21] Advertising exposure of the brand and the pack helps to make the brand more familiar and increase its salience. Repeated exposure of the pack in advertising makes it more familiar and hence gives it a better chance of being noticed earlier or faster than its competitor.

Figure 1.6: Visual salience—the 'pop-out' effect. Inclined letters 'pop-out' more than upside down letters.[22]

The importance of this marginal effect is seen in the finding mentioned above—that more than half of all purchases made in the supermarket are simply the purchaser locating what they want. Shoppers hardly pause at the display but simply reach out and pick up the item they are after. So in the supermarket a brand or pack has to cut through the clutter—to stop people walking at more than 1 mile per hour (2 km/h)—and get itself noticed.

Shelf displays, shelf 'talkers' and off-location displays are all ways to help a brand 'pop out' and get our attention. Advertising that we have been exposed to previously, however, also plays an important part in increasing the visual salience of a particular brand. The aim is to modify the degree to which the brand 'pops out' in the display and engages the shopper's notice earlier than other brands.

Measuring visual salience

Advertisers can quantify the visual salience of a pack or brand through market research in much the same way as they uncover the mental agenda. They give each brand in a supermarket display equal shelf space and then take a photograph of the display. They show the photo to a random sample of consumers and ask them to name the brands they see. The order and speed with which the brands are noticed provide a measure of their visual salience. (Actually, researchers use several photographs and control for position in the display by randomly changing the position of each brand.)

Summary

One reason we find it difficult to analyze advertising's effects intro-spectively and why advertising has remained a mystery for so long is that these effects are often so simple and so small that they fall short of outright persuasion. Advertising influences the order in which we evoke or notice the alternatives we consider. This does not feel like persuasion and it is not. It is nevertheless effective. Instead of persuasion and other major effects we should look for 'feathers', or minor effects. These can tip the balance when alternative brands are otherwise equal and, through repetition, can grow imperceptibly by small increments over time.

2 IMAGE AND REALITY: SEEING THINGS IN DIFFERENT WAYS

In Chapter 1 we considered the ways in which advertising can influence our decisions by influencing the order in which we evoke or notice the options. Now let us turn to advertising and focus on how it influences our *evaluation* of brand alternatives.

Human beings have a remarkable capacity for seeing things in different ways. The same physical stimulus, the same product or service, if you will, can be seen in more than one way. Look at Figure 2.1 . . . is it a rabbit or a duck? It can be seen either way.

Look at the next figure, 2.2. Think of it as a brand. You should be able to see it in two different ways. When you see a vase in the figure your mind is seeing 'white figure on black background'. When you see two faces, your mind is seeing 'black figure on white background'. This white-on-black or black-on-white that you are using to make sense of what you see is called the *frame of reference*. You overlay a frame of reference on a stimulus to generate a perception.

A brand, company or service can also be perceived in different ways

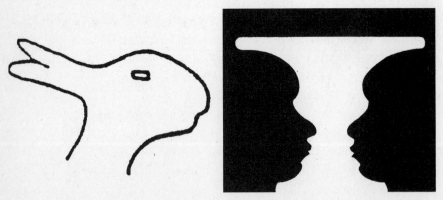

Figure 2.1: *Is it a rabbit or a duck?*[1]   **Figure 2.2**: *A vase or two faces?*

depending upon the frame of reference that people bring to it. Frame of reference is a psychological term that refers to a mind set or previous experience.

Evaluating a brand

When we evaluate brands we try to do so by evaluating their attributes or features. This is not always a straightforward task, for two reasons. First, there is the problem of what attributes the brand has. Second, there is the problem of how to interpret these attributes.

For example, with the brand Volvo you might think of heavy construction, safety, conservative styling and so on. Heavy construction is closely related to safety, which you rate positively. But you may also associate it with poorer fuel economy, a negative feature. Thus the same attribute, heavy construction, can be rated positively or negatively depending on how you look at it. Similarly, large size may suggest either comfort (a positive) or poor fuel economy (a negative). And fabric seat coverings are more comfortable than faux-leather but are harder to keep clean.

Our minds can interpret any attribute positively or negatively. For example, our attitudes towards ground beef vary markedly depending whether it is labeled '75 per cent lean' or '25 per cent fat'.[2] There are upsides and downsides to almost anything in life and a brand's features are no exception.

Positively or negatively charged features

'Choice between brands is driven largely by simple associations between the brand and attributes or **emotions** usually created and sustained through advertising.'[3] Attribute or emotional associations can greatly influence the way we feel about something. 'Cars are imaged variously as shields against accidents, reliable companions, virile athletes or purveyors of fun.'[4] Similar variations occur in our images of other types of categories. Think for example of the image you associate with these:

- professions (lawyers, advertisers, doctors, car salespeople);
- countries (France, USA, Australia);
- cities (Sydney, London, NewYork);
- organizations (International Monetary Fund, United Nations, OPEC);
- corporations (Apple, Microsoft, Wal-Mart, Neiman Marcus);

- brands (Toshiba, Sony, Hewlett Packard);
- services (Speedy Mufflers, Qantas, Virgin Atlantic, DHL);
- product categories (pearls, wine, motorcycles).

Consider the product category 'pearls'. Most people think of pearls as beautiful jewelry, whose salient associations are with gift-giving, attractive women, high fashion and expensiveness. But like any product, pearls also have non-salient features, aspects most people tend not to think of unless their attention is drawn to them for some reason.

Figure 2.3: An advertisement for Mikimoto pearls.

To pursue the example, a competitor of Mikimoto pearls (perhaps DeBeers diamonds) may seek to remind us of these other attributes because it wants us to buy diamonds instead of pearls. It may point out that a pearl is more easily damaged than a diamond (a small feather). Or it could point out that a pearl is an oyster tumor. Ugh! What unpleasant associations that statement triggers (a much bigger feather).

Under normal circumstances, however, we would never have cause to think about these aspects of pearls. Nevertheless, we would have to agree that both are true. The information that a pearl is more easily damaged than a diamond and that a pearl is an oyster tumor are both there in our heads. But they usually occur so far down on our mental attribute agenda that we would rarely, in the normal course of thinking about pearls, bring them to mind. Neither of them is a salient feature.

Calling a pearl 'an oyster tumor' plays the focal beam of our attention on an unpleasant aspect of pearls. This is a 'feather' but in this case a potentially large one and if it were repeated often enough its salience would be likely to increase. (In a sense, this is what animal rights group PETA has done by highlighting the cruelty involved in the product category of furs.[5]) It may not make us stop buying pearls but it might take some of the shine off our perception of them.

Under normal circumstances the focal beam of our attention is only wide enough to encompass a few of the attributes of a brand or product. By shifting the spotlight and playing the focal beam of attention on other attributes, it is possible to marginally change our perceptions. This is what the graffiti artists are trying to do when they write 'Meat is murder' on walls and bridges. Most people eat meat. We also know where it comes from. But we don't want to think about it too much. If we did, we would probably all consider becoming vegetarians. The killing of animals in order to eat their flesh is hardly an association that we want to be reminded of.

Advertising influence on our brand attribute agenda

When you think of Volkswagen you perhaps think 'economical', 'quirky', 'cute', 'reliable'. You could consider many other attributes, but your mind only has time to touch on a few. The advertiser wants fuel economy to be high on the Volkswagen attribute agenda. So its advertising traditionally used words and pictures to highlight the brand's association with that attribute.

A confectionery brand could focus on attributes like fun, popularity, self indulgence, color, taste, shape or texture etc. M&M for example traditionally played the focal beam of our attention on one specific attribute: 'Melts in your mouth, not in your hand'. Lifesavers focused on shape: 'The candy with the hole'.

With drinks, too, there are all sorts of attributes on which an advertiser can play the focal beam of attention. Some that will be familiar are:

- Health: *Another day, another chance to feel healthy*—Evian
- Unpretentious: *Image is nothing. Taste is everything*—Sprite
- Pretentious/exclusivity: *Stella Artois—reassuringly expensive*
- Sport: *Life is a sport. Drink it up*—Gatorade
- Taste: *Just for the taste of it*—Diet Coke
- Modern/up-to-date: *Pepsi—The taste of a new generation, Generation Next*
- Thirst quenching: *Heinekin—refreshes the parts other beers can't reach*
- Ethics: *Don't be evil*—Google
- Flavor: *7UP, the Uncola*
- Ubiquity: *Always Coca-Cola*
- Quality/flavor: *Good to the last drop . . . Maxwell House*
- Origin: *Fosters—Australian for beer, Columbia Coffee—100% pure Columbian coffee beans.*

The chain of associations (visual or verbal) that a brand automatically triggers in our mind can be ranked in the order in which they are triggered, with the most salient ones at the top. This is the attribute agenda.

One of the most important aspects of advertising, then, is to play the focal beam of attention on a particular attribute and make that attribute more salient for us when we think of the brand.[6] In other words, advertising influences the attribute agenda for a brand by rearranging the order in which we think of its attributes.

Using positively charged features: positioning

Words and images can be used to make the positive attributes of an advertiser's brand or product more salient; to increase the probability that when we think of that brand we will think of those positive attributes; to place them higher on the brand's attribute agenda.

What do you think of when I say 'Colgate'? Your stream of thought perhaps went something like this:

1. Toothpaste
2. Cleans teeth
3. Whitens teeth
4. Prevents decay
5. Long-lasting protection.

Now, what do you think of when I say 'Sensodyne'? Your stream of thought, heavily influenced by the name, elicits 'sensitive teeth' high up on the attribute agenda. Similarly the 'Close-Up' brand of toothpaste triggers a stream of thought that is heavily influenced by the name as well as the advertising which traditionally featured scenes of couples kissing. These play the focal beam of our attention on quite different attributes from those we associate with Colgate. Close-Up puts the brand's major selling point, the attributes associated with kissing, 'fresh breath' and 'sex appeal', high on our agenda of associations. Its attribute agenda is quite different from that of Colgate or Sensodyne.

Using negatively charged features: repositioning the opposition

Advertisers usually try to highlight the positive attributes of their own brand. An alternative strategy is to highlight the negative features of the opposition's product. We saw how this works with product categories when we discussed the examples of pearls and meat. Highlighting the negatives in the opposition brand is referred to as *repositioning the opposition*—repositioning the opposition brand in people's minds.

Sun OpenOffice software, for example, positioned its product against the competitor Microsoft Office by using the line 'Don't let a bully keep taking your lunch money', thus highlighting the dominant, almost monopolistic position that Microft held in the office software area. This is not dissimilar to what the famous Avis rental car advertising campaign did in its classic campaign with the line: 'Avis. We are number two, so why should you rent from us? We try harder!' In that campaign Avis acknowledged that it was not the market leader and scored points and credibility for its honesty. At the same time it indirectly and subtly highlighted a negative attribute often associated with strong market leaders and monopolies—that they can be complacent and give poor service; that they don't try hard enough. The proposition that Avis as number two in the market would be trying harder to deliver better service was the positive flip side of this. It was given more credibility by the company's apparent honesty in admitting it was not number one.

Thus, words and images can be used to make particular negative attributes of an opposition brand or product more salient: to increase the probability that when we think of the brand we will think of that negative attribute. It is a matter of advertising influencing which attributes our minds focus on when we think of the brand. When we think of pearls or brand leaders we don't usually think of the negative attributes, and this leaves them looking attractive.

The Sprite campaign: 'Image is nothing. Taste is everything' was another attempt at highlighting a negative attribute of opposition soft drink brands. Sprite positioned itself as 'unpretentious', focused on taste and not needing to play the focal beam of attention on image hype like other soft drink brands had.

It is the fact that our minds are usually focused on the positive attributes (like 'jewelry', 'good-looking', 'valuable', 'great gift') that makes them attractive. Just as there is a mental agenda of brands that we free-associate to the product category, so there is a mental agenda of attributes that we free-associate to entities like meat or pearls, or brands like iPod, Volkswagen or Google. Advertising can make certain attributes more salient and therefore higher on a product's attribute agenda. As a consequence, when we think of the product we think of the advertised features before, and perhaps instead of, other negative but less salient attributes.

Point-of-sale advertising: attribute cueing

Just as ads or signs at the point of sale can remind us of a brand, so too they can remind us of a particular attribute of the brand.

- Coke Zero: *Great Coke taste, zero sugar.*
- BA: *The world's favorite airline . . . British Airways.*
- M&M: *Melts in your mouth, not in your hand.*
- Evian: *Your natural source of youth.*

The words and pictures used to label and describe a brand can direct our attention to quite different aspects of the same thing; they can help us to see it in different ways.

To illustrate, what do you think of when I say 'Bill Gates'? A biography of Bill Gates could conceivably carry any of the following subtitles: 'World's greatest entrepreneur', 'Computer mogul', 'Business mastermind', 'Philanthropist', 'World citizen', 'Family man'.

Bill Gates is one person but he has all of these attributes. Depending which subtitle was chosen, the book would attract a slightly different audience and have slightly different appeals. The same man is being described but what we expect to see in the book would be very much influenced by which title or description was used. Whether people bought it would be influenced by a combination of their own attribute agenda for Bill Gates and how much they are interested in business or philanthropy or family life or the state of the world. If a cue is used in the subtitle of the book, whichever one is chosen focuses our expectations differently. Each description of Bill Gates plays the focal beam of our attention and our expectations on a different attribute of the same person. It consequently influences our perceptions and our expectations and does not leave them solely to our own mental agenda.

Point-of-sale advertising does the same thing. It influences us by playing the focal beam of our attention on the brand and the featured attribute at the same time.

Influenced by the brand name

As we saw with Sensodyne and Close-Up toothpaste, advertisers try to choose the name of a brand so the name itself can help direct attention, influence people's expectations, and help determine the brand's most salient features. Names like Safe-n-Sound (baby car seats), Posturepedic (matresses), BeautyRest (matresses), Revlon ColorStay (makeup), Head & Shoulders (shampoo), Chips Ahoy (cookies) and I Can't Believe It's Not Butter (margarine): these not only name the product but also make an implicit statement about its salient attributes. So we expect baby seats with the name 'Safe-n-Sound' to have features like quality and safety. We expect beds called 'Posturepedic' to be good for our back, and so on.

This has a very long history. 'Erik the Red named the country he had discovered Greenland, for he said that people would be more tempted to go there if it had an attractive name.'[7] Erik the Red obviously had an intuitive feel for what influences people's expectations even though he did not think of it in terms of a product's attribute agenda.

Another example from history: before the Civil War, anything labeled alcohol had no market in the areas of the US known as temperance regions because of the social taboo. Patent medicines, on the other hand, found a big market in these regions—especially medicines containing up to 44 per cent of the preservative alcohol![8]

Summary

How we evaluate a brand, a service or a product depends on how we perceive it. This in turn depends on the frame of reference we overlay on it. The frame of reference comes largely from our experience. Just as there is a mental agenda of brands that we associate with a given product category, so there is a mental agenda of attributes that we free-associate to a given brand.

Under normal circumstances the focal beam of our attention is only wide enough to focus on a limited number of the possible attributes of a brand or product. By shifting the spotlight and playing the focal beam of our attention on other attributes, it is possible to change our perceptions of the product. Words and images can be used to make its positive attributes more salient, to increase the probability that when we think of the brand we will think of those attributes.

Again, these may be 'feathers', but they may nevertheless be enough to tip the scales in favor of a particular brand—especially when all other factors are equal.

3 SUBLIMINAL ADVERTISING: THE BIGGEST MYTH OF ALL

Advertising is in an odd position. Its extreme protagonists claim it has extraordinary powers and its severest critics believe them.[1]

Andrew Ehrenberg

There are those who believe that advertising is all powerful and that the mechanism of advertising must be unconscious and subliminal and this is why its effects are not open to introspection. This chapter asserts that subtlety, not subliminality, is what is important and at the same time dispels the subliminal advertising myth. I also examine the reasons why 'embeds' which fan people's fears continue to appear in advertising from time to time.

The never-ending story

In 2007 during an episode of *Iron Chef America* on the cable Food Network, a single frame of the McDonald's golden arches was discovered, embedded in a part of the program.[2] Why was it there? The network later explained, 'It was a technical error on our part and not a subliminal message.'

When *The Lion King* movie was released Disney found itself under attack from accusers who said the word s-e-x could be discerned in one scene in the dust as the lions were playing. I saw the clip (before it was removed from YouTube) and there is no doubt it was in there.

Some time later in the USA, in print ads for Camel cigarettes the image of a camel was barely discernible, embedded in the patterns of exhaled smoke and in the arrangement of ice water droplets. And in a number of visual ads with no apparent message the Mercedes three-point star appeared embedded in a variety of obscure places (see the example shown below).

Figure 3.1: An ad for Camel cigarettes, where an image of a camel appeared in smoke.

Figure 3.2: Only one word, 'Speed', appeared on this ad. Note the Mercedes three-point star in the sole of the shoe.

Not surprisingly these things make consumers very uneasy. Things that we don't understand make us more fearful. The natural fear is that somehow these images are seducing us in some way without our knowledge.

Anxiety increases even more when the subliminal image is found in political communications such as happened when George W. Bush was running against Al Gore for the US presidency. A pro-Bush ad flashed the word 'Rats' subliminally just as the ad was denigrating Gore's drug prescription plan.

Rarely does anyone ever really provide a satisfactory explanation as to how these things get in there so it naturally makes people think 'Hmm . . . why is it there? Maybe I really should be afraid.'

There has been so much nonsense talked about 'subliminal advertising' that there is always a risk that writing about it will again fuel the uninformed hype. But by understanding its mythical origins we will see how subtlety, not subliminality, is what is important in advertising. The fears of subliminal effects have been grossly overblown while subtle effects that are not 'hidden' from consciousness have much more impact.

The original scare on subliminal advertising came from a marketing consultant in the USA, James Vicary, who flashed 'Drink Coca-Cola' and 'Eat popcorn' on the cinema screen during a movie so fast that nobody was supposed to be aware it was happening. He reported that sales of Coca-Cola and popcorn increased dramatically. This caused such a scare that legislation was quickly prepared to ban subliminal advertising.

If subliminal advertising did indeed have that kind of effect on our behavior, and without our knowledge, then we clearly would need protection from it. It is still widely believed that in the 1950s, subliminal advertising was made illegal in the USA. In fact, no such legislation was passed either federally or in any state. It was banned in a number of other countries including the UK and Australia, however, but as we will see, this was unnecessary.

That was a half century ago. Ever since, there have been numerous attempts—all unsuccessful—to replicate the substantial effect claimed by Vicary and more than 200 scientific papers have been published on the subject. Pratkanis and Aronson, after exhaustively researching that literature, concluded that 'no study has demonstrated motivational and behavioral effects similar to those claimed by the advocates of subliminal seduction'.[3] It is clear, in this case, enthusiasm and myth outweighed fact.

In 1984, when confronted with the overwhelming evidence against subliminal advertising, the marketing consultant James Vicary admitted to *Advertising Age* magazine that his original claim had been a fabrication.[4] So, subliminal advertising was just a myth all along.

Self-help tapes

If that is so, you may ask, then what about those self-help tapes? The ones that are supposed to contain subliminal messages to help you give up smoking, improve your self-esteem and so on? Are they nonsense also?

In the same way that a sugar pill will relieve pain in about a third of sufferers if they think it is aspirin, so too will such tapes work on a proportion of the people who use them—because they expect them to. Pratkanis and Aronson convincingly demonstrated this several times by giving experimental subjects tapes of classical music marked 'subliminally improve your memory' or 'subliminally improve your self-esteem'. A significant proportion of the subjects reported improvements in their memory or self-esteem, depending how their tape was labeled, but the proportion was the same whether the tapes actually had subliminal messages embedded in them or not.[5]

The practical jokesters: embedded words or images

What about the images and words like 'sex' that have been shown to be embedded in some advertisements? Don't they prove that subliminal advertising is being practised and that it must be working? They prove nothing of the kind! Despite the furore and the paranoia created by such books as *Subliminal Seduction* by Wilson Bryan Key, I believe this is nothing but visual graffiti and practical joke-playing by those who design the advertising.[6]

It is similar to Hirschfeld, the cartoonist for the *New Yorker* who put his daughter's name, 'Nina', in every one of his cartoons. You really had to look for them but they were there just the same.

Most of the examples Key cited have been in print advertising. It is very easy for an art director to put something in an ad, a caricature of his boss for example, without his boss being aware that it is there. An art director friend once pointed out to me a figure in a poster he had designed and which his boss must have seen hundreds of times. There, right in the middle of the crowd scene in the poster, was a caricature of his boss. Like the Waldo character in the children's books, he was virtually invisible— until you looked. After a hearty laugh this art director swore me to silence. These things are rarely discovered. The *London Daily Mirror* once owned by the infamous Robert Maxwell ran a cartoon in which the cartoonist inserted the words 'Fuck Maxwell' in tiny letters among the squiggles.[7]

When the word 'sex' is found disguised in the shadows of ice cubes in a Gilbey's gin ad, as likely as not it is an art director having a joke on his client or his boss or just seeing if he can get away with it without anybody noticing. This kind of thing, however, gives ammunition to the conspiracy theorists who interpret words or images as proof that subliminal advertising is practised and must therefore be seducing us without our knowledge.

Why did the subliminal myth take hold?

How, if subliminal advertising is just a myth, could the myth have been perpetuated for so long?

One reason is to be found in the fact that legislators in some countries moved so quickly to ban it. In doing so they lent a kind of legitimacy to unfounded beliefs about the power of subliminal advertising. The need to prepare legislation to ban it provided history with the *prima facie* evidence that subliminal advertising is a real threat. This helped enshrine and perpetuate the myth.

Another reason is that the myth fits the image of advertising that is perpetuated by the advertising industry. As we saw in Chapter 1, people believe that advertising has much greater powers to influence us than it really does. Once we started imputing witchdoctor-like powers to ad agencies, it was a small step to believing that they had the modern equivalent: the power to persuade us subliminally.

The media have also done their bit to foster this belief. Mystique makes for good copy and greater reader interest. Subliminal advertising taps into the same mystique as TV programs like *Heroes*, *The X Files* and *Ripley's Believe It or Not*.

But is that all there is to it? Just myth, hype and mistake? No. There is another important reason why the belief in subliminal advertising has persisted for so long. It is not totally without *any* effect. A high-jumper can leap 6 feet (2 metres) but this does not mean humans can fly. There are limits to how high we can go, unassisted. Similarly, as the earlier chapters of this book have shown, we are able to learn without full, conscious awareness—but only up to a point.

There is no doubt that we can be influenced without awareness, but as the earlier chapters show there is nothing necessarily unique or evil or manipulative about this. It is a quantum leap from here to believing in wholesale manipulation of people's minds through subliminal advertising. Just because we can learn without full awareness does not mean that advertising practises mass manipulation on us. People can jump 6 feet—but flying is something else.

Claims about subconscious learning had a kernel of truth. Claims about subliminal advertising were wildly exaggerated and they distorted this truth. Advertising often works without our being able to keep track of the process. There is no need for subliminal exposures on TV and cinema screens. The process happens naturally. It is what low-involvement communication is all about.

Thirty years of research later

So let's look at the claims a half century later—in light of the substantial body of scientific research on the human brain that has accumulated since then.

The notion of subliminal advertising was based on the belief that awareness was an all-or-nothing thing. That is, we are either aware of something or we are not. This is demonstrably untrue. Research in cognitive psychology over the past 35 years has shown that *conscious awareness is a dimension and not a dichotomy. It is a matter of degree.*

By way of illustration, let me draw your attention to the sounds around you right now. What can you hear? Were you aware of the sounds before I drew your attention to them? Probably not. The reason is a matter of degree of consciousness. You were not paying attention to the sounds but that does not mean they were 'subliminal' in the sense that they were unable to be heard.

A more useful way of thinking about this issue is in terms of depth of mental processing. Instead of subliminal we could use the terms 'peripheral', 'shallow' or 'implicit processing'.

The logic and illogic of subliminal advertising

The concept of subliminal advertising was based on the notion of a threshold. Subliminal meant 'below the limen, or threshold'. This was thought to be a fixed point below which awareness does not extend. This 'limen' was just another name for the threshold.

We know that for some sounds, dogs have a much lower threshold than humans. They can hear sounds that we can't. This is the principle behind the dog whistle.

When we have a hearing test, the loudness of a tone is gradually increased until we indicate to the doctor that we can hear it. This is the threshold at which sound enters our consciousness. The same applies to sight. If a word is flashed on a screen for 50 milliseconds we will not be aware of it. If the time of the exposure is increased, at a certain point the word crosses the threshold and enters our conscious awareness.

Subliminal advertising was supposed to be pitched just barely below the threshold of awareness. If it was too far below it would not work. The theory was that the exposure should be sufficiently long for people to register the message unconsciously but not long enough for them to become aware of it. Research has since shown that there is no absolute threshold below which we are always unconscious of something and above which we are always conscious of it. (For example, when we are hungry we recognize food words at much shorter exposures than non-food words. The threshold is lower for these words when we are hungry and higher if we have just eaten.)

Thresholds therefore turn out to vary in the same person from day to day and even from hour to hour. This is partly because sometimes we are more alert than at other times. They also vary as a result of tiredness, lack of sleep or drugs like alcohol or caffeine. And they vary from person to person.

For an advertiser always to pitch the ad message precisely at or just under the threshold would therefore seem impossible. Psychologists have now redefined the threshold of awareness in probabilistic rather than absolute terms—as the exposure level that enables a subject in repeated trials to detect a word 50 per cent of the time. To reach everyone, a message would have to be exposed for a relatively long period. But since this would put it above many people's threshold, the message could no longer be termed subliminal. Subliminal advertising as originally defined is therefore a myth.

Awareness and attention: limits to our capacity

Attention is not an all-or-nothing thing. Even though some people seem to be able to attend to more than one thing at a time, there are limits. Psychological studies show that the more things we allocate our attention to, the less the mental processing of any one of them.

Psychology experiments on shared attention show that there are real limits to our attention capacity when other things in the environment are competing for our attention. We only have a limited amount of mental processing capacity at any one time. Therefore some things are given shallow, implicit mental processing. Others are given deep attentional, or explicit, processing. There are just too many things around to process them all in the same depth.

Interestingly, the more attention that is paid to something, the easier it is for us to recall it later.[8] For example, while driving and conversing on a (hands-free) cell phone, eye tracking research shows that even when we look directly at objects we are less likely later to recognize having seen them.[9]

So what happens on radio or TV when some of our attention is directed away from the ad? What happens when we are barely aware of the advertising? To answer, let me take you into the fascinating world of the experimental psychologist and introduce you to what is known as the 'divided attention' experiment.

Divided attention

Divided listening experiments at first glance seem akin to a slow form of torture. Psychologists get subjects to listen through headphones to two different stories (or ads) simultaneously—one in the left ear and one in the right ear. (Experimental psychologists use stories while marketing psychologists might use radio ads.)

The subjects are tested immediately afterwards for what they remember. Not surprisingly, they recall only part of what they have heard and there is often a lot of confusion between what they heard in the right ear and what they heard in the left ear. Compared to subjects who are exposed to only one ad at a time, these people recall substantially less and their recollections are more confused. That is, the competition between simultaneous stimuli reduces the degree of recall.

This is not surprising. It is why many of us didn't do as well as we could have at school. And it's why television ads also have to be intrusive and interesting—to cut through and hold our attention, especially for low-involvement product categories.

Choosing what we attend to: selective processing

We can choose what to attend to and process deeply. The more interesting the stimulus the more we are likely to pay attention to it and the more of it we recall—in other words, the more impact it has.

What happens if the experimenter asks subjects to listen to the messages in both ears while 'shadowing' (repeating aloud) what they hear in one ear? In this way the experimenter can get the subject to direct even more attention to (process more deeply) the message coming into one ear. What happens when the experimenter tests for recall? It is no surprise that for the shadowed ear the degree of recall is very high. This illustrates that the greater the attention and the deeper the processing, the greater the recall will be.

But when the experimenter tests for recall of the message heard in the unshadowed ear, the result is zero. The subjects remember nothing—indeed, it is almost as if they have not been exposed to the other ad at all. (Poor recall of radio advertising is reflective of this phenomenon.) But if the subjects can't recall this message, does it mean it had no effect on them? Not necessarily.

The fact that some, albeit minimal, processing can occur at a very low level of consciousness is revealed by a further refinement of the divided attention experiment. In this version, the experimenter inter-rupts the subject while he/she is shadowing the ad in one ear and asks what he/she heard in the last second or two in the unattended ear?

Lo and behold, the subject recalls the previous 1–2 seconds of the unshadowed message. Perfectly! This is amazing, is it not? Especially since we know from the previous experiment that 30 seconds after the experiment the subject will remember nothing of that ad.

Thus the ad, even though it may not be recalled after the event, may nevertheless be processed, albeit at some very low level of attention.

Choosing what not to attend to: shallow processing

The problem is that the unattended message is not processed deeply enough. Its content is not retrievable after more than a few seconds unless we are induced to process it further by having our attention directed to it or by repetition.

It seems that a minimum level of attention is necessary for conscious awareness and recall to be retained. In glancing at ads as we scan through a magazine or newspaper, unless we spend at least three quarters of a second or more with the ad we will not even be able to recognize it later.[10] The more stimuli one is exposed to, the less attention is left for processing other stimuli. Advertising which receives only minimal processing, far from being frighteningly powerful, is actually likely to be very inefficient, and almost certainly has less impact than advertising which is processed at a more conscious level.

This is not to say that such advertising has no effect—just that its effects seem to be marginal, and the more abbreviated the processing of the ad the weaker these effects are likely to be.

What are these effects?

The evidence is that so-called subliminal advertising can influence mood and it can affect feelings by cueing a primary drive (e.g. remind us that we are hungry or thirsty or arouse us to feel sexy) or activate our existing goals.[11] As with hypnotism, subliminal ads cannot induce goals that we don't already have but it can activate goals that we do already possess.[12]

This is no different to ordinary advertising. Even at a low level of conscious processing we can be reminded that we are hungry or thirsty. The implication of it is that a subliminal cinema ad may be able to increase drink or food sales, but cannot *direct* the extra demand toward specific items such as Coke or popcorn—unless these items are the only things immediately available.

That's not to say that it can't act as a feather to help tip an otherwise equal brand choice but that amounts to jumping 6 feet, not flying. Even when a stimulus is 'subliminal' and nothing breaks through into consciousness, research shows that it can marginally increase brand familiarity that could act as a feather to swing an otherwise equal choice balance.[13] But why would advertisers do it this way, by flashing subliminal images, when, as Chapter 1 shows, there are less contentious and more effective ways to achieve even better results?

The late Anita Roddick reportedly put strawberry essence on the pavement outside her first Body Shop store.[14] A well-known producer of freshly baked biscuits is said to pump out baking smells from its stores in shopping centres.[15] Anyone who has ever walked past a Body Shop or a hot-bread shop knows that aromas can tweak our senses. There is nothing subliminal about it. Similarly it would be much more sensible for a cinema to use popcorn smells, or regular Coca-Cola advertising, to remind people that they are hungry or thirsty than to rely on less efficient stimuli such as so-called subliminal messages flashed on the screen.

Whether a stimulus is 'subliminal' or just subtle or whether it comes to us in the full glare of awareness, its main influence is on what enters the conscious mind.[16] It can remind us that thirst is high on our needs agenda or that we are nearly out of fuel or it can remind us of a brand that we should consider. In other words, it can influence what products and brands get weighed up and research has shown that this in itself can influence the probability of the brand being chosen even if its evaluation is not changed.[17]

'Subliminal' influence on evaluation of the brand: image, attitude and choice

The laboratory study evidence is mixed on the ability of implicitly processed advertising to swing the brand decision by influencing brand image, brand attitudes and brand choice. Two experiments seemed to show it could, but another which attempted to replicate one of the earlier ones failed to find the same effect.[18] Then another one found that in both high- and low-involvement situations, it added a decisive feather when everything else was equal.[19]

A problem with these laboratory studies is that subjects are usually exposed to only one or two repetitions of an ad. In the real world, the effect of one or two exposures may be too small to observe or even measure. Laboratory studies with substantial ad repetition are rare but they do show that an attitude can be conditioned to the stimulus (even at low levels of awareness) by *repeatedly* presenting a stimulus (like a brand) with positive or negative pictures or words.[20] And more recent experiments investigating what happens when we are exposed to but ignore web ads have revealed implicit effects on ad liking and brand salience (see Chapter 25, 'The web: advertising in a new age').

Tracking many TV advertising campaigns continuously over weeks, months and sometimes years revealed this picture. The influence of low-involvement messages on the image and salience of particular brands seems to be much the same as, but less efficient than, advertising that is attended to more closely and processed more deeply. Over time, advertising appears to be able to produce small but cumulative image shifts and salience increments. Often, the advertising needs to be continued to maintain these effects. When it stops, the reinforcement stops and the gains are eroded.

These small changes are like the 'feathers' we talked about in Chapter 1. With repetition, they can tip the balance—assuming everything else is equal.

Nike and Mercedes may draw comfort from their brand being triggered by just a swoosh or a three-point star in the ad. It can be an effective supplementary branding device and certainly means a brand has achieved presence.[21] That the brand can be recognized by this meagre cue testifies to and reinforces presence. It has more to do with that than any claims for subliminal effects in advertising.

When everything else is equal is when advertising is most effective

There is no evidence that low-involvement messages can directly influence or manipulate our conscious choices by *overriding* consciously received input or reasoning.[22]

Whether it is processed implicitly or explicitly, however, advertising of a particular product or brand is likely to have greatest impact when the alternatives weigh in equally and we don't care too much about the outcome. So its influence is in situations where we don't care much anyway. Or, in situations where we do care and it helps remind us of a favorable alternative or a nice thing to do that we might not have thought about otherwise, when it puts a favorable alternative on the agenda.

As the story of subliminal advertising shows, we need to be very careful that we don't jump to the wrong conclusion in evaluating advertising's effects.

Summary

Human beings can learn without full, conscious awareness, but there are real limitations to this. We only have a certain amount of mental processing capacity at any one time. Therefore some stimuli receive less mental processing. Others receive focused, deeper processing. So conscious awareness is a dimension, not a dichotomy. It is a matter of degree.

It is true that there are situations where it can be advantageous for advertisers to communicate outside the full glare of attention. It helps obviate the triggering of conscious defences and counter-arguing (see Chapter 5, 'The advertising message: oblique and indirect'). Advertisers have little need to bury obscure images in ice cubes or rely on things flashed rapidly at sub-threshold speeds, all for uncertain effect. Advertisers have other ways to do the same thing, ways that don't provoke the same controversy or social concern. Oblique messages are one way, and product placement is another (see Chapter 6). Fears of subliminal effects have been grossly overblown while subtle effects that are not so 'hidden' from consciousness have much more impact.

So-called subliminal advertising, which began as a hoax in the 1950s, has become enshrined in myth. Legislators reacting so quickly in some countries to ban it lent a kind of legitimacy to beliefs about its power. Far from being frighteningly powerful, it is likely to be very inefficient and is almost certainly weaker than advertising which engages us at a more conscious level.

4 CONFORMITY: THE POPULAR THING TO DO

In our society a celebrity is a person who is famous for being well known.

Lee Iacocca[1]

The same is true of brands. And companies!

Seeing things as others see them

I noted earlier that there are a number of different ways of seeing the same thing. What we perceive as 'reality' is very much influenced by how other people see it—the popular consensus. In making choices people are influenced by two things:

- what they think, and
- what they think other people think.

Let me illustrate this with an experiment (see Figure 4.1). Look at card 1. Imagine that the top line on this is a brand. Call it brand A. Brands have images and this one is no exception. I am going to ask you to compare this brand with others. The 'image characteristic' I want you to judge it on is its length.

Its competitors are the three lines below it on the card. Which one (of brand B, brand C or brand D) is most similar to the one at the top, brand A? Before reading any further, look at the card. Which one is closest in length to brand A? Brand B is the correct answer of course. It's so obvious that nobody is likely to give any other answer, right? Wrong!

What happens if we get several people together in the same room? Unbeknown to our subject, all of them except the subject are stooges who are going to say what we have told them to say—that brand C is the same length as brand A. Imagine yourself as the subject. Everyone who answers before you has given what you believe is the wrong answer. Now comes your turn. Imagine your dilemma. You break out in a sweat. Your senses are telling you that B is the right answer but all these other people seem so certain that C is correct.

How can this be, you ask yourself. What is wrong with me? Or them? What do you say? Can you resist conforming to the consensus?

This is a classic psychological experiment first performed by Solomon Asch many years ago. He showed that 75 per cent of people in this situation go against their own perception and give the popular response.

The thought process behind this will be familiar to anyone who has ever attended a business meeting. When we see things differently from others, do we always back our own perception and

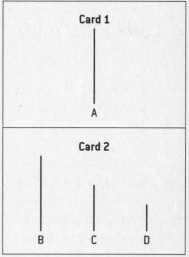

Figure 4.1: Card 1 and card 2.

go public? Or do we play safe and go along with the popular opinion? Very often we play safe. We conform. But how does the conformity so vividly illustrated in Asch's experiment operate outside the laboratory? Advertisers can't organize stooges or enforce conformity in everyday situations. So what relevance does this have for advertising?

To answer this, let's vary the experiment. We have demonstrated that when people make choice decisions, they do so on the basis of two types of information:

- objective evidence, and
- what they think other people think.

Popular opinion can influence not only compliance and conformity but indeed how we perceive reality.

When everything else is equal
In our experiment there was a real and noticeable difference between the brands (the lengths of the lines). When the difference is this obvious it takes a lot of peer pressure to get people to go against their own judgment

and conform to the popular view. What happens if we reduce the differences? After all, in the real world, brands are often virtually identical.

We repeat the experiment, but this time, we have our subject compare the original brand A with three brands which are closer to it in length: brands E, F and G (see Figure 4.2). Which brand (line) on card 2 is the same length as brand A on card 1?

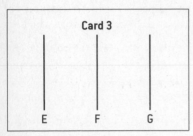

Figure 4.2: Card 3.

In fact, all of them are identical to brand A. But you have to choose, just as you do in the real world when faced with three identical brands (assuming you want to buy the product).

Imagine your surprise when everybody before you picks E (as they have been instructed to do). All the brands look the same to you. You must be missing something, you think. E looks about the same length as A—but so do the other lines. How is everybody else so sure the answer is E and not F or G or all of them?

In this situation people tend not only to conform by giving E as the answer but also to doubt the evidence of their own senses. This is the beginning of the belief in differences between brands.

It makes sense that in this situation the person will naturally have less conviction about the conclusion coming from his/her own senses. When there is less evidence to go on, or the evidence is ambiguous, people are less sure of their perceptions. The less sure they are, the more readily they will go along with other people's 'perceptions'. As the real differences between brands diminish, people rely more and more on outside cues to help them make judgments and decisions. This is when advertising seems to be most effective. When everything else is equal, it takes only a 'feather' to tip the balance and influence the choice.

The bandwagon effect: indicators of the norm

Conformity—being with the 'in' group, not being out of step—is a powerful human motivator. It can make the crucial difference in many brand choice decisions. When there is no real difference between brands or when the choice is not really important to a person, it takes much less than full consensus to influence their judgment. People will go with what they think the majority of other people perceive—the popular view.

This is known as the bandwagon effect. It occurs in situations as diverse as voting in elections and backing favorites in horse races.

Canned laughter, opinion polls and the Billboard Top 100 are all indicators of the norm. They tell us how others are reacting and thereby influence how we are likely to react. They provide signals about what to laugh at, what to think about and what to listen to.

How else do people form their impressions of what is popular or what is the norm? This is where marketing comes into play. TV and radio stations, newspapers and magazines frequently claim to be Number One. There is no doubt that this influences where media buyers and advertisers place their advertising. Some other indicators are even more subtle but nevertheless very powerful.

In the 1950s and 1960s the Billy Graham Crusades made a global name for this most powerful of evangelical preachers. How did he manage to get all these people to 'come forward for God'? Arizona State University researchers infiltrated the Billy Graham organization and revealed that: 'By the time Graham arrives in town and makes his altar call, an army of six thousand wait with instructions on when to come forth at varying intervals to create the impression of a spontaneous mass outpouring'.[2]

In the US, bartenders often 'salt' their tip jars with a few dollar bills at the beginning of the evening. This gives customers the impression that tipping with paper money is the norm.[3]

On telethons, inordinate amounts of time are spent reading out names of people who have donated money. The message is clear: everybody else has donated—what are you doing?

As real differences between choices diminish, people rely more and more on outside cues to help them make decisions. One such cue is what other people are thought to be choosing. Why do we *continue* to drink bottled water? On the streets, in the gyms, even in the movies, so many others are visibly doing it. When everything else is equal, the bandwagon effect may be the feather that tips the balance.

Insecurity: a motivator for conformity

People seem to have a natural aversion to being seen to be out of step with others, or different from the norm. This often leads us to take the safe course. We try to anticipate what others would do and then do the same. This can spare us embarrassment and it can sometimes save us from thinking too hard.

Management in bureaucratic organization is notoriously motivated by this. If a decision-maker does what everybody else would do, then if it turns out wrong, he or she won't be blamed. The personal risk is minimized. As the old saying goes: 'Nobody ever got fired for buying an IBM.'

People conform most when they are insecure. Adolescence is a time of great insecurity and uncertainty. It is no surprise, then, that teenagers are highly conformist. While rebelling against the out-moded values of their parents, they are at the same time the ultimate slaves to conformity—within their own peer group. Today, for reasons as varied as family breakdowns and longer working hours, the peer group has become even greater in influence. Adolescents increasingly define themselves by their friends and their possessions. Perceived popularity in the peer group determines and maintains success in the marketing of a widely diverse range of products such as music, cosmetics, jeans, fashion, sportswear, soft drinks, and radio stations.

Perceived popularity

How popular a brand is thought to be, or how familiar a company is thought to be, is an important dimension of image.

Popularity is a magnet. It attracts. And advertising can enhance its power to attract. Try to think of a single product of which the most popular brand is not advertised. Difficult, isn't it! Does this mean that advertising causes popularity? Not exactly. Advertising makes the brand appear popular. It influences its perceived popularity. The more a brand is advertised, the more popular and familiar it is perceived to be.

Advertising usually delivers specific messages that associate the company or brand with an image dimension or target attribute, such as 'reliability', 'environment-consciousness', 'value for money', 'good taste', 'ease of use'. Sometimes the attribute is 'popularity'. The advertiser may explicitly tell us that the brand in question is popular (e.g. 'British Airways—the world's favorite

Figure 4.3: *A Nivea ad promoting the brand as no. 1.*

airline', 'Budweiser—the most popular beer the world has ever known', 'Nickelodean—the #1 network for kids', 'Quicken—the world's #1 selling financial software').[4] Or the popularity may merely be implied (e.g. 'America spells cheese K-R-A-F-T').

The interesting thing about communicating popularity, however, is that the advertiser doesn't necessarily have to do so in so many words. We as consumers somehow infer that a product is popular simply because it is advertised.[5] The psychological mechanism behind this is known as the *false fame* effect.[6]

A supportive study

Some years ago I conducted a study in which people were asked which brand in various product categories they thought was the most popular.[7] Irrespective of which brand they named, they were then asked why they thought it was the most popular. Thirty-six per cent of the responses took the form 'It must be popular . . . because it is advertised so much'. (Others included 'because it has so much shelf space in the supermarket'.) This was compelling evidence that presence, and especially a sustained advertising presence, translates into an image of popularity.[8] It leaves a perception of popularity in our minds. Is it any wonder that advertisers are prepared to pay to have their brands appear as a 'natural' part of the script in movies, games and TV programs (see Chapter 6, 'Under the radar')? From such appearances our minds tend to infer that the brand must be popular or at least growing in popularity.

Advertising 'side effect'

Unlike other image dimensions (such as reliability, taste, price, etc) this perception of popularity is largely independent of the specific advertising message. In other words, it is a 'side effect'.

The graph in Figure 4.4 shows a brand which posiioned itself largely on the attributes of taste and suitability. Note, however, the effect of advertising on people's perceptions of its popularity. The mere fact of its being advertised significantly increased the proportion of people who associated it with the attribute 'everybody seems to be drinking it'.

So, whether advertising is designed to communicate the image of taste, style, reliability or whatever, it is also likely to increase the perceived popularity and the salience of the brand. This is a 'side effect' of the advertisement that influences which brands come to mind, which brands we think are popular and which brands we include in our consideration set.[9]

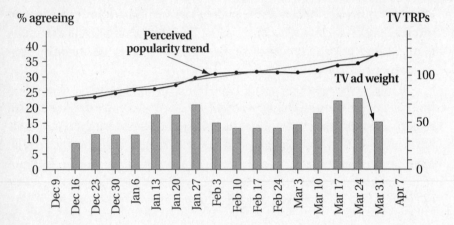

Note: The mere fact of something being advertised can increase its perceived popularity.

Figure 4.4: *Image of increasing popularity—everybody seems to be drinking it.* (*Source: MarketMind*)

Agenda setting

A mechanism behind this side effect is one we have already met. It is 'agenda setting'. The amount of media weight that an issue gets in newspapers, on TV, on websites and so forth indicates to people the degree of importance that the issue should have in their thinking. It sets their mental agenda. In marketing, the agenda that is set is not made up of political issues, but of the brands that are thought to be popular. For 'popular', read 'important'. Our agenda-setting mechanism is not necessarily logical or rational. After all, is a brand advertised because it is important? Or is it important because it is advertised? There is a circularity here which is difficult for logic and rationality to come to grips with. But logic and rationality do not reign here.

Familiarity

A particularly subtle mechanism in this advertising side effect is familiarity. With frequency of exposure of a brand comes a feeling of increased familiarity. Familiarity makes the brand 'stand out' (e.g. on store shelves) and that is important in determining its chances of getting weighed up in the choice decision.[10] However, familiarity not only increases a brand's chances of being noticed and weighed up, but importantly it can also influence brand evaluation and act as a feather that can tip the brand choice balance. This is because, other things being equal, familiarity itself is experienced as a positive.[11]

We feel more comfortable with things that are familiar. Moreover, brands that we see frequently become somehow 'easier on the mind'.[12] We recall them more easily and they spring to mind more readily than brands advertised less often. Crucially, when something springs to our mind readily, our minds assume not only that we must have seen it a lot[13] but that it must be popular and we like it marginally more.[14] Again we meet a circularity that is not logical or rational but is nonetheless real.

Is perceived popularity a plus?

If a brand seems to be popular, are people more likely to buy it? Yes.[15]

Advertising and media weight affect the perceived popularity image of a brand. They affect people's feelings of familiarity with the brand as well as their perceptions of the popularity of the brand. And that, in turn, can affect their buying of the brand.[16]

There is clear evidence that advertising can impact on the perceived popularity of a brand, and there are strong indications that perceived popularity also lends 'legitimacy' to the continued purchasing of a brand—in most circumstances. To understand why, we need to explore what 'having popularity' conveys about a brand.

Perceived popularity conveys notions such as 'a million people can't be wrong'; that the brand is tried and trusted; that we are choosing the best. We have no reason to doubt or question our choice of a popular brand. We are reassured by the knowledge that others use it, that we are swimming with the tide.

So popularity is a positive reinforcer. It helps to reinforce our continued, unquestioning buying of the brand. It makes us less likely to question ourselves as to why we continue to buy that brand. It is a feather on the scales of repeat buying. For advertisers, therefore, it can provide a basis for developing a kind of defense shield, to try to protect the established market share. Promotion of a brand as popular does not rely on persuasion; rather it represents a pre-emptive effort to fend off the inevitable competitors who will try to take over the brand's established mental territory. Used in this 'defensive' role, the popularity image of a brand is more akin to inoculation than to persuasion.

Popularity and the bandwagon effect

As we have seen, people tend to climb on the bandwagon of anything that seems to be gaining in popularity. If a new brand begins to acquire 'high visibility' and be seen as something that 'everyone is talking about' or that 'more and more people are using', this can be an attraction, a 'come-on', a temptation for us to try it too. Facebook, MySpace and YouTube took off exponentially when they passed a critical mass of users. The creation of high visibility can accelerate this take-off point and it has been the basis for many marketing fads over the years such as Ninja Turtles, Batman, 101 Dalmatians, Power Rangers, Teenie Beanie Babies, Tamagotchi virtual pets and so on, not to mention pop stars and politicians.[17] People are tempted to try 'the latest'—the one that everybody is talking about.

Overpopularity

The expression 'fast up . . . fast down' is particularly relevant in this context of creating popularity. If pushed too quickly, or to extremes, perceived popularity can go 'over the top'. The pole of the magnet can reverse and repel us rather than attract us. Advertisers have to guard against creating overpopularity, which can suddenly become a liability for their brand.

This is more often a danger when perceived popularity is used in an offensive role, to get us to try a brand initially, than when it is used defensively, as simply a reinforcer reminding us to buy the brand again. It is no accident that this type of marketing is often associated with products with short lifespans such as movies, children's toys . . . and, perhaps, politicians. As the saying goes, 'One day a rooster, the next a feather duster.'

Using high visibility to persuade us to try a brand is very different from using it to maintain the brand's position. High visibility can help persuade us to try a brand but the success of such a strategy risks being very short-lived. For the brand, it may well be a case of 'fast up . . . fast down' and it may go the way of things such as the Macarena dance craze, Pogs and Jennifer Aniston hair cuts.

Why popularity can become a turn-off

Perceived popularity is not always positive. When too many people use a brand, it risks becoming perceived as common unless its image is carefully managed. It is not just a case of familiarity breeds contempt. Overpopularity can degrade the currency.

Peter De Vries, an American novelist, once said in another context: 'Everyone hates me because I am so universally liked.' Astute advertisers have learnt to guard against this type of reversal. They know that simply giving a brand as much 'hype' as possible in as short a time as possible is not necessarily a good idea. Instead, they try to manage the perceived popularity of the brand as part of a long-term process of image development and ensure that they consolidate a lasting market share.

This is particularly true with brands aimed at adolescents. Adolescents are often prone to rebel—especially against parents and the rest of society. The grunge trend made it cool for youth to resist the notion of cool itself and treat marketing with derision. Since then, teen brands have been increasingly built virally and cautiously.

Also in adult 'social' product categories like wine and beer, if a brand becomes the most popular it risks becoming less and less acceptable to take to other people's places or serving to guests. Why? Since everybody drinks it, it begins to take on an image of commonplace. It becomes too successful. To take a bottle of it to a dinner party can become unthinkable because of what this signals about how you regard your host and the occasion.

Gifts and special occasions

We mark special occasions by the use of things out of the ordinary: a very old bottle of red wine, hiring a stretch limousine, eating out at a fine restaurant. Such symbols mark the specialness of the occasion. Similarly, when we want to express our caring and esteem for others, we give or do something special.

Hallmark cards, for example, reinforced this by using the tag line 'When you care enough to send the very best' and urged us to 'Turn the card over and make sure it's a Hallmark'. Specialness for a brand, once it is achieved, requires careful nurturing and reinforcement in order to maintain it in the face of mass popularity.

Positioning a brand or product as suitable for gift-giving or special occasions can therefore be a successful strategy, but if it becomes too successful it has within it the seeds of its own destruction. Overpopularity can 'devalue the currency'.

Price, exclusivity and popularity

Unless a prestige brand's image is kept up through high price or other image-lifting devices it risks gradual degradation from too much popularity (as seems to have happened to Pierre Cardin and Reebok).

International wine aficionados know that Veuve Clicquot champagne and Grange Hermitage (the premier Australian red wine) are 'popular' in a very different sense from brands like Gallow or Smirnoff. Because of their high price, Grange and Veuve Clicquot are most acceptable, but not very affordable—and this is the point. Like Lexus they have traditionally used price to try to protect the brand from the commonness that would otherwise go with great popularity. The high price and relative unattainability confers a degree of exclusivity, which in effect makes the well-known brand more an aspirational symbol.

Communicating popularity

Many advertising themes have tapped into the desire to conform. These include:

- *Fosters. Famous in Australia. Famous around the world.*
- *Why go with the number two when you can go with the number one in rental cars?*
- *The leader in digital audio . . . Sony.*
- *Nashua—number one in photocopiers.*
- *British Airways—the world's favorite airline.*
- *America's largest discount broker . . . Charles Schwab.*
- *America's number one nail protection . . . Hard-As-Nails.*
- *Oracle. World's #1 Data Base for SAP Applications.*

These are some of the more obvious examples. Others that are more subtle but work on the same principle include:

- *Wouldn't you like to be a Pepper too?* (Dr Pepper)
- *The word is getting around . . . Mitsubishi.*
- *The one to watch . . . Renault.*
- *Life Savers . . . a part of living.*
- *Chevrolet . . . Heartbeat of America.*
- *Join the 'regulars' . . . Kellogg's All-Bran.*
- *Tylenol . . . first choice for patients in pain.*
- *Going Ford is the going thing.*

Summary

As some wit once said, 'Conformity is something you can practice without making a spectacle of yourself.' In making choices we are influenced by two things:

- what we think, and
- what we think other people think.

Conformity is a powerful human motivator. Especially when everything else is equal, it can tip the balance in many brand choice decisions. We are more likely to go against our judgment and conform to the popular view if there are few real differences between brands. As the real differences become negligible, we rely more and more on outside cues to help us make our decisions. The more insecure we feel, the more likely we are to be influenced by others.

The more a brand is advertised or seen embedded in TV shows, games or movies, the more popular and familiar it is perceived to be. Popularity is like a magnet. Advertising can enhance its power to attract. We as consumers somehow infer that something is popular simply because it is advertised. If pushed too quickly or to extremes, perceived popularity can go 'over the top'. The pole of the magnet can reverse and repel rather than attract us. Overpopularity tends to 'devalue the currency'.

5 THE ADVERTISING MESSAGE: OBLIQUE AND INDIRECT

42.7% of all statistics are made up on the spot.

Anonymous graffiti

Like graffiti, advertising has moved a long way from simply imparting direct information messages. Advertising and graffiti often have succinct, clever messages that are not direct statements of information. Consider how much more powerful the above statement is compared to one that urges us to 'Be careful of quoted statistics because they can be easily fabricated'. The message that we take away from it is the same thing even though the words don't contain that literal message. Indirect forms of communication sometimes register a point with more impact.

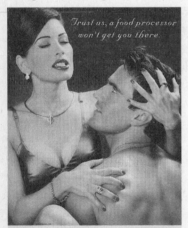

Trust us, a food processor won't get you there.

JEWELRY.COM

Figure 5.1: *Valentine's Day ad for Jewelry.com. Oblique communication can sometimes register a point with more impact. (By Robert Chandler & Partners of Los Angeles)*

For example, an ad that shows a Volkswagen Tourag towing a Boeing 747 along a runway does not need any words; it communicates very effectively that 'VW is compact but capable'. Or consider the print ad for Jewelry. com (Figure 5.1) used during the Valentine's Day buying season. These advertising messages are oblique and indirect. Oblique communication can sometimes register a point with more impact.

In management boardrooms advertisers traditionally ask their advertising agencies questions like: 'Are we getting our message across?'

or 'What message are buyers taking out of our ad?' This is based on the assumption that advertising is meant to be informational.

Usually consumers are asked something like: 'What was the ad trying to say to you?' or 'What was the message that the advertiser intended?' Even with the above type of indirect message, this process can provide valuable feedback to advertisers and quickly tell them if their commercial is communicating what they want it to communicate; if the commercial is an informational one, that is. However, the more the advertising moves away from *direct* message communication towards oblique message communication the less this makes sense. Entertainment commercials, including image, musical or drama commercials, are often oblique communications and very different from lecture-style commercials.

We mentally process 'image' ads, such as those for Honda, Nike, beer or perfume, quite differently from informational ads, such as those announcing this week's special at Macy's or Joe Blow's Valentine's Day sale. Indeed, it is difficult with many ads (especially image ads) to work out what message they intend to convey. Advertisers themselves find these ads the most difficult to evaluate, largely because there is little point in asking people what message they get from them.

There is a very real difference between advertising that has a clear, spoken, unambiguous message and advertising that is oblique, especially when it is more akin to drama or entertainment. We mentally process different types of ads in very different ways.

If you think of the current advertising for various image-advertised brands, you may find that the ad or the message, or both, is difficult to recall. What is missing from some of these ads is the sense that someone is trying to tell you something directly. This does not mean that they are ineffective—just that they do not work by way of clearly elaborated messages.

Australia has a brand of non-alcoholic drink called Clayton's which was traditionally positioned successfully with the tag line 'Clayton's—the drink you have when you're not having a drink'. Clayton's entered the vocabulary as a name for a 'social lubricant' substitute for alcohol acceptable for drinking on occasions when others are consuming alcohol. It predated Perrier bottled water which positioned similarly and other acceptable substitutes that have overtaken it today (like lime and bitters, etc) but the word 'Clayton's' remains linguistically generic amongst

Australians to mean 'the one you're having when you're not having one'. Hence many image ads could be said to have a Clayton's message i.e. the message you're having when you're not having a message.

What is a message?

Usually in image ads we are not being lectured to. Instead we are experiencing life or being entertained—but in the process, information gets in. If someone tells us 'Muhammad Ali was tough', that is a message. But what if, instead of telling us that Muhammad Ali was tough, you show an old video clip of him beating the hell out of someone? Answer: we get the same message! Yet if you asked 'What was that clip trying to communicate to you?' we would probably think the question quite odd. It is not obvious that the film clip is trying to communicate anything to us. Even so, after seeing it we would definitely be inclined to agree with the statement, 'Muhammad Ali was tough'.

In other words you get the same message. But it doesn't seem like a message. It's a Clayton's message . . . the message you're getting when you're not getting a message. Yet the impression, that Muhammad Ali was tough, is communicated just the same.

So, while advertisers frequently use *message take-out* (a.k.a. *message take-away*) as a measure of an ad's success, it is not necessary that consumers be able to parrot back the message for an ad to be working. Communication of impressions can be just as effective as communication of facts.

Window on the mind

Let me ask you a question: How many windows are there in your home? Answer before you read on.

Now think about the mental process you went through to retrieve this information. Did you visualize each room in turn and add up all the windows? If so, you are now more aware of a way in which our minds arrive at information other than by simple memory retrieval: by re-processing other information that we have mentally filed away.

The stored information may be verbal or visual. We put these previously unconnected bits and pieces together in our minds and arrive at something new. Sometimes the 'something new' is another piece of information (like the number of windows there are in your home). At other times, however, it may be a new attitude or a new feeling about something.

As consumers, we often construct our attitudes to brands out of stored information in this way. The attributes or images that have become associated with the brand may have lodged in our memory without ever having been part of a verbal message. They may have originated in visual images from advertising or experiential learning or input from other people. It is therefore a mistake to think about advertising communication solely in terms of conscious message take-out.

Ask yourself who you think is the typical user of Apple Mac, of Harley-Davidson or of Volvo? While you don't have a complete answer, you are not without impressions either. For example, do you think the typical owner of a Volvo would be more or less conservative than the owner of a Ford? More or less affluent? Most people would agree that the Volvo owner is likely to be more conservative and more affluent than the Ford owner. Yet they have not acquired those pieces of information through any direct message.

Advertising for many product categories, such as soft drink, beer, confectionery, or perfume is dominated by ads that appear to have very little message. Image ads convey associations and are totally different from informational ads that communicate 'news' (such as one that communicates the existence of a new product or one that announces what's on special this week at Safeway supermarkets). Associations are like individual windows. Images are like the number of windows. The number of windows in your home is not a piece of information that someone has communicated to you in a message. It is not directly stored in your memory. But you have the bits and pieces to generate it, nevertheless. In this way we can learn things or know things or develop attitudes without being particuarly aware of the process. There is nothing necessarily manipulative or devious about this. It happens all the time. It is part of life.

Learning without awareness

What is missing from some communications is the sense of someone trying to tell us something or trying to communicate a message. As we saw earlier this does not mean that they are ineffective—it is just that the learning is not by way of someone clearly elaborating messages.

Some psychologists have labeled this type of indirect learning 'learning without involvement'.[1] Others have called it 'implicit memory'[2] and still others have called it 'incidental learning' or 'learning without awareness'.[3] Strictly speaking this latter is inaccurate. It is not that people are unaware but rather that the 'focus of processing' is on something else in the communication. Our attention is focused on something other than the message per se.

In the venerable TV series *Sesame Street*, messages are embedded in entertainment. Messages such as 'cooperation' and 'sharing' are communicated through drama and song. Learning the alphabet or learning to count is not a chore for *Sesame Street* viewers, but an experience. These skills are effectively conveyed in an entertaining kaleidoscope of sounds and visuals.

We can easily process what we see and hear around us with the mind on autopilot and without any intent to learn. With repetition we can learn skills, information, image associations or almost anything by this implicit learning—provided it is not inconsistent with what we already know or believe.

We have thus discovered yet another reason why people find it hard to analyze introspectively the effects advertising has on them. Sometimes advertisements do not obviously impart information. Especially with ads based on image, emotion or drama there is a lessened sense of someone transmitting information—indeed if there is any sense of it at all. Such ads may communicate mood more than message; feelings rather than words.

Inconsistency—our protective shield

The mind on autopilot easily registers the identity of objects, people and events by a simple template-matching process and it registers or learns about relationships between them.[4] It makes sense that the mind's eye might also have some sort of protection device when our mind is processing like this on autopilot—a mechanism to alert us if the ID of something is not quite right, or our interpretation of the events is uncertain. And indeed, it does. We have a kind of inner alarm that, when activated, switches our minds to more conscious, explicit processing and the potential intruder gets the full focal beam of our attention.[5] As a leading researcher commented, 'When things match . . . the stream of consciousness flows smoothly . . . There may be fish in the stream of consciousness, but when an elephant swims by we sit up and take notice.'[6]

By switching on the full beam of attention, the learning situation is changed from implicit to explicit and any inconsistency is likely to invite rejection or reinterpretation. The importance of this is that, just as a person under hypnosis will not accept a directive that conflicts with their own values, so too our minds won't passively accept things that are clearly inconsistent with our existing beliefs or our knowledge of the world.[7] Communications that violate this principle risk being ineffective because they tend to trigger this 'intruder alarm'.[8]

Memory and association

As we saw earlier in the chapter, the number of windows in your home is not a message or a piece of information that someone has communicated to you. It is not directly stored as a piece of information in your memory. But you have the bits and pieces to generate it, nevertheless. Once again: How many windows are there in your home? That was quick! You didn't have to think about it this time; you already had the answer, because it is now stored in its own 'slot' in your memory in a more readily accessible form. Having put the component bits and pieces together, you can now access that piece of information much more quickly and efficiently at any time you want by accessing it directly. You don't have to go through the process. You have enhanced its 'availability'.

Just like a commercial, this chapter firstly helped evoke in you the necessary images or pieces of information to let you go through the process of arriving at that summary piece of information. Having arrived at it, you stored it yourself as a new piece of information in a memory slot of its own.

In the consumer world, what gets stored in memory slots like this is not just information. It may be an attitude, a judgment, a position or a conclusion. But once formed and stored, these things are more readily accessible and hence more available to influence future buying decisions—especially those types of decisions that tend to be made 'on the fly'.[9]

The all-important effect of a relatively subtle ad may rest on its ability to build the right visual or mood associations for a brand and lock them into memory; to put those associations on the brand's attribute agenda. Rather than communicating directly by a specific verbal message, the ad may be communicating indirectly, by associational imagery.

It is worth repeating that, strictly speaking, this is not learning without awareness. It is not that people are unaware but rather that the 'focus of processing' is on something else in the communication rather than the 'message'.

Learning by association

You visit a city for the first time, say Paris, and go to the top of the Eiffel Tower. What an experience! What a view! What is the view trying to tell you? What sort of a silly question is that? It is not trying to communicate anything. Views, just like some commercials, come across as an experience rather than an articulated message. Nevertheless, after just one or two exposures you may come to permanently associate a city with a wonderful visual experience. This splendid view is now higher up on the agenda of attributes that you associate with that city. An image can be built without any specific message. The process is not necessarily logical but it is real and natural, nevertheless.

In a sense it could be said that you have learnt much the same information as if you had simply been told 'Paris is a beautiful city'. In that case you would have received a clear verbal message. However, two things are different:

- You have learnt the information experientially instead of verbally. And this means that you probably have a much richer or deeper sense of it.
- You have learnt the information 'without awareness' i.e. without awareness of being taught something. There is no sense of any intended message.

This is not new. Years ago, the psychologist Charles Osgood demonstrated that when a given adjective is repeatedly paired with a given noun, the 'meaning' of the noun, as measured by a scale called 'the semantic differential', undergoes change—in the direction of the adjective.[10] For example, when the noun 'snake' is repetitively paired with the adjective 'slimy', we begin to think of snakes as slimy creatures (even though they aren't). Little is made of such findings today but the phenomenon seems to underlie much of the process by which image advertising works.

Image advertising's effects

To 'play back' the message from an ad we need to be able to articulate our experience—to describe what we see as the message. As an index of an ad's effectiveness, this playback (or message take-out) is more appropriate for ads that are designed to communicate 'news' about a brand.

For the more subtle types of ads our inability to play back much in the way of a message does not, in itself, mean that the ad is not working (though it may not be). How then, you may ask, does anyone detect these more subtle effects? How do advertisers know that any such effects are happening? How can the invisible be made visible?

The answer is, by inference—by looking at how the ad has influenced our image of, attitude to or behavior regarding the brand. We would be unable to see an invisible man but if he put on visible clothes we would know he was there. In the same way we cannot observe these invisible advertising effects directly but we can infer their existence by observing other things, such as:

- changes in brand image dimensions, as measured by questions such as 'Which brand do you most associate with …? (safety/best taste/ most popular, etc)'
- changes in brand attitudes, as measured by questions such as 'How do you feel about brand X overall?', 'How much do you like it?'
- changes in behavior, as measured by changes in sales and market share.

With image commercials, the invisible can be made visible by measuring the degree of association with image attributes; the degree to which the image feature appears in the brand's attribute agenda and how high up it is on that agenda. These measurements are often taken indirectly and calibrated in the form of belief statements about the brand (e.g. 'liked by everyone', 'best quality', etc).

A fairly typical image-building strategy is to make an ad (like those that were traditionally used for Coke, Fosters, etc) that featured the brand in a range of enjoyable situations. Blend in a mood soundtrack with appropriate lyrics and then serve with generous quantities of exposure. Again the important point to note about this type of advertising is that there is a lessened sense of someone transmitting information—indeed if there is any sense of it at all.

Communication by association

Some years ago a new brand was launched into a frequently purchased snack food category. The TV ad was musically based with a very catchy jingle. The words made musical reference to the glowing attributes of the new brand. Message take-out was measured by asking a random sample

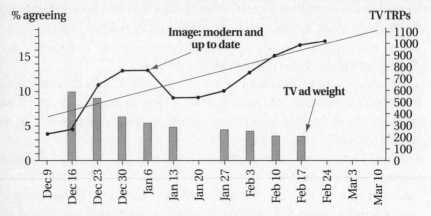

Note: Even though 'modern and up to date' was not part of the audio message that people 'took out', the association with this attribute is clearly affected by advertising.

Figure 5.2: *Image effects revealed—snack food product. (Source: MarketMind)*

of people what the message was. They responded with the attributes that were verbalized in the jingle. These were: 'better/best brand' and 'this brand is good for you'.

A subsidiary objective of the ad was to have the brand seen as 'modern and up-to-date' and 'a brand of today'. This was not expressed in words but was to be inferred from other pieces of information as well as the ad's tone, pace and fast-cut visuals. There was very little playback of this attribute. While some people said the ad was trying to communicate newness, almost no one mentioned 'modern', 'up-to-date' or 'a brand of today'.

However, as the graph in Figure 5.2 shows, a growing number of people were positioning the brand in their minds in association with this attribute. When they were asked: 'Which brand or brands do you most associate with the description "a modern, up-to-date brand"?', the associative linkages created by the ad became visible. The effect was more evident the longer the ad continued to be aired.[11]

The increased association of the brand with this attribute was also linked with a significant improvement in overall attitude towards the brand and, to a lesser extent, increases in market share. Any advertiser who relied only on conscious message take-out as a measure of this ad's effectiveness would be severely misled. People could articulate that the ad was trying to communicate 'better/best brand' and 'good for you'— the message of the jingle—but the 'modern and up-to-date' message was simply inferred. It was a Clayton's message. Yet it was in no way hidden; it was simply communicated visually rather than verbally.

Do you think in words or pictures?

When we are asked what message an ad is trying to communicate to us, the result is an index more than anything else of the success of the verbal communication in the ad. However, words are not the only way that we experience ads.

What does a television commercial communicate to you? Pictures, words or feelings? When you listen to a radio commercial, what goes on inside your head? Do you experience pictures or words? Or do you just experience the overall *feeling* of the commercial message?

Clearly, the answer depends to some extent on the type of commercial. An ad for Hawaii is vastly different from an ad for this week's specials at Safeway. But we now know from psychological research that different people tend to favor different modes of thinking. In other words, we differ in the way we mentally process information.[12]

You can start to get a feel for this by answering these questions:

- Do you think in words or pictures?
- Do you recall names better than faces?
- When you can't decide which way a word is spelt, does it help to write it down both ways and then choose the right one?
- When you hear a radio commercial, what do you experience? Pictures or words?
- When you remember a TV commercial, what do you remember first? Is it visual or verbal?

Compare your answers with those of your partner or a close friend. Most people are surprised to learn that the other person's answers are not the same as their own. We assume, without any real basis, that other people think the same way we do. Even advertisers tend to base their strategies on this assumption.

Individual differences

Over the years I have asked many groups of people the question: 'Do you think in pictures or words?' About a third say unequivocally that they think in pictures. Usually somewhat less than a third say unhesitatingly that they think in words. And the rest say either that they think both ways, or that they can't answer the question.

The proportions vary from group to group but the really interesting thing is the reaction of the 'word thinkers' to the 'picture thinkers' and vice versa. The strict picture thinkers become positively astounded with those who say they think in words and not pictures. 'How can you think in words?' they ask disbelievingly. 'How can you possibly think in pictures?' some of the word thinkers throw back at them, not so much as a retort but in equal puzzlement and disbelief.

So even in an informal research exercise like this, it becomes readily apparent that people are not in agreement on the way in which their basic mental processes work. There are very definitely those who believe they are primarily visualizers (picture thinkers) and those who believe they are primarily verbalizers (word thinkers).

The significance of whether we think in words or in pictures comes when we retrieve the commercial or its message from memory—say at the point of sale when we recall that we have seen a commercial for the brand. Do we hear the ad in our mind? Do we see in words what it said? Or do we retrieve the visual images or impressions that are associated with it?

The cues that advertisers use at the point of sale, such as pack design, shelf talkers, slogans, and so on, are designed to remind us of the verbal messages or to retrigger the visual associations that have been communicated by the ad.[13]

Summary

What is missing from some ads is the sense of someone trying to tell you something or communicate a message. This does not mean that such ads are ineffective—just that they do not work by way of clearly elaborated messages.

We mentally process image ads and visual experiences quite differently from informational ads or messages. We can learn or know things without being particularly aware of the process or the result. There is nothing necessarily manipulative or devious about this. It happens all the time. It is not that we are unaware of this in any subliminal sense but rather that our 'focus of processing' is often on something else in the communication rather than a verbal message per se. We can learn skills, information, image associations, or almost anything by this incidental learning—provided it is not inconsistent with what we already know or believe.

This is yet another reason why we find it hard to analyze the effects advertising has on us. As consumers we use the many bits and pieces which we receive from advertising, experiential learning or other people. They are put together as information, attitudes, judgments, positions or conclusions. Once stored in their own memory slots, these are more readily accessible to us and more available to influence other related decision-making. They have the potential to influence our future buying decisions—especially those that tend to be made 'on the fly'.

6 'UNDER THE RADAR': PAID PRODUCT PLACEMENT

As I pointed out in Chapter 3, advertisers have little need of subliminal techniques because there are other methods of advertising that don't provoke the same controversy or social concern. Fears of subliminal effects have been grossly overblown, while subtle effects that are not so 'hidden' from consciousness have more impact.

There can be advantages for advertisers in communicating their message obliquely or indirectly outside the full glare of attention, as we saw in the previous chapter. Despite a lessened sense of a message, we get the message just the same but it is less likely to trigger counter-argument. In a sense, it goes under the radar.

In this chapter I look at another form of advertising that goes under the radar: that of advertisers paying (either in cash or in kind) for their brands to be embedded in the storyline of movies, games, TV programs, song lyrics, music videos or books.

Sometimes called 'brand placement', 'product placement', or 'program integrations', this practice has grown explosively, driven along not so much by a need for stealth but as a reaction by advertisers to the threat posed by our newfound ability to fast forward through the TV ad breaks.

The scramble

When digital video recorders enabled us to fast forward through the ads, advertisers became more limited in their ability to engage us at a conscious level by using conventional advertising. This, along with a proliferation in the number of TV channels, was taking the 'mass' out of mass media audiences. Advertisers realized that they desperately needed to find other ways to reach consumers with their brand messages.

If consumers could increasingly screen out conventional TV ads by fast forwarding, what else could advertisers use to provide support for their brands? Companies scrambled for other ways to reinforce and defend their market positions.

The alternatives

One alternative was to change the method of advertising delivery. That is, delivering the same or similar video material via other media such as the cinema, the web (through YouTube, for example) and mobile devices (see Chapter 25: 'The web: advertising in a new age'). Another was to deliver the ads vicariously, for example, by viral email, and hoping that intriguing ads would be forwarded to friends thereby multiplying exposures.

Still another alternative was providing incentives for brands to appear in programs—product placement. For quite some years advertisers regarded this as very limited. Placing the brand in programs could help keep the brand in front of people's eyeballs to maintain its 'top of mind' presence. However, this was regarded as an inadequate substitute for conventional TV advertising as it did not carry any advertising messages. So, while there was a choice advertisers still preferred to spend their ad budgets on conventional TV advertising.

Finding new alternatives to match the effects of conventional advertising proved difficult and left advertisers with little choice but to make the best of what they had. That meant embracing and exploring more effective use of these things called paid product placements as well as making the best of any communication to be had when ads were fast forwarded.

Communication in fast forward

Importantly, to avoid the ads we don't skip them so much as we zip them—we speed them up. This difference is important. It is ironic that to avoid the ads, we end up watching and paying attention to sped up ad frames.[1] We are exposed to a stream of rapidly flashing ad content that is something akin to subliminal speed exposure. As we saw in Chapter 3, this is not something to be *too* worried about because the *exaggerated* claims made for subliminal exposure were a hoax from the beginning.

However, zipped ads are not completely without effect. They are at least akin to driving past a billboard or flicking through ads in a magazine. We know from the divided attention experiments earlier that the 'learning without awareness' effects are often quite small. An advantage that they do have, however, is that they fly under the defensive radar—we don't think of fast forwarded ads as having any effect on us at all.

Despite this, it has been shown that when an ad is already familiar to us from seeing it at normal speed, then playing it in fast forward:

- reminds us of the brand;
- reminds us of previously watched instances of the ad seen at normal speed;[2] and
- fleetingly retriggers a reminder of the emotional reaction we had to the ad previously.[3]

Fleeting and limited though such reminders are, they have a reinforcement effect that can still influence brand choice, because as we saw in Chapter 1:

- even a weak effect can be a feather and swing the balance of choice if everything else is equal;
- furthermore, small feathers can build over time, through repetition, into a bigger, cumulative effect (just like kids grow imperceptibly by a tiny amount each day).

So, while the effects of fast forwarded ads are small compared to normal-speed ads that manage to successfully engage us at a more fully conscious level, they still have some value to the advertiser. Advertisers have been slow to exploit this effect but as with paid product placements they have begun to find there is more to them than first meets the eye. Both are capable of doing more than simply reinforcing brand awareness. This is particularly true of product placement.

The history of paid product placement

Commercial products and brands have always appeared in movies and TV shows but until the last decade they were rare and often *not* paid for. Today, with the release of each new blockbuster movie and each new television episode comes another chance to play 'spot the paid product placements'. What's new is the rush of advertisers who are now willing to pay for brands to make appearances and the openness of producers to accepting, and indeed soliciting, these deals.

What is surprising is that it took so long for advertisers en masse to embrace product placement. The potential for movies and other media to influence what we do, what we wear and what we think has long been evident. When Clark Gable appeared without an undershirt in the 1934 film *It Happened One Night*, sales of undershirts fell by 40 per cent. In 1982, when Reece's Pieces confectionery was used to attract the loveable alien in the movie *E.T.*, sales of the brand increased by 65 per cent. Ray-Ban sunglasses claimed a 55 per cent gain in sales following prominent use by Tom Cruise in 1983's *Risky Business*, and in 1997 sales of Ray-Ban Predator 2 sunglasses are said to have tripled after Tommy Lee Jones and Will Smith wore them in the movie *Men in Black*. As a final example, when the 2005 movie *Sideways* eulogized pinot noir wine, sales of that variety in the USA shot up 22 per cent.

The wonder is that more brands and companies didn't seek out opportunities to *buy* into these types of appearances earlier, especially given the low cost of product placement compared to conventional advertising.

Product placement remained rare for many years even though it existed in the very early days of movie making. In the 1950s movie *The African Queen* starring Humphrey Bogart as the gin-boat captain, the company manufacturing Gordon's gin was said to have paid to ensure that the gin in the movie would be theirs. And in the movie *Superman II*, Philip Morris paid to have the truck that Superman destroyed be a Marlboro truck.[4] However, even by the time the 1990s came around paid product placements were still relatively rare.

Some suspicion prevailed amongst advertisers that many of the early success stories were hyped and indeed it was acknowledged that not all product placements worked. For example, Coors, which also appeared in the movie *E.T.*, reported that its appearance had no significant impact.[5] What gradually became clear, however, was that the success stories were not just exaggerated hype and that even if sales impact was not seen immediately, product placement did represent opportunity for advertisers to build, and not just reinforce, brand reputation.

Despite this, product placement was still ignored by many advertisers even as late as the early noughties. It was, however, becoming considerably easier to spot product placements in movies and TV shows. Nowhere were they more obvious than in reality TV shows (such as *The Apprentice*, *Survivor*, *Big Brother* and *American Idol*) and in the James Bond movies (which have always featured a proliferation of brands including Aston Martin, BMW, Motorola, Microsoft, Omega, and Bollinger).

When advertisers opened the door on the new world of product placement they discovered that it had more power than they had anticipated. They discovered more about how product placement really can work.

How product placement works

The main reason why advertisers were slow to embrace product placement was its inability to communicate *explicit* messages. The effect of brand appearances that placed the brand on an existing prop (e.g. an Apple logo on the notebook computer sitting on the TV newsreader's desk) was thought to be confined to reminding consumers of brands they were already aware of. It was acknowledged that advertisers could increase the sense of brand 'presence' (read 'brand importance')—but without any explicit message, what else could they do?

Product placement can, in fact, work much more broadly and it does so through a variety of mechanisms including implicit image association, reinforcement of familiarity, agenda setting and perceived popularity

Implicit image association

Our minds process movies and TV programs as experiences. We process such experiences quite differently to the way in which we process informational ads or messages. Even without any explicit message, the belief that Paris is a beautiful city can be built up from image associations such as experiencing the view from the Eiffel Tower or the Champs Elysées. So too can an image of a brand be influenced implicitly by images associated with it. Being seen in the same context as celebrities, for example, means that celebrity associations are likely to wash over onto the brand.

Because a brand can absorb its context associations despite no explicit message, advertisers are now using product placement to convey subtle associations and to communicate implicit messages. Brands, like people, are judged by the company they keep.

Research shows that the brand not only absorbs the image of celebrities but also absorbs the image of the program in which it appears.[6] Simply integrating the brand into the editorial content of a program (like *American Idol*) can have a significant effect on brand image. And as we watch more episodes of the program where the brand appears, the brand image tends to become more in agreement with the program image.

Additionally with product placement, when a brand appears in the same context as a celebrity, it is the nearest thing to an implied endorsement by that celebrity. So implicit image association works with product placement as it does with oblique and indirect messages in conventional advertising. It doesn't need any explicit, direct message to convey associations.

Reinforcement of familiarity

It has long been recognized that product placement can impact on our sense of familiarity with a brand. We feel more comfortable with things we are familiar with because, as we saw in Chapter 3, familiarity itself is experienced as positive.[7] Familiarity also has all sorts of indirect effects. It makes a brand 'stand out' on store shelves.[8] It even improves our tolerance of repetition for the brand's regular advertising because we seem to cut it more slack and tolerate ad repetition better with brands that are familiar.[9] Brands that remain unfamiliar are at higher risk of alienating us when they repeat their ads. So this is an important mechanism of broader impact for paid product placements.

Agenda setting

Agenda setting is yet another reason why product placement works. As we have seen in earlier chapters, the media *don't* tell us what to think. But they do tell us what to think *about*! They set the mental agenda. Paid appearances in the media raise the brand up on our agenda and increase the likelihood that it will appear in our consideration set and influence our choice.[10] Especially in parity choice situations (i.e. when everything else is equal) it has been shown that this can add a decisive feather (in both high- and low-involvement situations).[11]

Perceived popularity

A final reason why product placement works is the magnet effect that we met in Chapter 4. Popularity attracts. The perception of popularity, unlike other image dimensions (reliability, taste, price, etc), is a 'side effect' that is largely independent of any specific advertising message. Movies, TV programs, books, cartoons and pop songs don't tell us what to think but we infer from them what is popular and what we think other people think. Hence the product placement process is subtle and works partly by indicating what's popular or what's becoming 'cool'.

Each program appearance of a leading brand (like Coke, Nike or BMW) reaffirms its star status and helps maintain that leadership image. If smaller brands can afford the price of consistent appearances in this media limelight, they too may propel themselves into 'rising star' status.

Subtlety: under the radar

Paid product placements range from prominent to subtle.[12] For example, a Pepsi vending machine seen in Tom Hanks's living room in the film *Big* might be expected to be better remembered than something more subtle, say a Pepsi logo that appears in the background of a scene. Understandably, advertisers equated the effectiveness of the product placement with the likelihood that consumers would remember seeing the brand in the movie or the program. So, particularly in the early days of product placement, advertisers sought highly prominent placements. This form of thinking is now under challenge.

Where a product placement is prominent it usually means it will be more obvious to viewers that it is a paid appearance. In which case, there is more chance we will process it as an ad. When it is subtle, we don't; we process it as just another experience. To fly under the radar, product placement requires subtle positioning rather than conspicuous focus.

As we saw earlier, provided our defenses aren't triggered the effects (on brand image, on familiarity and on perceived popularity) can take place by implicit learning through associative memory without any explicit message. It doesn't matter whether we actually *remember* seeing the brand appear in the program.[13] Memory of the appearance is not necessary to influence our subsequent choice behavior.[14]

Indeed, remembering seeing the brand in the program seems to be relatively *un*important and there is evidence that product placement may have more effect on us when we don't become overly aware of it.[15] This makes sense. As we saw in Chapter 5, oblique and indirect messages are less likely to trigger defense mechanisms or counter-arguing. When there is less sense of receiving a message, there is less sense of persuasion intent and less to trigger our defenses. Nothing shows up on the radar for us to defend against—or to become defensive about.

To the extent that product appearances fly 'under the radar' our mental defenses are quiescent. Accordingly, product placements may be most effective when they position the brand subtly and they fit right in as a natural part of the program rather than overly prominent appearances.

Extensions of product placement

A brand that arbitrarily pops up in a program without linking much to the storyline risks triggering the reaction 'Ah ha . . . that's a blatant ad'. Such realization interrupts the viewer's immersion in the program and can detract from it. The mind dislikes mental interruptions so brand appearances in a program need to avoid being seen as a proxy 'ad break'.

This interruption annoyance effect of course applies to traditional ad breaks themselves. While watching a TV show about the pyramids, we are less likely to hit the fast forward button if the ad break goes directly to a 'Tour Egypt' ad for Harvey World Travel than something entirely unrelated like McDonald's. That's why advertisers usually try to place conventional ads in programs where they have at least some loose fit with the program content. Imagine, though, if the whole thing could be turned on its head and advertisers could cut deals with programs to modify the program's storyline and so engineer a better fit? It could enhance immediate engagement with the ad and probably minimize the likelihood of the viewer fast forwarding it. But how could this happen? Well, stand by because it is already happening.

Such a deal, for example, was engineered in 2006 by the Tease brand of body spray in the long running, popular Australian 'soap opera' series *Home & Away*. The program contracted with the Tease brand to create a new character in the series who would engage in flirtatious behavior. The idea was that the behavior of the new character would implicitly exemplify the positioning of the Tease brand. As part of the deal, the program would cut from these segments (starring 'Belle', who was the tease character) to commercial breaks with ads for the Tease brand.[16]

So, while the mind balks at interruptions, these deals can create a more natural 'tie-in' between the program content and the ad break. By lessening the sense of discontinuity such alterations exploit the fact that the mind embraces segues but dislikes interruptions. This is a potentially powerful way not only to reduce the likelihood of viewers fast forwarding, but also to enhance the effectiveness of the ad that appears in the ad break.

Summary

Subtlety is more powerful than subliminality and it is this subtlety of product placement that is blurring the distinction between programming and advertising. When brands pay to embed themselves in the media, such paid appearances are often indistinguishable from natural appearances.

Today, product placement is everywhere, even in books, cartoons, and games. Nobody is surprised any more that the media seek 'incentives' for allowing brands to make appearances in programs and editorial content. Just as journalistic war reporting has become 'embedded' with the military, so with product placement has brand advertising become 'embedded' with the mass media.

When companies make undisclosed payments to convey implicit messages and push their brands into the public's awareness, this is called 'product placement'. When record companies do the same thing and pay radio stations to play their records, it is prosecuted as payola! While regulators 'look the other way' as to 'who is paying the piper', we are accelerating down a slippery slope.[17] A mode of influence is emerging with product placement that has the potential to go well beyond what advertising has exercised previously.

7 SILENT SYMBOLS AND BADGES OF IDENTITY

Everybody repeat after me . . . 'We are all individuals.'

Anon.

In America wearing a Miami Dolphins sweater or a Green Bay Packers T-shirt makes a statement. In the UK the teams have very different names like Arsenal, Newcastle or Manchester United while in Australia, the teams that fans identify with have names like Collingwood, Sydney Swans or Brisbane Lions. Such names are brand symbols. Wearing them lets us, as individuals, make a statement about *our* association and *our* identification with that team.

Similarly, when we choose to consume a Perrier or a Pepsi or pull on

Figure 7.1: *Michael Schumacher for Omega.*

a pair of Calvins or Levis, whether we are aware of it or not, we can be making a statement about ourselves, though in a much more subtle way. In the brands that we choose, our consumption behavior goes beyond the simple 'quenching of thirst' or selecting of 'something to wear'. Football supporters don't wear the team cap and sweater just to keep them warm and nor do people wear designer clothes simply for that reason. There is much more to it. Our choice of brands can become an expression of self identity.

We have become accustomed to celebrities such as Paris Hilton, Tiger Woods, Charlize Theron, Brad Pitt, David Beckham and the like being used to endorse brands like Nike, Pepsi, Tag Heuer, Motorola, Loréal and Raymond Weil. When a brand is seen being consumed by these people, it becomes more than a brand—it can become a symbol of association with that person and with an 'in group'.

By consuming and displaying brand symbols which are associated with these entities we:

- reinforce in our minds our identification and closeness with the person or group they stand for; and
- make an expression of our own identity—a subtle statement or symbol to the outside world about ourselves.

In this way the act of consuming a brand can become a way for us to express our identity—who we are, what we are like, what our concerns are, what we enjoy doing, what we value, who our friends are and so on.

Look closely at the advertising slogans below. Consider the subtle but unmistakable allusions to how the brand reflects your identity . . . as part of a group, and how consuming that brand expresses something about you:

- *You don't have to be rich, just smart.* (Ikea)
- *Our country, our truck.* (Chevrolet Silverado)
- *What are you made of?* (Tag Heuer)
- *Join the first team . . . reach for Winston.*
- *It's More you.* (More cigarettes)
- *You've come a long way baby.* (Virginia Slim cigarettes)
- *The best a man can get . . . Gillette.*
- *Canada Dry Ginger Ale . . . for when your tastes grow up.*
- *Pepsi . . . Generation Next.*
- *Wheaties . . . Breakfast of champions.*
- *The most unforgettable women in the world wear Revlon.*
- *Wouldn't you like to be a Pepper too?* (Dr Pepper)

Above all, choosing these brands becomes a way of sharing, of participating, of representing or identifying with something. There is something about being part of a group. Even mental membership has its privileges!

Expression and self-presentation
One can identify privately with someone or something without needing to tell anybody else. In this sense identification can be a very private thing.

The flip side, however, is that very often we want to signal our feeling of identification—who we are and what we stand for—to the outside world. We do this non-verbally in our self-presentation and self-expression. We use symbols, mannerisms, gestures, idioms, flags, etc, to communicate non-verbal messages to the outside world. We can do this by displaying symbols (wearing Levis, Lee or Calvins; driving a Lexus, a Landcruiser or a VW Beetle), or using products that are symbolically associated with our favorite entities (Omega, Nike, L'Oréal).

In the US, more students wear their college T-shirts on the Monday following a football game when the college team wins (especially after a big victory) than when it loses.[1] The motivation is not simply the desire to bask in reflected glory. It is related to the reasons people wear branded jeans, designer clothes and branded sportswear. The broader, underlying motivation is one of personal identity and participation in (or association with) a larger, symbolic group.

Identification and conformity
As a motivator, identification is to be distinguished from conformity. Conformity is the need to avoid standing out from the crowd. It is partly based on the fear of being different: the need to go along with the ideas or choices of others for fear of the consequences that might happen otherwise.

Identification is a very different flip side to this. It is very similar to, but at the same time very different from, conformity. Most humans enjoy feeling part of something greater than themselves: their family, their school, their nation, their church, their football team, etc. This is more than just trying to avoid being different. It is a positive desire to be like something; to be part of it; to find identification with it. It is a desire for the secure feeling of knowing we are not isolated—that we are not alone. There is a warm feeling in sharing common values, common symbols, common ideas with others.

In valuing the same things others do, we reinforce to ourselves and make a statement to others about the degree to which we value our identity as part of 'the group'. Teenagers, for example, find a great deal of camaraderie in worshipping the same pop idols and movie stars as their friends.

Such identification and bonding becomes even stronger when we share the same emotions or experiences with others. The more powerful the common emotions or experiences, the greater the feeling of mutual closeness. As teenagers most of us share feelings of insecurity, of not knowing where we are going, and this brings us closer to those of our own age.

Pratkanis and Aronson adopted the term 'granfalloons', originally coined by American novelist Kurt Vonnegut, to refer to the entities we identify with.[2]

Granfalloons

Some granfalloons we are born into. The most important of these is our family. Most of us identify with our family and express this in our buying behavior at Christmas, Mother's Day and so on.

Other granfalloons we *choose* to identify with. Our choice here, however, is frequently influenced, if not determined, by the groups we already identify with. Many of us passionately support what we call 'our football team', but this often turns out to be the same team our family supported. Thus, identifying with one group such as our family can lead us to identify with other related groups such as a particular football team. The reason we consume certain products or display certain brand symbols (such as sweaters in the team's colors) can often be traced back through a chain of associations to the people and entities we identify with.

The stronger this feeling of identification, the more we defend the group and display its symbols. The more the group is attacked by outsiders, the stronger the feeling of comradeship within it. (This is why the promotion of nationalism, and even war, is sometimes used by politicians. It functions as a very powerful, cohesive mechanism.)

Even when our assignment to a group is random, such as in schools which have inter-house sporting competitions, identification takes place. When complete strangers are formed into groups on the basis of something as trivial as the toss of a coin, this same thing happens.[3] Though our reasons for belonging are unclear or meaningless, we nevertheless identify with the group. Any brand or product that associates itself symbolically with our group, family, team or values taps into this motivation.

This even happens with groups such as Amnesty International, in which most members never meet, and it also happens with individuals. We can be influenced in our own behavior by observing what another person does or imagining what they would do in the same situation. We identify with them and model ourselves after them. The closer our identification, the more likely it is that our behavior will be affected. In other words, the more similar we see the other person the more likely this modeling or copying influence is to take place.

Children who are terrified of dogs can be greatly affected by watching another child play happily with a dog for twenty minutes a day. In one experiment, after only four days of observation, 67 per cent of previously phobic children were willing to climb into a playpen with a dog and stay there alone petting the dog.[4]

The for and against position

Football team supporters often wear badges that say 'I support the New York Jets' or whichever team they identify with. They also wear badges that say 'I hate the Dallas Cowboys' or the team that they most love to hate in their country. Whether the hated team is called the Cowboys, Arsenal or Collingwood doesn't matter. It illustrates that one can find identity not only with being for something but also with being *against* something else. Our identification with something can be expressed either way.

Teenagers show their identification with their peer group by looking and acting like them but also by denigrating the tastes and preferences of the 'out group'—often their parents.

At its extremes this 'anti' motivation manifests itself in the form of jingoism and religious zealotry. In the super-strength, concentrated form it is a motivation sufficiently powerful for people to fight and die to preserve the integrity of the group and its values and symbols. Some people will even die in defense of the symbols alone (such as a country's flag).

At the opposite end of the scale the influence of this motivation is much more subtle and more difficult, though not impossible, to measure.

Reaction to symbols

Advertising has created some of the most recognized symbols in the world. Symbols such as the golden arches (McDonald's), the swoosh (Nike), the apple with the bite out of it (Apple), the cowboy (Marlboro) and the Nutrasweet swirl. Advertisers use symbols as shorthand communication and reap the benefits of investing for years in making the symbols mean something.

We react to symbols. At a red light we react by stopping. At a green light we react by going. When we see a swastika we feel revulsion. The 'man' symbol on a public toilet affects half the population one way and the other half another way.

Whether our reaction to a symbol is external (stop, go) or internal (revulsion) it is a learnt reaction. It is learnt by association of the symbol with other things. In this way a symbol gradually develops an ability to influence us in its own right and to evoke common reactions.

Meaning is an attachment

It is through a process that psychologists call 'discrimination learning' that a symbol or a brand acquires meaning. An odd thing about this is that once we have learnt via this process we become relatively unconscious of it. It is like our ability to drive to work without ever being conscious of having braked or being conscious of the process of changing gears. It takes place without much conscious awareness.

For example, when you see the letter

q

you are hardly likely to say to yourself 'Hey, that's romantic'. Nor do you say to yourself: 'This is a symbol that I am meant to decode as representing the letter q.' Instead you simply experience the letter q. You have become unconscious of the mental process whereby meaning is attached to the symbol. The meaning is experienced not as something that we attach to the symbol. The meaning is just there—in it.

Meaning is an attachment. It just appears as though the meaning is in the symbol. Another telling example is the word 'window'. Its meaning has in fact changed over hundreds of years from 'a hole where the wind comes in' to 'a hole where the wind does not come in'.[5]

A lesson in the origin of a kiss

Look at these symbols:

> <

What do they mean? Certainly there is nothing romantic about them. To us they mean 'greater than' and 'less than'. In primitive society, however, either one could be used to represent a bird's beak and, by extension, a mouth.[6]

If you bring these two symbols together what do you get? An 'X'. If the symbols are read as mouths, you also get two mouths together—a kiss. Hence the shorthand symbol for a kiss that we often use on text messages, emails and greeting cards is an X.

We all use this symbol and understand that it means a kiss, yet most of us don't know why it does. (This is a vivid illustration of how the meaning of a word or symbol, once established, can become divorced from its origins and operate independently of any knowledge of them.)

Our ancestors, looking at this symbol, decoded it as signifying two beaks in contact and deduced that this was meant to convey a kiss. As time passed, however, the intermediate associations gradually disappeared and the symbol came to elicit its meaning more directly.

The origins of such symbols and their meanings are often buried under layers of antiquity. But once a symbol's meaning is learnt, it is no longer necessary for us to know its origin or how our reactions to it came about. Even though we are no longer conscious of how it was learnt, we all use it and we all react to it just the same. That's why our consumption of bottled water is so hard to explain. Its symbolic statement about our identification with a healthy, active lifestyle was learnt in the late 1970s and hangs over in our behaviour today (see Chapter 1).

So symbols are like adults. We usually react to them as they are. But in order to understand them more fully we need to know something about their childhood and how they developed into and became what they are today. This is important because once learnt, we regard meaning as being in the symbol itself rather than an attachment process that takes place below the level of consciousness. Any sense of the mental process of attachment disappears.

To learn how brands are built into symbols we need to understand the way symbols acquire meaning and how we interpret that meaning. The real differences between brands such as Coke and Pepsi, or Perrier and Dasani, or Colgate and Close-Up may be quite small, but when the focal beam of attention is played on these symbolic aspects of the brand the differences may be significant.

Discrimination learning

Let's illustrate how crucial small differences can be. What do the following symbols mean?

q p 6 b d

To us they mean 'the letter q', 'the letter p', 'the number six' and so on.

When one of my daughters was about six years old she was learning numbers. She counted up eight toys. She was then given another one and

I asked her how many she had now. She was asked to write it down. She said 'nine' but wrote it like this:

ρ

This is not so uncommon when kids are learning to write. They sometimes get the symbol correct but write it back to front.

What happened next should teach us all a first-hand lesson about discrimination learning. I told her that she was correct but the number nine was written this way:

q

She looked at it, puzzled, then drawing on childlike logic said: 'But Daddy, that's a q.'

Father, after recovering his composure, explained to her: 'No darling, this is a q,' and drew a tail on her symbol, while realizing how small a difference it really was.

q

How subtle our learning of symbols and labels is! We take for granted that the same basic symbol is a nine when its tail is bent to the left but when it is bent to the right we are expected to have an entirely different reaction— it transforms it into an entirely different symbol.

Interestingly this is exactly the type of confusion that turns out to be the origin of the phrase 'mind your p's and q's'. Apprentice typesetters were urged to mind their p's and q's because of the similarity in the shape of the letters.[7] As adults we are so accomplished at making the distinction that we are too close to it. We are no longer conscious of how we come to instantly recognize:

q p b d g

as five quite different symbols.

Making brands into symbols

Brands are like letters. They can be transformed into symbols. They can become shorthand ways of communicating. They can be made to summon up or stand in for associations. In this way small differences can have big implications. They can become triggers for different mental associations.

The expression 'Just do it' cues us to think of Nike; the expression 'Take care' cues us to think of Garnier. In the same way brand names themselves can cue us to think of people and images that are closely associated with them. Nike may cue us to think of Tiger Woods, Shiseido may make us think of Angelina Jolie. Estée Lauder is more likely to trigger Gwyneth Paltrow.

If we want to identify with and feel closer to a particular image we can express it to ourselves and others by drinking, wearing, driving the same brand. Just as drinking alcohol can be to a teenager a powerful sign that he or she is now no longer a kid, so the consumption of other products can make powerful statements about us.

The importance of this as communication is as much for the user, the driver or the wearer as it is for the outside world. When an ad for Mercedes uses the line 'People will stare. Are you comfortable with that?' then owning a Mercedes lets you say something implicitly about yourself to the world. Drive a Prius and it says something entirely different—that you are environmentally concerned. Drive a Hummer and it communicates environmental 'nose thumbing' and that you are probably someone not to be messed with. One Hummer ad targeting female buyers used the headline 'Threaten the men in your office in a whole new way'. Think about it . . . the brands we buy and the brands we associate with often make powerful statements about us to ourselves as well as to others.

A brand can become a badge of identity in several different ways:

- by being a symbol of the group (e.g. football team logo);
- by being seen to be valued by members of the group (e.g. Mac owners are often passionately proud of others that make the switch from a PC to a Mac);
- by being seen as supportive of the group (e.g. sponsorship of a football team);
- by being seen as characteristically used or displayed by members of the group.

Summary

We react to symbols. Whether our reaction is external or internal it is a learnt reaction. It is learnt via association of the symbol with other things. In this way a symbol can influence us in its own right by evoking certain reactions. Symbols come to stand for other things in our mind and the act of consuming a brand can become a symbolic way for us to express our identification with the entities associated with it.

Our internal reaction to a symbol may be emotional or unemotional. Brands are initially unemotional marks; advertisers use advertising (and now product placement) to try to transform these (trade) marks into symbols that summon up certain mental associations. When a symbol elicits a cognitive or emotional response in us, we in turn can use it to express that idea or emotion to others.

We can identify privately with another person or a group without needing to tell anybody else. But often we want to signal this feeling of identification to the world. We do this by displaying and consuming symbols (such as football team badges, old school ties or brands symbols like Perrier or Prius), or using products that are symbolically associated with our favorite entities (Tag Heuer, L'Oréal). Identification is the flip side of conformity. It is not just the avoidance of seeming to be different. It is a positive desire to be like something; to be part of it; to find identification with it.

The difference between brands in the same product category may be quite small, but when the focal beam of attention is played on these symbolic aspects the difference can tip the balance. Consuming or displaying certain products can make powerful statements about us. The importance of the communication is as much for the user or wearer as it is for the outside world.

8 VICARIOUS EXPERIENCE AND VIRTUAL REALITY

The theater is a form of hypnosis. So are movies and TV.
When you enter a movie theater you know that all you are
going to see is twenty-four shadows per second flashed on
a screen to give an illusion of moving people and objects.
Yet despite this knowledge you laugh when the twenty-four
shadows per second tell jokes, and cry when the shadows
show actors faking death. You know that they are an illusion
yet you enter the illusion and become a part of it and while
the illusion is taking place you are not aware that it is an
illusion. This is hypnosis. It is a trance. [1]

Robert Pirsig

Virtual reality technology has been developed partly from video games, partly from cinema and partly from flight simulators. It is based on the concepts of illusion and immersion. It creates the illusion of being immersed in an artificial world.

Years ago Morton Heilig (the inventor of Sensorama), after he had seen Cinerama and 3D, said: 'When you watch TV or a movie in a theater, you are sitting in one reality, and at the same time you are looking at another reality through an imaginary transparent wall. However when you enlarge that window enough you get a visceral sense of personal involvement. You feel the experience and don't just see it.'[2] Anyone who has been in an Imax big-screen theater will relate to this. As Heilig put it: 'I felt as if I had stepped through that window and was riding the roller-coaster myself instead of watching somebody else. I felt vertigo.'

What has this got to do with advertising? Sometimes studying the extremes of a phenomenon can provide insights into its milder forms that would not otherwise be intuitively obvious. Ads that are mini-dramas work by mildly immersing us in a story rather than talking to us as viewers sitting out in front of the TV set or computer screen.

Just as there are technological ways (like 3D, Cinerama and virtual reality) to increase the feeling of immersion or involvement in movies and games, so too there are ways that advertising can be designed creatively and structurally to increase the immersion of the viewer in a commercial—and thereby enhance its effect.[3]

Ads as mini-dramas

Ads that are mini-dramas are those that depict a story or vignette. Mini-drama ads usually invite viewers to mentally migrate from their own reality and step into the fantasy world of the ad.

Take for example the ad that starts with a man on his morning run by the side of a misty lake. An attractive car sitting alongside the lake intrigues him and he can't help but stop to look. He reaches one hand out to touch the car and it falls over as it is actually a cardboard cutout. Immediately, a Loch Ness type sea monster strikes from the water and, in one hit, grabs the guy with its tentacle and takes him under. Meanwhile these words appear on the screen 'The irresistible Toyota Vios . . . you'll want one'. In the last scene, a tentacle comes back out of the water to stand up the cardboard cutout once again and reset the trap. This ad uses mini-drama to very effectively get across a message about this car's 'irresistibly attractive looks' but without ever actually saying it.

Take as another example the Land Rover commercial that starts with a little kid knocking on the door of a Land Rover to ask the woman who lowers the car window if his friend, Jason, is in there and can he come out and play. She says 'I'll check'. After about 20 seconds of silence in the ad she lowers the window again and says: 'I'm still looking'. Using mini-drama the ad very effectively gets across the message for Land Rover of a 'hugely spacious interior' but without ever actually saying it.

Perhaps the most famous example of mini-drama ads on TV was a series of ads that ran back in 1993 and then again in 2003 for Nestlé (Taster's Choice in the USA, Nestlé Gold Blend in the UK and the Nescafé brand in Australia). These featured two flirting neighbours whose relationship gradually developed over cups of instant coffee. Such ads invite us to step into the role of the characters in the same way as we would in a book or a movie. In fact the Nestlé ad series

Figure 8.1: *The characters from the (US version of) Taster's Choice coffee commercial.*

Figure 8.2: *In the 1990s Jerry Seinfeld starred in mini-drama ads with the American Express card as the hero.*

eventually inspired a best-selling novel called *Love Over Gold.*

Part of the reason for the popularity of drama is that it offers us a kind of out-of-body experience—a chance to be someone else for a little while—to experience life as someone else. Compared to movies and drama, TV ads offer a less complete out-of-body experience, but an out-of-body experience nevertheless. They offer a chance to experience life, if not as someone else, then at least as someone else experiences it.

The experiences may be those of celebrities like Robert de Niro or Kate Winslet in the 'My life. My Card' series of ads for American Express, or of Jerry Seinfeld's famous ads for the same company. Or they may be the experiences of fantasy characters like PC and Mac in the award-winning ads launched by Apple to counter the introduction of Microsoft's Vista operating system.

Stories as well as biographies and sketches often cast the product as hero or an essential part of the hero's life. In the Mac versus PC ads, the understated Mac character emerged as the 'cool' hero, able to accomplish things easily. The 'My Life. My Card' ads cast the American Express card as an essential and valued part of each celebrity's life.

Role-play

Children's games are full of role-playing. Kids pretend to be firefighters, truck drivers, doctors, and nurses. They also imagine themselves in the role of their favorite TV or movie characters: James Bond, Spiderman, Catwoman.

Television and PC video allow us to role-play and imagine ourselves in a character in the same way. With drama we have the opportunity to 'try on' other people's identities. We do this with TV serials and soaps, our favorite movies, and even advertisements. These ads often portray situations in which an individual experiences a problem where the product is part of the solution. In this way, we indirectly experience the self-relevant consequences associated with using or consuming the brand. We learn how the brand or product is (purported to be) instrumental in attaining the desired goal.

Identifying with a character

Our feeling of immersion in a drama or an ad seems to be greatly enhanced if we find ourselves identifying with one or more of the on-screen characters. This not only increases the feeling of involvement but also increases the likelihood that we will adopt the trappings of that character. These trappings may be the character's:

- lifestyle solution (American Express Card, Evian);
- behavior style (e.g. using Nestlé/Taster's Choice/Nescafé instant coffee);
- badges of identity (e.g. Nike, Harley-Davidson, Mercedes).

Because identification with a character in an ad is much more fleeting than with a movie character, it tends to be less conscious. It takes place quickly and evaporates. But it is fleetingly resurrected at the next exposure of the ad, and in this way permanent associations or links can develop between the feeling of identification and the brand itself. 'During identification with an ad character, empathizing consumers begin to feel as if they are participating in the character's experiences. That is, consumers imaginatively experience the story's events from the perspective of the character with whom they identify: consumers begin to perceive similarities between aspects of their own self-identity and that depicted by the characters.'[4]

Immersion and empathy

Identification with a character is not the only way immersion can take place, although it is probably the most powerful way. So what else might make these ads work? If you can't have identification, empathy is probably the next best thing. Some ads invite us to observe the character and take in what the character is experiencing without any expectation that we will necessarily identify with, or want to 'be like', that character.

Take for example the US insurance ads acting out the message that Geico.com is so easy to use that 'even a caveman could do it'. The caveman character, so upset at being demeaned in various Geico commercials, was such a hit with the public that in 2007 the ABC network gave a green light to making 'Cavemen', a sitcom based on the Geico character.

Empathy means that we understand at a deep level what the character is experiencing and feeling. It means that we have the impression we are experiencing some of the same feelings as the character. But we don't necessarily identify with the character. Identification goes one final step further in the process. It is a more complete projection. A viewer who identifies with a character desires to be like that character or feels like that character.

Immersion and image

Mini-drama commercials are not addressing us as the audience 'out there', but rather inviting conscious identification with the characters. Even if we don't identify with the characters, we are entertained by observing their interactions. Our 'vantage point' is not out front as audience but inside the character or somewhere in between. From this vantage point we are nevertheless able to immerse ourselves in the experiences of the characters and soak up the associations with the brand.

There are often no direct claims made. The focal beam of attention is not on a claim as such but on characters who are experiencing the brand and its attributes. This is particularly useful for advertisers in product categories like beverages, for example, where it is often very difficult to claim specific differences between brands and the differences are more associational (e.g. 'The Coke side of life', 'The real thing', 'The taste of a new generation', 'Time for a change').

Advertisers now have an alternative to creating mini-dramas as ads for the brand. As we saw in Chapter 6 it is possible for advertisers to use existing dramas and embed their brands (such as the James Bond movies where brands like BMW, Motorola, Microsoft, Omega and Bollinger have all appeared). Any existing drama, TV sitcom or reality TV show that is consistent with the desired image for the brand can be a candidate for paid brand appearances. If no program currently exists to suit the brand's image, it is even possible to do deals to modify an existing one to include a new character or a sub-plot storyline. Or indeed sponsor the creation of an entirely new program.

Emotions

Just as we experience life by observing the neighborhood out of our window, so too can we vicariously experience life through our television window, our YouTube window or our Xbox window. These frequently show characters experiencing life and experiencing emotions. In the midst of these situations the advertised brand is cast either in a feature role or as a central prop.

Such ads utilize qualitatively different channels of communicating which may be visual, musical or associational. They tap into our existing associations with things such as:

- personal desires (for fun, social recognition, achievement, dominance, power);
- belonging (acceptance);
- caring, human values (feeling good about and valuing others).

In other words, they tap into emotions and desires that we already experience.

Just as advertising can associate a piece of information with a brand (e.g. safety and Volvo), so too can it associate an emotion with a brand (excitement with Mazda Miata MX5). If we are concerned about safety then Volvo is a symbol of it. If we are interested in fun and good times then the 'zoom, zoom' of Mazda Miata MX5 is a better symbolic fit.

The connection of a brand with an emotion by means of characters experiencing life and that emotion increases the brand's relevance for us. It connects the brand with an emotion that is already there inside us. It may be something that was previously inactive in our mind or active but unassociated with the brand. The brand takes on associations and the more the brand takes on these associations, the more it can function as a symbol—one that expresses or stands in for that emotion and tends to elicit that emotional response. Instead of being connected to a piece of information, a brand may thus be connected, in our minds, to emotion. The emotion may be:

- a generalized positive emotion (e.g. *You can't beat the feeling*—Coke; *Oh, what a feeling*—Toyota; *Bud light . . . Bring out your best, Come to Marlboro country*).
- a specific emotion, like caring (*Reach out and touch someone . . .AT&T*; *Because there are other books that need doing*—Quicken), fun (*It's a good time for the great taste of McDonald's*), achievement (*Benson and Hedges*—*when only the best will do*; *Inter-Continental Hotels*—*the place to stay when you know that you've arrived*), power (*Feel the power*—Drakkar Noir; *The power to be your best*—Apple Computer), self reward (*You deserve a break today . . . McDonald's*; *You take life's disappointments on the chin, why dodge its rewards?*—Porsche).

The viewer's vantage point

Ads can work without generating identification or even without generating much empathy with the characters, but if so they usually rely on registering in our minds the claims or associations they convey about the product. The more entertaining ads invite us to immerse ourselves in the mini-drama and experience events from the vantage point of a participant or a bystander in the commercial.

These commercials vary in the degree to which they invite the viewer into a 'participant' or 'bystander' role. The role in which we are cast influences the way we are likely to mentally process the ad and what details of it we recall.

The implication of this is that in analyzing any commercial we should ask: What role are viewers being cast in? What character are they expected to identify with? Or empathize with? Are there structural aspects of the ad that enhance or inhibit identification? (Voiceover, for example, can be an inhibitor. Many narrative ads use voiceover to tell us what the character is thinking and feeling. This tends to interfere with the development of empathy by distancing us from the characters, in much the same way as does using the third person in a story rather than the first person.)

Immersion as attentional inertia

Observational studies of children watching TV indicate that for much of the time they do not actually watch the screen. In one study 54 per cent of all looks at the screen were for less than three seconds.[5] However, if a look lasts longer than about fifteen seconds, a child is very likely to become progressively 'locked in' to the program. After about ten seconds, the researchers often noted that the child's body relaxed, the head tended to slouch forward and the mouth to drop open.

This phenomenon is called 'attentional inertia', but at least one writer has directly related it to the 'hypnotic or trance-like quality of television watching'.[6] This 'attentional inertia' is not confined to children. It has been documented in adults as well.[7]

TV, hypnosis and reality

The quotation by Robert Pirsig at the beginning of this chapter likens TV watching to a mild form of hypnosis. TV and hypnosis do have some striking similarities.

A popular belief about hypnosis is that people have no knowledge of what they are doing while hypnotized; that they are compelled to do what is suggested to them; and that afterwards they can remember nothing of the experience. The truth is very different.

First, people do remember what happens to them under hypnosis and they feel completely conscious of it at the time. Only if the hypnotist gives them a posthypnotic suggestion to forget everything will they be unable to remember.

If they know what is going on, why, you may ask, do they follow the hypnotist's suggestion? This is an intriguing question. Most people who have been hypnotized will tell you that they felt as though at any time they could have ignored the hypnotist's instructions but went along with them anyway. In other words, they did not feel compelled to act as suggested.

However, this begs the question: Why do they go along? Most subjects say they just felt like it—that they could have acted differently if they wanted to, but they didn't want to. This is not unlike our own response when we ask ourselves why we have just spent several hours in front of the TV set. It is because we wanted to. We could have turned off the set and got back into reality at any time. We watched because we wanted to; because we felt like it. Just like the person under hypnosis.

The more an ad can immerse viewers (i.e. make the mediated experience momentarily more interesting, more involving, more immersing than what is otherwise going on around them), the more successful it will be. The best advertising does not remind viewers that they *are* viewers.

Tactics for increasing immersion

Immersion and identification are a matter of degree. The difference between reading a story written in the first person and reading a story written in the third person is that the former is like listening to somebody tell you directly about their own experiences, whereas the latter is like listening to somebody tell you about somebody else's experiences. The action is more easily experienced in the first person because we project ourselves into the identity. The difference is in the degree to which we are reminded of our own identity or the external reality.

This is related to virtual reality. By decreasing the awareness of stimuli other than those coming from the cinema screen, TV or book, we increase the 'reality' of the mediated experience and lessen the sense of it as mediated. It is like the difference between listening to music on headphones versus loudspeakers. With headphones one feels more immersed in the musical experience.

Advergaming

Things like Xbox, Wii and PlayStation immerse us even more completely because they are like headphones for the eyes as well as the ears.

The more complete the experience of virtual reality becomes, the more we can let go temporarily of one reality and become immersed in another. As a result, advertising is increasingly becoming part of that other world experience with electronic drama games. Product placement has extended to advergaming so that as we play games like *Grand Theft Auto*, part of that other world experience exposes us to brand names (like Mercedes). These product placements have increasingly become part of the gaming environment, again blurring the distinction between programs and advertising. Regulators are 'looking the other way' as paid product placement heads us down a slippery slope. What slippery slope? Play the game *First Person Shooters* and don't be too surprised to be exposed, as part of the experience, to ads for branded firearms (e.g. Mauser C96) in the form of product placements. Gaming drama represents the ultimate in 'switching off' from our own current reality and immersing ourselves in a fantasy world increasingly influenced by ad makers.

Summary

When we watch TV or sit in a cinema or play a computer game we are in one reality, and at the same time looking at another reality through an imaginary transparent wall. Just as we experience life by observing our neighborhood out of our window, so too can we vicariously experience life through our television, cinema, YouTube or PlayStation windows. Advertisements frequently show characters in 'real-life' and emotional situations. In these situations the advertised brand is cast either in a feature role or as a central prop.

Ads that are mini-dramas work by mildly immersing us in a story rather than addressing us as viewers who are sitting out in front of the TV set. We have the opportunity to 'try on' other people's identities. Identification with an ad character can build permanent associations or links between the experience and the brand itself. Some ads invite us to observe the character and take in what he/she is experiencing without any expectation that we will necessarily identify with, or want to 'be like', that character. Fantasy may not be true, but we can learn from it nevertheless, as is evident with shows like *CSI*, *Sesame Street* and *The Simpsons*.

Commercials vary in the degree to which the viewer is invited into a 'participant' or a 'bystander' role. The role in which we are cast influences the way we are likely to mentally process the ad and what details of it we recall. What we often recall is the association of a piece of information or an emotion with a brand. The more the ad immerses us—the more the mediated experience is momentarily more interesting, more involving, more absorbing than what is going on around us—the more we can feel the experience and not just *see* it.

Registering a claim or an association in our minds in this way does not necessarily imply anything about believing it. We will, however, recall differences being depicted between the brands and will recall the name of the brand that was cast as the best or safest or most exciting. These are 'feathers' that, when everything else is equal, may be enough to tip the balance of brand selection—even if only to prompt us to see if the association or claim is true.

9 MESSAGES, REMINDERS AND REWARDS: HOW ADS SPEAK TO US

With this chapter we begin to enter the mystical realm of the creative department of the advertising agency, whose art has traditionally been intuitive rather than encoded in any set of well formulated principles. The way an ad speaks to us can influence not only how the ad works but also *if* it works. The creative team's job is to design and make ads and good creative teams are paid a lot of money for their intuitive sense of what will be effective advertising. Their task is to make ads that are not only interesting and attention-grabbing but will also influence our brand choice and leave us feeling warm toward the brand and not alienated by it.

Articulating what makes for creative success in advertising is an underdeveloped science. In the past, researchers and psychologists who intruded on the creative team's domain risked finding themselves under hostile attack in enemy territory. However, their role has increasingly become more accepted, leading as it does to better understanding of the principles of psychological processing to underpin better predictions of ad effectiveness. In this chapter we bring these psychological principles to bear on messages, reminders and rewards and then in the following chapter we examine the individual elements of ads.

'News' advertising

As we saw in the previous chapter, we tend to process ads differently depending on whether we feel we are being talked to as prospective customers or whether we see ourselves as merely bystanders looking on. A related way of conceptualizing this is by asking, 'Am I being informed or entertained?' because we can process an ad as 'news'—or as 'entertainment'.

Some brands are heavily into 'news' commercials. Others are more 'entertainment' focused. There is evidence that ads seem to work best when they have something new to say.[1] As one US ad man put it: 'Ads are essentially about creating or broadcasting news about a brand' and 'News is the oxygen that lets brands live and breath and grow.'[2] ('News' advertising is closely related to, but not quite the same as, 'informational' advertising. The latter term is used in advertising in a very specific way.[3]) 'News' advertising provides news or information about the brand. It may be:

- a new formulation (new, improved Colgate);
- a new benefit about the brand (removes plaque, lemon-charged, sugar free);
- a new variant (100% Natural 7UP, Whiskas Organic, Fat free Pringles); or
- a price comparison (now half the price of the leading brand).

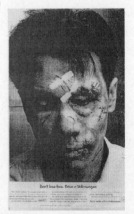

Our minds are invited to process 'news' advertising in the same way that we process the evening news on television or when we are reading the contents of the morning newspaper. The focus of processing is on what it is telling us that we don't know; what it is adding to our store of knowledge; how interesting the news is; how surprising it is; and how important it is to us or to people we know.

With news programs we don't necessarily have to enjoy what is being communicated. We watch news and current affairs programs for the information

Figure 9.1: You don't necessarily have to like this ad for it to be effective.

and not just for the entertainment. Evidence is emerging that the same applies to 'news' ads. It is not necessary that we like the experience of it provided the ad is imparting valuable information to us.

This explains why some ads which are disliked can still seem to work. Each country has its hated ad examples which, to the amazement of consumers, nevertheless seemed to work. The 'Ring around the collar . . . Wisk' commercials and the 'Mr Whipple . . . don't squeeze the Charmin' commercials irritated Americans for years. As did the Daz 'Doorstep Challenge' laundry detergent ads for UK viewers and the

'Mrs Marsh' Colgate ads in Australia.

When a 'news' commercial reveals a solution to a problem we have, then experience and enjoyment can take a back seat. For such ads to be effective it is not crucial that we like the ad if it gives us some news about the brand that is relevant to removing some irritation or problem we have with the product we are currently using.

In our society, the history and culture of advertising has its roots in communicating news about products and brands. Sometimes we see advertising messages delivered as though they are new when they are not. Unrequited expectations of being told something new tends to annoy us. News ads, by their very nature, are ads with messages formulated in such a way that they are almost guaranteed to irritate us if they keep being repeated. Yesterday's news, like yesterday's leftovers, is stale. So a problem for advertisers is that pure news advertising can wear out more quickly than other types of advertising.

Advertisers know they have to keep their brand salient in our minds and keep reinforcing its key attribute(s) so this inevitably leads to some degree of repetition, because there is a scarcity of new things to say about a brand. Even brand managers and ad agencies can run out of new things to say about humdrum, old products. They may then look for ways to 'create news' rather than reporting it. Trivial and often irrelevant differences are sometimes created in order to have something to say (e.g. caffeine-free cornflakes). In the past there has been a certain degree of reliance on 'beat-ups', as with 'new and improved' (yet again) laundry detergent! These pieces of 'news' are mostly harmless creations which ultimately risk boring us. There is a limit to how many times we can accept without questioning the idea that an old brand of laundry detergent can be once again 'new and improved' in any meaningful way.

Fortunately for us as consumers, news is not the only way that advertising can prevent a brand from becoming tired and boring while keeping it salient in our minds. Instead of messages that give us new information about the brand, advertisers can wrap up an old message in fresh, entertaining ways. They can reposition their message as an entertaining reminder rather than a new message. The essential difference is not in what they say but how they say it.

Some ads speak to us in a way that irritates us and we detest their repetition. Others can be appreciated and enjoyed, time and time again. The way in which we as consumers mentally process an ad is influenced by our individual interests, but it is also heavily influenced by how an ad speaks to us. It is not just what the ad says to us but how it says it. And the way the elements of an ad are blended can help determine which of our mental processes become engaged and which do not. In short they can help modify how our minds opt to mentally process the ad.

Liking of an ad

Liking of an ad doesn't necessarily make it work, but for the advertiser, all other things being equal, they would prefer to have us like it than not like it. There are two reasons for this:

- A brand's advertising is similar to its packaging in that it is part of the brand's personality wardrobe. Just as good clothes make a person more attractive, so a brand's advertising attire can make a brand more attractive. All other things being equal, we find ads that are dressed up as cute and enjoyable more acceptable than ads that speak to us in such a way as to grate on us and annoy us.
- Just as we feel more inclined to argue with someone we dislike and less inclined to argue with someone we like, our minds tend to react similarly with advertising. We are less inclined to counter-argue when we find ourselves enjoying an ad.

Entertainment

When brands have nothing new to say they do not have to irritate the audience by simply repeating yesterday's news. Advertisers have become very adept at wrapping up old messages in fresh, entertaining ways. So in product categories when brands are well established and there is little that is new to say, advertisers rely increasingly on reinforcement of the old message and the entertaining quality of their ads. These ads are not news and our minds do not process them as news. But when news is removed and the ad relies on entertainment and reinforcement, it becomes correspondingly more important that we, as consumers, like the brand's advertising.[4]

When the differences between brands are marginal or non-existent and the brands on the beam balance of choice weigh equal it only takes a feather to swing the balance. It is important to reiterate that the advertising for a brand is in fact one attribute of a brand's personality. If we like something about someone's personality, then the chances are greater that we will like that person. If we like a brand's advertising, the chances are greater that we will like that brand—however marginal this difference may be. It may be marginal but when everything else is equal, it can tip the scales

When we watch entertainment programs like *Desperate Housewives* or *The Simpsons* or feature movies, our interest is not in any information they may be communicating but in the entertainment they provide for us. It is important that we like the experience, otherwise why would we continue to watch? 'News' ads, like the news bulletins, clearly cast the viewer as the recipient of information. Entertainment commercials are different. We are not being addressed but simply experiencing. With entertainment commercials we react like an audience rather than a sales prospect.

Entertainment ads may take the form of 'drama' (see the previous chapter) or 'musical variety' (as used in Gap commercials) or 'animation' (the Geico gecko; Snap, Crackle and Pop; or the Keebler elves). Or they may be artistic, clever pieces of print or radio communication. As consumers we can and often do appreciate ads for their cleverness in wrapping up an old message in a fresh new way. While they may not communicate news about the brand in the sense of delivering a new message, they nevertheless create 'feathers'. They increase the salience of the brand and continue to reinforce the image or feeling that we have about the brand (or its users).

One of the crucial ways these entertainment commercials vary is in how integral the brand is to the execution and what role it plays. This can take various forms:

- the brand as a prop;
- the brand as a setting (e.g. various McDonald's and Pizza Hut drama ads);
- the brand as the hero (e.g. Mac vs PC).

Some ads relegate the brand to a bit part, while for others it becomes the star. The more integral the brand is to the ad the more likely the ad is to be effective.

Wrapping an old message in a fresh, entertaining way

After we have heard them, ad messages start to get boring. Most people already know for example that Asics make running shoes. And they know that Asics make running shoes for women as well as men. So how does a brand like Asics keep reminding people of its brand name and keep getting its message out to women?

Consider this print ad:

Visual: A picture of rural surroundings where women are jogging.
Headline: *We believe women should be running the country.*
Advertiser: Asics.

To take an advertising message and communicate it in this way is to re-package the message in a creative way. Shakespeare used the same technique. He was the master of the play-on-words and of course his plays are regarded as poetic works of art. At times ads are likened to aesthetic phenomena—just as though they were works of art (iPod ads or Absolut vodka ads for example).

Our conscious reactions to such ads are quite different to our reactions to straight ads. We typically react with at least mild appreciation of how 'cute' or 'clever' the ad is. And such ads do more than just entertain. Research indicates that all other things being equal we recall these ads better, we have greater liking for them and we are less inclined to engage in counter-arguing against them. Most importantly, when the brand is well integrated and communicated, it can nudge our attitude towards the brand in the positive direction.[5]

Why is this? What is the process going on here? An important point to note about such ads is that they often seem to stop us momentarily. There is a very brief 'interrupt' in the flow of our normal mental processing. Mostly we don't have to stop and think about an ad. Mostly we understand the communication immediately—usually automatically and without effort.

Techniques such as play-on-words, ambiguity or incongruity are used as creative material to force such an interrupt. Here is another example:

Visual: A close-up of a sandwich with a bite out of it.
Headline: *The next thing that gets eaten is your teeth.*
Advertiser: Colgate.

We are stopped fleetingly by a headline, 'The next thing that gets eaten is your teeth' when it is juxtaposed with a picture of a sandwich with a bite taken out of it. Our momentary reaction is likely to be 'Huh? What was that again?' But in virtually no time at all and almost without effort, we puzzle out its meaning. 'Oh . . . I get it . . . Colgate helps prevent the decay that begins to attack teeth immediately on eating . . . hey, clever!'

This ad, like many others, plays on the fact that words have multiple meanings and can represent more than one mental address in our mind. In this ad the word 'eat' is used to mean both 'ingestion of food' and 'something that decay does to your teeth'. One reason why there tends to be less counter-arguing with such ads is we expend more effort on understanding the ad and, consequently, less cognitive capacity is available to be used in contesting the ad's claims. This is a very fine line because if the puzzle is too hard it can fail completely as we are not going to be bothered . . . we just give up and turn the page.

However if we do successfully 'get it', then such ads are a brief mental diversion not unlike a crossword puzzle.[6] Making sense of something from limited clues is rewarding. We get a mild satisfaction when we are able to make sense of what is initially puzzling. The difference with ads is that we want to invest much less time on them and we are much less committed to puzzling them out than we are with crossword puzzles. So while ads and crossword puzzles that are too hard are likely to make us so frustrated that we escape from them, ads that puzzle us just momentarily, holding us just long enough so that we get closure on them and make sense of them, are accompanied by a mild positive sensation—a sense of fleeting reward.

Repeating yesterday's news

As I said, the problem with simply repeating yesterday's news is that it becomes stale. Creating and announcing new variants or new developments with the brand can provide the source for new messages about the brand. Otherwise, wrapping up the same messages in a fresh way provides a solution for the advertiser.

Consider with the Colgate sandwich ad discussed above that in the unwrapping process we are reminded of both:

- the brand—Colgate; and
- its key attribute—'protects against decay'.

The ad reinforces the strength of both. Furthermore, it does so in a mildly entertaining way. How much more boring and irritating would this ad be if it simply repeated the old message that we have heard so many times: 'Colgate provides protection against tooth decay'?

When exposed to an ad like this one, we immediately recognize it as an ad for Colgate. Then we store any 'new' information about Colgate (i.e. 'protects against decay') at that mental address. However, if we find we already know this—in other words we find it is already stored in our mental Colgate pigeonhole—our focus is on the message's clever wrapping rather than our otherwise reaction of 'Why are you telling me that? I already know it'. So we tend to appreciate ads such as this for their cleverness and are somehow more tolerant of seeing them repeatedly because they are much better than ads that simply assail us with the same information repetitively. The essential difference is in the way we process it.

How we understand ads

We are exposed to hundreds of ads like this every day but we fully process only a fraction of them. Some of them jump out at us immediately, others we miss completely and still others we deliberately ignore. When an ad catches our attention our minds automatically *try* to make sense of it. In this we may succeed or fail. We may fail because we find the ad 'too hard' to understand or there is not enough time or we are distracted by something else. Just how our minds go about trying to understand an ad goes something like this:

1. First, we recognize that it is an ad.
2. We then immediately try to identify what it is an ad for. To do this we look for something familiar. We look for something that corresponds to a memory address—something that already exists in our memory. (For example in the ad at Figure 9.2 we recognize Pringles. Aha . . . we know that name and we know this must be an ad for Pringles.)

Figure 9.2: 'New Fat Free Pringles taste just as good as Original because they are made with Olean. Tasting is believing.' (© The Proctor & Gamble Company. Used by permission.)

3. Once we have located this familiar memory address, our minds can then store any new information from the ad (such as 'fat free chips') in that (Pringles) pigeonhole.

Brand reminders

Before any new information (like 'fat free' or 'protects against decay') can be stored in our minds, a familiar mental pigeonhole or address has to be first activated (in this case Pringles). The opening of the mental pigeonhole, the triggering of that mental address, serves to remind us of the brand. This happens whether or not the information 'fat free chips' is new or is already stored there, and whether or not 'fat free chips' is important to us. In other words, it reinforces the salience of the brand in our mind and this result is independent of any new information. So brand reinforcement is one effect. Then, depending upon how important the new information is to us, the news itself may have an effect over and above the brand reinforcement effect.[7]

If there is no new information or if the information is considered trivial, this risks irritating us. This is where humor can deflect such irritation. Take as an example this billboard ad. A customer stands at a Burger King counter wearing a large trench coat and hat—he is clearly in disguise and wants to remain unnoticed. What we as viewers of the ad can see, however, is his trademark clown's red shoes, his red-and-yellow stripped socks and his very familiar 'Ronald' red hair. We locate the mental pigeonhole address immediately from the store and the Burger King logo. What is the new information to be stored there? Ronald McDonald buys his burgers at Burger King? No, we chuckle at the realization this is a joke. In successfully puzzling this out, it creates fondness for the ad as well as two reminders. It delivers a reminder of the Burger King brand and its oft cited claim that the burgers there are better. That's using humor to wrap up the same message in a fresh way.

Heralding

New information—a special promotion, a new deal, a new pack or whatever—can be announced by 'heralding' the new information. Some ads virtually scream the news at us (e.g. used car dealers shout 'Have I got a hot deal for you!'). The more heralding in the ad, the more it focuses our attention on the information as new. The more 'in your face' the ad message, the quicker the ad may impact on us. But once we have seen the ad and understood it, we don't really want to see it again. The more it is repeated the less affinity we are likely to feel both with the ad and the brand, and the more tired and boring they will start to look.

On the other hand, when the ad is pitched somewhat lower-key, and especially if it is done in a clever way that we can appreciate (such as the Burger King example), we are not only tolerant of its repetition but we can actually enjoy the information being repeated. The way in which an ad talks to us influences our reaction to it. Just as in our everyday interactions with people, *how* we are spoken to can heavily influence how we react. We like people who are fun, who make us laugh, and who don't harangue us. We feel more affronted by people who are strident; they put us in a less receptive state of mind to what they have to say and we are therefore more inclined to want to argue with them.

Non-heralding

As we have seen, when strident messages are used the more the ad heralds the new message, and the quicker the message becomes old. New information, once exposed and registered, is not new any more and repetition of it violates our cultural expectation that advertising is only supposed to communicate new information. That is why we encounter a lot of advertising that seems to persist in delivering old information as though it were new. 'Heralding' ads get the message across quickly but they also wear out very quickly.

Ads that communicate in a lower-key manner, aiming to get the information across more incidentally or as a reminder, tend to be longer lasting and less annoying in their effect. Once the new message has been communicated and before the repetition of the 'heralding' begins to annoy us, most advertisers would like to substitute more toned-down ads. But in order to reach the mass of people some degree of repetition of the heralding ad is almost inevitable.

An alternative for the advertiser is to use this lower-key form of communication in the first place. It does not get the message across as directly or perhaps even as quickly sometimes, but it does minimize annoyance and the ad will have a much longer life.

Even advertisers who do this would be hard pushed to articulate exactly what they do. Rather, advertisers can instinctively sense when an ad is in the consumer's face and when it is lower key and less likely to irritate. This result is governed in large part by the amount of focal stress placed on the newness of the information. In the lower-key commercial, often there is not the same focus on the newness of the information and there is much less heralding of this newness as would be found in a high-key commercial. The difference is often in how it is said rather than what is said.

Assertions and non-assertions

Information can be communicated by way of simple assertion—heralding—or with varying degrees of subtlety.

Consider for example the statement:

- Pringles are now fat free and taste just as good as Original.

There is no subtlety about this. It is a pure assertion and puts the focus on the information 'fat free' as being new, as well as that they taste as good as Original. Assertions like this wear out quickly because when they are no longer news, continual repetition risks the assertion becoming boring if not irritating.

But ads often use more oblique techniques such as descriptive adjectives or juxtaposition in place of assertion. These can slip in the same information more gently and with much less focal stress on the newness of the information.[8] For example, consider:

- Fat-free Pringles. As good as the original taste.

Using 'fat-free' as an adjective like this rather than using direct assertion (that Pringles are fat free) causes the focus of our processing to be directed on to the other part of the communication—'as good as the original taste'. Here 'fat free' is seen more as an identifying description than as an assertion. Adjectives are less like assertions of new information and operate more like matter-of-fact descriptions.

Granted, such differences are subtle and the smallness of the effect may risk a 'so what' reaction. However, these more oblique forms of expression can, by toning down the communication, soften the degree of assertion while communicating the same information.

The part of the ad we focus on

As we have seen, within a communication not everything attracts the focus of our attention equally. Indeed our minds tend to process information that we already know quite differently from things that are new. The content of any communication seems to get classified by our minds into two parts:

- Things that are already 'known'—called the 'given' information. We are being reminded.
- Things that are 'new'.

It is important to appreciate how our minds treat 'given' and 'new' information quite differently. Think about your school days. Did you ever ask the other kids trick questions like: How many of each species did Moses take with him on the ark? The unsuspecting kids always gave the answer 'two'. You laughed derisively and pointed out to the other kids' embarrassment that it wasn't Moses who went on the ark. It was Noah!

This schoolyard trick worked because you positioned Moses in the question *not* as new information but as 'given' i.e. already known. The kids assumed the given to be true and focused their processing elsewhere. It is easy for our minds to skip over something and take information as given, when it is positioned in this way.

The trick worked even though we were unaware of the mechanism underlying it. Similarly, while there are ads that to varying degrees may work because of this mechanism, very few advertisers would be able to articulate it or how it works. What we regard as 'given' simply registers in passing while we focus our attention on what we regard as new in the communication. Our minds tend to regard 'given' information merely as a reminder and assume the information to be true, leaving our processing capacity free to focus on verifying the truth of the 'new' information.

Reminders

There are various ways our minds pick up cues as to what is 'new' and what is already known or 'given' in the communication. In everyday conversation the prefix 'as you know' is frequently used. Consider the expression:

'As you know, Mac take less time than other computers to learn. Mac is the number 1 computer used worldwide in schools.'

The prefix 'as you know' has the effect of redirecting some of our focus of processing away from evaluating the statement 'Mac take less time than other computers to learn'. If we are going to focus on evaluating anything it is likely to be the statement 'Mac is the number 1 computer used world-wide in schools' because this is the new information that is being asserted in the communication.

The expression 'as you know' operates as a signal to the listener that this is a reminder—the information is just to be regarded as a lead-in to something else. It pre-empts any annoyance that we might otherwise have that might get in the road of the communication and avoids the annoyed reaction, 'I already know that! So why are you repeating it?'

More importantly, when something is signaled as a reminder instead of new information, we expect what is being said to be already stored in our memory. We expect it to be already known and therefore true.

Malleability of memory

When something is positioned as a reminder it has the effect that we expect it to already be in our memory. Just as we often see in people what we expect to see, so too do we often find in our memory what we expect to find. Why is this important? To answer this, let me tell you about the classic experiments concerning eyewitness testimony. They reveal a lot about how we as human beings process information differently when it is positioned as new versus when it is positioned as a reminder of something we already know.

In this famous series of experiments, psychologist Elizabeth Loftus showed people a videotape of a car accident and later asked them questions.[9] For example, 'How fast was the blue car going when it ran the stop sign?'

In fact there was no stop sign in the videotape. But the form of the question led people to assume it was there. People gave their speed estimates. When they were asked later if they saw a stop sign, more than half of them (53 per cent) claimed they had. The mental representation of the event had been 'altered' in their minds by the form of the earlier question.

Note that the information that there was a stop sign was positioned as 'given' information in the question. Using this technique of positioning the information as 'given', Loftus found repeatedly that we as human beings are prepared to add buildings, see people who aren't there, make cars go faster or slower, and in general witness actions that do not actually occur.

This is startling evidence of how we normally assume the given information in a communication to be true and concentrate on verifying what we see as the new information. As an aside, this is what lies at the heart of the controversy surrounding 'recovered memories' (of being sexually abused as a child, for example). The courts have to judge whether patients undergoing psychiatric therapy have been helped to 'recover' genuine memories or whether the memories have been accidentally created or altered in some way by the psychiatric questions themselves.

The general point is that expectations can be set up by the syntax or by other means that can significantly influence our focus of processing.

Silent signals

Our minds receive signals from communications indicating to us what we should presume to be new and what we should presume to be given. When we are listening to a radio ad, the amount of vocal stress in each part of the sentence helps signal to us what is new and what is given.

With written material and print advertising, it is the syntax as well as the graphics that provide the cues. For example, the use of an adverb rather than an adjective usually invites more focus of processing by signaling new information. Consider the statement 'Total clean Fab is gentler'. What is being signaled as new is that it is gentler.

Adverbs (like 'gentler') tend to signal that this is new information. Adjectives, on the other hand, do the opposite. They signal 'given'. Consider for example the statement: 'Gentler Fab gives total clean.' What is now being signaled as new is that Fab gives total clean. The gentler attribute is still being communicated but this time as an adjective. As an adjective, the fact that Fab is gentler is positioned more as a given—as something we already knew. So adjectives can communicate the same information more incidentally and more rapidly, with less focus on the information as new.

In an earlier chapter we saw how our minds mentally process image ads and visual experiences quite differently from informational ads. We can now see that information in ads can be processed by our minds in different ways depending on how directly or obliquely the information is asserted. What is involved here is a shift in our 'focus of processing' away from the information as new, to a focus on enjoyment, entertaining reminders or something else in the communication.

Oblique, less heralding ways have the effect of inviting less annoyance than when the information is repeated and they do not invite the same degree of counter-arguing. Wrapping up old information in fresh ways is just one form of rendering the information oblique and less heralding.

Summary

There are at least five ways that ads can minimize the likelihood of us counter-arguing with their messages and hence influence how we react overall to the ad:

- by not making assertions;
- by toning down any assertions made;
- by positioning the information as something that is already known;
- by packaging the information as entertainment; or
- by casting us, the audience, in a bystander role, 'overhearing' the information.

In Chapter 8 ('Vicarious experience and virtual reality') we saw how casting us as bystanders, rather than talking directly to us, can work for ads. In this chapter we focused on the other four points above—where instead of heralding the new information the ad is toned down or more subtly positions the information as a reminder.

Essentially, all communications work by triggering memories. Old images or concepts are triggered in our minds by something in the ad. We recognize various things as familiar. In the process, something new may be introduced and we are shown how to link this up with the old.

When something is positioned as 'new' the focus of our mental processing tends to be on evaluating: a) whether it is new and b) whether it corresponds to our own experience, knowledge, and beliefs.

The other parts of a communication, the 'given', we treat more casually. We assume we already know about it, so we tend not to spend as much time evaluating its validity. In other words we tend to take it as given.

Sentence construction, vocal stress and camera focus can be used to send signals as to what is given and what is new. While very subtle, these can also be very important. Don't let the subtlety distract you from their importance. Advertisers themselves are largely unaware of the mechanisms involved.

10 WHAT'S THIS I'M WATCHING? THE ELEMENTS THAT MAKE UP AN AD

In the last chapter we saw that the way an ad speaks to us affects our processing of it—that news is processed differently to reminders. Ads vary enormously even though their basic elements are much the same: sound, voice, music and pictures. A brand like Coke will often have several different ads exposed on TV in the same week, not to mention what's on YouTube etc. The message is often the same but the ads may all be executed in different ways. As we have seen, the way the executional elements of an ad are blended can help determine which of the consumer's mental processes become engaged and which do not.

Again, the art of the creative departments in ad agencies is traditionally intuitive rather than encoded in any set of well-formulated principles. Articulating what makes for creative success in advertising is an underdeveloped science and even more especially when it comes to analyzing the individual elements of an ad. This chapter draws on advertising findings and principles of psychological processing that are gradually coming to light, that jointly further our understanding of how the executional elements of an ad work, or don't work as the case may be.

Interaction of words and visuals[1]

It is important to note how elements can interact, such as music with visuals or words with visuals. For example consider the statement: 'The stripes expanded'. We can't effectively process it. What does 'The stripes expanded' mean? There is no mental address that is activated in our mind that corresponds to the stripes. Unless we can locate one we can't make sense of it. If on the same page, however, there is a picture of a man blowing up a striped balloon, we easily make sense of it.

In this way the visual element can be effectively used to manipulate what is 'on stage' in our minds and help us locate the appropriate mental address for a word. Ordinarily this interactive process is extremely fast and automatic rather than conscious. So we will rarely have any sense of having to expend any effort to put these elements together. At other times it takes just a minuscule amount of effort to make meaning out of it. Consider this example:

> Headline: 'This year, hit the beach topless'—Pepsi.
> Visual: The cap from a Pepsi bottle lies crumpled on the sand.

Our minds are easily able to discover the underlying connection that makes this ad comprehensible. The process is rapid but goes something like this. Our mind locates two addresses. One in response to the headline—appearing partially nude. The second is a soft drink bottle-cap. How to make sense of the two? We must first search for and locate an alternative address for the expression 'topless'—ah, the Pepsi bottle with the cap removed is, of course, topless. Suddenly the image of opening a Pepsi has been triggered by something linked to nudity, rebelliousness and risk-taking. The link is implicit and associative rather than explicitly asserted. And along with understanding it goes a fleeting satisfaction of having successfully puzzled it out and an appreciation for a cute or clever ad.

Such interactions and the minuscule effort we expend in the almost instant problem solving is partly what underlies our greater appreciation of such ads. But as consumers we are rarely motivated to expend much effort trying to puzzle out what a creative copywriter meant. So up to a point there is a certain reward that goes along with puzzling out the right meaning. But this works only if the ad first gets our attention.

Attention-getting devices

To maximize its effect, advertising has to get your attention. It has to 'cut through' the clutter of other advertising and be noticed. The first principal of advertising is that it needs to stand out. To this end, advertising uses a variety of attention-getting devices—the best known of which are sex and humor. In addition there are other more subtle elements that almost involuntarily capture our attention.

As Giep Franzen has written, 'People are social beings. Their attention often proves to be activated by other people, especially the portrayal of their faces and hands. Eyes in particular have an activating effect.'[2] Emotional characters, erotic stimuli, small children, and animals are just

Figure 10.1: *An ad for Lever body wash.*

some of the things that increase the probability of capturing attention. 'It is not for nothing they have frequently been used in advertising over the years—but not always functionally.'[3]

For example, advertisers who import sex into an ad and use it purely as an attention-getter when it has no intrinsic relationship with the product certainly gain attention, but contrary to popular consumer belief this stands little chance of being effective if it is not directly relevant to an advertisement's primary selling point.[4]

Many readers will be surprised to learn that ads they are highly aware of may nevertheless be ineffective. This is because getting attention is just one component of making ads work. Eggs are necessary for baking a cake but the cake will fail if you rely on using eggs alone. Attention alone will not necessarily make an ad work.[5] In fact, all too often in tracking I have seen that the very device being used to direct audience attention to the ad also serves to distract the audience from the brand and its message. Devices such as humor, sexual arousal and emotion can give an illusory impression to the audience that an ad is highly visible and therefore must be a great ad—but is it in fact working?

An ad that compels our attention but fails to register the brand and its message is next to useless for any advertiser. Though they stand out, such ads frequently don't work unless advertisers make sure that compensatory emphasis is given to strengthening of the brand and the message sufficient to outweigh this distraction effect. (See for example Chapter 17, 'The effectiveness of funny ads.')

Sex

Sex is a natural attention-getter that is fairly widely used. Various products are bought in part because we want to feel more attractive and they have a 'natural' association with our drive for sexual attraction. Products such as clothing, lingerie and fragrances often tie in to this 'natural' association—brands like Victoria's Secret (lingerie and swimwear), Fruit of the Loom (underwear) and numerous labels of fragrances for both males and females.

'Controversial' communicable ads

Some brands use attention-getting devices in a way that seems calculatingly designed to generate outrage. The effect is that they become 'talked about' ads and are passed on by word of mouth. Like communicable diseases they are spread, virus-like, by people who say to us 'Did you see that ad for . . .'.

Three examples of ads that became 'communicable' by using sex in an explicit or controversial way were:

Figure 10.2: *Victoria's Secret lingerie advertising.*

- *Nothing comes between me and my Calvins*—Calvin Klein jeans.
- *Are you wearing any protection?*—Bolle Sunglasses.
- Jaipur perfume ad showing a nude female from the back 'handcuffed' by Jaipur. The bondage overtones caused huge controversy.[6]

Humor

There are three main mechanisms by which humorous ads are supposed to work more effectively than straight ads:

- Humorous ads are noticed more i.e. they work through gaining greater attention.
- There is less counter-arguing with humorous ads because viewers process them as entertainment rather than engage in a true/false evaluation.
- They are liked more and there is evidence that ads that are liked have a higher probability of being effective.

These three points are dealt with in more depth in Chapter 17. Suffice to say at this point that while humor is another element that has the capacity to attract attention as well as entertain the audience and reduce counter-arguing, it does so at the possible risk of distracting us from attending to the brand and the message. Humor may hijack attention away from these other important elements. Consider for example this airline ad: a man bursts naked into his living room with a rose between his teeth, only to find that his wife has flown her parents over on a cheap weekend return flight.[7]

If you remember this ad, do you remember which airline was the advertiser? It is a very humorous commercial and while the message is well integrated, the brand is not. Nothing in the execution ties in to the brand itself. It could be used as a commercial for just about any brand of airline. In fact it was—because the same ad was used in different countries by *different* airlines. Where a brand is not inherently integrated into the execution, ads like this that use humorous executions have to make doubly sure the correct brand gets successfully registered in people's minds. Otherwise the commercial, while highly entertaining, may be doing a job for airlines generally but not the advertiser specifically.

Sometimes creative teams seem to feel a need to introduce humor almost gratuitously—for no functional reason other than because it appears clever—especially in sign-off lines at the end of commercials. Irrelevant throwaway lines at the end of commercials do little to attract attention to commercials. Furthermore they are likely to erase short-term memory and interfere with the main message of the ad.[8] These are to be contrasted with sign-off lines that *reinforce* the message e.g.

Volkswagen—it doesn't go in one year and out the other.

Such reinforcements at the end of a commercial are sometimes called 'klitchniks'. [9]

Testimonials

Testimonials can be used to increase attention, particularly with radio and print.[10] Though sometimes very effective as a form of advertising, they are not always done well.[11] The intention behind real person endorsements is to depict a simulation of word-of-mouth advertising. They may show an 'expert' (e.g. the 'doctor in white coat' technique) but more often they present 'typical people' who appear to be just like us. This is the 'satisfied customer' technique. For example, in the USA ads for Broadway musicals frequently show a lot of real people gushing about the show.

The process of empathy and identification indicates that the more like us the 'satisfied customer' appears to be, the more effective their testimonial. Consequently in many countries testimonials are often used by companies marketing to specialist occupational groups like farmers, plumbers or builders.

Music

Music is the 'rhythm method' of advertising. There was a time when music appeared in about half of all TV commercials.[12]

The inclusion in an ad of a tune that is already well known can help get attention as well as set the appropriate mood and act as a memory jogger. That's what Luv diapers were hoping for in buying the right to use the vintage Beatles hit *All You Need is Love*. They used it in an ad for their products with the lyrics suitably modified to 'All You Need is Luv's'. Consider these:

- The Resource, *Gimme That*—used in an iPod nano ad;
- Johnny Cash, *I've Been Everywhere*—used in a Choice Hotels ad;
- Louis Armstrong, *A Kiss to Build a Dream On*—used in a Visa ad;
- Hot Chocolate, *You Sexy Thing*—used in a Dr Pepper ad;
- Spice Girls, *Wannabe*—used in a Citibank ad.

Association of the brand with a popular piece of music increases the salience of the brand in our minds and makes it more likely that we will think of that brand whenever we hear the music.

When we are engaged in an entertainment experience, whether it be listening to a song or reading a novel, there is not the same motivation to *evaluate* 'information' as when we are told directly. *Persuasion by proxy* takes place when the focus is on the entertainment and not on the information.

Damping down the evaluative process and triggering emotion are not the only important effects of setting words to music. Rhyme, rhythm and repetition (the three Rs) give words a mnemonic quality, making the message more catchy and enduring in memory.

For years, Gershwin's *Rhapsody in Blue* serenaded us into seats for United Airlines. British Airways set the *Lakme* duet behind their famous 'face' commercial. The Partridge Family provided lyrics for Levi . . . 'I think I love you'. Later the Johnny Cash theme, *I Walk the Line*, provided the background for a whole series of Levis ads. Cell phone carriers often urge us to 'mentally migrate' to music. Dinah Washington gave us a rhythm-method reminder for Double Tree Hotels with 'Relax Max' while Budweiser urged us 'Don't hold back' with the musical assistance of the *Galvanize* track from the Chemical Brothers. Many thousands of advertisers have used hit tunes and other music to support their advertising.

Words to music: the jingle

Many ads set their own words to music. When Pepsi aired its first radio jingle in 1939, it was so popular that it was played in jukeboxes and became a hit record. In the 1970s Coca-Cola was so successful with its jingle 'I'd like to buy the world a Coke' sung by an international youth choir that it was extended, recorded and released to become an international chart hit called *I'd Like to Teach the World to Sing*.

Jingles have been around for over 80 years—the very first jingle was for Wheaties in 1926 at a time when sales were sagging and the brand was close to being discontinued. It turned the fortunes of the brand around and jingles took off. For about three quarters of a century, they flourished with many unforgettables such as:

- 'I am stuck on Band-Aids 'cause Band-Aids stuck on me'
- 'You deserve a break today. McDonald's'
- 'Just for the taste of it . . . Diet Coke'
- 'Stayin' alive . . . Volvo'
- 'Heard it through the grapevine'—California Raisins
- 'Take good care of my baby'—Johnson & Johnson baby shampoo
- 'You can tell a Wella woman by the way she wears her hair'
- 'Be all that you can be'—US Army
- 'A little dab'll do ya'—Brylcreem

Such jingles can easily be dredged out of our memories. A host of extraordinarily memorable campaigns owe much of their longevity in memory to the fact that the words were set to music. Music is a cutting edge that helps etch a commercial into long-term memory.

McDonald's even set to music the incredible line: 'Two all-beef patties, special sauce, lettuce, cheese, pickles, onions on a sesame seed bun.' A Canadian, Toronto-based pizza chain called Pizza, Pizza put its telephone number to a jingle so successfully that if you were to ask a Toronto resident what number they should call for pizza, they would 'sing': 'nine-six-seven, eleven, eleven/phone Pizza Pizza, hey, hey, hey!' On the strength of this, the company expanded to new locations across North America.

Wash-over effect of music

When words are set to music it can even create a *desire* for repetition. With great songs, we don't just want to hear them once; we want to listen to them over and over. Of course, most jingles hardly rate as great songs and that's part of the problem.

There is another effect that music seems to have. When the words of an ad are set to music they tend to wash over us rather than invite us to intellectualize. Why is it that when the words of an ad are set to music we do not have the same sense of somebody trying to convince us or sell us on something? By setting the words to music, somehow the edge is taken off what might otherwise be a strident message.

This is because we seem to process lyrics differently from spoken messages. As teenagers particularly, we seem to learn to process lyrics and music in a different way to other communications. And we do this in terms of 'enjoy/don't enjoy' rather than in terms of truth or falsity. We learn to process the experience as an experience rather than as a proposition which is supposed to faithfully represent real-world reality. Indeed much of the content of cable music television channels (like MAX or MTV), when processed in a rational way, is clearly unrepresentative of reality. It is designed to let fantasy and feelings in rather than shut them out.

Music is for appreciating and letting wash over us, not for arguing with. The mood that it sets can take the edge off potentially controversial topics. Words that might otherwise be processed in terms of truth/falsity get processed quite differently.

Musical commercials have become so much a part of our advertising environment that we almost forget they are there. We seem to respond to them as we respond to traffic lights: without thinking much about them. Putting words to music is a well-established creative technique— the rhythm method of advertising. In putting words to music it lessens the chance of us forming the idea that anyone is trying to tell us or sell us something and it reduces our tendency to counter-argue with what is being said.

Who is talking to whom?

It should be obvious that analyzing the executional elements in an ad requires some rather subtle analysis. An invaluable starting point to the process is to ask two questions:

- Who is the ad talking to? and
- Who is doing the talking?

The way we experience a commercial depends on what role the ad casts us, the viewers, in. This in turn influences who is seen to be talking to whom.

Lecture-style ads

Consider ads like 'This week only at Merv's supermarkets we have the following red-hot specials . . .'; 'I'm Joe Blow and have I got a deal for you'. Who is speaking to whom? These ads take a relatively traditional form in which it is clear that the advertiser (Merv's or Joe Blow) is talking to us, the viewer in front of the TV set.

We process these lecture-style ads in terms of the relevance of the information they convey. The advertiser hopes we will listen to what is said, find it of interest and see its relevance to us, then remember the information and act on it. For this to happen the ad has first to capture our attention and our interest. In advertising jargon, it has to *cut through the clutter*.

Look who's talking: face vs voiceover

Ads that reason with us often feature a presenter putting the case for why we should try or buy this widget rather than some other widget or why the presenter's brand is superior to the leading brand.

One important way in which lecture-style ads vary is in whether or not we can see who is talking; whether we can see the face of the advertiser. In the typical supermarket ad announcing the week's specials, the advertiser is usually unseen. The focus is on the specials. The person doing the talking is invisible. He or she is merely a 'voiceover'. If there is any real sense of a human being in the commercial it is merely a disembodied voice informing us how much we will save. Car dealer ads, on the other hand, often have the dealer as the on-screen speaker. The words come out of the dealer's mouth. In the advertising jargon, the ad has *lip-sync*.

These ads are like lectures and the person doing the talking is the lecturer. Some lecturers and some ads stick in our minds much more than others. Some lecturers like to work in a darkened room, hidden behind a lectern, with the audience's attention focused on a screen. Other lecturers are more lively. They work the audience from up-front, doing demonstrations and interacting with the audience or attempting to elicit participation from them.

So it is when we have a lip-synched, on-screen presenter like Jay Bush for Bush's Baked Beans or the now deceased Dave Thomas, who was the presenter for his own fast-food chain Wendy's for many years, or former Senator Bob Dole when he did the erectile dysfunction ads for Viagra. Advertising has gone more global over the years and because voiceover ads can be transposed more easily into other languages, such ads are seen more frequently. Nevertheless, it remains true that lecturers and present-ers who engage us with their person and are not just background voices communicate more effectively.

Voiceover commercials attract less attention.[13] I have personally found that in tracking lecture-style ads of this type over more than fifteen years, the ones with an on-screen human presenter and lip-sync almost invariably outperformed those with a disembodied voiceover. This is no doubt related to why many people don't like talking on the telephone and prefer to talk to people face to face. Talking to someone on the phone is just not the same when you can't see the other person's face and expressions. This type of news or lecture-style communication where the advertiser is imparting information usually comes across as more mean-ingful and more effective when there is a human face, a personality who is doing the talking either on the screen or in your mind. That is why so many car dealers are persuaded to appear in their own ads—because somebody whose face we can see is talking to us and becomes a known face. It helps when we can see the human face of the organization that is talking to us, whether it is Jay Bush for Bush's Baked Beans or August Busch IV for Annheiser Busch (Budweiser) beer.

Presenters

This raises the question of whose face? Some advertisers choose to use a human face but not their own. Just as governments use ambassadors to represent them overseas to be the human face of the government, some corporations prefer to use a presenter to represent the organization. So the presenter is not always the advertiser. He or she may be a model or actor with the 'right kind' of face (e.g. the Maytag repair man or Anthony Hopkins for Barclays Bank or Kathie Lee Gifford for Carnival Cruises).

The use of celebrity presenters is a global phenomenon. In Japan the majority of all commercials feature a celebrity. In the UK, Rowan Atkinson (alias Mr Bean) was the face of Barclays Bank for many years. More recently Barclays has used Anthony Hopkins. In Australia, where sport is almost a religion, Olympic medalists appear in ads for everything from breakfast cereals to cars.

Chances are you will recall one or more very old ad campaigns featuring the face of some celebrity—testimony to the durability of the memory trace that the use of such presenters can create. Celebrities and actors act as surrogates for the advertiser. They can put a human face on the image of an organization.

Apart from giving the advertiser a human face, the use of a presenter also acts as a mnemonic device to increase the salience of the brand. Who can think of Kirstie Alley without thinking of the ads she has appeared in for Jenny Craig weight loss programs? In years gone by, who could think of Karl Malden without thinking of American Express? In Australia Paul Hogan (Crocodile Dundee) was ultimately prohibited from doing Winfield cigarette ads because of his huge popularity with kids and his mnemonic association with the name Winfield. A similar ban was imposed on Camel cigarettes using Joe Camel, the animation character's face in the USA. Whether it be a face like Marcus Welby (Robert Young), Joe Camel, Paul Hogan or Kirstie Alley every appearance of that face in a movie, a variety show, or a TV interview inevitably reminds us of the brand.

The use of a presenter instead of the advertiser to do the talking in an ad seems to create a lessened sense of someone with a vested interest talking directly to us and doing a hard sell on us. We receive the message from the company but through a congenial and familiar figure who presents the advertiser and the product in a favorable light (e.g. Angelina Jolie pitched for luxury apparel brand St John and David Beckham pitches for Motorola).

The pros and cons of voiceovers

Whether the presenter is the advertiser in person or a hired face it is almost always more effective and more memorable than the use of anonymous, disembodied voiceovers. Why then do so many advertisers continue to use voiceover? One reason is cost. The ads are cheaper to make and as indicated they are more flexible, especially if they need to be modified (e.g. to dub in another accent or language for use internationally).

Advertisers sometimes have more success with voiceovers if they can vary them in some way. One way is the use of Hollywood's biggest stars as voiceover talent in major campaigns. When stars lend their familiar voices to ads, we say, 'I recognize that voice!' and we sometimes see the face in our mind rather than seeing the face directly in the ad.

Another way is if they can appropriately set the voiceover words to music. If we go out to an entertainment event like *Phantom of the Opera*, we clearly approach and assimilate the experience quite differently from a university lecture. When the voiceover of an ad is set to music it has a similar effect. These ads are more entertaining and enjoyable than they would be if spoken as straight voiceover commercials. They are processed differently—i.e. more as an experience—and their effects are more subtle. It seems to subtly change the way the ad is cognitively processed by the viewer, which becomes more akin to the way we mentally process musical drama.

Who is the ad talking to?

What is important in an ad is not just who is talking or singing but who they are singing or talking to.

Take the famous PC versus Mac ads that are really a dialogue between the two characters representing PC and Mac. Or cell phone ads with people talking to one another about the advantages of being with that particular telco supplier. Or an old spot for Chiffon margarine, 'It's not nice to fool Mother Nature'. A woman talks to the narrator about how nice and creamy the butter is, and the narrator corrects her that it's not butter; she gets angry and lightning and thunder flash around and she utters the famous 'not nice to fool Mother Nature' tag line.

Ask yourself who is the character on screen or the voiceover talking to? If we think carefully about this we will often find that the voice or character is not addressing us directly but some other character on the screen. At the same time we on our side of the screen are also experiencing the commercial and getting the message, but in the role of bystanders or passive observers.

The difference between being a bystander and being the obvious target of a communication was demonstrated way back in 1962 in an experiment by Walster and Festinger.[14] Subjects listened in on a conversation between two graduate students. Some subjects believed the students knew they were listening. Others believed the students were unaware of their presence.

The first group believed what the students said could conceivably have been directed at influencing them, the listeners. The second group were more influenced by the opinions expressed in the students' conversation. In other words, being in bystander mode seems to reduce the motivation for us to engage our defensive reactions and reduce our tendency to be as critical of what is being said.

We as viewers get messages from these ads indirectly rather than directly, much as we do when viewing a play or a soap opera or a movie. Our minds are not set to receive a message but to be entertained. This contrasts with the traditional type of ad which addresses viewers directly, such as the many retail supermarket ads in which the two main components are:

- voiceover and
- illustrative visuals (usually of the products).

Such ads clearly and unambiguously talk to the viewer. Most early TV advertising was like this, and we still tend to think of it as typical, probably because advertising's heritage is in the print medium. Straight words with illustrative visuals is an approach very much in the style of, and a carryover from, print advertising. But if you watch today's TV and video ads closely you will see that this style has mutated considerably. Often the (off-screen) voiceover appears to be talking not so much to the viewer but talking to, or about, an on-screen character.

Voiceover talking to, or about, an on-screen character
Having the voiceover in the ad appear to address an on-screen character is one of the primary ways in which a shift can be induced in our mental processing. It is one of several elements that invite us to take a bystander perspective. Oral B did this with the voiceover addressing Rob the dentist on screen and asking him to show us which toothbrush he used.

An Australian ad for Caro (a coffee substitute) illustrated the purer form of this technique where the voiceover throughout the whole commercial was not addressing the audience but addressing a product-user on-screen character. In it, the man on the screen was told by the off-screen voice-over that there are many people just like him who now drink and enjoy the product. The viewer is a bystander and the viewer's 'focus of processing' is the bystander's perspective.

The difference between being a bystander and a target is the difference between overhearing a conversation and being told something directly. What is different in overhearing information in a conversation between two other people is that our attention and cognitive processing are focused differently.

When we are being told something directly we are more likely to engage our defensive, counter-arguing mechanisms; we are more on the alert and ready for counter-arguing. The information gained from overhearing someone else's conversation may or may not be the same. However, the defensive processing applied to it is likely to be quite different.

Often this type of ad is very subtle and it is not immediately obvious that the primary role the audience is being cast in is bystander. The key to these ads is that they are addressing the people shown on the screen rather than addressing us sitting out front.

The on-screen character as receiver

An interesting question to ask is, who is the voiceover talking to? The long running Mastercard 'Priceless' ads use voiceover talking about the on-screen characters making purchases. Each commercial concludes with the line 'There are some things money can't buy . . . for everything else there's Mastercard'. The voiceover seems to be talking as much to the characters on screen as to the viewer sitting out front.

In the famous 'Gillette, Best a Man Can Get' commercials the voice sang to the on-screen character, 'You're looking good'. In the classic Dr Pepper commercial the off-screen voice sang to the people on screen, 'Wouldn't you like to be a Pepper too?'

When a commercial imparts a sense that it is the on-screen character who is being spoken to, or sung to, this further helps disengage the viewer from taking on the role of defensive customer. It engages the viewer more as a passive observer, a bystander enjoying the entertainment. The voiceover is not selling, talking or even singing to the viewer. Rather, it seems to be singing to the on-screen character.

To the extent that viewers identify with the on-screen character, they also receive the message indirectly and see it as relevant to themselves. Consider an 'erectile dysfunction' ad that depicts a mature age couple enjoying a romantic dinner with the headline 'Choose the treatment for him that suits your sex life'. It appears to be talking to *her* but not all is quite as it seems! While the message is *ostensibly* not directed at him, think about this: readers of this ad are *both* male and female. The message to her is 'overheard' by male readers. The difference is subtle but important.

In this type of ad, the pronoun 'you' or 'your' occurs often (e.g. 'You oughta be congratulated', 'Aren't you glad you use Dial?', 'When you care enough to send the very best'. This style engages us as passive observers and invites us to enjoy the ad while being invited to interpret the 'you' as referring to the on-screen character. However if we identify with the on-screen character, we can simultaneously interpret the 'you' as referring to us.

Tuning in to the on-screen character's thoughts

In some ads, it is as though the characters on screen are thinking the sentiments expressed in the voiceover or the song lyrics. Viewers have the impression of sharing what the characters are thinking or feeling. In these ads the words could be being spoken or sung by the characters, but they aren't. Instead the message seems to come from the characters' thoughts. Setting a message to music lessens the sense of being lectured to and this technique probably lessens that sense even more. We seem to be simply overhearing someone's thoughts. The on-screen characters in all these commercials are depicted doing other things while simultaneously we hear what seems to be their thoughts, desires or remembrances coming through the audio track. The style is frequently characterized by use of the pronouns 'I' or 'we'. To the extent that we find ourselves sharing the feelings of these characters and identifying with them, the pronouns 'I' or 'we' can be taken as referring to us as well.

Drama

Earlier we saw that people seem to process lyrics and music quite differently from spoken messages. Such processing, far from shutting out fantasy and feeling, deliberately lets it in.

'Drama' commercials are similar to music in this respect. Drama, like music, is supposed to be experienced and enjoyed. Experience and enjoyment are the focus of our mental processing. Our mental processing is not usually set to engage in analysis of the drama in terms of truth or falsity. Nor is it set to analyze what information goes into our heads in the process.

A classic drama commercial was Pepsi's 'archeological dig' which showed a bottle of Coke found at an archeological dig in the next century and the 'professor' admits that he doesn't know what it is. Another example is the delightful McDonald's ad that opens with a team of cute seven- to eight-year-olds preparing to play for their basketball championship.

They are discussing with their coach what to do because one of them is away ill. Overhearing them, Los Angeles Lakers basketball star Kobe Bryant walks over and offers to play for them. The kids don't have a clue who he is but they agree that 'he is tall' and so they decide to give him a go. One of them takes Kobe aside and whispers 'Hey, if we win, we get to go to McDonald's . . . so don't blow it. OK?'

These ads are like plays or dramas and they not only have people and faces but also characters and plots. All of these elements help the ads stick in people's minds. Classic long-running drama commercials include Impulse body deodorant (*If someone gives you flowers, it may be just 'Impulse'*), AT&T's 'Reach out and touch someone' and the Nestlé Gold/Taster's Choice/Nescafé serialized ads. These ads appeal to us emotionally. We can relate to them and they entertain us at the same time as 'educating' us.

They are mini-movies rather than ads that reason with us. There is a world of difference between listening to a lecture or a debate and attending a concert or a movie. The former are an invitation to reason; the latter are an invitation to experience. With drama commercials, this is the difference. We tend to record the incidental information or message that happens to be conveyed while the focus of our attention is on being entertained. Sometimes by putting both music and drama together we get musical drama. An example was the Pepsi commercial that starred Britney, Pink and Beyoncé as gladiators facing each other at the Colosseum while the emperor looks on drinking Pepsi. Instead of fighting, the three throw down their weapons to declare in song to the crowd 'We will . . . we will . . . rock you!' As the crowd get with the gladiators, the emperor's iced cans of Pepsi end up being drunk by the three gladiators on the Colosseum floor and the commercial closes with the emperor in the pit facing a growling lion.

Characters

When developing a commercial, ad agencies consider what is the target audience for the product (ie. who buys it) so they can make decisions about the characters. 'Young products' (e.g. jeans) usually feature young people and 'older products' (e.g. retirement plans) usually feature older people. Similarity in age between characters and audience is usually a plus.

The ad maker attempts to weave roles and characters into the ad that we will welcome, that are consistent with the way we see ourselves or would like to see ourselves, roles and characters that we can easily identify with.

The closer we feel to a character and the greater the similarity between that character and ourselves, the more effect a commercial is likely to have on us. This is why ads for Mattel toys usually star children, ads for Coca-Cola feature teenagers, and ads for All-Bran breakfast cereal show the whole family. The age, sex and lifestyle of the characters are chosen to maximize the probability that the target audience for the brand will identify with the character.

Multiple target audiences

Many ads have one specific target audience and the target character is designed accordingly. It is possible, however, for one commercial to address multiple target audiences and still achieve identification.

An example is a McDonald's ad that shows a working mom in a business suit showing her husband and kids everything in the refrigerator and freezer. She's going on a business trip and has color-coded all the plastic wrap around certain foods—blue is for broccoli, red is for . . . and the dad and kids are just looking at her, but paying attention. The ad then cuts to the dad pulling things out of the refrigerator for dinner and he asks the kids, 'What do you want for dinner, blue or red?' He then says, 'Let's go to McDonald's.' Lots of McDonald's spots work with multiple targets.

The point is that various people can identify with one or other of the character targets. Children can identify with the kids, males can identify with the dad while females can identify with the mum.

Two questions are pertinent when we examine an ad and its characters. First, are we members of the target audience for the ad? Or is it aimed at people in some other age, sex or socio-economic group? Tampon ads are not aimed at me, nor are women's fashion ads. Often, however, it is not that obvious. Assuming we are in the target audience for the ad, then which character or characters seem to be most like us? Which character in the ad do we feel some identity or empathy with? If the ad is working on us it is most likely to be through that particular character.

The person playing the character

Already admired characters generally have a head start in getting the audience to identify with, and project themselves into, the character. Almost every male adolescent in the USA 'wants to be' a Kobe Bryant or a Michael Jordan. Almost every female adolescent wants to be Beyoncé or maybe Pink. So the Colosseum gladiators mentioned in the Pepsi ad earlier has not one but three female characters that a young female audience might want to identify with. (Britney was also admired at the time, which underlines the risk of using celebrities who might turn out to be 'loose cannons'.)

What if that Pepsi commercial had used unknown actors? It would probably still have worked—but almost certainly not as well. Viewers would need longer to develop a feeling of familiarity with the characters. This would have necessitated many more repetitions of the ad (and possibly even the making of multiple ads). The identification process would not have been anywhere near as immediate or as intense. In other words, where the character has to be introduced and developed from scratch, the advertiser has to spend much more money for on-air time to elicit the same degree of identification effect.

When advertisers develop identities and establish characters in their ads they therefore regard these as an accumulating asset. They have an investment interest in the development of these characters. It is important for them to have in their ads attractive, recognisable characters that we the audience will want to identify with—whether these are known entities or (initially) unknown. This explains the advantage in ad campaigns of maintaining continuity in the star character. It is why we now see more sequels of successful ads. Advertisers are discovering that there are advantages to be gained in not changing the characters with every change of commercial. (See Chapter 23, 'Sequels'.)

Animated characters

Fictitious characters in shows like *Desperate Housewives*, *The Bold and the Beautiful*, *Neighbours* and even *The Simpsons* get fan mail all the time from people who empathize or identify with them. The fan mail is addressed to the character, not the actor. Why does this happen when everybody knows the characters are fictitious? It is because even though they are only characters they are real enough for us to identify with and empathize with.

We can even feel warm towards cartoon characters and puppets. A generation of people felt empathy, if not identity, with the 'Peanuts' character Charlie Brown, the born loser. A different generation warmed to Big Bird and the Cookie Monster. And then came the Simpsons and later Family Guy.

Animated characters have been used as both positive and negative role models. For example in *The Simpsons*, Mr Burns and Barney (the drunk) provide clear negative role models. As in *Sesame Street*, watching Oscar the Grouch is fun but acting like him is clearly absurd. Who wants to be perpetually grouchy? Oscar is the negative role model in *Sesame Street*; others, such as Big Bird and The Count, are positive role models.

Classic animated ad characters include the M&M characters, Charlie the Tuna and the Pillsbury Doughboy.

Ads starring animated characters, just like straight ads, seem to be most successful when the on-screen characters do the talking such as Bart Simpson did for the Nestlé confectionery brand 'Butterfinger', declaring 'Nobody better lay a finger on my Butterfinger'. In one ad, Bart is accosted by bad boy Nelson, who takes his money. Bart capitulates but when Nelson says 'I'll take that Butterfinger bar too', he snatches back the bar and escapes triumphantly up a tree to devour his Butterfinger bar.

Animation can be used to change the whole feeling and tone of a commercial. In particular it can be used to 'lighten up' what might otherwise be a serious, unpleasant message. Bug exterminators like Orkin and Terminex frequently employ the strategy of using animated or computer-enhanced bugs because they know that most of us are squeamish about seeing bugs on TV. AIDS campaigns around the world have used animated condoms to deliver a serious message. Similarly, many stomach-ache cures use drawings of the stomach to deliver their message.

In an ad for Kit 'N Caboodle cat food, advertising agency DDB needed to show a cat chasing a mouse. Instead of having cat owners watching their darling pussy on TV threatening the life of a real mouse, the ad agency used animation. The agency wanted people to respond to the realism of the cat so they mixed live footage of a cat with an animated mouse.[15] The ad was a delightful example of animation's ability to lighten an otherwise unpleasant scenario.

One appeal that animated characters have for advertisers is that advertisers are in total control of the characters' behavior. Their investment is protected. Advertisers using real people always have

Figure 10.3: The animated M&M characters don't 'age' like regular characters. (Reproduced with the authority of Mars Confectionery of Australia)

to hold their breath and hope. The character may get into trouble and develop a bad reputation which can cross over to the brand (today advertisers are acutely aware of disastrous examples like O.J. Simpson, Mike Tyson and Michael Jackson). With cartoon characters like Snoopy for MetLife or the M&M characters this can't happen. As one US film-maker put it: 'Animated characters are . . . appealing because they don't age like regular characters and won't be caught in a crack house and then try to gang rape the arresting officers . . . They give advertisers control.'[16]

Length of commercial

Sixty-second commercials are almost an extinct species today. Even the 30-second standard is threatened. Commercials on TV are getting shorter while on the web they tend to be getting longer. Think about this: a 60-second TV commercial is only about one-hundredth the length of a movie. This means that getting us to project ourselves into it and identify with a character is much, much harder to achieve than with movies. In the time it takes to screen a movie you could watch about one hundred 60-second commercials or two hundred 30-second commercials. So any identification that does occur is much more fleeting with advertising. This is one reason drama commercials seem to work better as longer commercials of 60 seconds or 45 seconds, rather than as shorter 30- or 15-second commercials. And it is another reason why there are now more longer ads on websites like YouTube where costs are much lower than TV advertising.

Time is both an enemy and a challenge for drama commercials. There is extremely limited time in which to develop the characters, depict the situation and get a message across. (See Chapter 18, 'Learning to use shorter-length TV commercials'.) It takes time to build involvement and identification with characters. This is why sequels can work so well—because the characters have already been developed in an earlier ad.

Negative roles or characters

Some ads deliberately use a character designed to be a negative role model. For example, in an attempt to get people to save water, a water utility used a thoughtless, mindless water-wasting character named Wally in its ads, the theme being 'Don't be a Wally with water'. It urged us not to be like this character. This use of characters in a negative role is one way to influence us not to engage in the same behavior.

Interestingly, some ads, in an attempt at humor, sometimes make the mistake of doing this inadvertently and depicting the target identification character as something of a 'goat'. Yet the advertiser still hopes that we will react positively to the character and what he or she is saying. These often fail and can sometimes be seen to have marked negative effects. An example of this is an ad showing a Fosters beer-drinker who is so naïve he fails to recognize the famous people he talks to in a bar. As the audience, if we squirm in embarrassment at a character's naïvety it makes it nigh on impossible for us to 'feel like' or want to 'be like' this character representing the brand user.

In another example, a one-time celebrity now regarded as something of a 'has been' appeared in an ad for a gas hot water service. Referring to his own fall from fame, he proudly announced that with this hot water service the water 'will still be hot when you're not'.

When we were kids we identified with the goodies, not the baddies. We wanted the attractive roles, not the embarrassing ones. Who wants to identify with the baddies, the 'has-beens', the losers or the naïve?

Some advertisers while not attempting humor can fall into this trap and be amazingly incautious or unthinking in their choice of characters. They are obviously not thinking of target identification. For example, in one country Toshiba inexplicably used a very obese individual in advertising its Toshiba notebook computer. While obese individuals might especially need lightweight portability in computers, not too many people want to identify with that image. Ads that contain negative characters are very risky for an advertiser when these characters are depicted as brand users.

A commercial is supposed to boost our positive image of ourselves, showing us as a user of that product, our positive self-image mirrored in the users of the brand: people we want to identify with. If on the other hand the users are people we reject any identification with, these ads start very much from behind the eight-ball.

So do ads like this work? I have not seen one that did, unless it was strongly informational. On the other hand I have seen a number of them have negative effects. It may seem surprising that ads can have a negative effect but in fact ads that have a negative effect are not so rare—especially if they are not pre-tested before they are run. In one study of 147 commercials, 45 per cent were shown to have had a negative effect and even if commercials were pre-tested, 6 per cent of them were still shown to have a negative effect.[17]

Negative role models is one of the problems here. Such negativity gets in the way of the identification process and can be the kiss of death for an ad—especially if the ad has nothing else going for it. The more that an ad has to rely on consumer identification with a negative character as the brand user, the stronger the risk that it will fail.

Comparative ads

Perhaps the best known of all comparative ads was the Pepsi Challenge, showing the blind taste-testing of two colas. It claimed that more people preferred the taste of Pepsi than Coke. Similarly, Duracell frequently advertises that it is longer lasting than Energizer. From pain relievers to automotive products we see many comparative ads that ask us, the viewer out front, to compare two brands. Especially in mature markets comparative ads are used by small brands to attack the market leader head on. For example, countless pain relievers have promoted themselves as 'More effective than Tylenol' or 'Longer lasting than Tylenol'.

Claims and counterclaims by the two brands may lead to such confusion that we as consumers give up trying to differentiate and simply buy the two brands interchangeably because we don't care which one we buy. We may be tempted to feel that this is another example of where advertising doesn't work on us . . . but wait. If as a result of this confusion the smaller brand is then purchased half the time, i.e. as much as the bigger brand, then this has paid off in a big way for (what was previously) the smaller brand. So even though we feel we weren't persuaded by either brand's advertising, nevertheless the smaller brand achieves its objective of increasing its sales.

Much comparative advertising says to consumers: 'Look, we're just like the leader, only cheaper.' It's not about building a brand personality, it's merely about setting a competitive framework and talking about one key attribute, which is often price. For example, Equal is a sugar substitute whose patent has long expired. So along comes NatraTaste, and creates similar packaging. It shows packs of Equal and NatraTaste side by side in its advertising with the line 'Same great taste as Equal. Half the price'. It maybe makes for unexciting advertising, but its appeal is simple: 'Hey, same stuff, half the price. What's not to like?'

Word of mouth and viral advertising

Marketing has always benefited from recommendation. Happy customers spread recommendation by word of mouth to friends. Ads too can become the subject of word of mouth. All of us have had the experience of a friend (or family member) exclaiming 'Hey, did you see that great ad for (insert brand) . . . that shows (insert description) . . . Isn't that so good/funny/ clever etc!' Advertisers know their ad has got attention when people are talking about it. Indeed, sometimes ads are deliberately engineered to try to trigger this and become 'performance enhanced' by being spread not only through TV but also by the web and word of mouth.

The web has facilitated this and viral advertising has been a growth phenomenon. The email that arrives from a friend with an ad attached or a link to the ad on YouTube or elsewhere is likely to be so entertaining, funny or clever that you, like your friend, forward it (or the link) on to other friends. Because they in turn forward it, the ad spreads similar to a chain letter. Like a flu virus, the spreading process is self-replicating as it is passed from person to person. Hence its name 'viral advertising'. Social networking sites (like Facebook, MySpace and Bebo) make it ever easier for us to share our discoveries of that which is new, exciting, outrageous or just plain titillating.

The key to word of mouth and viral advertising is to keep the chain or network going. It has to have some kind of 'wow' factor so that people feel compelled to share and 'pass it along'. This means the ad has to be novel, outrageous or uniquely entertaining in some way. The way the web is changing advertising and the implications of advertising in a new age are discussed further in Chapter 25.

Summary

The art of advertising creative teams is traditionally intuitive but principles of psychological processing are gradually coming to light that further our understanding of individual elements and how these work. The blend of executional elements can help the ad capture our attention as well as influence the way our minds process the advertisement.

Visuals interact with words to influence what is 'on stage' in our minds and determine what interpretation we give to those words. Setting words to music influences the mental processes we use on those words, in addition to making the ad more memorable.

Advertisers using sex, humor or other attention-getting devices have to be careful of the device stealing focus from other key elements of the ad and interfering with the registration of the correct brand and message. Nevertheless, elements that capture attention are important ingredients of ads. Sometimes they can be sufficiently novel, unique or outrageous that the ad becomes a topic of conversation in the community and becomes 'performance enhanced' as it is passed along, virus like, by word of mouth or passed along in links or emails to others via the web or social networking sites.

The type of ad also affects the focus of our processing. It is very different when we see drama or 'entertainment' advertising compared to when we see 'news' advertising. When there is no news, established brands often turn to entertainment commercials. With entertainment commercials we tend to record any incidental information or message that happens to get conveyed while the focus of our attention is on being entertained.

One important question to ask of any ad is this: 'Who is doing the talking?' Straight news ads and lecture-style ads have more effect when we can see the person talking to us on the screen with lip-sync. Using a presenter character as a surrogate for the advertiser seems to lessen our sense of a hard sell. The presenter character also acts as an important mnemonic device. In drama commercials, the choice of character is crucial for advertiser's hopes that we will want to identify with the character.

The second important question to ask of any ad is: 'Who is the ad talking to?' When it appears to be talking to an on-screen character, we tend to mentally process the ad as a bystander. The closer we feel to the character, the more effect the ad is likely to have on us. 'Overhearing' something can be more influential than being told it directly because we tend to apply less defensive processing to it.

Liking for a brand's advertising can be a feather—especially when everything else is equal. While ads don't necessarily have to be liked if they are imparting valuable news about the brand, a brand's advertising is nevertheless an intrinsic part of the brand personality. If we like its ads we have a greater chance of liking the brand. So, the more that things weigh equal the more important that liking of a brand's advertising is. Even as a feather, it can tip the balance of brand choice.

11 'BEHAVIORAL TARGETING': CONSUMERS IN THE CROSSHAIRS

This chapter introduces the practice of behavioral targeting, which is a way of targeting ads at us on the web so as to match what we are most likely to be interested in and most likely to respond to in a positive way.

To understand behavioral targeting, it is necessary to have an understanding of search engines and search advertising as well as ads that are placed on the web generally. There is more about these in Chapter 25, 'The web: advertising in a new age', so only the general concepts will be touched on here.

'Search' advertising

In this era of the Internet, most of us use a search engine like Google to access information from the web. The results of each query are displayed as a list of relevant links. Advertisers can buy the right to appear as a paid link (a.k.a. sponsored link) on that same page of results. *Search advertising*, as this is known, is not very exciting from a consumer's viewpoint but it does work and it has certainly been a growth phenomenon.

Of course, advertisers don't want their paid link to appear on the results page for any old query. This only works if their ad link is placed on results pages for queries that are related in some way to their product or service. That is, when search words are typed in that indicate that the searcher may be in a frame of mind to be interested in the advertiser's particular product or service.

So the paid links that are displayed are triggered by particular words or phrases that appear in our search query. Paid search advertising is sold to advertisers on the basis of keywords (Google calls them 'adwords'). Advertisers bid against each other for the right to have their link displayed whenever a particular keyword is searched in a query.

The point is that the keywords we search for indicate something about us. They are pointers to what our interests are, what we are concerned about and what we enjoy doing with our time as well as what we may be aiming to purchase. Just as the books you have in your bookcase can reveal a lot about you, so too can your search histories. Our extensive use of search engines generates an accumulating database of our individual search histories as a by-product.

Traditionally, market research by advertisers has been labor intensive using methods such as surveys, panels and focus groups to help advertisers know who best to target with their advertising. By contrast, search engine histories are a ready made, potential source of market research information that can indicate:

- who is in the market for a particular product;
- which people are likely to be most responsive to a particular message/appeal;
- which demographic group a computer user is likely to belong to.

But search engine information is just the beginning. What about the websites we actually visit and what about what we do there? Such information can also be revealing about what our interests are and to what things we are more likely to respond.

Visits to websites
Many websites are able to identify us (as a return visitor) if we come back to that website. They do this by placing a cookie (an identifier) on our computers on our first visit. Our search histories, plus the ability for websites to identify us when we return (using that cookie), open up a hugely expanded potential for web advertising to target us with the right kinds of web ads. If websites can utilize the information from our past visits to their site as well as information from our past search behavior, the site becomes well placed to pitch web ads to us that we are more likely to respond to.

Web ads (a.k.a. banner ads)
Web ads are sometimes called *banner ads* but they can in fact appear anywhere on a web page—not only at the top in the website banner. Historically, advertisers adopting the Internet as an advertising medium discovered their use of these web ads to be very problematic. That is

because we consumers more often than not seem to ignore them and click on so few of them to find out more information; at the time of writing, the average is something like one click for every five hundred exposures. This 'click-through' rate, as it is called, has been in decline for many years.

Technological advances have enabled web ads to become increasingly animated and this is having some positive effect. Movement gives web ads greater capacity to attract our eyes and to a degree, this results in greater click-through.[1] At the same time it can be really distracting and annoying.[2] Eye tracking data reveals that we try not to look *directly* at web ads and that we have to make a conscious effort to do this.[3] The same research indicates that web ads interfere with our reading and slow us down in finding information on the web page. So perhaps it is not surprising that we still click so few of them and that our opinion of them generally ranges from indifferent to negative. Many of us say that we rarely, if ever, find web advertising relevant.[4] However, this is likely to change as a result of behavioral targeting.

Behavioral targeting

Ever shopped at Amazon? If you have you will know that when you return to Amazon.com, the site recommends a list of books you might want to purchase. Amazon infers your interests from your past purchases and any titles you may have previously searched or inspected on Amazon. The practice of *behavioral targeting* is an extension of this.

When you search and browse the web and visit various sites from day to day, chances are that other online publishers and advertisers are also collecting information about your behavior. Increasingly this information is accessed and 'shared' (via middleman entities called ad networks).[5] Technically it is not you personally whose behavior they identify but mostly the behavior of your computer.[6] Behavioral targeting infers your interests from the behavior of your computer when it is on the web and what you (or others using your computer) type into search engines and websites.

The sites you visit, the searches you make, the articles you read, and the purchases you make are all data collected and potentially used for market research purposes. Advertising platforms like Yahoo can use this to profile visitors and say to advertisers: 'Looking for car shoppers, soccer moms or recent shoppers in any category? We have them.'

Such information is not restricted to a single website (as it is with Amazon.com) but can include data on what you search for in a number of search engines, which sites you actually visit and even what you buy at those sites. All this information is used to infer your interests, to enable advertisers to customize which ads to display to you when you are surfing or reading web pages. All this happens behind the scenes without you being much aware of it.

Those who sell web advertising space to advertisers have developed extensive capacity to merge and integrate this data that we reveal about ourselves on search engines and at web sites. To access many sites (like the *New York Times*, the *Guardian*, the *Washington Post*, etc) you are asked to register (or 'subscribe') and while this is usually free, it often requires you to enter demographic details like your age, sex and zip area code at the time of registration. Such sites can then use this information in conjunction with the broader data gathered from your general web surfing and search behavior to more precisely customize the ads they display to you on their pages.

On some sites, like social network sites such as Facebook, Bebo and MySpace, many people enter personal information that goes well beyond demographics. As part of their public profile, they include information such as who their favorite celebrities are, their favorite bands, favorite foods, their political views, their religious views, whether they are in a relationship, etc. This opens up a whole new dimension of potential targeting for ads to be directed at people based on their expressed interests, likes, and dislikes. Revealing such information about yourself makes it even easier to predict what appeals to you and which ads you will probably react to favorably.

Few consumers have any idea they are being tracked, profiled and targeted in this way. Like product placement, this is an area that is flourishing in the relative absence of regulation. And regulation has been slow in coming because in a sense this is regarded as an extension of ad targeting practices that have been accepted for many years.

Advertisers have always targeted advertising to particular segments of consumers. This is done by directing their ads into particular publications or into particular TV or radio programs that are known to attract a target group (e.g. eighteen- to 35-year-old males). The same can be done on the web. For example, if you frequently visit sports and car websites and read global warming articles on news sites and you bought tickets to a number of rock concerts recently then, statistically, the chances are pretty high that you are a male aged eighteen to 35 years.

But advertisers don't need to target their online advertising to *demographic* segments any more. Why should they, when they can directly target those who are in the market for their product. Are you in the market for a luxury car? If you recently searched for articles comparing the safety of Lexus versus Mercedes and visited various car comparison sites and one or more prestige car dealers' sites, then chances are pretty high that you are about to buy a luxury car. So, when you go on the web next time, don't be surprised if the ads on the pages you are reading turn out to be ads for luxury car brands. That is not too far removed from what has gone on in the past—except for one important difference: the extent of information collected about you that has been going on in the background without your awareness.

The ads displayed to you online can even be tailored on the fly, to match specific information about you. The technology to do this is very sophisticated. If, for example, you have recently searched information about coffee makers and you are now reading today's news headlines on your favorite website, you perhaps won't be surprised if an ad for a retail store (say Target) appears featuring coffee makers. You might, however, be taken aback that it lists the coffee makers in stock at the Target store *nearest to your address* and which ones are on special at that store this week.

Or, if you have been on a site comparing models of cars and researching the safety of various models, don't be surprised if, when you are reading today's news online, the ad displayed is not just any old ad but a Lexus ad—and not just any old Lexus ad but a Lexus ad that focuses specifically on safety. This is what the behavioral targeting information has pinpointed as your interest.

How much more precise can this get? In principle there is no real limit. In the absence of regulation, we are on a path of ever increasingly precise targeting.

Potential extensions

Applying pinpoint precision to messaging like this will inevitably be used for political campaigns. Political operators long ago learnt to target campaign ads into swinging seats or into key geographic battlegrounds. So tailoring local ads to feature local messages to run in local media (local newspapers, TV or radio stations) is nothing new. Indeed, these days key polling booth areas can even be targeted with direct-mail letters and specific cable TV ads that reach voters only in that micro-area and with a message that is highly relevant to it (e.g. a planned road redirection or a controversial high rise development plan for the area).

Behavioral targeting now increases this level of message precision to an even finer level. It enables political operators to target individuals not just in terms of locality but also in terms of interest and concern with particular issues (e.g. poverty, abortion or gender equality). As the chief marketing officer of a company providing this type of service explained: 'It becomes possible to identify people who are most engaged in and motivated by the issue based on sites they've visited, searches they've made, offers and ads they've been responsive to and communities of interest . . . Online there's a far richer pool of data to work with, including sites they visit, petitions, polls, or types of publications—and within those publications, specific articles they've read.'[7]

In the absence of regulation, this is another slippery slope. Tracking, profiling and targeting in order to accomplish pinpoint messaging doesn't stop with web advertising. If individuals can be targeted via their computer, there is no reason (except higher costs of production and delivery) why the same cannot be done with cable TV. Cable TV providers like Time Warner have already begun to move into this technology area by acquiring firms that possess this behavioral targeting know-how.[8]

Summary
Every new technology presents regulatory challenges and behavioral targeting is no different. We as consumers are increasingly in the cross-hairs as the web and web advertising assume more importance in our everyday lives. How will regulators respond?

And how will we consumers respond? After all, behavioral targeting is both a positive and a negative depending on how you look at it. The positive is that the ad spaces will, more and more, be filled with ads that we *want* to see. They will increasingly reflect products, brands, messages, and things that we are generally interested in. Less stuff of no interest to us will clutter up the web pages that we see.

The other side is the increasing temptation for us to spend that such targeting offers. And many people will be highly concerned about the privacy issue—the collection of information without our knowledge that goes on in the background. Privacy can be a very sensitive issue and nowhere more so than in the USA. The USA and indeed the world is grappling with policy in regard to the web and behavioral targeting.

As ads in cyberspace develop ever increasing allure, in more ways than one it will be imperative for us to 'watch this space'.

12 THE LIMITS OF ADVERTISING

It should be clear from previous chapters that traditional advertising's effectiveness has been much exaggerated. At the same time, newer forms of advertising, especially paid product placements, longer video commercials and web advertising (employing behavioral targeting) are all growing in potential influence and power. The exaggerated effectiveness of traditional advertising is based on what seem to be powerful psychological mechanisms: learning without awareness, making brands into symbols, having people see a brand in different ways, the influence of conformity and the use of brands to express identity. So why has traditional advertising not been anywhere near as powerful as many people feared?

This chapter explores the many factors that severely constrain and often frustrate the power of individual advertisers to influence us. It shows how difficult it is for advertisers to make these psychological mechanisms work and how their unbridled use in any wholesale manipulation has been virtually impossible. Just as democratic political systems are supposed to have various checks and balances to constrain the power of elected governments to dictate to us, so too are 'checks and balances' inherent in the competitive environment in which advertisers operate. In addition, we consumers vote with our feet—the most powerful constraint of all. When the brand or the product does not live up to its promise, when it does not meet the expectations created by the advertising, then we simply don't buy it again. So as we shall see, traditional advertising's power has been constrained as much by practical limitations as by absolute limitations.

Competitors' advertising
One of the most important limitations on any advertiser's power to influence us is the activity of its competitors. Competitors' advertising,

more often than not, severely blunts an individual advertiser's efforts. If McDonald's was the only brand that advertised in the fast food restaurant category, its advertising power and market share would undoubtedly be much greater.

For every advertiser there is at least one and usually several other advertisers in the same product category. This creates a lot of advertising 'noise' and clutter. The 'noise' of competing claims often neutralizes or at least greatly dilutes the effect of any individual campaign. It also makes it much more expensive for any individual company to advertise at a level and frequency that can be heard above the competitive 'noise'. This imposes a limitation of its own.

For example, in many countries ad wars between telecommunication brands have been in full swing for decades. In the USA and other major countries you no longer have to change numbers to switch phone carriers. Accordingly, if a company such as AT&T increases advertising spending, others like Verizon will correspondingly ramp up their spending to protect their customer base. So while AT&T has a huge budget and is usually one of the top ten advertising spenders, so too is Verizon. Quite a bit of this expenditure simply neutralizes or minimizes the effects of competitors' ads. Much the same is true of General Motors in competition with Ford, both of which, despite spending huge ad budgets, have been unable to prevent Japanese brands making long-term in-roads into their market share. While GM's ad budget is huge, the combined ad spending of Japanese vehicle makers is usually greater.

Money: limitations of budget

In the competitive environment it takes huge sums of money, sometimes over long periods, for mechanisms such as learning without awareness, making brands into symbols, having people see things in different ways, the influence of conformity and the use of brands to express identity to be really effective. Even the largest companies cannot afford the advertising that would be necessary to 'manipulate' us in the wholesale way that many opponents of advertising fear. This is especially true when the brand has no unique benefit or difference over other brands and the difference has to be created by advertising.

Even products that offer substantial real benefit over competitors must be prepared to spend very heavily to get that superiority message across.

Even dominant brands like Coca-Cola rarely account for the majority of advertising in their product category. In countries like the USA, the UK and Australia for example, Coke usually accounts for less than a third of the total soft drink advertising. The proportion is even smaller if we take into account other beverages which are less direct competitors of Coke, such as bottled water, fruit juice, milk, tea, and coffee. So even the huge brands rarely have the advertising field to themselves.

Creating needs

People who are 'anti advertising' often feel that advertisers create needs and manipulate us into buying things we don't really need or want. To what extent can the psychological mechanisms of advertising be used to create needs or manipulate us in such a way? Before answering, there are two related questions to answer. What do we really need, and what role does advertising play in bringing new products to our attention?

Advertising announces new products. It is generally quite effective in at least making us aware of new products and new brands. This is one role of advertising that people rarely object to—unless the new product is trivial. Most people see this as a positive role, informing us of new events. In this sense it is like news, which is valued because it is informative.

People who are 'anti advertising' do not focus on the awareness role so much as the persuasive role of advertising—on its ability to make us buy things that we don't need. I have largely dismissed persuasion in earlier chapters and pointed out that of the many psychological mechanisms underlying most advertising, persuasion is often the least relevant. If it were truly relevant its record would be rather poor. Estimates vary but everybody agrees on this much—at least 40 per cent of all new consumer products fail and some estimates go as high as an 80–90 per cent failure rate.[1] What advertisers and marketers would like to sell is influenced by what we as consumers can relate to, and in the end feel we want or need . . . and vice versa.

Advertising does not create these products. What it does do is help accelerate their diffusion into the mass market. The more truly new and beneficial a product is, the more informational its advertising tends to be. We have a choice: are we interested in this new benefit or not? Can we afford it? Are we prepared to pay the price?

Every household today needs a refrigerator, a washing machine and its TV sets. Even the severest critic of advertising is likely to have them.

What else do we really need? Heating, airconditioning, a microwave, dishwasher, DVD player? These are no longer regarded as luxuries. Digital cameras and mobile phones have also become pretty much universal. Wireless broadband also is becoming mainstream. And almost all homes in the developed world have a computer; twenty-five years ago almost none did. The list goes on and on. Yesterday's inventions and luxuries become tomorrow's necessities. Do we need these things? Those who argue that we don't are technically right. We could live without them. But do we want to?

These are acquired needs, not biological needs such as hunger, thirst, and sex. Were they created by advertising? No, they were created by inventors. Advertising's primary role is creating *awareness* of these inventions in the mass market. There is no doubt that without such advertising all these innovations (ranging from computers to low-fat foods and energy efficient appliances) would diffuse through each country's population very much more slowly.

How advertising accelerates mass markets

Communicating the existence of a new product (e.g. digital cameras, MP3 players, GPS navigators, satellite radios) to the mass market, even without persuasion, expands the demand for that product because just on the probabilities alone some proportion of us will always be interested in buying a new innovation. These purchases then have the effect of increasing the size of the production run for the new product, which in turn reduces the unit cost of production. This creates economies of scale in production and translates into a lower price tag on the new product that is offered for sale. When the product is advertised at a lower price, some of us who had previously decided against buying it because it was too expensive become interested. It has now become available to some of us who otherwise could not afford it. This expands sales further, which increases production runs further, which reduces price further, which makes the product more available and affordable for even more people. Electronic calculators, digital watches, mobile phones and personal computers are classic examples from the past. IPods, GPS navigators and digital video recorders are more recent examples.

The whole effect is circular. Advertising, in communicating first the product and then the affordable price, accelerates the diffusion of the innovation into the mass market. Without advertising the process would probably still happen, but at an infinitely slower pace and we might still be using wringer clothes washers and manual typewriters, and computers might still be something that only businesses could afford.

The critics of all this often seem to be nostalgic for the simplicities of the past. Nostalgia is an attempt to create an idealized past in the present.[2] It tends to gloss over the unpleasant aspects of the past and focus only on the pleasant aspects. However, there is no argument for staying where we are. Only the most naïve romantics would argue that as primitive humans we were happier living in our caves. Who wants to go back to washing dishes by hand and stovetop heating of foods without a microwave? Of course, as sustainability becomes an issue, curbing the growth in our consumption may well become unavoidable. But only the most nostalgic conservatives would argue that our grandparents were happier doing washing in a kerosene tin boiled over an open fire than we are with our modern washing machine, refrigerator, microwave, telephone and many other creature comforts.

Ads for brands or ads for products?

The vast majority of advertising attempts to get us to buy one brand instead of another and not new products per se. Earlier chapters focused on the low-involvement effects of advertising, which can tip the balance in the weighing up of brands when everything is equal or can influence which brands are weighed up. Only the rare category leaders (like Campbell's soup or Microsoft) can afford to advertise just to grow the category. Hence only a very tiny proportion of advertising is directly aimed at affecting our decision as to whether to purchase a product or not, as distinct from which of the various brands to buy. (The main exception seems to be advertising of primary food products—milk, pork, beef, raisins, mangoes, cheese, rice, butter, bananas, avocados, etc—and direct-to-consumer prescription drug advertising aimed at spurring visits to doctors to 'ask about' treatments for erectile disfunction, sleep disorders, etc.)

Persuasion is not involved in the great majority of *brand* advertising that we are exposed to. To the extent that most brand advertising does influence our feelings of need for the product category itself, then this result is more a side effect than a primary focus of the advertiser. That is not to say that it is unimportant. Clearly, enough people think it is important to have banned cigarette advertising and impose restrictions on alcohol advertising. And many believe that direct-to-consumer prescription drug advertising should also be restricted.

Research into the ability of brand advertising to create demand for the category as a whole is sparse. The strongest evidence is within the USA where the legalization of direct-to-consumer prescription drug advertising dramatically expanded the market for many pharmaceutical products. On the other hand extensive investigation into the role of brand advertising as a contributor to obesity, alcoholism and the like has remained frustratingly inconclusive. My own suspicion is that research will eventually show the spin-off effect to be substantial and that its mechanism is based primarily on agenda setting by creating an image of popularity and social acceptance for the product categories—but only if enough advertising for enough brands is aired for long enough.

If this turns out to be true, it still implies very severe constraints on the power of advertisers to foist just anything onto us. Unless a new product finds reasonable acceptance quite quickly, it is likely to be discontinued before the agenda-setting process has time to take hold. There are limits to how long advertisers are able or willing to keep advertising a product that is not selling enough to pay for the cost of production, simply in the hope that it will eventually 'catch on'. This is why market research tries to determine beforehand what consumers would like to have, or at least what is likely to meet with ready acceptance rather than resistance.

In influencing taste, trend, and social acceptance, the mass media has always been much more powerful than advertising. However, the rise of paid product placement, as we saw in Chapter 6, gives advertisers the ability to influence program content so that the previous distinction is blurring. In the absence of regulation, there is little doubt that product placement will deliver advertisers greater potential to influence us than previously.

Resistance to change
There is another limitation on advertising's ability to exercise unbridled influence and this is reflected in our resistance to change and the natural way our minds work. Our minds seem to have a strong inbuilt need for cognitive consistency. We tend to reject that which is not consistent with what we currently know or have come to expect. To succeed, an innovation usually has to find a line of least resistance.

For example, for years after it was developed many people rejected instant coffee, which was advertised on the basis of ease of use. Research revealed that household food buyers (mostly women in the 1950s) saw the so-called convenience benefit as reflecting directly on their performance. Buying instant coffee (as distinct from coffee beans) was seen as the mark of 'a lazy housewife who did not care for her family'. Remember, female role models in the 1950s were quite different from today's. This negative association slowed the rate of acceptance of many innovations pitched at convenience and time-saving, including dishwashers, microwave ovens and automatic washing machines.

Another example was a noiseless food mixer, which was rejected for quite a different reason—because it seemed not to have much power. We tend to believe powerful machines are noisy. A noiseless food mixer is a contradiction. A machine that is both powerful and quiet is inconsistent with our experience, so we find it difficult to accept.

Similarly many packaged cake mix products will have you add eggs to the mix. The eggs are not in any way necessary to the cake's success but were added to the recipe after research discovered people did not feel satisfied making a product they didn't put enough effort into, especially something as indulgent and nurturing as a cake.

Perhaps the most telling example of this effect is dishwashing detergent. Before detergent was invented, when we washed dishes in soapy water in the sink, it was lack of suds on the top of the water that we used as a cue to tell us when to add more soap. Dishwashing detergent does not naturally foam, but manufacturers eventually had to add foam to the product to get it accepted. Without foam the detergent was not seen to be working. Unless new products fit with, or at least do not clash with, what is already in our minds, their advertisers are likely to encounter substantial resistance to the innovation. They are likely to face a long, hard and very costly battle over many years before the product eventually, if ever, achieves widespread acceptance.

Dishwashing detergent as a new product initially clashed with (was not consistent with) something that was well established in our minds—namely that when washing up sudsing indicated water was working and lack of suds indicated when it was not and it was time to add more soap. For a product to gain widespread acceptance, the product may also have to be made consistent with consumers' existing beliefs or expectations. This reflects a more general psychological principle which is often known as cognitive consistency.

Cognitive consistency

Our minds seem to have a need for consistency, in our attitudes and beliefs, and between these attitudes and our behavior.[3] Let me illustrate the general mechanism that is at work here. If we drive a Toyota and believe that Toyotas are safe cars, and we read in consumer reports that more people have accidents in Toyotas than in any other car, what happens? A motivation is automatically set up in us to try to resolve the apparent contradiction. Either our original belief is wrong and we had better think again next time we buy a car, or there is something wrong with the report. We are experiencing the need for cognitive consistency. We either have to start to change our mind about Toyotas' safety or we have to find something wrong with the consumer report—to discredit it.

We humans try to keep our attitudes and beliefs consistent, as well as our attitudes and behavior. This is not a voluntary mechanism but more an unconscious one that goes into action automatically. It was first demonstrated by Leon Festinger in a classic series of experiments. During the Vietnam War, for example, Festinger gave experimental subjects who were opposed to the war an incentive to argue a position that was contrary to what they believed i.e. to argue in favor of the war. He found that these people's attitudes to the war tended to change in the direction that they had been paid to argue—in favor of the war.

This demonstrated that when our behavior becomes inconsistent with our attitudes, then those attitudes begin to change. Just as importantly, the same thing happens if we hold two attitudes or beliefs and then find out that they are not consistent. For example, what happens if you dislike large SUV vehicles because of their environmental impact and your closest friend, whose judgment you respect, tells you she has just bought one? You have two attitudes, one positive and one negative. Your attitude towards your friend is positive. Your attitude towards SUVs is negative. The two attitudes are inconsistent or out of balance. When this happens and we cannot avoid facing the inconsistency of two positions, then our minds automatically begin to change one or other of them in order to bring them into balance. It either weakens our prejudice against SUVs or weakens the respect we have for our friend and her judgment.

It is important to note that we don't have to be highly conscious of the discrepancy for the effect to be triggered implicitly.[4] Even if our minds are focused somewhere other than on the discrepancy, it can be triggered nonetheless. Indeed it has even been shown in people suffering amnesia i.e. even though they are incapable of retaining any explicit memory of the discrepancy, resultant change in their attitude or their behaviour takes place.[5]

Advertising is the weaker influence

Advertising is usually the weaker influence compared to what we already know or have in our minds. Any ad campaign is most likely to lead to advertising failure if the message is inconsistent with our existing beliefs and with what most other people believe. Advertisers have to strive to put forward a position that is credible, or at least is not inconsistent with what we as consumers already know and think.

For example, in a number of areas of the world light beer found great difficulty in gaining acceptance among young (eighteen- to 24-year-old) male beer drinkers. It tended to be much more accepted by older drinkers. The young tend to be searching for identity, and symbols of self-expression play a role in this. Despite successful efforts by advertisers to get light beer accepted, it was nevertheless strongly resisted by younger people for a number of years. For them, the image of light beer as a product was inconsistent with the strong male image that drinking beer was traditionally identified with.

Similarly, even where cigarette advertising was banned and health promotion ads urged our young people not to smoke, it took a long time to see any substantial effect—particularly amongst young females. As long as their friends smoked and it was seen to make you look 'cool', any messages that emphasized health consequences tended to fall on deaf ears.

It is rare that advertisers can afford to engage in protracted efforts to confront and change such entrenched attitudes or behaviour directly. Usually, they have to look for an approach that will be more readily accepted because it fits neatly with existing beliefs or aligns with more important motivations. When these anti-smoking health messages to young females fell on deaf ears, the advertising approach cleverly switched to making smoking 'uncool' (e.g. by emphasizing things like bad breath and smelly hair—things that can impact socially and romantically).

The point is that advertisers have to look for a message that is consistent with existing beliefs or motivations. An historical example is the famous 'Avis—we try harder' campaign discussed earlier. This capitalized on the widespread belief that monopolies and big companies tend to become complacent. Companies which are still trying to get to the top probably *will* try harder. The ad is cognitively consistent with what is already known, so it is more likely to be accepted.

Our need for cognitive consistency means that advertisers who simply try to persuade us against our will, who try to get us to accept something that goes against our existing information or attitudes, are almost certain to fail (unless they also have unlimited time and money to hang in for the long term). This is a big constraint on advertising's power that is contained in our psychological make-up. Like most of the other limitations, it is not an absolute constraint. Finding ways around it poses a real challenge to advertising agencies.

Positioning for cognitive consistency

Chapter 2 pointed out that humans have the ability to see the same thing (whether it be the same product or the same advertisement) in different ways depending on our frame of reference. The challenge for advertising agencies is to position the ad or product in such a way that it is seen to be consistent with, rather than to clash with, our existing mind set. All too often this is unsuccessful—as evidenced by the fact that so many new products fail.

It is a creative task and it is difficult to give examples of this 'creativity' at work without breaching client confidentiality, but let me illustrate how it works with a couple of hypothetical examples.

Consider Oscar Mayer, the Kraft-owned US brand heavily identified with 'food your kids will eat'. Suppose Oscar Mayer wanted to market a hot dog—one that is 'good for you'. However almost everyone knows hot dogs are made of leftovers—intestines and all the grossest possible parts of the animal. How can it be good for you? Even '100 per cent beef hot dogs' translates in our minds to 100 per cent leftovers from cows. Because there is an active predisposition not to believe it, positioning the product as 'good for you' would be most unlikely to succeed.

Consider another similar hypothetical example. This time a hypothetical brand of canned fish called Fine-C Foods, long established globally as a high quality brand, uses the slogan 'It's the fish that Fine-C rejects that makes Fine-C the best'.[6] The quality image of the brand is paramount in its positioning. The company decides to enter a new but related category. In certain parts of the world there is a product category known as 'fish paste', a spread that comes in a jar. Fine-C wants to get into this market with a quality fish paste to compete with the existing brands that are all of rather poor quality. Positioning it on the quality dimension 'Fine-C . . . superior quality fish paste' would make it consistent with the Fine-C quality image. It would fit with pre-existing beliefs and work in harmony with the pre-existing image of quality that the Fine-C brand has developed. So far so good. A real limitation, however, lurks below the surface. If there is a widespread belief among consumers (and indeed there is) that fish paste is made of leftovers—that is, all the good parts of the fish having been already used for something else (similar to the general image of sausages)—then 'Fine-C . . . superior quality fish paste' is likely to translate unconsciously in consumers' minds as 'Fine-C . . . superior quality leftovers'. This is hardly the desired image. It would also be disastrous for the product. The cognitive inconsistency is likely to doom the product to failure from the start.

What can an advertising agency do in this type of situation? One option would be to rename the product and market it as Fish-Paté. Paté is also a spread, but it has quite different associations that are consistent with the quality positioning of the Fine-C Food brand. This strategy is more likely to succeed than a strategy of directly confronting entrenched negative attitudes to fish paste.

Much of the art of advertising, then, lies in finding ways to play the focal beam of attention on the attributes of the product that are consistent with what already exists in our minds. That which already exists in our minds is a limitation or an inhibitor to what advertising can do.

When everything else is not equal

Advertisers are beginning to find that advertising seems to work best when it communicates some positive benefit, or when the brand is at least equal to other brands on the market and the advertising can tip the balance. Rarely can advertising succeed if a brand is inferior to the competition or if its qualities are cognitively inconsistent with the consumer's mind set. In other words, advertising is not magical. It is just one influence among many and when there are real differences between brands the truth generally wins out eventually. Advertising may get us to try a product, but our experience with the product then overrides anything that advertising may tell us. If the product does not live up to the promise, we don't purchase it again.

Conversion/persuasion vs reinforcement

This highlights the fact that advertising's principal effect is to reinforce rather than persuade. That is, it reinforces in us the decision we made to purchase the brand and increases the chances of us buying it again. Using panels of consumers reporting on what they purchase each week, Professor Andrew Ehrenberg in the UK has studied the effects of advertising on purchasing probably more than any other person in the world. His conclusion is that 'advertising's main role is to reinforce feelings of satisfaction for brands already being used'.[7]

This is consistent with my own observations from tracking many hundreds of ad campaigns in various parts of the world. Advertising has frequently proved quite ineffective by itself in convincing people to buy a brand for the first time. To achieve widespread trial of a new brand, advertising usually has to be heavily supplemented by promotions, in-store displays and free sampling. With supermarket brands this is very much influenced by simple locating behavior. The new brand has to stop us walking at more than 1 mile per hour (2 km/h) and cut through the clutter and get noticed. There are limits to how much advertising alone can do here. (Advertising does seem to be more effective at getting people to buy a truly new product for the first time than at getting them to try yet another 'me-too' brand in an established product category. But again, with supermarket products it often takes in-store displays and promotion to achieve widespread trial reasonably rapidly.)

Reinforcement is the reason why some ad campaigns, the ones conducted by the smart advertisers, talk to their own consumers. Users of a brand almost always react more positively to its advertising than non-users.[8] Toyota trucks used this to good effect in various parts of the world with the 'I love what you do to me' line. One US commercial for Toyota trucks featured vignettes of Toyota truck owners saying what they were doing at the time their truck clocked up 100,000 or 200,000 or 300,000 miles. It closed with an invitation to Toyota truck owners to phone a toll free number 'and tell us where you were and what you were doing' at these milestones. This ad undoubtedly reinforced the repeat buying of those who already owned a Toyota truck by reminding them of the durability of their truck and the number of miles it had endured. Just as importantly, however, it also got the message across indirectly to the 'bystanders', to those who had never bought a Toyota truck, that these must be very, very durable vehicles.

The long-running Dial deodorant soap campaign is another example of using a brand's own customers talking about their product in such a way that the viewer is cast as a bystander rather than the target of the message. 'Aren't you glad you use Dial—don't you wish everyone did?' Another example, this time from Australia, is the leading Australian margarine brand, Meadow Lea. For many years, its ads would sing to an on-screen buyer of Meadow Lea, 'You oughta be congratulated' (implying 'because of your good taste/judgment').

Such ads, rather than placing the focus of attention on what might otherwise be perceived as an empty promise or claim, address those of us already using the product, reminding us that we are happy with the brand. (Would we be buying it if we weren't? So who is going to argue?) Consider how greater the invitation to rejection is when it says: 'If you switch to our brand, you will be glad', or 'If you switch to our brand you will be congratulated'?

So instead of the typical promise style (i.e. 'Buy X brand and you will get Y result'), this type of advertising provides a verbal 'pat on the back' to its own customers. At the same time, it casts people not using the brand as bystanders who 'overhear' a communication between the advertiser and the buyers of that brand. Because they are bystanders, there is nothing in the ad likely to motivate them to try to refute it. As we saw earlier, this can be even more effective than when it is addressed to that person directly.[9] Of course should the bystander overhearing this be tempted to try the brand, he/she becomes a buyer and the commercial then becomes a verbal 'pat on the back' for them. The ad is a feather.

In a brilliant twist on this concept, Deighton pointed out that advertising tunes up our attention to a brand's key attribute(s) *at the time that we are consuming it.*[10] It is more likely that we will think of some aspect of the advertising at the time we use the brand, and consequently take greater notice than we otherwise would have of the advertised attribute. In the same way as I can direct your attention to the noises going on around you right now that you were previously not consciously aware of, so can advertising draw our attention to or remind us to notice the advertised attribute when we are consuming the brand. As a result of repetition of the advertising, when we consume the brand we may think to confirm that the brand does indeed have the advertised attribute. The advertising sensitizes us to experiencing those advertised attributes and confirming them. It therefore has the potential to *transform* the consumption experience.[11] Without first experiencing the advertising we might simply consume the brand without noticing the differences between it and its competitors.

Confirming that a brand has the advertised attribute has two effects:

- It reinforces the consumption experience and makes us more likely to buy the same brand again.
- It makes us feel more positively towards the advertiser and the truthfulness of their advertising. (People use their experience with the brand to judge an ad's truthfulness and therefore its informativeness. Whether people regard an ad as 'informative' is greatly influenced by their satisfaction with the brand.[12])

Ads that work or ads that win awards

Far from being omnipotent ogres who can manipulate us at will, companies which advertise often struggle desperately to get advertising that works. They are often frustrated by the inability to get a campaign that has a measurable impact on sales and market share. Getting something that is a clever piece of art is relatively easy, but they want to sell product.

The people who are primarily responsible for making ads for them, the creative directors in advertising agencies, are artistic people. A number of them are making ads not because they choose to, but because they can't do what they most want to do—make feature films.

Denied the opportunity to make full-length films, it is natural that they will get at least some satisfaction from producing 30-second feature films instead. The result is that advertisers can end up with 30-second feature films disguised as TV ads and many of these win awards. Such 30-second feature films may look nice and they may be very clever and entertaining, but if the brand is used merely as a prop and little regard is given to the main purpose as a commercial, then the chance of it succeeding in its real purpose is very small. If it does work, it is likely to be more by accident than design.

Traditionally advertising industry awards were not based on any measure of effectiveness but on subjective evaluation and artistic creativity. Objective measurement of effectiveness in selling the product has not been the primary consideration. As a result many advertisers in the past have not known whether these mini-films worked or didn't work. More often than not, advertisers are unable to gauge effectiveness by their sales alone because there are too many other things (price promotion, what competitors do) that also affects sales and, as we have seen, reinforcement rather than sales is often the primary effect. Advertisers have been able to do little more than grope towards effective advertising.

However, this is now beginning to change. With the advent of new market research technology and a more educated breed of product managers, marketing managers, and marketing directors, companies are becoming less and less reliant on their advertising agency simply winning artistic awards to reassure them that their advertising is working. Awards (such as the 'Effies') based on objectively measured evidence of advertising effectiveness rather than artistic merit are now operative in most major western countries. More and more, the advertisers themselves are putting in place the market research mechanisms which will allow them to assess what is working and what is not.

Summary

Most advertising tries to get us to buy one brand instead of another and much of it is not concerned with new products per se. It tips the balance in the weighing up of brands when everything is equal, and it can influence which brands get weighed up.

Advertising for new products announces more than it persuades. To the extent that persuasion is involved its record would be extremely poor, because at least 40 per cent of all new consumer products fail. When advertising does influence our feelings of need for the product category, this is more a side effect than something that the advertising is primarily focused on.

The effect of advertising is, therefore, more often not persuasion but reinforcement. That is, it reinforces in us the decision we made to purchase the brand and increases the chances of our buying it again.

Much of the art of advertising lies in finding a way to play the focal beam of attention onto the attributes of the brand that are consistent with our existing mind set. Positioning a product in this way is no easy task.

Advertising's power is constrained as much by practical limitations as by absolute limitations. These include:

- the fact that consumers vote with their feet;
- competitive advertising;
- money: limitations of budget;

- economic reality;
- resistance to change and need for cognitive consistency;
- the fact that advertising is usually the weaker influence compared to what we already know or have in our minds.

None of these limitations is absolute but taken together they make advertising much less able to influence us than has usually been thought by the average consumer. This notion will probably not convince those who want to believe in the manipulative power of advertising, because advertising is one of those things that some people love to hate. The reality, however, is that the power and mystique of advertising and the people who make it have been much exaggerated.

Nothing stays static, however, and the forms of advertising are now changing rapidly. Some of these, like paid product placement, are blurring the distinction between ads and mass media program content. When advertising masquerades as program content, some of our advertising defences are quiescent. Limitations that have protected us from undue influence of advertising in the past are not guaranteed to automatically protect us into the future. So, while the power of advertising has been much exaggerated, we should remember Thomas Jefferson's words that 'the price of freedom is eternal vigilance'.

PART B

WHAT WORKS, WHAT DOESN'T, AND WHY

INTRODUCTION

We saw in Part A that we can gain an important insight into advertising by asking the question, 'Who is the ad talking to?' The same applies to books like this one. Who is this book talking to? If it is aimed at the general reader it will have a different feel and style than if it is aimed at advertising practitioners or students of marketing or mass communication. Part A talked primarily to the general reader.

At this point in the book the general reader will sense a change of key. Many of the chapters that make up Part B had their origins in articles that were written for trade publications. The readers of these are advertisers and marketers who want to know more about how to make advertising work more effectively.

While this section talks primarily to these professionals, general readers should find it an interesting 'bystander' experience. In fact they may like to imagine themselves as advertisers. By looking briefly through the advertisers' eyes they will develop a greater understanding of advertising at work, and see the obstacles that advertisers strive to overcome in their attempt to influence us.

An understanding of only three technical terms is necessary for reading Part B. The first of these, *ad execution*, has already cropped up in Part A. A brand like Coke will often have several different ads on air in the same week. While the brand and the essential message are usually the same, the characters, dialogue or general scene may be different in each case. Each variation is referred to as an ad execution. Alternatively, you may see a 30-second ad and a fifteen-second one which is recognizable as a part of the larger ad. These are regarded as two different 'executions'. The creative execution, then, is the way that a particular ad is carried out or executed.

The second technical term is *flighting*. Some advertisers schedule their brand's advertising to appear every week. This is known as a continuous advertising schedule. Others prefer to 'flight' their advertising, in other words to have a burst of several weeks of the same advertising followed by a few weeks off air, then go on air again with another few weeks of the same advertising and so on.

This is known as a flighted ad schedule. Each new burst of advertising is regarded as a separate 'flight'.

The third technical term is TRP which is short for *target rating points*. This is known by different names in different countries. In the UK the term used is TVR; in Australia the term is TARP. But the concept is the same. Loosely speaking, it is a measure of the exposure that an ad gets. Indirectly, it reflects the amount of audience exposure and the number of exposures the advertiser pays for. The number of TRPs is a measure of how many people from the target market had an 'opportunity to see' because they were sitting in front of the TV set around the time when the ad was shown.

Let me explain this with an example. Kleenex might define its primary target market for tissues as females aged eighteen to 45 years old. If the ad for Kleenex tissues went to air on NBC at 8.50 pm last night and 5 per cent of this group were watching NBC at that time, the ad has 5 TRPs. If the ad is shown again multiple times in the same week in various programs on various channels, each time the percentage of the target market watching at the time is added to the accumulated TRP figure. So the ad might accumulate say 210 TRPs for the week. Note that this is merely the gross total of people who had an 'opportunity to see'. Some of these will have also seen the ad when it was shown earlier in the week but they are nevertheless counted again in the TRP figure. The total TRP figure can be calculated from the percentage of the target market that has had an 'opportunity to see' the ad at least once, or the net reach, and average the number of times they saw it, which is known as the average frequency.[1] A total of 210 TRPs for the week could represent a variety of combinations of reach and frequency. Table BI.1 shows only a few of the possibilities.

For example, the whole target market may have seen the ad during the week and they may have seen it on average 2.1 times. Or perhaps only 50 per cent of the target audience saw the ad but they saw it on average 4.2 times. This still accumulates to 210 TRPs. In other words an ad can accumulate 210 TRPs through any combination of net reach (percentage of the target audience who saw it at least once) and average frequency

Table BI.1: Calculation of TRP figure

Net reach	Average frequency	Total TRPs
100	2.1	210
50	4.2	210
35	6.0	210

(the average number of times these people did see it) that when multiplied together totals 210.[2]

The majority of ad campaigns run at 100 to 300 TRPs a week. Fifty TRPs would be a light weight while 400 TRPs would be a heavy weight of advertising in any one week.

13 CONTINUOUS TRACKING: ARE YOU BEING FOLLOWED?

An increasing number of advertisers now track their competitors' activities as well as their own with continuous customer surveys. These are not once a year or once a quarter surveys. They are conducted every week—on small samples each week which accumulate over the year into a large database and provide a total, continuous picture.

Every week these organizations capture, in their computers, fresh information on a new sample of consumers. The information covers all players in the market. Ideally it would cover the state of play for that week in regard to people's behavior, attitudes, brand awareness, brand image as well as direct communication effects such as advertising recall, advertising recognition and message take-out. This is then related to other information such as media data (indicating which advertisers were on air during that week, at what times and at what advertising weight) along with sales and market share data.

Continuous market research technology has rapidly become accepted as the best way to accurately assess advertising effects in terms of what works and what doesn't.[1] Continuous monitoring of *purchase* information can reveal if something worked or didn't. However, knowing *if* it worked is one thing, while finding out *why* or *why not* is another. This diagnostic information also needs to be continuous and comes from continuous surveying otherwise known as *continuous tracking*.

Market research is traditionally characterized by the large scale, large sample survey representing a single point in time. Known as 'ad hoc' surveys, these were sometimes conducted before an ad campaign and then again after it. Any differences in key measures between these two surveys (such as in the levels of people's brand awareness, ad awareness or the brand's market share) were supposed to indicate possible effects of the advertising. This 'pre/post' survey technique, as it was known, slowly but inevitably has been giving way to the new technology of continuous monitoring.

Conducting ad hoc surveys or pre/post surveys was the 'old' way of trying to understand what is happening in a market. It is like taking a couple of still frames from the beginning and end of a TV commercial and trying to get a sense of the whole commercial from just those two pictures. The difference between ad hoc surveys and continuous surveying resembles the difference between still photography and moving pictures: without continuous moving pictures, the dynamics of what is happening can only be guessed at.

Take this dramatic case of a shampoo brand in one country with around 2.5 per cent market share amongst females under 35. The brand launches a spectacular new commercial. The plot unfolds as follows: this new, different ad hits the TV. It is clearly an exciting and different commercial. The advertiser is putting quite heavy expenditure behind the commercial. Quickly we see, to no one's surprise, that this ad successfully breaks through the clutter of shampoo advertising and delivers a message. We see this in the first two weeks of data (see Figures 13.1 and 13.2). So far so good, but will the ad sell product? If you are a competitor, do you react? Panic? Sit tight? You recall a previous ad for this same brand which broke through very well, but ho-hum, it didn't sell. Maybe this will be the same. Let's not worry too much yet! The key issue is will consumer *behavior* change?

The continuous surveying that you are doing as a matter of course asks which brand the respondent last bought and the answers come in each week in the weekly sample data. You wait and watch agonizingly. Will brand purchase behavior move in response to the ad?

Figures 13.1 and 13.2 tell the story. Within a month of the ad coming on air, you know the hair-raising truth. By the third or fourth week of the new advertising, this brand's market share is clearly moving. By the fifth week it has doubled from 2.5 per cent to around 5 per cent. There is now no doubt this new ad is working. If this is a competitor, you had better move fast to try to find a way to counter it. Or start revising the annual market share projections for your brand *downwards*.

In fact, nine weeks after the launch of the new ad, the brand had successfully increased its market share in this target group to more than 10 per cent—a phenomenal achievement. If you are a competitor of this brand the news you are getting from your tracking is depressing. The upside of this, however, is that you know at the earliest possible moment. While it may be cold comfort, you do have more time to formulate a retaliation strategy.

I have also seen situations like this where the ad, while very visible and attention getting, did not sell the product (sometimes because there was no relevant message or the ad failed to correctly communicate the brand and link it with the message). In the absence of *weekly* information, it is sometimes an overwhelming temptation to react, when in fact there may be no need to. It is comforting to know at the earliest possible time whether you need to react to a competitor's move.

With the tracking results for this commercial, you have just received the clearest possible evidence that advertising can work in this market. Additional analysis over time allows you to draw conclusions as to the type of advertising that works and how it works in this market (because not all markets work the same way).

For example, in this market, did attitude change before behavior, or did behavior change before attitude? Did the advertising impact on image then attitude then behavior? What was the direction of the chain of events?

Product managers and marketing managers want to know what works in their market and what doesn't. If a competitor implements a new action, should they react? How do they judge what to react to and what not to react to?

While continuous surveying as a 'rear-vision mirror' has been around for a while, we can discern among advertisers a new trend in its use. The very astute advertisers are not just using it to see where their brand has been and evaluate the effectiveness of their moves, but to address the much larger question of how the market works. Increasingly, they are using it before making their important moves and to study their competitors' activities as well as their own. Their objective is to know what works and what doesn't before they make any important move in the market. The idea is to formulate the right move and ensure the maximum chance of success.

Not all are using it in this way—only the really smart ones. These advertisers are not just tracking their own brand. They are also tracking and studying their competitors' actions and the effectiveness of those actions. By getting a handle on what is effective and what is not, they move towards closure on the question of what works and what doesn't in their particular market. They address such questions as:

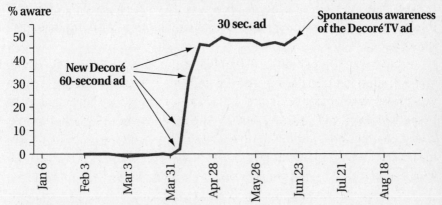

Note: Continuous tracking of people's spontaneous awareness of the Decoré advertisement.

Figure 13.1: *Shampoo advertisement awareness. (Source: MarketMind[2])*

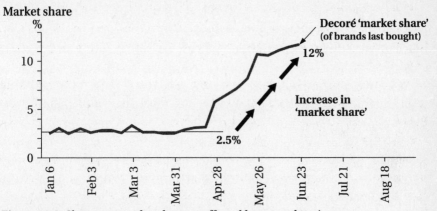

Figure 13.2: *Shampoo market share as affected by new advertisement. (Source: MarketMind)*

- Does advertising work in this market?
- What type of advertising works?
- How does it work?
- Does the advertising change attitudes and then behavior? Or behavior then attitudes?
- Should we have advertising that primarily reinforces behavior ('Aren't you glad you use Dial?')? Or do we need advertising that will primarily generate trial ('Four good reasons to try brand X')?

In other words, 'What works? And what doesn't?'

It is important to note that we are not just talking about advertising here. Product managers and advertising managers are also interested in promotions, changes in media flighting, different media weights, a switch to shorter length ads, new ads uploaded to YouTube, a free sampling campaign, a change in pricing, new positioning, a new presenter, or new creative advertising ideas. (The graph at Figure 13.1 shows what happened when this brand switched from 60-second to 30-second commercials. The flattening out of the growth in ad cut-through is very common after such a switch. It also happens after a switch from 30s to fifteens.) Almost any action or event that takes place in a market can be plotted on the time line and subjected to this type of effectiveness analysis.

Snapshot, single-point-in-time surveys do not cope with this. Dynamics are needed. Snapshot pictures are too slow, and they don't capture unexpected events—such as the launch of this new ad campaign by a competitor. Pre/post or periodic snapshot surveys of the market every quarter or half year or so are yesterday's technology. The problem with them is that the time dimension is missing.

With dynamic measurement, market modeling and market knowledge accumulate over time and let a company know much more than its competition about how the market works, what works in it, and what doesn't. The objective is to do more of what works and less of what doesn't.

It is no accident that Ronald Reagan was the most popular president than any before him—or that George Bush (the first) came from miles behind to take out the US presidency in 1989. The Republican party discovered very early the 'missing link' in research. This missing link was the time dimension: the use of continuous tracking. Bush was ultimately defeated in 1992 by Clinton which demonstrates the point made earlier—there are real limits to what advertising and promotion can do when the product does not perform or is looking old and tired. By the time re-election came around in 1996, Clinton and the Democratic party had mastered the new technology of continuous tracking, using it to great effect in evaluating and fine tuning the effectiveness of their ads—especially in swing states.[3] Such expertise was then 'loaned out' overseas, in the form of former Clinton experts assisting Tony Blair become elected as prime minister of the UK, and the rest is history. Continuous tracking research is now accepted as invaluable in the political campaign arsenal.

By contrast with such overtly successful results, traditional, single-point-in-time market research has often failed to produce actionable information. It has often been difficult to assess its value, precisely because the time dimension, reflecting the dynamic nature of markets, was either missing or very much mistreated. The time dimension has to be treated as a continuous variable and factored into marketing research methodology instead of being ignored or treated as a dichotomous variable.

Web tracking

In essence the concept of continuous tracking is the same with the web as with telephone. However in some ways the Internet makes continuous tracking easier and quicker, and can provide even better information.[4] Consider for example that:

- Measuring recognition of TV and print ads becomes better and easier, because visuals of the ads (or packs or displays, etc) are able to be shown so that people are reacting to the actual stimulus instead of verbal descriptions. Indeed, for your own ads the total ad can be shown in full video.
- People exposed to web ads are by definition on the web and potentially accessible using that (much less expensive) medium.
- The Internet enables very rapid, very cheap access to very large samples via random sampling (e.g. of people visiting a website) or via pre-recruited panels of respondents.
- Pre-recruited Internet panels enable targeting of even low incidence groups—such as whiskey drinkers, expectant mothers, psoriasis sufferers, etc.
- The low cost and super-fast turnaround of information means that web tracking has the capability of providing finer-grained information on a daily as well as a weekly basis.
- The use of 'control groups' is all too often cost prohibitive with telephone interviewing, but the Internet makes these much more affordable and much more feasible.
- It is also possible to continuously track visitors to your site. Who are they? Where do they come from? What pages do they visit? What are the most popularly visited places on your site? (See Chapter 11, 'Behavioral targeting'.)

Summary

The problem with traditional market research is that, with the time dimension missing, it is like taking still-camera snapshots. It is equivalent to taking the first and last frame of a television commercial and trying to guess from that what went on in between. With the time dimension included, you get the full dynamic picture. The research becomes richer and its value is much more easily demonstrable in terms of:

- its role as an 'early warning system';
- its ability to reveal changing patterns in a market;
- its ability to tease out inferences about causation and relate these to assessment of the effectiveness of advertising, promotions, etc;
- its ability to capture unexpected events; and
- its asset value as a cumulative database resource.

Markets are dynamic. They are a moving picture and they need dynamic—not static—techniques to capture their richness.

If you are not tracking your competition using continuous tracking, is your competition tracking you? In short, are you being followed?

14 NEW PRODUCT LAUNCHES: DON'T PULL THE PLUG TOO EARLY

Why do so many new products fail?

Over nearly two decades in many parts of the world I tracked advertising in hundreds of product categories. In many of these categories it was possible to observe a range of new brands or products being launched. There is no single reason for the high rate of new product failure but there is one fairly common one. This has to do with the fact that the care and attention evident at the pre-launch stage is not carried through after the 'go' button is pushed.

Not enough companies closely and continuously monitor what is happening at the product launch and in the immediate post-launch period. The result is that many of the all-important fine tuning adjustments necessary to marketing success fail to be made. And the product crashes.

Most companies these days put a lot of money and careful attention into development of a new product. They do the same with the development of the advertising and the promotional program to back it up. They pre-test the advertising and the acceptance of the product concept and try to put everything in place for the launch to succeed.

But then a funny thing happens. The launch button is pushed. And in this crucial immediate post-launch stage, the tendency is to do little more than take a deep breath, pray that they have done everything right, and wait anxiously for the judgment of the market. Will the product be a success or a failure? If NASA launched space shuttles the way manufacturers launch new brands, there would be fewer astronauts!

The advertising resources necessary to fuel these new product launches is huge and new product launches, like space flight launches, need continuous monitoring and adjustment.

Durable products

Many new durable products fail because early sales do not come up to expectation. Pessimism then spreads within the company and often results in management 'pulling the plug' too early and abandoning the product.

Figure 14.1 shows a new brand of durable product which was launched with a continuous advertising schedule for seven weeks. At the end of that time the company abandoned the advertising 'because sales were not up to expectation'. The whole mood of the company and its marketing team projected disappointment and an expectation of looming product failure. This is a real danger point in new product launches because the gloom is likely to be self-fulfilling.

Fortunately in this case, and for the first time in this company's history, not only sales but also the effect of the campaign on attitudes towards the brand were being monitored continuously. On the basis of the continuous tracking data, the researchers were able to argue that the company should keep going; that just because sales had not yet responded was no reason to abort the advertising or to give up on the new product.

As a result the company went back on air with advertising for the product. The graph clearly shows that since then, each time there was a burst of advertising, attitudes toward the brand improved (with one exception, when the launch of another new, competitive brand muddied the picture somewhat). Three months after the launch the brand, far

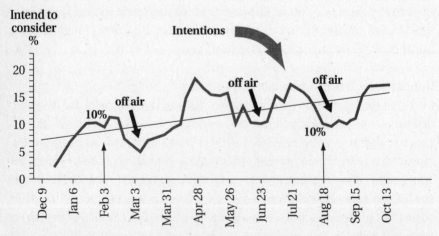

Note: Intention to buy new brand increases when on-air and decays when off-air, resulting in an overall upward trend.

Figure 14.1: *Advertising influence on intentions. (Source: MarketMind)*

from being a failure, had a 15 per cent market share. The same brand is alive and well today, but if the abort decision had been made it might well have ended up in the annals of product history as just another new-product failure.

This case clearly illustrates the importance of continuous measurement—not just snapshot surveys. The market is a movie and its richness cannot be captured by a couple of snapshot surveys with a Box Brownie. It needs continuous measurement.

Consider the situation in the first eight months of the product's life. If a snapshot-type survey had been conducted on 3 February, it would have shown that 10 per cent of people were prepared to seriously consider the brand next time they bought that type of product (i.e. were 'short-listers' for the brand). A good result. If another snapshot survey were conducted on 18 August after 6 months of advertising, it would have shown no change as a result of all that advertising. Without continuous measurement, these snapshot-type surveys might well have given the false impression that further advertising bursts were having no further effect on people's attitudes.

However, as the trend line in the continuous data clearly indicates, there was a long-term positive effect of continuing with the advertising for this brand. Each time it went on air it was developing and strengthening attitudes towards the brand—it was strengthening the brand's consumer franchise. Between those on-air times, the mental territory that the advertising had previously captured would begin to erode because of the lack of advertising reinforcement, but overall, in the long haul, the product was gaining more than it was losing.

Repeat-purchase supermarket products

Continuous information on sales and market share is important for any product—not just newly launched products. You need it to know if what you are doing is successful in terms of behavior. Such top-level information is, however, not enough to enable you to *diagnose* why things are going right or wrong. It may tell you what worked and what didn't and as such it provides an important rear-view mirror. But to be able to decide on corrective or future actions you have to focus on the diagnosis, *the why* of what is happening (see Chapters 26–27).

Especially during the launch of a new product, it is crucial to monitor various other things—among them awareness (the proportion of people who are aware of the new product) and trial (the proportion who have ever tried it)—and do this continuously. Why is this so important? Because a 10 per cent market share in supermarket-type products can be gained in either of two extreme ways:

- Ten per cent of people have ever bought the new brand and they are buying it 100 per cent of the time. That is, they are completely loyal.
- One hundred per cent of people have bought it, but they are only buying it 10 per cent of the time. That is, they are buying that brand only about once in every ten times they shop for that product category.

Depending which situation the new brand finds itself in, the strategic implications are quite different. In the first case the company needs to get more people to try the brand if it wants to increase market share. In the second case, the company has managed to get people to try it but the only way it is going to increase market share is to increase their repeat buying.

So it is vitally important in the lift-off stage to measure not just market share but also how many people have ever bought or tried the new product. Incredible as it may seem, some companies fail to do this. And in the cases when it is done, a reading is generally only taken in a survey repeated every six or twelve months.

This is not enough. Companies need to know how the trial is progressing continuously. NASA monitors its space launches *continuously*. It doesn't press the button and then come back after lunch to see how things are going. It knows that anything may have happened in the meantime. Things occur that need correction, adjustment or fine tuning! By the time some businesses come back and do a survey one month, two months or six months after launch, it is too late. What they frequently find is that the product is out of control or has crashed—or, sometimes, that it never even got off the ground.

A well-known cookie manufacturer used to launch new cookie products this way. The company spent huge resources developing new varieties of cookies and then conducting in-home placement tests in which consumers were asked which one(s) they liked best and therefore which were the best candidates to put on the market.

This type of testing revealed which varieties people liked, how much they liked them, and how likely they were to repeat-buy those varieties.

The problem that this company failed to come to grips with was how to get people to buy and *try* the cookies in the first place. This company looked only at sales and market share information.

Typically, after launching one of the new cookie products, the company would look at sales. If sales were not up to expectation in the first three months or so, it would simply abandon the product. While it had some successes, it had many more 'failures'. The main reason for the failures continued to go unrecognized and the company continued to make the same mistake over and over.

The problem in most cases was not that the new variety was rejected by the market. It was to do with the inadequate level of marketing support put behind the launch and the over-reliance on advertising alone without promotional activity to generate that key first trial. The company failed to monitor closely what was happening immediately after the 'go' button was pressed and the launch had begun.

Because it didn't know exactly what happened between the launch and the crash, the company kept having crashes, largely as a result of the same problems. This is what happens when businesses rely only on sales and market share to indicate new product performance and then make critical decisions on the basis of these indicators alone. This is a common cause of new-product launch failures.

In one case in point a new cookie was launched but discontinued after about four months. When the decision to abort was made this variety had about 3 per cent market share in its segment, which was regarded as 'not enough'. Like so many of its previous new product attempts, the company regarded this as a failure. But this market share was primarily because only about 10 per cent of people had ever tried it. Its repeat buying rate was in fact quite good. The people who had tried it were buying it about once in every three times they bought cookies—which is not bad in the cookie market, where there are so many varieties to choose from.

The company had tested the product by in-home placement, i.e. 'forced' trial, and this had accurately predicted that people would accept and like the product once they had tasted it. The key words are *once they had tasted it*. Remember, only 10 per cent of people had tasted it when the product was aborted. It was not the product that failed—it was the marketing activities that were designed to get it trialed that failed! Not enough resources were put into the launch to ensure successful communication of the product's qualities to enough people to prompt them to try it the first time.

The company aborted this variety and went off to develop a new one that it hoped would do better next time!

The point here is that initial trial is a key ingredient in new product launches for any low-cost product but particularly supermarket products. Even if the product was the greatest tasting cookie ever and got a repeat buying level of 100 per cent, it could not have gone above 10 per cent share if only 10 per cent of people had ever tried it. On the other hand with a 30 per cent repeat buying level, if the company had got another 60 per cent of people to try it the product would have gained a potential share of 18 per cent (i.e. 30 per cent of 60 per cent).

Our cookie manufacturer wasted a lot of money trying to find outstanding product formulations that would guarantee success. But once you look at its activity in the light of the very low trial figures for its new products, the lesson is clear. The world will not beat a path to any company's door, whether it develops a better mousetrap or a better cookie. The product has to be effectively marketed. The company has to get people to try it.

Fine tuning the marketing support

Instead of looking for ideal product formulations, the urgent need is more often to address the level and fine tuning of marketing support for new products. To ensure that these are adequate and functioning as they should requires that companies closely monitor their launches, making appropriate adjustments, fine tunings and corrections as required. Failure to do this is one of the most important causes of new product failure. Too often, marketers have too little information and pull the plug on the new product too early, i.e. before they have achieved the necessary awareness and trial.

Trial needs to be gained early, while the product has a newness and freshness about it. If it does not achieve good penetration in the first six months it is unlikely to succeed. This is particularly important for seasonal products such as new varieties of canned soup or chocolate cookies in winter or of ice confections in summer. If trial is not achieved quickly and in the first season, the 'new' product has to come back next season as an old product and this loses the 'newness' factor that can be so important in generating interest and trial. Generally, it doesn't work. (See Chapter 19, 'Seasonal advertising'.)

If the new product is going to succeed it has to get trial as quickly as possible before it loses its image of newness; that usually means in the

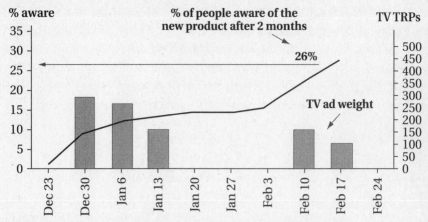

Figure 14.2: *Awarness of a new food product. (Source: MarketMind)*

season in which it is launched. An obvious part of getting this first-season trial is making people aware of the new product and getting them interested in it. This is a communications task and, like everything else, needs monitoring.

Figure 14.2 shows response to a new product two months after launch. Only 26 per cent of target consumers have heard of the brand, which means that advertising to this point has failed to communicate the existence of the new product to more than half of the potential market.

The implication is clear: it would be foolish to abort the product. What is needed is a change in the advertising or promotional strategy. Either the ad targeting and scheduling isn't effective enough, or the ad itself hasn't got the creative touch to break through clutter and get people to try the new product without more promotional support.

Launching new products should be like launching space shuttles— the successes should outnumber the failures. It is not an inevitable law of marketing that in the launching of products there needs to be more casualties than successes.

Summary
A key reason why so many new products fail is that the care and attention evident at the pre-launch stage is not carried through after the 'go' button is pushed. The fine adjustments so necessary for marketing success are missing.

Continuous information on sales and market share is crucial—but even this is not enough. In order to fine tune the marketing support, it is important to continuously monitor other key measures such as awareness, trial and repeat purchase. Otherwise, there is a real risk of 'pulling the plug' too early. All too often, new product 'failure' results from deficiencies in the marketing necessary to keep the launch on track.

15 PLANNING CAMPAIGN STRATEGY AROUND CONSUMERS' MENTAL FILING CABINETS

Ads are like alcohol: the more you have the less you remember. After only two or three drinks your faculties start to become impaired. After exposure to only one or two competing ads, your memory for the first one starts to become impaired.[1] What is true of alcohol is surprisingly true of consumer memory for advertising—at least for competing brands in the same product category.

Over a period of a week, the more competing commercials there are for a product category, the less the average person will remember about any one of them. Most people think that forgetting is simply the fading of memory with the passage of time. However, it is now well established that forgetting is due not to the passage of time alone, but to interference from additional learning that takes place in that time.[2] When time passes but little or no further (competing) learning takes place there is very little forgetting.

On the other hand, where a lot of activity and new learning, especially competitive learning, fill the time interval, these 'interference effects' become very great indeed. These effects are one of the clearest of findings on the way human memory works.[3] They are also one of the most frequent findings to emerge from continuous tracking of advertising.

Is implicit memory an exception?
Some will argue this only applies to explicit memory and does not apply to learning without attention because there is evidence that implicit memory (see Chapter 27, 'Measurement of advertising effects in memory') is much more durable. The argument is a false one, however, because it confuses learning in the absence of awareness, i.e. implicit learning, with implicit memory. They are not the same thing. Do you touch type? If so, then the location of the keys is stored in your implicit memory.

As John Anderson has written, 'Many people are not able to recall this information but . . . they can remember where a letter is by imagining themselves typing a word that involves the letter and seeing where their finger goes.'[4] The fact that this is implicit memory does not mean it was learnt without any attention. In fact it not only needed attention, it required repetition, persistence and hard work.

Implicit memory is not the same thing as learning without awareness and advertising effects in memory are rarely the result of learning totally without awareness. Explicit processing of a direct message is not the only way we receive a message. As we saw earlier, while we are paying attention to something else in the ad, implicit associations can be learnt. There is an interaction between the two. Robert Heath, who is perhaps the strongest advocate for implicit learning, acknowledges that: 'Implicit learning because it is subconscious, cannot access the analytical faculties within our working memory. It is only able to store what is perceived, along with simple conceptual meanings that are attached to these perceptions: it cannot interpret or decode messages, or draw conclusions from them.'[5] So the point remains that with advertising generally, the evidence is that our ability to retrieve an event or message can be severely impaired when we are exposed to other similar events within a short time.

While this is a well established finding in psychology, it is less widely recognized in marketing. Too few people take account of it in planning advertising media schedules or when they are assessing why their ad campaign may have 'failed'.

Models of memory and forgetting

At a crowded party, if you want to communicate you have to speak very loudly. The more voices, the more competition and the louder the din gets. You have to shout to be heard above the clutter. On television you also have to shout for your ad to be heard. The greater the clutter the more you have to shout. In other words, the more competitors you have advertising against you, the more effort and money you will have to expend to get your message into people's heads.

Even when you shout, your communication may still not register successfully, especially if the target is distracted or tuned in to someone else's conversation, or is musing on something else. How many conversations can you tune in to at one time? Two? Three? How many commercials for different brands in a product category can a consumer hang on to in his or her mind? There is no single threshold. Rather, each subsequent input progressively diminishes the memory for any and all others.

The popular view of memory is that a trace of the remembered thing is either there or it is not. You can either remember it or you can't. This model of memory is demonstrably wrong. How many times have you been unable to remember someone's name even though you *know* that you know it? Forgetting has more to do with 'inability to retrieve' than with failure to store the memory. It is usually not failure to store the memory that is the problem. It is inability to remember it when you want it.

It is sometimes helpful to think of memories as being stored in one of several mental filing cabinets. If you carefully file a new memory, a new ad, in a particular filing cabinet you should be able to retrieve it quickly and easily as needed. However, if you were distracted enough or unmotivated enough to casually stow the new memory away without paying any attention to what you were doing or which filing cabinet you were stowing it in, the chances are that you will have great difficulty retrieving it. More to the point, you will be unable to retrieve it quickly. The only way you can retrieve it will be to painstakingly look through every cabinet and every possible file.

With memory, the problem is usually not inability to retrieve, but inability to retrieve in any reasonable or functional time. So for all intents and purposes, the information becomes 'functionally lost'.

Information can become functionally lost because it is a long time since you filed it. It can also become functionally lost as a result of interference effects—the competing exposures discussed earlier. You can think of interference effects as the outcome of trying to store several similar memories all in the one file. The more cluttered the file becomes, the longer it is going to take to look through it and to retrieve any particular one.[6]

When a consumer is exposed to competing commercials, this is what happens. There is interference from previously stored ads which is exacerbated by the fact that the consumer is often fairly unmotivated or uninvolved when storing them. These types of memory inputs and the interference effect is all the greater when the viewer has low involvement.[7]

Advertising application

It is for this reason that the 'effectiveness' or impact of a commercial is very much influenced by how much competitors spend advertising against it. Especially when trying to get the message into people's heads in the first place, it is rarely just a simple function of how much an advertised brand spends on advertising time (its media weight).

An advertiser cannot effectively plan or monitor a brand's ad strategy without information about competing activity. This is why anyone who is serious about maximizing the effectiveness of their ad strategy needs to have access to weekly data (monthly or quarterly is not good enough) as to which competitors were advertising on TV, on the web and in print in that week and at what weight.[8]

It is always worth looking at the raw relationship between the amount spent on a brand's advertising and indicators of effectiveness such as sales, market share or advertising awareness. But don't be surprised or disappointed if you don't see any clear relationship. This does not mean that the advertising is not working. Try looking not at the total amount of advertising for the brand but at the brand's *share* of advertising in the product category, week by week. A strong relationship may then emerge. (This is more likely when you are trying to get your message into people's heads than with reminder/reinforcement advertising.)

Figure 15.1 illustrates the point. The bars indicate the weeks when this brand's advertising campaign was on TV. Their heights indicate the brand's *share* of the total TV advertising in its product category (share of media weight or share of voice).

The product is a consumer product and its share of voice is plotted against a measure of people's spontaneous awareness of the ad. This latter is a relative measure and is called the brand's TV ad share-of-mind. It is the brand's *share* of total ad awareness in the product category; in other words, memory for that ad relative to all other ads in the product category. It is indicated by the line graph.

A clear relationship is evident each time the brand comes on air with a flight of advertising. With each flight the brand's TV ad share-of-mind trends upward. (The graph also gives valuable indications of how quickly or how slowly memory of the ad decays between each advertising flight.) This performance graph can be compared with a similar graph for each competitor and inferences can then be drawn about whether the brand's advertising strategy is more or less effective than ads for the competing brands.

Components of clutter

This raises the question: what other ads does a particular brand compete with? In the broadest sense it competes with all other ads—even those

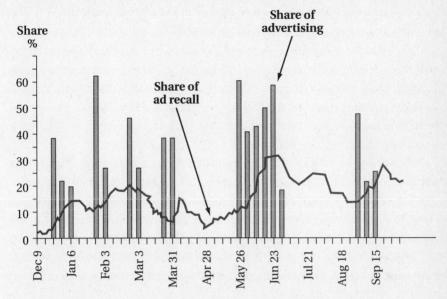

Note: For this brand a clear relationship is evident between its share of advertising and its share of advertisement recall.

Figure 15.1: *Television share of mind and share of voice. (Source: MarketMind)*

not in the same product category. This is known as the general level of clutter and any ad has to break through it. This general level of clutter is relatively constant, at least in the short term. However, it has tended to grow over the long term not only because of more time given to ads but also because of an increase in the use of shorter length TV commercials.[9] Shorter length commercials boost the total *number* of commercials on air and that people see in any given time period and this increases the general impression that there is more advertising on TV overall.

There is the general level of clutter but, even more importantly, there is also 'category clutter'. The ad in question competes with other ads in the same product category which is called 'category clutter', and this *does* vary from week to week.

What may be surprising to many readers is that the ad also competes with any other ads for the same brand which may be aired in the same week. That is, multiple but similar advertising executions for the same brand frequently compete among themselves and can set up interference effects that impede their individual effectiveness (especially with low-involved audiences).[10]

Can a company compete with itself?

Is your ad being limited in its impact by competition from other ads run by your own company? If you are a multi-product, multi-brand company, the answer is almost certainly 'yes'. A Toyota Corolla commercial competes against ads for other vehicles manufactured by Ford, GM, Nissan, BMW, Volvo, etc. It is not as obvious but nevertheless real, that it also competes with all other ads screened by Toyota itself in the same week. These are also competing for the consumers' mind and memory.

Commercials aimed at audiences with high involvement may be less subject to these effects than those aimed at audiences with low involvement.[11] This is because with high-involvement situations the consumer may consciously and deliberately process the message in such a way as to make it more resistant to forgetting. That is, it gets filed in a careful way that anticipates a future need to retrieve it. With high-involvement messages, unlike low-involvement ones, the viewer anticipates a future need to use the information.

The key point here is the level of involvement of the target audience. If vehicle ads are aimed at people intending to buy a new car in the next two or three months, then these people are likely to be highly involved. However, around a third of all new-car purchases are made by people who did not intend to buy a new car but were overtaken by events. These include people whose old car suddenly gave them problems and the growing number of people who separate from their spouse and find a need for another car. Such people are likely to be low involved at the time of exposure to the advertising—at least up to the point before the 'need' is triggered by the unforeseen event.

So advertising for high-involvement products (such as cars) doesn't just impact a highly involved audience. It generally impacts a relatively uninvolved one as well as the highly involved one. And this uninvolved one will at some time in the future become an involved one harboring memories of past advertising.

Summary

Successful advertising planning and evaluation demands detailed analysis of more than just one's own ad expenditure. It especially necessitates an understanding of consumer memory processes in regard to interference effects as well as memory decay. The on-air effectiveness of an ad is influenced by several things—not necessarily in this order:

- The execution. Is it a great ad?
- The dollar spend. How much 'weight' was put behind it that week?
- The reach. What percent of the target audience had at least one opportunity to see?
- The flighting. How is the ad being scheduled from week to week?
- The number of competitors who are on air in the same week and how much they spent.
- The number of different ad executions for the same brand that you have on air in any one week.
- The number of commercials for the same umbrella brand that you have on air in any one week.
- The level of involvement of the target audience and the complexity of the message that needs to be communicated.
- The ad objective. Is it a reminder of a message already established or communicating a new message?[12]

16 WHAT HAPPENS WHEN YOU STOP ADVERTISING?

In tight economic times, the pressures are always on to cut advertising. Can a company do this? Can it get away with it? What will be the effect on the company a bit further down the track? These are the questions that start to be asked when the recessionary animal starts to bite.

If the company stops advertising and sales stay at the same level, the cessation of ad spending generates an immediate improvement in the bottom line. Hence the strong temptation to cut advertising in tough times and make the company's profit performance look good. What are the consequences? What do we know about stopping advertising?

What happens when advertising stops?

We do not know a lot about what happens when advertising stops but what we do know is enough to warrant caution. Most companies don't know what happens when advertising stops because they only look at the immediate sales figures. If sales don't go down, they breathe a sigh of relief. But it is critical to look at what is going on underneath, at the brand image and 'brand value' level. Here is where the early warning signs of erosion in brand value are likely to be seen first.

For example, let's look at what happened when one US food manufacturer was forced to cut its advertising budget in half. Before the cut, ratings of the brand in taste testing studies differed greatly if the brand name was on the pack when tasted. While the brand was supported by advertising at adequate levels, the brand name provided a lift of 24 per cent over blind taste tests (24 per cent higher than respondents who tasted the exact same product, but without the brand name). Four years of greatly reduced advertising saw this differential erode so that there was only a 10 per cent lift over blind taste tests! The brand name lost more than half of its power. Consumers were less impressed with it as a brand and it lost much of its ability to influence people's impressions of quality and taste.

Another example. Some years ago a leading brand in another food category and the only major advertiser in the category decided to stop its previously consistent advertising. As might be expected this premium brand's share eventually deteriorated along with perceptions of its value and quality. It not only eroded on these indicators but also in market share and in association with an image of 'good value for the money' and 'high quality'. What was particularly revealing, however, was that ratings for the other brands, the low advertised, low price, so-called 'value' brands began to *increase* over that time. In the absence of advertising reinforcement by leading brands, consumers are freer to raise their perceptions of alternative products and base their decision on what is visible on the shelf. It took a long time but this once leading 'premium' brand ultimately came back to the rest of the market and today it is viewed as being at parity with the category bottom-feeder.

So stopping advertising could be a smart decision. But then again, it could be a time bomb. A doctoral thesis on milk advertising in the US some years ago revealed the delayed nature of the time bomb. In a prolonged series of test market experiments, it was found that when advertising of milk was stopped, nothing happened to sales. Nothing, that is, for twelve months! After a year of no advertising, milk sales suddenly went into a sharp decline and continued to decline at a sickening rate. This underlines the fact that maintenance of sales in the short or medium term after stopping advertising is no reason for complacency.

Advertising immediately re-started. But it was too late. It took another eighteen months to halt the decline and then begin to reverse it. So beware of the delayed time bomb. 'To regain a favorable position that is lost during belt tightening can cost more in the long run than to try to retain it by continuing advertising at a maintenance level.'[1]

For how long can a company afford to stop its advertising?
Rather than ask the question 'Can we stop advertising?', it may be more meaningful to ask 'can we maintain our advertising support of the brand but at the same time reduce advertising cost overall?' Capturing the mental territory for a brand requires much more effort and resources than holding it. The cost of funding your occupation forces can be significantly lower. It implies cuts in frequency, how many times people are exposed to the message within the week, rather than cuts to reach, how many people you reach with the message in the week.

However, in really tight recessionary times there may be no choice but to accede to a corporate board edict to pause the advertising. How long before you can you expect the effect of this to show up?

Much depends on how much residual or carry-over effect the current and past advertising has had. Some campaigns have amazingly strong residual memory effects. Other ads have almost none; they are forgotten almost as soon as they go off air. Continuous tracking of campaigns and advertising flights can reveal how much 'residual capital' has been built up and how quickly it gets eroded once the advertising is stopped.

Some experiences

Figures 16.1, 16.2 and 16.3 demonstrate some case experiences with stopping advertising. Compare the first two graphs. They show what happened when two brands (from different product categories) stopped advertising.

Brand A and its advertising had a lot of residual recall even after the ads stopped. There is almost no memory decay of the brand or the advertising after three months. In the case of brand B, on the other hand, the brand itself had good residual recall but the advertising didn't. When the advertising stopped, recall of the advertising declined rapidly while awareness of the brand held up well.

Brand A had been off air for four months. Brand B had been off air for seven months. Market share did not show any decline in either case. But that is where the complacency ends. When we look more closely, the indications are that other things are going on which could be very detrimental in the longer run.

Erosion of brand franchise

The third graph shows total advertising exposures (TRPs) in one of these markets. Advertising stopped in this market three months previously. There had been no marked changes in sales or market shares for any of the brands in this market *at that point*.

However, if we look further below the surface we find a worrying trend emerging. Brand loyalty is declining. People are still buying the brand but any feeling of 'commitment' that they may have to the brand is eroding.

The market shown in the graph has two major segments—'brand loyals' and 'habitual buyers'. The brand loyals believe there are differences between brands and always buy the same brand. The habitual buyers also

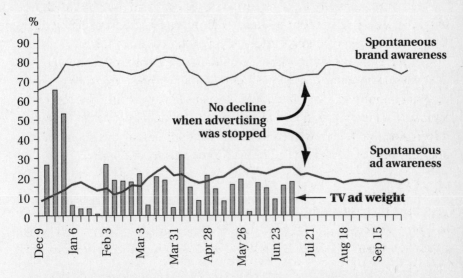

Note: When advertising was stopped for this product no significant decline was observed in spontaneous awareness of the brand or for spontaneous awareness of its advertising.

Figure 16.1: *Spontaneous awareness—brand A. (Source: MarketMind)*

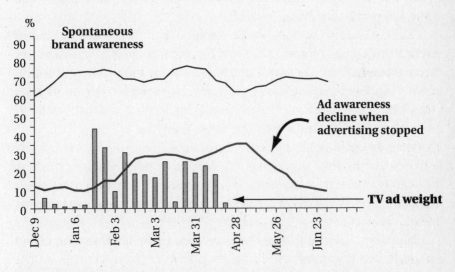

Note: When advertising was stopped for this product the spontaneous awareness of the brand did not decline significantly but a rapid decline in spontaneous advertising awareness took place.

Figure 16.2: *Spontaneous awareness—brand B. (Source: MarketMind)*

Note: When advertising stopped there was no visible effect whatever on sales. But after two months the 'commitment' of buyers eroded rapidly. The absence of reinforcement created habitual rather than loyal buyers, leaving the brand vulnerable to attack.

Figure 16.3: *Size of market segments. (Source: MarketMind)*

tend to buy the same brand each time but they believe there are *no real differences* between brands.

Habitual, repeat-buyers of a brand are not the same thing as brand loyals. Habitual buyers repeat-buy the brand for reasons of inertia rather than loyalty. With the cessation of advertising, the brand loyals diminish in the market and habitual buyers increase. While sales may not change immediately, the major brand(s) in the market become more vulnerable— more open to attack. They lose their brand franchise.

Even though sales and market share have not changed, if this trend is allowed to continue the market itself would be very different. Whereas the market in the past has been characterized by brands with strongly promoted brand franchises, it could well become more of a commodity market with little differences perceived between any of the brands. The market leader's sales could thus become wide open to a price attack from a new or existing competitor.[2]

Opportunity
William Moran has written that 'Rather than wait for business to return to normal, top executives can cash in on the opportunity that the rival

companies who are stopping their advertising create for them. The company courageous enough to stay in and fight when everyone else is playing safe in times of recession can bring about a dramatic change in market position.'[3]

Now we can see why. The above case illustrates how a market can be made vulnerable even though sales and market shares do not appear to have changed in the short term. For a company that is a smaller competitor in the market, this is the time to go after the market leader. Like a pilot taking off in an airplane and picking out holes in the cloud cover to climb through, the smaller advertiser can take advantage of these situations to steer its brand up to a higher level of market share and salience. At such times there is less advertising clutter and the smaller advertiser, even with a small ad budget, is more likely to be heard when the large advertisers are silent and mental commitment to these brands is beginning to erode.

Reinforcement effect of advertising
So the effects of advertising must not be looked at just in terms of increasing sales. To do so ignores the fact that advertising has a very important *reinforcement* effect.

One of the most important effects of advertising is consolidating and protecting what has already been built. It reinforces behavior. People are more convinced of the 'rightness' of their brand choice if they see the brand advertised. 'Good advertising provides people with the means to rationalize their brand preferences.'[4] And, all other things being equal, they are more likely to buy that brand again.

Some of the most avid readers of car ads are people who have just bought that brand of car. The ads provide reinforcement of their decision. This may not make a whole lot of rational sense, but that's the way we human beings are.

Alternatives to stopping advertising
In recession times, if the pressure is on, the key question should be how you can take surgery to the advertising rather than simply eliminate it. How can you improve the bottom line without jeopardizing the brand in the long run?

We have seen the dangers of stopping advertising altogether so, if you are not going to stop but are under budgetary pressure to economize, is there anything else you can do? Yes! You need to consider some belt-tightening strategies for tough times.

Some belt-tightening strategies for tough times
You need to make the ad budget that is available work more efficiently. Rather than stopping advertising, consider these ways of trimming the waistline and tightening the belt:

- A 'drip' media strategy, i.e. rather than stopping advertising altogether, use reduced exposures (reduced weekly TRP weights) to at least try to hold the ground you have already captured.
- Look for ways to trade off frequency while maximizing reach on the target market.
- *If necessary* examine the feasibility of having longer gaps in your advertising flighting pattern. How long can you afford to stay off air between flights without jeopardizing your brand franchise?
- If you are using several ad executions on air at the same time, cut back to just one ad and put all your media weight behind it. Be very single-minded. Most companies use too many executions anyway and have too few exposures (TRPs) behind each execution. In other words, avoid 'executional anorexia'. (See Chapter 20, 'Underweight advertising'.)
- If you want to cut back, consider shorter length commercials—but use them not as attack forces but as occupation forces to hold the mental territory that has already been captured. Make sure you build ad awareness to a high level with longer commercials before you switch to the shorter ones. Don't just use fifteens as substitutes for 30s. (See Chapter 18, 'Learning to use shorter-length TV commercials'.)
- Finally, if you have been successful with your TV and other attack forces and established a high level of ad awareness, consider switching to a more economical maintenance strategy using the occupational forces of lower cost media (print, web, outdoor, viral etc). The occupation forces come at a lower cost. Often it is surprising how long the mental territory that is already captured can be held by these lower cost, maintenance media. Remember, it is harder to get into the mind in the first place than it is to stay there.

Summary

In this financially driven world with so much emphasis on short-term performance, brands are often tempted to cut ad spending to improve the bottom line—not just during recession but at any time. When advertising stops, any effect on sales may not be visible for several months.

If, in response to cutting advertising, sales appear stable, it is critical to look at what is going on underneath those sales figures. Look at the 'brand value' level because this is where the early warning signs of insufficient advertising support are likely to be seen first. If the brand franchise erodes, it can take a long time to rebuild the brand's market position. An alternative to stopping advertising in tight economic times is to focus on ways to make the ad budget work harder—ways to guard the brand franchise and improve the bottom line at the same time.

17 THE EFFECTIVENESS OF FUNNY ADS: WHAT A LAUGH![1]

> A very young baby is sucking the side of his father's face like a teat. The only other thing in the ad is a picture of a Bic disposable shaver.

> An Argentine ad shows a pair of underpants on a washing line with a ragged hole burnt eloquently through the rear. (Advertiser: a brand of spicy tuna sauce)

I have had the opportunity to track many humorous ads. Increasingly we encounter them on YouTube or as viral ads but they are also still there on TV and radio. And every now and again a print campaign comes along that also makes people chuckle.

It is striking how little is actually written and known about humor in advertising and its effects. There is an amazingly small body of research on it, given how important it is to us. And what little laboratory research has been done has frequently produced contradictory findings.

Part of the problem is that it is so easy to treat all humor as the same and generalize about it—when it isn't the same. Slapstick humor for example is very different to wit.[2] And what is funny to one individual can be uninteresting or even irritating to another. So you can't assume something is funny. British humor for example is very different to American humor. It is not surprising therefore that research which treats humor as generic often produces confusing and sometimes contradictory findings.

This chapter will also generalize about humor but on the basis of what is different in the way people mentally process ads with humor in them. How is this different from straight ads? We will see why humor can have both positive and negative effects depending upon how it is used.

History of humor

To have a sense of humor is a good thing. Everyone agrees, right? To not have a sense of humor is a bad thing. Well, prepare yourself for a shock. Did you know that this idea is only about 400 years old? You don't have to go too far back in our history to find a time when laughter and humor were viewed negatively, not positively. Indeed, they reflected 'the satanic spirit of man'.

Figure 17.1: *Some humor relies on wit—this Suede-ish massage ad for Weatherproof brand clothing is an example.*

Greek philosophy depicted humor as a cruel and brutal affair. Plato thought it was based on an unfortunate lack of self-knowledge and that it was motivated by envy, which made it morally inferior and reprehensible. Aristotle described laughter as 'degrading to morals, art and religion, a form of behavior from which civilized man should shrink'. And Lord Chesterfield wrote that 'there is nothing so illiberal and so ill-bred than audible laughter'.[3]

The historical origins of humor lie in the darker side of humankind—in derisive rather than friendly, enjoyable laughter. If you don't believe this, then consider the expression 'pulling your leg'. It means having fun at your expense. It does today—but what's its origin?

Up until the nineteenth century public executions by hanging were a great source of entertainment. Often the victim's neck would not break and he/she was left to writhe and strangle slowly. Friends were allowed to pull down on their legs in order to put them out of their misery. This was an added source of amusement for the onlooker crowd.[4]

So much for the modern view that a sense of humor is something intrinsically good and has always been that way. Only 400 years ago laughter was 'seen as a socially disruptive force'.[5] Not exactly the stuff that ads are made of.

What has this got to do with commercials? Not much today perhaps—except that it should serve as a warning that humor is not as simple as it often seems. The more you study humor and the more you track the effects of humorous ads, the more that it emerges as a Jeckyll and Hyde phenomenon that can have negative and positive effects.

Anatomy of humorous ads

What makes ads humorous? Let us explore this with an actual ad. Readers may recall a classic ad that showed a lovebird pecking at what seemed like food but was really the keypad of a telephone. The beeps indicated it was accidentally dialing someone. Of course this had to be accidental. Everyone knows birds don't dial. And even if they did, who would they call? Ah, but then in the next scene we see a courier arrive, pick up the sleeping cat with delivery note attached and depart to the off-screen sound of the bird twittering—or maybe chuckling. We suddenly realize it wasn't just random food pecking behavior—the bird phoned the courier company to dispose of its nemesis, the cat.

So what makes a commercial like this one humorous? What's in it that makes us laugh? The key is in the incongruity. A bizarre combination of the bird pecking is mixed up with what we identify as a peculiarly human trait i.e. intelligent, manipulative behavior. Seemingly random pecking by a dumb bird at a telephone turns out to be cunning, manipulative behavior that you just don't expect from a bird.

So writers create humor by surprising us—but in a particular way. They force us to momentarily fuse together two things that already exist in our minds that are otherwise unrelated and incompatible (in this case food pecking and dialing). Incongruity is something of a general formula.

Our minds lead us up this garden path—a bird pecking at a phone is naturally interpreted in terms of buttons being mistaken for food. But only momentarily, before we are then forced to accept the alternative interpretation of the scene that the bird was purposefully dialing and not just pecking. This happens when we see the courier pick up the cat. This interpretation makes the two things consistent and while it is experienced as 'bizarre' it is also enjoyable. And therein lies the key to humorous ads.

The interesting thing is that jokes as well as humorous ads are often built intuitively by writers.[6] They notice the ambiguity in something (e.g. a visual scene, some word or phrase or some concept) and then create an incongruity. Instead of adopting the expected interpretation—which is the most obvious interpretation that everyone will take—they develop an alternative one, an interpretation that 'fits' but which is highly unlikely or bizarre in the context (i.e. the bird is dialing someone).

The conceptual elements that go into humorous ads such as this and induce a mental switch from information to humor and hence enjoyment of the ad are these:[7]

- two concepts (e.g. dumb bird and human intelligence);
- incongruity/incompatibility between them i.e. one violates the other;
- confidence that the stimulus elements occurring as depicted are impossible or highly unlikely; and
- a way of 'fusing' the two and making them momentarily 'compatible'.

The evidence suggests that the greater the degree of incongruity the funnier the humor is seen to be. The more impossible or incompatible the two things are that are fused together, the more enjoyment people seem to derive from it.

Humorists and scientists

Fusing incongruent ideas like this is part of the much broader process of creativity. Humor has a lot in common with scientific creativity, for example. Arthur Koestler pointed out that humor is 'the bringing about of a momentary fusion between two habitually incompatible frames of reference'.[8] The creativity involved in writing humorous commercials is not unlike the creativity of scientific discovery. One strives for the *'ha ha'* reaction, while the other strives for the *'ah haa . . .'* reaction. The difference is that scientific discovery is the *permanent* fusion of the ideas previously believed to be incompatible. Humor is only a temporary fusion.

Comedy writer Herbie Baker, who wrote for the comedian Danny Kaye, had an intriguing way of looking at incongruity. He believed that ideas struggle against each other to fight their way up to our conscious mind from the unconscious. But under normal circumstances, certain of these ideas are incapable of combining with one another. It is their incongruity that normally blocks these other ideas from making it successfully up into the conscious mind. Creatives, like scientists, are people who can somehow circumvent this and by various means bring incongruous ideas into their minds in spite of this otherwise natural blocking tendency. Marty Feldman, another of the great comedians of history, expressed this pithily when he said: 'Comedy like sodomy, is an unnatural act'.

Humorous ads

Ask the members of your family what advertisements make them laugh? Chances are they will spontaneously say 'Oh, lots of them!'—and then fall silent. If you persist, eventually they will dredge out of memory a specific commercial that made them laugh. You will probably note how difficult it is for them to immediately bring to mind such specific examples and when they do, it is even more striking how much difficulty they often have in remembering the brand name of the product advertised.

However, what emerges clearly from this as well as the tracking of numerous funny commercials of various types is the underlying Jeckyll and Hyde phenomenon. They are entertaining and a lot of fun, but when they come to mind why do they so often come without the brand? The first step in being able to make humor work effectively is to recognize these two faces; that such an approach to advertising has the potential for positive effects but it can have negative effects as well. You will see that much depends on precisely how the humor is executed.

How humorous ads work

There are three main mechanisms by which humor is supposed to work in advertising:

1. Less counter-arguing. Because we process it as entertainment (rather than engage in true/false evaluation of the content), there is less counter-arguing with humorous ads.
2. Humorous ads are noticed more i.e. they draw greater attention.
3. Humorous ads are generally *liked* more. Ads that are liked have a higher probability of being effective—all other things being equal.

Counter-arguing

The first mechanism is that humorous ads seem to invite less counter-arguing. When we read a fiction book we mentally process it differently to non-fiction. With fiction we engage in escapist enjoyment rather than a true/false evaluation of what we are reading. Humor is entertainment and tends to be mentally processed in a different way to informational commercials. We are less likely to process the ad in terms of a true/false evaluation.

Freud observed that the world of humor is 'a place to which we temporarily and symbolically return to the playful and happy mood of childhood'. When we switch into our enjoyment, humor appreciation mode, we switch off our attempt to process the ad in a normal, informational, or logical way.

The incongruous elements in the ad tip us off that this is meant to be humorous and triggers a re-set switch in our minds. We stop normal processing and sit back—hopefully to enjoy the absurdity and a momentary return to the playful, happy mood of childhood. But Mr Hyde is lurking because a reduction in counter-arguing can often be at the expense of correct branding of the ad. The risk with humor in advertising is always that we may be so focused on processing it as entertainment that little if any processing registers for the brand and the message.

Attention and recall

The second mechanism is the humorous ad's ability to draw greater attention. In helping the ad to get attention and break-through we see perhaps the most positive sides of humor. But Mr Hyde is never far away and whether that extra attention has a positive effect or a negative effect depends greatly upon *where* that attention gets focused.

People who are mugged at gunpoint often find it difficult to give the police much in the way of any description of the mugger. Why? Because if someone points a gun at us, the gun hijacks our attention. Understandably, we become so focused on the gun that we take little notice of anything else.[9]

Humor may provide big guns for advertisers to help them get noticed in amongst the clutter but humor can hijack attention so totally that people don't take in the message or even the brand that is in the ad—they are too preoccupied with the humor. Now we begin to see why it is not really surprising that a number of studies researching humorous ads have found that humorous ads were no more effective than straight ads or worse—they even impacted negatively on results.[10]

If you conduct your own 'family poll' as suggested above, chances are you will confirm that humorous ads have an unusually high risk of suffering a message and branding problem. Just as the use of high profile presenters can distract us from processing the important elements of the brand and the message, so too can humor. If not used properly it will hijack our attention from the brand and the message. That does not mean we should stop using humorous ads. We don't stop using high profile presenters because of this effect. But we do have to take deliberate actions to overcome this problem. We have to make sure that the brand/message communication in these commercials is *so much stronger* in order to compensate for this overshadowing effect.

Integration of brand and execution

How do you do this? Apart from making the brand *very* visible, the best answer is to try to heavily integrate the brand with the execution. How often do we see an ad produced that is an entertaining piece of film but where the brand/message is hardly integrated at all into the story? All too often the brand appears in the commercial—almost as a 'tag'—at the end of the ad.

Ideally, the brand should be made an integral part of the execution, not just with humorous ads but especially in the case of humorous ads because of the 'attention overshadowing' effect.

What do I mean by integration? To illustrate, consider the classic Budweiser frogs commercial in the USA. Three frogs croak in turn and at first it just sounds like nonsense croaking. But as the croaks speed up and run together, the camera pans so that a large Budweiser sign comes into view and it becomes clear that the sound the frogs are making is 'Bud', 'Weis', 'Er'. Here the brand is well integrated.

Here's another example. An ad for male fragrance brand Clix (made by Axe) shows an attractive male going through his day receiving admiring, amorous looks from various women. Each time this happens, he clicks a hand counter. As he gets into an elevator at the end of the day, he shows his click count for the day to another male but is disconcerted when the other guy's counter totals many, many more clicks. And the brand of male fragrance that he was using was of course Clix.

A good test of how integrated the branding is in any ad is to play a little game of imagine. Imagine the ad but with your competitor's brand substituted in it instead of your own. Does the ad still make sense? Does it do any violation to the ad?

If the competitor's brand could fit the execution just as well as yours, then you are at risk. It is especially likely to brand poorly (unless you are the market leader or take other steps to strengthen the branding in the commercial). The creator of the famous Volkswagen 'Beetle' campaign went so far as to say that if you take the brand out of the ad it should no longer be funny.

Consider an alternative example—the Land Rover ad where the little kid knocks on the door of the Land Rover, and when the woman winds the window down he asks 'Is Jason there—can he come out to play?' She says 'Hold on, I'll check'. This is another great ad but with the potential to 'slip' in memory to some other competitor such as Landcruiser or Jeep. There are no integrative branding elements.

Many ads have good integration of the product category with the execution but not with the brand. For example, consider the ad mentioned earlier with the lovebird who successfully disposes of the cat by pecking at the telephone keypad to dial a courier, who then comes to pick up the cat as a package. This was a great ad that ran globally and that many people will still remember. Which courier company was it for?

If you can't answer that question then you are among many who could not recall the brand even when the ad was on air. In fact the ad was for DHL couriers. Note that you could easily substitute FedEx into the commercial in your mind and it would do no violation to the ad whatsoever. The brand is not integrated with the execution. However, the product category is. You couldn't as easily change the product category to something else. A courier company is fundamental to the storyline and a key ingredient in making the humor work.

Poor branding is especially likely to happen in commercials where the humor is peripheral to, rather than integrated with, the brand message. This is because the audience is overly occupied with processing the humorous, executional elements of the commercial—things that have little if anything to do with the brand message—and this is hijacking attention from the brand.

Ideally the brand name itself should tie in, as in the Budweiser and the Clix commercials. This is rarely an easy thing to do. In fact some would argue that when it does happen it is pure genius. By way of illustration consider for example that the lovebird, courier ad would have worked much better with some kind of tie-in to the DHL company name. The ad would have worked wonderfully for a company called, say, Kruger Allstates Transport because it would have been much harder to confuse it with any other company (like FedEx). The K.A.T. courier brand could easily have been integrated as an executional element in the ad as Budweiser was in the frogs ad and Clix in the Axe fragrance ad. The cat, like the chorused croaks, would form an integral element of the commercial and act as a retrieval cue for the company brand. While it is much harder to do, if it can be done this works far better than simply tacking the brand on at the end.

So one of the guidelines is: wherever possible try to integrate the execution with the brand—not just the product. Ads like the DHL example, where only the product is inherently integrated with the execution, are very common and have to rely on other factors to stamp in the correct brand association. Unless the brand is integrated into the execution, even great humorous executions must be extra careful to make sure they get the brand across and register it in memory and guard against just doing a generic advertising job for the product category as a whole.

Liking

Liking of a brand's advertising is the third mechanism. Just as a brand's packaging is part of its brand attire, thereby adding to the liking of the brand, so too a brand's advertising reflects the characteristic way it communicates. Liking for the way it communicates can add to the liking for the brand. A brand's advertising is one dimension of its personality. Just as humorous public speakers are appreciated, so humorous ads are *liked* and this has the potential to wash over onto the brand itself.

As we have seen earlier, liking of a brand's advertising is a feather that can tip the balance towards that brand. In low-involvement categories where all brands in the category are virtually identical—where there is often nothing new to say about the brand—then the 'beam balance' theory comes into play. If all brands are equal then it only takes an additional feather on one side of the beam balance to tip the decision to that brand. Liking of the brand's advertising can be that feather. This is of somewhat less importance in high-involvement categories.

Humor therefore tends to be more effective in low-involvement categories because it can be an effective feather. But there is another reason as well why it does not usually work as well in high-involvement categories. To the extent that people are already highly involved, humor can be somewhat superfluous in attracting their attention. If the advertiser has some important information to tell people about a product that they are highly involved in, then they are likely to be all ears. It won't necessarily get any more of their attention if you include humor. Indeed it may distract them from the key message elements. So for both these reasons humor is less relevant to high-involvement categories than it is to low-involvement categories.

Wear-out

Conventional wisdom says that humorous ads wear out quickly and certainly wear out faster than other ads. But do they? It is nowhere near that clear cut. There are studies finding that they do wear out more quickly and other studies finding no difference between humorous and normal ads.[11]

In tracking I have seen situations where humorous TV ads worked very effectively for over a year without showing signs of wear-out. In one case, for example, the ad was on air for two years before showing any signs of wearing out. The advertiser and the ad agency would have pulled the ad off air eighteen months earlier but for the clear evidence coming from the tracking data.

Why do such contradictory results exist? One clue is in the social dimension. Laughter and humor is contagious—that's why laughter tracks are added in comedy shows. When we watch a funny ad our reactions are likely to be different depending upon whether we are viewing it alone or with others. Ads that are viewed by audiences that typically consist of just one person have less chance of being seen as funny. Studies are fairly consistent in showing that people laugh more if they are with other people and the more people, the more they laugh.[12]

One suggestion by two leading researchers is that this is why we get contradictory findings on wear-out of humor. As they put it:

> ... some [ads] seem to get better, as *anticipation* of what will be presented evokes an anticipatory humorous response. If in fact, a listener or viewer laughs because others do or have ... wear out of humor may be postponed ... certain television commercials seem to become 'funnier' over time as their punch lines enter the language of popular culture and are repeated by professional comedians, as well as the general public.[13]

This exposes the fact that humor not only helps an ad break through and get attention but it may also succeed in making the ad itself a point of discussion and attention of the social group. Quiz shows like *Who Wants to be a Millionaire?* owe a considerable amount of their success to this. Unlike most other TV programs they stimulate participation and discussion between members of the living-room audience ('I got that one right', 'Wow ... how did you know that?', 'I know the answer to this one!' etc).

This is not just a case of getting greater attention. The ad takes on a significance and an enjoyment that comes about by it emerging out of the TV to become the focus of a conversational interaction with others. ('Oh look ... here comes that great ad again ... Doesn't that just break you up! I love that ad.')

Summary

Humor remains one of the least understood elements in advertising and indeed one of the least understood sides of life. We have a lot to learn yet about how to maximize the chances of humorous commercials working effectively but we are getting there. The available research is thin and hardly provides anything like a clear view. The glimpses of insight can be extremely valuable, however—like peeking through venetian blinds. The view is not perfect but as someone once said, 'If it were not for venetian blinds it would be curtains for all of us'!

18 LEARNING TO USE SHORTER-LENGTH TV COMMERCIALS

Fifteen-second commercials were first introduced in the 1980s. They were attractive to advertisers previously unable to afford advertising on TV, with the result that money was redirected out of print into fifteen-second TV commercials. At the same time regular TV advertisers also began to experiment with changing from 30-second ads to fifteen-second commercials, hoping for better value for money.

At the time, when all this was beginning, I was continuous tracking all the ads in a client's product category and browsing through information on which advertisers were on air in the previous week. I noted one advertiser that went on air with a single ad but with a large media weight of 450 TRPs for the week. With such a lot of exposures you would expect the ad to be generating a reasonable return. However, I was amazed when I inspected the advertiser's ad awareness and market share information. Figure 18.1 shows that ad awareness and market share did not go up. They actually went down—despite all this weight of advertising! Crazy!

Intrigued by this, I played the ad to check it out. I wanted to see what ad could possibly be that bad. Fifteen seconds later I knew! It was a fifteen-second commercial, it had a fairly complex message and it was being aimed at a low-involved audience and being used as a solo.

I had increasingly observed in tracking fifteen-second commercials that when used on their own as a solo with low-involved audiences, they rarely seemed to work. Here was the starkest evidence yet. Even with heavy media weight this ad seemed all but invisible. It did not break through; it was doing nothing for market share and nothing in the way of reinforcing people's feelings about the advertiser. It was a waste of money. The advertiser might as well have not been on air.

Conventional wisdom at that time was that a fifteen-second commercial is 'about two-thirds as effective as a 30-second commercial'. Driven on

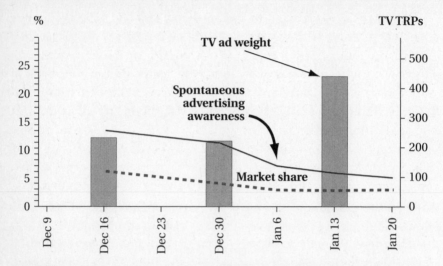

Note: The percentage of people spontaneously aware of this 15-second advertisement actually declined while it was on air as did the brand's market share.

Figure 18.1: *A fifteen-second advertisement failure. (Source: MarketMind)*

by this erroneous belief, fifteen-second ads grew explosively in number throughout the late 1980s and early 1990s before leveling off. Yet, my experience of tracking many of them was that all too often they just did not seem to work.

Tracking numerous ad campaigns provided me with the opportunity from time to time to compare the performance of a 30-second ad aired in one region with the fifteen-second version of the same ad running simultaneously in another region. The results emerged as generally clear cut. Simply trying to use fifteen-second ads as cut-down versions of 30-second ads rarely seemed to work, especially when they were used on their own as solos. *When* they work, fifteen-second commercials seem to work very differently from 30-second commercials.

At that time US researcher Lee Weinblatt also questioned the merits of fifteen-second commercials, making the point that 'You can't communicate a believable message in so short a time, unless you started with 30-second commercials and built a case of communication, then brought in a fifteen-second commercial as a reminder.'[1] This began to be supported by the research findings of others.[2]

Researchers Von Gonten and Donius concluded in 1997 from panel data: 'Wherever it has been possible to isolate the effect of 15's from 30's, the overwhelming majority of 15's have behaved as if off-air. Some few 15's perform strongly, but they are rare exceptions to the general finding.'[3]

When my 'early warnings' were first published in the first edition of this book, they aroused a lot of reaction. I was careful not to say that solo fifteen-second commercials cannot work. I did however emphasize that in my experience they almost never did. I had tracked a lot of commercials and it was the exception to come across a solo fifteen-second commercial that worked. Fifteen-second ads can work; but the ones that do are the exceptions and not the rule. However, studying exceptions can be revealing.

One exception is shown in Figures 18.2 and 18.3. This ad had a lot of media weight behind it but it did work exceptionally well. Why? How did this campaign differ from the overwhelming number that failed? One difference was that it was extremely simple and single-minded, both visually and verbally. It did not try to do too much. The message was strongly communicated in both the visual and the verbal medium and it was an extremely simple message.

As a result of observing exceptions like these, we now have a greater understanding of how shorter commercials work and how they *can* be used to effect if advertisers learn how to use them and also learn how *not* to use them. If you are going to use fifteen-second or ten-second ads successfully they need to be designed differently and used in a different way.

Getting into people's heads vs staying there

A general principle in the psychology of learning is that it is harder to get into people's minds than it is to stay there. In other words, there are two processes: the process of learning and the process of priming and reinforcement. One is original learning; the other maintains and reinforces the freshness of that learning. The process of reinforcement is not the same as the process of originally communicating something. It usually takes a longer commercial or more repetition to get an ad into people's minds in the first place than it does to keep an ad and its message there.

Familiarity

We know from psychology experiments that it takes much less time to recognize and process something that is familiar.[4] The more we prime

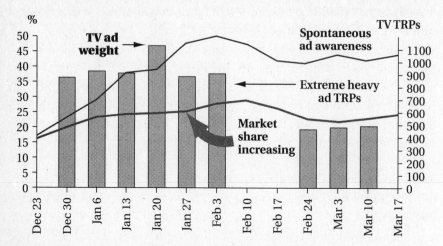

Note: This 15-second advertisement had an extremely simple and single-minded message along with extremely heavy advertising weight. It worked and market share increased—while it was on air!

Figure 18.2: *A fifteen-second advertisement campaign that worked!*
(Source: MarketMind)

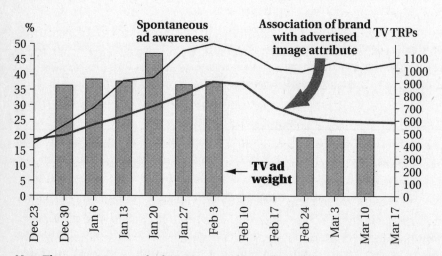

Note: The same 15-second advertisement also increased the percentage of people associating the brand with the advertised image attribute.

Figure 18.3: *Percentage of people associating the brand with the advertised image.*
(Source: MarketMind)

(or activate) something, the more familiar it becomes. It is like priming a pump. The more it is primed the quicker it works.

A new commercial with new images and new messages takes longer for our minds to process than an established commercial. Ten or fifteen seconds may be too short a time for our minds to process these properly. Like fast cut commercials they may just get lost. Even with words, the less frequently a word occurs in the language the longer it takes our minds to recognize it and process it.

Familiarity and speed of processing

Our minds process words and ads much more quickly and much more easily when they are familiar. Highly familiar words like 'book' and 'camel' are recognized up to three times faster than less familiar words like 'tome' and 'dromedary'. Similarly, our minds process highly familiar ads and brands more rapidly than less familiar brands. With more exposures, recognition becomes even faster as something becomes highly familiar.[5]

Hence, when we see shorter-length commercials (or we fast forward through ads on a pre-recorded program—see Chapter 25, 'The web'), we are nevertheless more likely to be able to pick up the communication if the ad is already familiar.

The general 'take-out' point here is that it is useful to advertisers to think about ads in terms of how much time our minds need to mentally process the elements of the ad and how many exposures it takes to develop a 'mental model' of it.

Shorter-length commercials are the occupying forces. They are best at occupying and holding the mental ground that has already been captured by the longer-length commercials. These longer-length commercials are the attack forces. They are good for bringing about learning. They are good for getting a message into people's heads in the first place.

My years of tracking research convinced me that shorter-length commercials can be quite effective in holding mental ground *after* longer length commercials have been used to capture it. However, when used on their own, as solos, they often prove disappointing and ineffective (see Figure 18.4, for example).

Lost in the clutter

Usually the first thing you want an ad to do is break through the clutter and get noticed. Shorter-length commercials, when used as a solo with

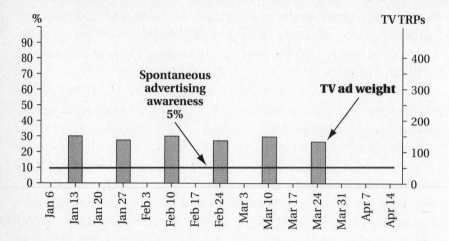

Note: The percentage of people who were spontaneously aware of this 15-second advertisement never rose above 5%.

Figure 18.4: *Another fifteen-second advertisement failure. (Source: MarketMind)*

low-involved audiences, have great difficulty breaking through the clutter. Time and time again, I have found that they are generally disappointing at breaking through on their own except when the audience is highly involved with the product.

This is despite the fact that shorter-length ads are usually screened at greater repetition levels than 30-second commercials. One of the seductive attractions of shorter-length commercials is that advertisers can get more repeat exposure for the same ad budget than they can with a 30-second ad. But even at very high exposure levels, shorter-length, solo ads often fail to register at the level of conscious ad recall. So if you are going to use them as solos, confine your expectations to conveying implicit association and make sure any explicit message is ultra simple.

There have been amazingly few exceptions. And the exceptions are usually due to the great creative idea in the commercial or to the audience being highly involved with the product category. Or to the shorter-length ads building on each other like 'sequels'. You need exceptionally creative ads or a highly involved audience or an extremely simple message, or you need to build them up in a series if you are going to use shorter-length commercials as solos. Otherwise they just seem to disappear into the ether.

Message communication

Capturing mental ground means not only breaking through but also correctly delivering a message or an impression. I have found shorter-length commercials when used on their own to be extremely weak in message communication with low-involved audiences. So when they do break through (which is rarely), they seem unable to communicate anything but the simplest of messages.

Table 18.1 shows the results of yet another fifteen-second ad campaign, compared with a 45-second campaign for the same product category but run at a different time. The fifteen-second ad's performance is abysmal.

This fifteen-second commercial campaign went for six weeks with a huge number of exposures (a total of 1850 TRPs, or over 300 TRPs per week). Despite this heavy media weight it achieved only 25 per cent prompted recognition and only 4 per cent correct message take-out.

Table 18.1: Comparison of advertisement campaigns

	45 seconds	15 seconds
Length of campaign	2 weeks	6 weeks
Total TRPs	400	1850
Execution cued ad recognition	49%	25%
Share of voice	28%	19%
Correct message take-out	30%	4%

Source: MarketMind

This dramatically illustrates that a key weakness of shorter-length ads is in getting across a message. They can effectively deliver a reminder, i.e. reinforce an already learnt brand message. But they won't communicate unless the message is extremely simple or it is a reminder ad or a sequel ad following from other commercials where the message has been exposed previously.

I stress that this is when used on their own, when the message is anything more than a visually supported, very single-minded state-ment, and when the audience is not highly involved. When the message is a very simple one and one that has been established before (usually by longer-length commercials), then shorter-length ads can work cost effectively.

Blame the creatives?

Some people take the view that the failure of so many shorter-length commercials is the fault of the creative teams. They argue that when these ads fail it's because of poor creative work, and not the length of the ad. This argument says that any commercial will work if the creative and the media are right.

In light of the many that I have seen fail, I think it is unjust and far too simplistic to blame this on the creative teams. To do so ignores what is now more widely acknowledged—that there are inherent limitations to shorter ads. It ignores the fact that ten to fifteen seconds may be an impossibly short time to get across the great majority of messages—at least from a standing start.

Yes, part of creative team's job is to cleverly package messages in such a way that they communicate easily, quickly and entertainingly and there are a few shorter-length commercials that do that. But ten to fifteen seconds is an extremely short time in which to successfully communicate anything. In those few instants the ad has to:

- tune people out of the previous commercial or program that they are watching;
- lock their attention onto the ad;
- communicate the brand name;
- get across an effective message;
- consolidate the memory trace before the next ad comes along (with the potential to interfere with the mental processing of what has just been said).

It takes time to tune in

The first and last of these are important reasons why so many shorter-length ads turn out to be less effective than expected. It takes time for people to tune out of one thing and into another. This applies to conversations or any other abrupt changes in our stream of thought. And it also applies to ads.

It takes us time, even though it is brief, to switch from what we are currently thinking about or attending to and re-tune our thoughts to something else. All of us can relate to the experience of being interrupted while doing something and then having to ask the interrupter to repeat what they have just said. That's because we were tuned in to something else and it took time to switch over.

It is easy to be deceived by the fact that we are talking about only very small amounts of time for this mental switching to take place. It may only be a couple of seconds, but this is a couple of seconds out of our mental processing time. And it is sobering to realize that in a fifteen-second commercial a couple of seconds represents 13 per cent of the total exposure time that may be down time for this reason alone. This is also a reason why in the new environment of digital video recorders commercials will increasingly become more focused on reminder and reinforcement. There is evidence that even when viewed at fast speed, the brand and the key reinforcement images can still register.[6]

It takes time to tune out

A problem may exist in the final seconds of the commercial as well. The 'interruption' interference effect on mental processing may also apply to the last second or two of the ad content. The memory trace for this has the potential to be interfered with by the next commercial. Psychological experiments show that interruption by, and switching to, the next event (the next ad) attenuates the mental processing and memory of what went on in the few seconds immediately before the interruption.[7]

So what this means is that for up to a quarter of the time of a fifteen-second ad, the viewer's mental processing may be subject to interference effects of one kind or another (at the start and finish).

Fifteens as cost-efficient reminders

Many of the shorter-length campaigns that critics cite as having worked turn out *not* to be solos or 'stand-alones'. Instead, they are often reminders reinforcing a previous campaign. This is not what I mean by 'solo' fifteens. This is building on or re-triggering what has gone before. It is advertising that ties closely back into, and re-occupies, the mental territory that has already been captured.

The point is that it takes more to get into people's heads in the first place than it does to stay there—or re-trigger memories that reside there and are well established. In such situations shorter-length commercials can work well.

The general implication is clear. If we need to get across a message then the preferred strategy is to use longer-length commercials to get it across, to firmly entrench it, before switching to shorter-length (*reminder*) commercials. Fortunately in the new YouTube world of video ads on the web, creative teams are being freed up to make longer-length commercials. These can achieve big bang effect by being virally disseminated and without the prohibitive cost of relying entirely on frequent screenings on TV. Cut down shorter, ten- to fifteen-second versions can then work well to effectively remind and reinforce established memories of the longer ad.

Shorter-length commercials can definitely give us reinforcement and reminders at lower cost, but only if the main communication has first been established with the longer commercial. This is because it takes less time and effort to reinforce a message than it takes to internalize it in the first place.

Table 18.2: Various ways shorter-length commercials have been used

As a *reminder*: e.g. a 30-second ad followed, after initial bursts, by fifteen-second reminder ads.	This works.
As a *fast-follower*: e.g. a 30 and a fifteen cut down from the first one that appear in the same commercial break. The 30-second commercial shown first up with the fifteen-second shortened version used last in the same break.	More often than not, this also works.
As a *'sequel'*: e.g. a fifteen- to 30-second commercial first up in the break with a fifteen-second sequel commercial appearing last in the break.	More often than not, this also works.
As a *mixture-ingredient*: e.g. 30s and fifteens randomly scheduled in the same week.	This seems to have little going for it.
'Back-to-back': e.g. two fifteens in a 30-second pod. Unlikely to work unless the ads are for two *related* products (e.g. toothbrushes and toothpaste for the same brand—say Colgate). These have the potential to appear as almost a seamless 30 seconds of advertising for the brand's dental hygiene products.	Unknown.
As a *solo*: fifteens used entirely on their own.	Usually don't work unless • highly creative • simple message • high involvement • confined to conveying simple associations.

Audience motivation

How does the level of motivation of the audience change things with shorter-length commercials? How are the principles any different if we use them to advertise to a highly involved audience? People who are highly involved are more attentive and also have lower thresholds. To go back to our flash-card experiments, people who have not eaten for several hours recognize food words (like apple, bread, cake, etc) faster than those who have just eaten. Hunger makes them process food words faster because their minds are more attuned to any stimuli that may be relevant to that immediate need.

It is less demanding to get through to an interested, motivated audience. The communicator has to put in less work to get the message across because the audience is predisposed to understand and internalize the communication. Highly motivated students are likely to pay more concentrated attention to the lecturer and work harder at trying to understand and internalize what he or she has to say. There is less onus on the lecturer because the students are more naturally attentive.

We rarely find this level of involvement in advertising. However, when aimed at highly involved groups, a shorter-length ad can work in its own right—if the message is simple. It may apply, for example, to a business ad with something new to say that is aimed at an involved audience watching a business program. Or a Toyota dealer advertising a red-hot price on Corollas to people actively shopping around for a Corolla. The key here is involvement, which affects not only attention but also the amount of work the recipient is prepared to do to take out the message.

Summary

Shorter-length commercials need to be used in ways that maximize the chances for effectiveness. Solo, stand-alone, shorter-length commercials are all too often used inappropriately and rarely work, especially with low-involved audiences. If the audience is not highly involved and/or the message is not visually simple, then don't use ten- to fifteen-second commercials as solos.

Consider shorter-length commercials as cost-efficient reminder ads after the mental territory has been captured with longer-length commercials. Or consider using a shorter-length ad as a sequel, topping and tailing it, preferably with a longer-length ad at the beginning and a shorter-length ad at the end of the break.

Remember that shorter-length ads have extreme difficulty breaking through the clutter. They also add to the clutter. (A three-minute ad break can consist of six 30-second ads or twelve fifteen-second ads.)

19 SEASONAL ADVERTISING

All advertising is not created equal. And all product categories are not the same. It is clear from tracking numerous ad campaigns in various parts of the world that there are important seasonal influences on advertising. Products that are to a greater or lesser extent seasonal include:

- **Summer:** ice creams, suntan lotions, soft drinks, swimwear, beer and charcoal.
- **Winter:** canned soup, chocolate bars, chocolate cookies, cough and cold preparations.
- **Seasonal events:** electric razors (most of which are sold for Father's Day and Christmas), children's shoes and school supplies (start of school year), champagne (New Year's) and greeting cards.
- **In addition:** some public-authority and utility advertising campaigns may be distinctly seasonal, for example: save water (summer), prevent forest fires (summer), drink driving, speed kills (holiday seasons) etc.

Sometimes these things are pretty obvious, but all too often we realize this only in retrospect. It is easy to fail to be aware of them or to be distracted from them in the product management process.

Perceived popularity

I referred earlier to the 'perceived popularity' of a product and the role that advertising plays in it. Brand popularity can be self-fulfilling. If people see something as popular the chances are enhanced that, provided everything else is equal, they will follow suit and buy the brand. Perceived popularity can tip the balance.

Sometimes products gather momentum through their advertising. The brand is seen as increasingly popular. And just when it is about to really catch on, the visibility and impetus suddenly stop. Why? Because 'the season' is over. This points to one key difference in marketing seasonal products—especially in the way one goes about developing a new brand.

The need for accelerated trial

With product categories that are seasonal, advertisers have limited time to build momentum. They have to make the product 'catch on' in much less time than they would normally have for a non-seasonal product. They are always racing to beat the seasonal clock.

Even with non-seasonal products there is an unwritten rule of thumb that you need to aim for maximum trial for a new brand in the first three to six months. Otherwise, it loses that sense of newness. It risks acquiring an image of having been around for a while and not having taken off. If this sets in, it makes gaining further trial all the more difficult to achieve.

With a seasonal product the problem is acute. If the advertising can't create a sense of the brand having taken off in the first season, chances are that by its return in the second season the brand will risk being perceived as 'old hat'. People will remember that it was around last season but 'didn't seem to catch on'. This can be the kiss of death.

Maximizing the proportion of people who try the product is crucial to success. Remember, a 20 per cent market share can be achieved in two very different ways:

- if only 20 per cent of people have tried the brand but they are buying it 100 per cent of the time;
- if 100 per cent of people have tried the brand but are buying it only 20 per cent of the time, i.e. once in every five times they buy the product category.

To give a brand the maximum chance of success it is important to aim for maximum trial as early as possible. If the trial rate at the end of the first season has only reached 25 per cent it means the brand is relying on a very high repeat-buying rate to achieve satisfactory market share and viability. More to the point, it will not be until next season that the brand will get a crack at the 75 per cent of consumers who have not yet tried the brand. By that time it may be too late.

The off-season pause

With seasonal products, the off-season period of inactivity is regarded by many advertisers as a temporary interruption. When it is over they expect to simply resume where they left off last season, in the same way as re-starting a video after pausing in freeze frame and expecting it to resume exactly where it left off.

But does it? It is dangerous to assume that even if it always has done that, it will do so again next time. Memories fade, attitudes change, people change and competitors may try to influence the market during the off season. If you have spent real effort and a lot of money during the season to capture the mental territory of the consumer's mind, can you leave the opening round of next season's battle to chance?

It is worth considering occupation strategies that attempt to hold on to the mental territory you captured during that off season.

Extending the season

Lipton in the US very effectively expanded the tea 'season' into summer by promoting 'iced tea' so that today, a majority of all tea in the USA is consumed cold. In Australia, the 'speed kills' and ' Don't drink and drive' campaigns were traditionally seasonal. Now they run throughout the year, with demonstrable benefits. Kit Kat, formerly a winter product, extended its season from winter to embrace summer through its 'Cool Kat' campaign that urged us to keep our Kit Kats in the refrigerator and enjoy them cold.

The idea is to find ways to maintain during the off season that which has been built up in the season. This may be in people's minds or behavior or both.

An example

Figure 19.1 shows one example of a highly seasonal campaign. This was a 'save water' campaign which ran over two months each year. It was very successful. Note that it achieved about 48 per cent spontaneous advertising awareness in the first season.

The campaign was very successful . . . *while it was on air*. But it was on air for only two months of the year. This campaign built extremely good awareness but five weeks after the advertising stopped its effect had decayed and was virtually gone. Like 'speed kills' campaigns, this water campaign was aimed at influencing people's behavior. The need for the

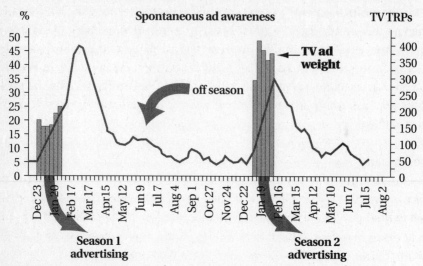

Note: A seasonal advertising campaign that is successful but its effect is very shortlived.

Figure 19.1: *Seasonal advertising campaign—spontaneous ad awareness.* *(Source: MarketMind)*

behavior change is more acute in the key period, but it is also present throughout the year—albeit at a lower level.

A better strategy would have been to build the awareness in the key months (to the same or higher level) in the first year and then, instead of going off air completely until the next year, to implement a low-cost maintenance advertising campaign to run through the other ten months of the year. Instead of using such large media weights in that second season, it could have deployed the same budget throughout the year to implement a maintenance schedule of shorter-length TV ads. This alternative maintenance schedule could have alternated by having:

* one week on air followed by
* one week off air followed by
* one week on air, etc.

At a low exposure (a maintenance weight of say 75 TRPs per week), and/or reminder ads in magazines and newspapers in that off season, this organization would have spent the same amount of money but to much more continuous effect.

The point is that if you build public awareness to a high level and then let it come all the way down again by going off air completely, it takes just as much effort to build it from scratch next time. It is usually much more economical to build the awareness and then try to maintain it with lowered advertising weight or support media. The principle is that it takes more expenditure to get into people's minds in the first place than it does to stay there.

Get in early

If your product category is truly seasonal and you and your competitors always start advertising in a particular month, consider jumping the gun. Get in first. This recommendation is based on the principle that it is easiest to get into people's heads *when there is little or no competing advertising clutter.*

If you can capture the mental territory before your competitors come on air, your job, when they do come on air, is easier—a maintenance task, not a building task. You have already captured the mental territory and it is easier and less expensive in the face of clutter to hold the ground you have won. Getting in early can be an effective strategy. (But be sure to send in the occupation forces in the form of a maintenance campaign when the competitors come on air.)

Who determines seasonality?

Is your product truly seasonal? For some products, seasonality is almost dictated by what the advertisers do—or don't do—in the off season. With some products, all brands seem to observe a conventional promotional seasonal cycle. The dictum seems to be: We only advertise in the season.

As some of the previous examples show, it is sometimes the marketers as much as the consumers who determine if something is seasonal. If marketers believe it is seasonal, this is likely to be a self-fulfilling prophecy. Products are rarely as inherently seasonal as we are inclined to believe.

Take the soft drink market, for example. Users consume primarily because they are thirsty. And it is true people get thirstier more often in summer. Hence the soft drink product is seasonal. However, brands like Coca-Cola and Pepsi Cola have been deliberately given a social overlay— an image that makes the drink function as a 'social lubricant' and not just as a simple thirst-quencher.

This adds functionality and at the same time reduces the seasonality of these two brands compared to ordinary soft drink. Like beer, they tend to be consumed more in summer but are also drunk in winter in substantial volume for social reasons.

The changeover-to-daylight-saving trap

Seasonal products have limited peak season time on TV. However at certain times of the year, often the times when seasonal products need to advertise, there is a peculiar problem. In the summer holiday season for example, there is significant doubt about how many people are going to be away on vacation and will therefore not be as exposed to advertising.

Another, not so well recognized problem that is important in some countries with seasonal products is the changeover-to-daylight-saving trap. This is especially a trap for any brand whose manufacturer might think about relying heavily on advertising in prime time during the evening news. The changeover to daylight saving in summer means that a number of people this week, who last week at 6 p.m. were sitting in front of their TVs watching the news, may no longer be watching TV at that time. They may be out kicking a football or swinging a bat with their kids or doing something else in the new-found hour of daylight. Especially with seasonal products, beware this 'changeover-to-daylight-saving' trap.

Summary

There is limited time to build advertising momentum with seasonal products. Consider ways to extend the season and ways to hold on to the residual effect of your advertising during the off season. An 'occupation-force' strategy during the off season can often hold much of the mental territory. Be sure to get the jump on competitors by commencing seasonal advertising early—before the season proper. New product launches require maximum awareness and trial in the first season. Unless the brand is seen as successful in the first season, it risks being regarded as 'old hat' on return. For scheduling media, be mindful of the changeover-to-daylight-saving trap.

20 UNDERWEIGHT ADVERTISING: EXECUTION ANOREXIA

How many exposures does an ad need to be effective? And in what period of time? No one knows for sure. Another way of putting it is: is there a minimum threshold of media weight needed to make an ad campaign work? The answer seems to be 'yes'.[1]

A case example

I once saw a new campaign come very close to being cancelled by the client. A whole battery of effectiveness-tracking measures said the campaign was having a disappointing and marginal impact. The client was close to the point of concluding that the ads were 'hopeless'.

The media weight for this campaign was around 150 TRPs per week. This means that the people who were the target market for the product were supposed to be exposed to it on average about 1.5 times a week.[2] At least that was what was planned. Before labeling any campaign a failure or concluding that 'these ads don't work' it is crucial to look at the actual TRP figures, the actual *delivered*, as distinct from the planned, media weight.

Sometimes ads do not go to air because of some mix-up. Sometimes the buying of air time is not as good as it should be. Sometimes (as in the changeover to daylight saving, holiday periods, etc) there are not as many people watching TV as there were the previous week. In this example, when these actual TRP figures were obtained (some two months after the campaign had started), it emerged that only about 60 per cent of the planned weight was in fact achieved (i.e. about 90 TRPs per week).

Corrective action was taken and in the subsequent weeks the planned exposure rate, the full 150 TRPs per week, was achieved. With this weight the campaign went on to perform amazingly well in the test market and later nationally. The reason the campaign was not working originally had little to do with the creativeness of the commercials. It was like listening to a signal from deep space. The signal was too faint. The volume had to be turned up.

Here was a perfectly good creative campaign which could have gone down in the annals of 'great advertising failures'. The problem was not the ads themselves but a level of exposure that was too low.

Execution anorexia

The difference between 150 and 90 TRPs a week may not seem like much. However, this campaign had three executions (three ads) being rotated on air in each week. This means that each ad was being exposed at the rate of only about 30 TRPs per week. This is a very low figure and evidently below a critical threshold for effectiveness—at least in that particular market.

There is a valuable lesson here. When planning a media schedule, the threshold TRP weights cannot be decided without taking account of the number of ad executions that will be used. The advertising weight must be set in terms of the number of TRPs per execution and not just in terms of an overall figure. Many advertisers use multiple executions (e.g. Coke, Toyota) but recognition of this point is all too often the exception rather than the rule. The rule is that in media planning it important to factor into the advertising schedule the threshold number of TRPs per ad execution in addition to the overall campaign weight. (That is even more especially important if the executions share little in common.) Otherwise the campaign can end up, like this one, with execution anorexia and underweight advertising.

One execution or many?

This raises an important question. What is the optimum number of ad executions to air in any one week? One? Two? Three? Is it better to have one execution or many?

I wish I could tell you that the answer was straightforward and simple. It's not. One thing is for sure, however. Multiple executions have to be considered carefully in terms of tightness of integration, media weight, flighting of each execution and particularly the degree of involvement of the target audience. Especially with low-involvement products, the use of multiple executions can be counter-productive. I have seen as many as six ad executions used for the same brand in one week. Were they effective? No! If there is a general rule that emerges it is this: for low-involvement products don't use multiple executions or if you do, make sure they are well integrated with each other and/or be prepared to back each one with substantial TRP weight in its own right.[3]

There are examples of tightly integrated campaigns where multiple executions have worked well but the general note should be one of caution. Being single-minded is usually best.

Low vs high involvement

How much media weight you need to get an effective response from advertising depends on the involvement of the audience as well as the number of ad executions you intend putting to air. Low- and high-involvement audiences process ads, and the information in them, quite differently.

Communicating to a target audience which is highly involved in what you have to say differs from communicating with people who don't care too much. How? Here is a potted summary:

- Highly involved target audiences are more motivated and actively looking for information.
- As a result the ad may require less repetition, and print media may often work very effectively.
- Advertising to highly involved audiences has been shown to be less subject to interference in memory when they see subsequent ads for competitive brands. The implication of this is that you should be able to get away with a lower share of voice (i.e. a lower share of the total ad spend in the product category) than would be the case for low-involvement products.
- Some evidence suggests that advertising to highly involved audiences is not as subject to minimum TRP thresholds as is advertising to low-involved audiences.
- Advertising to high-involvement audiences is less sensitive to the number of ad executions on air—but only relatively and it is important that the executions are integrated in some way. For example, a brand of door lock positioned on safety might have ad executions focusing on various reasons why it is safe i.e. one ad might focus on 'because it is drill resistant'; another 'because it is pick resistant'; and another 'because it has factory-only keys'.[4] The message 'safe' is the constant. Only the 'reason why' changes with each execution so this is good integration.

Some guidelines for the low-involvement audience

A crucial difference with low-involvement products is that the advertising has to capture the attention of the low-involved consumer. This is certainly the case with most packaged goods.[5] Advertising for low-involvement products puts a premium on highly creative and sometimes bizarre ad executions to make the advertising break through the clutter.

For low-involved audiences the overriding task is to break through the clutter of other ads and force people to notice the ad and its message. If you don't break through, the ad doesn't get noticed and the chances are that nothing happens. Consumers don't 'see' the ad and don't process the communication. (See Chapter 26, 'Mental reach'.)

The ad and the message needs to be very single-minded. Once you have forced attention, you have only limited time and tolerance to get your message across and have it processed effectively. The message has to be simple. The temptation to incorporate several messages in the same ad or in different ads needs to be cut off at the knees. An uninvolved audience just won't work hard enough to take in all the elements of your communication. If it requires anything other than easy processing, you have lost them.

Even when you get your message across with low-involved audiences, the way it has been processed makes it particularly subject to interference and memory degradation *through subsequent exposure to competitive commercials* for other brands. This is why, with low-involved audiences, repetition at that initial stage of getting into people's heads with the campaign in the first place is so necessary. With highly involved audiences the desired effect may often be achieved and maintained with much less repetition because a) the audience works harder on the message in the first place and b) this greater 'elaboration', as it is called, consolidates the information in memory, thereby rendering it less subject to subsequent interference and memory degradation from exposure to other competitive commercials.

With low-involved audiences you not only have to get the information in, you have to work to keep it there. This is where shorter-length commercials come into their own, along with print media and web ad tie-ins with the TV commercial—that is, to provide repetition and reinforcement. (See Chapter 18, 'Learning to use shorter-length TV commercials'.)

For all these reasons, the number of executions on air and the TRP weight behind each execution are critical for low-involved audiences.

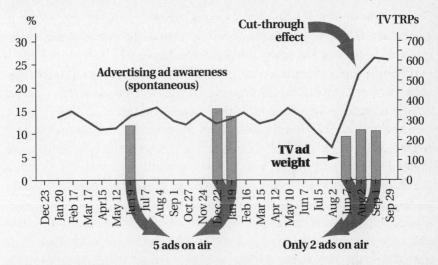

Note: This graph shows greater overall advertisement cut-through associated with fewer on-air executions for this brand. Executions reduced from five to two in any one week had a dramatic effect on advertisement awareness.

Figure 20.1: *The number of advertising executions. (Source: MarketMind)*

Another case example

Research has revealed a number of occasions on which multiple executions have been a problem in effectively communicating a low-involvement product. Figure 20.1 illustrates one such case. This is a frequently purchased, low-cost and relatively low-involvement product.

This brand was advertised with up to five different ad executions i.e. five ads on air for the same brand. The company then cut back on the number of different executions being rotated on air. The difference is dramatic (see graph).

Mixed-involvement audiences

To make things even more complicated, some product categories have mixed audiences—something that some ad agencies do not seem to explicitly recognize in the ad planning process. For example, with most durable goods (cars, computers, appliances, home entertainment systems, etc) you have at one time some people who are ready to buy and highly involved and some who may not buy for several months or years and who are relatively little involved.

Audiences are rarely homogenous. Some people will be highly involved and some will be less involved. In the planning process the advertiser needs to know the mix of the target audience.

To take one example, the audience for new car ads is often thought to be 100 per cent high involvement because only people in the market for a new car are thought to be worth targeting. This is a mistaken view. Something like a third of the people who will buy new cars in the next three months don't yet know they will do so. These people are unaware of what is just around the corner.

Some of them will find their present car starting to break down over the next three months; or if not their car, their marriage or long-term relationship. So some will separate from their partners and find themselves in need of a different car. Some will be relocated in their jobs; and still others will experience some unexpected windfall such as an inheritance or a lottery win.

These are just some of the many things that put people into a market when they didn't expect to be there. Right now they may be low involved but very soon they may well be much more highly involved. So like it or not, in these categories an advertiser needs to communicate with both the uninvolved and the involved consumer. The ad strategy can ill afford to assume that the only people worth targeting and communicating with are the highly involved ones.

Summary

Not every ad campaign is going to succeed. But don't let your ad campaign die from underweight advertising. Here is a small check-list:

- Check that your *planned* reach, frequency and media weights are in fact achieved.
- Especially with low-involvement products, use a single execution unless there is a very good reason for doing otherwise.
- If you are using multiple executions, make sure you check for the possibility of execution anorexia. Check the number of TRPs per execution per week. (Execution anorexia can be fatal to a campaign's health.)
- As a rough rule of thumb, if you can't afford to put a reasonable number of TRPs per week behind each execution, don't risk using a multiple execution strategy. Stay with a single execution and do it well.
- Check the involvement mix of your audience.

21 WHY RADIO ADS AREN'T RECALLED

Why is a lot of radio advertising so poorly remembered? It doesn't have pictures and it doesn't have the reach of television, but is there more to it than that? Even saturation campaigns don't seem to make it into the consumer's mental filing cabinet to the extent that one might expect. For example, one 'successful' saturation radio campaign which ran for a sixteen-week period in a specific target market was one of the highest-scoring campaigns I have seen in regard to radio ad awareness, yet it did not get more than 40 per cent of listeners to spontaneously recall the advertising.

Attention and pictures

Radio is not TV and it is not a substitute for TV. It could be used more effectively, but advertisers often seem to use it wrongly. The two main problems with radio seem to be listener attention levels and the fact that radio advertising doesn't have pictures. Advertisers can do something about both of these factors in designing more effective radio ads and media schedules.

Radio competes with its environment for the listener's attention—much more so than TV, which usually has its own, relatively quiet exposure environment. When people watch TV they more often do so with fewer distractions. That is not to say that TV audiences are glued to the set. Brands in low-involvement product categories particularly have to rely on very creative ad executions to grab and hold their TV audience's attention.

Radio, however, competes with all sorts of things. At breakfast it competes with the clatter of cutlery, the sounds of breakfast preparation and breakfast conversation. Again, in the morning and drive-time slots, radio has to work exceptionally hard to break through a different kind of 'attentional clutter'. This 'clutter' is made up of the peak-hour traffic, the business of driving, and passenger conversation, as well as the person's own thoughts.

So at certain times of the day, many listeners just aren't listeners in any full attentional sense. Radio's traditional listeners, who in its early days sat glued to programs like *Amos and Andy* or *The Goon Show* emanating from the bakelite mantle radio, have gone to television, MP3 players and the web. Nowadays, peak-time radio listeners are a low-involved lot. They are increasingly pressured from minute to minute by the many stimuli that compete for their attention.

Whether it is radio, TV, or point-of-sale advertising, the ad has to break through to deliver its message. At the same time it has to successfully register the correct brand. However, it is important with radio and low-involvement advertising generally not to look just for people's ability to recall the ad. Advertisers also need to look for behavior, attitude, image or salience effects before concluding simply from the lack of recall that the advertising is not working. (See Chapter 28, 'The buy-ology of mind'.)

Lessons for using radio

The message I want to communicate here is certainly not that advertisers should use less radio. That would be throwing out the baby with the bath water. Rather, the need is to use radio more intelligently and more effectively. Here are a few pointers:

- **Don't rely solely on recall as a measure of effectiveness.** Also look for other shifts, especially gradual image shifts and any influence on stimulating product-category consumption (as distinct from brand selection).
- **Use more selective time periods.** Clearly advertisers are likely to have more effect with radio (and TV) if they choose periods (or programs or stations) that offer less competition in the environment—less likelihood that the audience will be distracted. These may be the times when the listener base is at its lowest. So each spot may be more effective in itself, but amongst fewer people. This means using more spots but at a lower cost per spot.
- **Create better radio ads.** Put money into making better ads—ads that demand attention and break through. Too many radio ads are awful. There is a logical reason for this. Radio is regarded as the low-budget

medium. But keeping costs down at the expense of skimping on good writing and production seems to be the ultimate in false economy with radio.

- **Use TV, web, video (and perhaps even print) first to provide faces and visuals. Then generate reminder and reinforcement through radio.** Most people process something more easily and retain it better and longer when they associate pictures and faces with it. Pictures or 'visuals' act as memory hooks of the mind. This puts the focus on concrete messages and imagery. Use TV or the web or print media to give people the pictures and then use radio as a retrieval cue i.e. to *reinforce* the brand and the message that have already been associated with those pictures (for example you might use the soundtrack or audio excerpts from the TV commercial). Shorter-length TV commercials usually fail when used alone as attack forces. However, when used as occupation forces they can be remarkably effective. Radio can be used in the same way with low-involvement products. Establish the visual mental territory first with visual media and then tie in radio as a reminder/reinforcement. It takes more effort to get into people's heads than it does to stay there. Use the visual media for the attack. Use tie-in radio as a reinforcement/reminder.
- **Use radio to boost web ad effect.** The effect of radio when combined with web ads can be particularly attractive, as indicated by a number of research studies.[1]
- **Take advantage of the immediacy of radio.** Exposure to advertising is attended to more and has more effect the closer the customer is to the purchasing occasion. Schedule radio tactically where possible to hit the maximum number of consumers immediately before the purchase occasion (e.g. prior to people's supermarket shopping.)
- **Take advantage of the flexibility and immediacy of radio to stimulate consumption.** For example, Campbell's Soups in the US sets aside a substantial budget each year to run radio commercials on days when a storm threatens.[2] People are more likely to think of soup and eat soup when the weather turns bad.
- **Mention the brand name in the first eight seconds and a minimum of three times during the ad.** This finding emerged from studies in the US of 30-second TV commercials. My guess is that it is probably even more important for radio than for TV.

Summary

The aim must be to break through the clutter and get attention in order to deliver the ad message, or the chances are that your communication won't have anywhere near the desired effect. The more attention an ad gets, the more effectively it is likely to communicate and the more it is likely to be recalled. If it gets only a low level of attention it is likely to be at best inefficient and at worst ineffective. It will certainly require a greater level of repetition.

There is scope for using radio a lot more intelligently and to greater effect. Radio is a medium that is rarely well done!

22 MAXIMIZING AD EFFECTIVENESS: DEVELOP A UNIQUE AND CONSISTENT STYLE

Category conformity

Sameness, sameness everywhere! You can't see the forest for the trees. Too many product categories gravitate towards a single style of 'look-alike' advertising. The style becomes 'generic' to the category and we end up with entrenched category conformity.

For many years analgesics (aspirin, paracetamol) was one of these categories. Almost every brand's ad showed a glass with a tablet being dropped into it while the voiceover advised: 'If pain persists, see your doctor.' This is what I call the chameleon commercials syndrome. Instead of standing out from their environment, ads like this blend in with and virtually disappear into the background. The problem is that the ads are not distinctive enough to break through the clutter in the category and deliver the brand and the message.

In one dramatic case, before the commercial went to air I showed several still shots from it to respondents and they were asked if they had seen this ad recently. The ad was for a brand of pain reliever. Forty-three per cent of the group claimed to have seen the ad on TV recently—before the ad went to air. Not surprisingly, most of these people said they had no idea who the advertiser was, or thought the ad was for some other advertiser.

How can people claim to have seen a commercial that has never been aired? What does this mean? It means that the visuals (and the audio) in the commercial were generic. They were similar to those used by other brands in the category. They could belong to anybody. If the brand were changed, it would do no violence to this commercial. One brand name could have fitted this ad just as well as any other.

Beware of generic elements in commercials, whether these are visual or verbal. A high level of false recognition before the ad goes to air is a good early warning indicator of this. It is telling you that the advertising is 'look-alike' advertising i.e. an ad that people already have a mental model of. If such advertising is allowed to go ahead, many of those who do see the ad will not remember who the advertiser was.

So here's a suggestion to improve your advertising. Conduct a small test. Take your ad. If it is a TV ad turn down the soundtrack and, as you watch it, imagine a competitor's brand being substituted for your own brand. You can do the same thing with a print ad. Imagine a competitor's brand substituted for your own. Does it do violence to the ad execution? Or does the competitor's brand fit just as well as your own? If a competitor's brand would fit just as well, the chances are that your ad execution is lacking something and is suffering from 'category conformity'. The ad execution that works best is the execution that uniquely ties in to both brand and message.

Mistaken identity

One of my acquaintances wears a distinctive style of clothing. I can pick him out easily in a crowd. One day in a crowded airline lounge I caught sight of him, grabbed his arm and said 'Hi, Bob.' It turned out to be a case of mistaken identity: I realized that Bob had come to 'own' that style or position in my mind. Once somebody becomes inextricably associated with a particular style, it is natural to think of them whenever you see somebody dressed the same way.

Mistaken identity also occurs with commercials. If your brand is identified with a particular style, then anyone else who tries to use that style risks advertising for you.

'Owning' a style

In the USA, put a stage coach in a bank ad and you will communicate Wells Fargo. In bank advertising Wells Fargo 'owns' stage coaches. They are almost a surrogate for the brand just as the red and white bull's-eye is a surrogate for the Target department store brand.

As an example of another global style consider the iPod silhouette ads. In the category of sound devices, iPod owned this style. Any competitor copying it would very likely do a great job of advertising for iPod instead of their own brand.

The consistent style is helped by consistency in logo and packaging.

Figure 22.1: Consistency—MetLife advertising. (Reprinted with permission from Metropolitan Life Insurance Company 1999)

For example, capitalizing on the easily recognizable and always consistent brand-logo treatment that is on every wrapper, Snickers ran a billboard and bus sides campaign *without ever mentioning Snickers by name.* They featured a quirky word (like 'Hungerectomy' and 'Substantialicious') designed to amuse and trigger us to think about the ad and of course think about a Snickers. The brand was unmistakable because of this consistency of style.

Figure 22.2: Consistency—Absolut vodka

An example of using characters as the consistent style is a series of ads for MetLife in the USA which has for many years advertised using one of the Peanuts characters to put a happy recognizable face on something that would otherwise be really boring. MetLife 'owns' this style and if any other competitive company tried to use a Peanuts character in their advertising, they would risk doing an advertising job for MetLife.

This is exactly what happened in Australia when a soup manufacturer tried to use a similar style to that used for many years by the market leader, Heinz. The Heinz brand outside the USA has a high profile as a canned soup manufacturer and for many years used high-profile presenters. Along came competitor Continental soup which, for one year only, tried to use a similar high-profile presenter in the form of Dame Edna Everage (an alter ego of Australian entertainer Barry Humphries). What happened? The commercials broke through and people remembered the Dame Edna commercials. But almost as many remembered them as being for Heinz as for Continental. They were mistakenly recalled as being ads for Heinz because Heinz 'owned' that 'high-profile presenter' style of advertising in the soup category. When a brand comes to 'own' a unique and consistent style in its category, it prevents any attempt by its competitors to copy what it is doing without giving that brand free advertising.

Absolut vodka has been another classic success story of a brand that has capitalized on a unique and consistent style of advertising. Absolut used this unique and consistent style based on the shape of its bottle and its name, and until it recently changed Absolut managed to maintain this for over a quarter of a century.

Other examples include:

- In its own unique style Chanel No. 5 consistently features multiple bottles on a yellow 'see through' style background.
- Altoids. Through consistent use of a pale green background, the style instantly communicates the brand. The very first ad featured a strongman flexing his muscles with the headline 'Nice Altoids', followed by similar quirky representations of strength (such as the dominatrix, a girl with whip) and alluding to the strong flavor of the mints.

The award for boring sameness in ads probably has to go to the retail industry and in particular supermarkets. From time to time this changes a little but all too often we still see ads where there is nothing distinctive to differentiate one advertised store from any other. In department stores, apparel stores and home hardware stores there has been much more individuality. Target has been a standout.

To escape the category conformity trap it is useful to understand some of the key dimensions of style (see Chapter 10, 'What's this I'm watching?'), then apply this knowledge in your search for opportunities to differentiate your advertising and develop a unique style. A key dimension of style is constancy because of how constancy influences memory retrieval.

Style influences memory retrieval

Monet, Kandinsky and Picasso are all artists who painted. But their styles were totally different. A style implies some sort of constancy. That is, the execution varies but some element remains the same. As a result, you don't have to be told that a painting is a Monet. You don't have to inspect its signature. You know it from the style.

There is constancy in the style that acts as a memory trigger—a retrieval cue. It automatically retrieves from memory the identity (the brand) associated with it. Far too many advertisers have only one constant in their advertising from one campaign to the next and that is the brand or logo. The brand or logo is important: it is the equivalent of the advertiser's signature.

However, the most successful advertisers and the most successful artists don't rely on signatures alone: they have a unique and consistent style!

So what types of constants are on the menu? What should you be looking to include in your advertising? Here are some thought-starters on things that might potentially be constants you can use.

Slogans

A word, a phrase or a sentence can function as a constant. This is so common today that we even have a word for it—'slogan'. When we hear the expression 'Just do it' what do we think of? We don't need to be told who the advertiser is. We know the ad has to be for Nike. Similarly, when we see the expression 'The ultimate driving machine' we know it has to be BMW. In the USA the expression 'You're in good hands' can mean only one brand if it is an insurance ad and that is Allstate. Slogans are obvious constants. But there are other types of constants, discussed below, that we don't use as frequently. What makes it more difficult to discuss them is that we do not have any unique words, like 'slogan', to sum them up.

Symbols

Nike has come to own the 'swoosh' symbol so completely that it is synonymous with the brand. You need only see the swoosh on some article of clothing and it immediately registers Nike in your mind. This means that ad branding is not just dependent on the brand name. Indeed this advertiser has flaunted its ability to advertise effectively without actually using the word Nike by just using the swoosh as a sign-off in some of their ads.

In a similar way Mercedes uses the 3-point star symbol. At Grand Slam tennis competitions the symbol often appears embedded in the tennis

Figure 22.3: The Nike 'swoosh' symbol.

net and immediately communicates Mercedes. Disney ads always have the Mickey Mouse ears and/or Cinderella's castle included as constant symbols. The point is that symbols are one form of constant that can act as a powerful branding device in the total style mix.

Visual devices

An action is used very rarely as a constant but it can be quite effective. For example, Nestea always included in their ads someone falling backwards into a swimming pool. Tinactin treatment for athlete's foot used for many years the action of a foot on fire and the tag line 'Tinactin . . . puts the fire out'. Similarly in Australia, for several cough and cold seasons, ads showing people with sore throats could have been for any brand of lozenge except as soon as the people started 'breathing out fire', everyone knew it was for Anticol.

When a brand uses a visual device like these as a constant, it comes to establish it as something that brand 'owns'. We can't see the device without thinking of that brand.

It doesn't have to be an action. Milk has for years used the milk moustache successfully. The milk moustache device even carried through to chocolate milk. And globally the Energizer bunny represented a constant icon associated with longer lasting batteries ('Keeps on keeping on').

Sometimes these highly visual and dramatic action devices are used just as part of the sign-off in the brand's ads. For example in the USA, Sprint (the long distance telephone company) consistently used a pin dropping in slow motion, providing a visual for the telephone number to call, 1–800 PinDrop.

Figure 22.4: The Energizer bunny. (Used by permission of Eveready Battery Company Inc. Energiser Bunny® is a registered trademark of Eveready Battery Company Inc.)

The Toyota jump is a further example. The freeze-frame jump that often went along with the lyric 'Oh, what a feeling' was as an action constantly incorporated into the signature sign-off for Toyota in various parts of the world for many years.

Gesture

Sometimes these visual devices take the form of gestures. For example in the USA, ads for the insurance company Allstate featured an open uplifted palm in every commercial accompanied by the line: 'We're the good hands people . . . You're in good hands with Allstate.' This and the Sure deodorant campaign's 'Raise your hand if you're Sure' are examples of tying your brand to an action that is commonly observed in everyday life. (When Sure brand deodorant urged audiences to 'Raise your hand if you're Sure' there were pictures of people all over raising their hands without, of course, any perspiration marks on their clothing.) Something like 'raise your hand' can become a cue that almost involuntarily brings the brand to mind.

A simple gesture used as a constant can be very effective, especially if it can be easily mimicked by the audience. Mimicry can be performance enhancing and help broadcast an ad and its brand by giving it free registrations beyond the advertising itself. For example, in the USA at one time everyone was encouraged by introductory ads for a new Dodge Neon to say 'Hi' to the Dodge Neon, with the result that kids could be seen calling out 'Hi' as a Neon drove down the street. The technique is not new but it is effective. Way back in the 1960s, in Australia, the 'Hey, Charger' campaign for the Chrysler Charger did a similar thing. The ads showed people holding up two fingers in a V sign and saying, 'Hey, Charger!' Anyone driving a Chrysler Charger could expect to be greeted by people making the 'Hey, Charger' gesture. Kids in particular love such mimicry, which can range from V signs to hand raising to making a flapping wings action, as was used by the Chicken Tonight brand.

Presenter

Sometimes a presenter—often a celebrity—is used as the constant. If it is a celebrity, this also helps the advertising break through. In past years we have seen Michael Jordan for Gatorade, Kathie Lee for Carnival Cruise, and Cindy Crawford for Revlon Color-Stay. Despite the death of KFC presenter Colonel Sanders, KFC managed to resurrect the presenter icon by bringing him back as an *animated* character.

It is worth noting, however, that the person as constant does *not* have to be a ready-made celebrity. The alternative is the 'do it yourself' celebrity (or DIY celebrity for short) created by the advertising agency itself. Examples include the Maytag man and Wendy the Snapple lady. We may not know their real names, but they may become consistent visual properties for the advertisers. Another alternative is for a proprietor to consistently front the commercials such as Jay Bush and his dog Duke do with Bush's baked beans ads in the USA. Some of the original DIY celebrities were cartoon characters: Tony the Tiger for Kellogg's Sugar Frosties; Snap, Crackle and Pop for Rice Bubbles. There are many candidates for constants and many possibilities. Some have been used extensively; others represent untapped opportunities.

Characters
The constant may be characters who always appear but who are not necessarily presenters. Examples include:

- the Marlboro cowboy
- The Aflac duck
- Jack for Jack in the Box restaurants
- the Michelin man
- Rob, the dentist who uses Oral B toothbrushes
- identical twins for Wrigley's Doublemint gum, acting as a mnemonic to reinforce the slogan: *Double your pleasure double your fun with Wrigley's doublemint gum.*

Layout/format
Some brands make effective use of a unique layout. In remaining constant it may come to instantly identify a particular brand. Absolut vodka has been very successful using its bottle shape in various guises both as its branding constant and also its layout. Similarly, Altoids uses its packs on a pale green background as the context for its constant layout.

Music
Music can function wonderfully well as a retrieval cue. The table below shows some of the songs used by various brands in their advertising. While music is frequently used in commercials, it is used surprisingly rarely as a deliberate constant, across campaigns.

Sounds/sonic branding
It is sometimes amazing what can act as a retrieval cue. I discovered this while once tracking for Nabisco. The sign-off for each Nabisco commercial was the brand. The brand name was sung, Na . . . bis . . . co . . . followed by a little ping.

One could be forgiven for believing that the ping was irrelevant, incidental and hardly even noticeable. It was just a sound effect that punctuated the brand sign-off. However, when the ping was temporarily

Table 22.1: Some examples of popular music used in commercials

Song	Product	Song	Product
Beatles: *All you need is love*	Luvs diapers	Cole Porter: *Don't fence me in*	Embassy Suites
Dinah Washington: *Relax Max*	Doubletree Hotels	*Sing, sing, sing*	Nissan
The best is yet to come	Nestlé	Gershwin: *Someone to watch over me*	H&R Block
You are my sunshine	Johnson & Johnson	*I want to take you higher*	AT&T
The more I see you	Estée Lauder	Marlena Dietrich: *Falling in love again*	Mercedes Benz
Gershwin: *Rhapsody in blue*	United Airlines	*Peter Gunn* theme	Apple computers

dropped to make room for a promotional tag to be included at the end of the ad, an amazing thing happened. The ads did not break through as much. More importantly, they lost a lot of their ability to link the execution in people's minds with the Nabisco brand. The principle was crystal clear. Even a simple sound like a little 'ping' can have far-reaching mnemonic effects if kept constant. Intel harnessed this principle with their musical string of bleeps now unmistakably associated with Intel. In more recent years this tactic has been labeled *sonic branding*. Think of it as the aural equivalent of a graphic logo.

Color

What about color? Can color function as a retrieval cue? No doubt it can, but I can't think of many good examples of where it has been used in TV commercials as a constant. Chanel No. 5 uses yellow, as does Kodak. Pepto Bismol use hot pink. And De Beers used the black and white silhouette style commercial to good effect. But there seems to be surprisingly little use of constant color specifically related to commercials themselves, although color is more often carried across from the brand colors. For example BP has certainly used the masses of green and gold to great effect in the design of its service stations. Shell is similarly identified by yellow and red. While in soft drinks Coke is red and Pepsi is blue (Pepsi changed some years ago from green).

Others

Various other things could serve as constants but have rarely, if ever, been used. For example, there is no reason why one could not make more use of things like:

- a place i.e. always incorporating the same well-known place in the executions for the brand (as Transamerica does for insurance—see Figure 22.5)
- a feeling
- an emotion.

Figure 22.5: Transamerica ads show the landmark Transamerica building.

These are all potential memory cues that could enhance the ability of an ad to automatically trigger recognition of the brand identity. The general point is that the ad does not have to rely on the brand as the only constant.

When used consistently, such memory cues help develop a style that is unique to the brand advertiser because they become part of the brand identity—just as the flashy style of dress became part of our friend Bob's identity or image. They are symbols as well as memory hooks.

Voiceover . . . and over and over and over

One of the key dimensions of style is the use of voiceover. As discussed in Chapter 10, voiceover seems to be ubiquitous in TV advertising. While it has the advantage of being cheaper and, in an increasingly global world, more flexible, using voiceover is almost always less effective than using on-camera presenters, whether direct or indirect.

Voiceover does not break through anywhere near as effectively as using on-screen speech and I have seen this many, many times in the course of tracking various campaigns. However, there is voiceover and voiceover. And just so we don't toss out the baby with the bath water, let me be clear that I am talking about traditional voiceover with on-screen demonstrations or illustrations.

The traditional voiceover style

This traditional style uses voiceover with on-screen illustration. In its loud form with fast cuts this is the classic retail advertising style (e.g. supermarket weekly specials). In its more subdued form, with slower cuts and more extended scene shots, it is used by car manufacturers, perfume manufacturers and so on. This traditional voiceover, when used for packaged goods, cars and the like, does not break through anywhere near as well as the voice of a person speaking on-screen.

Musical voiceover with visual illustration

This is typified by someone singing for the commercial, but not appearing on screen. This style engages the viewer as a passive observer, a bystander enjoying the entertainment. The voiceover is talking/singing to the on-screen character/s. The viewer is expected to identify with the on-screen character/s and hence the message is received indirectly. The musical voiceover appears to be addressing the on-screen character/s rather than the viewer directly.

A subtle but important variation on this is where the on-screen character/s are not speaking but the voiceover is meant to represent what they are saying or thinking. The on-screen character/s are 'sharing their thoughts' with the viewer. Because these are in the form of a sung voiceover, the sense of being 'talked to' directly is very much reduced and there is a particular style and feeling to the ad.

The integral constant

The constant (character, gesture, sound or whatever) may become associated with the brand just through paired association. Ideally, however, it is better if you can find something that is, or can be made into, something that is integral to your brand identity.

For example, Aflac insurance in the USA had such success with the duck in their commercials that they added the duck into the brand logo so that the two would work integrally together. By contrast, the pink bunny in the battery ads is a constant character but is not integral to Energizer (except by simple paired association). It would be possible to take Energizer out of the commercial and substitute Duracell without doing any real violation to the commercial. Constants like these that rely entirely on paired association are potentially subject to more competitive memory interference and forgetting. (Is the bunny in those battery ads for Duracell? Or Energizer?) Others (like the milk moustache) are unmistakably for their particular product because they are more integral to the brand.

Ad style—the brand's attire

A brand's advertising needs to be thought of as one of its most visible features. It is an attribute of the brand, no less real than the price, the package, and what is inside it. A brand's advertising represents the brand's attire if you like. Imagine if your mother walked in with her eyebrow pierced, sporting a tattoo and dressed like a sixteen-year-old. Just as it would be disorienting if our family, friends and acquaintances suddenly became wildly inconsistent in the way they dress, so too do we expect the brands we value to maintain a reasonable degree of consistency in their substance, their image and their dress. If the brand keeps changing its style of attire capriciously every few months it is not only disorienting, it is difficult to get to know the brand. So we expect brands to remain true to themselves if we are going to get to know them and be attracted to them.

Traditionally, advertisers have not been encouraged by ad agencies to get involved in advertising style. Some creatives fear that constants like those discussed above can all too easily become 'creative handcuffs' that restrict their freedom and make it harder to come up with great ideas. There is some truth to this. Just as a constant strategy constrains the creative team to only those ideas which are *on-strategy*, so too does a constant style constrain the team to ideas that can be executed *on-style* i.e. consistent with the brand's style.

A brand's advertising style is a component of its ad strategy because it is part of the way the brand's communications are identified in people's minds. Advertising is part of a brand's wardrobe attire. The brand's advertising constants and its advertising style are therefore valuable equities that with successful brands become woven into the fabric of that brand, constituting part of its heritage and thereby lending stronger identification and presence to it. Hence it is a legitimate component of the strategy brief to build in a legitimate constraint in regards to ad style within which the creative team must work.

The winds of change are beginning to blow and an increasing number of advertisers and agencies recognize the benefits of maintaining a unique and consistent style. The style you choose can be a powerful form of nonverbal communication that identifies you and your ads.

Summary
Style is such a subtle characteristic of advertising that our language is hardly adequate for analyzing and discussing it. To maximize ad effectiveness, maintain a unique and consistent style. In order to do this it is useful to understand how style varies. Style is like hair: it needs careful grooming, it is crucial to your identity, and how you look depends on how you cut it!

> *A consistent brand strategy supported by a strong symbol can produce an enormous cost advantage in implementing communication programs. It is much less costly to reinforce an established image than to create a new one.*
>
> David Aaker[1]

23 SEQUELS

Sequels are a particular form of advertising style where the character/s are held constant and become associated with the brand. Sequels are something of a natural answer to the often over-exaggerated problem of 'wear-out'.[1]

Why is it that every new campaign for a brand has to be a total change? If your ad or campaign is worn out, it usually means people are bored with it or irritated by it. If you develop an entirely new ad that bears little if any relationship to the old one, then out goes another baby complete with the bath water!

Why change *everything* when your ad wears out? All too often, we seem driven to come up with an entirely new ad concept. The message may be the same but the new execution is a total departure from the old. We may have just spent a year and $30 million to break through the clutter—to build a strong awareness of the ad in people's minds. It has been a hard, competitive and expensive exercise but we have succeeded in taking the high ground. The ad campaign now dominates the category in share of mind. Then suddenly, for some reason, someone decides to change the ad. The focus is now on unleashing some other, entirely different type of ad execution. Why do so many advertisers make it hard for themselves by being intent on doing it all over again from scratch?

'Wear in'

Think of a new ad as having to 'wear in'. Like a new shoe, it may take a little time. The better the quality of the shoe the less time it should take to wear in. Some ads wear in very quickly. A great creative execution can capture the mental ground very quickly with a minimum of media weight. Other ads are of lesser creative quality and require more time and media weight to wear in. Unfortunately there are very few great creative executions.

Most ads are more pedestrian and reliant on many media bursts over a period of time to build the assault and then hold the mental territory.

Residual recall barriers to mental entry

The more successful an old ad is in capturing and holding the mental ground, the longer it remains in people's minds even after the advertising is removed. (This is one reason why it is difficult for a new competitor to break through in the face of a long-advertised market leader.) When a totally new ad for a brand is launched, it will be some time before the old one disappears from people's minds. In fact, the more successful and better-performing the old ad, the longer it will dominate and the longer it will take for the new ad to wear in.

A truly great ad execution does not take much time to wear in. But if it comes hard on the heels of another good performer, it will generally take longer. This is because it takes some time for the new ad to displace all those well-consolidated memories that surround the old ad and are linked to brand recall and recognition.

The consumer's mind is not a vacuum. It retains for some time the residual memories of the last ad for a brand. And this can act as an inhibitor or a 'barrier to entry' for the new ad.

An example of this is illustrated in Figure 23.1. An old ad dominated for seven or eight months after it had come off air even while a new ad was being aired. The bars represent the weekly media weight (TRPs). The lines represent advertising awareness for i) the old ad and then ii) a new ad for the same brand. There are a few points to note:

- The first ad peaked in August/September (at 32 per cent recall rate).
- With no further screenings, its recall rate declined.
- Despite not being on air it was still in people's minds five months later (at 12 per cent).
- In the meantime, an entirely new ad had been introduced and aired.
- Not until ten weeks later did the new ad break through and dominate over the old ad in people's minds i.e. the old ad held sway in people's minds for seven to eight months.

We might note that while this 'in-fighting between ads' is going on in people's minds, the sum total of ad recall for the brand (i.e. the old plus the new) is very low. It is not until the new ad breaks through and begins

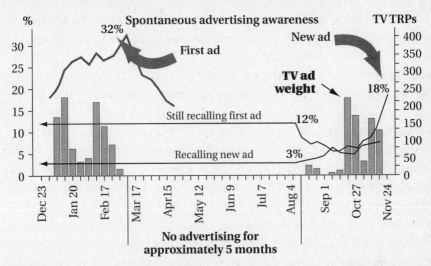

Note: Despite not being on air, the first ad was still in 12% of people's minds five months later. Not until about ten weeks after the new advertisement was introduced did it break through and dominate over the old one in people's minds.

Figure 23.1: Residual recall of old and new advertisements. (Source: MarketMind)

to dominate that net ad awareness for the brand starts to return to its previous levels.

The implication of this is that considerable time and media money could be saved if only the advertiser could somehow bypass or avoid this transition period when there is 'in-fighting' in memory between ads. Is there a solution? Yes!

Greater use of sequels

Modern movie-makers know that it is better to build on something you have already established than to start from scratch each time. In movie-making in the last quarter of a century there has been a multitude of sequels, including *Shrek, Pirates of the Caribbean, Spiderman, Superman, Batman, Indiana Jones, Rambo, Mad Max, Die Hard, Lethal Weapon, Star Wars, Star Trek, Jaws, Home Alone, Gremlins,* and *Terminator.* For longevity *Rocky I, II, III, IV, V* and finally, *Rocky Balboa* have been outstayed only by the inimitable *James Bond.* They all testify to the success of the sequel strategy.

The success of this strategy consists of harnessing the interest and familiarity that has already been built by a previous success with a movie (the equivalent of a successful ad 'execution') and tying in the next movie (the next execution) to the consumer recall of the previous one. This is such a clearly successful strategy, so why do we so often launch totally new campaigns after the old one has had its day? Why not make more use of sequels, as has proved to be successful for movies?

A few great sequel ads

One of the most successful sequel campaigns in the USA began in 2000 and was deployed for many years by the insurance company Aflac. All the commercials featured the live duck that became one of America's favorite brand icons.[2] The duck in the ads quacked an answer, 'Aflac' (that sounded like a double quack), whenever various characters asked 'Where do you get (supplementary) insurance?' The duck was the constant character and it was so successful over so many years that it became part of the brand logo.

A sequel offers continuity of style (see previous chapter) where one or more of the characters are held constant. Apple did this with its two characters PC and Mac representing the PC as a nerdy, stuffy, older guy and the Mac as a cool, creative younger guy. A decade before that, across the globe the budding romance between the character Gillian and her next door neighbor unfolded over convivial coffee and many sequels and the coffee just happened to be a Nestlé brand. This campaign started in the UK for Nescafé Gold and was used in the USA for Taster's Choice and in Australia for Nescafé. It portrayed an ongoing flirtation between two neighbors when one of them runs out of coffee and turns to the other to borrow some. Ultimately the campaign shaded into the next generation of characters as the focus shifted to Gillian's daughter.

Over the years there have been some great sequel ads like this—built around holding the characters constant. Wendy the Snapple lady in the USA was created by the advertisers as a receptionist character for Snapple drinks who read the fan mail sent to the company by consumers. Wendy's quirky New York attitude and humor ran for years as the many sequels drove Snapple along in the non-carbonated soft drinks category.

What the character Wendy did for Snapple, Mr Bean did for Barclays Card in the UK in a series of sequels that also ran for many years. And for Oral B toothbrushes, in a campaign that started in Australia and eventually went global for Oral B, the dentist character always brushing his teeth with his back to the camera was Rob ('This man is a dentist. . . . we can't show you his face on camera'). Eventually the ads showed Rob's young son alongside him, also back to the camera, using an Oral B toothbrush. Sequels in this way can offer a clever, smooth transition to the targeting of the next generation of buyers for the brand.

In the USA many sequels of white haired Orville Redembacher, a maker of popcorn, smoothly transitioned to his grandson. Orville appeared in all his own ads for many years, proud as he could be about his company and its popcorn, which had his image on the package. His grandson was introduced into the ads, appearing for a while with Orville in what was apparently a bridging campaign before Orville sadly died soon thereafter.

Resisting 'natural' forces

An anecdote often related in the ad industry tells of the head of a company complaining to his ad agency that fourteen agency people work on the brand but he never sees any changes. To which the canny punch-line response is: 'We have fourteen people working on your business precisely to see that nothing ever changes!'

Constancy in style in sequels such as this takes a lot of discipline on the part of the advertiser and the agency in order to keep them going. This is because the people involved tend to get bored with the characters and see them as 'creative handcuffs'. Also, brand managers frequently tend to move on after a couple of years and any new brand manager naturally would like to put his/her own 'creative stamp' on the brand through introducing a totally new campaign rather than continuing to develop the old one. It takes discipline from the top management levels for a company to resist these 'natural' forces and determine to keep things on track.

With a sequel the ad doesn't have to wear in. Nor does it have to displace what is already there. It just hooks in immediately to existing memories. No waiting. No delay!

Continuity is the key

Like a good soap opera program, such examples hold constant the main character/s and vary the situations. When new characters are introduced they are introduced through their relationship or relevance to the estab-lished characters. Each new ad is like a new episode. It provides continuity and the communications from the brand form a continuous unfolding story.

The important thing is that the new ad has a meaningful relationship with the one before; it is encoded or linked into the existing memory like pieces of a jigsaw puzzle which fit together. In this way people can file the two ads together in memory and retain both. I have previously likened this to storing things in a mental filing cabinet (see Chapter 15). Many people defer office filing. It's a chore. People are even less motivated to file ads in their mental filing cabinets, let alone file them carefully or correctly. They have little motivation to store a new ad in their mental filing cabinet at all—let alone under the correct brand name.

However, if something in the new ad immediately reminds them of something already stored there and then clearly presents a further development to it, the job is done almost automatically for the consumer. Instead of having to store everything that comes in as a separate file, we will store anything new that is related to an existing item in the most obvious existing file. This saves us having to create an entirely new file for every new thing, every new ad, that comes in.

The more closely the contents of a particular file are related, the more it can act as a chunk—an integral whole in memory. *Human memory works best when new things that are introduced have an integral fit with, or can be related in some way to, old things that already exist in memory.*[3]

Owning an ad style

Sequels are the epitome of maintaining a constant style. Absolut vodka had a unique style built entirely within print medium. This clearly illustrates how it is possible for a brand to own an advertising style and maintain it for over a quarter of a century.

The advantage in owning a style is that when a viewer sees that style of ad, it instantly triggers an association with the brand. The brand comes to stand for the style and the style comes to stand for the brand. So if a competitor should try to use the same style, he/she risks communicating the wrong brand (your brand) and doing an advertising job for you. It will be difficult for any other spirit brand to use the Absolut style without advertising Absolut, as it will be difficult for any other insurance company to use a cartoon character without advertising MetLife.

If you see an ad that shows a Peanuts character, which company do you think of? MetLife of course, which has been clearly associated with that style or mnemonic. It now owns that execution style. Not all ads are created equal. A sequel holds the character/s constant and varies the situations such that the unfolding brand communications are identified with the character/s. Sequels have a lot going for them. Too many ads start anew every time.

Summary

If your old ad has been successful but is now wearing out, consider a sequel rather than a totally new ad. If you do have to change horses and go for an entirely new ad, and if your past advertising has been very successful, then expect the new ad to take some time to 'wear in'. If you hit on a unique style that works, then continue it in the next ad. Strive to 'own' that style in the consumer's mind.

24 CORPORATE TRACKING OF IMAGE AND ISSUES

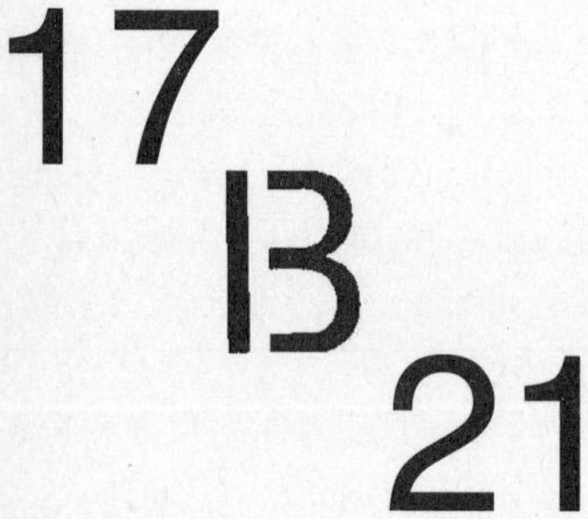

17

13

21

Figure 24.1: What do you see?

Look at the figure. I want you to think of the thing in the middle as a company. What do you see? You see the number 13 of course. Think of it as company 13. Note that it is surrounded by companies 17 and 21. Now read on and we will see the relevance of this when we come back to it later.

We saw in an earlier chapter that the same person, brand or company can be seen in different ways depending on the frame of reference we bring to it. Image is elusive. Your own image stares you in the face every morning, but do you have in your mind's eye the way you see yourself or the way others see you? Clothes, cosmetics, possessions and reputation can sometimes perform startling transformations of image and completely change the way others perceive us. Image is in the eye of the beholder!

The opponents of corporate image and corporate advertising argue that this is irrelevant for companies; that people buy products, they buy brands, but they don't buy companies. Even if it were true that corporate image has no effect on consumer behavior, how people perceive the company would still be important because a well-known and well-respected company will always enjoy advantages in at least two non-consumer markets.

First, it will attract and retain better quality employees. A well-known and well-respected company is very different from a nonentity. When you are asked where you work, the importance of a corporate image is quickly apparent. If there is an instant recognition of the name and what it stands for, the response is very different from a response like: 'Who are they? What do they do? Never heard of them.'

Second, corporate image can and does affect the company's stock price. Even the people the company uses in its advertising can influence it. Stock prices often increase when companies sign on a famous celebrity to endorse their brand.[1] People do buy companies! At least they buy shares in companies and the price they are prepared to pay for the shares is influenced by the company's profile, image and perceived respectability.[2] This is so basic it is difficult to see how it could ever be far from the minds of top management.

A company's share price, like any other price, is a subjectively derived value—what people are prepared to pay. People pay more for brand-name products than for generics. A Gucci toothbrush is 'worth' more than a Woolworths house brand toothbrush. The physical product may be the same but perceptions of its value can be significantly affected by image. So too can share prices. People perceive more value in, and expect the price to be higher for, something that has a substantial image. This has been very evident in the stock price of the high-flier companies such as Apple, Virgin, Disney, Microsoft, News Limited, Amazon, and eBay.

Companies increasingly recognize investors and the stock market as one of their key publics. In recent years it has for example become beneficial to be seen by the stock market as aiming to be 'green' and socially responsible. Investors know that, increasingly, consumers demand environmental responsibility from the companies they buy from, and they avoid brands associated with negative impact on the environment. Targeting this doesn't necessarily mean using corporate advertising exclusively aimed at investors. GE for example ran an extensive campaign around the theme 'Ecomagination' ostensibly aimed at consumers but which would be expected to impact investors also. Similarly the campaigns for Toyota with its Prius and Ford with its hybrid Escape (that starred Kermit the frog saying 'Maybe it is easy to be green') could be expected to impact buyers of stock as well as buyers of cars.

Defense as well as offence

Corporate communication plans and corporate image development can be used strategically for both offence and defense. In a protective sense, corporate image is like a condom—both need to be used discreetly. By rolling on a strong corporate image and managing it effectively, management can get the prophylactic protection needed to keep out unwanted corporate invaders. A healthy corporate image, along with a strong share price, is what keeps the corporate immune system intact.

Private equity companies make a science out of hunting companies with undervalued or undermanaged assets. So top management's attention must be tuned to corporate defense as well as corporate survival. To survive corporately, the management of listed companies needs to keep the share price up and be seen to be effectively managing the company's assets. If the company is undervalued by the stock market compared to the true value of its assets, this invites takeover attention.

Corporate raiders target undermanaged companies where changes in strategic direction can dramatically increase the value of the shares. Or they look for companies with high liquidation values relative to their current stock price. If the management of a company is seen to be weak, this can imply to the stock market that the company could be worth more under new management. This too could invite takeover attention. So it is important for the company not only to be well managed but also to *be seen to be* well managed. Perceived share value is not something traditionally thought of as a marketable entity. But there is no better means of avoiding a takeover than a healthy share price.

The most astute companies track the perceptions of their own shareholders—individual as well as institutional. They realize that it is important to know, week by week, month by month, how they and their management are perceived, what their strengths and weaknesses are. Is the company seen to communicate well with its shareholders? Is it vulnerable? At what price would shareholders sell out? To what types of communications do they respond best?

Forewarned is fore-armed. This type of tracking provides an early warning system of any weakness or vulnerability and forms the basis for managing the corporate image and the corporate communications plan.

The basis of image

Before you can change or create an image in people's minds you need to know what thoughts and associations are already there. The first step in image research is to find out:

- Which attributes are important in people's minds with regards to the (product or industry) category?

Figure 24.2: A Hyundai ad showing the diversity of its products.

- Which attributes differentiate your company from companies generally?

A key aspect of this is to establish what things people know about, or associate with, your particular brand or company.

Research may reveal, for example, that people know you only as a manufacturer of one product and they are relatively unaware of the much larger scope and size of your company or its product range, or that it competes in many other product categories. In some parts of the world Hyundai is known almost solely for cars. People have very little in the way of associations with the company other than as a car maker. The Hyundai ad featured above shows the company attempting to work on broadening that image by showing the various other products it makes (such as airplanes, ships, etc).

When researching people's knowledge and associations in regard to the company you may find that such associations may be blurred, half-formed or even plain wrong—but they exist nevertheless. So the next step is to determine how you want your organization to be seen. Which image attributes does the organization *want* to have dominate its perception? How does it want people to perceive it?

The same may be true of an issue that critically impacts on the organization's success. The organization needs to find out the consumer's current perception in order to then be able to 'engage the consumer in a dialogue' and put forward another way of seeing the issue. The timber and oil industries have for years engaged the environmental movement in a dialogue. More recently companies involved in producing genetically engineered foods have done the same thing. The objective is to begin setting the agenda by giving people specific facts about the issue and playing the focal beam of attention on those facts. The starting point is finding out how people currently perceive the company or the critical issue.

Attributes like size, credibility, stability, national interest, human, caring, responsible corporate citizen, non-polluter, environmentally conscious are all possible associations that a company might want to position on.

In choosing an attribute to position on, organizations need to develop a unique and consistent positioning around that attribute dimension and resist the temptation to chase every other positive dimension to its burrow. Trying to position on more than one or two at a time is fraught with the danger of image diffusion—trying to do everything and accomplishing nothing.

Being seen as a good corporate citizen is an increasingly common goal of many companies especially, but not exclusively, those working in environmentally sensitive fields. For example companies such as BP ('Beyond petroleum') and Toyota ('Aim: zero emissions') have tapped into the energy environment issue.

When an organization decides on the image it wants to communicate, and confirms that it can deliver on that image, it should then track public perceptions and closely monitor the effectiveness of its corporate communications. The image dimension may be of the 'good corporate citizen' type or it may be focused on more pragmatic platforms that address different types of customer concerns. Often it is a matter of keeping people focused on the positive side of what you offer corporately—keeping the perspective on the 'half full' rather than the 'half empty' aspect.

If you don't keep the focus on the positive perspective, the way is left open for your opposition to emphasize the negative. For example, Microsoft is a huge company and being number one can be a positive (see Chapter 4, 'Conformity: the popular thing to do'). But at the same time, people can also think of big companies in terms of abuse of that power.

Thus lurks a negative in the background potentially open to be exploited by competitors (e.g. the 'Stop giving a bully your lunch money' campaign for Sun OpenOffice software suite from Sun Microsystems).

Changing an image

There are three elements in an image, whether it is a brand or corporate image:

1. That image is a function of the attributes which are associated with it;
2. The degree of those attributes it is perceived to have; and
3. How important that attribute dimension is in people's minds when they make a decision.

    What advertising or corporate communications are trying to do is:

*   Move the organization along an attribute dimension e.g. honesty or corporate citizenship; or
*   Add a new attribute dimension to the image e.g. environmentally responsible, financially secure; or
*   Influence the perceived importance of an attribute dimension for the public in evaluating organizations i.e. change the importance that people place on a particular attribute.

By monitoring each of these three elements over time, an organization continuously knows how well groomed it is and this acts as an 'early warning system' for any changes. Image, like grooming, is something that needs continuous attention, not a once-a-year inspection.

Tracking the agenda of concerns

In this era of environmental concern and corporate responsibility, the 'green' movement has had a real impact on corporate communication philosophy. Some organizations deliberately undertook to keep their heads down. Holed up in the trenches, they hoped that by keeping a low profile they would avoid being targeted by environmentalists. Others took a more proactive approach and mounted specific ad campaigns that took their case to the people.

I would argue that whatever approach is taken, there is usually a need to know what is going on outside the trenches—to at least know how many people are out there firing at you, and what they are most concerned about. To this end, a number of organizations (corporate, government and industry groups) track what might be called the agenda of concerns among the general public in regard to their particular organization or industry.

By asking people what concerns if any they have in regard to organization X (or industry Y) an agenda of concerns is generated. For example, see Table 24.1.

Table 24.1: Agenda of concerns

Concern	% spontaneously mentioning the concern
Too big and uncaring	24%
Pollutes the environment	12%
Poor handling of its industrial relations	8%

This agenda is monitored continuously. It changes over time in response to the topicality of the environment, to strikes and to the organization's own news releases and radio and TV appearances.

The important thing about this is that the information allows the organization to detect events that have had a positive or negative impact on people's perceptions and concerns. Furthermore, it allows the detection of these at the earliest possible moment. This is crucial if an organization is going to take a proactive approach to managing corporate communications and corporate image.

Image: you can't leave home without it

Image is not something that companies can choose to opt out of. Nature abhors a vacuum, and so does the human mind. If an organization doesn't effectively communicate the way it sees itself and its beliefs and what it is associated with and what it stands for, then the public will do so for it. The environment will fill the vacuum and allow people to construct their own image of the organization based on whatever evidence is around and what things the company seems to be associated with.

To illustrate this, take a look at Figure 24.3 below. What do you see?

The image changes when its associative context is letters rather than numbers.[3]

In the middle is the same organization you met at the beginning of this chapter. Do you now see it in a different way? With a few changes to the associative context you now see this company as it sees itself. It is company B. Now with a few changes to the way the company presents itself you see it in its true light as company B—not to be mistaken for that unlucky organization 13.

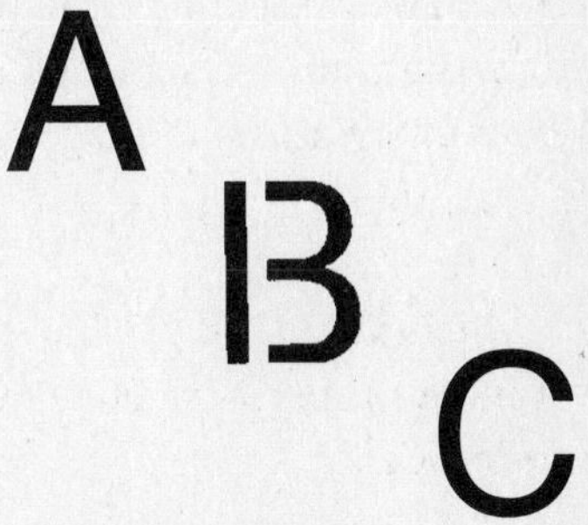

A

B

C

Figure 24.3: When the context is changed, the middle figure is now seen as a B.

Summary

Note that the two perceptions, the letter B and the number 13, are as different as you can get. Yet it is the same physical stimulus that you were looking at in the beginning of this chapter. What has changed is your perception of it—influenced purely by its associations, the things that it is paired with. Changes to the way that real companies are seen are not as immediately dramatic but over time can end up just as substantive. There is a lot to be said for a proactive, continuous tracking approach in the management of corporate communications and corporate image.

25 THE WEB: ADVERTISING IN A NEW AGE

Home is where you hang your @
Anon

The focus in the first two editions of this book was primarily on TV advertising. The way TV is watched has been changing since the last edition and not only because of the Internet but also because of the penetration of multiple screens into our everyday lives. Today, many of us not only have our own TV screen but our own personal computer and our own personal mobile-device screen, all of which are increasingly giving us ready access to the world wide web. Even the tradition of family television i.e. gathering together in the living room to watch the TV, is all but gone. 'Such viewing,' one newspaper article noted, 'now seems alien to kids, many of whom have their own TVs, computers and iPods. By the age of six, 33 per cent of American children have TVs in their bedroom.'[1]

The Internet is the medium of the current millennium. It affects the way we do almost everything. 'We write to our mums by email, we shop and bank online, we find new friends and hang out with them, play games, pursue passions, research products and flex our creative muscles, all via a keyboard.'[2]

Website: a 'home' on the web
For any brand of any substance today a website is a must. It is perhaps the brand's biggest ad of all and an important part of a brand's image. It also provides a point of contact with potential and existing customers and increasingly it focuses on ways to engage them and use the site to build closer relationships with them.

Having somebody visit your home is a form of traditional hospitality—a conventional and small but significant step towards building a closer relationship with them. Having people visit your website and inviting them to stay a while is also a significant step in hypertext hospitality. In this 21st century, the web has become the company's 'virtual' home. For many companies (in particular think Amazon, Dell, eBay, Microsoft, Yahoo) this is where people find the company and interact with it so this has become the company's real home as much as, if not more than, its physical address. The web is the primary point of contact—the place where people know where to find them. It is the place where the welcome mat is (in theory but not necessarily in practice) 'always out'.

Prior to the web, if a consumer wanted to contact a manufacturer for service or information on a product, or to complain or interact with that company, he or she would look for the physical address of the company. More and more consumers today locate the companies they want, not by contacting them at a physical address but at their virtual home on the web. Indeed for a growing number of companies, consumers have little idea of the company's geographic address and nor do they have any need to care or think about it. The company's primary home as far as the consumer is concerned *is* the web.

If you want any information on any product just click on a link to that company's front door and you can enter, browse around and generally make yourself at home. Jim Beam lives here at jimbeam.com. Jack lives over there at jackdaniels.com. Can't see what you are looking for? Google it or ask—interactively—or leave a message and someone will get back to you.

Web ads

Before search engines, the way to attract traffic to the company's website was primarily TV advertising. The rise of search engines has in a way partially displaced some of that TV advertising.

The other way of attracting traffic to a website was to take advertising space on other companies' websites. These are called website *banner* ads but they can in fact appear anywhere on a web page—not only at the top in the banner. Often they were not much more than cybernetic signposts that pointed readers to the advertiser's

Figure 25.1: An eBay cybernetic 'signpost'.

website and allowed the visitor to click through to it. These website banner ads also suffered some displacement from the rise of search engines and the inclusion of paid links in search engine query results.

Today the web address (the URL) of any company, product, brand or solution is easily found from a simple query typed into a search engine. However, such links on search engines, even when they are paid ads, generally incorporate only the barest of messages. The main message emphasis has customarily been *after* the person clicks through to the website.

This is changing for two reasons. The first is technology. Improvements in technology mean that more elaborate messages can today be incorporated into the rich media content of the web ads themselves—without having to first click through to another URL. Indeed, the online ad formats today already range from simple text ads to animated ads to dynamic rich media and broadband video ads. So, just as outdoor advertising improved its capability by becoming 'animated', so too are website banner ads improving. Just as outdoor ads were enabled to do much more than remind people of a brand, so too can these 'virtual billboards' increasingly display not just the brand name and a relevant link but also more elaborate brand messages.

Figure 25.2: Outdoor ads for Federal Express and Lotto.

The second reason why increased messaging is likely to become more incorporated in the ads themselves is that there is accumulating evidence that such messages seem to work implicitly even when they don't command attention. In the absence of click-through, there has been a strong tendency for advertisers to believe that these messages were not working and not really doing anything. This attitude is likely to change as the evidence further accumulates that web ads, even when static and even when 'ignored', can leave residual effects.

Residual effects without click-through

As this book goes to press, only about one in five hundred website banner ads are clicked on and that low level of click-through has given considerable impetus to paid search engine advertising. Higher click-through rates were easily obtainable from paid ad links on the search engine results pages so this shifted the advertisers' emphasis dramatically from website banner ads to paid search ads. But before abandoning website banner ads, be sure to take a closer look because you can't just assume that nothing happens in the absence of click-through.

Justifiably, most of us feel that we pretty much ignore web ads and we probably believe that in general they don't work on us.[3] However, the evidence is accumulating that this introspection fails us. Mostly the effects from website banner ads are not huge. The evidence is that they are usually feather effects and as we saw in Chapter 1, and feather effects by their very nature are hard to introspect. So curiously, even as we try to ignore web ads, they do seem capable of leaving residual effects that may influence us a little further down the track. Let me explain.

A number of research studies show that when we are exposed to ads while reading publications online (such as a news site like CNN or the *New York Times*), even though we probably don't notice the ads and we probably won't even recognize having seen them, there are likely to be residual effects. It has been consistently shown that readers of a web page where such an ad is placed are subsequently able to identify that *brand*, and perceive that *ad*, faster in the future as a result of the incidental exposure.[4] That is, it increases perceptual fluency without our awareness. Another way of saying this is that it tunes up the brain's processes that we use to identify the brand and its ads.

Not only do readers who are exposed in this way (i.e. incidentally or 'without awareness') identify the brand more quickly (important for the pop-out effect in cluttered product displays) but there is also an emotional 'knock-on' effect imparted to future displays of the ad. If we do notice the ad in the future, the research shows that we are likely to react more favorably to it. So although at the time we are 'unaware' of seeing it, our liking of a web ad marginally escalates after being incidentally exposed to it.

The effect is not great but research shows that people do *like* the ad more than they would had they not had the prior, incidental exposure.[5]

Importantly, this 'knock-on' liking response to the ad becomes progressively more positive as people are exposed (without much awareness) to additional repetitions of it.[6] So, as we saw in Chapter 1, even a small feather like this may be influential in swinging the balance of choice if everything else weighs equal . . . and small feathers can build over time, through repetition (just like kids can grow imperceptibly by a tiny amount each day). The bottom line is that despite website banner ads rarely being clicked on, there is reason nonetheless to believe that somehow they are curiously unique in having more brand building effect than we give them conscious credit for.

Some of this positive effect from website banner ads comes through *reminders* of the brand and the message and it is much the same as driving past a billboard or flicking through the ads in a magazine. Such fleeting exposures can deliver messages or reminders that are very short and compact and that communicate very rapidly. Similarly, web banner ads even in the absence of animation have been shown to reinforce existing messages provided they are packaged as short, sharp and very compact reminders. Like the real, outdoor billboards these are capable of impacting brand salience, perceived presence, image, and attitude.[7] So in addition to pointing the way to a company's site, website banner ads can:

- help build brand awareness and perceived advertising presence;
- reinforce/remind people with extremely compact, very simple messages that help consolidate the brand building process.

Click-through

For advertisers, click-through is understandably important but let's put it and its implications into perspective. Click-through has been likened by some people to a TV or print ad for say a brand of car that prompts some percentage of the people who see it to visit the company's showroom. Other people have likened it to when a TV or print or radio ad prompts people to dial the advertiser's 1-800 telephone numbers. All of these are about prompting a behavioral 'follow up' response. However, such behavioral responses vary in the amount of effort involved. A visit to a showroom involves considerable inconvenience and time to travel to the showroom. People are more likely to do something that takes less effort such as dialing a 1-800 number. Clicking on a banner ad or a search link is even lower on this effort scale. On a dimension of effort in making the response, click-through is more in company with things like opening a direct mail envelope or accepting a taste of a free sample in a super-market.

This begs the question that since it is such a minimal-effort response, why is it that click-through rates are so low? A key reason is poor ad place-ment. Another is that we develop a resistance to distraction as we become more experienced with using the web.

Figure 25.3: *Banner ads often focus on a behavioral response—click-through.*

If, for example, we are reading on a website a highly interesting news story about pets dying because of contamination in imported pet food, we try to suppress distraction from the ads on the same page. Whether they are for low rate mortgages, a new model Lexus or online retailers, our reaction is the same: we try to shut them out in order to maintain our focus on the story. If the ad is for pet food, however, our reaction is likely to be quite different. Rather than a distraction, it can become a bit of a segue to the pet food story we are reading. The difference in impact is illustrated by the following example. In April 2007, as pets were dying across the USA and panic-stricken pet owners flocked to the web for news about pet-food recalls, the results of their searches also displayed paid ads for brands of *natural and organic* pet food. These ads offered a solution to the problem and generated huge click-through traffic to the advertised websites along with significant sales of natural and organic pet food brands.

The organic pet food ads offered a segue slip-lane that was relevant to the current mind set. They were not a distraction requiring a switch in mind set but were able to seamlessly merge their message with people's current mind set. When there is a match between the ad and the story (or the search content), the two can work together because our minds easily segue from one to the other. No mental effort is needed and no suppression of distraction is involved because we don't feel that there is any real change in topic or mind set. Reading the ad becomes somewhat akin to reading another bit of the same story.

It is no surprise therefore that paid search engine ads that are displayed when we are looking for something on the web have been a big growth phenomenon. When there is a match between the ad and the person's mind set (indicated by the words typed into a search engine query), this segue slip-lane principle comes into play.

Paid search advertising

As this book goes to press, this type of paid search advertising accounts for around half of all Internet ad spending. Paid search advertising is sold and delivered on the basis of keywords that are typed into search engines when we make a query (Google calls them 'adwords').

A simple query may display tens if not hundreds (and sometimes even millions) of relevant unpaid links. The decision as to which links to click is not unlike the decision process we met in Chapter 1 where the outcome of buying decisions can be influenced by influencing the order in which the alternatives are considered. We saw that advertising's influence doesn't just come from influencing our evaluations but also from influencing the order in which these alternative brands are evoked/considered. The same principle applies with search queries. We don't consider every alternative link before making a decision as to which to click on. Rather it is more of a sequential process. We look at the first link and if that appears satisfactory, we will click. If it is not satisfactory, we consider clicking on the second link . . . and so on.

Clearly, only the top handful of search positions have much real chance of ever being considered, let alone clicked on, and that's why search engines sell paid links and why companies are happy to pay to have their ads listed as links at the top or in the side bar of the search results page.

The natural or unpaid links represent clutter with a capital C. (Type 'pet food' into Google and it presents you with at least 10 million unpaid links that would take two years to look through even if you only scanned each one for no more than two seconds without ever clicking.) This is a key reason why search advertising is so successful! It enables advertisers to influence the order of consideration by paying to locate their cybernetic signposts in positions that are more 'in your face'. But even then, a signpost won't get clicked if it is not clearly relevant to the person's search direction. Clues to that direction are contained in the words typed into the search engine and advertisers bid for these keywords (i.e. for the right to have their ads linked to them).

The rate of click-through for an advertiser's paid search ads is very much influenced by which keywords are bought by the advertiser and how well the ad matches the search direction indicated by those words. The closer the match, the more likely the ad will be seen as a segue slip-lane rather than a dead-end distraction to be ignored. The closer the match, the greater the click-through is likely to be.

A kitchen design company for example would want its ad to appear when someone types the keywords 'kitchen designers' or 'kitchen design' into a search engine. The click-through rate on their ad linked to those keywords is likely to be higher than it will be for other words that are not quite so close a match (e.g. the keyword 'cooking'). Nevertheless, there is business to be had from not so perfect matches like this when they are roughly pointing in the approximate direction.

Contextual advertising

A person's likely interests can be inferred not just from search words but also by editorial context. If the word 'cooking' works as a reasonable match for the ads of a kitchen design company on a search engine, then chances are the cooking section of online publications or articles about cooking will perform similarly. Therefore, instead of search words, another matching mechanism is editorial context and matching on this is known as *contextual advertising*. Just like paid search advertising, the closer the match of the ad with the page's editorial content, the greater click-through is likely to be.

To improve this match and determine what ads to display on a page, account can also be taken of profile information that is known about the site's typical visitors. For example, an ad for tampons on the cleo.com website makes much more sense than it does on the nytimes.com website. Females are Cleo's target audience whereas probably half the readers on the *New York Times* site are male and have no real interest in the product; the ad does not match the reader profile. It makes sense to match the ad where possible with both the editorial interest and the demographic profile of the likely readers of a page. And as we saw in the earlier chapter on behavioral targeting, the ultimate extension of this is to combine all this data with information about that visitor's past searches and past purchases at sites across the web generally and put all this together to get pinpoint precision matching. The more the ad matches the type of person and his/her need state at the time, the higher the likely click-through rate will be.

Contextual advertising, then, was the forerunner to behavioral targeting and indeed page content can be used as one of the refining elements in behavioral targeting to help achieve more pinpoint precision, as can demographic profile information such as gender or zip code. For example, a Californian kitchen designer operating only in that state might want to restrict the display of its ads not just to articles and editorial about cooking but where possible also restrict them to site visitors from Californian zip codes.

The times they are a-changing

TV's position as the dominant medium of delivery for advertising is now under relentless challenge by the spectacular growth of the Internet and 'new media'. The dollars spent on Internet advertising are anticipated to eventually overtake television advertising and the only question is, when? In the UK, where people already spend substantially more hours on the Internet than in most other parts of the world, it is projected this will happen as early as 2010.[8]

Unlike television where you can sit back and let it wash over you, the Internet is a different medium. It is a high involvement, interactive medium with an environment that demands a continual stream of decisions from you. What is called the *click-stream* is in reality a 'decision stream'. Each click is a decision. At every step you have to make a choice. Do I go here or will I click on this? Which of these will take me where I want to go? That link looks interesting but if I take it will I forget to come back? Will I click or won't I? Have I got time right now? Will it be worth it? I don't want to wait for fifteen seconds and find it is irrelevant anyway! The web is therefore very different to TV as we have known it traditionally. It demands very active involvement in a very cognitive way.

An advantage that the Internet does have is that when we are exposed to an ad online, it puts us but one click away from the advertiser's virtual home. It only takes a simple click-through and we are transported to the advertiser's 'door'. Television has been unable to do this but digital television will increasingly provide this same capability for us to click on a brand or product in a TV ad (or indeed in a program) and visit a website to purchase it or get more information. For online retailers and other advertisers who sell directly through the Internet, this ability to click through is a particular advantage. It is also an advantage for advertisers of information-intensive products (like finance, mortgages, phones, etc) that require active consideration before purchase. When digital TV has widespread web capability to enable such click-through, it will compete on a more level playing field with web advertising. This will likely serve as something of a brake on some of the migration of TV ad dollars that have been crossing over to the web.

The growth of advertising on the Internet in most countries has severely threatened print media advertising as well as TV advertising. By 2006 in the UK, the Internet's share of all advertising dollars overtook newspapers and the same is likely to happen in other countries. In many countries, amongst younger people, the habit of reading newspapers has been on the decline and some of the dollars previously spent on newspaper advertising have migrated to the Internet. Of course some of this decline in newspaper reading has been due to the fact that we are doing more of our newspaper reading online.[9] We can read the news of the day, or the latest on business, entertainment or whatever news on the websites of the *New York Times*, the *Guardian* or almost any other major newspaper in the world. Increasingly we can access these stories wirelessly by mobile (phone) devices as well as our computers. Advertising dollars have simply been following the migration trail across to these new technologies.

Newspaper content and newspaper reading are not the only things migrating to the new technologies. So too is the viewing of video and TV. The Internet is increasingly popular as a means of accessing video and TV content.[10] 'Internet TV plus mobile TV are liberating television from the domestic environment, enabling viewing in new situations: at the office desk or during commuting journeys.'[11] Far from being a threat to TV, some experts predict the Internet will prove to be a great ally of it and that the issue of TV audience fragmentation is only an issue 'about access points, not the content itself'.[12]

That ignores how bumpy this migratory journey of TV content to the new technologies might turn out to be . . . which is anyone's guess. Will it continue? One reservation as to its 'inevitability' relates to the interactive, active nature of the Internet. Whereas the major mode of TV watching is 'sit back and relax', the mode of the web is 'sit up and interact'.[13] Sometimes referred to as the 'lean back, lean forward' distinction, it means that whereas TV is a passive experience, with a PC or a mobile screen we lean forward and constantly interact with it via mouse, keyboard or keypad.[14]

And with a mobile phone screen we intensely scrutinize it for short bursts of time.

All of this means the viewing culture itself is changing and being changed by the new technologies. In tandem, the content of the mass media is being forced to struggle for survival by adaptation and change. To the extent that reading and viewing behavior migrates across to these other screens, the new environment in turn drives changes to both format and content. 'YouTube changed the way many people experience video but it typically involves short low-res bursts more suited to the highly interactive nature of the PC. It is not a TV type of thing.'[15]

Accordingly, this media migration is being accompanied by a trend towards shorter-length snatches of content that can be watched in just a few minutes.[16] 'We may watch snatches of TV highlights on mobile phones, or even longer stretches while we're waiting for a train or something, but we don't—and won't—settle down with a cold beer or hot coffee to watch a football game or movie on a mobile phone.'[17] As online video and 'on-the-go' video become ever more significant, media companies like Fox, Disney and Sony see opportunity in their vast archives of past programs and have begun to adapt by shortening them to fit the new technology viewing situations. Series like *Charlie's Angels* and *Starsky and Hutch* for example have been turned into 'minisodes' able to be viewed in five minutes on a PC or mobile phone screen.[18]

At the same time as the mass media migration is driving program content into short burst formats more suitable for viewing in snatches, the trend with ads is showing signs of going the other way i.e. getting longer. Traditionally the very essence of advertising has been super-short and super-compact communications and as such, it had no trouble fitting right in to the new-technology viewing situations as evidenced by its early popularity on sites like YouTube. The low cost of web delivery by contrast with the high cost of TV delivery led advertisers to experiment with longer ads for online viewing. These were often quirky ads that people would seek out for fun and spread the word about them through social networks, emails, blogs and word of mouth. This viral advertising phenomenon, as it is known, has meant a freeing up of the 30-second limit that was the standard length for most commercials.

On conventional TV, a four- to five-minute ad would generally not only be cost prohibitive but would test viewer goodwill. However, when the ad is sought out on the web, it doesn't interrupt the lean-back environment of TV program watching. And with an increasing number of programs being packaged for the web into snatches of 4 to 5 minutes so as to be more appropriate for viewing on the new screens, opportunity arose. Advertisers began to experiment with slightly *longer* ads that also began to blur the distinction between ad and program content. Entertainment hybrids known as 'webisodes' were developed and pioneered by advertisers like American Express. These short episodes (of just a few minutes) each hailed the American Express Card as the ultimate hero in the hilarious adventures of two unlikely close buddies, Superman and Jerry Seinfeld. Such webisodes were a merger of viral advertising and product placement into short, self-contained entertainment snatches.

Summary

The relentless pace of technological change is forcing much media to reinvent themselves. Adaptations to both program content and advertising formats have to be tried in a 'suck it and see' attempt to find what will work and what won't. Just what will prove unsustainable in the longer term is extraordinarily difficult to predict. With the pace of change as frenetic as this, inevitably a number of these adapted, new-media vehicles will crash and burn because no one really knows what is coming around the next technological corner. Which ones will survive and prosper for the longer term is anybody's guess. Being in technological hyper-drive means inevitably operating in a state of hyper-uncertainty. Or as Winston Churchill observed: 'If you are going through hell, keep going.'

26 'MENTAL REACH': THEY SEE YOUR AD BUT DOES IT GET THROUGH?

Whether communicating the corporate or communicating the brand, an ad must generally break through in order to work most efficiently. In this era of TiVo and digital video recorders (DVRs), when so many ads are fast forwarded, this remains true. Fast forwarded commercials may have an effect *if the ad has broken through and been noted previously.*[1] However, many ads are mediocre at breaking through in the first place. Others are compelling and involve us. Still others can be so boring that even if we don't fast forward them, we skip over them mentally or tune them out and we can't recognize ever having seen them.

Reach is a media term that simply means the percentage of people who have had an 'opportunity to see' that ad. But even if people are in front of the screen, to what extent does the ad reach them mentally and touch their minds as well as their eyes? And if it is does, just what gets through? This chapter focuses on the difference between 'media reach' (how many have an 'opportunity to see') and 'mental reach'.

Let us look first at what people generally do when they see an ad. We will focus on print ads for the moment and come back to TV and the web later in the chapter. In an earlier chapter we saw that in order to understand an ad, people seem to go through a process similar to the following:

1. First, they recognize that it is an ad.
2. They then immediately try to identify what it is an ad for. They look for something familiar that corresponds to a memory address that they recognize—something that already exists in their minds. Usually this is a brand or a product category.
3. When they have located a memory address, their minds can then store any new information that is in the ad in that pigeonhole.

For example, consider the print ad at Figure 26.1. Leafing through a magazine and seeing this, people would recognize they were looking at an ad. They would then quickly recognize it as an ad for Colgate toothpaste, which is a known memory address for most people. Now, if toothpaste is not high on their agenda of interests or concerns many at this point may flick over the page. They have identified it as:

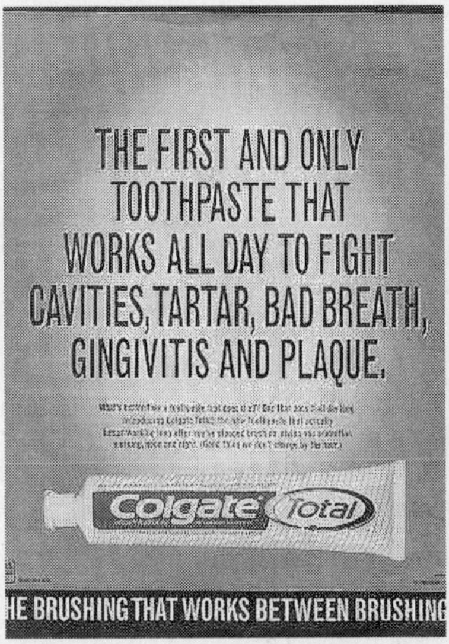

1. an ad;
2. extolling the virtues of Colgate toothpaste;

Figure 26.1: A print ad for Colgate.

so any curiosity they had is quite satisfied by recognizing these two things.

This is a very low level of mental processing and for many ads not much more than this low level of mental processing takes place. In this ad everything you need to know about the brand is included in the headline, so you might think that you don't have to work too hard to know what the ad is all about even if you just skimmed it. The message is pretty instantly communicated provided that you read it. As Franzen reports: *'When something in our minds decides we have enough information, we move our attention on to the next advertisement, or to another constellation of stimuli.'* That occurs after about seven eye fixations (about two seconds). *'The average reader never gets round to reading an entire sentence (longer-than-average headline, for instance).'*[2]

Recognition

However even with such minimal amounts of attention, an ad may nevertheless register enough to at least provide some brand reinforcement and help maintain the brand's salience in people's minds. The chances are reasonably high that they would recognize this ad if they saw it again. If after being exposed to an ad people can't even recognize having seen or heard it before, then chances are the ad is not doing much because this generally indicates the ad is not distinctive enough to 'cut through' the clutter and mentally reach its audience to this very minimal level. It implies that if there are *any* effects, they will be entirely dependent on implicit rather than explicit communication. To avoid distraction (as we saw in the last chapter) people try to ignore many web ads and hence these must depend relatively more on implicit, feather effects than must TV or viral ads.

So, to test for mental reach advertisers often show people the ad and ask if they recognize having seen it before. Web ads are an exception (see the previous chapter) but with other media, if people have been exposed to it chances are high that they will recognize it even though they may not have been able to *recall* it or describe anything specific about the ad. Recognition and recall are two somewhat different measures and we will be discussing this in more depth in the next chapter. Suffice to say here that advertisers can use ad recognition as an operational measure to validate that the ad is achieving at least some mental reach.

With print advertising, people are shown ads to see if they recognize having previously seen them. With radio, TV (and web) ads, the ad spot may be played to them in a web interview. However, it may be impractical because of time constraints to play all competitive commercials in the category so an approximation is often used whereby people are shown a series of still shots taken from the ad. (The selection of exactly which shots are shown is critical, as we shall see later.)

Mental reach is defined as the percentage of the target audience that we can demonstrate had at least some level of *mental* contact with the ad. In other words the ad registers with them, enough for them to at least recognize having seen it. It quantifies how many of the scheduled 'opportunities to see' in the media schedule actually translate into mental contact, recognizing that losses are caused by bathroom visits, attentional distractions and the simple act of mentally tuning out.

Reach vs mental reach levels

So what is important is not just the level of *media* reach ('opportunities to see') but the level of *mental* reach. An ad schedule that targets 28 per cent cumulative *reach* in a week will almost inevitably have a mental reach that is somewhat lower. Twenty-eight per cent reach means that 28 per cent of the target audience have the 'opportunity to see' the commercial on at least one occasion. If this produces say 14 per cent *mental* reach, it

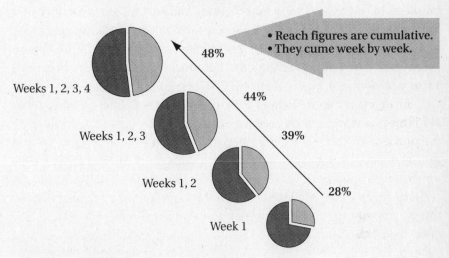

4-week cumulative reach 48%
All adults 18+

48%

• Reach figures are cumulative.
• They cume week by week.

Weeks 1, 2, 3, 4

44%

Weeks 1, 2, 3

39%

Weeks 1, 2

28%

Week 1

Figure 26.2: Cumulative reach over four weeks.

indicates that the ad has not only been exposed but also registered with half . . . enough for them to recognize having seen it.

So, an advertising media schedule quantifies the size of the audience that an ad is supposed to reach. A reach of 28 per cent means that is how many had an opportunity to see the ad—not that they actually saw it.

If the ad is shown several times over a period, the accumulated figure is known as *cumulative reach*. See Figure 26.2 for just one example of how an ad might cumulatively reach 48 per cent of the target audience over a four-week period.

Such measures as these (along with TRPs, GRPs, TVRs, TARPs and with web advertising 'impressions', etc) can be misleading unless it is clearly understood what they mean. It is most important to realize that such figures do not represent *actual* exposures. Much less do they represent mental reach. They are merely 'opportunities to see'.

Because the concept of mental reach is important, let's better understand the underlying psychology of it. What is not widely understood by advertisers or consumers is that in order for people to be able to recognize what they have seen or heard, they have to form a mental model of it. Comparison with this mental representation is what enables them to say if they have been exposed to it before—or if it is something new.

The representation may be just bits and pieces that are stored but these provide a basis for reconstructing the past event, 'much as a paleontologist reconstructs a dinosaur from fragments of bone'.[3]

There are many print ads that people just flick over and ignore and would not be able to recognize again. Similarly with TV ads people's minds have the capacity to mentally 'flick over' them as demonstrated by the work of researchers Thorsen and Zhao, who unobtrusively videotaped people while they were watching TV in a naturalistic setting when they were free to read, watch TV or chat.[4]

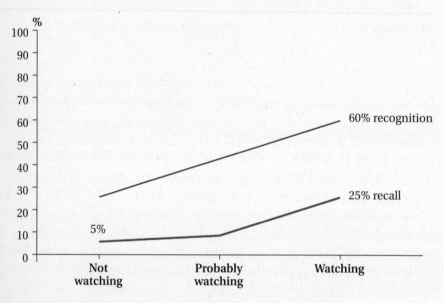

Figure 26.3: *How 'eyes on screen' impacts on memory for TV ads. (Source: Adapted from Thorsen & Zhao 1994)*

Immediately after the program the people were given a surprise test to see which ads they were aware of that had been shown during the 90 minute program. Figure 26.3 shows the relationship between people having their 'eyes on screen' while an ad was being aired (as evidenced by the videotaping) and subsequent recognition (and recall) of the ad, immediately following the 90 minute program.

Remember these were people who had their eyes on the screen when the ad was being shown. As the figure shows, only 60 per cent of these people were able to recognize having seen the ad. This is an average level across about 50 commercials. It *quantifies* what we knew intuitively, that even if people have their eyes on the screen and have resisted the urge to go to the bathroom or make a cup of coffee, an ad may nevertheless still fail to register mentally. (As expected the percentage who were able to free recall the ad without being prompted was substantially lower at 25 per cent.) Clearly there are a lot of other things going on in people's heads when they are exposed to ads—things that can neuter the effect of an ad.

Problem diagnosis

If an audience, shortly after being exposed to an ad, can't even recognize having seen or heard it, they have either not noticed it or have been unable to take in enough to form a mental model of it. The main barriers and reasons for this are:

1. **Poor creative.** Boring ads that fail to get people's attention may not be distinctive enough. Or complex ads that may make mental processing too difficult.
2. **Insufficient processing time.** Many scene switches in TV commercials, or very brief commercials or fast forwarding all limit the amount of processing time for understanding. Time pressures and constrained reading time can do the same thing for print ads.
3. **Distractions.** Even when the person is in front of the screen, they are often subject to distractions. While watching TV, people are frequently doing other things (such as talking, reading, using the phone, doing handicrafts, ironing, playing with kids or pets, etc). Naturally, when people are doing something else at the same time they don't have their eyes constantly on a screen. The ad has to be compelling enough to 'break through' and engage people in the face of these distractions. Preoccupation with congested traffic and road conditions can have the same effect with radio commercials.
4. **Resistance to distraction.** Particularly with web and radio ads, people will at times deliberately need to resist distraction.
5. **Lights on but no one home.** Even when people have their eyes on a screen, they may be thinking of something else, perhaps reflecting on the events of the day or listening in to another conversation. Even with eyes on the screen people don't necessarily mentally process the ad. Again it is the ad's job to 'break through' against *internal* distractions as well as external.

Overcoming the barriers

It is the creative execution, the creative elements of the ad as well as movement and sound that are designed to 'break through' and capture attention. However as estimated from the Thorsen and Zhao study, with only one single 'opportunity to see' the TV ad about 40 per cent of the time this breakthrough doesn't happen on that occasion. In the next scheduled 'opportunity to see' the ad, the minds of some of these people who missed it on the first occasion may not be as pre-occupied or as distracted. This is a common justification for repetition of the ad—though usually a weak one and less compelling in these days of DVRs and fast forwarding.

Repetition and better media placement may go some way to improving the situation but you wouldn't like to bet the farm on it. Good creative ads compel your attention and there is a lot of evidence to suggest that repetition (in the form of more media exposures) will not make up for an ad if it is the commercial itself that fails to engage people's interest and attention on the first occasion.[5]

Relying on repetition alone to try to fix this problem is not only expensive but it is also risky. There is no guarantee that the ad will 'mentally reach' them on the next occasion or the next. So these single exposure results are a strong argument for the power of creativity and the need to design distinctive ads that do not have to rely on repetition to break through.

Summary

In this chapter I have focused on the difference between 'reach' (how many have an 'opportunity to see' an ad) and 'mental reach' (how many can recognize having seen it). Measuring mental reach is best done through the ad recognition measure. But this is only one of a number of measures that are used in the diagnosis of where an ad is breaking down if it is not working. Ad recognition doesn't tell us if the ad is working. But it does pinpoint if the ad is being seen—if it is getting at least the bare minimum of attention.

How then do we tell if the ad is working? In the next chapter ('Measurement of advertising effects in memory') I show how to assess this through brand focused measures (like brand purchasing and brand awareness, etc) rather than ad focused measures (such as ad recognition). Then, in Chapter 28, 'The buy-ology of mind', I revisit ad recognition but this time in the context of the other ad measures (such as ad recall and message take-out) and show how they are used to pinpoint other critical areas where the ad may be breaking down.

27 MEASUREMENT OF ADVERTISING EFFECTS IN MEMORY

Traditional measures of advertising effectiveness such as ad recognition, ad recall, ad liking, message take-away,[1] brand awareness, brand image, and purchase intention confuse many advertisers.The question often posed is: What do these all mean? Which one should I use? Do they really indicate how effective my advertising is? This chapter and the next focus on these mental measures. I look at what they mean, relate them to measures of purchase behavior and put them clearly into the modern perspective of how our memories work.

Diagnostic complementary measures

Mental measures are essentially diagnostic. They help with the problem of sorting out what is going on underneath the observed purchasing behavior. When there are changes in sales or market share they help us in sorting out what changes are due to what causes. How much is due to the advertising and how much to other things that happened at the same time (such as promotion, pricing, competitors' actions, etc)? Advertisers want to know more than just whether their ad worked or not. They need to know how and why it worked. If it didn't work they want to know why, in order to avoid the same mistakes next time.

Let me make it as clear as possible that I firmly believe some form of purchase behavior measurement is crucial whether this be sales, market share, scanner data or self-report. Mental measures won't substitute for these measures of purchase behavior. But measuring purchase behavior by itself cannot provide the necessary diagnostic ability to know what is happening with them unless they are combined with mental-response measures. Mental-response measures in providing this diagnostic ability don't substitute for behavior-change measures; they complement them. They help sort out what is causing what. They provide understanding of how and why the ad works or doesn't work.

Indeed using purchase behavior alone can prove to be misleading and result in perfectly good ad campaigns being mistakenly jettisoned simply because they haven't led to any increased sales or market share (yet). This is especially a problem for brands that already have large market shares. Increases in market share become harder to get the greater the existing brand share. Maintaining existing customer behavior is not necessarily a bad thing when you are a large, well-established brand. An important role for advertising is to continually defend the established sales and market share levels against the many would-be attackers. For established, larger brands, advertising's role must increasingly focus on defending or holding its established share. Judgment of advertising effectiveness *solely* in terms of increases in sales or market share is naïve because amongst other things, it fails to come to grips with the role of advertising as an 'occupational force'.

To fully understand the way these other, mental measures work, to understand what they mean and how to use them, we need to discard the traditional, old-fashioned view of memory. There is often a gap of ten to twenty years between new developments in psychology and their dissemination and use in marketing. The past half-century has seen significant developments in psychological research on memory, some of which have still not been built into the thinking of some marketing and advertising practitioners.

One reason for this is that some aspects of it are not all that easy to explain. It takes some effort to understand the full implications. The effort will be repaid however because an understanding of the modern view of memory is fundamental to understanding advertising's effects and to using mental measures diagnostically in the evaluation of an ad campaign.

Towards the modern view of memory

In 1959, a neurosurgeon by the name of Wilder Penfield inserted a microscopic electric probe into a patient's brain while the patient was conscious. This will make your eyes water, but Penfield used local anesthetic and the patient was able to converse with him while this was happening. The patient reported various 'memories' being activated, like watching *Gone with the Wind* years earlier—complete with the smell of cheap perfume in the cinema and the beehive hairstyle of the person in front.[2]

When Penfield touched the brain at one spot the patient reported 're-experiencing' a piece of music. Penfield then shifted the probe slightly and into the patient's mind suddenly came the vivid 'memory' of an old childhood experience that the patient claimed had long been forgotten. Depending on the exact location in the brain that Penfield touched with the electric probe a different 'memory' might be reactivated. Whether these were true memories or not, they were often things the patient claimed not to have thought about in many years.[3]

Penfield's experiments eventually led psychologists towards what is called the 'spreading activation' theory of memory.[4] Cast in the framework of neural networks and distributed representation,[5] this has become the best-accepted theory of how memory works today (notwithstanding that the strength of the original interpretation of the Penfield results appear to have been somewhat overstated).[6]

Implicit memory

As we ended the last millennium, another memory concept had emerged— 'implicit' memory.[7] A brand or an ad can trigger a feeling without it necessarily retriggering full awareness of how, when, and where you have encountered that object before or where the feeling about it came from.

Conventional memory refers to retriggering some residue of a past experience. It means re-activation of that past experience as a conscious (explicit) memory which shows up as either recall or recognition. However, if one has been exposed to an ad but cannot recognize ever having ever seen it, can it still have an effect? Yes. Instead of a re-activation of the memory, the effect may be implicit which simply means we have processed it to some extent but without being able to recall or recognize ever having seen it. We saw in earlier chapters that feather effects can be produced in this way by:

- subliminal exposure (Chapter 3)
- oblique messages (Chapter 5)
- ignored web ads (Chapter 25).

In other words sometimes effects shows up indirectly. While we can't recognize that we have seen the ad, the effects might show up in brand image or in a marginally increased liking for the brand or increased liking for its advertising. Research indicates that the mental measures that implicit processing can influence are:

- salience (brand or ad)
- attitude/affect i.e. liking (for ad or brand)
- image shift.

A complication however is that these measures are not only impacted by implicit (unconscious) processes. They can be impacted by explicit (conscious) processes as well. So the only way to infer that the causal process was implicit and not explicit is to look at ad recognition. If the person doesn't recognize having ever seen the ad before, then the strong implication is that any effect must have resulted from implicit processes. What does this tell us? Not much except it underlines how important it is not to simply rely on ad recognition (or ad recall) as hard and fast criteria of advertising effect. Mental measures need to include more than recognition or recall. Indeed, you need an armory of mental measures including those above, as well as others that I will discuss shortly.

First though, let me put in a few words of caution about implicit effects. It does appear that implicit and explicit learning are parallel learning processes and this means some learning can take place through automatic, implicit processing, even in the relative absence of attention. The operative word here is 'can'. You need evidence from the tracking (or other research) that the ad is indeed influencing behavior, and if not behavior then attitudes. And if not behavior or attitude, then image or brand salience. You can't just *assume* an ad is working implicitly. Only after one or other of these effects is established (for the ad that people don't recognize seeing) can you conclude that it is working implicitly. In other words, in the face of definite behavioral, attitudinal, image or salience effects, you can rule out explicit communication explanations by showing that people don't recognize ever having seen the ad. Any conclusion that the ad must be working implicitly is arrived at by a process of elimination. Unless you have the evidence that the ad is clearly working, then claims that it must be working implicitly are nothing more than 'smoke and mirrors'.

Actually, my view is that learning is rarely either wholly implicit or wholly explicit. In many ads there are elements of the two processes at work. My guess is that the accumulating evidence will eventually reveal that while explicit and implicit processing systems can and do work independently, they also often work together interactively. For example, touch typists' knowledge of where the keys are on a typewriter is largely implicit (often they can only tell you where the keys are by moving their finger) but that doesn't mean it was learnt unconsciously or without any attention. Nor indeed does it mean that it didn't require a huge amount of repetition.

Another caution is: beware of exaggerated claims for the power of implicit processing.[8] There is no doubt that ad exposures can have effects through associative processes even though there is no retrievable memory trace of the actual exposures. But in my experience those associative effects are more often feather effects and even then they have to be evidenced and not assumed.

Another caution is that communicating purely by association usually requires substantial repetition. As discussed in Chapter 3 ('Subliminal advertising: the biggest myth of all') and in Chapter 5 ('The advertising message: oblique and indirect'), repetition is often important for measureable effects to show up. White says of implicit advertising: 'This kind of advertising seems to put a premium on repetition and ubiquity.'[9] Indeed, relying totally on implicit learning (low levels of attention) usually means slower learning and hence significant repetition.

This conclusion, as to limitations of learning without attention, is also supported by the tracking experience of others. Mundell, Hallward and Walker for example, using the Ipsos-ASI system, agree that implicit (low attention) processing can influence brand preference, but when ads are processed with high attention 'it has a profoundly more significant impact'.[10]

We have to conclude that high attention advertising is still the rapid route to learning.[11] So, despite the fact that we can and do learn implicitly by association (especially with product placement, see Chapter 6), advertisers will nevertheless continue to try to capture consumers' attention. To the extent that implicit associations work best with low (rather than high) attention, then techniques like oblique and indirect messages (see Chapter 5) can enable the ad to do double mileage. That is, by deliberately engaging the consumer's *explicit* processes, it can simultaneously draw attention away from other elements of the ad in order to communicate associations more obliquely, outside the full glare of attention.

Association
When you hear 'MmmmmmMmmmmm', what do you think of? Chances are that it immediately brings to mind Campbell's soup. As already

mentioned, when someone says to you 'Just do it' the chances are you immediately think 'Nike'. This is because our minds work by association.

Things remind us of other things. For example we are often reminded, in the course of listening to someone else in a conversation, of something that we want to say. This association process lets our minds 'fill out' more complete memories from fragments of information. We see the back of a head at a friend's party and before the person turns around we remember their face and if we are lucky, also their name. While walking past the television we hear the words 'priceless' and 'for everything else' and we immediately think 'oh another MasterCard commercial' even though we did not actually see or hear the word 'MasterCard'.

Our memory system can be cued with a fragment of a memory and to the extent the connections and associative strengths are there, then our minds tend to 'fill out' the rest through spreading activation that travels through the mental connections.[12] Brain neuro-imaging studies show us exactly what parts of the brain are active at any time (e.g. when we recall a person's face versus a person's name). This reveals the surprising fact that the various features or fragments of a memory are not stored together. The bits and pieces of a memory are distributed throughout different parts of the brain. They are bound together as cliques by their connections and the associative strength of those connections.[13]

If you want to really appreciate the pervasive and spontaneous nature of associative connections try this exercise:

- Read out to a few people these words: candy, sour, sugar, bitter, good, taste, tooth, nice, honey, soda, chocolate, heart, cake, eat, pie.
- Then ask them to write down as many of the words as they can remember.
- Finally, ask them if any of the words 'taste', 'point' or 'sweet' were on the list.

Chances are that they will say (incorrectly) that 'sweet' was on the list (up to 90 per cent of people do).[14] Why? The association is so strong that people mistakenly think they were actually exposed to the attribute 'sweet' instead of generating it themselves. 'Sweet' is an attribute which is strongly associated with a number of the words on the list (candy, honey, sugar, etc) and it appears to activate the general category of 'sweet' in our mind.

Mental network

Recognizing something involves us in linking together the fragments we have seen—linking them by associative strengths into a 'coherent' representation in our mind. We 'bind' the distributed features of the memory together. This representation of the memory is in the form of a mental network which may include not only things that we actually saw or heard but also (as with the word 'sweet') things that are very closely associated. This applies not just to memories but also to the meanings of things.

For example, when I say the word 'cars', what do you think of? You may have thought immediately of 'roads' or you may have thought of a brand of car such as Toyota, Ford, or Volvo. What underlies these associations in our minds can be thought of as a gigantic neural network of interconnected associations.

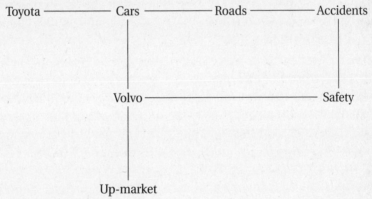

Figure 27.1: A memory network.

These billions of neurons are all connected, some directly and others circuitously, through other neurons. But the connections have different strengths. This is illustrated in Figure 27.1. It shows an over-simplified version of what part of this network might look like.

Just as the touch of Penfield's electric probe might activate his patient's networks and cause the apparent recall of some memory, so may a picture that we see, or a word that we hear, activate a part of our mental network. The activation spreads through the distributed representation of that thing and causes us to recall what it is and what is its meaning. For example, seeing a picture of a car or hearing the word 'car' activates their meanings. The activation is like an electric current spreading outwards and activating other close things that are associated with 'car'.[15] This is why an expression such as 'Just do it' is likely to trigger not only its own meaning but also any things that are closely associated with it, like 'Nike'.

When we are exposed to words and pictures, each one activates a clique of neurons that collectively represent that thing in the network.[16] As I demonstrated with the word 'sweet' this does not have to be activated directly, however. It can be triggered by 'spreading activation' from some close associate.

This is one of the main reasons why ad campaigns like 'Mmmmmm Mmmmmm', 'Priceless' and 'Just do it' have been successful. They are frequently recurring expressions that crop up all the time in the normal course of our lives. So when we come across them in conversation it is the equivalent of inserting a probe into our minds and activating our mental memory network. The activation then triggers off any close associates, such as 'Campbell's' or 'MasterCard' or 'Nike' that may have become connected to the active representation. It gives the brand 'free registrations' and helps the brand stay 'top of mind'.

Meaning and brand image

The fact that our memories work through this process has far-reaching implications for advertising and marketing. It means much more than simply keeping something top of mind. In fact, it is the whole basis for the meanings things have for us, including the meanings of brands.

As Figure 27.1 implies, when 'Volvo' is activated it in turn activates any attributes that are closely associated with that brand, such as 'safety' and 'up-market'. These things that 'Volvo' activates in our mind, the things that are closely associated with it, collectively represent the meaning of 'Volvo' for us. This meaning takes in the resonances of all the associations that are closely linked with 'Volvo' and activated by it. This is the underlying essence of meaning as well as the underlying essence of brand image. It is why Volvo is seen as safe and Coke is seen as fun. It explains the ability of a brand name to activate (at least partially) these attributes in our minds. They are close associates of the brand.

Closeness of connections

Activation spreads though the mental network like an electric current.[17] When there is low resistance between two points (synapses), these two things have high associative strength and a high probability of the connection being made—the association being completed. On the other hand, when two things have low associative strength there is high resistance in the flow. So things with low associative strength are less likely to be activated. The stronger the associative strength between an attribute like 'safety' and the brand Volvo, the more likely it is that activating 'Volvo' will spread activation to the attribute 'safety'. Conversely, the weaker the associative strength the less likely it is to be activated by that trigger.

Another way of thinking about this is in product positioning terms. Simply, it means Volvo 'owns' the safety position in people's minds. That is, Volvo is more closely connected to 'safety' than any other brand (in its class). This associative view of memory thus gives advertisers a much richer way of thinking about product positioning as well.

Reinforcing connections

Connections are like muscles. When they are exercised they get stronger. When they are not exercised they get weaker. We all have leg muscles, but if we want to use them for running long distances they need to be strengthened and exercised. Like leg muscles, connections that are not exercised may be too weak to perform.

When we encounter the American Express card today those of us who experienced the 'Don't leave home without it' campaign that featured Karl Malden rarely, if ever, think of it. That is not to say we are unaware that he once advertised American Express. Similarly we are only vaguely aware that Jerry Seinfeld appeared in a number of American Express ads also. We don't think about these ads any more. Yet the connections in a sense still exist except they have become so weakened by lack of use that they don't work of their own accord.

Contrast with the traditional view of memory

This all contrasts with the traditional view of memory that dominated much of marketing practice until recently. In that view, a memory trace is laid down. The memory is either there or it is not there. Either you remember it or you don't.

It is amazing that this model of memory survived at all, because it was always demonstrably wrong! How many times have you been unable to remember someone's name even though you know that you know it? Forgetting more often has to do with our 'inability to retrieve' the memory (or some fragment of it) and we are unable to activate it again. Sometimes we may have failed to store the memory in the first place but more likely we just 'forgot where we put it' or that part of it. In other words, our mind has lost the connections.

Retrieval cues

Our memories get triggered by retrieval cues. These are things that prompt us to remember other things. When we are trying to think of somebody's name, for example, and the name won't come to mind, we use retrieval cues. We may deliberately bring to mind the situation in which we last saw the person. That may help us remember the name. Why? Because we are hoping that the activation which spreads from the memory of that situation will activate the name of the person and allow us to recall it.

If that doesn't work, we may try other related cues to help us spread enough activation towards the person's name to trigger recall of it. What we are doing is looking for a retrieval cue that will help us activate the name. Strong retrieval cues are things strongly connected with something and tend to remind us of it. They help pop that thing into our mind.

The relevance of this to advertising is that advertisers want their brand to be cued into people's minds when they think of making a purchase from that product category. If you are an advertiser, you would no doubt like to tie your brand strongly to a retrieval cue that is often in people's minds or in their environment—and ideally is also around at the time they buy the product category. This could be almost anything. It could be something visual (e.g. the pack or a dispenser label that we are likely to see at the point of sale). Or it could be something verbal (e.g. 'MmmmmmMmmmmm'). Or it could even be a piece of music. So one test of the effect of an ad is to ask, is it strengthening the association between a relevant retrieval cue (such as the product category) and the advertised brand?

Association measurement

As marketers, the retrieval cues we are interested in are brands, products, messages, and image attributes. We have the ability to measure and track the changing strength of associations—to tell us how closely two or more things are connected in buyers' minds and how that strength increases with repetition.

Given the word 'fingers', 46 per cent of people immediately think of 'hand' and very few (less than 1 per cent) think of 'glove'. Fingers and hand have high associative strength. Fingers and glove have very low associative strength.[18]

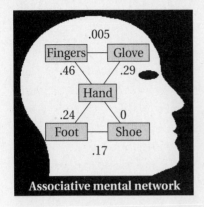

Figure 27.2: We are more likely to be reminded of 'hand' by the word 'fingers' than 'glove'. Given the word 'finger', 46% of people immediately think of 'hand' while very few (less than 1%) think of 'glove'. Fingers and hand have high associative strength. Fingers and glove have low associative strength.

(Adapted from: Postman L. & Keppel G, Norms of Word Association, *Academic Press, 1970)*

The essential method was pioneered years ago by psychologists exploring relationships between words and asking large samples of people 'What is the first thing that comes to mind when I say . . .'. The inserted word is the retrieval cue and this might be for example the word 'fingers' or the word 'glove'. From the responses the researchers can derive some picture of that part of our associative mental network and the strengths in the associative mental network can be mapped (see Figure 27.2).

When advertisers use products and brands and image attributes as the retrieval cues the principles remain the same. The connection strength is measured by the percentage of people giving each response. Direction is important e.g. the likelihood of the expression 'credit card' triggering 'Visa' is not the same as 'Visa' triggering 'credit card'.

But how do you relate associative mental networks and strength of connections to advertising effectiveness? Exactly what associations should be tracked and which ones indicate effectiveness?

An example

Let me illustrate using an old print ad for Minute Maid fruit juice that will serve as an example (Figure 27.3). A young girl with plaited hair is holding up her juice glass and asking 'Mom, can I have some more calcium?' The copy explains that Minute Maid is enriched with calcium—as much calcium as milk has and that 'it's one delicious glass your kids will actually drink'. This implies images of Minute Maid being:

- 'healthier' (fruit juice); and
- a more delicious way for kids to get their calcium than drinking milk.

When this ad is run, the ultimate test of it is this: are more buyers purchasing Minute Maid fruit juice? If not, are they at least more disposed to purchasing Minute Maid? The underlying logic of the process is this:

- if people, when they think of fruit juice, are more likely to think of Minute Maid (*brand awareness*);
- and when they think of it, they think of it as 'healthier/good for you' (*brand image*);
- then, if 'healthier/good for you' is important in fruit juice purchasing (*attribute importance*);
- we can expect a greater likelihood of people buying Minute Maid fruit juice will follow.

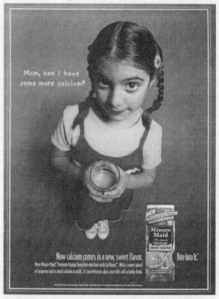

Figure 27.3: '*Mom, can I have some more calcium?*' *Ad for Minute Maid fruit juice enriched with calcium. (© 2000 The Coca-Cola Company. 'Minute Maid' is a registered trademark of The Coca-Cola Company.)*

Additionally, the ad very cleverly attempts to tie the brand to milk as a retrieval cue and remind people of the fact that some kids don't enjoy the taste of milk and are reluctant to drink it. In other words, the hope is that when they think of milk, this will tend to trigger Minute Maid fruit juice as an association and as a possible substitute that parents might entertain as a way for their kids to get their calcium. This is a mechanism that could generate perhaps a bigger effect than the simple one of giving Minute Maid the image of a healthier fruit juice. So we should also ask: is it strengthening the association between milk as a retrieval cue and Minute Maid fruit juice as one of the other alternative ways their kids can get their calcium? Because this is another way the ad could be working and having its effect in addition to making the brand into a 'healthier' fruit juice brand. To keep things simple for the purposes of illustration here, we will ignore the 'milk substitute' mechanism in the explication of the measures that follow and focus only on testing for evidence of the healthier fruit juice mechanism. It should be noted, however, that the same type of analysis procedure can be very easily extended to test the associations involved in building up the milk substitute mechanism—in other words, positioning Minute Maid juice as a more acceptable way for kids to get their calcium than milk.

Whether a greater likelihood of purchasing Minute Maid does result is a question to be answered by sales, market share or other forms of behavior data (such as self-report.). Table 27.1 summarizes the primary measures that need to be available. Note that in addition to behavior (1), we need to look at attitudes (2). People may feel more predisposed to buy Minute Maid but, if they get to the supermarket shelf and find their regular brand of fruit juice on cut-price special they may postpone their trial of Minute Maid until next time. That does not mean that the ad has failed.

Table 27.1: Primary measures of effectiveness

1. Are more buyers purchasing Minute Maid?
2. If not, are they more predisposed to purchasing it?
3. At point of sale, what is the likelihood they think of or notice the brand?
4. When they do notice or think of the brand, what is the likelihood that the image information (from the ad) is activated?

Behavior: Do sales, market share, scanner data, or survey self-report show more people buying Minute Maid juice?
Attitudes: Has disposition or intentions towards buying Minute Maid juice improved?
Awareness: Has *spontaneous* brand awareness for Minute Maid increased?
Image: Is Minute Maid juice now more associated with 'healthier' (because it has calcium) than it was before?

Measure 3 (brand awareness) and measure 4 (image) are not meant to substitute for the behavior and attitudes measures, but they are diagnostic—they help us analyze why the ad is or is not working and, if it is not they give us pointers as to what to do about it. Figure 27.4 depicts measures 3 and 4 as two diagnostic connections that need to be measured in the associative mental network.

Do people, when they think of fruit juice, think of Minute Maid? The connection strength of measure 3 represents the likelihood that people will think of (or notice) Minute Maid when they get to the point of sale. Pack displays, special promotional material, and all sorts of other things can influence this as well, but these things aside and other things being equal, the product category is one thing that is always present in the situation.

The other connection is the brand image connection: when people think of Minute Maid juice do they think of it as healthier? There is nothing too complicated in measuring the strength of this brand-attribute association. It is simply a matter of asking something like, 'What brands of fruit juice do you most associate with "healthier"'? or 'What attributes do you associate with Minute Maid juice?'

Note that none of these four measures asks questions about the ad. They are all focused on the brand itself. If the tracking shows that both the brand connections get stronger when the ad is being run then, all else being equal, we expect more people to be buying Minute Maid. Of course 'healthier because it contains calcium' would need to have been pre-researched and established as a potentially important attribute in fruit juice choice. If that has been done and these two connections are strengthening, then purchase behavior in the form of sales or market share (or at least attitudes) should also be moving in consequent response.

Under such circumstances where these four *brand*-focused measures are moving as expected, analysis of *ad*-focused measures such as ad recognition, ad recall, and message take-out are rather irrelevant. The ad is working and even if such additional analysis showed the ad with poor recognition or poor message take-out (which is rather unlikely), nevertheless the *brand* connections that you want to influence are somehow strengthening and the key outcomes are happening. Something is working. Unless it can be accounted for by some other activity (such as brand-building promotion or PR), the ad must be working and, while this may be in a way that you don't fully understand (i.e. implicitly), nevertheless it is working.

This is an important point because,

Figure 27.4: Brand associative mental network.

while we know how a majority of ads work, we don't understand everything about the way that all ads work. In my experience, it is the exception for them not to work through conscious ad recognition processes but, as discussed earlier in the section on implicit memory, it does happen. We should *never* throw out an effective ad that is working just because we don't understand exactly *how* it is working. Poor ad recognition or poor message recall should never be allowed to override the stronger evidence of movement in the strength of the *brand* connections (together with sales, market share and attitudes, of course).

But what if purchase behavior and attitudes to the brand have *not* changed? This is when the ad-focused measures like ad recall and message take-out, as well as ad liking, can become really important because they give further diagnostic aid in working out what is going wrong.

When an ad isn't working

It is when these key indicators (of sales, market share, brand attitudes, and the two primary brand associations) reveal that an ad isn't working that the ad-focused questions become valuable diagnostics. This is when we need to delve deeper into the underlying related associations in an attempt to diagnose why the breakdown might be occurring.

We need to answer questions like 'Are they seeing the ad?' and 'Is it communicating the right message?' We know that an ad can work despite its apparent failure on one or both of these questions, but that is the exception not the rule. If an ad is clearly not working (as indicated by the behavior and attitude evidence discussed above), then ad-memory questions may help to identify whether the problem is one with mental reach (getting attention) or branding or message registration.

With a high degree of confidence, this will point to a key reason why the ad is not working and hopefully allow us to do something about it. We take this up again in the next chapter.

Summary

Mental connections are like muscles. When they are exercised they grow stronger and when they are not used they get weaker. The primary role of mental measures as an indicator of connection strength is essentially a diagnostic one. Measuring the strength of connections can help with the problem of sorting out what is going on underneath the observed purchasing behavior.

These are all brand-focused measures. They measure performance and associations with the brand. Measures that are focused on the ad itself (ad recognition, ad recall, ad liking, message take-out, etc) are important when the ad is not working; they aid the diagnosis and supplement the brand-focused measures. As we see in the next chapter, they help to pinpoint exactly where an ad seems to be strong and where it seems to be weak and what actions we need to take to fix it. Understanding this can help advertisers do much more of what works and less of what doesn't.

28 THE BUY-OLOGY OF MIND

The suffix '-ology' is used to mean either 'the study of' or 'the science of'. This chapter is about the science of consumption (or buying). In particular we address the role of the mind, how it influences buying and brand choice, and how to go about measuring it.

The last chapter peeked inside our 'necktop' computer to see how memory works. Memory consists of the firing or activating of an interconnected network of neurons. If our brain is touched internally at any point with a probe, a picture or a word, some part of our mental network is activated and we may recall a particular memory, meaning or feeling about that word or picture.

Like an electric current, the activation spreads out in all directions from the original point of activation, gathering up the meaning of the stimulus as it goes. The meaning of a thing is represented by the total pattern of the activation that the word or picture initiates. Knowledge is retrieved (or recalled) by activating the appropriate network in memory.

What we haven't discussed is the fact that there is more than just knowledge in these networks in our brain. Not all memory is knowledge. There is also memory for things that happen to us—of autobiographical events that are not knowledge per se. We remember episodes in our life—like driving to work this morning. Or perhaps we remember tasting a new brand of coffee yesterday. And we remember watching *The Simpsons* last night and seeing that great Missy Elliott ad for Pepsi again.

These are autobiographical events or episodes that are retained in our memory, at least for some time. They form memory networks that can be activated later to be re-triggered in our mind. Psychologists label memories for episodes like this 'episodic' memory, to be distinguished from remembering that is in the form of knowledge which is called 'semantic' memory.[1] The two are seen increasingly to be related.[2]

When we are exposed to an ad that gets our attention, such as the Minute Maid fruit juice ad discussed in the previous chapter, there are usually four distinguishable components or fragments that can potentially be stored in memory. Under normal ad-exposure circumstances it is all too rare that we remember all four of them. These fragments are:

1. the ad execution (girl with glass asking for more calcium);
2. the product category (fruit juice);
3. the brand (Minute Maid);
4. the message (healthy/good for you—kids ask for it).

The first component, the execution, is the creative vehicle that we hope will make the audience sit up and take notice; that will make the ad break through the clutter so that, having captured some attention, it can deliver its message. The ads shown in Figure 28.1 for Volkswagen (the 'Save Face' ad that we saw earlier) and for Dairy Soft spread are good examples. These executions almost compel us to stop and take a closer

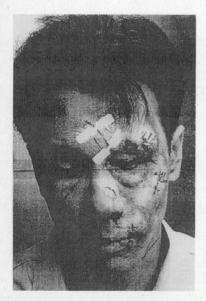

Two ways to make
butter easier to spread

If you love the delicious, natural taste of butter, you'll love Devondale *Dairy Soft*. *Dairy Soft Dairy Spread* is simply pure Devondale butter blended with Canola oil so now you can enjoy the taste of real butter and get easier spreading.

No wonder so many butter lovers are going *Soft*.

Figure 28.1: The ad executions for VW and Dairy Soft spread grab attention and, having done so, can then deliver a message.

look at what they have to say. Once the execution has got our attention, it has a better chance of delivering its message and linking this to the brand.

If the ad execution does its job of successfully breaking through the clutter, that is an important but just a first step. Getting attention is the first stage but the other elements are also important. Having broken through the clutter, what message does the execution register in memory? Is it what the advertiser intended? And if it is, did the consumer connect all of this in memory with the correct brand and the correct product category? If not, the advertiser could be doing a great job of advertising for some other brand or product.

These four elements of any ad experience that need to be represented in memory as fragments bound together by connections can be depicted as shown in Figure 28.2. The ideal is to have all four of these elements highly integrated in the ad so that they mutually reinforce each other. However, this is all too rarely achieved and 'different elements of the ad compete with each other for the attentional resources available'.[3] Even some integration is better than none. The Volkswagen ad, for example, goes part way in that the visual execution reinforces the verbal message ('Volkswagen puts safety first').

Similarly, the visual execution of the Dairy Soft ad dramatically reinforces its verbal message—'easier to spread'. Here, two of the elements (the execution and the message) are highly integrated and work very effectively to reinforce each other. To remember the execution is almost certainly to remember the message and vice versa. Compare this with the Minute Maid fruit juice ad, which has much less integration. Few ads

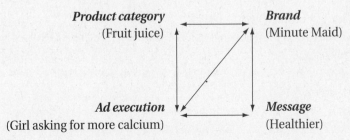

Note: Four elements need to be represented in memory and bound by connections.
Figure 28.2: An ad experience memory network.

manage to have all four elements highly integrated. The more integration there is the higher the chances of the ad's success.

The most common problem in advertising is, without doubt, registering the (correct) brand in memory. It is staggering how much advertising fails because it doesn't successfully connect up everything else with the (correct) brand in memory.[4] Back in Chapter 22 I showed how to use 'constants' to help in this task of binding the brand into the memory network. It is a real advantage if you can use elements that are strongly and uniquely associated with that brand because they act as effective retrieval cues for the brand over and above the brand name itself. For example, when you see an ad with Fergie (the Duchess of York), chances are you think of Weight Watchers whereas an ad with Kirsty Alley may make you remember the line 'Have you called Jenny yet?' and trigger recall of Jenny Craig Weight Loss Centers. You don't have to see the brand but you get the brand all the same. And you only have to hear the words 'For everything else, there's . . .' and you think 'MasterCard'.

Looking at this another way: when your memory network is activated at two points simultaneously (i.e. the product category and an execution fragment like Kirsty Alley), the activation spreading from those two points and activating any other strong connections should trigger the brand. This is epitomized in some of the Nike commercials that are able to 'sign off' with the 'swoosh' and nowhere in the ad is there any explicit mention of the brand 'Nike'.

So, one point that can be strongly connected to the brand is the ad execution. Another is the message (e.g. 'I'm lovin' it' and McDonald's). If the brand has a unique message that has remained constant for some time, just the message itself should trigger the brand. For example, 'Where's the beef?' and 'Just do it'. These are unique retrieval cues that immediately communicate their respective brands (Wendy's and Nike) even without any explicit mention of the brand name.

Ad effect measures

In the past, some advertisers placed great store on people being able to recall their ad. Others did not believe in ad recall but thought it important that people be able to indicate they had seen the ad by at least recognizing it. Some advertisers have put the focus on communication of the message rather than people remembering the ad itself, while others have argued that consumers' ability to parrot back a message is not relevant to the ad's sales effectiveness. There is a resolution to all this. To arrive at it we must first understand that *the effect of an ad is a process*, and that evaluating the effectiveness of an ad using continuous tracking data is also a process.

The process of evaluating an ad

Suppose that an ad like the Minute Maid ad, when first exposed, is not showing clear and obvious effects on changing behavior (as measured by sales, market share, or other behavior measures such as trial, repeat buying, etc). The first part of any doctor's diagnosis is to determine whether there is a *real* problem and, if there is, to locate the source of it.

As has been made clear in earlier chapters, advertising does not just make us 'run out and buy'. In order to capture its intermediate effects we need indicators of its impact on more than just behavior. For each strategic point in this attempted influencing process, we should aim to have an appropriate measure to indicate what is happening. When sales and market share movements as well as other behavior measures do not react immediately to advertising, the advertiser needs urgently to diagnose what is happening. It is at this point that the other measures assume center stage, because it is necessary to trace back through the intermediate effects to see where the ad is having an impact and where it is not, so as to make a judgment about what to do.

In the last chapter we touched briefly on the four important brand measures—brand behavior, brand attitude, brand awareness and brand image. Now it is time to extend this and look at the full range of measures, including ad-focused measures.

The main measures

The second set of measures (see Table 28.1) focuses on the ad itself—ad recognition, ad recall, message take-out, and liking and believability of the ad. These measures fit together with the brand-focused measures in the total picture of advertising evaluation because they are used in a process of elimination to try to assess, first, whether the ad is working and, if it is not, to isolate what is going wrong. The questions that are asked about the effectiveness of an ad (e.g. the Minute Maid ad) will call for information derived not only from the brand-focused measures but also from the ad-focused measures.

Table 28.1 Measures of advertising effectiveness

Brand-focused	Ad-focused
Brand-purchasing behavior	Ad recognition
Brand attitudes/purchase intentions	Ad recall
Brand awareness	Correct branding
Brand image	Message take-out
	Ad liking
	Ad believability

The crucial difference is that having all these measures enables the pursuit of a full diagnostic interpretation.

Use of the brand-focused measures

The brand-focused measures that we met in the last chapter are primary. The questions they answer are shown again in Table 28.2.

Table 28.2 Brand-focused measures

1. Are more buyers purchasing it?	Measure **brand behavior**
2. If not, are they more predisposed to purchase it (but perhaps being prevented by something like a competitor's cut-price promotion)?	Measure **brand attitudes or intentions**
3. What is the likelihood they think of or notice the brand? (If they don't think of it at the appropriate time this can prevent them buying it.)	Measure **spontaneous brand awareness**
4. When they do notice or think of the brand, what is the likelihood that the (image) information from the ad is activated?	Measure **brand–image association**

I need to elaborate a little more on these four brand-focused measures.

1. *Are more buyers purchasing it?* (Or are the same people buying more of it?) The earlier it is in the campaign, the less likely that *purchase-behavior* evidence will show clear, unequivocal evidence of movement, especially for products such as durables where the

purchase cycle may be months or years, and movements cannot be expected instantly.

2. *Is the ad showing any signs of affecting people's overall attitude to the brand or, in other words, their disposition towards purchasing it?* (Another way to think about this is in terms of their attitudinal commitment or loyalty to it.) The answer can be provided by brand-attitude (or purchase-intention) measurement. It can often be revealing to see how much brand attitudes are changing even though behavior itself may not (yet) have changed. Note, though, that the earlier it is in the campaign the more likely that the evidence from this too may be 'fuzzy' and inconclusive because the effect may (as yet) be only small.[5]

So, especially during the early period, the next level of diagnostic measure comes into play, requiring information from the next two brand-focused measures. When, initially, there is only fuzzy information on changes in the behavior and attitude measures, these next two, somewhat more sensitive, measures provide 'early-warning' indicators as to whether the ad has a *likely* problem.

3. *Is spontaneous (category-cued) brand awareness increasing?* The one thing that is almost always in our minds when we are about to buy something from a particular product category is the name of the product category itself. So the product category (e.g. fruit juice, cars, computers, margarine, beer) is almost always an important retrieval cue that should bring the brand to mind in the purchase situation. When market researchers measure spontaneous brand awareness, they ask people what brands in the product category they can name. Which ones can they easily bring to mind? This is a gauge of the degree to which the product category acts as a retrieval cue in bringing the brand to mind; it indicates how closely the brand is connected to the product category. An increase in spontaneous brand awareness therefore provides an indicator of a strengthening in the connection between the product category (as retrieval cue) and the brand (shown as connection *a* in Figure 28.3).[6]

If spontaneous brand awareness is increasing, the ad is achieving at least that part of its aim. But if it isn't, then it signals the need to explore why the ad seems to be failing to produce this part of its effect.

4. *Is brand image association strengthening?* The brand's association with the key image attribute featured in the advertising (e.g. 'healthy')

should also be showing signs of strengthening. If the image attribute association is strengthening (connection *b* in Figure 28.3) then the ad is doing this part of its job. But if it is not, it signals the need to explore why the ad does not seem to be achieving this part of its intended effect.

Pinpointing where an ad is breaking down

Establishing that either measure 3 (the category-brand association) or measure 4 (the brand-image association) is not strengthening will raise the question *why?* It is in order to explore the 'where and why' of something breaking down that we need the ad-focused measures. The ad-focused measures are diagnostic supplements. As we said, ad recognition, ad recall, message take-out, and ad liking do not substitute for brand-focused measures but complement them. They assist in pinpointing which components of the ad are not performing and which ones are. They also indicate something about the nature of the remedial action/s that might be taken to redress these problems.

For example, suppose we found that the connection (in Figure 28.3) between the retrieval cue—the category (fruit juice)—and the brand (Minute Maid) was not being strengthened. In other words, spontaneous (category-cued) brand awareness was not increasing. Naturally, the advertiser wants to know why. There are two possible reasons.

First, as we saw in Chapter 26, the ad may not be achieving 'mental reach'. It may simply not be capturing attention. Alternatively, the ad may be capturing attention and being seen but it may be weak in communicating the link between the product category (fruit juice) and the brand (Minute Maid), perhaps because people remember the ad but don't remember the

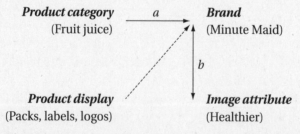

Note: The two key memory connections, and how product display may act as a supplementary retrieval cue.

Figure 28.3: *Associative mental network connections.*

brand. To take remedial action, the advertiser needs to know whether it is the attention-getting characteristics of the ad that need to be changed or the communication content itself. At this point, the ad-focused measures assume center stage and allow us to trace back through the cognitive effects to see exactly where the ad may be falling down.

Episodic memory and knowledge memory

When we store experiences such as ads as events in episodic (autobiographical) memory, we can learn from the experience. A non-advertising example illustrates this nicely. If a fox terrier bites us we remember the episode but we also learn that this cute type of dog can be fierce and to be more cautious of it next time. In other words, the events in our episodic memory feed into our 'knowledge' memory, as represented in Figure 28.4.

The experience may be one of being bitten by a dog, which is a highly emotional knowledge memory. Or it may be an experience with a brand (such as enjoying a cold glass of Minute Maid fruit juice after school—a memory with some but not the same emotion). Or it may be an experience with an ad for that brand (such as seeing the Minute Maid ad in a magazine we read last night—again a memory with perhaps some but not the same emotion).

So there are:

- memory networks that represent *brand experiences,* and
- memory networks that represent *ad experiences,*
  both of which feed into
- 'knowledge memory' networks.

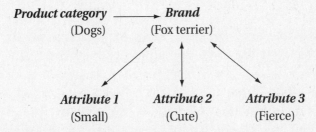

Note: The fox terrier part of the network affected by experience.

Figure 28.4: *Dogs' knowledge memory network.*

Ad experiences and brand experiences also percolate through to affect the strength of the various connections in our 'knowledge memory' network. We don't know *exactly* how these two types of networks interact and affect each other but we do know that activating two items simultaneously in one network affects the other. For example, strengthening the connection between the category (e.g. fruit juice) and the brand (e.g. Minute Maid) in our memory for the ad experience, as represented in Figure 28.3, also strengthens the corresponding connection between the same two items in our 'knowledge memory' (Figure 28.4). The 'activation' primes or strengthens that connection as well as any other closely associated connections.

Armed with our newly acquired perspective on the modern view of memory, we can now resume our examination of how the ad-focused measures perform as diagnostic aids. It is time to examine, one by one, the more common measures that focus on the ad itself and outline the role of each, how it is used, its strengths and weaknesses, and where it fits into the overall diagnostic armory.

Ad recognition

We visited ad recognition in Chapter 26. 'Ad recognition' is the conventional name for this measure but, in line with our modern view of memory, it should really be called 'execution-cued ad awareness' because it is recall that is prompted by the ad execution. Whatever we choose to call it, however, it is measured by showing people the ad execution (or describing the execution)[7] and asking if they recognize having seen it before.

For example, people may be shown the ad for Volkswagen which shows the man's horribly scarred face (Figure 28.1). When asked whether they have seen the ad, and they say 'no', this has a clear implication. Either they have not been exposed to it or, if they have, it has failed to command enough attention to get noticed. As a result it will very likely fail to show any observable effects on behavior, As discussed in Chapter 26, this is a good measure of 'mental reach' and indicates whether the ad is at least being noticed.[8]

It is not a very demanding test but is useful because it provides an indication of the proportion of the audience that has been 'mentally reached' by the ad. The Thorsen and Zhao laboratory research referred to in Chapter 26 indicates that when a TV ad is aired once, we can expect about 60 per cent of the people who have their eyes on the screen to be able later to recognize having seen it before.[9] When people are given multiple 'opportunities to see' an ad, as happens in campaigns of several weeks, tracking results indicate that 70 per cent is the absolute minimum figure this should reach and it should preferably be much more. Note that this is among those who have had an opportunity to see it—this, of course, must be quantified by the cumulative reach media figures for the ad that pertain up to that point (see Chapter 26).

It is in cases where recognition turns out to be low that this measure is especially helpful for diagnosis. If people don't recognize the ad after a few weeks on air (and none of the other measures are moving), the advertiser can be certain there is something very wrong—because recognition is such an 'easy' test. The question is, is there something wrong with the ad or with the media schedule? We can eliminate the possibility of it being a media scheduling problem by checking on the media figures that show what the cumulative reach of the ad has been (the percentage of people who have actually had at least one opportunity to see it). If cumulative reach is okay, then the low recognition figure reveals that this ad is 'wallpaper'—that is, it does not capture enough attention to get noticed.

In reality you will find that low recognition figures and 'wallpaper' ads like this are rare—for TV at least. Most often, 70 to 90 per cent of people who have been exposed to an ad a number of times in a TV campaign do recognize they have seen it—unless there is something very wrong with the ad or they have not actually been exposed to the full length ad because of fast forwarding through the commercials. A high recognition figure shows that the ad is capturing enough attention to get noticed and may give the advertiser warm feelings—but keep it in perspective. It is important to emphasize that this reveals nothing about the *strength* of any mental connections that have been established. This is because ad recognition is, in a sense, an 'easy' test, merely testing that a connection is there. It confirms that the ad execution does have some representation in consumers' memory networks. It has been seen. Establishing this is one thing. Measuring the *strength* of the mental connections within the network is another.

This difference can be demonstrated with old ads—but it applies to new ones as well. As pointed out earlier, those of us who are old enough will recognize that we still have a mental connection between Karl Malden and American Express. We remember that Karl Malden was the presenter for many years of the original American Express 'Don't leave home without it' commercials. That is, we can remember when prompted, so the connection is there in our minds, but ask yourself how many years it is since that memory saw the light of day. How long is it since it was last activated in your mind? In the same way, those of us who remember the famous commercial 'I'd like to buy the world a Coke' rarely, if ever, think of that song or that ad when we encounter Coke today. The connections still exist but they have become so weakened by lack of use they don't work of their own accord. The connections are dormant.

So the recognition measure can tell us that the connections exist but tells us nothing about their current strength or the likelihood that these connections will be activated by everyday events, especially at the point of purchase. The fact is that there are many, many connections in our minds that lie dormant and never influence us because they are never spontaneously reactivated. Even though we may recognize an ad, it reveals nothing about the likelihood that the right connections will be activated in the purchase situation. Ad recognition (execution-cued ad awareness) is therefore a diagnostic measure to check whether the ad has been seen—nothing more. In saying that, let me not take away from the fact that it is a very valuable measure for that purpose and consequently needs to be included.

But, in addition to it, we need to provide diagnostic indicators as to the strengthening of the connections that the ad is attempting to influence.

Spontaneous ad recall (category-cued ad recall)
Suppose, as a consumer, you are asked to describe any ads for 'cars' that you have seen recently. You describe an ad showing a man's horribly scarred face. This provides evidence of a mental connection between the product category and the ad execution in your mind—one that is strong enough to be triggered by the product category as a retrieval cue. This is conventionally known as 'spontaneous ad recall' but, in the modern view of memory, it is more accurate to call it '*category-cued* ad recall' as it is recall prompted by the product category. (Remember that the more appropriate label for recognition is 'execution-cued ad recall' because it is prompted by the ad execution.)

After you have described the ad, you are asked which brand was being advertised and you answer correctly 'Volkswagen'. This is 'ad execution-brand association'. It provides the evidence that the execution is connected to the correct brand in your memory.[10]

When you are asked to recall and describe ads for product categories like this, which ones do you describe? Those which are activated in your memory by the 'spreading' activation moving outwards from the two points in the network that have been activated (i.e. from the product category 'cars') and from a point representing the general notion of advertising.[11] The ads you describe are those that have the strongest memory connections to the product category at that point in time. These will be ads with already high activation (e.g. those exposed very recently) and ads that have established high strength (those that have been exposed more frequently).

When consumers are cued only by the product category and they spontaneously recall an ad along with the correct brand and the correct message, it tells advertisers more about the likely strength of the connections in consumers' memories than if they are merely able to recognize the ad. It requires a stronger connection for us to be able to recall details like this rather than simply being able to recognize the ad.

If, in response to the product-category cue, a respondent can recall and describe the ad execution and also correctly recall the brand, an advertiser can deduce two things. First, the ad has undoubtedly been seen.[12] Second, it is strengthening the interconnections in memory between the product category, the brand, and the execution.

Advertising tracking has demonstrated that increases in category-cued *ad* awareness almost always lead to increases in spontaneous (category-cued) *brand* awareness (unless the memory of the ad is not being linked up with the correct brand).[13] This is because activation spreads out in all directions from the initial point of activation and reinforces or strengthens any other close connections to it. Spontaneous (category-cued) ad recall is therefore a check to see that the ad is doing this part of its job—strengthening the connection between the brand's ad and the product category (the purchase-situation retrieval cue). (We consider some other, supplementary retrieval cues at the end of this chapter.)

Ad-brand association

The strength of the connection between the ad execution and the brand is revealed in the answer to the second part of the questioning procedure outlined above—namely, what brand was being advertised? This measure of correct brand association with the ad is important because it is perfectly possible for us to recall and describe an ad in detail but have it mistakenly connected in our memory with the wrong brand.

When this happens, some other brand (e.g. Volvo) may be benefiting from a brand like Volkswagen's advertising.

This is not an uncommon cause of 'leakage' in the effectiveness of many ads. It means that everything is working except that the advertised brand (in this case Volkswagen) is not being successfully connected to the memory network. Consequently, its association with the product category ('cars') or the attribute ('safety') is therefore not being strengthened. Some other competitive brand (Volvo) may be connecting to the memory network instead and getting the benefit of the advertising.

Failure to connect up the (correct) brand in the memory network is an all too frequent problem. A check on ad-brand association is therefore a crucially important procedure in the total armory of diagnostic checks.

Message take-out

Let's look at the Minute Maid ad again (Figure 27.3) and assume the ad is:

- being seen (as revealed by execution-cued ad awareness); and that
- the connections between the product category and the ad and the brand are all strengthening (as revealed by category-cued ad awareness and correct ad-brand association).

Suppose Minute Maid discovered that its ad did not strengthen the association between the brand and the attribute 'healthier'. We would expect it to strengthen because this is an objective of the ad. What else could be going wrong? We know that the ad-brand association is okay so there is little if any brand 'leakage', so why isn't Minute Maid increasing its association with the attribute 'healthier'?

The problem may lie with the quality, or clarity, of the message and this is where 'message take-out' assumes center stage to determine whether this is the problem. Message take-out is usually measured by asking, 'What was the main message that the ad was trying to communicate to you?' Suppose consumers answer, 'It is healthier because it has calcium and kids ask for it/like it'. This tells us that the message take-out is in line with the objective of the ad, and would effectively eliminate this as the source of the problem. Note how these measures are used as part of a process of elimination to close in on 'causes'. If we had found that people were seeing the ad and associating it with the correct brand but that the message take-out did not conform to what we intended, this would reveal the ad's weak link. But in this case we assume that the message take-out is okay.

If message take-out is okay and the communication is successful, what could possibly be causing the failure of Minute Maid to strengthen its association with the attribute 'healthier'?

Believability

Failure to strengthen the brand's image on the attribute can happen if people have cause to disbelieve the message. For example, what happens if people saw a *Reader's Digest*-type article about calcium that says its health benefits are overrated and that it can cause unwanted health problems in itself? (I am making this up merely to illustrate the point.) These people may still recall the message of the ad but it will be much less likely to translate into a strengthening of the connection between Minute Maid and the attribute 'healthier'.

A direct inconsistency between two ideas is a signal for our minds to stop and examine the ideas and decide which one is correct. The consistency of the message with what is already in our minds is crucially important (see Chapter 5, 'The advertising message: oblique and indirect'). If the ad or its message is inconsistent with what is already in our minds, if there is motivation for our minds not to accept what is being said, then simply remembering the message will not necessarily influence our underlying 'knowledge' network. This is where a measure of believability of the ad is a helpful aid to detect whether this is the problem.

Message recall can be neutralized by our minds actively rejecting the proposition. It is therefore imperative to keep the diagnostic nature of message take-out in clear perspective. Many people have argued over the years, and much evidence has been presented, that recall is unrelated to advertising effectiveness. The fact is that in many cases it *is* related—but recalling the message of an ad does not in itself mean the ad is effective. It is perfectly possible for us to parrot back the message that the ad is trying to communicate even though the strength of the connection between the brand (Minute Maid) and the attribute ('healthier') remains unaffected.

We can now see why so many people have been led to argue that no relationship exists between ad recall and ad effectiveness.[14] To hear and remember something is not necessarily to accept it and build it into our network of underlying 'knowledge'. Message recall is only one component of the process. Cognitive consistency is another.

Message recall is nevertheless a valuable diagnostic tool to have in the advertiser's armory because, when an ad is going wrong, it can help the advertiser to analyze why or how. Like other measures, it may be limited in what it reveals but it can, nevertheless, be particularly revealing at times of where and how the ad is falling down. Specifically, if an ad is not working, message recall can help answer these questions:

- Is it because the ad failed entirely to communicate the message that was intended?
- Or did it communicate the message but was just not accepted? (Ad believability helps to sort this out.) A third possibility also exists:
- Is the attribute (e.g. healthier) relevant?

The message may be successfully communicated and accepted, and strengthen the brand's connection with the attribute. But if the attribute itself is not relevant to the consumer's decision-making processes, then the ad still won't affect behavior. So the degree to which the attribute is relevant is also important.

Attribute importance

Which attribute does the advertiser choose to emphasize? Clearly, different brands put their faith in different attributes. In the beer market, for example, one beer might rely on forging a connection with the attribute of 'reward for a hard-earned thirst' by showing people consuming the brand in a variety of thirst-raising, physical exertion situations. In contrast, another brand may rely on creating connections with 'natural brewed'—a very different attribute. And still another brand may focus on communicating the fact that their beer is 'less filling'.

Like the Minute Maid ad, these try to connect the brand with an attribute that the manufacturer thinks will be important or at least relevant to the consumer's decision-making process. If it is relevant, then the advertising maximizes its chance of being successful. If it is not relevant, then even if the ad successfully breaks through the clutter and communicates the message and the message is accepted, the advertising may still be ineffective in influencing behavior.

If the message is not right, if the attribute is not relevant to the consumer, then effectiveness may be limited or non-existent. To have any effect at all in that situation, the ad will be totally reliant on increasing the salience of the brand in people's minds (i.e. strengthening the connection of the brand with the product category). Just creating greater salience of the brand may not be a big enough feather in itself to tip the beam balance and lead to sales increases for the brand. Much depends on whether the opposition brands that are ranged up against it are seen as otherwise equal (see Chapter 1).

Attribute relevance, or attribute importance, is or at least should be researched up front as part of the 'message engineering' at the time an ad campaign is being developed. The aim is to convey a message that has some relevance to the consumer, or one that has some chance of influencing the choice decision. (The relative importance of attributes may also be tracked by asking people to rank, or rate, how important each attribute is to them in their purchasing of that particular product category.)

Ad liking

In a substantial number of product categories where transformational advertising is the norm, liking the ad is critical to making people feel good about the brand—especially where there is not much else to differentiate it from other brands.[15]

This is the last of the ad-focused measures and simply asks people to what degree they liked or disliked the ad. On the beam balance of choice, if everything else is equal, liking for the brand's advertising can tip the balance. As was made clear earlier, a brand's advertising is similar to its packaging in that it is part of the brand's personality wardrobe. A brand's advertising attire can make a brand more attractive and make the essential difference when everything else is equal. With certain types of products and certain types of advertising (especially web advertising—see Chapter 25), ad liking can be an important diagnostic aid.[16]

Supplements to the category retrieval cue

Before concluding, let me round out the picture by considering the notion of supplementary retrieval cues. The main retrieval cue we have looked at is the product category itself. This is why category-cued brand awareness provides an important diagnostic measure of advertising effect. However, smarter advertisers also build other retrieval cues into their advertising which may need to be considered in the measurement of that advertising's effectiveness.

To illustrate, during the work day or some other extended activity many of us have said, 'Have a break' or 'Give me a break'. If we weren't aware that we were feeling 'snackish' before we said this, we probably would be afterwards. Drinks and snacks are closely connected in the mental network to the notion of taking a break. 'Have a break' or in some countries 'Time for a break' and/or 'Gimme a break' are retrieval cues that not only remind us we might be hungry but, as a result of advertising, also activate a particular brand that became closely connected to the expression. That brand is, of course, Kit Kat. 'Have a break. Have a . . . Kit Kat.' 'Time for a break. Have a . . . Kit Kat.' 'Gimme a break. Have a . . . Kit Kat.'

Another way of thinking about this is to be aware that a brand can tie itself to some connection, some retrieval cue, that helps it break through the mental or visual point-of-sale clutter and pop into mind, especially at the point of sale or point of consumption. The clutter that it has to fight against may be just mental clutter or it may also include the visual clutter that is presented by a product display crowded with brands and assorted variants. The brand wants to 'own' the occasion, or the moment or the feeling.

The advertiser wants the advertised brand to be more strongly connected with something that is likely to be in our mind or in the product display at the time of purchase—something that will remind us of the brand or help it to be noticed for long enough to gain our consideration.

The main retrieval cue is the product category (name) because, almost by definition, this is in our minds when we are about to make a purchase. However, there are other cues—especially those that are likely to be encountered near or at the point of purchase (or sometimes consumption). These supplementary cues can be visual or verbal. The important thing is that something is included in the advertising that is also likely to be encountered at the point of purchase. Signs that tie in with the advertising, or a distinctive logo, pack shape or designer label that are included in (or tie in with) the advertising can all function in this way.

As an example of a visual cue let me cite one very convincing experiment. A brand of breakfast cereal took a single-frame shot from its TV commercial and incorporated it prominently on the pack. This acted as an effective retrieval cue connecting the pack and the brand to what was in people's minds about the ad. It gave it a boost that helped that cereal break through the shelf-display clutter.[17]

Advertisers who have built strong supplementary retrieval cues into their advertising rely correspondingly less on the connection between the product category and the brand to do all the work. The brand can be brought to mind by a trigger from the product category or the supplementary retrieval cue or both. This has implications for measuring the strength of not just one but all of these connections to the brand. In the evaluation of Kit Kat's traditional advertising, for example, monitoring the strength of the association between the expression (e.g. 'Have a break') and Kit Kat was important as well as the association of Kit Kat with the product category itself.

Summary

This and the previous chapter have covered the main measures of ad effectiveness. This coverage is not completely exhaustive. There are other, less used ad measures but the main measures have been covered.

As I said at the outset, advertisers can get understandably confused about measures of ad effect. In the end it is behavior that they want to influence and therefore measures of behavior such as sales and market share are what they want to see moving. However desirable, changes in sales and market share are rarely sensitive enough and rarely *sufficient* in themselves to measure ad effectiveness. To capture advertising's immediate effects, it is necessary to have indicators of cognitive and affective impact as well as behavioral impact. For each strategic point in this attempted influencing process an appropriate measure is needed that can indicate what is happening.

Behavioral measures can't diagnose why an ad works or why it doesn't. Without mental measures, advertisers can develop very little understanding of this buy-ology of mind and the real effects of advertising. These measures provide diagnostic tools that are all-important if advertisers are to translate the knowledge that something worked into a wider learning experience that generalizes to help formulate new effective advertising for the brand. Unless a brand is tracked on a wide range of mental measures it is difficult, if not impossible, to say how and why it worked and to use that knowledge to design better advertising in the future.

29 CONCLUSION

When we die we will have spent an estimated one and a half years just watching ads either on TV or the web. No matter which way you look at it, advertising today takes up a significant chunk of our lives. For that reason if for no other, advertising is an important phenomenon in our society.

As children we wonder about how car engines work, how aircraft fly, or how it is possible to transmit voices invisibly through the air. We also wonder about advertising as we are growing up—but for a quite different reason. Unlike cars and aircraft, ads seem deceptively simple—indeed so blatant and so transparent that it is difficult to understand how they could really persuade anybody. What really puzzles us, then, is why such advertising continues to survive. Is there some secret that advertisers are not telling us? It seems irrefutable that advertising must be doing something to somebody—but what, how and to whom?

This is the traditional view of advertising that has held sway in our society for as long as we can remember. It is a view that has been based on intuition and introspection and which gets fanned from time to time by books alluding to 'the secret' in terms of hidden persuaders or subliminal seductions. This book has tried to present a fuller understanding of the subtleties and complexities of advertising as revealed through the systematic, continuous tracking of advertising campaigns as well as by scientific developments in psychological research into memory and behavior.

This book has tried to demystify advertising by developing an understanding of some of the real psychological mechanisms underlying it. Not all of the mystery is solved because as we have seen, advertising, far from being simple, turns out to be more complex than the traditional view suggests.

To some extent this complexity reflects simplicity in disguise. If you bolt together enough simple things, you get something that appears complex. So the way to begin to understand such seemingly complex things as radios or car engines or advertising is to start breaking them down into their simpler components and functions and looking at them at a micro level before moving up to the macro perspective. Understanding how advertising works on a macro level comes from understanding how all these micro-bits fit and function together.

I readily embraced the opportunity to track the effects of advertising over the years because it provided a window through which I could observe first-hand the effects of one of the childhood 'mysteries'. Looking at advertising through this window has led me to several conclusions:

1. Advertising works on people just like you and me—not just on those 'other more gullible people' out there.
2. The typical world of advertising that we may have envisaged where advertisers always knew exactly what their advertising was doing turned out to be very far from the truth.
3. The reality is that there are still more ads that fail than there are ads that are outstandingly successful. The great majority of ads are at best mediocre in their effect.
4. The fourth realization was that much of the myth and mystique of advertising has come from the 'tribal' ad agencies—many of which know less than they would like us to think, about how or why advertising works. As with medicine men, their powers and methods have seemed all the greater because of the mystery that surrounds them. By imputing witch-doctor-like powers to advertising agencies, books like *The Hidden Persuaders* and *Subliminal Seduction* helped enshrine and perpetuate this mythology.
5. The fifth realization is that persuasion per se is a mechanism that is rarely involved in advertising. If it were, this book probably could have been called *The Not-So-Hidden Persuaders*.
6. Finally, the real mechanisms underlying advertising effects turn out to be more subtle than they are mystical.

This book, in revealing the much more benign nature of these so-called 'unconscious' effects of advertising, has I hope dispelled many of the myths and much of the over-claiming that have been associated with advertising. At the same time, it has tried not to downplay the subtlety of these influences, or the effect they can potentially have on the success or failure of one brand over another *especially when everything else is equal.*

We are still very much in the process of discovering how the new forms of advertising work i.e. advertising on the web, mobile devices, viral advertising, and paid product placement. What we do know is that advertising in the future is likely to look very different to its past.

In fact, the advertiser and the consumer have been closer bedfellows than they knew. Both have been frustrated by not knowing more about the effects of advertising. All too often advertisers have known little more than consumers about how, why or when their advertising was working. This is beginning to change with new tracking and research techniques but again, as our understanding of the mechanisms of advertising grows, so too does greater recognition of its limitations as well as its effects. This knowledge probably lessens rather than heightens the anxieties people may have about advertising having unbridled power.

One message that both consumers and advertisers can take from this book is that just because advertising doesn't seem to be working doesn't necessarily mean it is not working. It takes sensitive measurement to gauge the often small, subtle but cumulative effects. At the same time, any fears that we may have had of being exploited by wholesale subliminal manipulation are way off the mark.

The reality is that advertising has most impact on us in those areas:

- where we are otherwise disinterested in the choice between alternatives;
- where the effects are subtle and we don't feel any effects. (Subtlety is what we need to look out for rather than subliminality. In this regard, I have singled out paid product placement and behavioral targeting as the two new practices that we need to be especially aware of.)

Individual advertisers who have felt for a long time that they don't know enough about what their advertising is doing should be prompted by this book to stiffen their resolve to overcome this. In an era that is now coming to an end where ad agencies enjoyed and exploited their mystique as the wise medicine men, the state of knowledge remained primitive. But increasingly, the better agencies are coming to realize that like modern-day doctors, they must be accountable. Appeals to faith or mysticism only work on people who are in a primitive state of knowledge. Effectiveness today has to be proven and established by observation and careful measurement. Mysticism eventually gives way to scientific reality.

By continuously tracking their advertising over time advertisers are coming to understand much more about what works, what doesn't, and why. Accordingly, they are much better placed to brief their ad agencies. In being better equipped to articulate exactly what they want from their advertising, they are in a position to demand and confidently expect advertising that is successfully directed towards faithful implementation of their communication strategy.

The message of this book to both consumer and advertiser is that it is time to forget the mystique and focus on the real effects. Human beings have the ability to see the same thing in different ways, depending upon the frame of reference that we bring to it. This book represents a frame of reference that it is hoped will allow us to see advertising in a different perspective. For consumers, this perspective should be a more balanced and less fearful one. Understanding advertising and its real effects should make us less suspicious of it. Its power has been much exaggerated but at the same time we should note how advertising is changing and remember that 'the price of freedom is eternal vigilance'. Or as someone else put it: 'When you jump for joy, beware that no one moves the ground from beneath your feet.'[1]

Advertisers, on the other hand, should take the attitude that we now know a lot more about what works, and what doesn't, and why. As a result they can more confidently reject attempts to obscure their inquiries or fob off their concerns about whether their advertising is working. Belief in the exclusive power and province of the tribal medicine man belongs to an era that has passed. Accordingly advertisers should be able to get much more effectiveness out of their advertising budget and out of working with their advertising agency. At the same time consumers should be able to accept, without necessarily feeling threatened, that advertising does influence which brands they choose especially when the choice of brand doesn't matter to them personally.

APPENDIX: HOW TO PROMPT AD AWARENESS

In this appendix I address the ways that ad awareness questions can be asked and clarify some of the confusion that abounds as to exactly what is being measured. It provides an understanding of how different ways of asking the question may result in different figures. It also explains why that occurs and which way/s of asking it are best for your purpose.

Since the second edition of this book, broadband penetration has enabled web interviewing to become mainstream. It is now feasible to play the complete ad on the web and measure recognition by asking respondents if they have seen it before. Yet, time and other interview constraints mean it is usually impractical to assess all the opposition commercials in the product category in the same way. For this reason, there is usually still value in asking respondents to say what commercials they can remember seeing within the product category. This means that there are still a number of alternative forms of asking about ad awareness that use different cues. It is important to understand the differences between these different cues.

What is the cue?

Every ad awareness question has a prompt or what is more technically called a cue. Sometimes people mistakenly use the term *unprompted* ad awareness. There is no such thing! There *always* has to be some kind of prompt in a question in order to tell people what it is you want them to try to remember. It would be absurd to simply ask people do they 'remember'? Remember what?

You have to tell them something about what it is you want them to remember. You have to prompt them with some kind of a retrieval *cue*. So the issue is not whether you use a cue but exactly which cue you use. Should you use:

- the ad execution
- the brand, or
- the category?

The box on this page shows full definitions and illustrative question wordings for each of these.

Questions like the ones shown in the box above are designed to trigger the memory in some way. Like giving an actor a cue from offstage, the cue in the question is designed to act as a starter that jogs the memory. Any ad awareness question has to have some kind of cue built in. The various forms that the question can take, therefore, mostly amount to variations in the type and richness of the cue that is used.

Practicality

For most product categories it is impractical to measure recognition for each ad by playing all the ads in the category, one at a time. Similarly it is usually impractical to describe the ad execution for *every* ad and *every* brand. There can be dozens of brands and an impossible multitude of ads. Consider the huge number of brands and ads in categories like financial services, fast food or computers for example. If you tried to do this, it would fill up the whole questionnaire, overly tax the respondents and leave no room in the questionnaire for the many other important things you need to cover.

For the purpose of measuring awareness of *your own* ad/s as an indicator of their mental reach, execution-cued ad awareness is a highly valuable measure and is most appropriate for this purpose (see Chapter 26, 'Mental reach').

While it is important if you can do it, to be able to compare your ad's performance with competitors' ads, it is rarely practicable to do this for mental reach. 'Execution-cued ad awareness' (recognition) is rarely practical for competitive comparison for the reason outlined above—even though it definitely should be used to indicate the mental reach of your own ads.

The other two forms of cueing are by category or by brand. As discussed in Chapter 27 ('Measurement of advertising effects in memory'), these also give some idea of the strength of associative connection. However as we shall see, only one of these two lends itself to complete coverage of all ads and all brands in the market.

Brand vs category cueing

For comparative purposes then, which question is best to use—the one with the category cue or the one that uses the brand cue?

The controversial alternatives

1. **Category cued:** Describe for me any advertising you have seen for *credit cards* on TV recently.
2. **Brand cued:** Have you seen any advertising for Diners Club on TV recently?

One prominent company has always favored brand cueing and has long been critical of category cueing.[1] Others take strong issue with their unsupported assertions on this, pointing out that their claims are not based on empirical evidence.[2] Let us look a little more closely at the two.

When the two are compared, you will find that the brand-cued advertising awareness figure is usually *higher* than if the question is category-cued. In other words more people claim awareness when the question is cued by the brand. This is apparent in the case examples in Figure A.1 and Figure A.2. In case 1, the brand-cued ad awareness figure

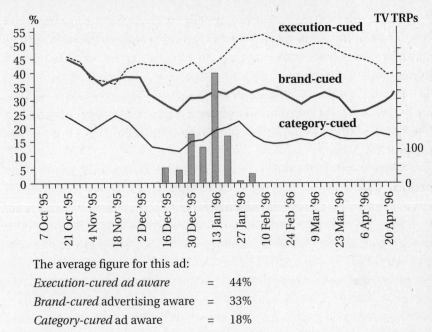

The average figure for this ad:

Execution-cured ad aware = 44%

Brand-cured advertising aware = 33%

Category-cured ad aware = 18%

Figure A.1: *Case 1—category vs brand-cued advertising recall. (Source: MarketMind)*

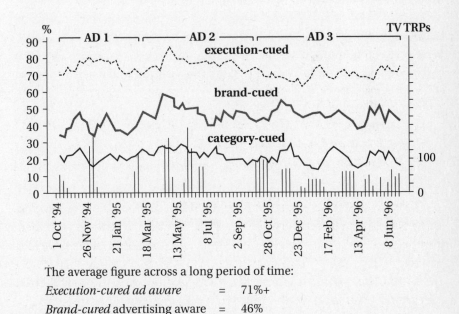

The average figure across a long period of time:

Execution-cured ad aware = 71%+

Brand-cured advertising aware = 46%

Category-cured ad aware = 22%

Figure A.2: *Case 2—category vs brand-cued advertising recall. (Source: MarketMind)*

averages 33 per cent compared to category-cued of 18 per cent. In case 2, brand-cued is 46 per cent and category-cued 22 per cent. Such differences are reasonably typical.

So, why is brand-cued generally higher? Is it just that brand cueing focuses the memory on a more specific question that people find it easier to wrap their minds around (i.e. 'Have you seen any advertising for Diners Club on TV recently?')? Or is there more to it than that?

The nature of the output

There is indeed more to it than that. Note that there is a difference in *expected output* from the two types of questions.

Category cueing ('Please describe any advertising you have seen for charge cards on TV recently') expects people to recall and describe what happened in the ad. Compare this with brand cueing where you provide the advertiser's name (or pack or logo) and ask 'Have you seen any advertising for Diners Club on TV recently?' As Staplehurst has noted, 'A simple yes/no is recorded for each brand, hence this measure is also known as claimed TV ad awareness, as the respondent does not have to prove or describe an execution.'[3]

Now, think about this for a moment. If the respondent 'does not have to prove or describe an execution', what does it mean, if for example 46 per cent of people say 'yes' to the question 'Have you seen any advertising for Diners Club on TV recently?' What does the figure tell you about the current Diners Club ad?

Ad awareness

Not until respondents are asked a follow-up question like '*Describe the ad* (you have seen recently for Diners Club)' can you begin to uncover how this claimed, (brand-cued) 'advertising awareness' is made up. When you do this do you find that it will invariably reveal those claimed advertising recalls are made up of not one thing but at least *four* things. As shown in the box on p.329 this includes false recalls, old ads and ads where they can only remember the brand. Typically if you have, say, 46 per cent level of (brand-cued) advertising awareness then maybe half or less are valid recalls of the current (Diners 'frequent flyer points') ad.

The four components outlined in the box should make it crystal clear that when you are using the brand cueing type question, then only if you also ask the follow-up question and ask people to 'describe

Asking people to describe the ad they claim to have seen for the brand will reveal that claimed advertising recalls are made up of at least four things:

1. *Current ad*: Valid recalls of the current ad (e.g. 'I remember the ad that said Diners earns you 1.5 frequent flyer points for every dollar spent').
2. *Past ads*: Recalls of past ads (for Diners Club) that are mistakenly remembered as being on air recently.
3. *False recalls*:
   a) Brand 'slippage': These are recalls or descriptions of competitor's ads (like American Express, MasterCard or Citibank) mistakenly recalled as being ads for Diners Club (e.g. 'I remember the ad where Kate Winslet tells us that Diners Club is part of her life').
   b) Category 'slippage': These are recalls of advertising from some other product category that are mistakenly recalled here e.g. an ad for an airline (like American Airlines Mileage Miles) might be mistakenly recalled.
4. *'Don't knows'*: 'I can't describe the ad but I know it was for Diners Club.' (But is this correct? And if it is, is it a past ad or the current ad? There is no way of knowing.)

the ad' can you quantify the level of ad awareness of the current ad. When you do this and use the information to subtract from the claimed awareness those that are not valid recalls of the current ad, it lowers the result. The result is likely to be much more like the figure that you would have obtained from category cueing the question instead of brand cueing it. That is because after these extraneous items are subtracted it then represents a measure of *ad* awareness. Before that it is a figure for claimed *advertising* awareness and this is naturally higher because it has all this other extraneous material in it.

Ad awareness vs *advertising* awareness

Too often people use the terms '*ad* awareness' and '*advertising* awareness' interchangeably.[4] If 46 per cent of people claim to have the perception or belief that they have seen a Diners Club ad recently, this is *advertising* awareness. It simply means that the brand has an image, among 46 per cent of people, of having been advertised recently. Advertising awareness is an image in the person's mind. It is not *ad* awareness. It is not a measure of awareness of any specific ad or campaign.

Ad awareness and advertising awareness are not the same. One is an image dimension of the brand. The other is the level of ad recall for a specific ad (or campaign). One quantifies the brand's perceived advertising presence. The other helps you diagnose how people are processing the *current ad* (inferred from the questions on content, message, branding, etc; see Chapter 27, 'Measurement of advertising effects in memory').

The bottom line

The bottom line is: if you want to use ad awareness as a measure—if you want to use it to help diagnose what's working and what's not in your current ad (or campaign)—then you have to ask people to describe the ad anyway, whether you ask them to do this using a question that is:

- category-cued: 'Describe for me any ads you have seen recently on TV for charge cards' or
- brand-cued: 'Have you seen any advertising for Diners Club on TV recently?' and making sure that it is followed by 'IF YES, describe the ad you saw'.

Debating which *way* you ask this (category-cued or brand-cued?) is something of a red herring. It is not as material as making sure that you *do* ask it and therefore making sure you get a measure of *ad* awareness, not just an image measure of *advertising* awareness.

So this is a key reason why brand-cued *advertising* awareness figures almost always *appear to be* higher than category-cued ad awareness. It has all this extraneous material in it.

Evaluating ads

Let me emphasize yet again that in evaluating ads, awareness is a *diagnostic* measure. Ads should not be judged on whether they can get high ad awareness but on their ability to change behavior and attitudes (see earlier chapters). It is therefore important to always keep in mind exactly what the diagnostic objective is of including ad awareness in the measures.

It is a perfectly valid objective to quantify the brand's perceived advertising presence (see Chapter 4, 'Conformity: the popular thing to do'). For this specific purpose, brand-cued advertising awareness does the job well, although it would be more helpful if it were called 'perceived advertising presence' instead. This is because it is roughly equivalent to asking in an image bank a question like this: As I read out each brand please tell me for each brand if you think it is:

- recently advertised on TV   yes/no
- good value for money   yes/no
- often on promotion   yes/no
- etc.

But for the objective of evaluating the *ad* itself and diagnosing why it is or is not working, you cannot escape asking people to describe the ad and what message they took out of it, etc, whether you begin with category cueing or brand cueing.

Three measures move together?

At the risk of too broad a generalization, it is my experience that all three measures of ad awareness (category-cued, brand-cued and execution-cued) tend to *move* in a similar way, more often than not. Figures A.1 and A.2 on p. 327 illustrate this and show how they tend to move together.

But note that there is a major difference in their *absolute* values (as discussed earlier).

While more often than not they tend to move together, it would be unfortunate if any reader took out of this that they *always* do, or that they *necessarily* do. They *don't* and there are very good reasons.

Let's look closely at the three measures in turn.

Recognition

Why is the figure highest when this type of cuing is used? It is because it is a richer cue than the other two.

It is a well established principle in psychology that memory is most effectively triggered if the cues at time of retrieval are identical to those at the time of exposure.[5] What this means is that in an ideal world we would show the video of the ad and ask if they recognize it and have seen it recently.

As we have pointed out, in the real world of survey research cueing memory by the ad itself in this way can only be done using web interviewing. If it is impractical to play the actual ad, the alternative is to trigger the memory with some surrogate, some substitute cue. The more this cue approximates the full ad itself, the more likely that it will effectively trigger the person's memory.

Showing photo-stills from the ad execution or describing the ad verbally is the next best thing to playing the ad. While rarely practical for use with *all* brands and *all* ads in a market, execution-cued ad awareness is valuable to use for your own ad/s. There are some important things to note about exactly how this is measured.

Execution-cued ad recall

For *web interviewing*, the best method is to show the full video of the ad and ask the respondent if they have seen it before. This is ad recognition.

If time or other constraints prevent this then the fallback position is to show photo-stills from the ad *which should always have some of the words from the audio track underneath*. Let me repeat: you *must* provide cues taken from the 'audio' track as well as cues taken from the video. It is amazing how often this is overlooked and yet it makes a huge difference to the level of recall.

When you show photo-stills or describe the ad, strictly speaking this should not be referred to as recognition. Even though the person is being asked if they recognize having seen the ad previously, it is not the full ad that they are being exposed to but a surrogate—some representation of it. So to avoid the possible confusion it is better to refer to this as execution-cued ad awareness (though admittedly it does not trip off the tongue so easily).[6]

For *telephone interviewing*, execution-cued ad awareness usually goes something like this: 'Have you seen an ad telling you about a brand of charge card where you receive 1.5 frequent flyer points for every dollar spend on the card?'

For most ads the ad execution may be described to the respondent in words. Clearly, however, there are some executions—some ads—that are so complex they defy verbal description. In which case, the best way around it is to use web interviewing.

Execution-cued is usually highest

Note in the graphs that executional-cued ad awareness produces the highest ad awareness figure of all three measures of ad awareness.[7] This is not surprising since this usually provides the richest set of cues. If the objective is to find out what percentage of the target population has been mentally reached by the ad, then this is the best measure of the three to use. It gives the best estimate. (As discussed earlier it is mainly the practicalities that get in the road of using it for brands other than your own brand.)

What this measure, execution-cued ad awareness, does is to establish if there is *any evidence* that the person has been *mentally exposed* to the ad, irrespective of whether the person can spontaneously retrieve it or what details they remember and irrespective of whether they paid it scant or a lot of attention. It addresses the question: in what percentage of the target market does the ad appear to have any 'mental reach'?

Problem with the media or the ad?

As discussed in Chapter 26, this percentage figure needs to be compared against the percentage of people who have had the 'opportunity to see' the ad according to the cumulative reach in the media schedule.

This cumulative reach figure from the media schedule for the client's ad sets the ceiling that you can expect for recognition or execution-cued ad awareness. The degree to which ad recognition falls short of it quantifies something meaningful.

Large gaps between the level of ad recognition and the cumulative reach indicate either:

- *A media schedule problem.* People without an 'opportunity to see' the ad; or
- *An ad problem.* People who had an 'opportunity to see' it, but who failed to notice it—at least enough to recognize it again.[8] Advertising that people have been exposed to but don't recognize having seen is usually like advertising that they have never actually been exposed to.

As part of the diagnostic process of elimination you have to rule out the possibility that the media schedule is the problem *before* you can start concluding that the ad is a problem. The ad recognition measure is immensely valuable for this for your own ad/s.

When an ad doesn't track well on this measure (i.e. there is a large gap between it and the cumulative reach), my experience is that it most often identifies a problem with the media schedule i.e. that it is not delivering on its cumulative reach objective. It is much rarer that it turns out to be a problem with the ad itself—i.e. the ad being just 'wallpaper' and just not getting noticed—especially after multiple exposures.

Include the ad recognition measure before the ad goes to air

The ad recognition measure must go into research before the ad goes to air, for two reasons:

1. Sometimes when a new ad is very similar to other ads in the category, people can indicate they recognize having seen it even before it goes on air.[9] This problem of 'generic content' is an important reason why *the recognition question should be put into the tracking before the ad goes to air* so that the degree of false claiming can be quantified. When false claiming like this does happen, it almost certainly indicates that the ad is *not* going to be successful (except in promoting the category itself).[10]

2. There is one other circumstance where false claiming can occur. That is when the ad is a sequel or it contains elements similar to the brand's previous advertising—such as using the same presenter, character, verbal expression, scenes, etc—as were included in some previous ad for that brand. This type of continuity can be a positive so some small degree of false claiming in this situation is tolerable and not necessarily negative. But it should not be large and again *it needs to be quantified by incorporating the question in the tracking before the ad goes to air.*

Brand cueing

This suffers from a similar limitation to execution-cued ad awareness. As we saw with execution-cued ad awareness it is mostly not possible to get complete coverage of all ads for all brands in the market. There are just too many and this makes it impractical. The same applies although to a slightly lesser extent with *brand cueing*.

This limitation of rarely being able to get full coverage is reasonably apparent when you think about it but it is rarely drawn to advertisers' attention. To use brand cueing, there is a need to specifically ask about each brand. This means a separate question for every brand. *Have you seen any TV advertising for brand X recently?* This can mean a lot of questions.

The situation is even worse because it means in fact that two or three questions must be asked for each brand, not just one, because there is the need to follow up each one by asking people:

- Describe the ad;
- What message was it trying to communicate?

So unless yours is a market with a very limited number of brands it will be impossible to ask about every brand in the market if you use brand cueing. If you use brand cueing you will have no choice but to use a *subset* of brands, which means yet again the tracking compromises on getting coverage of the full competitive ad spectrum. (Category cueing does not suffer from this problem and therefore usually represents a more attractive alternative.)

Ads for new brands and new variants

It is also important to note that with brand cueing, if a new competitor enters the market you will miss out on its advertising because any new brand or new variant will not be specifically included in the list of brands that the interviewer has to ask about each week. You only become aware of this omission after the new advertising has been launched. And then you have to decide if the brand is going to be important enough to warrant putting it into the questionnaire. This is a difficult decision because if the new brand is going to have substantial impact then the answer is yes. If it is not, then the answer is no. But predicting this is exactly why you want to capture the ad awareness in the first place. You want it to act as an early warning system to indicate to you how much impact its advertising is likely to have.

With category cueing on the other hand, if the new brand's advertising is salient enough, it will be recalled and will be automatically picked up by the category-cued question—without any need to manually intervene and change the questionnaire. So category cueing as well as offering full brand coverage also has the advantage of this automatic capture of new brand advertising by the questionnaire.

Category cueing

It should be apparent that in most cases, using category cueing is about the *only* practical way to get coverage of the full competitive spectrum in the ad awareness question. Hence it is generally the recommended choice for that reason as well as the automatic capture of new brand advertising.

There are however some limitations of category cueing that you need to watch out for. One difficulty for category cueing is that the definition of the category may sometimes be contentious. There can be contention as to whether the category is best described one way or some other way. (For example in our earlier example for Diners Club, would it be better to describe the category as 'charge cards' or 'credit cards'? This is a fairly trivial example but it helps to make the point.)

Some categories are easier to define than others. Ones like banks, shampoo, cookies are fairly clear cut. Others are not—sometimes because they are at a higher level of aggregation and sometimes because they are not well formed as categories in people's minds. For example, consider the following:

- financial services
- hair treatment products
- snacks.

What exactly does each of these mean? 'Categories' like financial services, hair treatment products, snacks, etc are at a much higher level of aggregation than banks, shampoo, and cookies and are consequently less well formed as categories in people's minds. It is not entirely clear exactly what falls into that category. For example, is an ice cream a snack? Is an insurance company a financial service? Is a hair dryer a hair treatment product?

When categories are specified like this at a higher level of aggregation, it is more difficult to define the category and on some occasions it may be impossible. Fortunately this tends to be more the exception than the rule. But there are times when category cueing will have its limitations. In particular it will have problems with ill formed categories and it possibly misses out on some low salience ads, but on balance the positives of category cueing more often outweigh the negatives.

The positives of category cueing can be summarised as follows:

- It allows complete coverage of the ads for all brands—not just a subset of brands.
- It does not miss out on ads for new brands or variants that inevitably come on the market.
- It is clearly the easiest to manage from a questionnaire point of view and avoids the problem of the questionnaire being made out of date by new product/variant entries.

Recommendations

1. Where the category is relatively well defined (e.g. banks, shampoo, cookies) there is therefore strong argument to use category cueing rather than brand cueing. This measures the strength of connection of the brand to the product category (see Chapters 27 and 28).

2. With categories that are less well defined (e.g. financial services, hair care and hair treatment products,) where you don't feel completely comfortable with category cueing and especially if there are only a small number of brands, then brand cueing may be preferable to use in that minority of cases. *But be sure to include the follow-up question asking people to describe the ads they claim to have seen so that you can come up with a measure of ad awareness and not just an image measure of advertising awareness.*

3. In addition, it is important to include a measure of execution-cued ad awareness for your own ad/s in order to be able to quantify the absolute level of 'mental reach'. It tells you nothing about the strength of any connections but will tell you if your ad is not capturing enough attention and how many people it has 'mentally reached' (see Chapter 26).

NOTES

About the author

1   NFO acquired MarketMind in 1998. The brand was later sold to Interpublic and eventually acquired by (and folded into) Taylor Nelson Sofres.

Part A   Introduction

1   David Ogilvy, *Confessions of an Advertising Man*, Atheneum, NY, 1963 and 1984, p. 96.

2   Variously attributed to John Wanamaker in the USA and to Lord Lever-Hulme in the UK.

3   John Philip Jones, *When Ads Work: New Proof that Advertising Triggers Sales*, Lexington, NY, 1995, p. 28.

4   William Lutz, *Doublespeak*, Harper Perennial, NY, 1990, p. 74.

5   Vance Packard, *The Hidden Persuaders*, Mackay, NY, 1957.

6   Alec Benn, *The 27 Most Common Mistakes in Advertising*, Amacom, NY, 1978, p. 5.

7   As Kover has pointed out: 'Copywriters have a "reputation" in the folklore of the advertising business. They are charged with defending their work and its integrity against any change, no matter how small. They do this against account management, against their own creative department managers, and often in opposition to research findings and the urging of clients.' Arthur Kover, 'Copyrighters' implicit theories of communication: an exploration', *Journal of Consumer Research*, Vol. 21, March 1995, p. 604.

8   Jones 1995, op. cit., p. 27.

9   John Rossiter & Larry Perty, *Advertising and Promotions Management*, McGraw-Hill, NY, 1987, p. 558.

Chapter 1   Influencing people

1   Referring to this effect as a 'feather' is not meant to deprecate its importance. On the contrary, it is meant to give consumers an intuitive *feel* for why we often find it difficult to introspect on how advertising affects us. We don't feel the effect because it is below the JND (just noticeable difference), but that doesn't mean that feathers aren't important or effective. They are! If an ad has real news to convey, it can become a very big feather, in which case we don't need an explanation of the effect. Mostly, however, they are much smaller feathers.

2   William E. Baker, 'When can affective conditioning and mere exposure directly influence brand choice?', *Journal of Advertising*, Vol. 28, No. 4, winter 1999, pp. 31–46.

3   John Deighton, 'The interaction of advertising and evidence', *Journal of Consumer Research*, Vol. 11, No. 3, December 1984, pp. 763–70.

4   Scott Hawkins & Stephen Hoch, 'Low involvement learning: Memory without evaluation', *Journal of Consumer Research*, Vol. 19, September 1992, pp. 212–25. Scott Hawkins, Joan Meyers-Levy & Stephen Hoch, 'Low involvement learning: Repetition and coherence in familiarity and belief', *Advances in Consumer Research*, VXXII, 1995, p. 63.

5   Especially when the repetition comes from various sources such as different publications—even for low plausability claims—see A.L. Roggeveen & G.V. Johar, 'Perceived source variability versus familiarity: Testing competing explanations for the truth effect', *Journal of Consumer Research*, Vol. 12, No. 2, 2002, pp. 81–91.

6   Even though it may be perceptibly small, a single reinforcement/reminder exposure can have substantial effects on short-term sales and market share for well established brands with established ad campaigns. See the pioneering work by John Philip Jones, *When Ads Work: New proof that advertising triggers sales*, Lexington, NY, 1995 and Colin McDonald, 'From "Frequency" to "Continuity"—is it a new dawn?', *Journal of Advertising Research*, Vol. 39, No. 5, July/August 1997, pp. 21–5.

7   M. Von Gonten & J. Donius, 'Advertising exposure and advertising effects: New panel based findings', *Journal of Advertising Research*, Vol. 37, No. 4, July/August 1997, p. 59.

8   In this section I am heavily indebted to Charles Fishman's excellent account that appeared in C. Fishman, 'Message in a bottle', *FastCompany.com.*, July–August 2007.

9   C. Fishman, 'Message in a bottle', *FastCompany.com.*, July–August 2007.

10   ibid.

11   S. Shapiro, D. Macinnis & S. Heckler, 'The effects of incidental ad exposure on the formation of consideration sets', *Journal of Consumer Research*, Vol. 24, No. 1, June 1997, pp. 94–101.

12   M. Sutherland & J. Galloway, 'The implications of agenda setting for advertising research', *Journal of Advertising Research*, Vol. 21, No. 5, 1981, pp. 25–9.

13   Food Marketing Institute as reported in *Businessweek*, 7 January 1996.

14   Andrew Ehrenberg, Neil Barnard & John Scriven, 'Differentiation or salience, *Journal of Advertising Research*, Vol. 37, No. 6, November/December 1997, pp. 7–14.

15   J.A. Bargh, 'Losing consciousness: Automatic influences on consumer judgment, behavior, and motivation', *Journal of Consumer Research*, Vol. 29, No. 2, September 2002, pp. 280–5.

16   M. Sutherland & S. Holden, 'Slipstream marketing', *Journal of Brand Management*, June 1997.

17 R. Fazio, P. Herr & M. Powell, 'On the development and strength of category-brand associations in memory: The case of mystery ads', *Journal of Consumer Psychology*, 1992, Vol. I (1), pp. 1–13.

18 P. Nedungadi, 'Part list cuing effect', ACR Conference 1991. A POS prime will inhibit the recall of other brands. It especially inhibits the elicitation of subcategories and most of the inhibition effect on other brands comes from this.

19 P. Dickson & A. Sawyer, 'The price knowledge and search of supermarket shoppers', *Journal of Marketing*, July 1990, pp. 42–53.

20 W. Wells & L. Losciuto, 'Direct observation of purchasing behaviour', *Journal of Marketing Research*, August 1966, p. 227. M. Sutherland & T. Davies, 'Supermarket shopping behavior: An observational study', Caulfield Institute of Technology Psychology and Marketing Series, No. 1, August 1978.

21 P. Winkielman, N. Schwarz, R. Reber & T.A. Fazendeiro, 'Affective and cognitive consequences of visual fluency: When seeing is easy on the mind', in *Visual Persuasion* (ed. R. Batra), Ann-Arbor, Michigan, 2000.

22 Guisberti et al. 1992 as reported in C. Cornaldi et al., *Stretching the Imagination: Representation and transformation in mental imagery*, Oxford University Press, NY, 1966.

Chapter 2   Image and reality

1 Duck/rabbit figure as used in various psychology experiments.

2 I.P. Levin & G.J. Gaeth, 'How consumers are affected by the frame of attribute information before and after consuming the product', *Journal of Consumer Research*, Vol. 15, No. 3, 1988, pp. 374–8.

3 Richard Elliott & Larry Percy, *Strategic Brand Management*, Oxford University Press, London, 2007, p. 13.

4 G. Hughes, *Words in Time*, Blackwell, Cambridge, 1988, p. 174.

5 People for the Ethical Treatment of Animals, www.peta.org.

6 Scott MacKenzie, 'The role of attention in mediating the effect of advertising on attribute importance', *Journal of Consumer Research*, Vol. 13, No. 2, September 1986, p. 174. Meryl P. Gardener, 'Advertising effects on attribute recalled and criteria used for brand evaluations', *Journal of Consumer Research*, Vol. 10, No. 3, December 1983, pp. 310–18.

7 The Greenland Saga, as reported in Hughes, *Words in Time*, p. 155.

8 Stephen Fox, *The Mirror Makers: A history of American advertising and its creators*, William Morrow, NY, 1984, p. 16.

Chapter 3   Subliminal advertising

1 Andrew Ehrenberg, 'Repetitive advertising and the consumer', *Journal of Advertising Research*, Vol. 40, No. 6, 2000, pp. 39–48.

2 View it at www.sutherlandsurvey.com/Column_pages/subliminal_advertising.html.

3   A. Pratkanis & E. Aronson, *Age of Propaganda*, W.H. Freeman, NY, 1991, p. 201.

4   W. Weir, 'Another look at subliminal "facts" ', *Advertising Age*, 15 October 1984, p. 46.

5   Pratkanis & Aronson, op. cit., p. 203.

6   Wilson Bryan Key, *Subliminal Seduction*, Signet, NY, 1972.

7   Roy Greenslade, *Maxwell's Fall*, Simon & Schuster, London, 1992, p. 99.

8   John R. Anderson, *Cognitive Psychology and Its Implications*, Freeman, NY, 1990, pp. 183–8.

9   D.L Strayer & F.A. Drews, 'Cell-Phone-Induced Driver Distraction', *Current Directions in Psychological Science*, Vol. 16, No. 3, 2007, pp. 128–35.

10   Giep Franzen, *Advertising Effectiveness: Findings from empirical research*, NTC Publications, Oxfordshire, 1994, p. 45.

11   G.V. Johar, D. Maheswaran, et al., 'MAPping the frontiers: Theoretical advances in consumer research on memory, affect, and persuasion', *Journal of Consumer Research*, Vol. 33, No. 1, 2006, pp. 139–49. A.B. Aylesworth, R.C. Goodstein, et al., 'Effect of archetypical embeds on feelings', *Journal of Advertising*, Vol. 28, No. 3, 1999, pp. 73–81. A. Dijksterhuis, P.K. Smith, et al., 'The unconscious consumer: Effects of environment on consumer behavior', *Journal of Consumer Psychology*, Vol. 15, No. 35, 2005, p. 200.

12   J.A. Bargh, 'Losing consciousness: Automatic influences on consumer judgment, behavior, and motivation', *Journal of Consumer Research*, Vol. 29, No. 2, 2002, pp. 280–5.

13   G.V. Johar, D. Maheswaran, et al., *Journal of Consumer Research*, loc. cit.

14   HBS case: 9–392–032, 'The Body Shop International', Harvard Business School, Cambridge, MA, 1991, p. 2.

15   Alan Hirsch, 'Nostalgia: A neuropyschiatric understanding', Association for Consumer Research Annual Conference, October 1991.

16   S.L. Coates, L.T. Butler, et al., 'Implicit memory: A prime example for brand consideration and choice', *Applied Cognitive Psychology*, Vol. 18, No. 9, 2004, pp. 1195–211.

17   P. Nedungadi, 'Recall and consumer consideration sets: Influencing choice without altering brand evaluations', *Journal of Consumer Research*, Vol. 17, December 1990, pp. 263–76.

18   Gerald Gorn, 'The effects of music in advertising on choice behavior: A classical conditioning approach', *Journal of Marketing*, Vol. 46, Winter 1982, pp. 94–101. William J. Ruth, H.S. Mosatche & A. Kramer, 'Theoretical considerations and an empirical test in advertising', *Psychological Reports*, Vol. 60, No. 2, 1989, pp. 1131–9. James Keflaris & Anthony Cox, 'The effects of background music in advertising: A reassessment', *Journal of Consumer Research*, Vol. 16, No. 1, June 1989, pp. 113–18.

19   W.E. Baker, 'When can affective conditioning and mere exposure directly

influence brand choice?', *Journal of Advertising*, Vol. 28, No. 4, 1999, pp. 31–46.

20   M.A. Olson & R.H. Fazio, 'Implicit acquisition and manifestation of classically conditioned attitudes', *Social Cognition*, Vol. 20, 2002, pp. 89–103.

21   W. Moran, 'Brand presence and the perceptual time frame', *Journal of Advertising Research*, Vol. 30, No. 5, October/November 1990, pp. 9–16.

22   B. Gawronski, E.P. LeBel, et al.,'What do implicit measures tell us? Scrutinizing the validity of three assumptions', *Perspectives on Psychological Science*, Vol. 2, No. 2, 2007, pp. 181–93. S.M.J. van Osselaer & C. Janiszewski, 'Two ways of learning brand associations', *Journal of Consumer Research*, Vol. 28, No. 2, September 2001, pp. 202–23.

Chapter 4   Conformity

1   Lee Iacocca, *Iacocca: An autobiography*, Bantam, NY, 1984, p. 286.

2   D. Altheide & J. Johnson, 'Counting souls: A study of counselling at evangelical crusades', *Pacific Sociological Review*, Vol. 20, No. 3, 1977, pp. 323–48.

3   Robert Cialdini, *Influence: The new psychology of modern persuasion*, Quill, NY, 1984, p. 118.

4   L. Urdang et al., *Every Bite a Delight And Other Slogans*, Visible Ink Press, Detroit, MI, 1992, p. 50.

5   Merely hearing a new, hypothetical brand name is sufficient to increase the probability of that same name being mistakenly judged as an established, known brand 24 hours later. See S. Holden & M. Vanhuele, 'Out of mind influence: Incidental and implicit effects on memory', Association for Consumer Research Annual Conference, 1996, Tucson, AZ. And as referred to in a summary prepared by M.T. Pham, 'Really-low involvement consumer learning', *Advances in Consumer Research*, Vol. 24, 1997, pp. 121–2, Provo, UT: ACR.

6   L.L. Jacoby, C. Kelley, J. Brown & J. Jasechko, 'Becoming famous overnight: Limits on the ability to avoid unconscious influences of the past', *Journal of Personality and Social Psychology*, Vol. 56, No. 3, 1989, pp. 326–38.

7   Unpublished survey conducted by Caulfield Institute of Technology students, Melbourne, 1978.

8   W. Moran, *Journal of Advertising Research*, loc. cit.

9   S. Shapiro, D. Macinnis & S. Heckler, *Journal of Consumer Research*, loc. cit.

10   S. Shapiro, 'When an ad's influence is beyond our conscious control: Perceptual and conceptual fluency effects caused by incidental ad exposure', *Journal of Consumer Research*, Vol. 26, No. 1, June 1999, pp. 16–36.

11   A.Y. Lee & A.A. Labroo, 'The effect of conceptual and perceptual fluency on brand evaluation', *Journal of Marketing Research*, Vol. 41, No. 2, May 2004, pp. 151–65. G.V. Johar, D. Maheswaran, et al., *Journal of Consumer Research*, loc. cit.

12 P. Winkielman, J. Halberstadt, et al., 'Prototypes are attractive because they are easy on the mind', *Psychological Science*, Vol. 17, No. 9, 2006, pp. 799–806.

13 Amos Tversky & Daniel Kahneman, 'Availability: A heuristic for judging frequency and probability', *Cognitive Psychology*, Vol. 5, 1973, pp. 207–32.

14 X. Fang, S. Singh, et al., 'An examination of different explanations for the mere exposure effect', *Journal of Consumer Research*, Vol. 34, No. 1, June 2007, pp. 97–103.

15 Nigel Hollis, 'They said my brand was popular—So what?', Proceedings of the Advertising Research Foundation 1996 Advertising and Brand Tracking Workshop, pp. 105–22.

16 A. Rindfleish & J. Inman, 'Explaining the familiarity-liking relationship: Mere exposure, information availability, or social desirability?', *Marketing Letters*, Vol. 9, No. 1, 1998, pp. 5–19.

17 Irving Rein, Philip Kotler & Martin Stofier, *High Visibility*, Dodd, Mead, NY, 1987.

Chapter 5   The advertising message

1 Herbert Krugman, 'The impact of television advertising: Learning without involvement', *Public Opinion Quarterly*, Vol. 29, 1965, pp. 349–56.

2 Daniel L. Schacter, *Searching for Memory*, Basic Books, NY, 1996, pp. 161–91.

3 L. Postman & R. Garrett, 'An experimental analysis of learning without awareness', *American Journal of Psychology*, Vol. 65, 1952, pp. 244–55.
E. Philbrick & L. Postman, 'A further analysis of learning without awareness', *American Journal of Psychology*, Vol. 68, 1955, pp. 417–24. F. Di Vesta & K. Brake, 'The effects of instructional "sets" on learning and transfer', *American Journal of Psychology*, Vol. 72, 1959, pp. 57–67.
B.D. Cohen et al., 'Experimental bases of verbal behavior', *Journal of Experimental Psychology*, Vol. 47, 1954, pp. 106–10.

4 D.W. Zaidel, 'Different organization of concepts and meaning systems in the two cerebral hemispheres', *The Psychology of Learning and Motivation*, Vol. 40, 2000, pp. 1–21.

5 M. Sutherland, 'False alarm theory: How humourous ads work', at www.adandmind.com, August 2005.

6 M. Lieberman, R. Guant, et. al., 'Reflection and reflexion: A social cognitive neuroscience approach to attibutional inference', *Advances in Experimental Social Psychology*, Vol. 34, 2002, pp. 199–249.

7 B. Gawronski, E.P. LeBel, et al., 'What do implicit measures tell us? Scrutinizing the validity of three assumptions', *Perspectives on Psychological Science*, Vol. 2. No. 2, 2007, pp. 181–93. Leon Festinger, *A Theory of Cognitive Dissonance*, Stanford University Press, Stanford, California, 1957.

8 G.S. Berns, J.D. Cohen, et al., 'Brain regions responsive to novelty in the absence of awareness', *Science*, Vol. 276, 1997, pp. 1272–5.

9   Russell Fazio, Martha Powell & Carol Williams, 'The role of attitude accessibility in the attitude-to-behavior process', *Journal of Consumer Research*, Vol. 16, No. 3, December 1989, pp. 280–8.

10 Charles Ozgood, G. Suci & P. Tannenbaum, *The Measurement of Meaning*, University of Illinois Press, Urbana, Illinois, 1957.

11 It is necessary to be wary of simple 'halo' effects in such cases. That is, when a brand is advertised it is frequently seen in a more haloed light generally, i.e. across a wide range of attributes. This happens simply because it is advertised. What needs to be shown is that there is greater movement on the target dimension than is evident in all the other more peripheral 'halo' dimensions.

12 John Grinder & Richard Bandler, *The Structure of Magic*, Science and Behavior Books, Palo Alto, California, 1976.

13 Kevin Keller, 'Memory factors in advertising: The effect of advertising retrieval cues on brand evaluations', *Journal of Consumer Research*, Vol. 14, No. 3, December 1987, pp. 316–33.

Chapter 6   'Under the radar'
1   E. DuPlessis, 'DVRs, fast-forwarding and advertising attention', *Admap*, September 2007, pp. 39–42.

2   Robert Gilmore & Eugene Secunda, 'Viewing in the distracted environment: A VCR zipping study', Advertising Research Foundation workshop on electronic media, 1991.

3   A. Goode, 'What happens at x30 fast-forward?', *Admap*, 2006, pp. 46–8.

4   R. Levine, *The Power of Persuasion*, Wiley, Hoboken, NJ, 2003, p. 23.

5   C.A. Russell & M. Belch, 'A managerial investigation into the product placement industry', *Journal of Advertising Research*, Vol. 45, No. 1, March 2005, pp. 73–92.

6   E.A. Reijmersdal, v. P.C. Neijens, et al., 'Effects of television brand placement on brand image', *Psychology and Marketing*, Vol. 24, No. 5, 2007, pp. 403–20.

7   A.Y. Lee & A.A. Labroo, *Journal of Marketing Research*, loc. cit. G.V. Johar, D. Maheswaran, et al., loc. cit.

8   S. Shapiro, loc. cit.

9   M.C. Campbell & K.L. Keller, 'Brand familiarity and advertising repetition effects', *Journal of Consumer Research*, Vol. 30, No. 2, September 2003, pp. 292–304.

10 S.L. Coates, L.T. Butler, et al., 'Implicit memory: A prime example for brand consideration and choice', *Applied Cognitive Psychology*, Vol. 18, No. 9, 2004, pp. 1195–211. S. Auty & C. Lewis, 'Exploring children's choice: The reminder effect of product placement', *Psychology & Marketing*, Vol. 21, No. 9, 2004, pp. 697–713.

11 W.E. Baker, loc. cit.

12 Product placement is sometimes combined with cross promotion (e.g. Shrek

movies deals with the toy-maker Mattel) and these usually work quite differently. They are more like sales promotions than subtle product placements.

13 E.A. van Reijmersdal, P.C. Neijens, et al., loc. cit.

14 S. Law & K.A. Braun, 'I'll have what she's having: Gauging the impact of product placements on viewers', *Psychology & Marketing*, Vol. 17, No. 12, 2000, pp. 1059–75.

15 ibid.

16 Neil Shoebridge, 'Tease tactics work for spray', *Australian Financial Review*, 26 March 2007, p. 48.

17 Max Sutherland, 'Product placement accelerating on a slippery slope', www.sutherlandsurvey.com, 31 October 2005.

Chapter 7 Silent symbols and badges of identity

1 R.B. Cialdini, et. al., 'Basking in reflected glory: Three field studies', *Journal of Personality and Social Psychology*, 1976, Vol. 36, pp. 463–76.

2 A. Pratkanis & E. Atonson, op. cit., p. 168.

3 H. Tajfel, *Human Groups and Social Categories*, Cambridge University Press, Cambridge, 1981.

4 A. Bandura, J. Grusec & F. Menlove, 'Vicarious extinction of avoidance behavior', *Journal of Personality and Social Psychology*, Vol. 5, 1967, pp. 16–23.

5 Nicolas Humphrey, *A History of the Mind*, Harper Perennial, NY, 1993, p. 119.

6 R. Brasch, *How Did It Begin?*, Fontana Collins, NY, 1985, p. 28.

7 R. Brasch, op. cit., p. 273.

Chapter 8 Vicarious experience and virtual reality

1 Robert Pirsig, *Lila: An inquiry into morals*, Bantam Press, London, 1991, p. 364.

2 Morton Heilig, as quoted in Howard Rheingold, *Virtual Reality*, Secker & Warburg, London, 1991, p. 56.

3 S.M. Leong, S.H. Ang, et. al., 'Using drama to persuade: The effects of involvement and ad form of persuasion', *Asia Pacific Advances in Consumer Research*, Vol. 1, 1994, pp. 261–4.

4 Gregory Boller & Jerry Olsen, 'Experiencing ad meanings: Aspects of narrative/drama processing', *Advances in Consumer Research*, Vol. 18, Association for Consumer Research Annual Conference, 1990, pp. 172–5.

5 D. Anderson, L. Alwitt, E. Lorch & S. Levin, 'Watching children watch television', in G. Hale & M. Lewis (eds), *Attention and the Development of Cognitive Skills*, Plenum, NY, 1979, pp. 331–61.

6 Pirsig, *Lila*, p. 364.

7 D. Anderson, L. Alwitt, E. Lorch & S. Levin, loc. cit.

Chapter 9   Messages, reminders and rewards

1   'Advertising Research for Bottom Line Results', Proceedings of the Advertising Research Foundation Key Issues workshop, November 1991.

2   Larry Bisno, 'News, news and more news', Breakthrough Marketplace Advertising Research for Bottom Line Results, Proceedings of the Advertising Research Foundation Key Issues workshop, November 1991, p. 75.

3   See Rossiter & Percy, 1997, op. cit., pp. 120–2, for clarification of the terms 'informational' and 'transformational' motives in advertising.

4   John Philip Jones, *When Ads Work: New proof that advertising triggers sales*, Lexington, NY, 1995, pp. 66, 225, 229. E. DuPlessis, *The Advertised Mind: Ground-breaking insights into how our brains respond to advertising*, Kogan Page, 2005.

5   See, for example, E. McQuarrie & D. Mick, 'Figures of rhetoric in advertising language', *Journal of Consumer Research*, Vol. 22, March 1996, pp. 424–38.

6   Elsewhere John Rossiter following Werner Kroeber-Riel has conceptualized this in terms of RAM-Conveyor Theory; see J. Rossiter & S. Bellman, *Marketing Communications: Theory and applications*, Pearson Prentice Hall, Sydney, 2005.

7   In a study of 87 print ads tested against a pure 'no information' ad, it was revealed that only about one third of the ads were substantially more effective than the pure brand reinforcement ad. Eric Marder, *The Laws of Choice*, Free Press, NY, 1997, pp. 308–9.

8   See for example McQuarrie & Mick, *Journal of Consumer Research*, loc. cit.

9   E. Loftus, *Eyewitness Testimony*, Harvard University Press, Cambridge, 1979; E. Loftus, 'The Maleability of Memory', *American Scientist*, 1979, vol. 67, pp. 312–20.

Chapter 10   What's this I'm watching?

1   I am indebted to the insightful work of McQuarrie and Mick in this section. See E. McQuarrie & David Mick, 'On resonance: A critical pluralistic inquiry into advertising rhetoric', *Journal of Consumer Research*, Vol. 19, September 1992, pp. 180–97.

2   G. Franzen, op. cit., p. 35.

3   ibid.

4   Terence Shimp, *Advertising, Promotion and Supplementary Aspects of Integrated Marketing Communications* (4th ed.), Dryden Press, Orlando, Florida, 1997, p. 299.

5   J. Severn, G. Belk & M. Belk, 'The effects of sexual and non sexual advertising appeals and information level on cognitive processing and communication effectiveness', *Journal of Advertising*, Vol. 19, No. 1, 1990, pp. 14–22.

6   See Terence Shimp, op. cit.

7   Thanks to Simon Anholt for some of the examples used in this section.

8   John Rossiter & Larry Percy, *Advertising Communications and Promotions Management* (2nd ed.), McGraw Hill, NY, 1997, p. 288.
9   Rossiter & Percy, 1997, op. cit., pp. 242, 288.
10   Rossiter & Percy, 1997, op. cit. pp. 285, 295.
11   See G. Franzen, op. cit., p. 189.
12   Rossiter & Percy, 1997, op. cit., p. 282.
13   G. Franzen, op. cit., p. 64.
14   E. Walster & Leon Festinger, 'The effectiveness of "overheard" persuasive communications', *Journal of Abnormal and Social Psychology*, Vol. 65, 1962, pp. 395–402.
15   'New animation', *Marketing News*, American Marketing Association, 6 August 1990.
16   James Wahlberg, Celluloid Studios, Denver USA as reported in *Marketing News*, American Marketing Association, 6 August 1990.
17   Laurence Gibson, 'What can one exposure do?', *Journal of Advertising Research*, April/May 1996, pp. 9–18.

Chapter 11 'Behavioural targeting'

1   M. Burke, A. Hornof, et al., 'High-cost banner blindness: Ads increase perceived workload, hinder visual search, and are forgotten', *ACM Transactions on Computer-Human Interaction (TOCHI)*, Vol. 12, No. 4, 2005, pp. 423–55. W. Hong, J.Y.L. Thong, et al., 'How do web users respond to non-banner-ads animation? The effects of task type and user experience', *Journal of the American Society for Information Science and Technology*, Vol. 58, No. 10, 2007, pp. 146–82.
2   W. Hong, J.Y.L. Thong, et al., loc. cit.
3   M. Burke, A. Hornof, et al., loc. cit.
4   K. Kozlen, 'The value of banner advertising on the web', Graduate School of Arts, University of Missouri-Columbia, 2006.
5   Network BlueLithium was gobbled up by Yahoo, Tacoda by AOL and Doublelick by Google; 24/7 Real Media by WPP.
6   Via a cookie placed on your computer that makes a note of your online behavior.
7   P. Leggiere, 'BT: Ready for prime-time politics', *MediaPost's Behavioral Insider*, 2007.
8   In 2007, AOL acquired behavioral targeting firm Tacoda.

Chapter 12 The limits of advertising

1   P. Kotler, *Marketing Management* (9th ed.), Prentice Hall, NJ, 1997, p. 309.
2   Alan Hirsch, loc. cit.
3   Leon Festinger, *A Theory of Cognitive Dissonance*, Stanford University Press, Stanford, 1957.

4   A. Dijksterhuis & P. K. Smith, 'What do we do unconsciously? And how?', *Journal of Consumer Psychology*, Vol. 15, No. 3, 2005, pp. 225–9.

5   M.D. Lieberman, K.N. Ochsner, et al., 'Do amnesics exhibit cognitive dissonance reduction? The role of explicit memory and attention in attitude change', *Psychological Science*, Vol. 12, 2001, pp. 135–40.

6   This quality positioning line is actually used very successfully in Australia for the brand John West.

7   A.S.C. Ehrenberg, loc. cit.

8   M. Schlinger, 'A profile of responses to commercials', *Journal of Advertising Research*, Vol. 1, No. 2, 1979.

9   E. Walster & Leon Festinger, loc. cit.

10 John Deighton & Robert Schindler, 'Can advertising influence experience?', *Psychology & Marketing*, Vol. 5, No. 2, Summer 1988, pp. 103–15. John Deighton, D. Romer & J. McQueen, 'Using drama to persuade', *Journal of Consumer Research*, Vol. 16, No. 2, December 1989, pp. 335–43.

11 Elizabeth S. Moore & Richard J. Lutz, 'Children, advertising and product experiences: A multimethod inquiry', *Journal of Consumer Research*, Vol. 27, No. 1, June 2000, pp. 31–48.

12 Raymond Bauer, *Advertising in America*, The Graduate School of Harvard, Massachusetts, 1968, p. 290.

Part B   Introduction

1   Note that this is merely the average frequency figure. The fact is that some people will have seen it only once, others will have seen it twice and still others will have seen it three or more times. The overall average for the number of times seen is, however, a single figure and this figure is known as average frequency. The more astute advertisers today are demanding that their media plans and media schedules be looked at in more than this simplistic way. They are demanding information on the full frequency distribution of these figures rather than the simple overall average, so that they can see exactly how many people were exposed once, twice, three times, etc., rather than having just a single overall average figure.

2   Same comment as for note 1.

Chapter 13   Continuous tracking

1   John Philip Jones, *When Ads Work: New proof that advertising triggers sales*, Lexington, NY, 1995. J. Rossiter & S. Bellman, *Marketing Communications: Theory and applications*, Pearson Prentice Hall, Sydney, 2005, p. 320.

2   Subsequently acquired by Taylor Nelson Sofres.

3   Richard Morris, *Behind the Oval Office*, Random House, NY, 1997.

4   Like telephone in the early days, the web does not have everybody online.

However any skew in samples will diminish as more and more of the population get hooked up to the Internet.

Chapter 15   Planning campaign strategy

1   Raymond Burke & Thomas Srull, 'Competitive interference and consumer memory for advertising', *Journal of Consumer Research*, Vol. 15, June 1988, pp. 55–68. A. Kumar & S. Krishnan, 'Memory interference in advertising: A replication and extension', *Journal of Consumer Research*, Vol. 30, 2004, pp. 602–11.
2   Alan Baddeley, *Your Memory*, Prion, London, 1996, pp. 141–3.
3   Michael Anderson & James Neely, 'Interference and inhibition in memory retrieval', Chapter 8 in Elizabeth Bjork & Robert Bjork (eds), *Memory*, Academic Press, San Diego, 1966, pp. 237–313.
4   John R. Anderson, *Learning and Memory* (2nd ed.), Wiley, NY, 2000, p. 303.
5   R.G. Heath, *The Hidden Power of Advertising*, World Advertising Research Centre, Henley-on-Thames, 2001, p. 115.
6   John Anderson, *Cognitive Psychology & Its Implications* (3rd ed.), W.H. Freeman, NY, 1990, pp. 164–70.
7   'Competitive interference and consumer memory for advertising', Raymond R. Burke & Thomas K. Srull, *The Journal of Consumer Research*, Vol. 15, No. 1, June 1988, pp. 55–68. Burke and Srull suggest that 'competitive advertising would have the strongest inhibitory effect on the memory of consumers who are not in the market for a product, or who do not have the ability and/ or the motivation to process ads in a manner that will enhance information retrievability'.
8   Such data is available in most developed countries—at a price.
9   Giep Franzen, *Advertising Effectiveness*. NTC, Oxfordshire, 1994, p. 20.
10 Under conditions of forced attention it is not uncommon to find research that appears to contradict this and supports multiple executions but this is very different to the normal low involvement conditions. See for example H. Rao Unnava and Robert Burn.
11 Burke & Srull, op. cit., p. 65.
12 M. Sutherland, 'To build a brand, use something old as a link to something new', *Journal of Brand Management*, Vol. 3, No. 5, April 1996, pp. 284–6.

Chapter 16   What happens when you stop advertising?

1   N.K. Dhalla, 'Advertising as an anti-recession tool', *Harvard Business Review*, Vol. 58, No. 1, January–February 1980, pp. 158–65.
2   William Moran, 'Relating the product line to market needs and wants', *Handbook of Marketing* (2nd ed.), McGraw Hill, NY, 1986.
3   ibid.
4   Kenneth Longman, 'To build brand equity, it pays to advertise', *Journal of Brand Management*, Vol. 5, No. 5, 1998, p. 366.

Chapter 17   The effectiveness of funny ads

1   I am grateful to Simon Anholdt for some of the international ad examples used in this chapter.

2   As Charles Gruner points out, wit deals more often with real events while humor more usually deals with fantasy. Charles R. Gruner, *Understanding Laughter: The workings of wit and humor*, Nelson-Hall, Chicago, 1978.

3   See Tony Chapman & Hugh Foot (eds), *Humor and Laughter: Theory, research and applications*, Wiley, London, 1976.

4   Eric Smith, *An Accidental History of Words*, Bay Books, Sydney, 1998, p. 83.

5   Chapman & Foot, op. cit., p. 1.

6   A study of highly successful comedy scriptwriters in the USA found that humorists were not able to provide much in the way of conscious insights about their technique. Most 'showed a charming and convincing naiveté about humor theory per se'. Chapman & Foot, op. cit., p. 251.

7   Adapted partly from P. McGhee, 'Development of the humor response—a review of the literature', *Psychological Bulletin*, Vol. 76, pp. 328–48.

8   Arthur Koestler, *The Act of Creation*, The Macmillan Company, NY, 1964.

9   Daniel Schacter, *Searching for Memory*, Basic Books, NY, 1996, p. 210.

10   G. Belch & M. Belk, 'An investigation of the effects of repetition on cognitive and affective reactions to humorous and serious television commercials', *Advances in Consumer Research*, Vol. 11, 1984, pp. 4–10.

11   McCollum/Spielman research report 1978. Also B. Gelb & G. Zinkhan, *Journal of Advertising*, Vol. 14, 1985, pp. 13–20. Belch & Belk, loc. cit.

12   G. Zinkhan & B. Gelb, *Advances in Consumer Research*, Vol. 17, 1990, p. 440.

13   ibid.

Chapter 18   Learning to use shorter-length TV commercials

1   Lee Weinblatt, 'People meters for print', *Print Media Magazine*, March 1990, pp. 35–7.

2   'Improved Marketing Productivity or Advertising's Vietnam?', Association of National Advertisers, NY, 1990. Analysis of the distribution of Day-After-Recall scores revealed that a majority of all fifteens scored at the low end of the DAR scale. J. Walter Thompson publication: *A Closer Look at 15-Second Commercials in the Nineties*.

3   M. Von Gonten & J. Donius, 'Advertising exposure and advertising effects: New panel based findings', *Journal of Advertising Research*, July/August 1997, p. 59.

4   L. Jacoby & M. Dallas, 'On the relationship between autobiographical memory and perceptual learning', *Journal of Experimental Psychology: General*, Vol. 110, 1981, pp. 306–40.
L. Jacoby & C. Kelley, 'Unconscious influences of memory for a prior event', *Personality and Social Psychology Bulletin*, Vol. 13, pp. 314–36.

5   Up to a point.
6   E. DuPlessis, 'DVRs and advertising attention: The case for inadvertent attention', *Admap*, 2007, pp. 31–42.
7   The technical term for this effect is 'backward masking'. For a formal definition of it, see M. Eagle, 'The effects of subliminal stimuli of aggressive content upon conscious cognition', *Journal of Personality*, Vol. 27, 1959, p. 578–600.

Chapter 20   Underweight advertising

1   Two writers independently have suggested 50 TRPs per week as the minimum threshold. See John Philip Jones, op. cit. and M. Von Gonten & J. Donius, loc. cit. (50 TRPs means that at best only half the target has an opportunity to see the ad during that week.)
2   150 TRPs could mean 100 per cent of people exposed on average 1.5 times. In this case it was more like 93 per cent of people exposed on average about 1.6 times in the week.
3   Note that laboratory research using *forced attention* is quite different to natural viewing, low-involvement conditions (see E. McQuarrie, 'Have laboratory experiments become detached from advertiser goals? A meta analysis'). Not infrequently laboratory forced attention studies produce findings that might *appear* to support the use of multiple executions. We believe these are applicable only to high-involvement conditions. See for example H. Rao Unnava & Robert Burnkrant, 'Effects of repeating varied ad executions on brand name memory', *Journal of Marketing Research*, Vol. XXVIII, November 1991, pp. 40–417. Also S. Hawkins, S. Hoch & J. Meyers-Levy, 'Low-involvement learning: Repetition and coherence in familiarity and belief', *Journal of Consumer Psychology*, Vol. 11, No. 1, 2001, pp. 1–12.
4   S. Hawkins, S. Hoch & J. Meyers-Levy, loc. cit.
5   It is important to note that brand buyers are relatively more involved with that brand than non-buyers of it. By implication brands with low market shares have a communication 'handicap' compared to brand leaders—especially if the brand leader is talking to its own buyers. For empirical evidence of this see B. Rice & R. Bennett, 'The relationship between brand usage and advertising tracking measurements: International findings', *Journal of Advertising Research*, Vol. 38, No. 3, May/June 1998, pp. 58–66.

Chapter 21   Why radio ads aren't recalled

1   J. Plummer, S. Rappaport, et al., *The Online Advertising Playbook: Proven strategies and tested tactics from the Advertising Research Foundation*, Wiley, NY, 2007. J. Peacock, 'Radio and the consumer's mind', *Admap*, July/August 2007.

2   John Rossiter & Larry Percy, *Advertising and Promotion Management*, McGraw-Hill, NY, 1987, p. 447.

Chapter 22   Maximizing ad effectiveness
1   David Aaker, 'Resisting temptations to change a brand position/execution: The power of consistency over time', *Journal of Brand Management*, Vol. 3, No. 4, February 1996, pp. 251–8.

Chapter 23   Sequels
1   C.L. Nordheilm, 'The influence of level of processing on advertising repetition effects', *Journal of Consumer Research*, Vol. 29, December 2002, pp. 371–82.
2   L.K. Thaler & R. Koval, *Bang: Getting your message heard in a noisy world*, Currency Doubleday, NY, 2003, pp. 19–24.
3   Max Sutherland, *Journal of Brand Management*, loc. cit.

Chapter 24   Corporate tracking of image and issues
1   Jagdish Agrawal & W. Kamakura, 'The economic worth of celebrity endorsers', *Journal of Marketing*, Vol. 59, July 1995, pp. 56–62.
2   Alan Cleland & Albert Bruno, *The Market Value Process: Bridging customer and shareholder value*, Jossey-Bass, San Francisco, 1996.
3   When seen in the context of the numbers 16, 17, 10 and 12, 83 per cent of people see this stimulus as the number thirteen. When seen in the context of the letters L, M, Y and A, 92 per cent see it as the letter B. Jerome Bruner & L. Minturn, 1951 as reported in J. Grivas, R. Down & L. Carter, *Psychology*, Macmillan Education, South Melbourne, 1996, p. 128.

Chapter 25   The web
1   P. Edgar, 'The day the television died', *The Age*, 28 July 2007, p. 9.
2   T. Alps, 'The future of TV', *Admap*, July/August 2007, pp. 22–5.
3   X. Dreze & F.X. Hussherr, 'Internet advertising: Is anybody watching?', *Journal of Interactive Marketing*, Vol. 17, Autumn 2003, pp. 8–23.
4   X. Fang, S. Singh, et al., 'An examination of different explanations for the mere exposure effect', *Journal of Consumer Research*, Vol. 34, June 2007, pp. 99–103.
5   ibid.
6   ibid.
7   B. Hilliard, 'Beyond click-through: The internet as an advertising medium and more', Paper presented to the American Academy of Advertising Conference, Albuquerque, New Mexico, March 1999 accessible at www.utexas.edu/coc/admedium. R. Briggs, 'A road map for online marketing strategy', *Admap*, March 1998, pp. 27–30.
8   L. Story & E. Pfanner, 'The future of web ads is in Britain', *New York Times*, 4 December 2006.

9   T. Alps, 'The future of TV', *Admap*, July/August 2007, pp. 22–5.

10   R. White, 'Where is TV, and TV advertising, headed?', *Admap*, July/August 2007, pp. 20–1.

11   T. Alps, loc. cit.

12   T. Alps, loc. cit.

13   R. White, loc. cit.

14   G. Philipson, 'Devices put to a screen test', *The Age*, 18 September 2007, p. 7.

15   P. Edgar, loc. cit.

16   G. Philipson, loc. cit.

17   ibid.

18   P. Edgar, loc. cit.

Chapter 26 'Mental reach'

1   E. DuPlessis, 'DVRs and advertising attention: The case for inadvertent attention', loc. cit.

2   Giep & Franzen, op. cit. p. 20.

3   Ulric Neisser as quoted by D. Schacter, *Searching for Memory*, Basic Books, NY, 1996, p. 22.

4   Esther Thorsen & Xinshu Zhao, 'Television viewing behavior as an index of commercial effectiveness', Association for Consumer Research, Advertising & Psychology conference, 1994.

5   John Philip Jones, *When Ads Work*, Lexington Books, NY, 1995.

Chapter 27 Measurement of advertising effects in memory

1   This is referred to in the USA as 'message take-away' but in other parts of the world it is more commonly known as 'message take-out'.

2   Wilder Penfield, *The Mystery of the Mind: A critical study of consciousness and the human brain*, Princeton University Press, Princeton, NJ, 1975.

3   The question of whether these 'experiences' are memories of actual incidents or mere fantasies or hallucinations has been raised by Daniel L. Schacter, op. cit., p. 77.

4   For an excellent account of 'spreading activation' theory see John R Anderson, *Cognitive Psychology And Its Implications* (3rd ed.), Freeman, NY, 1990, pp. 150–209.

5   S. Greenfield, *Brain Story*, London, BBC Worldwide, 2000. J.Z. TSein, 'The Memory Code', *Scientific America*, July 2007, pp. 34–41.

6   Daniel L. Schacter, op. cit., p. 77.

7   Daniel L. Schacter, *The Seven Sins of Memory*, Houghton Mifflin, NY, 2002. Larry Percy, 'Advertising and the seven sins of memory', *International Journal of Advertising*, Vol. 23, 2004, pp. 413–27.

8   Robert Heath, *The Hidden Power of Advertising*. Admap Publications, Henley-on-Thames, 2001, pp. 57–8.

9   R. White, 'Engagement, involvement and attention', *Admap*, Vol. 487, October 2007, p. 24.

10 J. Mundell, J. Hallward, et al., 'High attention processing: The real power of advertsing', *Admap*, Vol. 474, July/August, 2006.

11 S.M.J. van Osselaer & C. Janiszewski, 'Two ways of learning brand associations', *Journal of Consumer Research*, Vol. 28, 2001, pp. 202–23.

12 Technically this is known as 'content addressability'.

13 J.Z. TSein, loc. cit.

14 Daniel L. Schacter, op. cit., p. 103.

15 Brain imaging technology reveals that things that have high connection strength do not necessarily have to be physically close but are often widely distributed throughout the brain. See for example Schacter et al., 1998, ibid.

16 J.Z. TSein, loc. cit.

17 Although the primary method of transmission is chemical rather than electrical.

18 L. Postman & G. Keppel, *Norms of Word Association*, Academic Press, NY, 1970, pp. 1–38.

Chapter 28   The buy-ology of mind

1   For an excellent account of episodic memory, see Mark H. Ashcroft, *Human Memory and Cognition*, Scott Foresman, NY, 1989.

2   One view is that the residue of repeated information from similar episodes forms semantic (knowledge) memory. See Francis Bellezza, 'Mnemonic methods for storage and retrieval', in E.L. Bjork & R.A. Bjork (eds), *Memory*, Academic Press, San Diego, 1996, pp. 356–7.

3   Scott McKenzie, 'The role of attention in mediating the effect of advertising on attribute importance', *Journal of Consumer Research*, Vol. 13, No. 2, September 1986, p. 178.

4   This is based on my MarketMind experience over more than 15 years of tracking numerous campaigns and also strongly supported by the publication of the work of Eric Marder, *The Laws of Choice*, Free Press, NY, 1997.

5   Extensive studies by Marder (ibid.) indicate that the effect attributable to a *single* placement of a print ad is small and below the order of magnitude that can be detected in many research sample designs (p. 287). However, with TV the average effect, while still small, is many magnitudes (8 or 9 times) greater (p. 319).

6   R. Fazio, P. Herr & M. Powell, 'On the development and strength of category-brand associations in memory: The case of mystery ads', *Journal of Consumer Psychology*, Vol. I (1), 1992, pp. 1–3.

7   For example, people may be questioned about the Volkswagen ad by asking whether they have seen an ad for cars that showed a close-up of a man's face that is badly scarred.

8   Ad recognition (execution-cued ad awareness) can be a good measure of 'mental reach' only if precautions are first taken to set benchmarks and control for the tendency towards 'yeah'-saying. A new ad can look or feel familiar even when people have not actually seen it before—particularly if the new ad is generically similar to other ads. We have observed as many as 43 per cent of people in benchmark periods claiming to have seen an ad, before it even went to air. It is amazing how many market research companies ignore this and fail to benchmark these types of measures.

9   Esther Thorsen & Xinshu Zhao, loc. cit.

10 It is possible to do this an alternative way by asking people if they have seen any advertising for the brand and, if they have, to describe the ad. This is known as brand-cued ad recall. This is discussed in more detail in the Appendix.

11 In fact, people are more likely to recall TV ads than print ads like this but we have used the print example for clarity of illustration.

12 Note that this is not a good estimate of the percentage of people who have seen and noticed the ad, which will be significantly greater and more appropriately indicated by the execution cued (recognition measure). Movements in the two measures are usually correlated (see Appendix). Here, what is being indicated is the percentage of people for whom the connection has not only been established but is strong enough to be triggered into mind spontaneously by the product category.

13 There is also some tendency for the reverse to be true. Increasing brand recall can also lead to an increase to some extent in advertising recall for that brand. If more people become involved with that brand they may be more likely to notice its advertising. But this relatonship is much weaker and not a necessary one at all.

14 Jack B. Haskins, 'Factual recall as a measure of advertising effectiveness', *Journal of Advertising Research*, Vol. 4, March 1964, pp. 2–28.

15 Advertising that is not designed to solve a problem or remove a dissatisfaction but depicts consumption of the brand as a source of reward in its own right. For a fuller understanding of tranformational advertising, see John Rossiter & Larry Percy, op. cit., p. 121.

16 It is important to recognize that brand users are usually more favorable to that brand's advertising than non-users of it. This needs to be borne in mind, especially when comparing one brand's ads with another smaller brand's ads. See B. Rice & R. Bennett, op. cit.

17 Kevin Keller, 'Memory factors in advertising: The effect of ad retrieval cues on brand evaluations', *Journal of Consumer Research*, December 1987.

Chapter 29   Conclusion

1   Lec J. Stanislaw, Polish writer (1909–66).

Appendix

1   Graham Staplehurst, 'Effective research for effective campaign results', paper presented to Australian Market Research Society Annual Conference, 1996.

2   See for example Frank Simper, 'A response to effective research for effective campaign results', Paper presented to Australian Market Research Society Annual Conference, 1997.

3   G. Staplehurst, op. cit., p. 12.

4   M. Sutherland & L. Friedman, 'Do you model ad awareness or advertising awareness?', *Journal of Advertising Research*, Vol. 40, September/October 2000, pp. 32–6.

5   This is known as the encoding specificity principle: see E. Tulving, E. Thomson & D. Thomson, 'Encoding specificity and retrieval processes in episodic memory', *Psychological Review*, Vol. 80, 1973, pp. 352–73.

6   Frequently the brand will be masked out of the photo-stills and the description—in which case it is called 'masked, execution-cued ad awareness'.

7   A study by Stapel provides evidence that all recall comes from the much larger group of people who recognize the advertising. J. Stapel, 'Recall & recognition: A very close relationship', *Journal of Advertising Research*, Vol. 38, No. 4, July/August 1998, pp. 41–5.

8   When consumers look at your advertising communications, what do they think about? Some are daydreaming—staring while their minds are 'off elsewhere'. An hour later 40 per cent or more won't even recognize having seen it. See E. Thorsen & X. Zhao, loc. cit.

9   One complication is that when an ad is very similar to other ads in the category it is possible for people to say they recognize having seen it before it goes to air. This usually signals that it is a problem ad because it is not distinctive enough—its content or style is too 'generic'. It is crucial to quantify this level of 'false claiming' by including the question in the tracking *before the ad goes to air*. This then becomes a diagnostic in its own right.

10   See Chapter 22, 'Maximizing ad effectiveness: develop a unique and consistent style'.

INDEX

CHINA'S
CIVILIZATION

CHINA'S CIVILIZATION

A Survey of its History,
Arts, and Technology

by Arthur Cotterell
and David Morgan

PRAEGER PUBLISHERS
New York

This book is dedicated to
Joseph Needham, F.R.S., F.B.A.
Master of Gonville and Caius College, Cambridge,
whose studies of China have done so much to foster
international understanding

Published in the United States of America in 1975
by Praeger Publishers, Inc.
111 Fourth Avenue, New York, N.Y. 10003

Library of Congress Cataloging in Publication Data

Cotterell, Arthur.
  China's civilization: a survey of its history, arts, and technology
  Bibliography: p. 314
  Includes indexes.
  1. China—Civilization. I. Morgan, David, 1947—joint author. II. Title.
  DS721.C83   915.1'03   74-17887
ISBN 0-275-33550-X
ISBN 0-275-85140-0 pbk.

Printed in the United States of America

Preface

This book attempts to provide a context for understanding China's current re-emergence as a leading world power. It aims to make accessible to the general reader and mature student the kind of information that will provide some answers to the questions often asked about the Chinese. We have adopted an integrated approach because China should be seen in the round, if any real insight into its nature and historical experience is to be gained.

For assistance with translations and invaluable advice on 'how it appears to a Chinese' we should like to thank Mrs Yong Yap Cotterell. Also, we are greatly indebted to Dr Needham for his encouragement when we were beginning the 'impossible' task of surveying Chinese civilization within a single volume.

A.B.C. and D.W.M. 1974

Acknowledgments

For permission to use copyright material, thanks are due to the following: Messrs George Allen and Unwin, Ltd, for an extract from *Monkey*, by Wu Chêng-ên, and for the verses 'To Tan-chiu', by Li Po, and 'On his Baldness', by Po Chü-i, all translated by Arthur Waley, the verses appearing in *More Translations from the Chinese*; Messrs Constable and Co., Ltd, for 'Fighting South of the Ramparts', by Li Po, and 'The Chancellor's Gravel Drive', by Po Chü-i, both from *One Hundred and Seventy Poems*, translated by Arthur Waley; the Hong Kong University Press, for 'The Spin-dance Girl', by Po Chü-i, translated by Shih Shun Liu, from *One Hundred and One Chinese Poems*; Grove Press, Inc., and Mrs. J. K. Rideout for permission to print an extract from 'Memorial on the Bone of Buddha', by Han Yu, translated by her late husband, appearing in *An Anthology of Chinese Literature*, also to Grove Press and to Mr A. C. Graham for translations of 'On Wine', by Li Po, and part of 'Autumn Meditation', by Tu Fu, both being by Mr Graham and appearing likewise in *An Anthology of Chinese Literature*; 'The Chancellor's Gravel Drive', 'To Tan-chiu', 'Fighting South of the Castle (Ramparts)' and 'On his Baldness' from *Translations from the Chinese*, by Arthur Waley. Copyright 1919, 1941 by Alfred A. Knopf, Inc. Copyright re-newed 1947 by Arthur Waley, 1969 by Alfred A. Knopf, Inc. Re-printed by permission of the publisher.

Where efforts to trace the holders of copyright material have proved unavailing, apology is offered for any inadvertent infringe-ment of rights.

The authors also wish to thank the following for their permis-sion to reproduce copyright illustrations: *An Introduction to Chinese Art*, by Michael Sullivan (Faber and Faber), pp. 108, 286; Bodleian Library, pp. 215, 224; British Museum, pp. 67, 104, 162, 167, 235, 237; Camera Press, pp. 84, 163, 170, 223, 271, 293, 296, 298, 299, 300, 304; *China: a short cultural history*, by C. P. Fitzgerald (Cresset Press), pp. 37, 96, 240; Cultural Properties Commission, Tokyo, p. 112; Dominique Darbois, p. 107; *Every-day Life in Imperial China*, by Michael Loewe (B. T. Batsford, Ltd), p. 73; Field Museum of Natural History, Chicago, p. 137; *Happiness Pictorial Monthly*, pp. 17, 33, 165, 166, 171, 213; J. Allan Cash, p. 151; *Japan: a short cultural history*, by G. H. Samson (Cresset Press), p. 184; John Hillelson Agency, pp. 88, 89, 174, 175, 223, 273, 274, 278, 285; Mansell Collection, pp. 210, 222, 243, 249; National Maritime Museum, p. 239; National Palace Museum, Peking, pp. 119, 130, 134; National Palace Museum, Taipeh, Taiwan, pp. 23, 132, 133, 135; Dr Joseph Needham and Allen and Unwin, pp. 27, 35, 39, 53, 57, 65, 74 (top), 81, 86, 126, 173; Dr Joseph Needham and Cambridge University Press, pp. 74 (bottom), 76, 80, 138, 139, 141, 145, 154, 155, 156, 159, 164, 169, 261; New York Public Library, pp. 143, 144; Nicholas Bouvier, p. 157; Paul Popper, Ltd, pp. 50, 51, 69, 172, 174, 175, 195, 221, 280, 294; Radio Times Hulton Picture Library, pp. 218, 238, 263, 267, 270; Royal Geographical Society, p. 217; St Louis Art Museum, p. 168; Victoria and Albert Museum, pp. 69, 227.

Contents

8

INTRODUCTION

Prehistory

In 1971 the People's Republic became a member of the United Nations. Her population approaches 800 million and when her leaders have something to say, then the world listens. The Chinese form a large part, about one quarter, of mankind, but outside China little is known generally about the way these people think and get on with the business of living together. What does the Chinese citizen expect from life? How does he see the place of his own country among the present-day community of nations? Where would his hopes for the future lead us? What contribution can China make to the last third of the twentieth century?

For these urgent questions some answers will be found in our study of China. In order that they do not seem strange and incomprehensible we have tried to provide a background for the Chinese viewpoint, as far as possible keeping a balance between Chinese and non-Chinese sources. This book attempts to discover what it has been like to be born and brought up within the Great Wall. The tense change, from present to past, is deliberate, because no understanding of China would be complete unless the historical experience of the Chinese people has been taken into full account. This is the case for several reasons. Firstly, the Chinese see themselves as the direct descendants of an ancient civilization. It is a fact that China is the oldest continuous civilization surviving today. Secondly, this great tradition was isolated from the rest of the world for centuries at a time so that many of its developments are unique and require our special attention. Thirdly, the influence of even remote times is evident in the happenings of the 1970s; old ways die hard in China. What we hope this book will offer is a 'context' for the current re-emergence of China as a world power. The emphasis is on the historical development of Chinese civilization because this is not the first occasion that its greatness has been acknowledged by the rest of mankind.

WHO ARE THE CHINESE?

Although we think of the Chinese as people who live in, or come from China, the present political boundary of the People's Republic encloses a much larger area than the first Chinese Empire. It embraces many diverse races, each having its own history and culture. So where did China proper originate? When can it be said to have begun? And, most important, why has it become such a powerful country?

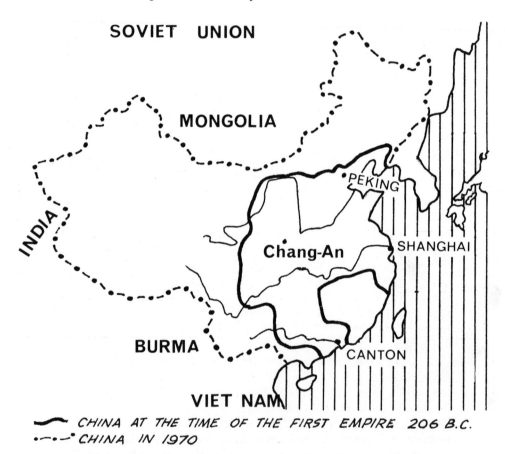

SOVIET UNION

MONGOLIA

INDIA

PEKING

Chang-An

SHANGHAI

BURMA

CANTON

VIET NAM

CHINA AT THE TIME OF THE FIRST EMPIRE 206 B.C.
CHINA IN 1970

THE HEARTLAND OF CHINA

The original centre of China lies along the middle course of the great Yellow River. The river is so called because of the large amount of yellow silt it carries from the high plateau lands of Inner Mongolia. From the Desert of Ordos to the North China Plain, squeezed between the Lu Liang and Chin Ling Highlands, lies an area known as 'The Land within the Passes.' The earliest Chinese settlements developed here over 5000 years ago. By 1000 B.C. the Chinese had spread eastwards along the Yellow River valley and southwards to the valley of the Yangtze. Many different races were absorbed, while others were repelled to the highlands and wastelands of Yüeh and Yunnan.

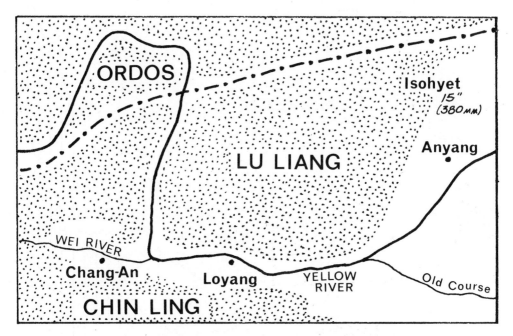

The Land within the Passes showing ancient capitals

The Land within the Passes
The physical environment of this area had a great formative effect on Chinese culture. Early man was totally dependent on the natural elements, the seasons, rainfall, the régime and flow rate of the river. As a result his whole way of life, his beliefs, superstitions, fables, his work and leisure, were all dominated by them. The physical environment not only determined the basic nature of Chinese culture but ensured its preservation by the formidable barriers it imposed between the unique civilization of

11

the Yellow River valley and the other great civilizations of the ancient world.

Ancient Cultural Centres
a—Egypt   b—Babylon   c—Indus Valley   d—China

Major Physical Barriers
1 Gobi Desert and Mongolian Plateau
2 Himalayas, Pamirs and Tibetan Plateau
3 Yunnan Plateau

The Isolation of China

THE MAJOR PHYSICAL INFLUENCES

- The continental (inland) situation
- The highly seasonal and erratic nature of rainfall
- The loess covering of the region
- River flooding
- Earthquakes

The inland nature of the Land within the Passes affects life in two main ways. Monsoon rains starting over the Indian Ocean have been largely deposited by the time they reach North China. The resulting decrease in cloud cover makes for great ranges in both daily and seasonal temperatures, since insolation is lost. If winter comes early, or is prolonged, the whole cycle of agriculture is affected. The winters are bitterly cold with the dominant winds coming from Mongolia. The second result is of course *the problem of light and erratic summer rainfall* which scarcely exceeds 762 millimetres, which leads to drought and crop failure. In effect, the limit of settled agriculture is roughly the line of 15 inch (380 mm) isohyet. Beyond this live the nomadic stock rearers. But it should not be forgotten that excessive rainfall can be equally disastrous to the easily eroded soil.

The region is covered by *thick deposits of windblown yellow earth called loess*. This soil originated on the Mongolian Plateau at a time when it was well watered and fertile. Changes in climate, brought about by a glacial period and the uplift of the Tibetan plateau which cut off monsoon rains from the Indian Ocean, reduced the soil to a fine dust which was carried southwards by

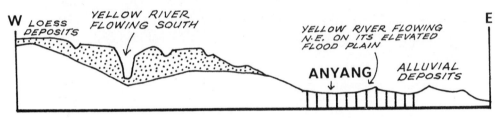

W–E Sketch—section through site of Anyang.

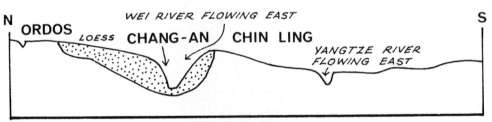

N–S Sketch—section through site of Ch'angan.

the cold winds. It was deposited over a large area of North China in depths over 75 metres in some valleys. Not only was the soil fertile but it was laid down on successive growths of grass, creating a capillary effect. Agriculture could be supported by the utilization of underground moisture even where rainfall was limited. High population densities were maintained but unfortunately the loess suffered from wind and rain erosion. Sheet and gully erosion have carved steep-sided gorges and denuded whole hillsides.

MISFORTUNE This is the character for calamity or misfortune. The original meaning is dramatically clear since the strokes show a large river with some form of obstruction across it, thus causing the calamity of floods. The character has two distinct elements, a river 𝄫 and a bar — : it is pronounced *tsai*. It is shown in its ancient form, the general practice adopted for Chinese characters in this book.

The loess is carried by the Yellow River and its tributaries in exceptional amounts. This has been gradually deposited on the flood plains of the river, raising its level above the surrounding land. This has led to *periodic flooding and complete changes in river courses.* The last major flooding of the Yellow River in 1931 caused nearly 4 000 000 deaths. The factors mentioned so far have been aggravated by *earthquakes.* Cave houses built in the loess cliffs were cool in the hot dry summers and warm in the cold windy winters. But they rapidly disintegrated during earth tremors. As late as 1920 a quarter of a million deaths resulted from earthquakes in this region.

The effect of these physical influences on the way of life of the Chinese is particularly reflected in the Yin-Yang philosophy. Rituals and ceremonies to avert disaster recognized the delicate balance of the extreme forces of nature.

Yin-Yang

This design illustrates the interaction of the Yin and the Yang. The harmony of the universe was thought to depend on the balance of these two natural forces—Yin, negative, female and dark; Yang, positive, male and light. They were not fighting each other, but rather existing together in precarious balance, which if disturbed would bring disasters to mankind.

Heaven, the sky, was Yang, while Earth, the land on which man dwelt, was Yin. Heaven, the origin of weather, was looked upon as a chief god whose goodwill had to be ensured with sacrifices made by the chief man, the ruler, the Son of Heaven.

This perception of the natural forces stems from the everyday experience of the early farmer of the Yellow River valley. The loess soil is fertile with adequate rainfall, but in time of drought little more than dust. A sudden deluge, or flooding from rivers, can alter the landscape itself. The ancient kings preserved the people by maintaining a proper relationship with the heavenly powers and undertaking practical works in the countryside. They were priests as well as kings.

Yin-Yang has remained a basic concept of the Chinese mind. The natural world is seen as a single intricately balanced organism in which mankind must find the way to play its own correct part. Harmony, attunement, is vital. This very old idea has had a tremendous influence on Chinese thinking—in politics, science and the arts.

THE MOVEMENT SOUTH

As population pressure built up in the middle valleys of the Yellow River there was a movement eastwards to the flat alluvial plains. Here the problems of river control were greatest, but more reliable rainfall and the fertility of the soils encouraged a more diverse agriculture, and the population continued to expand. As the Chinese moved south into the Huai and Yangtze valleys they encountered a different climate and different cultures. Subtropical rain forest was the natural vegetation cover. Rice replaced millet as the staple food. The problems of erosion and flooding were not as destructive in the south, since rice growing involved water control through the use of ditches, canals and basins. The point is that despite a movement into another climatic region the basic elements of traditional Chinese culture remained unchanged. Moreover, the South like the North was cut off from other centres of civilization by the Tibetan and Yunnan Plateaux. Between 221 and 206 B.C. both North and South China adopted a standardized form of writing, coinage and weights.

PREHISTORIC CHINA

Our knowledge of 'Prehistoric China' is dependent upon archaeological excavations. As yet there are many gaps in our knowledge. Evidence of human habitation can be divided into three main groups:

- Palaeolithic, or early Stone Age finds;
- Neolithic or late Stone Age finds;
- Bronze Age finds.

15

Early Sites

The earliest evidence of human-type culture was found in the
1920s at Chou Kou Tien. Peking Man as he is called lived between
300 000 to 500 000 years ago, and was a hunter with a knowledge
of fire. Similar evidence of such encampments has been discovered
in the Desert of Ordos, the Upper Yangtze Valley, and Kwangsi in
South China.

Late Stone Age Settlements

There is a great gap between such finds and later ones. During
such time the climate factors changed considerably and many
sites are probably buried beneath loess and alluvial deposits.
Certainly northern China has had a far more benevolent climate
in the past, with lush pasture supporting a wide variety of wild
animal life. A Stone Age settlement buried under loess at Chou
Tong Kou has been dated at 50 000 B.C. Evidence of later
cultures shows them to be largely located in the river valleys of
North China. These are of much more recent origin, being around
5 000 years old. There were two main cultural groups—the Yang
Shao and the Lung Shan, named after important sites illustrating
their ways of life. They were sedentary agriculturalists as well as
hunters, fishers and collectors of wild vegetation. Yang Shao on
the loess plateau is the older of the two. This culture spread
throughout the middle course of the Yellow River and its tribu-
tary the Wei.

At Pan Pei, near ancient Chang-an, further information on the
form of these settlements has been revealed. At its height Pan Pei
had over two hundred houses with a population of between five
and six hundred people. Such a population could only be supported by the cultivation of cereal crops, such as millet, and
domesticated swine. Their cultivation often accelerated the process
of erosion by the removal of tree and grass cover. One of the
major features of the Yang Shao people was their painted pottery,
none of which was turned on a potter's wheel. Remains of three-
legged cooking vessels called *li* have established a link with later
Chinese cultures. The Lung Shan were more advanced and lived
on the eastern coastal and river plains. Their settlements were
surrounded by defensive walls not ditches and their agriculture
was more diverse including cattle, sheep and goats and wheat and
rice where conditions were favourable. The best known artifact of
the Lung Shan was a highly polished, very hard, wheel-made
black pottery.

16

Reconstructions of the types of houses discovered at Pan Pei, near ancient Chang-an.

Cookery and medicine. The *li,* three pots joined as a tripod, dates from the neolithic period and is peculiar to China. It represents an immense advance in terms of using heat, as the hollow legs both provide support and present a greater surface to the fire, while the internal division allows the preparation of several things at once. Chinese skill in cooking would seem very old. Today the Chinese housewife knows a great deal about medicine. In meals she makes for the family she uses herbs and special ingredients intended to ensure the health of all members. Should this connection between cooking and medicine be an ancient tradition, as the discovery of the *li* suggests, then we may have found one of the reasons for the large size of the Chinese population from early times. A proverb runs: 'The beggar is an Emperor when he eats.'

17

The Bronze Age

The Lung Shan take us to the Dawn of Civilization, from the Stone Age to the Bronze Age. Our knowledge of the descendants of the Lung Shan is supplemented by legend. The first dynasty, the Hsia, was supposedly founded by Yü, the great tamer of the Yellow River, but little evidence as yet exists to back up its historical authenticity. The following dynasty, the Shang, were regarded as mythological until 1928 when the last of their six capitals was uncovered at Anyang. Shortly after another at Cheng Chou was discovered. Important elements of these finds include:

- their large scale organization, and architecture;
- the sophisticated use of bronze;
- the highly complex record of pictogram writing on oracle bones and turtle shells.

Anyang was founded in 1300 B.C. It had a carefully planned, almost extravagant royal palace and carefully segregated semi-subterranean dwellings for the lower orders. The consecration of new important buildings required ritual sacrifices of both animals and humans.

Ancient symbol for sacrifice to ancestral spirits. The ancestor is standing above a hand offering food.

Language. A factor which may have contributed to the age-long unity of China despite marked geographical differences between regions is the unique nature of the Chinese language. An ideographic script, the individual characters have value as ideas rather than sounds, so that the meaning is accessible to speakers of different dialects. For example, the character for king, 王 , is pronounced *wang* in Mandarin, *ong* in Hokien dialect and *w'ong* in Cantonese dialect. No difficulty of understanding can exist once the character has been written down, since the character is exactly the same for each dialect. All pronunciation given in this book is Mandarin, now the national speech.

18

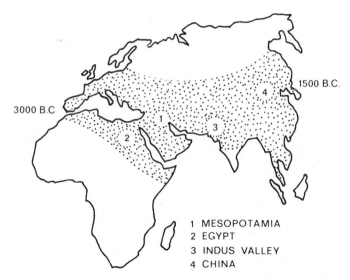

Bronze Cultures of the Prehistoric World.

We have learned much from the complex and sophisticated writing found on the oracle bones which were used to foretell the future. Animal bones or turtle shells were heated with a live coal or a red-hot bronze poker, the resulting cracks being interpreted as the reply of the gods and carved on the bone. The beginning of the pictogram writing came later than that of Mesopotamia and Egypt but as the basis of the Chinese language it has outlived them to the present day. Over 2000 different characters have been noted for the Shang period. Similarly, the use of bronze spread to China much later than to the West, from its Middle Eastern origins. Yet the Chinese became technically more advanced than other bronze users. Alongside the diffusion of bronze by about 1500 B.C. came wheat cultivation; the spread of the two was closely linked.

China, then, had links with the West but was sufficiently isolated to develop a very original form of civilization and science. Anyang proved myth to be reality.

CHINA—AN ECOSYSTEM

China has a unique culture which has been maintained despite changes in boundaries. It is not that China has lacked communication with the outside world, despite the formidable mountain barriers. The Chinese had overland trading links with the Middle East and Europe before the birth of Christ. They were exploring

19

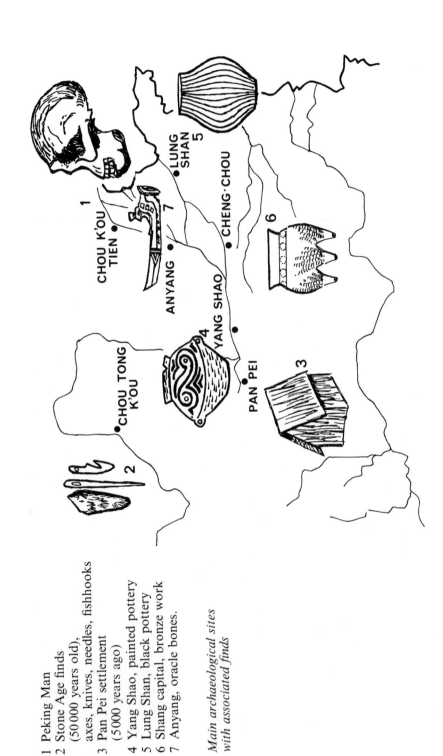

CHOU K'OU TIEN 1

LUNG SHAN 5

CHENG·CHOU

ANYANG 7

YANG SHAO

PAN PEI

CHOU TONG K'OU

2

4

3

6

1 Peking Man
2 Stone Age finds
  (50000 years old),
  axes, knives, needles, fishhooks
3 Pan Pei settlement
  (5000 years ago)
4 Yang Shao, painted pottery
5 Lung Shan, black pottery
6 Shang capital, bronze work
7 Anyang, oracle bones.

*Main archaeological sites
with associated finds*

the East coast of Africa long before the Europeans rounded the
Cape of Good Hope. They were not static, their territorial
boundary ebbed and flowed, generally at the expense of immediate neighbours. The mobile nomadic peoples from the Mongolian steppe swept through the valleys and plains on several
occasions in spite of the natural physical barriers and man-made
walls. But such movements seem incidental when compared with
the unbroken traditions of China, the language, philosophy,
architecture, cooking, and the status of teachers and peasants as
twin pillars of society. Because of the basic stability of Chinese
culture in the face of continual inflows and outflows of ideas and
people, we can call China an ecosystem. An ecosystem is a state
of equilibrium between nature in all its forms and man in all his
works. Man has learned to survive by working with nature just
as Yü the Great Engineer succeeded in controlling the floods, not
by building dams, but by deepening the river beds. China has
always been self-sufficient and remains so today. At times the
ecosystem has been disturbed, even severely shaken, but always
it has succeeded in absorbing what was useful and rejecting the
unhelpful or irrelevant. More than most countries China has
pursued its own distinct way.

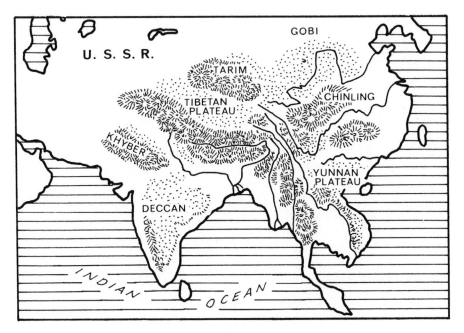

MYTHOLOGY AND LEGENDARY FIGURES

Since ancient China was isolated from the other early centres of civilization, Egypt, Mesopotamia and the Indus valley, the first thoughts of the Chinese, their legends, are worth our attention. They belong to China alone. From them we may be able to identify what are the original and distinct elements in the Chinese consciousness.

A legend of the creation of the universe concerns Pan Ku, primeval man. At the beginning the universe was an egg. One day the egg split open. The top half became the sky and the bottom half the earth. Pan Ku, who emerged from the broken egg, grew three metres taller every day, just as the sky became three metres higher and the earth three metres thicker. After eighteen thousand years Pan Ku died. Then, like the original egg, he split into a number of parts. His head formed the sun and moon, his blood the rivers and seas, his hair the forests, his sweat the rain, his breath the wind, his voice thunder and, last of all, his fleas became the ancestors of mankind.

What stands out most in this story for a Westerner is the lowly position the Chinese have ascribed to man. Not the centre of creation, not a colossus in the landscape, but rather a small figure in the great sweep of natural things. This view of the world is expressed in Chinese painting where men are set down amid the magnificence of Nature, mountains and valleys, clouds and waterfalls, trees and flowers. The first inhabitants of the Yellow River communities must have regarded themselves as members of a vast order of living things, with whose processes they had to seek a harmonious relationship. Life was a matter of reciprocity, mutual interchange between its many parts.

After Pan Ku came a series of emperors, largely divine, since Huang Ti, the Yellow Emperor, is considered by Chinese historians to be the earliest human ruler. Under the Yellow Emperor and his four successors, Chuan Hsiu, K'u, Yao and Shun, the people learnt the ways of civilized life. Arts and crafts flourished; government and moral conduct were established; the gods received regular sacrifices. The throne was not passed on to the next emperor according to birth, but each successor was chosen by merit. Yü the Great Engineer, selected for power by Shun, was the founder of the first dynasty, the Hsia.

Around Yü many stories have collected. They all praise his devotion to duty. Thirteen years Yü spent 'mastering the waters' without once returning home to see his wife and children. By his

A Mountain View *by Hsia Kuei (A.D. 1190–1230) shows Man in a Chinese landscape: it is a small section of a large scroll.*

large scale conservancy schemes he made the country safe from floods and well irrigated for agriculture. The legend of Yü reveals that from very early times the Chinese began to develop a technology capable of transforming their homeland into a region suited to a settled pattern of life. The Hsia dynasty ended with the defeat of its last king, Chieh, a cruel tyrant, by a people and nobility driven to rebellion. The new dynasty, the Shang, had a similar fate in store for it, though Chou Hsin, the last Shang king, is reputed to have outdone Chieh with his viciousness. Much later the philosopher Mencius was to construct a theory of the Right of Rebellion from this event. But records of Hsia and Shang times are scarce; the historical period in China does not start till the Chou dynasty.

WORLD CHRONOLOGY 3000–1000 B.C.

3000 B.C. 2900	2800	2700	2600	2500	2400	2300	2200

EUROPE

WEST ASIA and NORTH AFRICA

EGYPT
- 2900 Unification of the country under Narmer
- 2700 Cheops' pyramid at Giza
- 2626 Death of Imhotep the Great Builder

MESOPOTAMIA
- 2600 Cities with ziggurats for their gods
- 2370 Sumer under Sargon becomes powerf state controlling valley

ASIA MINOR
- 2225 Troy bu

SOUTH ASIA

INDUS VALLEY
- 2500 Great cities Mohenjo-Daro and Harappa flourish – each a masterpiece of town planning
- 2100 Seals sugg contact with Sume

EAST ASIA

CHINA
- 2200 Yü the Great Engineer founds the Hsia dynasty

ENGLAND
● 1850 Stonehenge,
a Neolithic monument

GREECE
● 1700 Mycenae
and Tiryns

● 1500 The coming
of the Dorian Greeks

CRETE
● 1900 The great
palace at Knossos

● 1400 The destruction
of Knossos

● 1700 Hyksos
invade Egypt

● 1570 Hyksos
expelled

● 1480 Pharaoh
Tuthmosis III conquers
Palestine and Syria

● 1250 Moses leads
Israelites from Egypt

● 1750 King Hammurabi
of Babylon introduces
his code of laws, first
known in history

● 1400 Hittites
develop iron

● 1123
Death of
King
Nebuchadnezzar I

● 1500 Aryan invasion of
India – a new people and
a new civilization; the
Rig Veda, ancient book of
Hindu religion, dates from
this time

● 1500 Shang period
in China. Notable
achievements in bronze
working

1027 ●
Chou
dynasty
founded

1 Classical China

From early times to 221 B.C.

HISTORICAL OUTLINE

One of the first events which can be said to be certain was the overthrow of the Shang kingdom by Chou, a vassal state on the western frontier. About 1027 B.C. Anyang, the capital, fell to the rebel armies and the last Shang king was slain. The new dynasty, the Chou, was destined to have the longest rule in China's history, and even though the last centuries were filled with civil wars, this was the 'Classical Age'. Chinese society found its pattern during this period. Great thinkers appeared, leaving their mark on the minds of all future generations. Science and technology developed; cities and towns multiplied.

The second ruler of the new dynasty was too young to take charge of the government on his father's death so Chou Kung, or the Duke of Chou, acted as regent. This man firmly established the new kingdom and seems to have found a way of saving the best things from Shang times. There was no abrupt break, but continuation and improvement. Two of his actions illustrate the smoothness of the change-over. The descendants of Shang were awarded the tiny state of Sung so that they would have sufficient revenue to keep up the sacrifices such a princely family had to make to its ancestral spirits. And the officials of the defeated kingdom were added to the Chou civil service. Looking back on these early years from the confusion at the end of the Chou dynasty many people, the philosopher Confucius among them, came to look upon this period as a lost ideal. The Duke of Chou had shown proper respect for the Shang family and his treatment of the scholar officials was a sign of the value he attached to peace. Order, balance, respect for elders and learning—these were the virtues they thought they saw. How correct these wistful glances into the past were it is not possible to know. Though the Chinese were one of the first people to write history as we know it today, accurate records do not survive before the last four

Here the Duke of Chou is seen making an announcement to the officials of the defeated Shang kingdom. The drawing comes from a nineteenth-century edition of the Shu Ching (Historical Classic), *a work dating from 850 B.C. and a main source for details of the Chou dynasty.*

hundred years of the Chou kingdom. What the rise of Chou most probably represents is a major expansion of Chinese civilization, for there is mention of the Yangtze valley, not then considered to be part of Chou, or the Middle Kingdom, a name still used to denote China.

27

The Period of the Warring States (481–221 B.C.)

This last part of the Classical period, known as the Warring States, marks the breakdown of the feudal system and ends in the unification of all China, the foundation of the first Chinese Empire. The royal house of Chou gradually lost control of its vassal states. In 771 B.C. the ninth ruler was expelled from his capital by a mounted army from the Mongolian steppe. This barbarian invasion was an unexpected setback for the Chou dynasty and, though they rebuilt their capital on a new site at Loyang, the old authority over the other feudal powers was permanently weakened. Ch'u and Ch'in, large semi-barbarous states on the fringes of the Middle Kingdom, steadily became more developed and acquired greater military strength. There was an overall tendency for the smaller and weaker states to be absorbed by the stronger ones, particularly after 500 B.C.

THREE These three strokes stand for the number of heaven, earth and humanity. Therefore, the king is the one **|** , the man who connects together heaven, earth and humanity. The title for king, pronounced *wang,* was restricted to the supreme monarch during the Classical Age. It was borne only by the king of Chou, the leading feudal power. From 221 B.C., the accession of the king of Ch'in as first emperor, the term *huang* was introduced for the idea of the sole ruler of an empire. On top of the character for king the sign for antiquity was added.

KING

Although the 'Tiger of Ch'in' overthrew the feudal states and dispossessed the noble classes, he claimed to be an emperor, a ruler like the famous figures of ancient times, Huang-ti, Chuan Hsui, K'u, Yao and Shun.

EMPEROR These renowned ancestors were looked upon as 'the five sages', ideals for following ages to respect and emulate. The Chinese consciousness of being part of a long civilization existed even before the birth of Christ.

Soon the Chou kings were rulers of little more than their own city, powerless to prevent Ch'in in the west and Ch'u in the south from gaining territory through the quarrels of their Chinese neighbours. Although Sung was annexed by Ch'i in 286 B.C., the King of Ch'u had gained the greater share of the spoils with Wu, Yüeh and Lu.

But a real shock went through Chinese society when the ambitions of Ch'in were translated into action on the battlefield. In 259 B.C. the army of Chao was starved into surrender and the Ch'in commanders ordered the slaughter of all prisoners. It is said that 400 000 heads were cut off. Then, three years later,

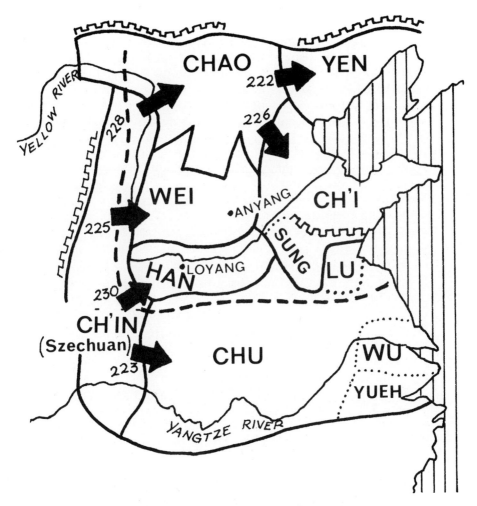

LINES OF FORTIFICATIONS

BOUNDARIES OF RECENTLY
ABSORBED STATES

LIMIT OF CHINESE STATES, ORIGINAL
MEMBERS OF THE MIDDLE KINGDOM

CH'IN CONQUESTS WITH DATES

Map showing the growth of Ch'in power 230–221 B.C.

Ch'in attacked the remaining possessions of the royal house of Chou and the Son of Heaven was dethroned. The Chou dynasty passed into history, its ancestral spirits into neglect. From this point onwards all eyes apprehensively watched as Ch'in reduced one state after another, like 'a silkworm devours a mulberry leaf.' There seemed to be an exceptional force behind the advance of Ch'in. Several factors that contributed to the ultimate Ch'in victory can be noted:

● Unlike Ch'u, its chief rival for supreme power, Ch'in occupied the loess areas and had need of vast irrigation schemes. Organizing such public works greatly strengthened the authority of the king at the expense of the nobles. A more streamlined state emerged, a predecessor of the bureaucratic system to be developed in the Chinese Empire.

● There is evidence to suggest that Ch'in was well advanced in terms of industry and may have been the first state to use iron.

● The School of the Law, the official philosophy of Ch'in, was a severe military code that made the people virtually slaves. Society had only two purposes—agriculture and war. Nothing else should be tolerated by the monarch. Cruel and merciless punishments were reserved for anyone foolish enough to disagree. Ch'in has been called a 'fascist state.'

● In 246 B.C. the future First Emperor, Shih Huang Ti, became King of Ch'in. He was a very determined man. Besides defeating all the other feudal states and unifying China for the first time, he was responsible during his reign as emperor for another event of lasting significance, namely the building of the Great Wall.

● The early conquest of modern Szechuan provided Ch'in with additional manpower resources and turned the flank of Ch'u.

● The Chinese kingdoms were always divided and involved in wars with each other. Moreover, the general decay of feudalism had encouraged internal conflicts as the old loyalties were forgotten. Confucius himself had resigned his office in his native state of Lu on account of the goings-on at court.

The 'Tiger of Ch'in' took just a quarter of a century to make himself the First Emperor in 221 B.C. After a decade of preparation the Ch'in armies were ready to devour the other states. Han went down in 230 B.C., but the decisive encounter did not occur till 223 B.C., when the great rival state of Ch'u was completely overrun. Another year saw remote Yen fall and the end of all serious resistance to the will of the Ch'in monarch.

SOCIETY

At the apex of Chinese society was the feudal hierarchy, before
the First Emperor swept away this highly privileged class. The
titles held by its members are usually translated duke, marquis,
count, viscount and baron. After the foundation of the Empire
this aristocracy was to be confined to the relatives of the reigning
imperial house, and its members, carefully watched and kept out
of the civil service, were never a powerful force in public affairs.
Below this feudal group the rest of the population was divided
in the famous four estates:

- *shih*, lesser nobility, that is the gentry and scholars;
- *nung*, the peasant farmers;
- *kung*, the artisans;
- *shang*, the merchants, the last of all.

The low social position given to the merchants was the natural
outcome of economic development in the Classical Age, for the
feudal kings had assumed most of the responsibility for industry
and public works. Irrigation schemes have already been mentioned. Metal working had come under royal control too. In the
Han Empire, the Chinese dynasty that was to oust the Ch'in in
207 B.C., there were further extensions of nationalization,
placing under imperial care the making of wine and beer. Another
emphasis unusual to people brought up in the West was the
Chinese attitude to the military. 'Good iron is not made into nails,
nor good men into soldiers,' a proverb that indicates soldiers
were also put at the bottom of the social scale. Experience of
the harshness of Ch'in rule confirmed this view, though the
philosopher Mo Tze had earlier taught the folly of war and
insisted upon the brotherhood of all men. Yet the importance
attached to learning, the respect for one's teacher, ensured that
the pattern of Chinese society was based on a civil ethic. Good
behaviour meant knowing how a citizen should behave. The poor
status of merchant and soldier has remained down the centuries.
Most important, perhaps, there was no enormous slave class.
The institution of large-scale slavery as understood in the Ancient
World—Egypt, Mesopotamia, Greece and Rome—was unknown
in Classical China. Society rested on the peasant farmers, whose
comparative freedom was confirmed after the Ch'in dynasty by
the early Han emperors. The absence of slavery seems to have
had an influence on the social outlook of the philosophers,
except the School of Law. But the barbarous actions of Ch'in
were greeted with universal disapproval.

The Family

Large families were preferred. Confucius stressed the duties of children to parents, seeing loyalty as the cornerstone of the whole social structure. 'The hundred families' had long been a name for the Chinese people. Primitive ancestor worship was gradually transformed into a ritual observance ensuring the continuation of the family. 'Five generations in one hall' became the great aim. Custom and tradition were enshrined in the Chinese family.

GOOD This is the ancient way of writing the character which means 'what is good'. It tells us a lot about the way Chinese people think too. On the left side of the character the strokes represent a woman, a wife, and on the right they show children. So important in China is the continuation of the family that the word for good is a drawing of a mother with her children. The character is pronounced like the English word 'how' and today it is written 好.

What might be called an off-shoot of large families, or clans, were the numerous secret societies. These associations may have grown in response to the general decay of society during the Warring States period. They offered protection in uncertain times, such as the decline of a dynasty, and were often directly connected with popular rebellions.

'BUYING A DEAD HORSE'

BUYING A DEAD HORSE A fable of the Warring States period tells how one of the kings desperately wanted a fast steed. For three years he sought after such a horse but without success. One day an official asked to be entrusted with the task and the king agreed. This official searched for three months before he heard about a place where a very fast horse was kept. But when he got there he found the horse had died. He considered the situation for a while and then purchased the dead horse for 500 pieces of gold. Returning to court with a dead horse made the king very angry, but nonchalantly the official said: 'I have spent five hundred pieces of gold and bought this dead horse on your behalf so that all the people under heaven will learn of your love for fast horses. This news will bring horses to court.' And so it happened that before a year had elapsed the king possessed three fast steeds.

IDEAS

The centuries of ever-increasing political confusion down to the triumph of Ch'in were accompanied by great intellectual ferment. Men cast about for explanations of contemporary failure. This was the time of the 'Hundred Schools,' when roving philosophers offered advice to any ruler who chose to listen to them. The kingdom of Ch'i welcomed philosophers of every school but Confucius was ill-used in Lu. Of the many different schools there were two that became the main currents in Chinese thought:

- Taoism, the philosophy of Lao-tzu (? born 604 B.C.) and Chuang-tzu (350–275 B.C.);
- Confucian philosophy, the ideas of Confucius (551–479 B.C.) and Mencius (374–289 B.C.).

Taoism

Lao-tzu, the Old Philosopher as he is known in China, may have been keeper of the royal archives at Loyang, the Chou capital, but few details are known of his life. He was 'a hidden wise man,' reluctant to found a school and gather a following. 'When he foresaw the decay of Chou,' the Han historian Ssu-ma Ch'ien tells us in the oldest biography, 'Lao-tzu departed and came to the frontier. The customs official, Yin-Hi, asked the sage to write a book before he retired from the world. So Lao-tzu wrote a book consisting of five thousand words, in which the proper way to live was set forth. Then he went on. No one knows where he died.'

The book mentioned here is *Tao Teh Ching*, or *The Way of Virtue*, a collection of profound sayings, many of which date from the earliest times. It is significant that in the legend about Lao-tzu's departure he was only persuaded to leave a record of his wisdom at the very last moment. Saddened by the short-sightedness of his fellow men, their tragic perversity, their inability to follow natural goodness, Lao-tzu decided to leave so-called civilization behind him. Making statements, trying to explain his ideas, would only add to the current confusion, since words have an unpleasant way of limiting what should really be said. Unlike the philosophers of the Confucian school, the Taoists held written words in mean respect.

Though the figure of Lao-tzu is wreathed uncertainly in the mists of legend, the characters in his book stand out with pristine strength. 'Conduct your triumph as a funeral': this saying has lost nothing since it was first applied to the senseless rivalry of

Lao-tzu meeting Yin-Hi on the frontier.

the Warring States. 'He who feels punctured must have been a bubble.' What concerned Lao-tzu most was man's rootedness in Nature, the inner power that made all men wiser than they knew. 'Knowledge studies others; wisdom is self-known.' The artificial demands of society had disturbed the natural abilities of men. Instead of following the Way, the *Tao*, codes of love and honesty were introduced. Learning and charity became necessary. Men have to return to the natural way of behaviour:

> As the soft yield of water cleaves obstinate stone,
> So to yield with life solves the insoluble:
> To yield, I have learned, is to come back again.
> But this unworded lesson,
> This easy example,
> Is lost upon men.

This verse may partly explain China's age-long survival. To yield and then come back again. The conquest of Ch'in was neither the last nor the worst invasion that the country was to suffer. When Marco Polo reached Cathay over a thousand years later the government was in the hands of the Mongols, fierce descendants of Genghiz Khan. Yet Chinese civilization endured the Mongols as well as other warlike peoples from the steppes. Water's being a strong element is an interesting thought, so different from firmness of rock praised in the West. The formidable rivers of China were there for everyone with eyes to see, but the humility of water, ever seeking the lowest level, was an appropriate route for the descendants of Pan Ku's fleas to tread.

Taoist philosophy received its classical form in the works of Chuang-tzu. By then it was a tradition for Taoist hermits to shun human society in order to contemplate Nature. A story about him illustrates the point. Because of intrigue and dishonesty at court a certain Prince determined to send two high officials to ask Chuang-tzu to take charge of the government and become Prime Minister. A long and weary journey brought them to the remote valley in which the sage's hut was situated, but they did not mind the hardship since they were sure that the new leader would reward them once in office. They found Chuang-tzu fishing. Intent on what he was doing he listened without turning his head. At last he said: 'I have been told there is in the capital a holy tortoise which has been dead for over a thousand years. And that the Prince keeps this tortoise carefully in a temple there. Now would this creature rather be dead but considered holy, or alive and wagging its tail in the mud?' The two officials answered that it would prefer to be alive and wagging its tail in the mud. 'Clear off from my valley then—you and your offer!' shouted Chuang-tzu. 'Like the tortoise I will wag my tail in the mud here.'

Chuang-tzu had turned down the highest office of state, something a member of the Confucian school would never have done. 'A thief steals a purse and he is hanged,' Chuang-tzu wrote, 'another man steals a kingdom and becomes a Prince.' From the Taoists came the conviction the government was a necessary evil. China needed some form of organization, they admitted, but it should be reduced to the minimum, lest restrictions hinder the natural way of doing things. Another legacy could well be Chinese science, which was far in advance of the West till the Renaissance. It has been suggested that Taoist experiments in alchemy were the beginnings of science.

Confucian Philosophy

Historically younger than Taoism, the school of philosophy that derived from Confucius' ideas became the dominant one from the Han Empire onwards. Confucius himself was a descendant of the Shang kings. His family were related to the rulers of Sung, whose Shang ancestors had been awarded this small state by Chou Kung, near the beginning of the Chou dynasty. He felt himself to be an active member of the feudal system but the

An engraving of Confucius. Contrast the formality and correctness of his clothes with the attire of Lao-tzu riding on the ox.

37

abuses prevalent during his lifetime set his mind on a course of reform. Finding his own state of Lu uninterested in what he had to say, he became the first of the 'wandering scholars,' moving from one capital to another seeking a monarch who would listen to his instructions and put his philosophy into practice. Often the reception at court was cordial enough. Yet there was always hesitation over taking virtuous advice. By Mencius' time the prolonged struggle between the Warring States had closed royal ears altogether. Mencius found that the sole concern of the King of Wei was any scheme likely to harm his rivals.

Still, Confucius collected numerous followers and his philosophy took shape in words. It was a feudal ethic, an attempt to shore up the breaches in the society of his own day, but, above all, it was essentially social-minded. The monarch must rule with benevolence and sincerity, avoiding the use of force at all costs. He should manage affairs so that justice was enjoyed by every subject. Soldiers were a sign of bad government. The virtue of the king would call forth the virtue concealed in all men. For the breakdown of society had caused men to be corrupted from their natural goodness. The duty of the subject was loyal service to the king.

The *shih*, the scholars and gentry, were responsible for the maintenance of morality too. They must display an independence of mind in the service of their king. When Confucius was asked how a Prince should be served, he answered: 'If it becomes necessary to oppose him, withstand him to his face, and don't try roundabout methods.' This firmness of principle was destined to be the cardinal rule of the imperial civil service; officials were to perish at the hands of impatient emperors, only to be admired for generations afterwards. Mencius went further in propounding the theory of justified rebellion against wicked rulers. The Mandate of Heaven was withdrawn from a corrupt dynasty whenever a successful rebel arose. This theory has been called the Chinese Constitution.

Although Confucius agreed with the Taoists over the natural goodness of men, his remedy for the times was quite different. He placed the emphasis on nurture, not Nature. Men had to learn how to conduct themselves properly. Education was given a central place in society. Young people were to be nurtured in the ways of virtue—loyalty, respect for elders, attention to ceremonies and rites, decorum. Referring to the Taoists Confucius said: 'They dislike me because I want to reform society, but if we

38

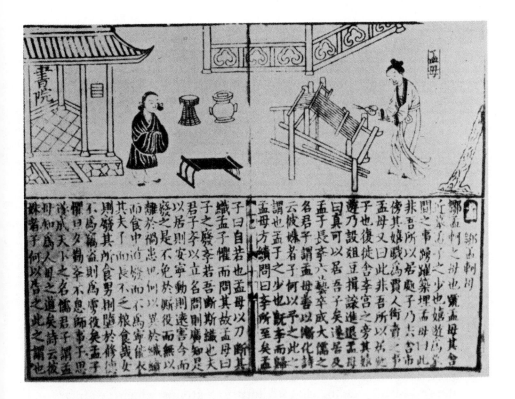

Mencius' mother. This popular story explains how wise the mother of the philosopher was in knowing how to bring him up. It is the classic account of the importance of nurture.

At first they lived in a cottage near some tombs. Finding young Mencius interested in funerals and tomb construction, she moved to a house by a market. But the activity in the market attracted the boy and she moved house again. Next to a college she was pleased to see Mencius watching the comings and goings of scholars. She said: 'This is the right place for my son'.

Returning from school one day Mencius found his mother weaving on her loom. 'Have you learnt everything now?' she asked. 'Yes', he replied, 'I know enough.' Immediately she picked up her scissors and ripped across the cloth. Mencius was shocked and worried. 'Your stupidity about learning is like my cutting through this unfinished piece of work. Men only attain fame for their knowledge after hard work and great effort. Wise men possess a breadth of learning, live in peaceful places, and shun bad things. Realize this and you will come to no harm. . . .'

are not to live with our fellow men with whom can we live? We cannot live with animals. If society was as it ought to be, I should not be wanting to change it.'

Finally, the Confucian school of philosophy introduced a sense of balance in the supernatural world as well as on the earthly level. 'I stand in awe of spirits,' Confucius said, 'but keep them at a distance.' This rational attitude ensured that a certain amount of scepticism was always available during religious crises. The T'ang scholar, Han Yu (A.D. 768–824), drew on this tradition when he composed his famous *Memorial on the Bone of Buddha*, a stinging attack on the excesses of the court. Han Yu was exiled, not executed. Taoism tended to shade too easily into magic. In the Chinese mind, however, there was room for elements from both of these main schools of thought. This capacity to retain diverse viewpoints at the same time is a notable feature of Chinese thought.

TECHNOLOGY

Major developments in technology helped to transform China into a centralized, well-organized state by 221 B.C. Furthermore, they ensured that China could maintain its independence, thus preserving the cultural pattern they had helped create. The improvements can be divided into five groups which are inter-related:

- building;
- agriculture;
- communications;
- hydraulics;
- metal working.

Improvements in these fields must be seen against changes occurring in the Chinese economy. An increasing number of people were non-food producers. Because administrators, scholars, craftsmen and soldiers depended on others to provide their food, the traditional subsistence agriculture had to be made more productive in order to guarantee a regular surplus. Increased state taxation, levied in grain, was a further stimulus to agricultural improvement. The specialists congregated in the growing number of cities which acted as administrative and military centres as well as market and service centres. In exchange for loyalty and the payment of taxes the cities were built for the benefit of the country peasants, providing winter shelter for them and giving protection from marauders. To speed the flow of food between producers and consumers, and to maintain state security and protection, improved transportation by land and water was introduced. Metallic money became acceptable instead of cowrie shells and barter for transactions and a merchant class developed. But the foundation of the whole system remained the peasant food producer.

Building

Wall building was particularly important to the early Chou since it was the foundation of both house construction and city defences. Subterranean wattle and daub cave dwellings remained in use but 'earth' walls became increasingly important in the construction of dwellings. A wall could be built of layers eight to ten centimetres thick. Each layer would be added with the use of a wooden frame into which earth was rammed until solid. This wooden shuttering would then be removed and the process repeated at the next level. Bamboo might be placed between each layer to absorb moisture, and rubble stone was often used as a foundation.

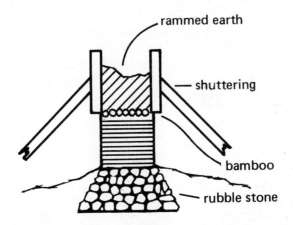

Method of wall building

These walls were particularly useful where little weight had to be carried or where protection from erosion could be obtained from overhanging eaves. In the later Chou period adobe, or sun-dried bricks, were used to construct or 'face' walls and in the Warring States period fire-baked bricks were introduced. These were often skilfully inscribed for ornamental and burial purposes.

Rival powers in the Warring States period constructed large defensive walls along their boundaries to halt invasions. The First Emperor, Ch'in Shih Huang Ti, linked and extended a number of these in order to thwart potential cavalry attacks by the nomadic peoples of the North. This was a prototype for the later Great Wall of China, which marked the border between the steppe and the sown lands. City walls date back to 1500 B.C. Prior to this the nomads and primitive hunters had used ditches or earth mounds for protection. By the Shang period city walls were up to twenty metres thick at the base and later Chou capitals had similar dimension. Hantan founded in 386 B.C. had walls over 1350 metres long, 15 metres high and 20 metres wide at the base. Some of the city walls built before the First Empire were still in use at the beginning of this century.

Agriculture
The basic foodstuff of the early Chinese farmers of the Yellow River valley was millet. By the time of the Chou dynasty this was supplemented by the other indigenous crops, kaoliang and buck wheat. The ancient method of clearing land was 'slash and burn' which accelerated erosion. The only fertilizers were ash and silt. The peasantry were obliged to work on the lord's land and spent the winters in the shelter of the cities. Along the flood plain of the Yellow River the field system was geometric with an equal re-distribution of land each year to each family. The final amount they received depended on the relative fertility and nature of the land. Livestock such as pigs, dogs, cattle, sheep, goats, water buffaloes and elephants probably originated in the forests of the South.

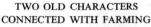

TWO OLD CHARACTERS
CONNECTED WITH FARMING

 Chiang, meaning bounds. The two fields ⊞ were separated by barriers.

 Tzu The uncultivated areas; a field exposed to floods.

The population of China may have grown fivefold to around fifty million in the Chou period. This was supported partly by an extension in farming land along the coastal lowlands but also by improvements in technique. Irrigation was first recorded around 560 B.C. and manuring seems to have become common-place by the late Chou period. New forms of livestock and crops were assimilated from the South whenever climatic conditions allowed. The northern limits of China became increasingly identified with the marginal agricultural lands on the edge of the Mongolian Plateau. This was an area of continual friction between the settled farmers who eked out a living from the dry and easily eroded soil, and the nomadic herdsmen of the steppes, the Hsiung Nu, who encroached southwards. At the same time the Chinese themselves were moving southwards into different climates. Rice had penetrated from India by about 3000 B.C. but until the Chinese had moved south of the Chin Ling mountains they did not encounter it. Rice was initially considered as having medicinal value. It was a very productive cereal which could support high population densities. As a result the southern states of China became increasingly influential. Rice could not easily be adopted north of a line drawn east from the Chin Ling for climatic reasons, but there was a definite two-way movement of agricultural knowledge between these differing economies. A great amount of organization was required for the efficient growing of rice; there must be careful control of stored water at vital times in the growing cycle. After the land had been divided into small rectangular basins, it was ploughed and harrowed before being flooded. The seeds were then sown and when the plants were thirteen to fifteen centimetres high they were planted out. The water was drained off before flowering and seeding, and flooded again afterwards. Thus co-operation was essential to the success of the rice farmers.

Communications
Good communications were necessary for strong, centralized government. The ancient *Book of Odes* records:

> The roads of Chou are smooth as whetstone,
> Straight as an arrow

and this probably helped account for the long reign of this feudal dynasty. As the stability broke down so each individual state took charge of its own road system, and it was not surprising that the eventual dominance of the Ch'in was related in part to its engineering skills.

In the early Chou period the main routeways ran east–west along the Yellow River valley and then south to the Huai and Yangtze valleys. Chinese road-building techniques were quite different from those used by the Romans. While the latter favoured enormous foundations and heavy surfacing, the Chinese relied on the use of thin, convex, watertight 'shells' over ordinary subsoil as the base. (This technique was to be adopted by McAdam in Britain over 2000 years later.)

'The radiation of virtue,' Confucius is reported to have said, 'is faster than the transmission of imperial orders by stages and couriers.' The Posting System was used for the speedy relay of royal orders and to obtain systematic intelligence reports from frontier regions. Ch'in became skilled in building roads as they forged southwards over the Chin Ling barriers towards the important area of modern Szechuan. The 'five-foot [1·5 metres] way' was a remarkable feat, which included many kilometres of 'hanging galleries,' suspended along the sides of precipitous slopes.

Hanging galleries.

Great importance was attached to bridge building and several forms were developed. The simplest was the wooden-beam bridge which was seldom more than 6 metres long. This could be extended into a trestle bridge resting on partly submerged piers. Records exist of bridges over 600 metres long with 68 spans and a deck 17 metres wide. Since these lay close to the water they were often submerged in floods. Stone-arch bridges were also constructed.

Hydraulics
In the Yellow River basin eighty per cent of the rainfall falls in the three summer months when the cold dry continental winds are replaced by the warm moist monsoons. However, the quantity and timing of rainfall was so irregular that drought or flooding were equally likely. The Yellow River was the most difficult to master, followed by the Huai and Yangtze rivers. It carries up to 1 000 million tons of silt every year and deposits much of this on its flood plain, elevating it above the surrounding lowlands, and making it very vulnerable to changes in course and flooding when the banks burst.

Yü the Great Engineer initially controlled the waters by deepening the existing channels rather than building dams. Before 600 B.C. Duke Huan of Ch'i built levels or dykes along the nine branches of the flood plain. Usually the policy of containing the river has failed because it proved impossible to control nature.

One scheme carried out in the Ch'in State stands out as being highly successful. In 246 B.C. the Cheng Kuo Canal was built parallel to the Wei river. It was the organization of this scheme which consolidated the power of Ch'in. The scheme still operates today.

The importance of controlling floods and drought was not seen purely in agricultural terms. Political considerations were present too. An official might have reasoned along these lines: If floods should break the dykes along the rivers, this would cause drowning and distress among the people. Distress leads to a disregard for morality and increases the problem of maintaining order. Hence, it is in the interests of political stability to encourage hydraulic engineering developments. The way out of the problem is for men to act in disciplined unity. Reaching such a conclusion, the official would see to it that the labour was organized through the *corvée* (obligatory unpaid labour for the state) and engineers appointed.

Metal Working
Though bronze reached China as late as 1500 B.C., the Chinese reached a far higher level of technique than other bronze users. Iron arrived in China about 700 B.C. and the earliest examples of work include cauldrons inscribed with the code of law. We know that the King of Wu had weapons of iron by 500 B.C., but the use of iron probably permeated eastwards via the passes of the Tarim Basin. This could account for the development of iron in Ch'in, a factor in its military superiority.

Iron was used for tools, such as hoes and ploughshares, besides weapons. What is important about iron production in China is the fact that it was smelted and cast almost as soon as it was known. In the West iron working was to be limited to the forge until A.D. 1350. Possible reasons for this great advance were:

● high phosphorus content of Chinese iron which lowered the melting point of the ore;

● good refractory clays for making crucibles for steel production and moulds for casting;

● the development of double acting piston bellows which maintained high and constant draughts into the furnaces, thus keeping temperatures high;

● the extremely advanced traditions of copper and clay working.

In China this knowledge did not fundamentally alter the nature of society as it did in the West.

2 One Empire Under Heaven

The unification of China under the Ch'in and Han dynasties, 221 B.C.–A.D. 220

HISTORICAL OUTLINE

By 221 B.C. the Ch'in armies had crushed all remaining pockets of resistance and the King of Ch'in was able to proclaim himself Shih Huang Ti, 'the First Emperor.' In place of the old feudal system of government belonging to the Classical Age a centralized monarchy was established. For the future development of China the significance of the revolutionary change that Shih Huang Ti began and Liu Pang, the founder of the following purely Chinese dynasty, the Han, completed cannot be underestimated. Under the Han Emperors the political structure assumed a pattern that was to serve China right down till 1912, when the Empire was overthrown and the Republic founded.

The Triumph of Shih Huang Ti

The ruthless determination that had directed the 'Tiger of Ch'in' in his defeat of the ancient feudal kingdoms soon became evident in the organization of the new Empire. Indeed, Shih Huang Ti was one of the great destroyers of history. He was conscious of the insecurity of his Empire, which lacked any degree of economic integration. Strict military control he decided was the quickest and most efficient way of bringing stability. Insecurity came from two sources:

● In the east there was an internal political threat from the aristocracy of old feudal states.

● In the north the Hsiung Nu nomads, probably the Huns who invaded the Roman Empire in the fourth century A.D., were a continual danger.

To break the power of the nobility Shih Huang Ti abolished all the feudal states and divided the Empire into new administrative areas, under military governors. Great landowners lost their estates and all the nobles were forced to reside at the Ch'in capital, where isolated from their supporters they remained without influence. The *nung*, the peasant farmers, were given greater rights over their land, but were liable for taxes.

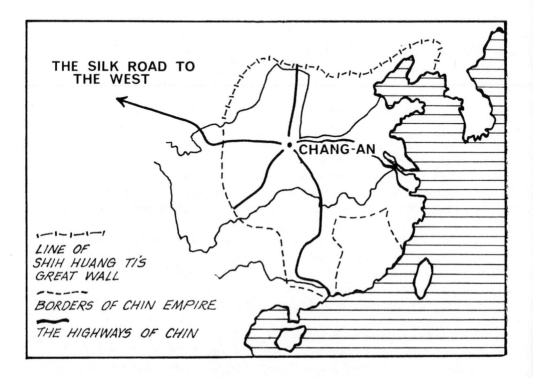

China 206 B.C.

Unification and centralization were synonymous for Shih Huang Ti. Since the capital could hardly be considered central to the Empire, a good communication system was essential both for dispatch of messages and for transport of armies and taxes. To ease communication between previously independent provinces it was not sufficient merely to extend the superior roads and canals of the Ch'in State. The written language was standardized as were currency, weights and measures. These eased the collection of the all-important grain taxes on which prosperity depended. It was impossible to have a large administrative capital without a constant supply of foodstuffs to feed it. The Emperor made it his policy to visit all points of the Empire in order to check on the work of his administrators, though his movements were always kept secret. The first Emperor was a harsh ruler, but his policy of centralization helped foster a feeling of national identity among the Chinese.

The location of the imperial capital itself, near Chang-an, in the heart of Ch'in, caused deep resentment. The Ch'in, inhabiting the Wei Valley, were disliked by the lowland Chinese because of their contact with the nomad peoples, which had led to some intermarriage, and because they were essentially a war-orientated society with distinct military advantages. They had adopted cavalry and obtained iron weapons in the preceding centuries. From their favoured geographical position, protected on three sides by mountain or desert, the Ch'in could sweep down into the lowlands and retire into an almost impregnable stronghold whenever the forces of the Great Plain were organized. Thus in choosing Chang-an, Shih Huang Ti increased his chances of holding the capital and, by extending the highly efficient radial road system to link the extreme points of the Empire, he could ensure his orders were transmitted rapidly to the farthest outposts.

Perhaps most important the First Emperor refused to grant fiefs, feudal holdings of land, to his sons or relatives, since he felt they might revive the local divisions which had caused rivalry in the period of the Warring States. When the *shih*, the scholars, argued for the maintenance of the boundaries of the feudal kingdoms, Li Ssu, Shih Huang Ti's tough minister, made it clear that the Empire was going to last for 'ten thousand years' because the throne had reduced everything 'in a uniform manner.'

Although Confucius had not condemned empire, he had been unaware of such a possibility, so that his followers at this moment in time were opposed to the end of feudalism. Finding this alliance between the dispossessed nobles and the scholars dangerous for the régime, Li Ssu made his infamous proposal to Shih Huang Ti. Throughout the Empire, on pain of death, teaching should be banned and all books except those dealing with technical subjects like agriculture burnt. Only the history of Ch'in was to be read. In this way, Li Ssu hoped, the people would have to adopt the philosophy of the School of Law.

The Burning of the Books was the death-blow for feudal ideals: it caused a definite break in consciousness. When, in Han times, the ancient texts were painfully reconstructed, from memory and the badly tattered copies that had been hidden at great personal risk, the feudal world seemed remote. Education, not birth, appeared the important social qualification. Li Ssu had dealt a decisive blow at the aristocracy, but he had weakened the Ch'in dynasty too. The *shih* were united in hatred against the imperial house. Only the official class of Ch'in remained loyal.

The Great Wall of China

It was *the measure introduced to deal with the Hsiung Nu,* namely the Building of the Great Wall, that unified the ordinary people against the Ch'in dynasty. Along the northern boundaries of the feudal states walls had been constructed as a means of defence against raids from nomadic tribes. Such an invasion had shaken the power of the Chou kingdom in 771 B.C. To give the Empire permanent protection, to divide the steppe from the sown, Shih Huang Ti ordered that the old walls be joined together as a continuous 'Great Wall.' The completed line of the wall ran from the western frontier of Ch'in to the sea in the east, a distance of 2 250 kilometres. It has close proximity to the 15 inch (380 mm) isohyet which effectively marks the limits of settled agriculture and may have moved further south since the second century B.C. through desiccation of the region.

'A wall between is a mountain' runs an ancient Chinese proverb.
The Great Wall of Shih Huang Ti did act as an immense barrier
between the steppe and the sown. The construction was rubble filled
walls faced with stone, topped by a brick roadway edged with a
parapet and battlements. Towers were sited at strategic points and
gateways had additional defensive walls.

Hundreds of thousands toiled on the immense task of construction, prisoners of war and conscripted labourers, working and dying in the cold mountains of the north. The terrible lot of these people has remained a constant subject for Chinese folksong ever since. Forced labour on the Great Wall and the road network became an everyday fact of life for the people under the harsh rule of the School of Law. Ch'in governors, backed with large garrisons, enforced one severe decree after another. But not all the reforms of Shih Huang Ti were pitiless. He standardized weights and measures, transport, currency and the written script. As an administrator he worked hard, handling 'fifty-four kilos of reports' daily, and he travelled widely.

The Fall of Ch'in
No rebellion occurred during the eleven stern years that Shih Huang Ti ruled, but his less able successor was soon engulfed with risings in every province. Heavy taxes, forced labour, unjust laws, cruel tortures, widespread crime—all the ingredients for popular rebellion were there awaiting an opportunity: it came with an intrigue over the succession. Li Ssu concealed the fact of the First Emperor's death in 210 B.C. long enough to force the Crown Prince to commit suicide by a forged imperial command. The Crown Prince had objected to the treatment of the scholars and had been banished to the northern frontier. Fearing for his own safety now his old master was dead, the minister had the second son declared Er Shih Huang Ti, or the Second Emperor. He proved too young and incompetent to deal with the rebels.

As soon as the Ch'in generals put down one rising another broke out. Soldiers mutinied, peasants took up arms, and rebel armies gathered strength. The civil war was a long contest between several leaders, who at first pretended to restore the old feudal kingdoms, till Liu Pang gained overall control in 207 B.C. A man of obscure origins, possibly the son of a village headman and certainly illiterate, he was forced into active rebellion by the excessive rigour of Ch'in law. Having lost a group of convicts and being doomed to execution for this failure of responsibility, Liu Pang deserted and became the leader of a band of such fugitives.

The Foundation of the Han Empire
That a part of the inspiration for the popular rebellions against the Ch'in dynasty was a desire to put the clock back to feudal

一日萬幾圖

Here the legendary Emperor Shun is shown going carefully through piles of reports and other documents brought to a terrace by his secretaries. The drawing comes from a Ch'ing edition of the Shu Ch'ing. *Shih Huang Ti was an efficient ruler too.*

53

times cannot be doubted. 'The Avenging Army of Ch'u' was the name of one rebel force. But so thorough had been Shih Huang Ti's measures against the old order that in the hour of Ch'in's collapse all attempts to re-establish feudal authority were unsuccessful.

However, Liu Pang, as the Emperor Han Kao Tsu, or 'High Ancestor,' sought a compromise. He saw that though Ch'in policy was correct in reducing everything 'in a uniform manner,' it was necessary to go about it more tactfully. He was prepared to move slowly and undermine feudal institutions over a number of decades. Fiefs were permitted and a few of the old royal houses received small territories, but future Emperors could only come from his own family. Besides, the principal areas came directly under the Emperor's control through the appointment of imperial officers in the Ch'in manner. To make completely sure of his position the Emperor Kao Tsu steadily eliminated possible rivals, loyal generals included, so that his successors inherited undisputed sway over 'the Empire of all beneath Heaven.'

Two things hastened the decline of what was left of feudal influence:

● In 144 B.C. it was decreed that all the sons of a feudal lord were co-heirs of their father, and his estates must be divided among them. This measure accelerated the breakdown of large feudal holdings into little more than substantial country estates.

● Then it was decided that many of the aristocrats should live on their rents in the capital, Chang-an. This measure combined with the threat of dispossession for misconduct caused ties between feudal families and their traditional localities to wither away.

By 100 B.C. the Court was the undisputed centre of power and authority.

The Court

As the Liu family enjoyed great prestige and produced a succession of excellent rulers, the Han Empire was not much troubled by rebellions. Where political difficulties arose was in the palace, with plots and intrigues centred on the Consort Family, the relations of the Empress. With the passing of the feudal kingdoms a China isolated from the rest of the world could not provide royal brides for each new Emperor. The advantage of a foreign Empress or Queen, as European states have found, is that she has no relatives in the country and cannot readily become the centre of a faction. Since in China marriage within the same

family was strictly forbidden by immemorial custom the choice
of a new Empress became a matter of immense importance. As
relatives of the imperial house her kinsfolk automatically became
'the Second Family.' They expected high offices and rewards.
Each new Empress would wish to see her people enjoying the
status they deserved and the Emperor could be expected to grant
her requests. The conflict became intense when two Consort
Families were struggling for position. This situation occurred
when the new Consort Family, the relatives of the Emperor's
young bride, were opposed by the old Consort Family, the
relatives of the Emperor's mother.

Such court intrigue remained a permanent feature of the
Chinese Empire. Only the sixth Han ruler, Emperor Wu, 'the
Warlike,' who reigned from 140 to 86 B.C., ever solved the
problem. He took a desperate course; he executed all the members
of the Empress' family. Though this left his court free from
family strife, later Emperors did not follow his example. As a
result the Wang family succeeded in temporarily taking over the
Empire for fourteen years (from 9 to A.D. 23). But the usurping
uncle, Wang Mang, found the provinces solidly against his rule
so that at last another branch of the Liu family was able to
reinstate the Han dynasty in a new capital at Loyang.

Away from the imperial city itself these intrigues, short of civil
war, were hardly noticed. Governors might change but the
system of government went on unaffected. Liu Pang had founded
the Empire well. The Han dynasty (207 B.C.–A.D. 220) made
united China a reality for centuries and an ideal for which in
times of later division men would always strive. 'Men of Han,'
in fact, became one of the names for the Chinese thereafter.

The End of the Han Empire

Not surprisingly the Han dynasty lost the Empire through a
struggle with an all-too-important Consort Family, the Liang.
In A.D. 159 the Emperor Han Huang Ti used the palace eunuchs
to oust the Liang from office. Yet this dependence on the eunuchs
eventually proved more disastrous than the old trouble with the
Consort Families. Unable to found families of their own and
recruited from the lowest levels of society, the eunuchs took
advantage of their new power to gather personal wealth. Weak
Emperors failed to check their activities and corruption became
rife. When a loyal general, the brother of a dowager Empress,
was assassinated by the eunuchs in A.D. 186, his infuriated
soldiers stormed the palace and massacred them. The ensuing

civil war destroyed the Han Empire and split China into the Three Kingdoms.

THE CIVIL SERVICE AND THE REVIVAL OF LEARNING

Despite his lack of education the first Han Emperor did not persecute the *shih*. He allowed the scholars to reconstruct the ancient texts and reopen their schools. Employment for large numbers of them was provided in the body of government officials that became necessary for the smooth running of the Empire. In 206 B.C. the harsh Ch'in laws were repealed, and gentler ones introduced. The growing influence of Confucian philosophy can be observed from this event onwards. An episode concerning the Emperor and his chamberlain, Lu Chia, reveals the civilizing efforts of Confucian scholars.

Lu Chia constantly quoted from the ancient books to the Emperor, who ended by becoming exasperated. 'I conquered the empire on horseback,' he cried, 'what is the good of these sayings?' Lu Chia replied: 'That is true, but it is not on horseback that you will be able to govern it. War and peace are two aspects of an eternal art. If the Ch'in, having become masters of the empire, had governed it in humanity and righteousness, if they had imitated the ancient sages, you would not have got it.' The Emperor changed colour and said: 'Show me then what it is that lost the empire for Ch'in, and how it was I got it, and what it was that won and lost kingdoms of old.' So Lu Chia wrote a book about the causes of the rise and fall of states. There were twelve chapters in all. He read them one after the other to the Emperor, who never failed to praise them.

The School of Law was identified with the worst excesses of Ch'in rule. Those who believed in the values of this stern code soon disappeared from imperial service. During the long reign of the Emperor Wu not only did a regular civil service become the accepted basis of organization for the Empire, but the means of selection for entry into its ranks included the examination of a candidate's understanding of the teachings of Confucius. The ideal candidate was distinguished by 'abundant talents,' respect for family, moral rectitude and learning. In 124 B.C. the Poh Shih Kuan, or the Imperial University, was set up, with a department for each of the ancient books. Many of its students were recruited as government officials. Provincial centres of learning were founded at this period too.

A photograph taken in 1925 of the old examination cells at Nanking.

Under the system of imperial examinations candidates who had won their bachelor's degrees locally used to assemble at the provincial capital for the examinations for the master's degree. Each candidate spent his days in one of a vast range of cells like riverside changing-cabins, guarded by invigilators and supplied with frugal meals brought in from the outside. In the Ming and Ch'ing Empires, the subjects were confined to orthodox literature and philosophy; but during the T'ang and Sung Empires the examinations were more concerned with concrete administrative, governmental and economic problems, while technical subjects such as astronomy, engineering and medicine could be taken too.

The ruling *shih* were recruited through this examination system, whose origins date from the Han Empire. In the nineteenth century European countries adopted the idea of competitive entry to their own civil services. Today, the People's Republic has moved away from such a system—it is considered élitist and undemocratic.

Inevitably the socially well-placed families were able to take the most advantage of this system. They could afford for their sons the many years of education necessary to obtain literary success. At first there were built-in advantages for these people, special exemptions and other rights, but gradually the examination system gained authority and served as 'an open door' for the gifted son of humbler parents. The members of the civil service became a learned élite; families rose into this estate and sank out of it. It was not hereditary. These cultivated officials and lesser gentry, the *shih*, and the peasant farmers, the *nung*, formed the two great pillars on which the structure of the Empire rested till its final overthrow in 1911. The *nung* supported the system, while the *shih* made it work.

The assimilation of the *shih* into the very heart of the Han Empire was possible through the disappearance of feudalism. The followers of Confucius, with their strong sense of duty and their desire to have an orderly society, were naturally drawn into government service. Confucian philosophy was applied to Empire and founded the 'most glorious of the hundred schools.' The Han Emperors encouraged the process for good reasons, not least connected with their own humble origins and lack of noble blood. A system of promotion based on education, not blood, was not inappropriate for a family that had raised, by its own efforts, a member to the exalted position of Son of Heaven.

A revival of learning sprang directly from the tolerance of the Han Emperors. The ancient texts were reconstructed, from memory and surviving fragments. New commentaries were written. Historical writing became a major interest. Ssu-ma Tan, the father, and Ssu-ma Ch'ien, the son, wrote their *Shih Chi* (*Historical Memoirs*). As officials at the court of Emperor Wu they had access to the imperial library and archives. Ssu-ma Ch'ien also travelled the length and breadth of the Empire. The invention of the brush pen began to make a notable change in the style of the characters when used on silk. The beginnings of later achievements in calligraphy, the writing of Chinese characters, and painting date from the Han Empire.

ECONOMY AND SOCIETY

The law honours farmers, yet farmers have become poorer and poorer; the law degrades merchants, yet merchants have become richer and richer.

The view of a shih *in the second century B.C.*

Feudalism had not been destroyed for the benefit of the fifty million peasants but to create absolute power for the First Emperor and his descendants. Political changes were immaterial to the *nung* until they actually prevented them from earning a living. This could occur through greedy administrators, high taxes or an abuse of the *corvée*; or through inconsiderate or non-existent government action to ease periodic famine. But since Confucian philosophy interpreted natural disasters as a sign that a régime had lost the Mandate of Heaven, only a foolish ruler did not consider the feelings of the *nung*. They were the vast majority of his subjects and they provided the food for the maintenance of cities and armies.

The King Emperor and the Peasant Emperor

Shih Huang Ti did a creditable job in uniting the Warring States during his eleven years as Emperor. He did reduce a great deal 'in a uniform manner.' The standardization of cart axles is a good example of Shih Huang Ti's attention to detail. Previously the cart-wheels of one state would not fit the ruts made by the cart-wheels of another state. Loads had to be transferred at borders, where reweighing slowed down transport considerably. Common weights and measures, coupled with a reduction of local corruption and inefficiency, encouraged the growth of trade throughout the Ch'in Empire. The freer interchange of people and goods gave impetus to the Chinese nationalist movement, which came to maturity in the Han Empire.

Although Liu Pang followed this policy, there was a funda-mental difference in his attitude towards the four estates of society. The first Han Emperor avoided the harshness of the School of Law. It should not be forgotten that each great feat of Ch'in civil engineering from the Great Wall to the reconstruc-tion of the capital at Hsien Yang (near to Chang-an) required hundreds of thousands of labourers who were conscripted in an outright abuse of the *corvée*. Such large-scale projects completely disrupted the agricultural cycle of entire regions. Up to 700 000 coolies had been involved in the construction of Shih Huang Ti's palace, which towered above the two hundred and seventy other palaces built at Hsien Yang to house the exiled nobles from the Warring States.

Liu Pang was a man of the people; he ruled by obtaining their support. He is remembered also as a lover of women and wine. When he had to leave his homeland of Chou in order to take residence at the new capital Chang-an, he left with tears after throwing a farewell party for his poorer friends. Such stories reflect the human image of a man who was called the Great Ancestor, 'Kao Tsu.'

Commerce in Chaos

Liu Pang was disturbed to see merchants filling the power gaps left in the provinces after the collapse of feudalism, but he found this process hard to check. Because the merchant had a local monopoly he could buy grain at very low prices at harvest time, then hoard it until scarcity forced the price up. In periods of famine the monopolists could become extremely wealthy. A policy of discrimination and taxation against these speculators failed to alter this situation and it was repealed soon after the death of Emperor Han Kao Tsu.

The economy had come under stresses that are quite familiar to us, today.

● Government reserves were drained by maintaining forces in the North. As a result taxes had to be increased.

● The minting of money by private individuals led to a continual rise in the price of grain and also threatened to make such people financially stronger than the Emperor.

● In salt and iron production too the manufacturers became increasingly richer, through virtual monopolies.

● Because a few were wealthy there was only a veneer of prosperity, concealing underlying chaos.

● The *nung* were suffering at the hands of the grain speculators and their incomes were always falling behind the level of prices.

Nationalization

In 140 B.C. Emperor Wu came to power and in his incisive manner attempted to wrestle the wealth from the merchants and industrialists in order to finance his military expeditions. At first he courted them, taking the most able into the civil service, a course of action that upset the *shih*. Always short of money, Wu subjected China to heavy taxation and increasing production of worthless coinage. He nationalized the iron and salt industries, employing their former owners to run them. By 100 B.C. all iron was supposedly produced in forty-nine government factories. Later in the Han Empire beer and wine production were nationalized too. None of these measures had the desired effect of reducing rampant inflation. Barter began to replace cash transactions and eventually the sheer low value of each unit of currency led to a cessation of the illegal minting of coins, which had become something of a business for many families.

A Notable Success

To prevent fluctuation in food prices provincial officials were ordered to establish public granaries, to buy grain when prices were low, and to sell in times of shortage. This was the *p'ing chun* or 'levelling system,' specifically designed to break the monopoly of local merchants. Of all Emperor Wu's measures the 'ever normal' granary was admitted to be most effective, even by the traditional *shih*. The merchants remained wealthy enough to be able to buy titles and positions with grain or livestock, but the *nung* were safeguarded against heavy speculation.

After Wu's death the Empire tottered on the verge of economic and military ruin. From the signs of famine and war it could be interpreted that the days of the Han Empire were numbered, and Wang Mang, a highly esteemed member of the Empress's family, considered that he had received the call from Heaven to save China. Establishing himself as the founder of the brief Hsin dynasty (A.D. 9–23), he was popular and unpopular by turns. A great rebellion ended his reign of fourteen years and named him posthumously 'the Usurper.' But his controversial efforts deserve our attention.

The Revolutionary Reformer

Increasingly, great landlords were dominating agriculture, buying out smaller farmers, who could not compete. The Ch'in and Han dynasties had not prevented this trend for two reasons. First, it permitted an increase in productivity, which a growing population needed. Secondly, the landowners were influential and some account had to be taken of their interests.

A small farmer in debt through a bad harvest might mortgage his land, eventually being forced to give it up when debts could not be repaid. A tenant farmer had to pay half his produce in rent and the rest was split between his family, the government and seed for the following year.

Wang Mang decided on the following reforms:

● no buying and selling of land was allowed, as it belonged to the nation;

 ● each farmer was to be allocated land in proportion to his needs;

 ● idle land should be triply taxed;

 ● there should be a reintroduction of the 'levelling system,' which had been allowed to lapse;

 ● government banks were to give small loans to farmers at low interest;

● administrative expenses were to be met out of the existing monopolies of liquor, salt, iron and coinage;

● no buying and selling of slaves should be allowed.

Thrust upon an ill-prepared country the administration of these schemes created chaos and bitterness on all sides. Eventually the *nung*, who were suffering as much as anyone from the measures intended to help them, joined with the landowners and the outraged *shih* to overthrow the Hsin dynasty.

CHINESE EXPANSION AND THE DISCOVERY OF THE WORLD

The area occupied solely by Chinese within the Empire was limited to the flood plains of the Yellow River. From 'The Land within the Passes' the Chinese had continually moved southwards, particularly from 400 to 200 B.C. when the population expanded rapidly with improved agriculture. This movement was always accelerated by famine, whether caused by drought, flood or war.

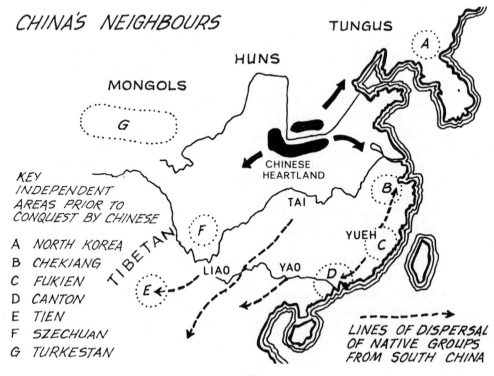

CHINA'S NEIGHBOURS

TUNGUS

A

HUNS

MONGOLS

G

CHINESE HEARTLAND

KEY
INDEPENDENT
AREAS PRIOR TO
CONQUEST BY CHINESE

TAI

B

A NORTH KOREA
B CHEKIANG
C FUKIEN
D CANTON
E TIEN
F SZECHUAN
G TURKESTAN

TIBETAN

F

YUEH

C

LIAO

YAO

D

E

LINES OF DISPERSAL
OF NATIVE GROUPS
FROM SOUTH CHINA

Often conflict with the indigenous peoples of the South was limited, for the most primitive were hill-forest dwellers, while the Chinese farmed the plains. Shih Huang Ti encouraged such movements southwards but discouraged any movement to the North fearing that the farmers of the northern outposts might abandon their often marginal farms to take up stock raising and join the nomadic herders.

China's Neighbours in the South
The main groups of non-Chinese peoples in contact with the Empire were as follows:

● *The Liao* These were a very primitive tribe originating in the forested hills of Hupei and Hunan to the south of the Yangtze River. The Chinese tended to avoid them because of their backwardness.

● *The Yao* These too originated in Hunan but spread throughout the hill country of South China. They practised primitive agriculture unlike the Liao, who were entirely hunters and collectors.

● *The Tai* They came from the flatter lands of the Yangtze valley and later spread throughout South-East Asia, particularly in Thailand and Burma. They had a sophisticated agricultural system based on rice and it was through contact with these people that the Chinese improved their own agriculture, adopting many new crops and animals like the water buffalo.

● *The Yüeh* The greatest resistance to Chinese encroachment was displayed by the Yüeh. They were a well-organized people who may have been related to those previously mentioned. As the inhabitants of the south-east coastlands they were masters of maritime enterprise. Their supremacy in coastal waters, coupled with the mountainous terrain encircling their coastal states, gave them greater protection from Chinese dominance.

China's Neighbours in the North
To the north and west of the Empire dwelt tribes of nomadic herdsmen. They were all regarded by the Chinese as 'barbarians,' but formed basically four geographically distinct groups. These were:

● *The Tibetans*, whose economy depended on sheep. Although not highly organized as a military and political force, they came into conflict with the Chinese during the Han dynasty. They usually fought on foot as their horses were inferior to the cavalry chargers of more organized armies. However, in their fastness of

63

high mountains they remained largely undisturbed. Altitude sickness always hampered later imperial forces sent from China.

● *The Mongols* They inhabited the steppes and plateaux which rolled down from the Tarim Basin to North China. Their economy was based on cattle, though like the Turkish group they also had sheep, camels and goats. Since they lived across the overland trade routes to Central Asia, the Chinese had contact with them over a long period.

● *The Turks* These were the Hsiung Nu, or Huns, that were a constant threat to the northern frontier of China. Horses comprised the basis of all wealth in their economy, though other animals were kept. They were highly mobile and well-organized. Their reputation as fierce fighters was fully deserved. After 200 B.C. they abandoned what little farming they had done and became involved in barter trade as well as pillage of neighbouring agriculturalists, such as the Chinese.

● *The Tungus* of Manchuria and Hopeh. These differed in many respects from the other northern peoples. As forest dwellers with an economy based on pigs they had little occasion for fighting the Chinese.

The Great Wall and the Huns
The success of Shih Huang Ti's wall was noticeable between about 200 and 140 B.C. when the Hsiung Nu were persuaded to adopt a policy of peaceful coexistence and trade with the Empire. They accepted gifts of silk and other luxuries, and even copied some Chinese customs. But in 141 B.C. the Han Emperor, Wu (the Warlike), tried to ambush the Chief of the Hsiung Nu at a frontier post on the Great Wall. The Chief escaped and a very long war broke out in which the Chinese had greater success than in earlier encounters due to their increasing competence as horsemen. Two pieces of technology gave the Han Empire security in the north—the fortifications of the Great Wall and the longer range of the crossbow, invented at the end of the Chou dynasty but developed by the Han—yet for Emperor Wu this was insufficient. He wanted to dominate the steppelands too.

The struggle came to a temporary halt in 51 B.C. following civil conflict within the nomad nation. It resumed in A.D. 73 as nomad raiders took advantage of discord in the Empire. But the significance of the feud with the Hsiung Nu lay rather in China's attempts to obtain allies and outflank them. An era of exploration and conquest was stimulated by these goals and was to expand China's political boundaries far beyond the valleys of the Yellow

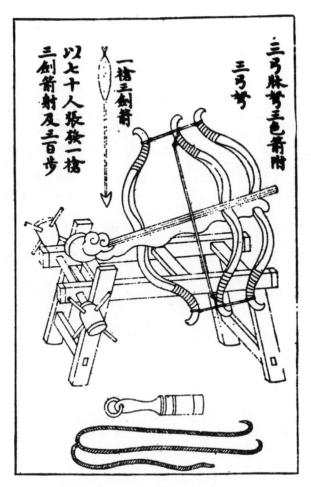

Large-scale use of the crossbow, from a handbook
(A.D. 1044).

and Yangtze Rivers. The Han Empire extended its authority over large areas of Central Asia, a relationship that persists even today, and by annexing Lak Lang province, now North Korea, Chinese culture came to flow down the peninsula and, eventually, across the sea to influence Japan. Incidentally, China discovered the West.

The Discovery of the West
Searching for allies against the Hsiung Nu in 138 B.C., Emperor Wu dispatched Chang Ch'ien to find the Ta Yueh Chi, nomads living to the west. In spite of being held prisoner by the Hsiung Nu for a decade Chang Ch'ien eventually located the Ta Yueh

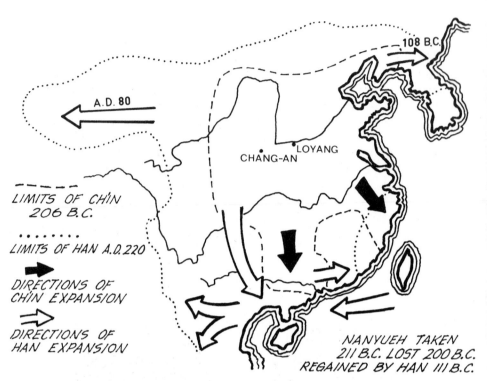

108 B.C.

A.D. 80

LOYANG

CHANG-AN

LIMITS OF CHIN
206 B.C.

LIMITS OF HAN A.D. 220

DIRECTIONS OF
CHIN EXPANSION

DIRECTIONS OF
HAN EXPANSION

NANYUEH TAKEN
211 B.C. LOST 200 B.C.
REGAINED BY HAN 111 B.C.

Imperial expansion 220 B.C.–220 A.D.

Chi, far removed from China and uninterested in returning. They had settled in Ta Hsia, now part of Russian Turkestan and Afghanistan, but what had been a few years before the Chinese envoy's arrival the Greek kingdom of Bactria.

Chang Ch'ien was amazed to discover a settled population: his report of the journey speaks of 'cities, mansions and houses as in China.' Here was another civilization, beyond the nomad lands. The description excited the Court in Chang-an, as did his news of India and Persia. But what interested Emperor Wu were the fine horses Chang Ch'ien had seen on his journey through Ta Yuan. These large animals could carry heavily armed men against the Hsiung Nu who rode the smaller Mongolian pony. Embassies and military expeditions were sent to Ta Yuan, the incredible distance of two thousand miles, until by 102 B.C. the forceful Emperor had obtained enough horses for breeding purposes.

Contact with states in Bactria and northern India was interrupted by troubles at the Han Court, the usurpation of Wang Mang (A.D. 9–23), and the Kushan invasion of India. When the second phase of Han discovery of the West took place at the end of the first century A.D., the chance of cultural exchange between European and Chinese civilization had gone. The Greek element in that region, with the exception of the arts, was submerged in Buddhist India and the ruling Kushans, a nomadic tribe recently converted to Buddhism, had adopted Indian culture. Between A.D. 73 and A.D. 102 General Pan Chao established Chinese overlordship of Central Asia, even reaching the shores of the Caspian Sea with an army of seventy thousand men, but his envoys did not open up relations with the Roman Empire. The other civilization that was to touch China, now that the 'Empire of all under Heaven' had learnt of other advanced worlds, was not Europe, but India. The transplanting of the Buddhist faith to China confirmed the oriental frame of Chinese society and continued it along its separate course, so remote from the historical experience of Western Europe.

Coin of King Menander. This silver coin was struck by Menander, King of North India; it has a bilingual inscription in Greek and an Indian language. After the death of Alexander in 323 B.C. the eastern provinces of his empire were ruled by the Seleucid dynasty from Antioch in Syria. But about 250 B.C. they broke off as an independent Greek kingdom. Under Demetrius I Bactrians, Greeks and Indians merged as a single people in the Buddhist kingdom of Bactria. His general Menander invaded the north of India around 190 B.C. and was made a separate king. A famous Indian book, the ancient *Milinda Panha*, records Menander's own conversion to Buddhism. Other Greek kings appeared in north-west India but they were swept away by the great invasion of the Kushan tribes during the first century B.C. Bactria and Ferghana, to the north, had many magnificent cities and towns at this time. Large-scale irrigation schemes permitted agriculture while international trade brought in commodities and wealth. The present-day desolation is largely due to the fury of the Mongols. Early in the thirteenth century A.D. Genghiz Khan devastated the entire area.

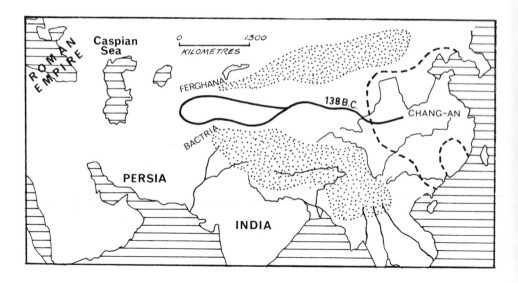

Probable route of Chang Ch'ien (138–126 B.C.) during his mission to the Ta Yueh Chi.

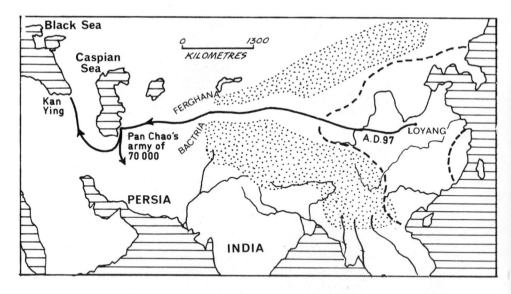

General Pan Chao reached the shores of the Caspian Sea in A.D. 97. This is the closest point that a Chinese force has ever approached Europe. But the majority of Pan Chao's troops were raised in the kingdoms of Central Asia which had accepted Han overlordship on the march westwards. An ambassador, Kan Ying, was sent towards the Roman Empire but he returned to Pan Chao's camp without making contact.

A tea caravan on a pass near Tachienlu on the borders of Tibet.

A clay model of a horse (A.D. 220–589). It is one of the heavier breeds that the Han Emperors sought for their cavalry regiments.

The Coming of Buddhism

The only significant foreign influence on the Chinese people has been the teachings of the Buddha. Nothing else, till the nineteenth century, has ever modified the way of life followed by the 'Men of Han' to the extent achieved by this religion. The Han Empire officially noticed Buddhism in A.D. 65, though it is likely that some of Buddha's teaching had earlier travelled back along the path trodden by Chang Ch'ien. An embassy was sent to India to collect copies of the *sutras*, or holy books, and Indian scholars to help translate them. Centuries of labour and many pilgrimages to India were necessary before the Buddhist scriptures became generally available in China. It was in the fifth and sixth centuries A.D. that Buddhism developed into a great popular religion.

The legend of Bodhidharma, the monk who is reputed to have introduced the Ch'an school of Buddhism from India around A.D. 520, retains something of the initial shock that many Chinese must have felt from the impact of this Indian religion. Arriving at the southern court, where the Chinese Emperor Liang Wu Ti not only strongly supported the new faith but had retired from the world himself on more than one occasion, to the dismay of his subjects, Bodhidharma, a fierce-looking fellow with a bushy beard and wide-open, penetrating eyes, baffled nearly everyone. His interview with Emperor Wu was brief and abrupt. For the Emperor described all that he had done to promote the practice of Buddhism, and asked what merit he had gained thereby—taking the popular view that Buddhism is a gradual accumulation of merit through good deeds, leading to better and better circumstances in future incarnations, or lives, and finally release in *nirvana*, or eternal bliss. But Bodhidharma replied, 'No merit whatever!' This so undermined the Emperor's idea of Buddhism that he asked, 'What, then, is the sacred doctrine's first principle?' Bodhidharma replied, 'It's just empty; there's nothing sacred.' 'Who, then, are you,' said the Emperor, 'to stand before us?' 'I don't know,' was the final reply.

After this interview, so unsatisfactory from the Emperor's point of view, Bodhidharma retired to a monastery in Wei, where he is said to have spent nine years in a cave, 'gazing at the wall.' The replies of Bodhidharma must have seemed very strange to the *shih*, the scholar officials, in the court, but their emphasis on inner values and the limits of what can be expressed in words about eternal truth is not very far removed from Taoism. Confucian philosophy consistently opposed the rising tide of the

Buddhist faith, while Taoism paralleled and competed with it in the hearts and minds of the *nung*, the peasant farmers. Ch'an Buddhism, a fruitful interaction, even amalgam, of the teachings of Lao-tzu and Gautama, was to reach its climax in Japan as Zen.

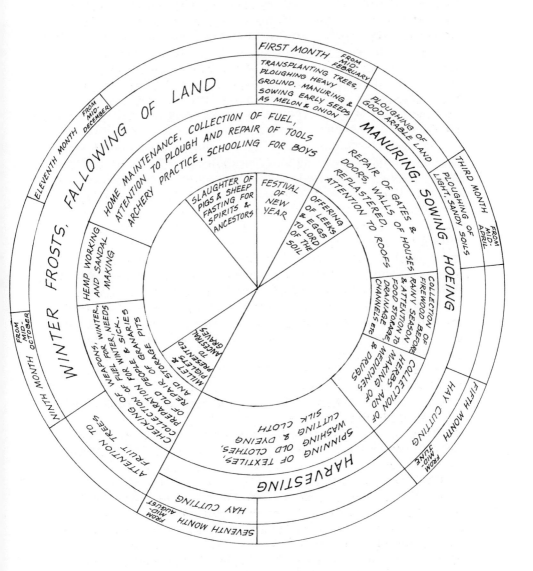

An Agricultural Calendar from one by Tsui Shih (A.D. 100–170) for Loyang.

71

SCIENCE AND TECHNOLOGY

Because of the fundamental role of Nature in Chinese culture, specialists such as astronomers, engineers and magicians were absorbed into the civil service. Science and sorcery could exist side by side because natural phenomena, like flooding or eclipses, were related to supernatural powers. It would have been silly to confine efforts for their control to practical measures.

By the end of the Han Empire, China had acquired much experience in science, accumulated a mass of information, formulated some fundamental principles, and anticipated many discoveries associated with the West. In the past it has been fashionable to criticize Chinese advances as being unscientific in their methodology and for being practical rather than theoretical. We are now reassessing this view. Science and technology were inevitably linked. Without engineering precision scientific instruments could not be used to record accurate data; by the first century B.C. Chinese craftsmen were using sliding callipers graduated in decimals.

Chang Heng (A.D. 78–139)

An example of a government official well versed in science was the mathematician and astronomer from Hupeh, Chang Heng. Among his notable achievements were:

- the most accurate calculation of the value of π at that time;
- the improvement of the armillary sphere and other precision instruments used in the plotting and understanding of heavenly bodies;
- the modification and clarification of existing astronomical theory in the light of his findings;
- the introduction of the grid system of co-ordinates in cartography;
- the construction of a seismograph to record the direction of earthquakes.

Magnetism

The very first dial and pointer readings, the magnetic compass, was developed in Han China. It evolved from a piece of lodestone embedded in a wooden fish floating in water. A needle projecting from it indicated South. The 'South controlling spoon' was used by diviners, being carved from lodestone which rotated on highly polished plate used to foretell the future.

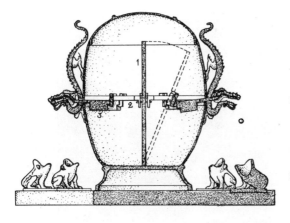

A cross section of Chang Heng's seismograph. A tremor would disturb the pendulum (1) causing the arm (2) to open the dragon's mouth (3) and releasing a ball which fell into the mouth of the frog below, thus indicating the direction of the tremor.

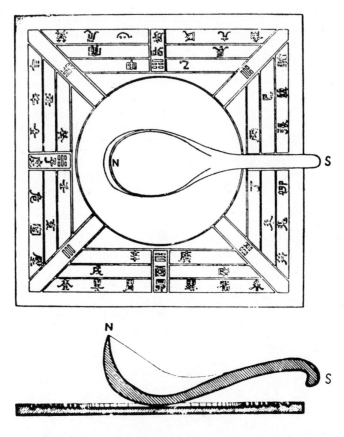

The diviner's board and south-pointing spoon.

73

The Iron and Salt Industries. From the fourth century B.C. cast iron hoes, ploughshares, axes, swords and picks are recorded. Cast iron was produced at a very early stage aided by man- and water-powered double-acting piston bellows, as illustrated. The picture also shows production of wrought iron by 'puddling,' a technique not developed in Britain until the eighteenth century. Steel making was undertaken as early as the sixth century A.D. by the forerunner of the later Siemens-Martin method, known as co-fusion—both wrought and cast iron were heated together, thus 'averaging' out carbon content.

Salt production utilized steel drilling bits to extract brine from underground sources up to 600 metres. Extracted through bamboo tubes it was evaporated in large iron pans. In Szechuan natural gas was used for this as early as the second century B.C. The illustration below shows a deep drilling operation for brine and natural gas.

An invention often confused with magnetism was the 'South pointing carriage.' Invented by Ma Chun around A.D. 260, the carriage carried an indicator which always pointed South on journeys. This was not magnetic. It rotated by means of a simple differential gear and therefore utilized toothed wheels or cogs.

Chinese Inventions of Daily Significance

● *The harness.* Down to A.D. 1000 in Europe a 'throat-and-girth' harness was used, giving inefficient haulage. Only China had developed the 'breast strap' harness as early as 200 B.C. This forerunner of modern collar harness increased the haulage capacity of horses. Chinese chariots were larger and carried more passengers than either Greek or Roman chariots.

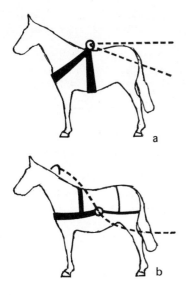

a. Western 'throat-and-girth' harness.
b. The more efficient 'breast-strap' harness of ancient China.

● *The wheelbarrow.* No evidence exists of this labour-saving device in the West until the thirteenth century. In China it was used for supplying the armies of Chu Ko Liang, a Shu general, in the third century A.D.

● *Stirrups.* Probably stimulated by the Indian toe stirrup, the foot stirrup appeared in China in the second century B.C., a thousand years before it reached Europe. It made Chinese cavalry a rival force to the Huns for the first time, fusing horse and rider into one immovable force.

● *The rudder*. The stern-post rudder is found in model boats dating from the first century B.C. in the Canton area, though Chinese boats did not have a stern post as such—it was rather box shaped. The rudder reached Europe in the twelfth century (about the same time as the magnetic compass).

A pottery model of a ship from a Cantonese Han tomb, showing stern-post rudder.

● *Paper*. First announced by the eunuch Tsai Lun, the Director of Imperial Workshops in A.D. 105, the use of paper may have led to the loss of many important Chinese records that might have survived if written on cruder parchment or bark. Printing probably developed by the sixth century A.D. under Buddhist influence.

Technical Education

Medical examinations date from the Han period. State education in general originated in Szechuan under Governor Wen Ong. In 145 B.C. he founded a teacher's training college in Cheng Tu in order to spread civilization among the uncultured masses of the Red Basin. Scholars received special privileges and they obtained key government posts. In 124 B.C. the Po Shih Kuan or Imperial University was founded with a chair for each of the classical books. When Wang Mang was Chief Minister, he inaugurated the first assembly of scientific experts. More than a thousand attended the conference at Chang-an. Scientific bibliographies, dictionaries

and encyclopaedias were all drawn up by the end of the Han
dynasty.

The Development of Medicine

Although the functions of priest and doctor were separated early
on, the basis of medicine remained the balancing of the forces of
yin and yang within the body's main organs. The Yellow Emperor
is traditionally accredited with a systematic study of medicine,
including the invention of acupuncture, but the Han period witnessed most of the earliest writings and personalities.

Diagnosis was developed in 255 B.C. by Pien Chiao. His work
was furthered in the *Pulse Classic* of Wang Shu Ho in 280 A.D.
On each wrist six pulses could be examined indicating the condition of each of the twelve internal organs. Pulse types could be
superficial, deep, slow or fast. Altogether, over fifty-two chief
varieties were recorded, including seven which signified impending
death.

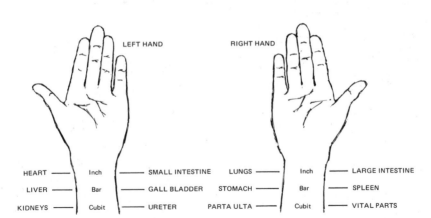

The twelve pulses of the body.

Acupuncture was the use of hot or cold needles of silver, brass
and other metals which could be long or short, coarse or fine, to
puncture the twelve invisible channels of the body. This was to
release the yin and yang. Three-hundred-and-sixty-five points of
puncture were recognized.

Three great medical men emerge in the Han period:
● Tsang Kung (around 180 B.C.) who was known as Father
Tsang, developed the use of drugs rather than palpation or
acupuncture.

● Chang Chung-ching, who was called the Hippocrates of China, graduated in medicine in A.D. 168. He was exceptional in his belief in clinical treatments, having no time for supernatural or magic cures. His most famous work was on typhoid and related diseases.

● Hua To, who was born in A.D. 190, became a famous surgeon with great knowledge of anaesthetics, despite the pressures of the orthodox *shih* who were against dissection of bodies. It is said that with his death surgery came to an end.

THE AGRICULTURAL BASIS OF THE FIRST EMPIRE

In A.D. 2 the first reliable census revealed that three-quarters of the total population of around fifty-eight million lived in the Wei and Yellow River valleys. The only other densely populated area was the Red Basin of Szechuan, while the Lower Yangtze valley was still a sparsely populated pioneer-frontier.

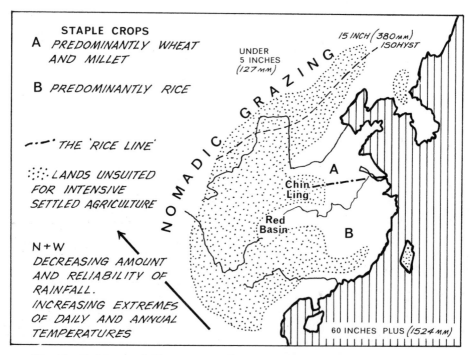

The physical basis of Chinese agriculture showing the relationship between climate, relief and subsistence types.

The Northern Farmer

By abandoning wasteful and destructive shifting cultivation the peasants of the Wei valley were able to increase output from the fragile loess soils of the hills and the easily-breached alluvial soils of the valleys.

A complex system arose based on:

- co-operative use of labour for irrigation and dyke building;
- high and continuous inputs of labour in the care of land;
- intensive use of fertilizers;
- adoption and development of new crops and techniques.

Irrigation and Flood Control

While many indigenous northern crops were drought resistant, yields could also be increased by the provision of summer water. This was initially supplied as a by-product of strategic military and transport canals. Experience gained in their construction proved valuable when rice was introduced from the sub-tropical South, for this needed complicated irrigation when taken from its natural environment.

The strength of Chang-an depended entirely on the canal systems of the Wei valley. Emperor Wu was criticized for developing them to the benefit of one corner of the realm only, as he neglected to repair the breached dykes of the lower Yellow River valley after disastrous floods.

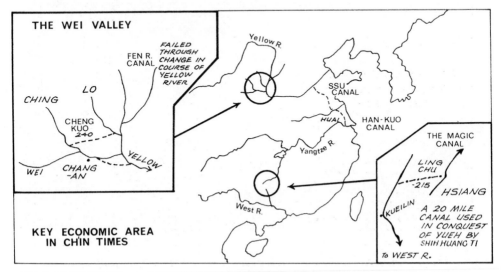

Some major canal schemes of the Han dynasty.

Some important schemes were the *Cheng Kuo Canal*, constructed in 246 B.C., which increased the power of the Ch'in State by watering over 182 000 hectares and increasing productivity in the Wei valley fivefold. The *Chang-an Canal* of 129 B.C. reduced the distance from the Yellow River to the capital by half and irrigated a further 182 000 hectares on land formerly fit only for sheep. An improvement of the Cheng Kuo Canal was made in the *Po Canal* (95 B.C.). A significant achievement outside the Wei valley was the *'Magic Canal,'* linking the Yangtze and West Rivers in 215 B.C. This allowed Shih Huang Ti to send troops into Yüeh and was a spearhead for the agricultural colonization of the South.

Tenure and Technology
Traditionally the Chinese were accredited with the 'well-field' system of farm-holding. Farms would be grouped in nines. Eight would be operated as family units and the ninth exploited jointly for the benefit of landlord or ruler. But this ideal may never have been attained, because the small farmer was frequently

A Han tomb model of a rotary mill (foreground), a pedal tilt-hammer, and a rotary winnowing fan with a crank handle (the oldest known illustration of a crank).

under pressure to sell his land and surrender his independence as a tenant of a great estate. Laws were introduced to prevent the handing-over of intact estates from father to son but this did not

Agriculture around the city wall. Fertilizer from the city helps explain why such fields had the highest yields.

prevent wealthy merchants from accumulating land at the expense of the farmer. Technically their estates were more advanced. Ox-drawn ploughs were fitted with iron ploughshares and moulding boards. Water and animal power were harnessed for the milling of grain by tilt hammers and circular stone grinding wheels. Prototype seed drills are mentioned. Water-buffalo, introduced from the south, worked in the increasing number of paddy fields, the small square basins used for rice growing. These contrasted with the long narrow strips winding around the loess hillsides on which dry crops would be grown. The 'endless chain' was devised for raising water by footpower from canal and well. The estate could boast all these and an impressive array of fruits and ornamental shrubs from far afield. The *nung* however were forced to retain the ancient methods and crops, depending on millets and beans, wooden hand hoes, and manually-operated grain mills, and carrying their water by yoke and bucket.

Fertilizers
River silt and canal mud were an initial source of fertility readily available to the Chinese. Up to twenty-eight tonnes per hectare were applied as it was recognized as essential to put back into the soil what had been taken out. All waste material was saved, including ashes, manure, silkworm debris and human excrement. The daily collection of city 'night soil', rich in phosphorus, potassium and nitrogen, was a major commercial enterprise. It could be stored as a liquid in stone jars for feeding to plants, or reduced to a fine powder for manuring soil prior to planting. Fertilizers were generally processed by composting and mixing with soil before application as it was thought the growth of the plant foods from it would compete with plant growth itself. This prior processing was an important time-saver. Plants such as clover and beans may have been ploughed into the earth as 'green fertilizer' and it is likely that crop rotation was developed to prevent soil exhaustion.

> In 1905 a peasant farmer in Shantung was keeping his family of ten, plus one pig and one donkey on two-thirds of a hectare. This is equivalent to 240 people, 24 donkeys and 24 pigs on 16 hectares, which at that time was considered too small an area to support the average American farming family.

The Oriental farmer has been called a 'time economizer beyond any other.' By careful use of the calendar and his spare time he should not need to rush or panic in any season. In the essential task of ploughing he was exhorted to attend to it during a drizzle or after rain thereby conserving moisture which would be invaluable in the summer. As early as the first century B.C. Chao Kuo, an agricultural minister, evolved the system of ploughing called 'tai-tien.' The traditional field was about 240 paces long by 1 pace wide, a pace being equivalent to about 1·5 metres. Each farmer would own several of these unenclosed strips. Chao Kuo advocated the digging of 3 shallow trenches or furrows separated by 3 raised ridges along each field. Improvements were immediate:

- seed previously sown broadcast was now efficiently channelled into the furrows;
- the position of ridge and furrow was alternated each year;
- the ridges would slowly be flattened during the growing season as weeding took place, giving extra support to the crop;
- the system could be adapted for growing two complementary crops at the same time, one on the ridge, the other in the furrow.

Another system of the period was the 'ou-t'ien' or shallow-pit system by which good land could be obtained from bad. Barren slopes or wastes could be made fertile by removing the earth, taking it to the village, composting it with organic refuse, and then replacing it. The method was also used to grow crops in very shallow soils.

Crops and Stock
The Chinese remained primarily crop growers even when imperial expansion gave control of the grasslands and new livestock, such as camels, were introduced. Shih Huang Ti was aware that the poor peasants of these semi-desert lands would become nomads, if given half a chance. Fearing the infiltration of the Huns southwards he created many settlements to act as focal points for agriculture. Discouragement of large-scale livestock raising had sound economic as well as political motives. Overgrazing was highly likely in an area of little and infrequent rain and this could hasten the whole cycle of erosion which so affected agriculture in the Wei valley. Further, livestock were poor 'converters' of vegetable products. In other words the end products in foodstuff terms did not justify the high vegetable inputs.

The Chinese regarded cows' milk as the drink of barbarians, and cattle were raised mainly as draught animals. Smaller, more economical livestock such as dogs, chickens, geese and pigs supplemented the largely vegetarian diet. The indigenous cereals of the north such as millets and wheat were supplemented by beans and root crops. Cereals, such as kaoliang, provided not only bread and porridge but also thatch, fuel and fertilizer. Soya beans were another versatile crop, having a high protein content,

Terraced and flooded paddy fields.

and being capable of having flour and paste made from them. (Today synthetic plastics and non-meat steaks are made from soya beans.)

Rice

This had been introduced successfully in the North by the first century B.C. North of the Yangtze River it could only be grown in the summer and with careful irrigation. As a result it was mainly a luxury crop accredited with medicinal value. But with improved techniques its productivity exceeded all other crops, and above all others it depended on co-operation and joint action by the farmers.

The rice would be planted by experienced sowers in seed beds covered with carefully smoothed liquid manure. A seed bed of one hectare would supply enough shoots to fill ten hectares after thirty to fifty days. Before transplanting, the paddy fields would be prepared by ploughing in clover or composted refuse and mud. Paddy fields and terracing are first recorded in the North, where farmers were exhorted to build small rice fields to allow greater control of standing water. Terracing was essentially designed to minimize erosion in hilly areas and probably preceded the introduction of rice. As the rice plants grew the water level of the fields went down until the final harvesting took place in dry fields.

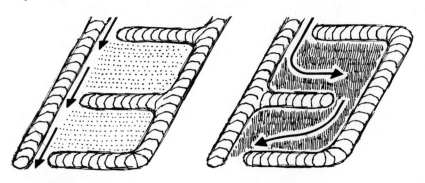

A Movement of water
in rice paddies in
early growing season

B Movement of water
at hottest part of
growing season

Water circulation in paddy fields. To keep water temperature up at the beginning of the summer growing season, water circulation was minimized. At the summer peak, temperatures were kept down by increasing the circulation.

Silk

Linen made from hemp was the commonest and cheapest form of clothing. Wool was used mainly as a protective padding between two layers of linen to combat the bitter northern winters. Other materials included rice straw for rain-resistant capes and sun shade hats. Cotton was introduced via the South much later.

Silk had been known from 1000 B.C. and the Chinese had a monopoly of its production until silkworm eggs were smuggled to Korea in the second century A.D. Cocoons spun by wild silkworms could be unravelled into a single thread of fibre of long staple and high tensile strength. These silkworms were domesticated and reared wherever mulberry trees could be grown for food. Each single thread could stretch for several hundred metres. The cocoons had first to be soaked in hot water before the silk was wound on to reels by means of a quilling wheel.

Spinning wheel possibly used for making thread from broken cocoons. Machinery for cloth production was far ahead of Europe by the first century A.D.

It has been recorded that, at hatching, seven hundred thousand silk-worms weigh just under half a kilogram. They shed their skin four times in thirty-six days before reaching maturity. By this time they weigh over four kilograms. In that time they have eaten nearly twelve tonnes of mulberry leaves. The cocoons they spin weigh up to nine hundred kilograms. About one-twelfth of this, i.e., seventy-five kilos becomes raw silk.

Silk was an extremely valuable luxury commodity. Ceremonial robes and 'best suits' would be made from it. The Romans valued it highly and the Chinese used it to 'buy off' potential enemies. It became an important element of taxation and was regarded as worth its weight in gold. Weaving and dyeing were developed to a high level at a very early stage. It was of course trade in silk which encouraged East–West contact and kept open the major trade routes via the Jade Gate and the Tarim Basin.

NEW TERRITORIES AND THE MOVEMENT SOUTH

During the Han dynasty military colonies were established in two directions:
- the northern arm of Kansu leading through Sinkiang to the Tarim Basin, and
- the lowland river valleys of the South.

The northern oasis settlements maintained garrisons to protect and extend Chinese influence along the Silk Roads. The southern settlements were intended to 'civilize' the native populations by spreading Chinese culture. As agricultural settlements both areas had limited initial success for climatic reasons. However, a two-way flow of crops and techniques was facilitated.

The South—'the land of rice and fish'—was peopled by two main groups of agriculturalists, the shifting cultivators of the hills and the settled farmers of the coast and valleys. The Chinese had most contact with the latter who were said to be lazy but never hungry thanks to the warm climate and abundant rainfall throughout the year. They could grow two crops of rice, and in the extreme South East a third crop of cabbages, beans, or other vegetables was possible. Tea growing was referred to by A.D. 273 and sugar-cane had already been established for four hundred years by then. Sea products and domesticated fish also figured commonly in the diet. By A.D. 150 there had been a major population shift away from the overpopulated Wei valley. The

Fragmented holdings, kitchen gardens, and fish ponds in a southern village.

overall population had remained at around fifty million after disastrous floods, famine and civil wars, but the heartland of the empire had lost eighteen million people while the South gained nine million. The rest were found in the Shantung peninsula and the Red Basin. As a result the lower Yangtze valley became the new key economic area of China, as a major supplier of grain to the imperial capitals.

Paddy fields and peasant farmers in the South.

The middle Yangtze valley. The watery landscape helped to make it a new key economic area of the later Han dynasty.

WORLD CHRONOLOGY A.D. 200–630

CHINA	'The Three Kingdoms' succeeded the Han Empire: the long struggle between these contending powers ended with the victory of Wei over Shu (264) and Wu (280). The older 'core area', the northern region in which the Middle Kingdom originated, had reasserted its control over the west and south, two newly developing economic regions. The advanced agricultural and communication systems of Wei were the decisive factor. But the new dynasty, the Tsin, proved unable to unify China in the face of pressure from the steppes. The Hsiung Nu, and other nomad tribes brought in as allies during civil wars proved impossible to expel or control. By 316 everything north of the Yangtze watershed was lost to Tsin. ● In the North, the most populous region and the stronghold of Chinese culture, the Tartar tribes set up a series of dynasties, but they were not able to alter the pattern of life. The sown quickly began to absorb the steppe. Chinese agriculture and administration continued. Intermarriage was general. Confucian and Taoist thought was too rooted in the mass of the people to be lost even though the presence of non-Chinese rulers did facilitate the growth of Buddhism. In 500 a decree was actually issued banning Tartar speech, dress and customs. ● In the South, Chinese dynasties were secure after the invading Tartar army was defeated in the battle of Fei Shui (387). The Yangtze Valley, in fact, proved entirely unsuited to the Tartar cavalry. The Court of Emperor Wu, of the Liang dynasty, was an impressive cultural centre when Bodhidharma visited it in 520. Reunification came from a movement starting yet again in the north region of China. Seizing the throne, Yang Chien, a Chinese general with Tartar blood, invaded and easily conquered the South. The new Sui dynasty (589–618) was welcomed by the southern population since it offered the return of the ideal, lost at the end of the Han dynasty, of a united China, 'One Empire of All under Heaven'. Over three hundred years of division had ended.
INDIA and WEST ASIA	
EUROPE	● The Roman Septimius Severus died in York after campaigning in Scotland against the fierce tribes there and rebuilding Hadrian's Wall, the northernmost frontier of the Empire. ● 410 Rome sacked by the Goths. The British cities were told that they must fend for themselves: the legions were needed closer to the capital. By 450, the Anglo-Saxons had overrun the province. ● 476 The last Roman Emperor in the West abdicated. Unlike the Tartar invaders in China (316–590), the 'barbarians' who overran the Roman Empire could neither maintain their own cultural traditions nor fully adopt those of the Empire. Roman culture had been spread thin in the Western Empire; the Eastern Empire was more compact and urban. Also the large slave element meant that there was no cultural reservoir equal to the Chinese peasant farmers. The Church was a unique survival.

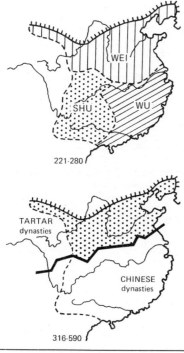

221-280

316-590

But the Sui dynasty, not unlike the Ch'in at the end of the Warring States period, overstretched itself and caused a popular uprising that ended in the establishment of the great T'ang dynasty (618). The second Sui emperor, Yang Ti, undertook vast projects. Communications between North and South were improved by canals linking the Yellow and Yangtze rivers; later this became the basis of the Grand Canal and effectively united the two key economic regions of China. Forced labour on this scheme and military failure in Korea precipitated rebellion.

● 455 Emperor Skanda Gupta repelled White Huns but the Empire was seriously weakened. By 550 it had disintegrated. Lacking a defence system, like China's Great Wall, the great plains of northern India were open to invaders from Central Asia.

● 399 Fa Hsien, a Chinese monk, set out for India and returned via Ceylon and Java. Pilgrimage to Holy India became a familiar event in China.

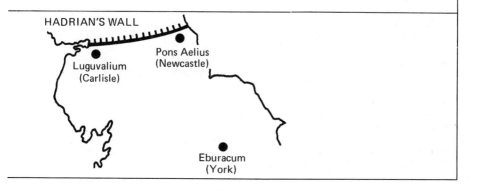

CHINA	Major canal development in China 1 Cheng Kuo Canal, opened in 246 B.C. It irrigated a vast area of land and provide excellent water-transport facilities: Ch'in gained a decisive advantage over the oth Warring States by this project, unusual for its time. 2 Chang-an Canal, completed 129 B.C., was used for navigation and the movement silt-laden water, a rich fertilizer, downstream to the lower middle course of the Yello River. 3 Suen Fang Canal, and others in this area, formed part of a strategic network dug Wei during the Three Kingdoms period and later Tartar dynasties. 4 The Old Pien Canal was dug partially by the King of Wu, one of the Warring Stat (486 B.C.). It was intended to facilitate the northern expansion of this state. 5 The New Pien Canal, built A.D. 616–18, effectively joined the North with the South This involved the re-opening of older sections of existing but derelict water courses well as the cutting of extensive lengths of new canal. It was the product of Sui author tarianism. 6 Cheng-tu Canal System was begun by Li Ping, a Ch'in governor of Shu, and Pa, cap tured from Ch'u in 316 B.C. Although it was originally constructed for water-transpo purposes, the numerous canals were extensively used for irrigation. Soon the Cheng-t plain was called 'sea-on-land' and the agricultural prosperity of the area was firml established. The Red Basin took advantage of this economic base to assert its indepen dence whenever the central authority declined: it was known as Shu in the Thre Kingdoms period too. 7 Yuan Grand Canal was dug by the Mongol conquerors as a means of connecting the capital at what is now Peking with the Yangtze Valley, the stronghold and econom base of the defeated Sung dynasty. Its route was followed by the larger Ming Gran Canal, which is still in use today.
INDIA and WEST ASIA	● Persia under the native Sassanid dynasty grew powerful. King Shapur attacked India and Rome in the West.
EUROPE	● Emperor Justinian (died 565) found it impossible to reunite permanently the Mediter ranean provinces of the former Roman Empire. The old language cleavage, West speakin Latin and East Greek, was decisive. A single language, as prevailed in China, was lackin There was internal conflict within the eastern provinces too. Islam (after 636) was t release the region from the last vestiges of Roman rule.

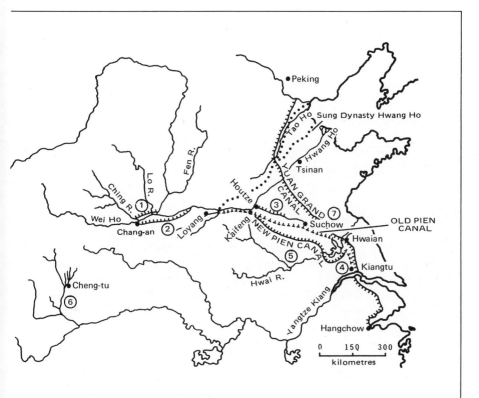

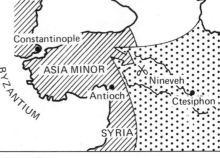

● 627 Emperor Heraclius defeated the Persians at the Battle of Nineveh. But both the Byzantine and Sassanid Empires were exhausted. Islam was about to overwhelm West Asia. Byzantine Egypt and Syria were restive under heavy taxation and religious persecution.

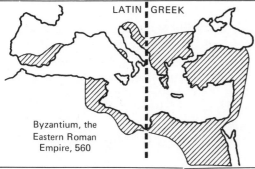

Byzantium, the Eastern Roman Empire, 560

3 A Golden Age

The restoration of unity under the T'ang Dynasty, A.D. 618–907

HISTORICAL OUTLINE

The successful way in which the T'ang dynasty built on the foundations laid by the short-lived Sui not only restored the Empire but ensured that the Chinese would always prefer unification during future generations. Henceforth, the country was united for far longer than it was divided either by internal conflict or external conquest. In the Chinese mind it is the T'ang Empire that has become the Golden Age.

Yet the restored Empire was not the same as the Han Empire. It was a more open society. Internally, the re-establishment of the examination system for entrance to the civil service on a more regular basis than the largely oral tests used since the Han period led to an enormous expansion in education. The invention of block printing some time in the eighth century A.D. met the demand for textbooks as well as encouraging the spread of literacy. Recommendation continued as a slight advantage for the relatives of the *shih*, but it became a familiar event for a group of *nung* to club together and pay for the education of a promising village boy. Literary achievement was the hallmark of the T'ang Empire, with its Confucian prose writers like Han Yu and its Taoist poets like Li Po. The Empire evolved a bureaucratic system in place of the lesser aristocratic one that had replaced feudalism.

Externally, too, a more flexible attitude appeared in the ready acceptance of foreign peoples and their ideas. The streets of the capital, Chang-an, were thronged with priests from India and South-East Asia, merchants from Central Asia and Arabia, and travellers from Persia, Korea and Japan. The second T'ang Emperor, T'ai Tsung or 'Supreme Ancestor,' came out to meet personally the famous Buddhist monk Hsuan Tsang when he returned from India with scriptures in A.D. 645. Although the

A block-printed scroll found at Tun-huang. It shows Buddha addressing his disciples. This copy of the 'Diamond Sutra' was made in 868; the earliest known example of block printing is a Buddhist charm (770). The demand for copies of the Scriptures as well as Confucian Classics led to this invention. For centuries the Chinese had used ink and paper besides being expert in stone engraving: put together they made block-printing, which may have been brought to Europe by the invading Mongols in the thirteenth century A.D.

Emperor was a Taoist, he supported the Confucians for the sake of the civil service, besides welcoming Buddhism and other foreign faiths. This distinction between the Han and T'ang Empires is expressed today in two common forms of address for the Chinese people. 'Men of Han' embodies a sense of exclusiveness, Chinese as opposed to Hsiung Nu or barbarians, while 'Men of T'ang' incorporates the diversity of a China stretching from the steppes to the tropics on one hand and from land-locked mountains to the sea on the other.

The Imperial Administration
A strong civil service, recruited by examination, was the foundation of the hundred-and-fifty years of peace and prosperity that the reign of Emperor T'ai Tsung (627–49) inaugurated. It shifted the power centre from the military to the civil. During the Three Kingdoms and the Tartar partition a military aristocracy had developed at the expense of the old alliance between the ruling

An engraving of the Emperor T'ai Tsung.

house and the *shih*. The Li, T'ai Tsung's own family, belonged
to this class so that as Emperor he was well aware of dangers
from this quarter.

Until the rebellion of An Lu-shan in 755 had severely shaken
the Empire, the central administration effectively controlled
every province. Regular censuses informed the Emperor of the
exact population and resources available. The T'ang Empire was
certainly the largest and most populous state in the world. In 754
there were nearly 53 000 000 persons living in over 300 prefectures.

Empress Wu

To the horror of traditional Chinese historians, members of the
shih class, the continued success of the T'ang dynasty was largely
due to an ex-concubine who finally usurped the throne itself.
That Wu Chao, concubine to T'ai Tsung, could escape the
Buddhist convent where the concubines of a dead Emperor were
required to live, win the favour of the new Emperor Kao Tsung,
and then dominate the government for fifty years, tells us a lot

96

about the power structure of the T'ang Empire. It reveals that the Court, supported by an improved civil service, was supreme.

Emperor Kao Tsung was an indifferent ruler but he had the sense to let his consort, now Empress Wu, deal with affairs of state during his long reign (649–83). After his death she dethroned two of her sons, both ineffectual: her official reign began in 690 and lasted for fifteen years; at the age of eighty, her health failing, Empress Wu, 'Holy and Divine,' was forced to abdicate (705). This was the first and last occasion on which a woman occupied the Throne of the Emperors.

Although Empress Wu was ruthless towards her political enemies, the period of her ascendancy was a good one for the Empire. Government was sound; no serious revolts occurred; the army was reorganized; and Korea was conquered, a task that no previous Chinese had ever managed. One of the few favourable comments on her reign by Chinese historians pinpoints her desire to find new blood for the Empire. We read:

> The Empress was not sparing in the bestowal of titles and ranks, because she wished to cage the bold and enterprising spirits of all regions. Even a wild reckless fellow who said something which she thought apt would be made an official without regard to the normal order of the degrees of rank; but those who proved unfit for their responsibilities were forthwith, in large numbers, cashiered or executed. Her broad aim was to select men of real talent and true virtue.

The T'ang Empire avoided civil disturbances over the succession through the emergence of the third great ruler of the dynasty, Emperor Hsuan Tsung, known as Ming Huang, 'the Brilliant Emperor,' the grandson of Empress Wu, whose court became a splendid cultural centre admired by later times. However, there was to be a terrible revolt near the end of his reign.

The Rebellion of An Lu-shan

Poets and playwrights have made the tragic events of An Lu-shan's rebellion famous. Every Chinese knows how the aging Emperor fell in love with a beautiful concubine, Yang Kuei Fei, who clouded his judgment and persuaded him to foolish policies. Through her urging Ming Huang bestowed undeserved honours on An Lu-shan, a barbarian general serving on the northern frontier. An Lu-shan was appointed commander-in-chief of the army, and this ambitious soldier took advantage of the idleness of the Court to make a bid for power. Almost unopposed, he captured Chang-an in 755; the Emperor had fled westwards. When the disheartened troops of the imperial bodyguard demanded that Yang Kuei Fei should be executed as a traitor, and backed their demand with a threatened mutiny, Ming Huang was obliged to consent.

Beneath these human episodes of the rebellion, the very stuff of character drama, there was an economic conflict. For An Lu-shan, though a Turk of the Kitan tribe, had the support of the eastern provinces. The burden of supplying grain to the upland capital may have been a root cause of the strife. In the reign of Emperor T'ai Tsung the annual shipment was around 10 000 tonnes, but by this time it had topped 160 000 tonnes. The cost and waste of transporting such amounts up-river for the benefit of an indolent Court may well have been too much for the *nung* to stomach.

The civil war was long (755–66) and bitterly fought. The North was devasted: the T'ang Empire lost most of its dynamic force. A Tibetan army was able to break through the weakened frontier defences and sack Chang-an, just recovered from the rebels.

The Last Years of the T'ang Dynasty

Though the Empire experienced general peace for another century, its organization was less efficient and less satisfactory. The central administration declined as military leaders became more independent of the throne; at Court the eunuchs became a political force again; the Tibetans in the East and the Turkish tribes to the North pressed hard; heavier taxation and levies were required to meet the various crises. Perhaps a crucial neglect was that of the hydraulic works, the traditional unifying factor in Chinese history. After the rebellion of An Lu-shan few projects were undertaken and many old schemes fell into decay. When the last T'ang Emperor was deposed in 907, the country fragmented into more than a dozen separate states. New methods of warfare might have accounted for the unusual extent of the disunity too. The first reference to the use of gunpowder is in 919.

EXPANSION AND ABSORPTION

Imperial expansion reached farther under the T'ang dynasty than under the Han. Most of the gains were made before the rebellion of An Lu-shan, whose victory at the battle of Ling Pao (755) opened the pass to the Wei Valley and placed Chang-an at the mercy of his rebel forces. The ensuing civil disturbances and contraction of the Empire may give the impression of decay, but these related events were really a function of two factors: internal economic changes and over-expansion.

● Internal conflicts were largely a result of the movement of the key economic area of China from the North to the Yangtze Valley. By 742 Chang-an and its satellites had a population approaching 2 000 000. The strain on the easily exhausted loess soils in supporting such an urban concentration could only be offset by imports from the South. At first this was feasible with the construction of the Grand Canal network, built by the Sui dynasty, but eventually the operation proved unworkable. Grain transport increased from 10 000 tonnes to 160 000 tonnes between 627 and 742. Consequently the capital was very insecure in event of civil war and every decade made it increasingly distant from the chief economic regions.

● The Empire had tended to overreach itself. The major gains before 755 were:
—pushing the Turkish tribes back to Inner Mongolia, where they accepted Chinese overlordship (648);
—obtaining control over Turkestan, where Sinkiang ('the new dominion') was established;
—the repenetration of Vietnam;
—the annexation of Korea and Manchuria;
—the alliance with Tibet through royal marriage of a Chinese princess, which did not ensure perpetual peace but caused an inflow of Chinese cultural influence;
—the acceptance of 'protection' from China by many states in Central Asia.

Only the hill-tribesmen of Yunnan remained obstinately independent of the Empire. But such a far-flung border was not easy to defend. It was impossible to maintain security on every frontier once civil wars broke out, and other imperial powers were eager to expand at China's expense. The Arabs, having crushed the Sassanid Empire in Persia (642), initially formed an alliance with the Chinese, but then began to take over the weaker states in Western Turkestan. A confrontation came just before the rebellion of An Lu-shan. In 751 the Chinese armies in the West were decisively beaten at the battle of Talas River, and Central Asia ceased to be Buddhist and became a part of the Moslem world. Slightly later Mongolia broke free, while in Korea the semi-independent state of Silla absorbed the Chinese territories there.

The Tibetans actually sacked Chang-an during An Lu-shan's revolt. After 750, in effect, the T'ang Empire contracted.

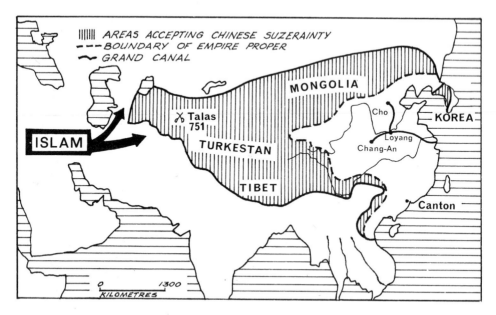

The T'ang Empire at its peak—A.D. 700.

Cross-cultural Assimilation

Besides the large numbers of scholars and diplomats welcomed in Chang-an there were many alien groups who were absorbed by Chinese society. With the fall of the Sassanid Empire, a colony of Persian refugees was established. Muslim soldiers, recruited against An Lu-shan, settled as permanent residents at the end of the fighting. In the South the city of Canton became a centre of international trade after the northern 'silk roads' came under pressure (751 onwards). There were colonies of Arabs, Jews, Persians and Christians. A similar openness existed with respect to foreign religions, though national crises towards the end of the T'ang dynasty were marked with the temporary restriction of alien creeds and occasional riots.

The Ecosystem Maintained

The T'ang Empire can be seen as the reassertion of China's natural unity. In the Introduction, the continuity of Chinese civilization was stressed because it remains a remarkable fact that China has a history of four thousand years. Our description of this unusual historical phenomenon as an ecosystem was put to the test following the fall of the Han Empire. The T'ang restoration at the end of three hundred years of division was a part of the self-adjustment of the ecosystem. The basic stability was evident in several ways:

- the balanced relationship between man and the natural world as a function of dependence on agriculture;
- cultural continuity from the ability to absorb and modify new ideas or innovations, such as the imperial control of early capitalist iron technology, or the introduction of Buddhism;
- geographical integrity despite changes in inputs and outputs, such as imperial expansion and contraction, alterations in key economic regions, and the growth of the Chinese 'core area' through large scale hydraulic works.

For the *shih* and the *nung* the pattern of production and the system of philosophy which had evolved slowly from ancient times still held good. A change of dynasty or a civil war did not change the necessity of providing food for the next day. Military exploits did not outlast the words of the sages. Moreover, early state influence over the capitalist activities of merchants and industrialists maintained the equilibrium of the ecosystem, ensuring that China was not fundamentally changed by the development of technology. Printing did not encourage a Reformation, the spur failed to elevate the knight, gunpowder was about to cause little more than an extra fragmentation between the T'ang and the Sung Empires, and the magnetic compass would not lead to overseas colonies. In short, China has always pursued its own distinct way.

RELIGIONS

Confucian philosophy had become a strictly moral code of conduct during the Han Empire. In the hands of the official class of scholars it was transformed into the yardstick for measuring correctness of behaviour in the 'Empire of all under Heaven.' But its appeal was confined largely to the *shih*, the gentry and the scholar officials themselves. Though the mass of the people agreed with Confucius about the importance of the family and respect for ancestors, they wanted something less austere and clung to Taoism, at this time absorbing the magical rites and practices of the countryside. The local gods of ancient tradition found room under the spreading umbrella of Taoism; the followers of Confucius respected Heaven, but showered the cold water of ridicule over spirits and lesser deities. What completed the transformation of Taoist ideas into a popular religion was competition with the new faith from India, Buddhism.

Later Taoism

Both Taoism and Buddhism had little patience with the world that Confucian philosophy admired. Inner space, the mystical elements in man's nature—these became their main concern. Lao-tzu had tired of life in the Chou capital and gone into the west. Chapter nineteen of his book, the *Tao Teh Ching*, runs:

> Rid of formalized wisdom and learning
> People would be a hundredfold happier,
> Rid of conventionalized duty and honour
> People would find their families dear,
> Rid of legalized profiteering
> People would have no thieves to fear.
> These methods of life have failed, all three,
> Here is the way, it seems to me:
> Set the people free,
> As deep in their hearts they would like to be,
> From private greeds
> And wanton needs.

Since Chuang-tzu's time there was a strong tradition for Taoist sages to live in retirement from the world.

> Who will prefer the jingle of jade pendants if
> He once heard stone growing in a cliff!

'The jingle of jade pendants' stands for the Court, its beautiful women and splendid life, which is a hollow-world for a person who has experienced the *Tao*. This was the highest form of Taoism, the holy man quietly living at one with Nature on a remote mountainside, but another aspect, alchemy, caught the imagination of many Chinese. Chang Tao-ling, the first T'ien Shih, or Heavenly Teacher of Taoist religion, spent most of his long life (A.D. 34–156, according to legend) in retirement studying alchemy. His purpose was to obtain the elixir of life, a drug capable of bestowing immortality. Gradually the Taoist adept became in the popular mind the magician. Wang Pi (A.D. 226–49) wrote an excellent commentary on the *Tao Teh Ching*, entirely in tune with its original spirit, and numerous *shih* embraced Taoist ideas as an alternative to Confucius, but the popular response was the decisive factor.

During the Tartar partition one royal house, the Wei in Shansi, sought a new book of charms on the accession of each ruler. Astrology only added strength to the Confucian opposition to Taoism. Yet it now seems likely that major scientific inventions and discoveries originated from Taoist experiments: new medical knowledge, the magnetic compass which was used to determine favourable positions for graves, and gunpowder which was used in ghost-scaring firecrackers. While Taoism was becoming more concerned with magic and identified with popular superstition, Buddhism did make a serious and sustained challenge to Confucian philosophy in the Court itself.

Buddhism
At every level in Chinese society the teachings of the Buddha have had a profound effect. Until the modern period only India, 'the Holy Land of the East,' has influenced China. Yet that singular Chinese ability to absorb and transform foreign peoples, whether Tartar, Mongol or Manchu conquerors, was active in the development of Buddhism too. In the end the Buddhist faith was adapted to suit Chinese society, rather than China being altered by the new religion.

Gautama (died 479 or 477 B.C.), the prince from North India who became the Buddha, 'the Enlightened One,' required his followers to be fully conscious of the nature of the universe and to exercise full self-control. The saffron robe worn by Buddhist monks represents the death of themselves to a worldly life: the colour was chosen because condemned men used to be dressed in such material on the day of execution. What was demanded from the individual believer was nothing less than the death of self, freedom from all desires and fears. A hard and lonely path to tread, for Buddha said, 'no man can help another.' To prevent himself becoming a god in the eyes of later followers after he had died and gone into *Nirvana*, or 'eternal bliss,' the Buddha prohibited pictures or sculptures of his life or deeds. An empty seat or a footprint was to be the only sign of the way he had discovered and taught. Enlightenment, like the *Tao* of Lao-tzu, could not be explained in words or represented visually. It was ineffable, something 'no man can help another' to experience. It was an individual quest.

Head of Buddha, a fine example of Gandharan sculpture, the Greek
tradition in India (second century A.D.). The lips are folded into
the cheek with the Enlightened One's consciousness of the heavy
weight of the Flesh; skin sags laden with experience; and inner
freedom lies deep down the channels of the sightless eyes, far below
the weary drooping of the lids. India is the inwardness of the Vision
as well as the acceptance of universal misfortune. The West, carved
in the Greco-Roman modelling of the face, is the outer presentation
of world-weariness. It is as if the descendants of Alexander's great
army, the generations settled and reinforced on the shadowy edge
of his vast imperial dream, had reached the same fundamental insight into life as prevailed in the country they inhabited.

The Buddha's consciousness of suffering is basic. As an infant
prince it was prophesied that he would not be a great king, but a
great holy man, if he became aware of the sufferings of the world.
The king his father did his utmost to prevent him from having any
contact with the outside world; a special palace was constructed in
which all possible pleasures were offered to beguile the young prince's
mind. However, one day Gautama saw a sick person, on another
a tottering old man; these experiences troubled him considerably,
but it was an encounter with a corpse that jolted him into active
discontent with 'soft' living. The serene calm of a hermit suggested
a course for him and, leaving throne, family and offspring, he became
a wandering ascetic, bent on discovering Truth. Having tried the way
of self-mortification for a number of years without success, Gautama
resolved to sit in meditation till he finished his quest. His Enlightenment followed, whereby he became the Buddha.

But as Buddha foresaw his teachings became another religion over the centuries. The great tradition of Greek and Roman sculpture may have been an untimely influence, for marvellous statues of Buddha were carved in Bactria and the other regions where the Greeks had settled. The immense rock carvings to be found in China are an offspring of Greco-Indian tradition. A late Buddhist proverb explains what had happened: 'To mistake a finger for the moon.' When a man was asked by another to show him the moon, he pointed it out in the sky. But the questioner mistook the man's finger for the moon. The monasteries, the places of pilgrimage, the stories of Buddha and the saints had become accepted as the essence of Enlightenment.

By the time, then, that China received Buddhism it was a highly developed faith. The older Hindu beliefs of the Indian people had added much. Two distinct branches were evolved, Hinayana and Mahayana. And it was the more complicated and less other-worldly Mahayana version that had been introduced into Han China in A.D. 65. For Mahayana Buddhists Gautama was a single incarnation in an almost infinite series of Buddhas. Saints and gods had appeared capable of securing the believer a place in the 'Western Heaven.' Merit from good deeds in the world accumulated in better reincarnations till complete bliss was obtained in an after-world. Against this manageable system of belief, quite properly held by Emperor Liang Wu Ti in his capital at Nanking, the uncompromising doctrines of Bodhidharma came as a terrific shock.

The Ch'an school held contemplation to be the way to achieve Buddhahood. Everyone had this potential in him but most people failed to realize it. Although Bodhidharma is supposed to have brought this true version of the Buddha's teachings direct from India, the parallels with early Taoism are quite obvious. The Buddhist monk and poet Han-shan, living in the eighth century A.D., was very like a Taoist hermit. In a preface to his poems Yin Lu-ch'iu wrote:

No-one knows just what sort of man Han-shan was. There are old people who knew him: they say he was a poor man, a crazy character. He lived alone . . . at a place called Cold Mountain [Han-shan]. . . . He often went down to the Kuo-ch'in Temple. At the temple lived Shih-te, who ran the dining hall. He sometimes saved leftovers for Han-shan, hiding them in a bamboo tube. Han-shan would come and carry it away; walking the long veranda, calling and shouting happily, talking and laughing to himself. Once the monks followed him, caught him, and made fun of him. He stopped, clapped his hands, and laughed greatly—Ha Ha!—for a spell, then left.

He looked like a tramp. His body and face were old and beat. Yet in every word he breathed was a meaning in line with the subtle principles of things, if only you thought of it deeply. Everything he said had a feeling of the Tao in it, profound and arcane secrets. His hat was made of birch bark, his clothes were ragged and worn out, and his shoes were wood. Thus men who have made it hide their tracks: unifying categories and interpenetrating things. On that long veranda calling and singing, in his words of reply Ha Ha!—the three worlds revolve. Sometimes at the villages and farms he laughed and sang with cowherds. Sometimes intractable, sometimes agreeable, his nature was happy of itself. But how could a person without wisdom recognize him?

Cold Mountain was more than the name of a place or a man; it was a state of mind. Han-shan's verse tells us that he read 'Huang and Lao,' the ancient Taoist book of the Yellow Emperor and the *Tao Teh Ching*. These lines communicate what the hermit monk felt:

> Cold Mountain is a house
> Without beams or walls.
> The six doors left and right are open
> The hall is blue sky.
> The rooms all vacant and vague
> The east wall beats on the west wall
> At the centre, nothing.
> Borrowers don't bother me
> In the cold I built a little fire
> When I'm hungry I boil up some greens.
> I've got no use for the kuluk
> With his big barn and pasture—
> He just sets up a prison for himself.
> Once in he can't get out.
> Think it over—
> You know it might happen to you.

Tun-huang, the great Buddhist cave complex at the western end of the Great Wall, was started in A.D. 366. Although it has not always been within the Chinese Empire, the remoteness of the site and the dry conditions in that area have saved its marvellous frescoes and sculpture from destruction. It was a religious centre, with monasteries and schools.

107

A Buddhist Paradise, copy of the central section of a wall-painting at Tun-huang, painted during the T'ang dynasty.

The Confucian Reaction

The growing strength of Buddhism in China alarmed the *shih*, who considered the ideas and practices it was introducing to be entirely 'un-Chinese.' The rational, sceptical outlook of the Confucian philosophy reacted strongly to the mass excitement which the new faith generated. Opposition became explicit in Han Yu's (768–824) famous defence of traditional values and behaviour, the *Memorial on the Bone of Buddha*. Addressing the credulous Emperor Hsien Tsung, the scholar official wrote:

I humbly submit that Buddhism is but one of the religious systems obtaining among the barbarian tribes, that only during the later Han dynasty did it filter into the Middle Kingdom, and that it never existed in the golden age of the past . . .

It was not until the reign of Ming-ti of Han that Buddhism first appeared. Ming-ti's reign lasted no longer than eighteen years, and after him disturbance followed upon disturbance, and reigns were all short . . .

When Kao-tsu succeeded the fallen house of Sui, he determined to eradicate Buddhism. But the ministers of the time were lacking in foresight and ability, they had no real understanding of the way of the ancient kings, nor of the things that are right both for then and now. Thus they were unable to assist the wise resolution of their ruler and save their country from this plague. To my constant regret the attempt stopped short. But you, your majesty, are possessed of a skill in the arts of peace and war, of wisdom and courage the like of which has not been seen for several thousand years. When you first ascended the throne you prohibited recruitment of Buddhist monks and Taoist priests and the foundation of new temples and monasteries; and I firmly believed that the intentions of Kao-tsu would be carried out by your hand, or if this were still impossible, that at least their religions would not be allowed to spread and flourish.

And now, your majesty, I hear that you have ordered all Buddhist monks to escort a bone of the Buddha from Feng-hsiang and that a pavilion be erected from which you will in person watch its entrance into the Imperial Palace. You have further ordered every Buddhist temple to receive this object with due homage. Stupid as I am, I feel convinced that it is not out of regard for Buddha that you, your majesty, are praying for blessings by doing him this honour; but that you are organizing this absurd pantomime for the benefit of the people of the capital and for their gratification in this year of plenty and happiness. For a mind so enlightened as your majesty's could never believe such nonsense. The minds of the common people, however, are as easy to becloud as they are difficult to enlighten. If they see your majesty acting in this way, they will think that you are wholeheartedly worshipping the Buddha, and will say: 'His majesty is a great sage, and even he worships the Buddha with all his heart. Who are we that we should any of us grudge our lives in his service?' They will cauterize the crowns of their heads, burn off their fingers, and in bands of tens or hundreds cast off their clothing and scatter their money and from daylight to darkness follow one another in the cold fear of being too late. Young and old in one mad rush will forsake their trades and callings and, unless you issue some prohibition, will flock round the temples, hacking their arms and mutilating their bodies to do him homage. And the laughter that such unseemly and degenerate behaviour will everywhere provoke will be no light matter.

The Buddha was born a barbarian; he was unacquainted with the language of the Middle Kingdom, and his dress was of a different cut. His tongue did not speak nor was his body clothed in the manner prescribed by the kings of old; he knew nothing of the duty of minister to prince or the relationship of son to father. Were he still alive today, were he to come to court at the bidding of his country, your majesty would give him no greater reception than an interview in the Strangers' Hall, a ceremonial banquet, and the gift of a suit of clothes, after which you would have him sent under guard to the frontier to prevent him from misleading your people. There is then all the less reason now that he has been dead so long for allowing this decayed and rotten bone, this filthy and disgusting relic to enter the Forbidden Palace. 'I stand in awe of supernatural beings,' said Confucius, 'but keep them at a distance' . . . ; and to my shame and indignation none of your ministers says that this is wrong, none of your censors has exposed the error.

I beg that this bone be handed over the authorities to throw into water or fire, that Buddhism be destroyed root and branch for ever, that the doubts of your people be settled once and for all and their descendants saved from heresy. For if you make it known to your people that the actions of the true sage surpass ten thousand times ten thousand those of ordinary men, with what wondering joy will you be acclaimed! And if the Buddha should indeed possess the power to bring down evil, let all the bane and punishment fall upon my head, and as heaven is my witness I shall not complain.

In the fullness of my emotion I humbly present this memorial for your attention. *(Copyright © 1972 by Grove Press, Inc.)*

The Emperor was very displeased. But Han Yu was saved by the Confucian scholars of the day. They rallied behind him on the issue and his sentence was reduced to banishment. He was posted to the South.

Han Yu had behaved responsibly. His outspokenness may have been dangerous in terms of his personal safety and his own career, but it was in the classic mould of the honest Confucian official. It should be remembered that the Censorate was a Chinese institution. The officials of this department had the difficult duty of reporting to the Emperor all cases of misgovernment. Opposition to a court favourite or an unreasonable ruler called for moral courage. Censors, Chinese ombudsmen, often perished.

On his recall to Court Han Yu was to use his resoluteness for the benefit of the tottering T'ang dynasty in 822. As an official of the War Office Han Yu was sent, by a harassed Emperor, to persuade a rebellious governor in Hopeh not to plunge the Empire into another civil war. With only a token bodyguard he went to the rebel's camp and spoke his mind. The officers there wavered when they heard what the eminent Confucian scholar had to say. As a result the rebel leader, uncertain of the strength of his support, agreed to terms and the revolt was over. Discipline in the imperial armies greatly improved under Han Yu's watchful eye. As one common soldier put it: 'A person who is prepared to burn the holy finger of Lord Buddha himself will not hesitate to chop the heads from mere soldiers.'

Other Foreign Faiths
Christianity, Islam and several other religions entered China during the T'ang dynasty. In A.D. 635 a Nestorian monk, in Chinese named O Lo Pen, was granted an audience by the ever tolerant Emperor T'ai Tsung. Afterwards the Emperor issued an edict in which he gave permission for Christianity to be preached freely. For 'the Way has more than one name. There is more than one sage. . . . This religion does good to all men.' And the Nestorian Church flourished despite some persecution under Empress Wu, who was a fervent Buddhist. However, it did not really put a strong root down into the Chinese soil, for it was unable to recover from the proscription of all foreign creeds in 845. The Taoists were jealous of the power of the Buddhists and induced the Emperor Wu Tsung to ban all alien faiths. Possibly the Court was worried about the resources tied up in the numerous monasteries, both in terms of land and people, for the eventual compromise let Buddhism keep only one temple with thirty monks in each city of the Empire. The Christian Church in China faded away. When Jesuit missionaries arrived in 1581, the Chinese had forgotten that the Nestorians had already brought the teachings of Jesus Christ.

Such a lapse of memory is not surprising. The Chinese approach to religion was different from that of the West. There was room for a variety of faiths; 'the Way has more than one name.' Exclusive religions, creeds with a single deity like Christianity and Islam, have never made much headway in China. The inclusive habit of mind coupled with Confucian scepticism has tended to keep religion and the priesthood a minor element in Chinese society. The severe, though short, repression of foreign faiths in A.D. 845 was a symptom of national unease and uncertainty connected with the decline of the T'ang dynasty.

THE T'ANG POETS

While the Han Empire was distinguished for prose, particularly in historical writing, and the coming Sung Empire was to be the era of painting, the T'ang dynasty acted as patron for China's finest poets. The three great names are the two friends, Li Po (699–762) and Tu Fu (712–70), and the later Po Chü-i (772–846). In many respects the T'ang Empire was the romantic age. Confucian scholarship was comparatively weak. The importance of the imperial civil service was qualified by the tolerant atmosphere of the Court, especially during the reign of Emperor T'ai Tsung.

Li Po reciting a poem.
A painting by Liang K'ai,
thirteenth century A.D.

112

By the middle of the dynasty Taoism was accepted in the civil service examinations: in 742 it was decreed that Chuang-tzu and other Taoist works should be regarded as Classics, like the Confucian Classics. Above all, the long reigns of Empress Wu and Ming Huang, 'the brilliant Emperor,' provided the social stability necessary for the development of refined literature.

Li Po was, in fact, a Taoist. Though his verse is not colloquial like Han-shan's unusual style of writing, Li Po had a similar longing for the wilder aspects of Nature, vast mist-filled valleys, tumbling waterfalls, bare mountains, deep gorges and jagged cliffs. To the dismay of his relatives the young poet did not proceed to the civil service examinations and high official rank, but dwelt for a couple of years with a Taoist recluse before taking to a wandering life on the road. During his travels he met the other writers of the day, making a lifelong friendship with the younger poet, Tu Fu.

Imperial notice of Li Po's poetry came when he was summoned to the Court in 742. For three years Li Po enjoyed a sinecure given to him by Ming Huang, composing verse by command and recording his own feelings about life in Chang-an, but Court intrigue made him resign the post and travel again. In the capital his drinking may have caused difficulties, but wine often was, and still is, a part of creativity for the Chinese calligrapher, poet and painter. The long years of training and discipline necessary for accomplished brushwork—twenty years would not be considered as much more than a moderate preparation—tended to induce self-consciousness. The wine cup relaxed the heart and hand. After leaving Chang-an Li Po studied Taoism at the residence of the current T'ien Shih, in Shantung, till the rebellion of An Lu-shan drove him southwards to the Yangtze valley. There he became entangled with another rebel group and on the T'ang restoration only escaped the death sentence through the intercession of the loyal general Kuo Tzu-i, whom Li Po had helped on his early travels. Li Po was banished to the South, not far from his own native Szechuan. Several years later a general amnesty allowed him to return along the Yangtze River, in which he is supposed to have drowned in 762. Not far from Nanking a temple to Li Po marks the place where legend says the poet was drowned when trying to embrace the reflection of the moon in the water.

The following poem brings into focus the conflict Li Po must have known so well during his stay in Chang-an. It is that ancient dispute between Taoism and Confucian philosophy concerning the naturalness of urban life.

To Yüan Tan-ch'iu

My friend is lodging high in the Eastern Range,
Dearly loving the beauty of valleys and hills.
At green spring he lies in the empty woods,
And is still asleep when the sun shines on high.
A pine-tree wind dusts his sleeves and coat;
A pebbly stream cleans his heart and ears.
I envy you who far from strife and talk
Are high-propped on a pillow of grey mist.

Again his rendering of an old song in *Fighting South of Ramparts* places human destructiveness in a universal context, Time. The poet's vision of the futility of war, his civilized detachment and resigned quietness, rests on Taoist belief in the value of non-action as much as Li Po's personal experience of civil strife. The final lines are a quotation from the *Tao Teh Ching*.

Fighting South of the Ramparts

Last year we were fighting at the source of the Sang-kan;
This year we are fighting on the Onion River road.
We have washed our swords in the surf of Parthian seas;
We have pastured our horses among the snows of the T'ien Shan.
The King's armies have grown grey and old
Fighting ten thousand leagues away from home.
The Huns have no trade but battle and carnage;
They have no fields or ploughlands,
But only wastes where white bones lie among yellow sands.
Where the house of Ch'in built the Great Wall that was to keep
   away the Tartars,
There, in its turn, the House of Han lit beacons of war.
The beacons are always alight, fighting and marching never stop.
Men die in the field, slashing sword to sword;
The horses of the conquered neigh piteously to Heaven.
Crows and hawks peck for human guts,
Carry them in their beaks and hang them on the branches of
   withered trees.
Captains and soldiers are smeared on the bushes and grass;
The general schemed in vain.
Know therefore that the sword is a cursed thing
Which the wise man uses only if he must.

As a final example of Li Po's verse here is a poem of his about drinking:

On Wine

Have you not seen
How the Yellow River, which flows from heaven and hurries
    toward the sea, never turns back?
Have you not seen
How at the bright mirrors of high halls men mourn their
    white hairs,
At dawn black silk, by evening changed to snow?
While there is pleasure in life, enjoy it,
And never let your gold cup face the moon empty!
Heaven gave me my talents, they shall be used;
A thousand in gold scattered and gone will all come back again.
Boil the sheep, butcher the ox, make merry while there is time;
We have never drunk at all till we drink three hundred cups.

Master Ts'en,
Friend Tan-ch'iu,
Here comes the wine, no standing cups!
I have a song to sing you,
Kindly turn your ears to me and listen.
It is nothing to feast on jade to the sound of bells and drums.
I ask only to be drunk for ever and never wake!
They lie forgotten, the sages of old;
Only the great drinkers have left us their names.
In time gone by, when the Prince of Ch'en feasted in the hall of
    Peace and Joy,
At ten thousand a quart he never stinted the revellers.
Why must our host say he is short of money?
Send to the shop at once, keep the cups filled.
My five-flower horse,
My fur which cost a thousand,
Call the boy, send him out to change them for good wine,
And let me forget with you the sorrows of ten thousand ages!

Tu Fu, the contemporary and friend of Li Po, is regarded by many Chinese as the greatest poet of all. His poetry is stricter, paying more attention to conventional forms; it has a Confucian outlook too. Unsuccessful as a career official, Tu Fu held a number of minor posts in the capital and the provinces. His much appreciated *Autumn Meditation* was composed when he was away from Chang-an. In this poem many aspects of T'ang Empire were fixed forever in the imagination of succeeding generations of Chinese readers. These three stanzas give an impression of Tu Fu's undoubted quality as a poet:

Autumn Meditation

Gems of dew wilt and wound the maple trees in the wood:
From Wu mountains, from Wu gorges, the air blows desolate.
The waves between the river-banks merge in the seething sky,
Clouds in the wind above the passes meet their shadows on the
  ground.
Clustered chrysanthemums have opened twice, in tears of other
  days;
The forlorn boat, once and for all, tethers my homeward thoughts.
In the houses winter clothes speed scissors and ruler;
The washing-blocks pound, faster each evening, in Pai Ti high on
  the hill . . .

The thousand houses, the circling mountains, are quiet in the
  morning light;
Day by day in the house by the river I sit in the blue of the hills.
Two nights gone the fisher boats once more come bobbing on the
  waves,
Belated swallows in cooling autumn still flutter to and fro.
K'uang Heng writing state papers, which earned me no credit,
Liu Hsiang editing classics, my hopes elsewhere . . .
Yet many of my school friends have risen in the world.
By the Five Tombs in light cloaks they ride their sleek horses.

Well said, Ch'ang-an looks like a chessboard—
Won and lost for a hundred years, sad beyond all telling.
The mansions of princes and nobles all have new lords,
And another generation wears the caps and robes of office.
Due north on the mountain passes the gongs and drums shake,
To the chariots and horses campaigning in the west the winged
  dispatches hasten.
While the fish and dragons fall asleep and the autumn river turns
  cold
My native country, untroubled times, are always in my thoughts . . .

(Copyright © 1972 by Grove Press, Inc.)

Po Chü-i, the son of a minor provincial official, hailed from the northern province of Shansi. Unlike Li Po and Tu Fu, the later poet had a distinguished career in the imperial civil service and rose to high rank. He retired in 831, settling at Lung Men, a Buddhist shrine in the country near Loyang, where he had had his official residence as governor of Honan province. As a

116

thorough-going Confucian scholar, Po Chü-i wrote a number of
sharp political poems, like *The Spin-dance Girl*.

The Spin-dance Girl

Spin-dance girl! Spin-dance girl!
She danced to the music of drums and stringed instruments;
She lifted her sleeves as the music sounded;
And, revolving like whirling snow and floating blades of grass,
She turned this way and that, untiring,
In seemingly endless gyrations.
Nothing in the world could equal her speed,
Not even fast-moving wheels and the whirlwind.
When the music ended, she bowed to the Emperor,
Who responded merely with a faint smile.
'Spin-dance girl, born in Sogdiana,
Your eastward trip covering over ten thousand *li*
Was a waste of time. Here spin-dancers abound.
You may not know that they have vied with one another
Since the end of T'ien-pao, when times began to change,
Ministers and concubines have sought to learn
The art of revolving smoothly.
Of these there were two—T'ai-chen and Lu-shan,
Who succeeded best of all. The one was made
Imperial concubine in the Garden of Pear-Blossoms;
The other became Lady Yang's adopted son.
Lu-shan, revolving, deceived the Emperor's eyes;
His revolt was not suspected even after
His troops advanced past the Yellow River.
The Lady, revolving, beguiled the Emperor's heart;
Her death at Ma-wei made his recollections more poignant.
Since that time heaven and earth have changed places;
And for fifty years no ban has fallen on the whirling.
Spin-dance girl, do not dance in vain;
Sing this song often to stir the well-meaning ruler.'

The purpose of the appeal is plain; China needs an Empire
undisturbed by violent alterations of policy and changes of
powerholders. Po Chü-i is looking at a weakened T'ang dynasty,
still recovering from the rebellion of An Lu-shan, mentioned as
Lu-shan in the same line as T'ai-chen, or Yang Kuei Fei. T'ien-pao
is Ming Huang, whose heart was beguiled by Lady Yang. But the
tremendous popularity of Po Chü-i's poetry in his own lifetime
did not entirely please him. The lines he had written were 'on the
mouths of kings, princes, concubines, ladies, plough-boys and
grooms,' but usually they were not those with the really serious

meaning. For as a poet Po Chü-i favoured content above form; his style is deliberately simple and direct. He thought he had something to say to his contemporaries, as this satire shows:

The Chancellor's Gravel Drive
(A Satire on the Maltreatment of Subordinates)

A Government-bull yoked to a Government-cart!
Moored by the bank of Ch'an River, a barge loaded with gravel.
A single load of gravel,
How many pounds it weighs!
Carrying at dawn, carrying at dusk, what is it all for?
They are carrying it towards the Five Gates,
To the West of the Main Road.
Under the shadow of green laurels they are making a gravel-drive.
For yesterday arrived, newly appointed,
The Assistant Chancellor of the Realm,
And was terribly afraid that the wet and mud
Would dirty his horse's hoofs.
The Chancellor's horse's hoofs
Stepped on the gravel and remained perfectly clean;
But the bull employed in dragging the cart
Was almost sweating blood.
The Assistant Chancellor's business
Is to 'save men, govern the country
And harmonize Yin and Yang.'
Whether the bull's neck is sore
Need not trouble him at all.

As a member of the Censorate, he tells us in another poem, his 'bluntness did not suit the times.' Firm memorials had caused his banishment to Hangchow in 822. Po Chü-i was a 'loyal' *shih* and, like Han Yu, his career was marked by a series of ups and downs. Yet his personal poems do communicate to us today as they must have moved his contemporaries.

On His Baldness

At dawn I sighed to see my hairs fall;
At dusk I sighed to see my hairs fall.
For I dreaded the time when the last lock should go. . . .
They are all gone and I do not mind at all!
I have done with that cumbrous washing and getting dry;
My tiresome comb for ever is laid aside.
Best of all, when the weather is hot and wet,
To have no top-knot weighing down on one's head!

I put aside my messy cloth wrap;
I have got rid of my dusty tasselled fringe.
In a silver jar I have stored a cold stream,
On my bald pate I trickle a ladle full.
Like one baptized with the Water of Buddha's Law,
I sit and receive this cool, cleansing joy.
Now I know why the priest who seeks Repose
Frees his heart by first shaving his head.

*Emperor Ming Huang teaching Yang Kuei-fei to play the flute, by
Ch'ien Hsuan (1235–90).*

CHINA

The period of division between the T'ang and Sung Empires is known as the 'Five Dynasties', after the short-lived military dictatorships which controlled the provinces of North China. The length of the longest of these dynasties was seventeen years.

● In the North only three events during this period of instability were to have lasting significance.
1 The capital was moved down-river from Loyang to K'ai Feng, outside the Land within the Passes. This shift may well have been a recognition of the economic changes which had been in progress during the T'ang dynasty. The site was closer to the Yangtze valley.
2 There was an exodus of many T'ang officials to the South, which weakened even more the remaining central administration. They chose not to serve the Northern Emperors who were mostly adventurers of barbarian stock.
3 The cession of large tracts of Hopeh, including the gates in the Great Wall and what is now Peking, by the first ruler of the Later Tsin (936) to the Kitan nomads. In this key strategic area, these people established the Liao kingdom (936–1168); the region was to remain outside China for four hundred years, and through it foreign invaders, the Mongols, were to conquer all China.

● In the South the traditions of the T'ang Empire were preserved. The influx of scholars considerably advanced the culture of the region. Nan T'ang and Shu were particularly distinguished. Being weak the Southern kingdoms were not able to inflict much damage on each other. Printing became widespread.

960 ended fifty-three years of division. General Chao Kuang-yin seized power in the North, then conquered the South, like the earlier Sui reunification. When one king begged independence, the first Sung Emperor asked, 'What wrong have your people done to be excluded from the Empire?'

INDIA and WEST ASIA

900 onwards

EUROPE

● The westward sweep of Muslim arms was halted at the Battle of Poitiers (732). Spain remained the frontier until Italian fleets beat off attacks from Sardinia (1016) and, gaining control of the Mediterranean, allowed a counter-attack. This was to be 'The First Crusade', launched to aid a struggling Byzantine Empire, now reduced to an eighth of its original size, and free the Holy Land from Islam. Although Pope Urban II found a useful outlet for restless warrior nobles in the Crusade, its success was transitory. A feudal army of quarrelling barons had taken on a sophisticated civilization. Charlemagne (768–814) had failed, like Justinian, to restore Roman power; the Crusader kingdoms, an alien growth in the Holy Land, soon fell through the disunity of Christendom.

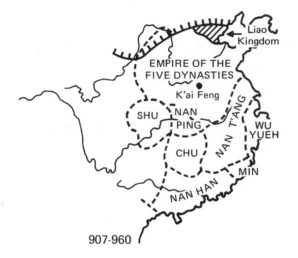

EMPIRE OF THE
FIVE DYNASTIES

K'ai Feng

Liao
Kingdom

SHU

NAN
PING

NAN T'ANG

WU
YUEH

CHU

MIN

NAN HAN

907-960

● The Hindu Kingdoms of North India were dominated by the Rajputs, who had kept the Arabs at bay since their occupation of Sind (712). But new Muslim forces were building up in Central Asia: the Turkish tribes made serious inroads after 1000. Hindu India was under siege. Only the far South was to maintain the tradition when Islam conquered the sub-continent.

● In the West the Muslim world passed on to Christendom the Greek heritage and, by transmission, Chinese achievements. Spain and Norman Sicily were the points of cultural interchange.

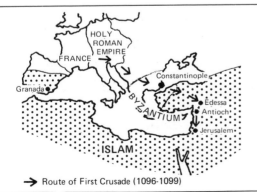

→ Route of First Crusade (1096-1099)

4 A Second Golden Age

The Northern Sung, A.D. 960–1126, and the Southern Sung Dynasties, A.D. 1127–1279

HISTORICAL OUTLINE

The founder of the third Empire, the Sung, was a northern general named Chao Kuang-yin, whose mutinous troops forced him to don the yellow gown, the colour reserved for Emperors. Such a military revolution was an unusual beginning for a successful dynasty in Chinese history. But the reluctant Emperor was a shrewd ruler. He spared the fallen imperial family, gained the goodwill of the *shih* by restoring the civil service to its dominant position, and, not least, rid himself of those military leaders who had put him on the throne. An early historian has recorded how the vicious circle of suspicion and mutiny that had raised and degraded the five brief dynasties in the North was broken:

> In the first year of his reign the new Emperor summoned all his military officers—the men responsible for the mutiny to which he owed his throne—to a banquet. When the company had drunk deeply and were in cheerful mood, the Emperor said:
> 'I do not sleep peacefully at night.'
> 'For what reason?' inquired the generals.
> 'It is not hard to understand,' replied the Emperor. 'Which of you is there who does not covet my throne?'
> The generals made a deep bow, and all protested:
> 'Why does Your Majesty speak thus? The Mandate of Heaven is now established; who still has treacherous aims?'
> The Emperor replied:
> 'I do not doubt your loyalty, but if one day one of you is suddenly roused at dawn and forced to don a yellow robe, even if unwilling, how should he avoid rebellion?'
> The officers all declared that not one of them was sufficiently renowned or beloved for such a thing to happen, and begged the Emperor to take such measures as he thought wise to guard against any such possibility. The Emperor, having brought them to this point, promptly made his proposals known:
> 'The life of man is short,' he said. 'Happiness is to have the wealth

and means to enjoy life, and then to be able to leave the same prosperity to one's descendants. If you, my officers, will renounce your military authority, retire to the provinces, and choose there the best lands and most delightful dwelling-places, there to pass the rest of your lives in pleasure and peace until you die of old age, would this not be better than to live a life of peril and uncertainty? So that no shadow of suspicion shall remain between prince and ministers, we will ally our families with marriages, thus, ruler and subject linked in friendship and amity, we will enjoy tranquillity.'

The officers and generals immediately vowed to follow the Emperor's wishes, and the next day, pretending imaginary maladies, all offered their resignations. The Emperor accepted their offer, and carried out his part of this strange bargain. All were given titles of honour and richly endowed with wealth and land.

The Northern Sung Dynasty

The southern kingdoms watched these developments with interest and sympathy. Nan P'ing and Shu submitted to the Sung dynasty through diplomatic arrangement. Nan Han (971) and Nan T'ang (975) surrendered after short wars, while the last independent state, Wu Yueh, held out only till 979. Except for the Liao kingdom, China was reunited for the third occasion as 'one Empire under Heaven.' There was an overwhelming consciousness among the Chinese that unity was natural and deserved the sacrifice of local autonomy. The early part of the tenth century A.D. had witnessed a revolution in communications. Block-printing made the Classical Books of China generally available for the first time. Not only did the number of scholars greatly increase but the cultural heritage contained in literature became more widely spread through society. To be a Chinese meant—even for the illiterate *nung* who listened to some one read from the newly available books—belonging to a great cultural tradition as well as an Empire.

The second Sung Emperor attempted without success to recover the territory occupied by the Liao kingdom. Defeat and a long war ended when the third Emperor agreed to tolerate the Kitan presence and pay a large annual subsidy to Liao (1004). Unlike the Han and the T'ang dynasties, the foreign policy of the Sung was never imperial in design. Containment of the nomad peoples, the *status quo*, not expansion, was the fundamental rule. Foreign invasion remained the perpetual threat and was the cause of final overthrow of the Sung Empire. Apart from the Kitans on the northern frontier another group, the Tungus, Tibetan tribesmen, had secured in Hsia a power-base

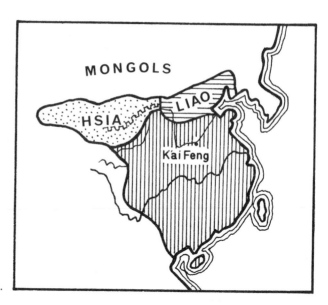

*Empire of
Northern
Sung Dynasty
(till A.D. 1126).*

from which to exploit any Chinese weakness for southern expansion (1032).

The Sung administration was modelled on the T'ang. The civil service reached its zenith, completely overshadowing the military arm of government. Organization and recruitment procedures were perfected. At Court two groups of officials vied with each other for power, the Conservatives and the Innovators. During the reign of Emperor Shen Tsung (1068–85) a revolutionary economic policy was introduced by Wang An-shih, the leader of the Innovators. Although it did not outlast the ministry of Wang An-shih, the new measures seem to have been beneficial to the *nung*, as was intended. Political failure brought banishment to a distant provincial post, nothing worse. Indeed, the pacific atmosphere of the Sung Empire, particularly from 1004 till 1126, has led not a few people to regard this period as the climax of Chinese civilization. Philosophy, painting and science reached levels before unknown, while the pattern of urban life became the envy of later ages.

Disaster struck the Sung Empire in the form of the warlike Kin. These untamed nomads were originally vassals of the Kitans, but ten years of conflict with the Liao kingdom gave them mastery of the region and direct contact with the Chinese. The Emperor Hui Tsung, the painter and patron of art, mis-judged the strength of the Kin army and tried to recover the Liao territories by force. In 1126 the Kin besieged and captured K'ai Feng; they took prisoner three thousand of the *shih* as well as the Emperor, who died in captivity.

124

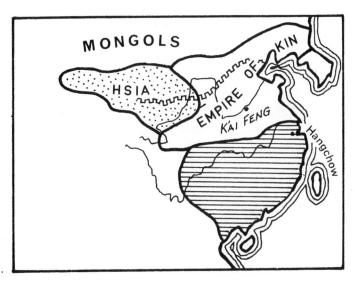

*Empire of
Southern
Sung Dynasty
(after A.D. 1126).*

The Southern Sung Dynasty

Kin cavalry crossed the Yangtze in 1129 and captured the city of Hangchow, where new Sung Emperor Kao Tsu had established his capital. The situation looked grave but the Empire rallied, finding in Yo Fei a general capable of defeating the Kin (1131). When fighting had restored Sung control over the Yangtze valley and the southern provinces, Emperor Kao Tsu decided to come to terms with the Kin (1141). To the anger of Confucian historians, Yo Fei was secretly executed and China divided between two powers, the Sung and Kin Empires. Their frontier was almost identical to the line drawn across China during the Tartar partition (316–590). It was the northern boundary of the wet, rice-growing valleys of southern and central China, country unsuited to the military tactics of nomad cavalry.

Despite a further Kin invasion in 1161, which was repulsed, the Sung Empire continued on its pacific course, at home and abroad. Painting and philosophy came into their own, though Chu Hsi (1130–1200) found his ideas neglected by the Court. His re-interpretation and development of Confucian ideas bear the stamp of the concern that a 'loyal' *shih* must have felt when he reflected upon the reduction of the Empire. Since he died before Genghiz became the Great Khan of the Mongols (1206) and started his nation on their world-shattering course of conquest and destruction, Chu Hsi was spared seeing the agony of civilization savaged by the Mongol horde. The Kin Empire fell first (1210) amid scenes of appalling ferocity. But it was the cold-blooded extermination of the Hsia kingdom, in 1224, that proclaimed the inhumanity of the Mongols. So thorough was that

125

devastation the region became a permanent wasteland, while the language and culture of the Hsia was lost forever.

In 1235, after Genghiz Khan's death, the Mongols turned their attention to the Sung Empire. Nearly half a century of war was necessary before the last member of the Sung dynasty perished in a sea battle off what is now Hong Kong (1279). The terrain of the South, valleys, forests, mountains, hindered the Mongols. And, though a pacifist dynasty, the Sung was technically the best equipped for warfare in the world. Gunpowder had been adopted by the imperial armies. Explosive grenades and

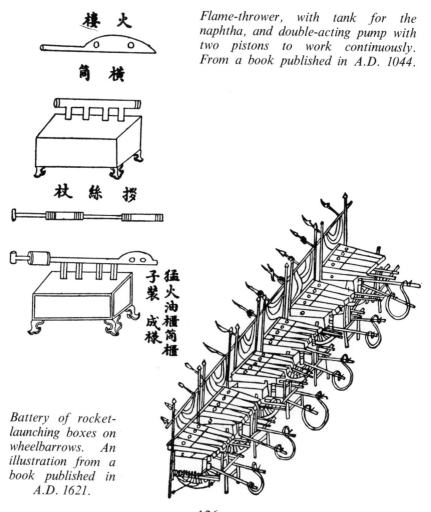

Flame-thrower, with tank for the naphtha, and double-acting pump with two pistons to work continuously. From a book published in A.D. 1044.

Battery of rocket-launching boxes on wheelbarrows. An illustration from a book published in A.D. 1621.

bombs were launched from catapults; rocket-aided arrows and flame-throwers were in service; poisonous smokes could be deployed too. Yet there was another factor involved. The Kin Empire had provided the Mongols with scholar-statesmen like Yelu Ch'u-ts'ai, a Kitan admirer of Chinese culture. He did what he could to temper the furious determination of the Mongols, converting an urge to destroy into a desire for a regular empire. The absolute hatred of sown lands typical of Genghiz Khan was transformed into Kubilai Khan's great foundation, the city of Peking (1263). The grandson of Genghiz and the first Yuan, or Mongol Emperor (1279), had transferred his people and his capital from steppe to sown lands.

NEO-CONFUCIANISM

> The educated believe nothing,
> the uneducated believe everything.
> —*Chinese saying*

The names of Chu Hsi and Confucius are always linked together because the Sung philosopher recast the sage of Lu's teaching in a form that has been accepted as orthodox ever since. The Sung Empire was a time when Confucian philosophy was debated, re-interpreted and transformed into a more modern system of ideas. Perhaps the continued development of Buddhism caused this rethinking of Confucius, though it seems likely that scientific discoveries and applications may have influenced Chu Hsi too. His views have been called 'a kind of scientific humanism.' The traditional Confucian contempt for popular religion, whether Taoism or Buddhism, was taken a stage further by Chu Hsi, who denied that there was a personal deity. 'There is,' he said, 'no man in heaven judging sin.' Instead a moral force, an impersonal power, ruled the universe; the duty of mankind was cooperation with its workings, since they were the laws of Nature.

The Confucian Classics contained few references to divine powers so that Chu Hsi had little difficulty in removing the supernatural realm altogether. The good life, proper conduct as a citizen, was to be expected because the nature of man was good. Decent behaviour did not need to depend on a sense of sin and fear of punishment. Evil was simply the result of neglect and the absence of a proper education. These ideas were to impress profoundly the European scholars of the Enlightenment who first became aware of Chinese thought at the end of the seventeenth century. They responded to a morality that managed without supernatural sanction. The social emphasis pleased them too. According to Chu Hsi, there was no real reason why human society could not become perfect. It was a question of attunement to *li*, or the moral law. A favourite comparison used by Chu Hsi was between man in society and a pearl in a bowl of dirty water. Although the pearl appears grey and spoilt, it has lost nothing essential. Taken from the bowl it shines forth in all its original brilliance. Should man seek his true nature and live in harmony with it, then his original goodness will become clear likewise. His natural purity has become clouded through the false values of social life. The way is to follow the Mean, a balanced style of living. The idea that men have been led astray by the distortions of the society in which they live is not far from present-day Chinese Communism, which has adopted a policy of re-education for those 'who have taken the capitalist road.' After the 'Hundred Flowers' episode in 1957, when Mao Tse-tung relaxed censorship and encouraged the educated classes to voice their views, those 'rightists' who did criticize the government from mistaken viewpoints were sent to the country districts for re-education among the revolutionary *nung*.

Despite Chu Hsi's considerable reputation in his own lifetime the relation between the Sung Court and the philosopher was often strained, even antagonistic. He experienced the inevitable ups and downs in the series of official appointments that were forced upon him. For Chu Hsi was loath to serve in a capacity which compromised his philosophy. The tone of a memorial he addressed to Emperor Hsiao Tsung in 1180 concerning the Court favourites was less than tactful:

> As the power of these people waxes and as their prestige becomes established, throughout the land everyone bends before them like grass before the wind, with the result that Your Majesty's edicts, promotions, and demotions no longer issue from the Court, but from the private houses of these one or two favourites. Ostensibly these acts are Your Majesty's individual decisions, but in fact it is this handful of men who secretly exercise your power of control.

What Chu Hsi wished to see was an Emperor surrounded by true and virtuous *shih*. A memorial of 1188 stated: 'Know those who are worthy and employ them.' His role, as that of all 'worthy' *shih*, was teacher to the Emperor. Scholarship and moral character were required in those who would serve the Empire. They had to follow the Mean. To register protest against things he disliked at Court, Chu Hsi would decline official posts. But it was a negative gesture and he failed to find ways of applying his philosophy. In fact, Chu Hsi's influence was on succeeding generations of Confucian scholars.

SUNG PAINTING

> When you are planning to paint, you must always create a harmonious relationship between heaven and earth.
>
> —*Kuo Hsi*

China's tradition of painting, like much else in her civilization, differs considerably from what we are used to in the West. Artists were not professional in the sense that they did nothing else apart from painting. Just as good handwriting, or calligraphy, and the ability to compose verse became an expected accomplishment of the *shih*, so painting was added by Emperor Hui Tsung to the minimum qualifications of would-be officials of his Court. A good painter himself, the Sung Emperor introduced painting in the Palace examinations, those designed to select candidates for the most senior posts in the imperial civil service. The examination question consisted of a line or phrase taken from the Classics or a well-known poem, which had to be illustrated in an original way. Thought, the idea behind the composition, was more important than fidelity to natural objects. One year Emperor Hui Tsung chose for illustration the line:

> When I return from trampling flowers,
> the hoofs of my horse are fragrant.

The candidate judged to have produced the best work offers an insight on what is valued in Chinese art, for his painting showed a horse walking along a path with a pair of butterflies fluttering around its hoofs. Neither field nor flowers could be seen—Spring was implied. The observer had to discover for himself the artist's intention. Like a great deal of Chinese poetry, paintings were appreciated for their inexplicit quality, a reticence on the part of the artist.

129

In the Sung Empire Chinese art found its perfect mode of expression, namely landscape painting. Later dynasties, the Ming especially, were to be patrons of famous artists but the surviving scrolls of the Sung masters have rarely been equalled. T'ang painters tended to prefer figure painting but the period of the Five Dynasties and the Northern Sung witnessed the rise of

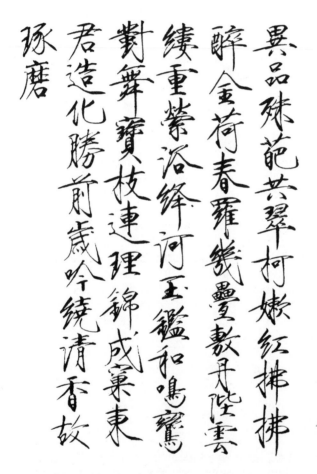

A poem written by the Sung Emperor Hui Tsung. He called this style of calligraphy 'Slender Gold.'

landscape as the pre-eminent form. The shift from human subjects to Nature continued with the growing interest in birds and flowers. From Emperor Hui Tsung's brush came a number of much prized bird paintings as well as fine examples of calligraphy, before the unfortunate ruler was carried off as a Kin prisoner (1126).

Sung landscape painting grew from the spontaneous delight Chinese people took in the splendid natural scenery with which the Empire abounded. The popular Chinese proverb 'Mountains make great trees' expresses the idea that significant landscape moulds men of great character. T'ang poets had put into words the traditional pleasures of the hermit, remote from the bustle of cities, so that a romantic appreciation of landscape became a general sentiment among the literate classes. Religion contributed to this movement; the Ch'an school of Buddhism had no small influence on individual Sung painters.

Kuo Hsi (1020–90) was one of the founding masters of Sung landscape painting. Not only did he paint numerous large-scale scrolls and wall paintings, but he left a record of his views on the purpose of such art. His *Advice on Landscape Painting* explains how he hoped his own works would be used:

It is human nature to resent the hustle and bustle of society, and to wish to see, but not always succeed in seeing, immortals hidden in the clouds. In times of peace, under a good Emperor and kind parents, it would be wrong to go off alone and try to find oneself. For there is duty and responsibility which cannot be ignored. . . . But the dream of a retreat to forests and springs and finding the company of saints in retreat is always there. We are usually excluded from the sights and sounds of Nature. Now the artist has reproduced it for us. One can imagine oneself sitting on rocks in a gully and hearing the cries of monkeys and birds; while in one's own sitting-room the light of the mountains and the colours of the water dazzle one's eyes. Is it not a joy, a fulfilment of one's dream? That is why paintings of landscapes are so much in demand. To approach such paintings without the requisite state of mind would be committing a sin against such natural beauties. . . .

It should be noticed that we are expected to prepare ourselves, to acquire 'the requisite state of mind,' as much as the artist had to prepare himself in order to catch and record the unique character of a landscape. Kuo Hsi tells would-be painters that they must study every aspect of the natural world, for true vision should transmit the life within all things. Two landscapes by an older contemporary, Fan K'uan (990–1030), could serve as illustrations here. One depicts the immensity of rugged mountain peaks, while the other has a winter landscape softened by a covering of snow.

131

Fan K'uan (c. 990–1030): Travelling Among Mountains and Streams.
Ink on silk.

Winter landscape by Fan K'uan.

Perhaps the perspective seems odd, but Western eyes have been trained to see things from a single point. The Chinese artist imagines himself to be looking from the top of a small hill so that he has a total vision of every part. Another surprise may be the restricted palette, the sparse use of colour. But the Chinese saying 'Black is ten colours' indicates the importance of the brush, whose strokes give vitality to the composition. Skill with the brush had become an art in calligraphy since the Han Empire, and its techniques were transferred into painting. Notice the variety of brushwork in the following painting by Ma Yuan (1190–1224): it is simply ink on silk.

Landscape by Ma Yüan.

Indian ink was condensed to a solid state in China. Then it was rubbed on an ink-stone with the required amount of water in order that the artist could obtain a range of colour strengths.

The most celebrated Sung landscape painter was Hsia Kuei (1180–1230). In his scrolls, often long panoramas measuring several metres, the romantic spirit of Chinese art finds full expression. His brushwork has remained the admiration of later generations of painters and connoisseurs.

Distant View of Rivers and Hills *by Hsia Kuei. Large panoramic scroll, another part of which is reproduced in the Introduction.*

Finally, Mu-chi (early thirteenth century A.D.), a monk, represented the Ch'an school of Buddhism in painting, for which reason most of his works are to be found today in Japanese temples and collections. Traditional Chinese critics have consistently underestimated Mu-chi's paintings because the outlook they embody did not remain central to either Chinese thought or Chinese Buddhism, whereas the Japanese who turned Ch'an into Zen prize his work.

135

SCIENCE AND TECHNOLOGY IN THE T'ANG AND SUNG EMPIRES

Whenever one follows up any specific piece of scientific or technological history in Chinese literature it is always at the Sung dynasty
that one finds the major focal point.

—Joseph Needham

The freedom and stability afforded by the T'ang and Sung
dynasties was responsible for a great expansion in scientific and
technical knowledge, which culminated in a minor 'Industrial
Revolution' by the twelfth century. Enquiring minds were not
suppressed and new, or alien, ideas were not rejected. An increasing flow of knowledge between East and West was facilitated
by the tolerant attitude towards foreign travellers in China.
Neo-Confucianism rejected the idea of a deity being responsible
for earthly phenomena and sought 'down to earth' empirical
explanations of them. The resulting spirit of scientific enquiry,
permeated to the West only slowly, but technological developments travelled faster. Even so, some Chinese inventions such as
the 'magazine' crossbow were never used outside China.

Printing

Between the invention of paper in the first century and the
emergence of block-printing in the eighth century little written
material survives. The origins of block-printing were in the stone
and bronze seals and rings engraved with raised inscriptions
which could be reproduced on wax. Larger inscriptions on stone
tablets could be copied by rubbing techniques (cf., brass rubbing
in churches). As early as the fifth century B.C. records were
being engraved on stone and Confucian and later Buddhist works
were recorded in this way to avoid distortion in their retelling,
and to popularize them. After the invention of paper, books
could be made by binding together a number of rubbings.

Although the first reference to printing comes in A.D. 593,
hand copying was most common until the ninth century. In 932
the government ordered the printing of nine Confucian classics
consisting of 130 volumes. This took twenty years to complete
for block-printing was slow and expensive. Each page had to be
carved on to a separate piece of wood or stone. In the mid-
eleventh century movable type was introduced by Pi Sheng.
Each Chinese character was represented on a separate piece of
clay (later porcelain and tin). To print a page, the type was

glued together on an iron plate. Subsequently, the pieces could be removed by heating the plate. Block and movable type printing existed side by side until the twentieth century.

This rubbing comes from a monument of A.D. 1107 and shows Confucius and a disciple. The stone carving was a copy of a famous eighth-century painting.

Mechanical Engineering

The development of mechanical engineering was closely tied to the harnessing of water power, initially in the metallurgical industries.

The earliest use of water power was probably in the *spoon-tilt hammer*. Water would be channelled into a succession of spoons which on filling would tilt, empty and operate a hammer which could be used for forging metal or operating an air blast. The spoons could be arranged side by side or as a continuous bucket wheel. References to this technique go back to A.D. 20. Gradually such machines were adopted for milling purposes, such as grinding corn or hulling rice. A twelfth-century poem by Lou Shou gives a beautifully apt description of them in operation.

The graceful moon rides over the wall,
The leaves made a noise 'sho, sho, sho' in the breeze;
All over the country villages at this time
The sound of pounding echoes like mutual question and answer;
You may enjoy at your will the jade fragrance of cooking rice
Or watch the water flowing in and out of the slippery spoon
Or listen to the water-worn wheel industriously turning.

137

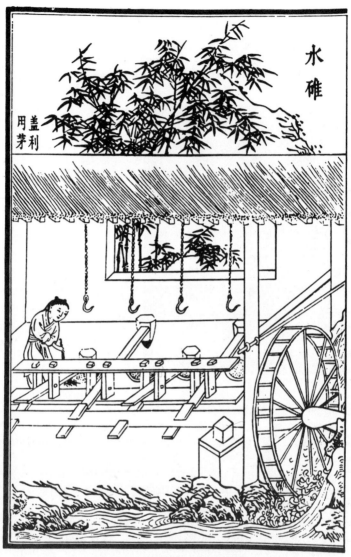

Water powered trip hammers.

The bucket wheel developed into the *water-wheel* as we know it. In China they were often arranged horizontally not vertically. By the thirteenth century water power was being applied to textile machinery for throwing silk and spinning hemp.

Such machines combining crank or eccentric, connecting rod and piston rod, and depending on toothed cogs and gearing apparatus, contained many of the features of later western steam-powered engines.

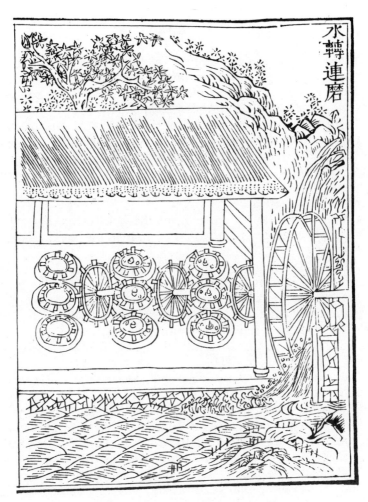

Mill on a river. This system of milling by interconnecting cogs had been invented by the early fourteenth century.

Clockwork

Water power was the basis of mechanical timekeeping devices in the absence of weighted pulleys and springs. In the twelfth century four methods of timekeeping were recorded:

- clepsydra or water clock;
- the burning of incense sticks;
- the sun-dial;
- the 'revolving and snapping springs.'

The first and last of these were connected. The simple clepsydra had developed beyond recognition by the tenth century. The principle of regular and controlled water flow had been linked with the armillary sphere, a model of the heavens used in astronomy. It allowed the sphere to turn slowly keeping pace with the apparent movement of the heavens. This obviously necessitated accurate timekeeping but the machine was not regarded as a clock. In 1090 an astronomical clock tower was constructed in K'ai Feng powered by water-flow. This actually struck a gong to indicate the hours by the system of bamboo 'revolving and snapping springs.'

Marine Developments

It is highly relevant to move from the field of astronomy and mechanical engineering to that of shipping and navigation developments.

In A.D. 118 Chang Heng, the astronomer, said 'there are in all 2 500 stars, not including those which the sea people observe.' By sea people he meant sailors who relied on astronomy for navigation. By the tenth century the *magnetic compass* had been perfected, though it had been around in various forms since Han times. The first clear description comes in *The Dream Pool Essays* of Shen Kua in 1080.

While the Chinese were initially a continental rather than a maritime nation, the significance of inland waterways and coastal trade was so great by the T'ang Empire that many marine developments ensued. The Chinese craft, typified by the 'sampan and junk,' were very different from western craft. They had no keel, no stern or stern post, no framework of ribs, and they were flat-bottomed. The junk's side planking ended at the stern with a solid transom of planks. Rigidity was maintained by solid bulkheads, of which the bow and stern transoms were the terminal ones. These could be made watertight thus establishing a principle not found in western vessels until much later.

The origins of these vessels may derive from observation of split

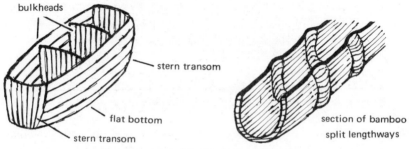

Key features of hull of Chinese junk.

140

bamboo which contains many parallels. Also, some features may have developed from the large ocean-going bamboo sailing rafts still found in South East Asia.

Methods of propulsion were far ahead of the West. Three important developments were:

- the self feathering 'propeller' or sculling oar;
- the use of multiple masts as early as the third century A.D.—usually of mat and batten, their arrangement and shape were so developed by the ninth century as to be aerodynamically very efficient;
- treadmill-operated paddle warships. Their origins lay in the mounting of water wheels in ships which were moored in river currents. Such ship-mounted mills were known in Europe by A.D. 500 but already the Chinese had man-powered paddle boats. The Sung navy developed warships with up to twenty-three wheels (eleven on each side and one stern wheel). These carried crews of 200–300 men, a complement of marines and crossbow-men, and an artillery of catapults for throwing bombs and grenades. From 1100 to 1230 the Yangtze was successfully defended by these vessels from the Kin.

Shantung freighter exhibiting classical features of multiple mat and batten sails and abrupt termination at stern transom.

The stern-post rudder has been mentioned in Chapter 2. By 900 it had ousted the steering oars, which were up to fifteen metres long on even the small sea-going and lake vessels. The steering oar maintained its use on the rivers as it was useful in countering strong currents and rapids. In a rough sea its use was very limited. In 940 one of the earliest specific references to the stern-post rudder was made thus: 'The control of a ship carrying 10 000 bushels of freight is assured by means of a piece of wood no longer than one fathom.'

Cartography
Just as the scientific cartography of the Greeks was disappearing from Europe, to be replaced by religious and symbolic inspiration, the same science was being developed in China. From the first century to the seventeenth, Chinese cartographical development was uninterrupted. Chang Heng (A.D. 78–139), the astronomer and seismologist, was said to have 'cast a network about heaven and earth, and reckoned on the basis of it.' The first principles of scientific cartography were laid down by P'ei Hsiu (224–71) who was Minister of Works in A.D. 267. In drawing up a map of the short-lived Tsin Empire he established six principles:

1 the use of scale based on graduated divisions;
2 the use of a rectangular grid to 'depict correct relationships between different parts of the map';
3 the pacing out of the sides of a right angled triangle to determine the length of the third side where the terrain made it impossible to do a physical measurement;
4 the measuring of the high and the low;
5 the measuring of right angles and acute angles;
6 the measuring of curves and straight lines.

These principles were passed down to later mapmakers such as Chia Tan who in 807 completed a map nine metres long and ten-and-a-half metres high entitled *Map of both Chinese and Barbarian Peoples within the Four Seas*. At a grid scale twenty-five millimetres to 100 *li* this map must have been of the whole of Asia. The T'ang period also contributed early contour maps and the adoption of a mercator-type projection borrowed from astronomy. The application of celestial co-ordinates to the world may have provided the first evidence of a spherical Earth. Moreover, the Chinese put North at the top of their maps unlike the Arabs who placed South at the top. The oldest printed map in the world was of Western China in 1155.

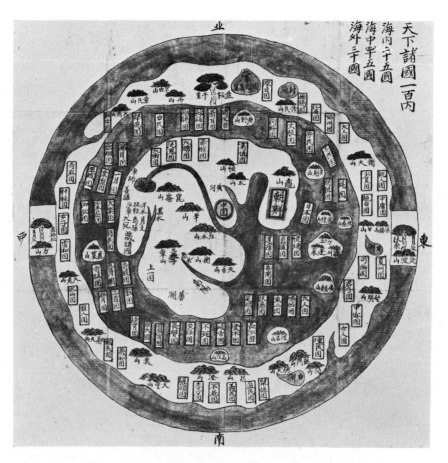

An ancient Chinese view of the World. China is at the centre—the outer ring of land has such names on it as 'Country of the Giants.' The inscription says: 'There are 100 Nations in the World, 25 surrounded by the 4 Seas, 45 on the 4 Seas, and 30 beyond the 4 Seas.'

The knowledge accrued in the T'ang and Sung periods was inherited by Chu Ssu-pen (1273–1337). He added to it the products of cross-fertilization with Arabs and Persians and the Mongol knowledge of West Asia. His work was the basis of the Chinese view of the Asian continent until the nineteenth century. By the time the *Enlarged Terrestial Atlas* was printed in 1555 the shape and alignment of Africa was known. The Atlas was based on a two-metre map divided into sheets as follows: 16 on various provinces; 16 on border regions; 3 on the Yellow River; 3 on the Grand Canal; 2 on sea routes; 4 on Korea, Annam, Mongolia and Central Asia.

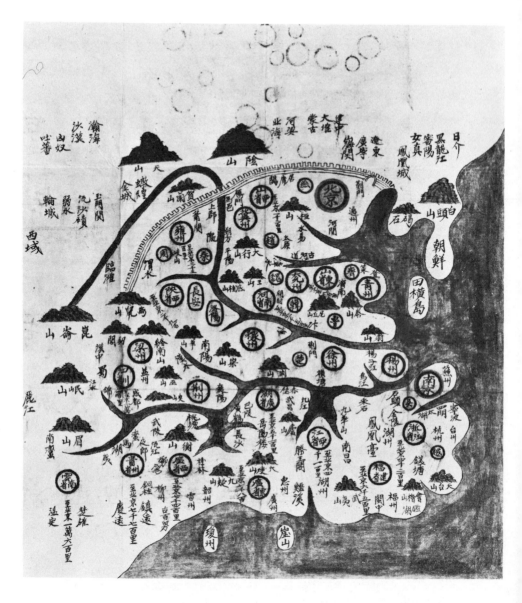

A Ming map of North China showing clearly the Great Wall, the Yellow River and the Yangtze River.

Although at this point China's geographical knowledge became fused with Western knowledge it was not until the work of the intrepid field geographer Hsu Hsia-kho (1586–1641) that the source of the West River was discovered; it was proved that the

Chin Sha Chiang River was the upper reaches of the Yangtze, and that the Mekong and Salween were separate rivers.

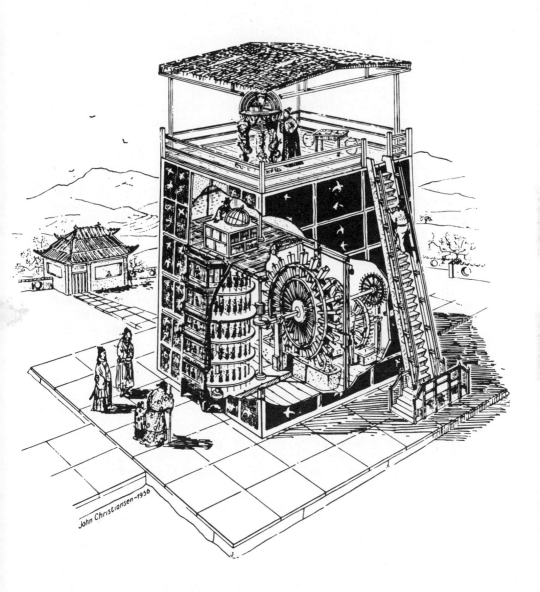

Su Sung's astronomical clock at K'ai Feng (built 1088–92). This reconstruction shows clearly a celestial globe and an armillary sphere. The striking mechanism is to the left: there was no outside dial.

ECONOMY AND SOCIETY

The Growth of a Cash Economy

Before the tenth century the amount of cash in circulation was limited for three basic reasons:

- most taxes and dues were paid 'in kind';
- metals such as copper were generally in short supply;
- there was a problem of maintaining a coinage free from debasement and counterfeiting.

The basic unit of money, the circular copper 'cash' coin with a central square hole, was of very low value (equivalent to about ·028 of a gram of silver). State accountants only dealt with units of one thousand 'cash,' while in everyday trading one hundred was a standard unit. By the eleventh century the 'hundred' was still the common unit but in fact its value had fallen to about seventy-seven 'cash' and by the end of the dynasty was worth only fifty 'cash.' (Just as the Pound Sterling maintains its name but falls in value.) Metal-based, low value, money was very inconvenient, since a 'thousand cash' weighed over half a kilogram.

The Sung dynasty saw a great increase in currency mainly in the form of paper money. Merchants who stored their copper 'cash' with wealthy families received receipts in exchange. These could be cashed in other towns by other members of the wealthy family or their friends. This system was called 'flying money.' The state extended this service in the eleventh century, initially by accepting receipts in exchange for its monopoly products of salt and tea. By the twelfth century the number of notes issued in a single year amounted to twenty-six million strings of 'cash.' Notes were only valid for a certain length of time and in certain areas. But from 1265 to 1274 the government put out notes backed by gold and silver; they were valid throughout the Empire. The great increase of money in circulation led to general price rises and reduced even further the value of 'cash.' The penalty for counterfeiting notes was death.

The Economic Reforms of Wang An-shih

Wang An-shih was Chief Minister in the reign of Emperor Shen Tsung (1068–85). He saw the dangers of disintegration in the Empire as the affluence of K'ai Feng increasingly contrasted with rural poverty. His measures were unpopular with his court rivals, the conservative *shih*, on the grounds that they were 'new.' Despite their fears of peasant rebellion similar to that

146

which overthrew another reformer, Wang Mang, a thousand years before, his measures tended to unify and strengthen the Empire.

The key points of his 'New Laws' were:

● *'Equalization of Loss.'* State granaries were established throughout the provinces to store grain tribute. This was then resold to the population in times of need at low prices. The money was then forwarded to the capital. Prior to this grain was transported to K'ai Feng. Not only did this add to its price, but also there were often great surpluses there when the provinces were starving.

● *'Young Shoots' Law.* State loans to farmers were introduced at low interest rates. This reduced the power of local money-lenders and merchants, thus encouraging farmers to extend the area of land under cultivation.

● *'Remission of Services' Law.* Forced labour (the *corvée*) was commuted for money payments.

● *Rationalization of Court Expenditure.* 40 per cent of the national budget was saved.

● *Control of Trade.* Taxation was reformed. Hoarding of commodities by merchants was reduced and production of luxury goods restricted. Prices were fixed and profits limited.

● *'Pao Chia System.'* Families were grouped in units of ten, all members being responsible for the misdeeds of any one. Each group was forced to provide conscripts to the army. Wealthy families had to maintain a standing supply of cavalry mounts for army use. By increasing the military reserve, Wang An-shih was able to reduce the size and power of the standing army.

● *Reform of Examination System.* The Classics and poetry were replaced by more practical subjects including geography, economics, law and medicine.

The criticisms aroused by these reforms stemmed from the growth of bureaucracy and policing of the population. The existing administration had neither the ability nor experience to organize the New Laws. Furthermore, there was popular opposition to conscription and the Pao Chia system. When Wang An-shih died in 1086 his policies had not caused rebellion and most of his measures were continued by his successors.

The Growth of Trade and the Rise of Merchants
The Sung Empire was a great period of trade expansion. As the key economic area of China shifted to the Yangtze valley and the South-East coast a 'national' market was developed based

on 3200 kilometres of the navigable Yangtze river, the Grand Canal, and ever increasing coastal traffic. The great southern ports of Canton, Ch'uan Chou, and Fuchow had contact with Africa, Arabia, India, the Pacific Islands and the South-East Peninsula. Chinese porcelain and 'cash' of the period have been found in Cairo, Bengal, Annam and South India.

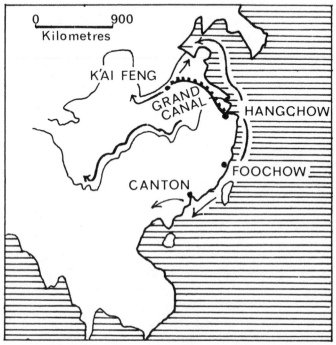

Expansion of a national market in the Sung dynasty.

The government monopoly on the trade of tea, salt, liquor and incense did not prevent the actual transportation and warehousing of these goods from being in the hands of private merchants. Merchants traditionally were entrenched in the lower orders of society, but by the Sung Empire their growing wealth could neither be controlled nor ignored. Increasingly, wealthy merchants were allowed to buy titles to join the ruling *élite*. Mercantile activity, theoretically forbidden to individuals in government service, was undertaken by civil servants on a large scale in Hangchow. The same administrators leased warehouses, shops and dwellings. Nepotism and patronage were common. It even became respectable for well-to-do families to buy businesses for their sons who failed the imperial examinations.

Retail and wholesale organization in Hangchow was highly organized and controlled by guilds. Each trade, such as rice, jewellery, or even medicine, had its own guild. Some parts of the city were areas of specialized trades. The 'Pearl Market,' a jewellery centre, was located between the 'Sweet Harmony District' and 'South-of-the-Market.' The money-changers were to the north between 'Five Span Pavilion' and 'Official's Lane.'

Despite the Chinese desire to prosper, the merchants were regarded as being scrupulously fair in payment of debts and other financial transactions. The guilds enforced standards of quality and behaviour. The determination of merchants to be accepted socially led them to distribute great sums of money on charity, on outward signs of culture like painting, and on great banquets.

Rural Peasantry to Urban Proletariat

The rapid growth of southern cities was characterized by two features:

- a growing inability for the city to support itself;
- a great immigration of poverty stricken peasants from rural areas.

Being dominated by the desires and needs of a wealthy *élite* the economy of the city was based on expansion of luxury trades at the expense of necessities. In short, cities consumed more than they produced. The difference was increasingly made up by the flow of money and foodstuffs from the great estates in the North. The increased demands of the landowners put increasing pressure on an already impoverished peasantry. Similarly, government expenditure was being financed by higher taxes and increasing pressure on the large numbers of employees in state industries. 280000 families in the salt marshes of Huai lived in semi-slavery and perpetual debt. Interest rates were as high as 20 per cent per month. Men were forced to sell their own land to pay debts and became landless labourers. One eye-witness account runs:

> The man is hired for the season, generally from the first moon [February] until the ninth [October]. His wage is one 'load' [about 8 bushels] of cereals [corn and millet] per month. His employer undertakes to furnish him with free clothing, a 'spring' outfit, a shirt and trousers for summer, and a pair of leather shoes. In exchange he must work without stopping, from morning until evening. . . . If he falls ill, payment for the days when he is not at work, is deducted from his wages. If he loses or damages the agricultural goods entrusted to him [wicker baskets, sacks, knives, hoes and spades] he has to see that they are replaced.

149

The final alternatives for men who had sold their land, sold their children as servants, and not committed suicide or become hired labourers, were to become brigands or to migrate to the city.

The cities swarmed with the poor searching for freedom and employment. Many were homeless. Labour, being plentiful, was extremely cheap. A man or woman could only survive by a mixture of cunning and intense specialization. The main areas of occupation available were:

● *Servants and employees of wealthy families.* These families maintained large retinues of dependants, including jewellers, tutors, private soldiers, and a whole range of services to maintain a large household. Such employment was relatively secure as long as the family maintained its wealth.

● *Street vendors and labourers.* These lived from 'hand to mouth' and were their own bosses. 'Poor and honest' pedlars collected a few cheap goods, such as sweets, from 'factory work-shops' in the morning, and received a 10 per cent commission on their sales. The labourers included navvies, water-carriers, scavengers and night-soil removers.

● *Entertainers.* A vast number of mimics, comedians, jugglers, animal trainers, singers and dancers were found in covered bazaars, known as 'pleasure grounds.' Also a large number of tea-houses provided singing-girls and the amount of prostitution in Hangchow amazed visitors, Marco Polo included.

● *Vagrants and thieves.* Petty crime was common throughout the cities, so that many gangs of vagabonds were openly able to defy the police.

The urban proletariat had no feeling of unity. Many were totally dependent on the continuing wealth of their employers. While everyone belonged to a guild, even beggars, they were too numerous and diverse to present a common face on their members' behalf. Occasional crises such as the fire which destroyed 50000 houses in Hangchow in 1201 prompted officials and wealthy members of society to increase their charity in an attempt to reduce panic and unrest.

THE CHINESE CITY

Development of Walled Settlements
Walled settlements developed as early as the Shang dynasty. They were the most efficient means of protection from marauding

nomads. They also allowed easy collection and storage of grain taxes and helped reduce the impact of famine. The permanent residents were largely administrators, civil servants, the military and those providing food and services for them. Intensive agriculture was carried out within the walls and immediately around them for the residence population.

Among the earliest settlements in the 'Land within the Passes' were the cave dwellings of the loess country. These were photographed in Honan province.

Such settlements were most numerous in areas of high population density, namely the most fertile parts of the river valleys. However, numerous garrison towns were 'planted' along the almost deserted northern boundaries.

Distribution of the chief cities referred to in this section.

Craft industries developed as winter occupations of farmers but the larger settlements soon had permanent segregated industrial and commercial sectors. The administrators imposed strict controls on these for fear of the growing power of the merchants. Shih Huang Ti was to use the city to hold the Empire together. He centralized power at the capital Hsien Yang and instituted thirty-six provincial capitals and hundreds of prefectures called *hsien*. The hsien were miniature capitals controlling the small towns and large villages. By Han times the number of settlements recorded indicates that most of the population lived in one of these types of settlement for at least part of the year. Some settlements became cultural centres, places of worship or education, and trade, but all were dominated by their function as administrative centres. Each carried the stamp of government

152

uniformity, from Anyang and Cheng-chow up to the nineteenth-century growth of the Western commercial Treaty Ports. Where they grew around mining, industry or fishing, government control was obtained by nationalizing the industries and recruiting the powerful entrepreneurs into government service.

Today's pattern of Chinese cities was largely established by the fourteenth century A.D. when Kubilai Khan finally organized forty-five hsien in the previously independent area of Yunnan. The coast was relatively neglected until the eighteenth century and the Chinese have remained a continental people as the vast majority of present sites indicates, with a preference for river valleys.

Town Planning
The ancient Chinese considered that heaven was round and the earth square. Human organization of space was supposed to repeat this cosmic pattern. Thus, the basic unit of the classical Chinese settlement was the square. It had to be surrounded by four walls facing the points of the compass. Each wall was identified with the changing position of the sun or with the four seasons. As the Polar Star dominated the universe so the Palace or Official Residence should dominate the city, being centrally located with its rear facing the North Wall, allowing the ruler or his representative to look southward down the main north/south avenue leading to the main gate. This pattern was followed, with allowances for natural conditions, in all sizes of settlement.

The settlement was a microcosm of the natural order. The Chinese were determined to ally themselves with Nature rather than oppose it and to reach this end the initial siting of any settlement involved complex calculations by geomancers, whose knowledge of *Feng-Shui* (Wind and Water) would ensure that evil spirits in the form of flooding or attack would be repelled. 'Without harmony nothing lasts,' according to an old Chinese adage. (The north/south axis of the city and the south-facing main gate had a logic in North China considering the major climatic and barbarian onslaughts came from the north.) The ceremony involved the accurate measurement of sun and shade and the direction of running water. The final decision would be checked by consulting an oracle. Once a site was chosen the construction would be done with great speed during the winter months from October to January, when labour was available. The walls were built first, followed by gates and towers, sometimes a moat, then the ancestral temple and altar of the soil, and, last of all, the official residence at the centre. The places of worship were located south of the Palace and the market place to the north; thus the sacred and profane were separated.

Selection of a city site.

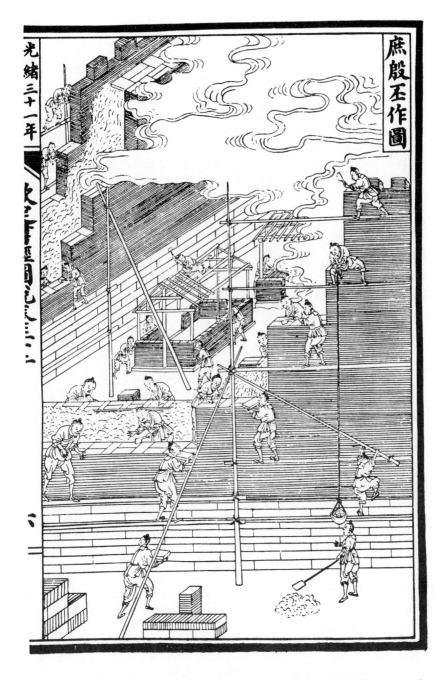

The construction of the walls of the capital of the Chou Dynasty. An illustration from the Ch'ing period. Note the solid foundations and tamped earth walls contained by brickwork.

A royal city's outer walls contained twelve gates to represent the months of the year. Smaller cities had four gates. Gates were of great importance in controlling the urban population. The Han city of Chang-an was divided into 160 *li* or wards, each containing up to 100 households. Each ward was surrounded by a wall controlled by a single gate. Each household in turn was surrounded by a smaller wall with one gate. Each of the three sets of gates was guarded and closed at night, thus a close watch was kept on the movement of the population.

A royal tomb of the Shang built in the fourteenth century B.C. Excavated in the area of the capital Anyang.

The rigidity of the Han system was later relaxed as a result of population expansion, less totalitarian régimes, and the enforced movement of large numbers to less typically Chinese cities in the South, as the North collapsed under Mongol attack. By the Sung dynasty the fastest growing cities were south of the Yangtze and were largely commercial centres. Even so the Mongol capital of Khanbaluc (Peking) in the North, despite being designed by a Muslim architect, displayed all of the classical Chinese features although construction did not begin until 1267.

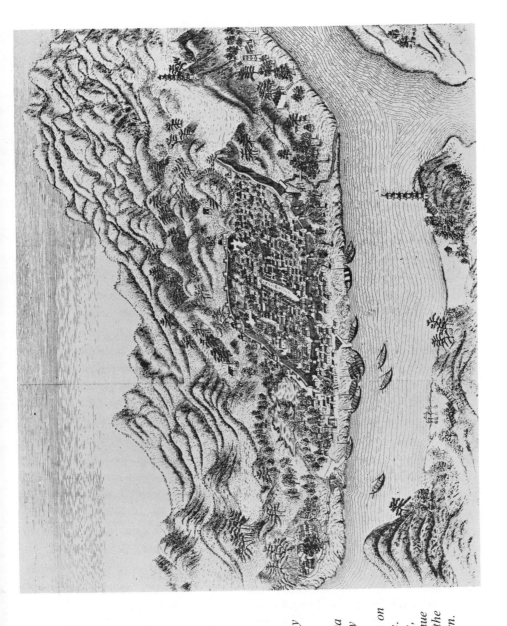

This
eighteenth-century
illustration of
a small town
in Southern China
illustrates clearly
the impact of
planning traditions on
later settlements.
The walls, gates,
towers, main avenue
are all clearly in the
traditional pattern.

The City as a Centre of Change

Cities in Europe have been great centres of social change. Through trade and industry they have been wealthy enough to maintain their independence and have rejected established political, legal and religious ideals. The Chinese city is obviously different. Western university towns have traditionally been centres of provincial dissent against metropolitan ruling. Chinese universities have acted to support centralization by feeding their graduates into the civil service, via the examination system. Chinese rulers have seldom relied on the support of wealthy urban merchants. If anything they discriminated against them, particularly in the sphere of taxation, and absorbed the most able and influential into government service. Change in China could only be obtained by successful peasant rebellions and even then it was not the nature of the political social and economic system that was attacked, only its administrators.

Traditionally, craftsmen and merchants were segregated, often being forced to live outside city walls. Their position was relaxed with the shift of the national centre of gravity to the South, the growth of population in the eleventh century, and the overall expansion of trade in the T'ang and Sung dynasties. An increasing number of cities developed as 'break-of-bulk' points and transport termini on rivers and coast. The rigid-grid pattern was neglected and suburban sprawl became common. In some areas commercial cities developed as twins to existing administrative cities, like: Chengtu and Chungking in Szechuan, K'ai Feng and Chengchou in Honan and Peking and Tientsin in Hopeh.

Chang-an and Hangchow

Chang-an

The site of Chang-an has been developed as a strategic city location from early Chou times to the present day. Hsien Yang, Shih Huang Ti's capital, dominated the fertile Wei Valley which could then be easily defended from attacks from the east. Hsien Yang was razed to the ground to be replaced by Liu Pang's seat, Chang-an. The new city had ramparts over 24 kilometres long, 18 metres high and up to 15 metres thick. The centre and south of the city were occupied by Emperor and Court while the craft and service quarter lay to the north-west and the rest of the population to the north-east. The 160 *li* were served by 9 markets located on each side of the main north/south thoroughfare.

City life in Ka'i Feng about A.D. 1125. The painting emphasizes the bustle of commercial areas of the cities with numerous refreshment houses to the foreground. The painting celebrates the Spring festival and gives a great feeling of merrymaking. The bridge is of bamboo with a multi-angular cantilever construction no longer found in China.

Chang-an was sacked in A.D. 25 and Emperor Kuang Wu chose Loyang in the east as his capital. In the sixth century the Sui reunified the Empire which had collapsed in A.D. 220 and again chose Chang-an as the capital. The architect, influenced by barbarian adaptation of traditional planning built the Royal Palace against the North Wall with government offices directly to the south. These were entirely separated from the rest by walls. The residential and market areas were split by a main north/south highway over 145 metres wide, into two administrative sections each with its own police force. One-hundred-and-eight separate wards were defined, each with its own brick-paved, tree-lined avenues up to 36 metres wide.

159

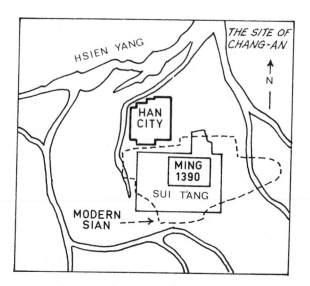

Chinese city sites in the vicinity of modern Sian.

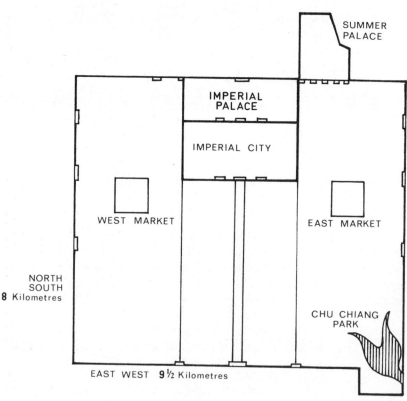

Chang-an during the T'ang dynasty.

160

The market occupied 9 squares, the central one being used by government officials for checking weights and measures, fixing prices and collecting taxes. Each market had 220 trading units and each market street had its own specialized merchandise. 300 drum beats heralded the opening at noon while 300 bell chimes gave warning of closure nearly 2 hours before sunset. Population distribution was uneven. Hence the largely middle-class eastern sections could not maintain sufficient support for their market which gradually declined. The densely populated western section supported a very lively and cosmopolitan market.

About one million people lived in the 77 square kilometres of Chang-an by the seventh century A.D. Large areas were devoted to parkland and open space and the city was used as a model for many others including Nara, an early Japanese capital. The present city of Sian shares the same site as Chang-an.

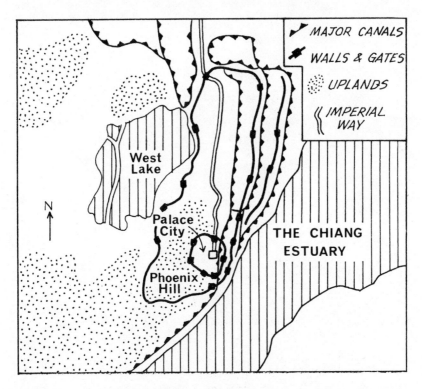

Hangchow, capital of the Southern Sung dynasty in the thirteenth century. Note the irregular form and the contravention of many classical town planning traditions.

Hangchow

K'ai Feng was the capital of the Northern Sung dynasty from 960 to 1126. Attacks from the Kin, coupled with a continued southward movement of surplus population led to the adoption of the southern city of Hangchow as the new capital. Hangchow failed to follow any of the major planning precepts of classical China but came to symbolize a golden age in Chinese history.

Life along the river *by Chang Tse-tuan, a Sung artist.*

162

Why Hangchow differed from the northern cities:

● Its shape was irregular and the walls were pierced by thirteen equally irregular gates.

● The palace was located to the south while the centre was occupied by a pig market.

● Commerce was uncontrolled and spilled out of its allocated quarters.

● There was great freedom of movement for all and the streets were alive with people and entertainment well into the night.

● Increasing use was made of multi-storeyed dwellings through lack of space. These faced directly on to the street rather than into courtyards.

● Great fortunes were made by individual merchants who were increasingly influential.

Houses adjoining waterway, a typical city scene in South China. Population growth and the shortage of land are reflected in the crowding of dwellings along the brinks.

A street in K'ai Feng, shortly before its fall to the Kin.

Hangchow substituted irregularity and human charm for the order and grandeur of the cosmicized cities of the North. The city walls enclosed 10 square kilometres compared to Chang-an's 77 square kilometres. The population of $1\frac{1}{2}$ million was crowded into 26 square kilometres including the immediate suburbs. There were few open spaces. The ten markets were not large enough to cope with all the trade created. Marco Polo was astonished at the city which he called Kin-sai. Life in the capital could be hectic and exciting. There was a continual danger from fires in the densely populated sectors but also a continuous and large selection of entertainments available from music halls to tea houses and state-run taverns. The charms of its singing girls were one of the reasons why it obtained its nickname of the City of Heaven.

Gardens

Poetry, painting and garden art have always been closely inter-related in China. Appreciation of Nature led to attempts by all three at expressing the beauty of the landscape as well as the contrasts to be found in it. Rocks and gnarled stones are often juxtaposed with the soft leaves of plants, like bananas. Because of Taoism water has been a fundamental element in the garden, while water lilies remain one of the favourite subjects for painters today.

Snowscene at the Five Dragon Pavilion, Peihoi Park, Peking. Notice how the formal style of architecture is softened by the snow.

During the Sung Empire both landscape painting and the garden reached a high point, which has rarely been equalled again.

Snow at the Ye Ho Garden, Peking.

But the country house had been a favourite resort, a kind of 'hermitage,' for the *shih* from the Han period onwards.

Opposite is the house and garden of the T'ang painter and poet Wang Wei (609–759), probably by his own hand.

Flowers have always fascinated the Chinese too. Either seeking cherry blossoms in the snow or gazing on chrysanthemum flowers at home the scholar has taken delight in the delicate beauty of the living world around. Failure to do so would have been regarded as a serious shortcoming in the 'cultured' person.

The Japanese garden is a development of the Chinese model, though it may not have been a direct import. Korea could have acted as a half-way stage for its transfer.

166

Enjoyment of the Chrysanthemum Flowers by Hua Yen, 1753.

The Chinese House

The House. The house below is typical of a prosperous family of the Sung period. The connecting courtyards were arranged in accordance with the classical pattern. Regional variations in house-type varied from caves on the loess plateau to stilt houses in the South-East. The poor often had to dispense with court-yards. As population pressure increased in towns an increasing number of dwellings became multi-storeyed.

The Courtyard. Passing through the outer gate from the street, a visitor entered the first courtyard, which might contain shrubs and a goldfish pond. Into this 'public' yard traders might be invited. The rooms along the side might be used as libraries, rest rooms, or guest rooms. The inner courtyard was reserved for the family, side rooms being allocated to in-laws, concubines and other relatives. The main building contained five rooms for the head and his first wife. Behind this were the kitchens and servants' quarters. Gardens would surround the building within the confines of the outer wall. Circular doorways and terracotta reliefs added visual effect to the whole household unit.

The Walls. The buildings were characterized by a rigid wooden structure which supported the whole of the roof weight. The walls could be completely remodelled without danger of collapse Inner walls were usually of pounded earth or bamboo wattle, sometimes plastered with clay and white-washed. Outer walls might be of sun-baked brick. Wood was often in short supply but stone was not favoured in construction as it was an 'unnatural' pillar between earth and heaven. Wood was also more likely to withstand earthquake tremors. Houses were not built as monuments. 'One can create something, it is true, which will last a thousand years, but no one can tell who will be living after a hundred.' Great stability was derived from the use of the corbel bracket, allowing a slight wooden framework to support a heavy roof. Eventually these became a great source of ornate decoration.

The Roof. Most Chinese houses had ridge-pole roofs, overhanging eaves, and gable ends. Curved roofs originated in the South where split bamboo was used as roofing material. The natural sag in these long bamboo strips was incorporated into roof design when curved tiles provided a more durable agent. Poorer houses were often thatched with cereal straw, but this was a great fire hazard in towns. Tiles were colourful, safe, durable, but expensive in comparison.

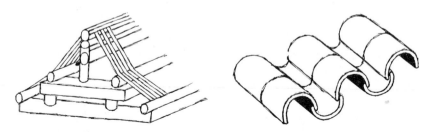

A Land of Bridges
In a country dominated by waterways and mountains it is easy to exaggerate the number of bridges. However, their military and economic importance could not be overrated. Marco Polo estimated that Hangchow alone had over 12000 bridges, mainly of stone.

Bridge at the Summer Palace, Peking.

The earliest bridges were of wooden planks on semi-submerged pillars but by the early Han dynasty stone was the major material. The style was a direct copy of the wooden plank bridge although the stone trusses were up to fifteen metres long. By the later Han dynasty the stone-arch bridge was seen more frequently in North China. These were both ornamental and functional as they allowed junks to pass along the canals. The stone trusses were used mainly for ornamentation and light traffic, over shallow water not used for transport.

The oldest extant stone-arch bridge in China was built in A.D. 605–16 at Chao-hsien in Hopeh. The An-chi bridge has a span of thirty-seven metres but rises only seven metres from foot to crown. This gave a very flat crown which was not emulated in Europe until the sixteenth century. It was in use until 1954 and is the earliest segmental arch bridge in any civilization. The arch bridge reached a peak of perfection in the Sui dynasty and has been adopted for the ornamentation of lakes in major cities such as Peking.

The stone-truss bridge was developed for commercial purposes in the south-east particularly during the Sung period. These were up to 1 200 metres long, composed of twenty-one-metre sections each weighing up to 200 tonnes.

The oldest segmental arch bridge in the world. The An-chi bridge at Chao-hsien, Hopeh.

173

A suspension bridge across the Mekong.

In western China, mountain gorges demanded bigger spans at greater heights and the arch was replaced by the cantilever and suspension bridges. Wooden cantilever bridges were tunnels with resting houses at each end. Suspension bridges were initially supported by cables of twisted bamboo hung from towers on opposite sides of a gorge. The towers contained winding gear to keep the cables tense. Iron-chains were used as early as the sixth century and were extended into the south-west throughout the Sui and T'ang dynasties. Such mountain bridges became important market and communication centres.

Ornamental marble bridge at the Summer Palace.

174

A Moon bridge in the Summer Palace at Peking.

Pavilion bridge at Wan Hsien.

Daily Life in Hangchow

The inhabitants of thirteenth century Hangchow were early risers. Monastery bells and the cries of the monks touring the streets shouting details of the day's weather would waken them between four and five o'clock. The city would already be busy. The rice wharves operated continuously to provide the 200 tonnes and more of rice needed to feed the population each day. The abattoirs would be killing and preparing the day's meat. Shop-keepers arranged the day's displays by six o'clock and the Imperial Way was thronged with farmers and street traders coming in from the suburbs. The aroma of fried tripe and other breakfast delicacies would emanate from the large number of kiosks and the portable stoves of the food vendors. By seven o'clock the whole city, from refuse collectors to the officials of the Imperial Court, would be well into their day's work.

The running of the individual households would be supervised by the elders of the family. Servants would be commissioned to buy and prepare the day's food. Cleaning and housecare would be aided by the simplicity of interior decor and furnishings. Beds were of wooden planks, covered in rush mattresses and covers lined with silk floss. The pillows were cylinders of plaited rushes,

The pillow of wicker, wood or porcelain.

lacquered wood or porcelain with a hollow in the centre for the head. Curtains were used to screen the bed. Wealthy homes made use of black lacquer to cover furniture which might also be engraved or inlaid with precious stones or metal. Chairs were an innovation from India. In the T'ang Empire people sat on them crosslegged. By Sung times lighter 'barbarian seats' with crossed legs were common, as were circular stools. Tables were low and rectangular for dining, but circular pedestal tables were used for flower arrangements and antiques such as vases. Flowers were a common form of decoration and great prestige was obtained by the growing of delicate and fragrant blossoms. The walls of wealthier homes were covered with scrolls and paintings of landscapes, or examples of fine calligraphy.

In summer the houses could be stifling, although the waxed-paper windows could be removed. The wealthier families moved to cooler altitudes outside the city. In winter the thin partition walls gave little protection from the cold and there was great heat loss from the charcoal fires. Coal was very expensive and the main protection from cold was probably obtained from thicker quilted clothes. In rural districts hollow brick seats and beds (*k'ang*) were heated with hot air from the cooking stove.

Water was delivered daily from the freshwater lake to the west. Bathing was very popular in Hangchow unlike the northern cities. Liquid soap made from peas and herbs, and perfumes, was available. The poor who did not own bathing facilities could use one of the hundreds of bathing establishments open to the public for a small fee. Hot water was always on sale in the streets. The city was hygiene conscious. The wealthy had their own cesspits and all refuse and excrement were collected in vessels and carried to the suburbs by the night-soil man. Most visitors were impressed with the cleanliness of both the city and its people but Arab traders found the Chinese use of toilet paper as early as the ninth century quite distasteful.

Mosquitoes were a common pest in the house, particularly in summer, but fumigants could be purchased along with incense. Cats kept down the rodents. The markets had stalls specializing in toys and other goods as well as pets, like Pekingese lapdogs and crickets which were kept in cages.

The kitchens of the houses contained charcoal stoves and

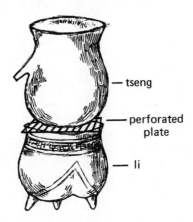

— tseng

— perforated plate

— li

cooking implements of copper and porcelain such as the three-legged li and the tseng. Cooking by steam heat was recognized as being rapid and effective in preserving the goodness of foodstuffs. There were few taboos on foodstuffs. In Hangchow specialized restaurants provided foods as diverse as snakes, dogs and snails. Little beef was eaten for the simple reason that oxen were too valuable as draught animals and there was little tradition of consuming milk or dairy products. Pork was the main meat together with poultry. The wealthy could afford venison or game birds, while the poor consumed large amounts of offal or horse flesh. Per capita consumption of rice in the city was about a kilo per day. Both freshwater and saltwater fish were commonly available. Water was seldom drunk on its own. It had to be boiled to avoid contamination and tea was usually made. Many varieties were known. Vying with tea as the most popular drink was rice wine flavoured with spices. Drunkenness was quite common.

In the evening the wealthy family might entertain friends, relatives or guests. A large number of courses would be served over several hours. Food would be presented on the low tables in many dishes. All meat was cut up in advance, allowing the guests to eat with chopsticks and spoon. Entertainers would be hired to amuse the company. Meanwhile, the streets would be teeming with the evening's pleasure seekers as they visited the numerous tea houses and restaurants until the early hours.

5 The Mongol Conquest

The Yuan Empire, A.D. 1279–1368

HISTORICAL OUTLINE

Although the date of the beginning of the Yuan or Mongol Empire is considered to be 1279 by Chinese historians—that is, the year in which the last member of the Sung dynasty was killed—there had been a Mongol Empire in China since the accession of Kubilai Khan. From 1263 Peking, not Karakorum in Mongolia, was the centre of Mongol world power.

The Mongol Terror

The Mongol Terror was unleashed on the world by Genghiz Khan, who laid down the rule that any resistance shown to Mongol arms should be punished by total extermination. Whenever a city put up a defence or delayed its surrender, the fate of the inhabitants was certain death—every man, woman and child. Genghiz Khan was a man incapable of feeling pity. On occasions his fury even extended to animals and plants. During a campaign in 1222, Mutugen, the favourite grandson of Genghiz Khan, was killed laying siege to a fortress in Bamiyan, a valley within the folds of the Hindu Kush. To appease the grief of the boy's mother, he took an oath to put to death every living soul in that rich and populous valley. Accordingly, Genghiz Khan set out with his army, devastating villages and towns, until Kakrak, the chief city, had been reduced to rubble. The present-day obscurity and unimportance of Bamiyan is an impressive monument to Mongol ruthlessness. Yet the Mongols exulted in such ferocious actions. 'The greatest joy,' Genghiz Khan said, 'is to conquer one's enemies, to pursue them, to seize their property, to see their families in tears, to ride their horses, and to possess their daughters and wives.'

Every Mongol male was a soldier. Hunting and battle were his sole occupations. Slaves performed the few domestic duties the restless Mongols considered necessary. When these fierce

179

A portrait of Genghiz Khan by a Central Asian artist.

horsemen fell on the Kin Empire in 1220, their physical appearance struck terror into the Kitans, for they were unkempt. In fact, Mongols were expressly forbidden to wash themselves, or have anything washed in running water.

What the Mongol conquest represents is the greatest clash in Asian history between the nomadic culture of the steppe and the civilization of intensive agriculture. There is a revealing incident recorded in *The Secret History of the Mongols*, commissioned by Genghiz Khan's son Ogodei around 1240. After one of his campaigns in Central Asia, Genghiz Khan summoned to his court two people from the city of Khiva, Turkestan, to explain to him 'the sense and significance of the cities.' To the Mongol emperor, the city was something alien, an encroachment upon a world which once belonged to the nomads alone, a world which during the thirteenth century for the first and last time came very close to being dominated by a nomadic empire. But to Genghiz Khan understanding was not condoning: cities were plundered and laid waste by his hordes.

Yelu Ch'u-ts'ai

When the Mongols overran those areas of China under the control of the Kin Empire and the Hsia kingdom, the nomad fear and hatred of settled life was indulged to the utmost. The brunt of this fury fell on the 'Land within the Passes,' whose ancient importance as the centre of Chinese civilization was eclipsed forever. The decimated *nung* were no longer able to maintain the extensive hydraulic works, and many northern frontier towns had to be abandoned. One man, however, spoke out against the Mongol devastation and, fortunately for China and the world, his words convinced Genghiz Khan. Here is an account of the discussion leading up to this momentous alteration of policy:

When Genghiz invaded the western countries, he did not have in his stores a single measure of rice or a single yard of silk. When [they came to the first Chinese provinces] his advisers said 'Although you have now conquered the men of Han, they are no use to us; it would be better to kill them all and turn the land back to pasture so that we can feed our beasts on it.' But Yelu Ch'u-ts'ai said 'Now that you have conquered everywhere under Heaven and all the riches of the four seas, you can have everything you want, but you have not yet organized it. You should set up taxation on land and merchants, and should make profits on wine, salt, iron, and the produce of the mountains and marshes. In this way in a single year you will obtain 500 000 ounces of silver, 80 000 rolls of silk and 400 000 piculs of grain. How can you say that the Chinese people are no use to you?' . . . So Genghiz agreed that it should be done.

Yelu Ch'u-ts'ai, a Kitan, had been summoned by Genghiz Khan to Mongolia in 1218. The Mongol Emperor expected that such a nobleman from the old kingdom of Liao would welcome service in Mongol cause. When Genghiz Khan met Yelu Ch'u-ts'ai for the first time in his court, he said: 'Liao and Kin have been enemies for generations; I have taken revenge for you.' To which Yelu Ch'u-ts'ai replied: 'My father and grandfather have both served Kin respectfully. How can I, as a subject and a son, be so insincere at heart as to consider my sovereign and my father as enemies?' Pleased by the frankness of this reply as well as the demeanour of Yelu Ch'u-ts'ai, the Mongol Emperor found a place for him in his retinue. The Kitan nobleman became secretary-astrologer to Genghiz Khan and, finally, Chief of the Secretariat under Ogodei Khan.

The attitude adopted by Yelu Ch'u-ts'ai in his initial interview with the Mongol Emperor and expressed in his later advice on state affairs was the direct result of a Confucian training. As in the earlier period of the Tartar partition, the Kitans and the Kin had been profoundly influenced by Chinese culture. Through Chinese sympathisers, like Yelu Ch'u-ts'ai, there was a constant attempt to mitigate the harsh Mongol rule in North China as well as to provide an administration for the unwieldy nomad empire. While Yelu Ch'u-ts'ai was prepared to play on Mongol cupidity in an emergency, he hoped that wisdom and learning would triumph at last. In his diary we find this entry:

> The teachings of the Three Sages are all of benefit to mankind. When I read the book of Lao-tzu, my admiration was deeply roused. I wished to make Our Sovereign [Genghiz Khan] tread loftily in the footsteps of the ancient worthies. This is the reason why I supported Ch'an-ch'un, who, of course, I also intended to be an advocate of Confucianism and Buddhism.

Ch'ang-ch'un, a leading Taoist, had been called to the Mongol court because of a rumour that he had found the elixir of life. But at this time in China there was a general belief in the common origin of the Three Ways, the teachings of Buddha, Lao-tzu and Confucius. To follow all of them meant 'to stand firmly in the world like the three legs of a tripod.' Although Ch'ang-ch'un proved a disappointment by using his relationship with Genghiz Khan to further the fortunes of his own sect in China, Yelu Ch'u-ts'ai achieved other successes in the Mongol court. At the election of Ogodei Khan he introduced a number of Chinese practices designed to stabilize the dynasty, but, more important, he opened the civil service to Chinese scholars by having examinations re-established in 1237. This measure alone freed more than a thousand *shih* from being Mongol slaves. Yet agitation from the anti-Chinese faction at Court soon stopped the practice and the influence of Yelu Ch'u-ts'ai on government came to an end in 1239 when tax-farming was permitted by Muslim business men. Yelu Ch'u-ts'ai died of a broken heart in 1243. The Mongol dynasty, which he believed had the Heavenly Mandate, went on to become an entirely non-Chinese régime, supported by a civil service recruited from foreign adventurers. Had the wish expressed in the diary come true, the Mongols might have saved themselves from the great Chinese rebellion that was to drive out the last Mongol Emperor in 1368.

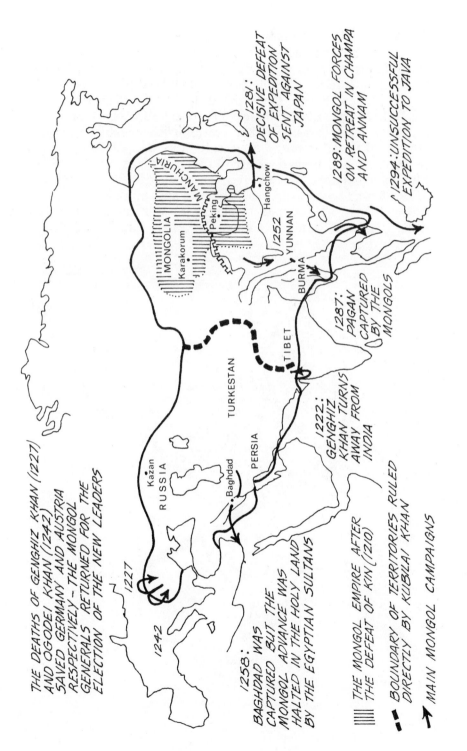

The Mongol World Empire on the death of Kubilai Khan (1294).

THE DEATHS OF GENGHIZ KHAN (1227) AND OGODEI KHAN (1242) SAVED GERMANY AND AUSTRIA RESPECTIVELY—THE MONGOL GENERALS RETURNED FOR THE ELECTION OF THE NEW LEADERS

1227

1242

1258: BAGHDAD WAS CAPTURED BUT THE MONGOL ADVANCE WAS HALTED IN THE HOLY LAND BY THE EGYPTIAN SULTANS

1222: GENGHIZ KHAN TURNS AWAY FROM INDIA

1287: PAGAN CAPTURED BY THE MONGOLS

1281: DECISIVE DEFEAT OF EXPEDITION SENT AGAINST JAPAN

1289: MONGOL FORCES ON RETREAT IN CHAMPA AND ANNAM

1294: UNSUCCESSFUL EXPEDITION TO JAVA

RUSSIA
Kazan
Baghdad
PERSIA
TURKESTAN
TIBET
BURMA
YUNNAN
1252
Hangchow
Peking
MANCHURIA
MONGOLIA
Karakorum

THE MONGOL EMPIRE AFTER THE DEFEAT OF KIN (1210)

BOUNDARY OF TERRITORIES RULED DIRECTLY BY KUBILAI KHAN

MAIN MONGOL CAMPAIGNS

The Mongol World Empire

Kubilai Khan had been on the Mongol throne for twenty years when the last member of the Sung dynasty died (1279). Nominally he ruled an empire spanning Europe and Asia, from the Danube to the Yellow River. Only the death of Genghiz Khan had recalled the generals for the election of his successor and spared Germany from invasion. That year English merchants decided not to sail to Baltic ports: they feared the Mongol Terror might be there by the time they arrived. But the vast extent of the Mongol conquests, spread over so many diverse peoples and places, forced successive Great Khans to appoint rulers for distant provinces. By 1270 it was beginning to split up into the four distinct Mongol states of China, Turkestan, Russia and Persia.

A Mongol bowman, as seen by a Japanese artist.

184

Ogodei Khan ruled 1229–41

Ogodei was considered a benign ruler, particularly before the fall of Yelu Ch'u-ts'ai. However, he became addicted to alcohol—he preferred grape wine from the West to kumys, the alcohol obtained from fermented mare's milk that Mongols had always drunk. His wife became increasingly powerful as he withdrew from active leadership before finally dying of drink. Kubilai was more sober and stable, though his successors indulged in women and drink, leaving the non-Chinese Yuan civil service to run the Empire for its own benefit.

The conversion of the western Mongols to Islam in 1295 completed the process of fragmentation, because the Muslim Khans refused to recognize Buddhist Kubilai Khan or his successors.

Despite the steady break-up of the Mongol World Empire, the reign of Kubilai Khan has remained a marvellous image in the mind of West. The chief reason for this very odd view of

185

Kubilai Khan ruled 1260–94

Chinese history is that China during the Yuan Empire was better known to Europe than at any time till the twentieth century. Mongol control of so much of the world ensured that roads were safe and travel easy, while the Mongol prejudice in favour of war meant that foreigners with any useful skill or ability could make a career for themselves in China. Marco Polo served in the Yuan civil service from 1271 to 1297.

Military ventures undertaken from the Yuan Empire had a mixed success. Yunnan and Burma were quickly annexed, but serious reverses were sustained in Indo-China and Japan. The Mongol army sent against Champa, modern South Vietnam and South-east Cambodia, found the guerrilla tactics employed by the Chams utterly exhausting. Fever and jungle warfare forced the invincible Mongols into a difficult withdrawal, not unlike the experience of Western powers since 1945. The invasion of Japan was a complete disaster (1281). A storm wrecked the fleet and

186

those who managed to wade ashore were cut down by Japanese samurai. Little more success was achieved by a sea-borne expedition against Java in 1294, though the Mongols avoided a massacre.

Kubilai Khan ruled an empire already showing signs of decay. The violence of the initial Mongol attacks on China had impoverished whole provinces. The administration was unconcerned with the welfare of the people; the state officials were corrupt and unreliable. The *shih* and the *nung* found themselves steadily coming together as a united opposition to the Yuan dynasty.

The End of the Mongols

In 1315 the reintroduction of the examination system for entrance to the civil service came too late to rally support from the long-excluded *shih*. The Yuan dynasty was clearly in decline with a series of mediocre Emperors. The last ruler, Togan Timur, was advised by his chief minister, Bayan, that the only hope for the Mongols was wholesale massacre of the Chinese. Open rebellion began in 1348 and for twenty years rival groups and secret societies jostled for position in the fight against the struggling Yuan dynasty. Taoism, a politically subversive philosophy ever since Lao-tzu rode off into the West, played a considerable part in the expulsion of the Mongols through the 'White Lotus' secret society. Foreign dynasties such as the Mongols and the later Manchus were always suspicious of Taoism on account of its ancient opposition to the pomp and ceremony of government. At last Chu Yuan-chang, a peasant, assumed the lead of a national movement and the last Yuan Emperor fled from Peking without a fight (1368).

Chu Yuan-chang, later the Ming Emperor Hung Wu, had great ability as a leader. Indeed, his success derived from the way in which he was able to unite both the *shih* and the *nung*, those two pillars of Chinese society. No other peasant rising has obtained the support of the scholars.

A popular festival today incorporates a legend about this rare event. 'Moon cakes,' the chief item of offering in celebrations for harvest, are said to have been used to co-ordinate action against the Mongols. One version of the story runs like this:

It was not easy for a weaponless population, just ordinary citizens, to overthrow the Yuan dynasty, with a fully armed Mongol soldier billeted in every house. A scholar hit on a simple and effective idea. Every Chinese family must act together and at the same moment. To do this a secret message had to be sent to every house without arousing suspicion. Since the harvest festival was approaching in the autumn and one of the celebrations was eating special cakes by all the members of the family as soon as the moon had climbed into the sky, he and his trusted friends decided to get the bakers to put the message inside these cakes. Throughout the cities of China 'moon cakes' were baked with a tiny piece of paper in the middle; not a word was breathed to outsiders.

On the festival night the Chinese families and their unwanted Mongol lodgers gathered round the table. The moon rose and the head of the household picked up the table knife to slice the cake. As each man cut a cake he was amazed to see the paper within. The message was clear, an order: 'Kill the Mongol.' Knife after knife was grasped hard, then plunged into the chest of the unwary soldier. By the morning panic had seized the remaining Mongols and the last Khan fled.

MARCO POLO AND THE WESTERN IDEA OF CATHAY

The Pope sent Franciscan friars to convert the Mongols to Christianity in the middle of the thirteenth century. After the hordes had turned back from the borders of Germany and Austria, Europe began to see the Mongol Terror not as a new 'scourge of God' but a possible ally against its chief foe, the Muslim powers. The missionaries had no success, though Kubilai Khan asked for the assistance of a hundred men of learning. Marco Polo, as a young man, accompanied his father and uncle on the mission dispatched by the Pope in reply to this request (1271). Although the two learned Dominican friars sent with the Polos were faint-hearted and dropped out of the journey at the first sign of danger, Kubilai Khan received the Venetian travellers kindly and found employment for Marco in the Yuan administration. Twenty years' service gave him a unique opportunity for observing and collecting information about the Yuan Empire. *The Travels,* the account of his experiences, provides us with interesting details about Mongol rule but it lacks real insight concerning the situation of the Chinese. He did not learn the Chinese language and seems to have moved only in Mongol social circles. His writings gave Europe a glimpse of another world, the splendour and power of the Yuan Empire. Kubilai Khan is portrayed as a great ruler, presiding over a magnificent court, to which all men of worth were welcomed, regardless of origin, race or creed. While the amazement and praise at this liberal atmosphere expressed in *The Travels* is understandable in the light of the narrow, closed world of Europe at this period, the Yuan Empire was a pale imitation of what had been a general

Chinese practice since Han times. And lost on Marco Polo was the political motive behind the employment of foreign adventurers, namely the Mongol desire to exclude the *shih* after the fall of Yelu Ch'u-ts'ai.

Ignorant of Chinese history and culture, Marco Polo divides the Yuan Empire into two regions: Cathay, or Northern China, where the Mongol capital was situated at Khanbaluc (Peking), and Manzi, the lands to the south of the Yangtze valley. But his description of Hangchow, which he calls Kin-sai, is valuable because this city, the capital of the Southern Sung dynasty, capitulated to the Mongols and so avoided destruction.

OF THE NOBLE AND MAGNIFICENT CITY OF KIN-SAI

At the end of the three days you reach the noble and magnificent city of Kin-sai, a name that signified 'the celestial city,' and which it merits from its pre-eminence to all others in the world, in point of grandeur and beauty, as well as from its abundant delights, which might lead an inhabitant to imagine himself in paradise. . . . According to common estimation, this city is an hundred miles [160 kilometres] in circuit. Its streets and canals are extensive, and there are squares, or market-places, which, being necessarily proportioned in size to the prodigious concourse of people by whom they are frequented, are exceedingly spacious. It is situated between a lake of fresh and very clear water on one side, and a river of great magnitude on the other, the waters of which, by a number of canals, large and small, are made to run through every quarter of the city, carrying with them all the filth into the lake, and ultimately to the sea. This, while it contributes much to the purity of the air, furnishes a communication by water, in addition to that by land, to all parts of the town; the canals and the streets being of sufficient width to allow of boats on the one, and carriages on the other, conveniently passing, with articles necessary for the consumption of the inhabitants. It is commonly said that the number of bridges, of all sizes, amounts to twelve thousand. Those which are thrown over the principal canals and are connected with the main streets, have arches so high, and are built with so much skill, that vessels with their masts can pass underneath them, while, at the same time, carts and horses are passing over their heads—so well is the slope from the street adapted to the height of the arch. If they were not in fact so numerous, there would be no convenience of crossing from one place to another.

Beyond the city, and enclosing it on that side, there is a fosse about forty miles [64 kilometres] in length, very wide, and full of water that comes from the river before mentioned. This was excavated by the ancient kings of the province. . . . The earth dug out from thence was thrown to the inner side, and has the appearance of many hillocks surrounding the place. There are within the city ten principal squares or market-places, besides innumerable shops along the streets. Each side of these squares is a half mile [0·8 km] in length, and in front of them is the main street, forty paces in width, and running in a direct line from one extremity of the city to the other. . . . In each of the market-places, upon three days in every week, there is an assemblage of from forty to fifty thousand persons, who attend the markets and supply them with every article of provision that can be desired. . . . Each of the ten market-squares is surrounded with high dwelling-houses, in the lower part of which are shops, where every kind of manufacture is carried on, and every article of trade is sold; such, among others, as spices, drugs, trinkets and pearls. In certain shops nothing is vended but the wine of the country, which they are continually brewing, and serve out fresh to their customers at a moderate price. The streets connected with the market-squares are numerous, and in some of them are many cold baths, attended by servants of both sexes, to perform the offices of ablution for the men and women who frequent the baths, and who from their childhood have been accustomed at all times to wash in cold water, which they reckon highly conducive to health. . . . All are in the daily practice of washing their persons, and especially before their meals.

In other streets are the habitations of the courtesans, who are here in such numbers as I dare not venture to report; and not only near the squares, which is the situation usually appropriated for their residence, but in every part of the city they are to be found, adorned with much finery, highly perfumed, occupying well-furnished houses, and attended by many female domestics. These women are accomplished, and are perfect in the arts of blandishment and dalliance, which they accompany with expressions adapted to every description of person, insomuch that strangers who have once tasted their charms, remain in a state of fascination, and become so enchanted by their meretricious arts, that they can never divest themselves of the impression. Thus intoxicated with sensual pleasures, when they return to their homes they report that they have been in Kin-sai, or the celestial city, and pant for the time when they may be enabled to revisit paradise. . . .

The inhabitants of the city are idolaters, and they use paper money as currency. The men as well as the women are handsome. The greater part of them are always clothed in silk. . . . Among the handicraft trades exercised in the place, there are twelve considered to be superior to the rest, as being more generally useful; for each of which there are a thousand workshops, and each shop furnishes employment for ten, fifteen, or twenty workmen, and in a few instances as many as forty, under their respective masters. The opulent principals in these manufactures do not labour with their own hands, but, on the contrary, assume airs of gentility and affect parade. Their wives equally abstain from work. They have much beauty, as has been remarked, and are brought up with delicate and languid habits. The costliness of their dresses, in silks and jewellery, can scarcely be imaged. . . . Their houses are well built and richly adorned with carved work. So much do they delight in ornaments of this kind, in paintings, and fancy buildings, that the sums they lavish on such objects are enormous. The natural disposition of the native inhabitants of Kin-sai is pacific, and by the example of their

190

former kings, who were themselves unwarlike, they have been accustomed to the habits of tranquility. The management of arms is unknown to them, nor do they keep any in their houses. Contentious broils are never had among them. They conduct their mercantile and manufacturing concerns with perfect candour and probity. They are friendly towards each other, and persons who inhabit the same street, both men and women, from the mere circumstance of neighbourhood, appear like one family. In their domestic manners they are free from jealousy or suspicion of their wives, to whom great respect is shown. . . . To strangers also, who visit their city in the way of commerce, they give proofs of cordiality, inviting them freely to their houses, showing them hospitable attention, and furnishing them with the best advice and assistance in their mercantile transactions. On the other hand, they dislike the sight of soldiery, not excepting the guards of the grand Khan, as they preserve the recollection that by them they were deprived of the government of their native kings and rulers.

On the borders of the lake are many handsome and spacious edifices belonging to men of rank and great magistrates. There are likewise many idol temples, with their monasteries, occupied by a number of monks, who perform the service of the idols. Near the central part are two islands, upon each of which stands a superb building, with an incredible number of apartments and separate pavilions. When the inhabitants of the city have occasion to celebrate a wedding, or to give a sumptuous entertainment, they resort to one of these islands, where they find ready for their purpose every article that can be required, such as vessels, napkins, table-linen and the like, which are provided and kept there at the common expense of the citizens, by whom also the buildings were erected. It may happen that at one time there are a hundred parties assembled, at weddings or other feasts, all of whom, notwithstanding, are accommodated with separate rooms or pavilions, so judiciously arranged that they do not interfere with or incommode each other. In addition to this, there are upon the lake a great number of pleasure vessels or barges, calculated to hold ten, fifteen, to twenty persons, being from fifteen to twenty paces in length, with a wide and flat flooring, and not liable to heel to either side in passing through the water. Such persons as take delight in amusement, and mean to enjoy it, either in the company of their women or that of their male companions, engage one of these barges, which are always kept in the nicest order, with proper seats and tables, together with every other kind of furniture necessary for giving an entertainment. . . . And truly the gratification afforded in this manner, upon the water, exceeds any that can be derived from the amusements on the land; for, as the lake extends the whole length of the city, on one side you have a view, as you stand in the boat at a certain distance from the shore, of all its grandeur and beauty, its palaces, temples, convents, and gardens, with the trees of the largest size growing down to the water's edge, while at the same time you enjoy the sight of other boats of the same description, continually passing you, filled in like manner with parties in pursuit of amusement. . . .

191

CHINA AND THE WEST UNDER THE 'PAX MONGOLICA'

The establishment of a World Empire stretching from the Don to the Mekong greatly facilitated overland travel from West to East. A merchant's handbook of the fourteenth century says 'the road which you travel from Tana [at the mouth of the Don] to Cathay is perfectly safe, whether by day or by night, according to what the merchants say who have used it.' The main reasons for safe and speedy communications were:

● the establishment of an efficient system of relay stations about forty-eight kilometres apart on the main routes, where horses could be exchanged and provisions obtained;

● the benevolent attitude of the Khans to Western travellers. At first Genghiz enslaved foreigners to gain their knowledge and craftsmanship, but Ogodei and Kubilai encouraged the free movement of travellers and employed many of them as administrators.

Western Debts to China
But in the two-way flow of information between East and West China gave far more than it received. As Mohammed once said, 'seek for learning though it be as far away as China.' Even before the unification of Asia under the Mongols the Old Silk Road had been a major source of communication. However, little information about Chinese technology had been directly transmitted, possibly because of the self-containment of the Chinese Empire. Only with the breaching of China's isolation by the Mongols did a flow of technical information actually influence the technological development of the West. This may have happened in two ways:

● the records of increasing numbers of literate and knowledgeable western observers such as the Polos;

● information carried by Tartar slaves for domestic service in Italy in the first half of the fifteenth century.

The granting of Venetian citizenship to Peter the Tartar, Marco Polo's own servant, began this influx of people in 1328. Yet Chinese science was largely neglected in this information flow, though for three years Marco Polo had been governor of Yangchow, a regional capital specializing in the production of armaments and military provisions. By the beginning of the thirteenth century Europeans were using the magnetic compass, the stern post rudder and the windmill, and in the fourteenth century mechanical clocks, blast furnaces, gunpowder, segmental arch bridges, and block printing are all recorded. Although the exact origin of these inventions was unknown to the inhabitants of Europe at this period, their significance as agents of social and economic change was not altogether unnoticed. In the early 1600s Francis Bacon, Lord Verulam, Lord Chancellor to King James I, was aware that the vast transformations of Europe stemmed from the application of these scientific advances. He wrote:

> It is well to observe the force and virtue and consequences of discoveries. These are to be seen nowhere more conspicuously than in those three which were unknown to the ancients, and of which the origin, though recent, is obscure; namely printing, gunpowder, and the magnet. For these three have changed the whole face and state of things throughout the world, the first in literature, the second in warfare, the third in navigation; whence have followed innumerable changes; insomuch that no empire, no sect, no star, seems to have exerted greater power and influence in human affairs than these mechanical discoveries.

This acute observation is interesting. For printing had ended the monopoly of the Church over education. Knowledge became readily available in printed form whereas previously only the very rich layman could afford the long, tedious and expensive process of hand-copied manuscripts. The Renaissance and the Reformation followed. Gunpowder inaugurated large-scale warfare, eclipsing both knight and castle. The Thirty Years' War, which raged shortly after Bacon's death, was the closest experience of total warfare in Europe before 1914. The magnetic compass had sent Columbus to America in 1492 and helped Magellan circumnavigate the globe in 1520. What Bacon was pointing out—his scientific interests provided him with an important clue—was a crucial watershed in European history. Modern times, in fact, were beginning, and Europe was acquiring technological knowledge from China that would give it such an immense advantage over the 'Empire of all under Heaven' in the nineteenth century.

Some Western Travellers to the Orient

Apart from the Polos there were other travellers who were attracted to the Mongol Court. Not all of them have left records of their journeys, but we know something of the following men and their motives:

● *Friar John of Pian di Carpine.* An Italian Franciscan, he set off in 1245 as an ambassador from Pope Innocent IV. The Catholic Church was worried at the ease with which the Mongols were sweeping westwards, claiming to be both universal and divinely inspired. John was joined by Friar Benedict, a Pole, in Breslau. They passed through Kiev in mid-winter shortly after its devastation by the Mongol horde. On their arrival in Mongolia they discovered that a new Khan, Guyug, was being elected at the Shira Ordo, or the Yellow Camp, near to Kara-korum, where they were amazed to find a large number of Westerners already in residence. These were mainly the envoys of East European rulers, and slaves. Having exchanged gifts and letters with Guyug, they met Cosmos, a Russian goldsmith, who introduced them to some Nestorian Christians. They arrived back in Lyons bearing Guyug's answer on 18th November 1247.

The earliest travellers heading East were really entering the unknown. Legend, folklore, and superstition were the main sources of information on the East. Fabulous monsters and strange men with dogs heads, or single feet, or faces between the shoulder blades, lived there. Oddly enough the Chinese had the same sort of idea of the West as this illustration of a headless Westerner shows (early fifteenth century).

● *Friar William of Rubruck*. He travelled as a missionary, not as a political ambassador, and his aim was to obtain converts and establish contacts with the groups of enslaved Catholics known to exist in the East. He reached Karakorum in late December 1253. Guyug had just died and been replaced by Mongke who interviewed the Friar shortly after his arrival. William was amazed at the international nature of court society, recording the presence of an Englishman named Basil. After contacting Boucher, a famed Parisian artist and architect, one of the involuntary army of technicians employed at Karakorum, he was able to record more comprehensively the life of the tented city. (Boucher's adopted son spoke Mongolian.) He recorded that Chinese craftsmen were esteemed for pottery manufacture and building and made the first report of their use of paper money and calligraphy. He co-operated with the Nestorian Church,

Life at the Court of Genghiz Khan.

celebrating joint masses, in the hope of gaining court support for Christianity. However, competition for favour was strong as Buddhists, Taoists and Mohammedans were all attempting the same. The Mongol leader always encouraged any faith that would contribute its prayers to his spiritual well-being but found William too zealous and uncompromising. At one point a debate between the Christians, Buddhists and Moslems was arranged as an entertainment, the only rule being that no abusive language was to be used. Few converts were made and William returned to France in 1255.

● *John of Montecorvino.* An Italian Franciscan, he set off for Cathay in 1290, before the Polos returned. He knew the Khan gave protection to Christians but all that was known of China itself was that it was the ancient Seres (from Serica, Latin for silk). He departed from Venice to preach for several months in Tabriz, where he was joined by a Dominican, Nicholas, and an Italian merchant Peter of Lucalango. They left Persia by sea to avoid the war between Kubilai and his cousin in Central Asia. After preaching in Southern India, where Nicholas died, and surviving a hazardous journey round what is now West Malaysia, they arrived at Peking in 1294, just after Kubilai's death. The new ruler's son-in-law, Prince George of Ongut, was converted to Catholicism, to become the first Catholic ruler of East Asia. Two churches were opened, one paid for by Peter of Lucalango out of his profits, and forty slave boys were bought and trained as choristers in Latin. John of Montecorvino became first Archbishop of Khanbaluc (Peking), dying as first Patriarch of the Orient (1328).

● *Odoric, the Roving Friar.* He reached Peking in 1325 and, while fulfilling less of a political or religious function, was the keenest observer of the Chinese. He mentioned for the first time the binding of women's feet, the long nails of Chinese gentlemen, and the use of cormorants for fishing. On his return to Europe many of his stories were greeted with incredulity and ridicule.

● *Ibn Battuta* (1304–77). He was the greatest traveller of Islam and his reports on China were more perceptive and influential on technological changes than his predecessors'. He described the construction of Chinese ships, the making of porcelain, machinery for raising water, and even old-age pensions. Zaiton (Ch'uan Chou) had a large Moslem community largely from Persia and it contained the oldest Mosque in China.

6 The Chinese Revival

The Ming Dynasty, A.D. 1368–1644

HISTORICAL OUTLINE

The Mongols were thrown back to their homeland. In 1372 general Hsu Ta crossed the Gobi desert, sacked Karakorum, and pursued what Mongol forces remained into the fastness of Siberia. By the time the first Ming Emperor, Hung Wu, died (1398) the Chinese Empire had enjoyed thirty years of peace at home and successful conquest abroad. Ming armies annexed Yunnan and Liaotung, besides re-establishing Chinese authority over much of Central Asia, while Annam and Korea became tributaries. 'Rule like the T'ang and the Sung' was the advice Emperor Hung Wu had carved on his tomb. His successors did restore Chinese unity and tradition but the Ming Empire was bright rather than golden. The administration was neither as efficient as the T'ang nor as enlightened as the Sung. The harsh punishments meted out to rebels during the Ming Empire suggests that a legacy of the Mongol invasion was a less humane standard of war and politics. Entrance for the civil service examinations was still theoretically open to all candidates, though the development of costly associated customs made advancement the privilege

日月 *Ming* means bright, clear or brilliant. Chu Yuan-chang chose this name for the dynasty he successfully established in 1368. Usually an ancient name connected with the first emperor's birthplace or background was adopted—Liu Pang had called his house the Han from territories held by him at the downfall of the Ch'in dynasty—but the Ming Emperor Hung Wu departed from the traditional practice. It has been suggested that his obscure origins may have prompted this innovation, but the need to revive China and recreate the civilization so badly mauled by the Mongol invasion could be responsible for the choice. The Ming period was a time of brightness for Chinese culture, an era of restoration in which efforts were directly concerned with reviving the glories of the T'ang and Sung Empires.

of the rich. As estimate for 1469 seems to show there were over 100 000 civil and 80 000 military officials in the imperial service. Moreover, the use of eunuchs eventually led to serious clashes within the administration, though the *shih* made vigorous attempts to check the growth of eunuch influence through the permitted criticisms of the Censorate, and a number of child emperors gave unscrupulous eunuchs ample scope to repeat the worst experiences of the Court at the close of the Han Empire.

Emperor Yung Lo

The Emperor Yung Lo, uncle of the second Ming ruler, was commander of the northern armies at Peking when he usurped the throne (1402). Nanking, the capital of Hung Wu, was badly damaged in the civil war and Yung Lo decided to transfer the Court to Peking, where he felt most secure. The present imperial palace, or Forbidden City, is his work. Building the new capital and deepening the Grand Canal took immense resources in terms of both manpower and materials.

LANGUAGE AND THE MOVEMENT SOUTH
Old Forms   Present day

YUEH, meaning to speak, to tell. The mouth ☐ exhales ∟ a breath, a word.

TA, meaning piled up or crowded together. It also means flow. A flow 劜 of words 曰. So 沓 is used to denote a babbling flow of talk.

The process by which Chinese civilization absorbed the indigenous peoples of the South was a natural extension of the economic penetration that had been in progress since earliest times. During the Kin and Mongol periods large-scale population movements were common, but the southern expansion of the Chinese people is an historical event that has lasted several thousand years. The Chinese trader was followed by his family and their language gradually converted the native tongue into a semi-Chinese dialect. The wealthier natives became bilingual, and later their children started to speak Chinese as a first language. Speech and custom are closely bound together, hence the assimilation of these people into 'the hundred families'. An important function of the Chinese language, with its neutral script, has been this capacity to accommodate non-Chinese peoples: it has maintained the ecosystem.

One million workmen are said to have completed the Forbidden City in just ten years, so that it has been likened to the 'Great Leaps' undertaken in the People's Republic. The northern site of the capital was to prove a grave disadvantage towards the end of the dynasty. Peking, forty miles from the Great Wall, was unnecessarily exposed to attack from the steppes and an extreme distance from the now dominant South. Preoccupation with the defence of the northern frontier may have been a cause of the cessation of naval operations (1433), which has left China vulnerable from the sea for the last four centuries. Opposition from the *shih* was certainly another factor—Cheng Ho, appointed admiral of the fleets by Emperor Yung Lo, was a eunuch.

Although there were many military and naval expeditions—Emperor Yung Lo died on the way back from a campaign in Mongolia (1424)—the reign was a period of internal peace and prosperity. Building activity was conspicuous: city walls, paved roads, bridges, temples, shrines, tombs, villas, palaces, gardens and other monuments were built throughout the provinces of the Empire. Writers and painters flourished, their works form today a major part of the Chinese heritage. China seemed to have not only recovered but reached new heights of achievement. However, it is during the Ming dynasty that for the first time China lagged behind the progress made in other countries, and particularly Western Europe. Marco Polo had taken back tales of wonder about the Yuan Empire, but the final hundred years of the Ming Empire were marked by a steady decline, a fact not lost on the Europeans, who sailed along the Chinese coast; the Portuguese came first in 1514, the Dutch in 1622, and the English in 1637.

The Decline of the Ming Empire

The disaster of Huai Lai (1450) was the turning point for the Ming Empire. The eunuch Wang Chin had gained the confidence of Emperor Cheng T'ung during his youth and he used this influence to persuade the inexperienced ruler that a Mongolian expedition was necessary, despite protests from senior generals. Wang Chin wanted to display his power by entertaining the Emperor in his hometown, Huai Lai, near the northern frontier. The eunuch was given command of the forces raised for the campaign and his generalship proved disastrous. A nomad host destroyed the Chinese army outside Huai Lai and Emperor Cheng T'ung was carried off as a prisoner. Though the nomads were not strong enough to exploit this sudden victory, they had gained the military advantage over the Ming Empire. In 1644 another northern tribe, the Manchus, were to find an entrance through the Great Wall and found a new foreign dynasty.

Cheng Ho, the eunuch admiral, had been a loyal supporter of the imperial house. His skill as a naval commander and a diplomat became legend. Unfortunately, the rise and fall of Wang Chin was a sign that the times had changed. In 1510, when Liu Chin, another favourite, was disgraced, officials discovered that the greedy eunuch had amassed an immense fortune. His private stock of precious metal included the equivalent of 251 583 600 ounces of silver in unminted pieces of gold and silver. Corruption had become a widespread feature of the administration, an activity that not all of the *shih* could resist as well. The old ways were breaking down. Ineffectual government was aggravated by a series of economic crises, partly the result of pressure upon the land by a rising population of about two hundred millions. Famines began to recur, accompanied by popular rebellions. The long reigns of Emperor Chia Ching (1520–66) and Emperor Wan Li (1572–1620) helped the declining Empire, though the improvement in administration was due to the work of 'loyal' *shih* like Chang Ku-ching.

The Shun Dynasty and the Manchu Invasion
In 1618 the Manchu tribes united and invaded Liaotung. Ming armies remained continually engaged against the growing Manchu power, which reached the Great Wall itself by 1629. That vast fortification might have been sufficient to have withheld the Manchus, had not internal discord given them an entrance. For the Manchus were not the same kind of people as the Mongols. Their proximity to Chinese culture had begun the process of conversion from nomads to settled agriculturalists even before Nurhachu made them a single nation. What provided the Manchus with their chance of conquest was the civil war that ended the Ming dynasty in 1644, when Li Tzu-ch'eng, an ex-bandit, had captured Peking with his rebel army, whose numbers were increased by famine refugees, and proclaimed himself the first Emperor of the Shun dynasty. But general Wu San-kuei, the commander of the Ming army defending the Great Wall, refused to acknowledge that the Mandate of Heaven had passed to the Shun. Repeating the error of the Tsin dynasty in the third century A.D., Wu offered the Manchus an alliance against Li and opened the gate at Shanhaikuan. Perhaps he intended to gain time by this policy of friendship with the Manchus, thereby using his forces to defeat the usurper and gain the throne himself. Li was soon vanquished but the complicated struggle that followed gave the Manchus the opportunity

to make themselves masters of all the Empire (1682). In this they had greater success than the Hsiung Nu, called in by the Tsin Emperor.

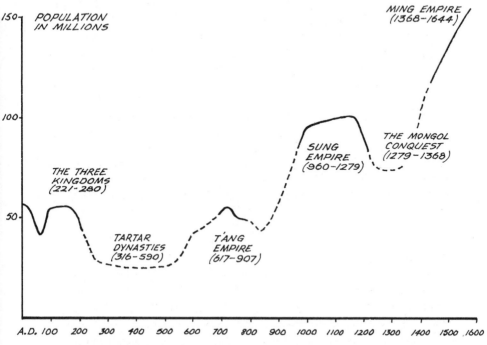

A Han census figure for A.D. 2 gives the population of the Empire as 58 million, which may be somewhat overlarge as a figure. Civil strife, floods and disease soon reduced this number, though during the stability of the Later Han just over 50 million was maintained. Tartar invasions (316–590) reduced the numbers of Chinese people living in Chinese-controlled territories by half, though the reunification under the Sui (589–618) led on to the T'ang Empire and a stable population of over 50 million. In the same way the Sung Empire permitted population growth, which was only arrested, temporarily, by the Mongol Conquest (1279–1368). The Ming Empire topped 150 million. However, the T'ang and Sung figures may prove an underestimate because only those people liable to tax were included in the census.

ECONOMY AND SOCIETY

The Ming dynasty began in a strong, purposeful and ruthless spirit and for a hundred years or more provided an efficient framework for economic advance, particularly in trade and

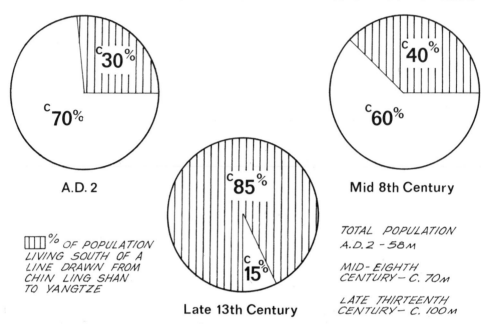

A.D. 2

Late 13th Century

Mid 8th Century

$^{c}30^{\%}$

$^{c}70^{\%}$

$^{c}85^{\%}$

$^{c}15^{\%}$

$^{c}40^{\%}$

$^{c}60^{\%}$

☐☐☐ *% OF POPULATION LIVING SOUTH OF A LINE DRAWN FROM CHIN LING SHAN TO YANGTZE*

TOTAL POPULATION A.D. 2 - 58M

MID - EIGHTH CENTURY - C. 70M

LATE THIRTEENTH CENTURY - C. 100M

agriculture. After 1500 it was increasingly affected by conservatism, nepotism and corruption in which increased wealth was achieved not by innovation and improvement but by extortion and parasitical exploitation of the rural masses, the *nung*.

Agricultural Development

The Khans had recognized the danger of having a capital in the north which was dependent on southern grain supplies. Sea transport was affected by pirates and storms. The Grand Canal was a great engineering feat but was frequently damaged by floods and changes in the course of the Yellow River. Frequent attempts were made during more stable periods to increase the agricultural efficiency of the North. The harsher climate of the North with the frequent catastrophes of drought, flooding and continuous erosion, combined with its frequency as a theatre of war, had led to a continuous movement southward of its population. To counteract this and to try to make Peking self-supporting, government land was distributed as a reward to Ming supporters. Free seed, oxen and tools were made available and plantations of Chinese settlers reached as far north as the fertile South Manchuria plain. These measures successfully increased output but also stimulated a rapid population increase which nullified its impact.

Rice provided about seventy per cent of China's grain needs and the Ming sought to diversify grain production to reduce this reliance. Contact with the Western countries, who were familiar with the crops of the Americas, led to the introduction of groundnuts, the sweet potato and maize in the sixteenth century. However, these did not become widely accepted until the eighteenth century. Groundnuts were particularly suited to sandy soils unfit for rice and they were most easily adopted in the newly developing territories of Yunnan and western Kwangtung. Maize entered by the ports and also overland via India and Burma; before 1650 it was largely found in the South West. The sweet potato had similarity to existing Chinese crops, yams and taros. Being drought-resistant and high yielding the sweet potato was assimilated more rapidly and widely.

Early European visitors in the sixteenth century were impressed with the efficiency of Chinese agriculture. A Portuguese merchant-writer Pereira wrote: 'Not one foot of ground is left untilled' and 'the dung farmers seek in every street by exchange to buy this dirty ware for herbs and wood. The custom is very good for keeping the city clean.' He also called the 'Chins' the 'greatest eaters in the world.' Fish formed a substantial part of the diet in South China. Tame, trained cormorants were used to catch fish in rivers and at sea, while many artificial ponds had been created where the fish were 'farmed.' Mendes Pinto, another Portuguese who was captured as a pirate and transported from Nanking to Peking along the Grand Canal, noted the hard working peasantry, the careful use of manure, and the extremely common activity of duck raising.

Population Growth and the Movement South
Whether agricultural improvement stimulated population growth or population growth stimulated agricultural development is still debated. What is certain is that population rose rapidly from around 80 to 150 million and that a great amount of land was brought into cultivation for the first time. A conscious policy of colonization was carried out particularly in the south-western areas of Yunnan, Kwangsi and Kweichow.

The south-west had been controlled by the Kingdom of Nanchao which developed its strength thanks to an early alliance with the T'ang. Having come to dominate other kingdoms of the area, it took on and defeated the armies of its former ally and turned westwards to invade Burma. The people of Nanchao were mixed tribal groups dominated by the advanced rice-

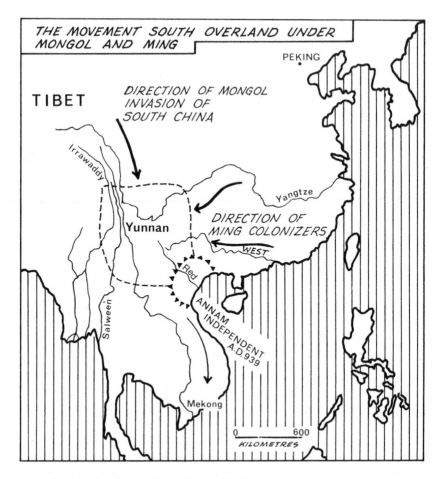

THE MOVEMENT SOUTH OVERLAND UNDER MONGOL AND MING

PEKING

TIBET

DIRECTION OF MONGOL INVASION OF SOUTH CHINA

Irrawaddy

Yangtze

Yunnan

DIRECTION OF MING COLONIZERS

WEST

Red

Salween

ANNAM INDEPENDENT A.D. 939

Mekong

0   600
KILOMETRES

growing Pai of the Tali plain. Tali was an important strategic site and lay on a fertile plain which seldom suffered drought or flood and whose tropical latitude was modified by the altitude of 2 000 metres. They expanded their territory eastwards absorbing areas of Chinese settlement and gradually became increasingly sinicized. In the tenth century the kingdom was overthrown by a grandee of Chinese descent who formed the Tali Kingdom. Tali maintained an allegiance to the Sung dynasty, which left it largely alone. Gradually the kingdom consolidated itself in Yunnan. The Mongols invaded South China in 1252, through Tali, taking it by surprise after marching 960 kilometres over difficult terrain. A hundred years later it was the last Mongol stronghold to hold out against the Ming. It was reduced and incorporated officially into China in 1382.

With the inflow of troops came many settlers from the Yangtze valley. They rapidly established themselves on the plains and fertile river valleys, driving the more primitive shifting cultivators on to upper slopes and forcing the stone-age hunters and collectors into the highest and most inaccessible areas. Cities developed as miniatures of Peking. The region was connected to the capital by paved roads, and iron-chain bridges crossed the valleys of the Salween and Mekong. Emperor Yung Lo had great slabs of marble transported by road and river from Tali in 1405, for the construction of the Imperial Palace at Peking.

Not all the settlers were voluntary pioneer farmers, many were forced exiles from many parts of China. As they would tend to go to areas occupied by others from their own home provinces they maintained their own dialect and regional customs. The inhabitants of K'unming, the provincial capital, speak with a close affinity to Peking colloquial speech, while those of Paoshan,

THE STRATEGIC LOCATION OF TALI

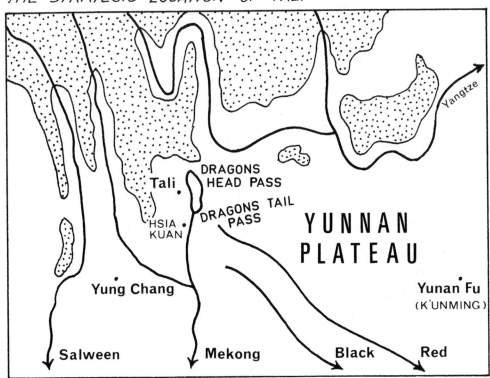

LAND OVER 3000M (10 000 FT)
THE TALI PLAIN LIES AT 2000M (7000FT) WHILE THE
YUNNAN PLATEAU FALLS TO 1200M (4000FT) IN THE EAST

between the Mekong and Salween rivers, speak the dialect of Nanking. The people of Tali have strong native Pai or Tai accents. Little attempt was made to integrate the 'raw' or un-civilized tribes of Yunnan but those which were considered 'ripe' for improvement were allowed employment and acceptance after receiving some Chinese education.

The settlement of Yunnan by the Chinese ensured that it remained part of the Empire. Wherever territories were merely administered by imperial officials there was always a danger that independence movements would form. Vietnam, centred on the Red River Basin, was a Chinese province for a thousand years but in the tenth century freed itself. It was peopled by the fiercely nationalistic Yüeh peoples who had been decimated or pushed southwards from Chekiang, Fukien and Kwangtung. Since the Chinese were busy colonizing the Yangtze Valley and the coastal areas, they never really sinicized the Red River Basin. Emperor Yung Lo's invasion and occupation from 1407 to 1427 was the last attempt to incorporate Vietnam as a province of China. After this the Vietnamese continued to pay tribute, while begin-ning their own southward policy of colonization which excluded Chinese from directly controlling the south-east peninsula.

Decline in the North
By the mid-sixteenth century the Ming dynasty was in decline.
● Pirates were virtually controlling the sea coast south of Hangchow.
● Corruption was increasing as more power was placed in the hands of the eunuchs. Offices were created or maintained after the need had passed. Some superintendents of rivers had no rivers to supervise since they had changed course.
● Taxation was increasing to support the wasteful bureauc-racy.
● Famine was increasingly common, particularly in the North.
● Tenant farmers were increasingly exploited by the great landlords.
Ming supporters had been rewarded with estates or 'planta-tions' at the beginning of the dynasty and subsequent Emperors adopted this means of reward. The plantations varied from around 400 hectares to nearly 40000 hectares at a time when a farmer owning 6 hectares was considered prosperous. The land-lords used threats to expand their plantations at the expense of small surrounding farms and were able to use their influence to abuse the protection offered in law. They often lived in the

major cities, squandering the wealth of the countryside on luxurious living and leaving a manager to extort the highest profit from the labouring *nung*. The Emperors were given warning as early as 1489 when the Minister of Finance, Li Min, in a memorial to the Emperor wrote:

Within the capital area there are five royal plantations with a total area of 12800 *ch'ing* [c. 77500 hectares]. Besides these, there are 332 plantations with a total acreage of 33000 *ch'ing* [c. 199700 hectares] owned by royal relatives and eunuchs. Plantation managers and their subordinates hire hoodlums and ruffians to do their bidding. They forcibly take over people's land, extort their money and other valuables, and debauch their wives and daughters. If people dare to make the slightest protest, they find themselves being sued on fabricated charges. The sheriff comes to arrest them, and their whole families tremble with fear. This is why people hate the plantation managers to the marrow of their bones.

Taxes were so crippling, even in the richest parts of the Yangtze Valley, by the mid-seventeenth century that people were being forced to sell their children to meet tax payments. In assessing taxes the government made sure to include all land owned by a tenant even where used for ditches and roads and therefore nonproductive. In 1628 a terrible famine in Shensi was recorded in this memorial to the Emperor:

Your humble servant was born in Anse subprefecture, Shensi province. I have read many memorials submitted by Your Majesty's officials in connection with the present state of affairs. They say that famine has caused fathers to desert their children and husbands to sell their wives. They also say that many people are so starved that they eat grass roots and white stones. But the real situation is worse than that which they have described. Yenan, the prefecture from which your humble servant comes, has not had any rain for more than a year. Trees and grasses are all dried up. During the eighth and the ninth moon months of last year people went to the mountains to collect raspberries which were called grain but actually were no better than chaff. They tasted bitter and they could only postpone death for the time being. By the tenth moon month all raspberries were gone, and people peeled off tree bark for food. Among tree bark the best was that of the elm. This was so precious that to consume as little as possible people mixed it with the bark of other trees to feed themselves. Somehow they were able to prolong their lives. Towards the end of the year the supply of tree bark was exhausted, and they had to go to the mountains to dig up stones as food. Stones were cold and tasted musty. A little taken in would fill up the stomach. Those who took stones found their stomachs swollen and they dropped and died in a few days. Others who did not wish to eat stones gathered as bandits. They robbed the few who had some savings, and when they robbed, they took everything and left nothing behind. Their idea was that since they had to die either one way or another it was preferable to die as a bandit than to die from hunger and that to die as a bandit would enable them to enter the next world with a full stomach. . . .

The starving *nung* were joined by mutinous troops from South Manchuria whose pay had not been forthcoming, and also a large number of redundant coolies who suffered from the disbanding of the Imperial posting system. This made the North more vulnerable than ever and the Manchus were able to sweep down towards Peking with little opposition.

MARITIME EXPANSION IN THE EARLY MING DYNASTY

The Background to Expansion

We have stressed the 'continental' and anti-commercial nature of early Chinese culture and yet by the Southern Sung dynasty China was obviously the home of the world's largest mercantile and maritime cities. This dualism had developed for many reasons:

● the continual and accelerating movement of Chinese to the once sparsely populated and hostile south-east coast (Yüeh);
● a high level of nautical technology and science;
● a decline in prejudice against trading as an occupation when its profitability was realized. Kao Tsung, accredited founder of the Chinese navy, said in 1143: 'Profits from maritime commerce are great; if properly managed they can amount to millions. Is this not better than taxing the people?'

Long before Kao Tsung, Chinese vessels had plied the Indian and China Seas. The Persian Gulf and the Red Sea were frequented before the eighth century A.D. From this time until the fourteenth century Arabs dominated these routes, establishing settlements in the Chinese ports and monopolizing the spice trade to the West. But the fifteenth century saw a Chinese recovery that was both spectacular and short-lived.

Cheng Ho's Mission to the Western Oceans

'In the third year of the Yung Lo reign period (1405) the Imperial Palace Eunuch Cheng Ho was sent on a mission to the Western Oceans.' Thus, a Chinese historical work of 1767 introduces a chapter of Chinese history that fully indicates the potential of the fifteenth-century Chinese mercantile marine, which, if it had been backed by a 'crusading mentality,' might have put the Chinese in Europe before da Gama reached India.

Cheng Ho was a Muslim from Yunnan who became an admiral, ambassador and explorer responsible for seven major voyages between 1405 and 1433. These voyages were made on behalf of the Emperor and the reasons were manifold.

● It was commonly thought that the Emperor was searching for his predecessor who had supposedly fled westward in 1403.

● More likely the voyages were designed to magnify and extend the grandeur and prestige of the Imperial Court both at home and abroad.

● They may have been an attempt to counteract a reduction in overland trade with the West following the break up of the Mongol Empire.

Each voyage combined diplomatic functions, such as the exaction of 'tribute,' with commercial enterprise and scientific discovery. Local rulers felt little compunction about giving tribute to the distant Chinese Emperor when they received in exchange much wanted gifts of porcelain, jade, lacquer, silk and cotton.

The voyages of the Imperial Fleet were as follows:
1 1405–07 to Champa, Java, Sumatra, Ceylon and Calicut;
2 1407–09 to Siam and Cochin;
3 1409–11 to Malacca, Quilon and Ceylon;
4 1413–15 to Bengal, Maldive Islands and Hormuz;
5 1417–19 to Java, Brunei, Hormuz, Aden, Somaliland and Malindi;
6 1421–2 to South Arabia.

The Emperor then died and his successor, Hsia Yuan-chi, reversed this policy with the following statement in 1424: 'If there are any ships already anchored in Fukien or Thai-tshang they must return at once to Nanking, and all the building of sea-going ships for intercourse with barbarian countries must cease at once.' His early death provided a short reprieve for Cheng Ho and the seventh voyage was commissioned between 1431 and 1433 going to Java, Nicobar, Mecca and Al Zaij.

Cheng Ho's initial fleet of 62 treasure-ships contained the

largest ships known to the world. They were over 134 metres long and 55 metres in their broadest beam. They had 3 super-imposed decks and up to 9 masts. The upper decks and poop

A seventeenth-century European view of junk construction at Kowloon. Hong Kong is in the background. By this time junks were much smaller than Cheng Ho's.

could override the beams by up to 30 per cent. The rudder was about 6 metres long. (In 1962 a rudder post 10 metres long was discovered from one of these ships.) They carried cannon, and a crew of over 400.

Chinese and Portuguese Voyages Compared
While the 'Three-Jewel Eunuch' was exploring the east coast of Africa, the Portuguese were edging southwards down the west coast. Diaz rounded the Cape in 1488, about sixty years

after the Chinese. There were fundamental differences in the voyages of the Europeans and the Chinese.

● The Chinese voyages were an extension of a pattern which had occurred before (even if a long time before). The Portuguese voyages were unprecedented.

● The Chinese vessels were larger versions of traditional craft. The Portuguese were experimenting with triangular, lateen sails borrowed from the Arabs, with the marine compass and stern-post rudder which had originated in China, and multiple masts which were a common feature of Asian craft.

● The treasure-ships of Cheng Ho weighed up to 1 500 tonnes compared with 300 tonnes for da Gama's ships.

● The Portuguese maintained a 'conquistador mentality' with large-scale slaving and warring. Although Chinese fleets were armed and threats were commonly used to exact tribute, they had few skirmishes. They established no forts and founded no colonies.

● Portuguese mercantile activity was based on a private enterprise search for personal fortune; the search for the mythical El Dorado. The Chinese voyages were an extension of state bureaucracy with incidental, if somewhat large, trading. Portuguese hopes lay in the slave trade and the breaking of the Arab spice monopoly. Chinese ambitions lay in the collection of drugs and medical knowledge and materials such as rhino horn, and exotic beasts like giraffes and zebras.

● The Portuguese were in the position of wanting goods from the East but of having nothing the East wanted in exchange; thus, they had to pay in gold bullion which was not very satisfactory. On the other hand, China had lots to offer the countries to the West but found little it needed there, and so never had the same bullion problem.

● Except where an alliance with heretics suited them, the Portuguese extended the reign of terror associated with the Inquisition into their colonies and trading ports. The Chinese were 'all things to all men,' distinguishing the different religions, and making gifts to leaders of all.

Why the Chinese Voyages Ceased

Thirty-six countries in the Western Ocean sent tribute to China, acknowledging the Mings' overlordship. These included eight from the East Indies, eleven from India and Ceylon, five from Persia and Arabia, and five from the east coast of Africa.

However, such returns were not sufficient to placate the Confucian scholar-landlords who felt the Emperor was devoting too much attention and money to the ventures of the eunuchs. Confucianism was losing its scientific humanism to an anti-scientific idealism which was to encourage lethargy and conservatism, particularly under the next dynasty, the Ch'ing.

East–West maritime exploration in the fifteenth century.

Furthermore, the northern frontier was under attack from the Mongols and Tartars, making Peking very vulnerable. By 1474 only 140 warships out of 400 survived after a long period of neglect and hostile legislation. In 1500 it became illegal to build a sea-going junk with more than two masts and in 1551 it became treasonable to go to sea in a multiple masted ship. It was decided that the Chinese lost more than they gained through such maritime contacts and a period of withdrawal from maritime intercourse ensued until the Europeans prised China open. One effect of this was to weaken the south coast defences, virtually handing over the seas to an increasing number of Japanese pirates. At the same time there was a reversal of migratory trends towards that area. The further development of the Grand Canal reduced the amount of coastal traffic and tended to reinforce the role of the North as the focal point for Ming internal development.

A Ming carved lacquer cup-stand of the type highly valued in the West. The arrival of such treasures in the West stimulated a whole range of copies known as 'Chinoiserie' which became extremely fashionable.

213

THE COMING OF THE EUROPEANS

By 1440 the Ming dynasty was reducing contact with barbarian merchants by the force of law. At the same time the Renaissance spirit was sweeping Europe, stimulating a desire for knowledge, and bizarre luxury. Coupled with this in southern Catholic Europe was the Inquisition with its fanatical desire to convert all to the Church of Rome. These two forces conspired to put the Portuguese in Canton harbour for the first time in 1514.

Since they were dealing with pagans the Portuguese and Spaniards had no scruples about using violence in the interests of profit. They had no wish to return from such hazardous voyages empty-handed. Naturally the Chinese came to the conclusion that Westerners were merely marauding pirates. As the barbarians had no manners or understanding of Chinese etiquette it was difficult for them to be accepted as 'bearers of tribute,' which had become virtually a euphemism for traders.

The Portuguese established themselves as intermediaries between Malacca, their colony in the southern archipelago, and South China. They were also involved in smuggling. Since the cities of the Southern coast were dependent on trade for their survival they increasingly argued for a relaxation of government restrictions. In 1557 Macao was allocated to the Portuguese as a base for their 'factories' or warehouses. It was hoped that this would confine their activities and keep them out of the other ports such as Canton and Ch'uan Chou.

The growing wealth of the Portuguese encouraged rivalry from other European states. The Dutch were twice refused permission to trade in the early seventeenth century and operated as smugglers from Taiwan. In 1636 the first British China expedition began as a rival to the East India Company. They arrived at Canton a year later to be rebuffed by the governor of the city. The captain of the fleet, John Weddell, was determined not to return empty-handed. Naturally, they received no co-operation from the Portuguese at Macao and when the Chinese made the mistake of firing a few badly aimed cannon balls at them, they landed and took the city without much trouble. The Chinese garrison's feeble defence amazed the sailors. A compromise was achieved after two English merchants were captured. One cargo of ginger, silk and porcelain was allowed to be loaded on condition that the fleet left rapidly.

While the traders were considered ignominious barbarians, many Jesuit missionaries who accompanied them became

Sketches from the notebooks of Peter Mundy, a Cornish sailor who visited China in 1634.

215

accepted. Matteo Ricci landed in China in 1583 at the age of
31. He had studied mathematics, astronomy and cartography
and took the trouble to learn the language, philosophy and
customs of China. He preached near to Canton, dressed as a
Mandarin, until he was allowed to go to Peking in 1607. His
gifts to the Emperor included a crucifix and paintings of Christ
and the Virgin Mary—they were not well received. However,
two clocks sufficiently impressed the court to grant him a favoured
position as a scientist and translator rather than as a preacher.
Some influential converts were made, and increasingly Jesuits
were entrusted with the preparation of maps, translations of
such books as encyclopaedias and Galileo's writings. In 1611
Father Adam Schall headed a team of priests in revising the
Imperial Calendar. Before Ricci died in 1610 he had observed

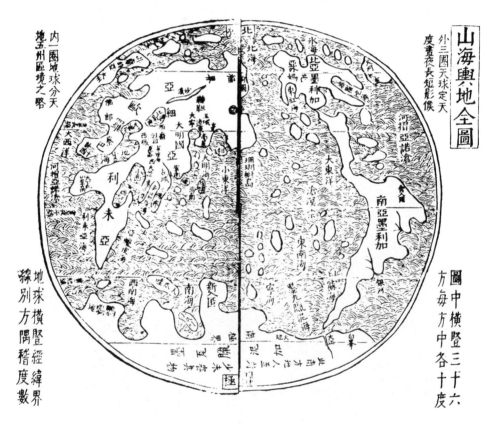

*Matteo Ricci's map of the world sensibly placed China at the centre and
thus overcame their prejudices against it.*

that the Chinese army was underpowered. Although gunpowder was a Chinese invention dating back several hundred years, its main use was for fireworks. Their cannon were inefficient and small in number. Later Jesuits designed and cast better cannon after European models. An order for 500 was placed with Schall in 1640, only four years before the Ming dynasty fell. It was obviously too late.

Father Adam Schall as a mandarin of the first class.

The success of the Jesuits and the privileges of movement they obtained from the Court, encouraged other missionary groups from Europe. However, the Dominicans and Franciscans failed to appreciate the need for pragmatism and compromise over deep rooted cultural traits and criticized the Jesuits for doing so. The long debates and increasing rivalry between the different orders did little to encourage the Chinese to change their views and overall few converts were made (perhaps 200 000 in the seventeenth century).

Foreign devil, 1839:
Chinese sketch of a
fire-breathing English sailor.

YANG KUEI TZU or 'Ocean Devils' was the nickname the Ming Chinese used for Europeans. It has been unfortunate for international relations that the first impressions of people from Western Europe gained by China were so uniformly bad.

Albuquerque, the second Portuguese viceroy in the East, who captured Goa (1510) and Malacca (1512), told the Sultan of Calicut that he had come 'for Christians and spices.' Possibly the Ming Court was warned by Arab traders—whose activities had been tolerated for over 700 years—but the piratical behaviour of Portuguese visitors at Canton, Ningpo and Ch'uan Chou (1549) only served to confirm Chinese suspicions. It was not until 1598 that Ricci was permitted to travel to Peking and explain the Catholic faith. But the Protestant nations behaved in much the same way. The Dutch and the English were quick to seize opportunities for plunder.

PEKING

Under the Ming rule there was a definite reaction against the unplanned, sprawling, mercantile cities of the South, such as Hangchow and Ch'uan Chou. Traditional town-planning concepts were re-introduced and the walls of 500 cities were entirely reconstructed by the New Ministry of Public Works. The centre of gravity in political and economic terms shifted north and inland towards the cradle of Chinese civilization. Symbolic of this change was the choice of Peking as capital to replace Nanking in 1409.

Peking was on the site of Khanbaluc, the Yuan capital. Kubilai had followed the classical chessboard pattern on a north–south axis when he commissioned the city. The walls were over 25 kilometres long and up to 12 metres high. While the Ming had little to do but extend this existing pattern little now remains of the Yuan city. The Bell Tower which lay at the centre of Khanbaluc today lies to the north of the Imperial Palace which indicates a southward expansion of the city under the Ming.

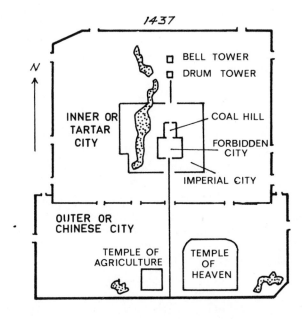

Peking in the Ming Dynasty.

219

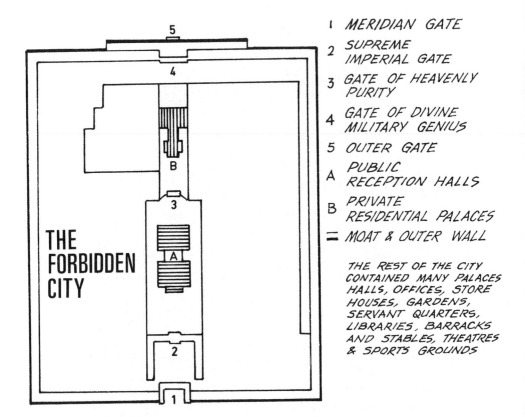

THE FORBIDDEN CITY

1 MERIDIAN GATE

2 SUPREME IMPERIAL GATE

3 GATE OF HEAVENLY PURITY

4 GATE OF DIVINE MILITARY GENIUS

5 OUTER GATE

A PUBLIC RECEPTION HALLS

B PRIVATE RESIDENTIAL PALACES

= MOAT & OUTER WALL

THE REST OF THE CITY CONTAINED MANY PALACES HALLS, OFFICES, STORE HOUSES, GARDENS, SERVANT QUARTERS, LIBRARIES, BARRACKS AND STABLES, THEATRES & SPORTS GROUNDS

The city walls enclose four distinct sections. *The Inner, Tartar, or Northern City*, enclosed in 1437 by a wall 24 kilometres long. This in turn surrounds the *Imperial City* with its wall 10 kilometres long. Within this section lies the *Purple Forbidden City* containing the Imperial Palace, again protected by its own wall. The growth of suburbs to the south led to the incorporation of *the 'Outer' or Chinese* city in 1544 by a wall 22 kilometres long. The latter contained the important Temples of Agriculture (from 1422) and Temple of Heaven (1420). These temples were parks containing halls and altars for prayers and sacrifice. The Outer city was very congested particularly along the avenues from the main gates. The noise, smell, and volume of traffic, amazed visitors. Commercial activity was as intense as one would expect in a city of 500 000.

The Temple of Heaven This has been called the 'noblest example of religious architecture in the whole of China.' It lies within a 300-hectare walled enclosure just inside the southern Gate. To the south is the Altar of Heaven where each winter solstice the Emperor offered sacrifice. This was the only time the Emperor faced north to worship instead of facing south to be worshipped. At the northern end lay the Hall of Prayer for Good Harvests where the Emperor prayed on a spring day chosen by the astronomers. This is a magnificent temple with a triple tiered roof covered in blue tiles. The walls, beams and pillars are richly painted in red, blue, gold and green. The three terraces on which it stood were of marble. Both buildings were circular and were surrounded by square courtyards. This symbolized the journey from earth to heaven as one approached the Altar.

The Imperial Gardens and menageries on Coal Hill, protecting the Palace from evil northern influences.

If the main north–south avenue was taken from the outer wall the visitor would pass from the Outer to Inner City and be headed directly for the Imperial City. The Inner City appeared just as busy, but away from the main avenues lived the *shih* and the *kung* who worked in the Imperial City. The public were not allowed access to the latter unless on business. Having crossed a moat and passed through the Gate of Heavenly Peace the whole pace of life changed. Few people were about, it was quiet and there was a spacious distribution of classically arranged parks, lakes, halls, pagodas and pavilions. Here the officials and scholar bureaucrats would be at work. At the northern end of the main avenue was the Meridian Gate. Here the Emperor sometimes received tribute from foreign ambassadors.

Within the Forbidden City few were allowed. The southern part was dominated by three aligned halls. First came the Hall of Supreme Harmony where the Emperor gave his audiences; behind this was the Hall of Middle Harmony which was a waiting chamber; the third, the location for state banquets, was the Hall of Protecting Harmony. Beyond these lay the Offices of State, palace workshops and gardens and finally the private quarters which were accessible only to the royal family and their eunuchs. This area contrasted sharply with the rigidity of form elsewhere;

Inside the Imperial Palace. Behind the Hall of Supreme Harmony (see below) lay the Hall of General Harmony. In the northern wall of the public part of the Palace was the Gate of Heavenly Purity leading to the private quarters.

Ambassadors at the Meridian Gate in the seventeenth century.

it contained a complex and informal maze of courtyards, alleys and gardens—a perfect setting for palace intrigue.

It is considered that Ming architecture was less adventurous and experimental than that of the Sung. Buildings were plain rectangles, rigidly laid out. However, some features were very striking:

- the sheer scale of construction;
- the increasing use of durable materials such as marble;
- the great increase of colour, particularly through the use of porcelain tiles, the painting of eaves, and the use of gold leaf, while marble bridges and steps contrasted with the pink, red and gold walls, yellow and blue-tiled roofs, and blue, red and gold eaves;
- widespread use of curved roofs in which all four faces of the roof swept down to the eaves thus eliminating the east- and west-facing gable ends typical of the Sung;
- the corbel brackets were increasingly decorative rather than functional in the largest buildings.

Ming architecture was far more durable than its predecessors. Even where fire or age created a need to replace an official building the increasing conservatism of later Chinese architects preserved the styles and techniques of the period.

224

PLAYS, NOVELS AND POTTERY

The exclusion of the *shih* from the imperial civil service during the Yuan dynasty stimulated the development of two new forms of literature, the play and the novel. Preoccupation with the Confucian Classics was relaxed while the examinations were discontinued. Scholars found themselves free to venture beyond

Papercut of an opera character.

the confines of history, philosophy and poetry and they took up the popular play and novel. In a similar way the potter's art so outstripped painting that the European importers of Ming wares called all porcelain china, after the country that made the finest products. A kind of creative split appeared in Chinese culture, which lasted till 1911. The Ming and Manchu Courts became traditional, antiquarian, backward-looking, as the *shih* wistfully

A noble character of the opera, and (below) the opera's version of a mother-in-law.

recalled the lost splendours of K'ai Feng and Chang-an, while the more vital and exciting artists worked without imperial patronage.

A fine example of Chinese porcelain.

During the T'ang Empire the manufacture of porcelain was perfected. China clay and china stone were fused at high temperatures to give a hard but translucent ware. Coloured glazes became common as copper, iron and cobalt were added to the colourless lead silicate in order to produce reds, yellows and blues. The North was the major area of innovation.

The fall of K'ai Feng to the Kin (1127) caused refugee potters to set up kilns in the South. Imperial factories were dotted around the Yangtze and associated canals, allowing easy transportation, internally and for export. In the Ming period cobalt blue was the most popular colour. From late Ming times mass production methods steadily reduced the individuality of the potter's art.

227

Monkey by Wu Ch'êng-ên (1505–80) illustrates the colloquial power of both new forms, since it is a novel that draws on the folk stories and plays that had collected around Tripitaka's pilgrimage to India. The historical Tripitaka, Hsuan Tsang, was greeted by the T'ang Emperor T'ai Tsung in A.D. 645 when he returned to Chang-an with the Buddhist scriptures. By the Southern Sung dynasty (A.D. 1127–1279) a whole cycle of fantastic legends was in existence and the various episodes from the pilgrimage were constantly represented on the Chinese stage. Possibly, *Monkey* is the most widely read book in Chinese literature. Below is a comic extract relating the worsting of the dominant Taoists in Cart Slow Kingdom, where Tripitaka and his three companions, Monkey, Pigsy and Sandy, are not well received. Ingenious and resourceful, Monkey devises a plan to disconcert the religious opponents of the Buddhists and have the pilgrims' passports stamped with travel visas. The knock-about humour may surprise Western readers, though the wisdom of laughter was appreciated by Chuang-tzu long before the foundation of the First Empire and the sceptical tradition of Confucian thought discovered in ridicule a potent weapon against religious fanaticism. Indeed, the humorous story is something close to the Chinese heart.

'Get up and come with me,' said Monkey. 'We're all going to have a treat.' 'Who wants a treat in the middle of the night,' said Sandy, 'when one's mouth is dry and one's eyes won't stay open?' 'The Taoists are celebrating a Mass in their great temple,' said Monkey, 'and the whole place is littered with offerings. There are dumplings that must weigh a quart, and cakes weighing fifty pounds, and all kinds of dainties and fruits. Come and enjoy yourself.' Pigsy, hearing in his sleep something about things to eat, at once woke with a start. 'Brother, you're not going to leave me out of it?' he cried. 'If you like the idea of something to eat,' said Monkey, 'don't make a fuss and wake up the Master, but both of you come quietly with me.'

They dressed quickly and followed Monkey. As soon as they came into the light of the torches, Pigsy wanted to rush in and get to work. 'There's no hurry,' said Monkey. 'Wait till the congregation disperses; then we'll go in and set to.' 'But they're praying for all they're worth,' said Pigsy. 'They have evidently no idea of dispersing.' 'I'll see to that,' said Monkey; and reciting a spell he drew a magic diagram on the ground. Then standing upon it he blew with all his might. At once a great wind rose, which blew down all the flower-vases and lamp-stands and smashed the ex-votos hanging on the walls. The whole place was suddenly in darkness. The Taoists were frightened out of their wits. 'I must ask the congregation to disperse,' said the Tiger Strength Immortal. 'The wind will no doubt subside, and tomorrow morning we will recite a few more scriptures, so that the prescribed number may be reached.'

As soon as the place was empty, the three of them slipped in, and that fool Pigsy began to stuff himself with victuals. Monkey gave him a sharp rap over the knuckles. Pigsy drew back his hand and retreated, saying, 'Wait a bit. I've hardly had time to get my tongue round the things, and he begins hitting me!' 'Mind your manners,' said Monkey. 'Let's sit down and enjoy ourselves decently.' 'I like that,' said Pigsy. 'If we're to sit down and behave ourselves decently when we are stealing a meal, what pray should we do if we were invited?' 'What are those Bodhisattvas up there?' asked Monkey. 'If you don't recognize the Taoist Trinity,' said Pigsy, 'what deities would you recognize, I wonder?' 'What are they called?' asked Monkey. 'The one in the middle,' said Pigsy, 'is the Great Primordial, the one on the left is the Lord of the Sacred Treasure, and the one on the right is Lao Tzu.'

'Let's take their places,' said Monkey. 'Then we can eat decently and comfortably.' The smell of the offerings made Pigsy in a great hurry to begin eating, and scrambling up on to the altar he knocked down the figure of Lao Tzu with a thrust of his snout, saying, 'You've sat there long enough, old fellow. Now it's Pig's turn.' Monkey meanwhile took the seat of the Great Primordial, and Sandy that of the Lord of the Sacred Treasure, pushing the images out of the way. As soon as he was seated Pigsy snatched at a big dumpling and began to gobble it down. 'Not so fast!' cried Monkey. 'Surely, brother,' said Pigsy, 'Now that we've taken our places, it's time to begin.' 'We mustn't give ourselves away just for the sake of a small thing like a bite of food. If we leave these images lying there on the floor, some Taoist monk may come along at any minute to clean the place up, and trip over them. Then he'll know at once that there is something wrong. We had better put them away somewhere.' 'I don't know my way about here,' said Pigsy. 'There may be a door somewhere, but I shouldn't find it in the dark. Where am I to put these images?' 'I noticed a small door on the right as we came in,' said Monkey. 'Judging from the smell that came from it, I should think it must be a place of metabolic transmigration. You had better take them there.' That fool Pigsy was uncommonly strong. He hoisted the three images on to his back and carried them off. When he reached the door, he kicked it open, and sure enough it was a privy. 'That chap Monkey finds some wonderful expressions,' he said laughing. 'He contrives to find a grand Taoist title even for a closet!' Before depositing them, he addressed the images as follows: 'Blessed Ones, having come a long way, we were hungry and decided to help ourselves to some of your offerings. Finding nowhere comfortable to sit, we have ventured to borrow your altar. You have sat there for a very long time, and now for a change you are going to be put in the privy. You have always had more than your share of good things, and it won't do you any harm to put up with a little stink and muck.' So saying, he pitched them in. There was a splash, and, not retreating quickly enough, he found that his coat was in a filthy state. 'Have you disposed of them successfully?' asked Monkey. 'I've disposed of them all right,' said Pigsy, 'but I have splashed myself and my coat is all filthy. If you notice a queer smell you'll know what it is.' 'That's all right for the moment, come and enjoy yourself,' said Monkey. 'But you'll have to clean yourself up a bit before you go out into the street.' That fool Pigsy then took Lao Tzu's seat and began to help himself to the offerings. Dumplings, pasties, rice-balls, cakes . . . one after another he gobbled them down. Monkey never cared much for cooked food, and only ate a few fruits, just to keep the others in countenance. The offerings vanished swiftly as a cloud swept away by a hurricane, and when there was nothing left to eat, instead of starting on their way, they fell to talking and joking, while they digested their food. Who would have thought of it? There was a little Taoist who suddenly woke up and remembered that he had left his handbell in the temple. 'If I lose it,' he said to himself, 'I shall get into trouble with the Master tomorrow.' So he said to his bed-fellow, 'You go on sleeping. I must go and look for my bell.' He did not put on his lower garments, but just threw his coat over his shoulders and rushed to the temple. After fumbling about for some time, he succeeded in finding it, and was just turning to go when he heard a sound of breathing. Very much alarmed, he ran towards the door and in his hurry slipped on a lychee seed and fell with a bang, smashing his bell into a thousand pieces. Pigsy could not stop himself from breaking into loud guffaws of laughter, which frightened the little Taoist out of his wits. Stumbling at every step he dragged himself back to the sleeping-quarters and, banging on his Master's door, he cried, 'Something terrible has happened!' The Three Immortals were not asleep, and coming to the door they asked what was the matter. 'I forgot my bell,' he said, trembling from head to foot, 'and when I went to the temple to look for it, I suddenly heard someone laughing. I nearly died of fright.' The Immortals called for lights, and startled Taoists came scrambling out of all the cells, carrying lanterns and torches. They all went off to the temple to see what evil spirit had taken possession there. . . .

Monkey pinched Sandy with one hand and Pigsy with the other. They understood what he meant and both sat stock still, while the three Taoists advanced, peering about in every direction. 'Some rascal must have been here,' said the Tiger Strength Immortal. 'All the offerings have been eaten up.' 'It looks as though ordinary human beings have been at work,' said the Deer Strength Immortal. 'They've spat out the fruit stones and skins. It's strange that there is no-one to be seen.' 'It's my idea,' said the Ram Strength Immortal, 'that the Three Blessed Ones have been so deeply moved by our prayers and recitations that they have vouchsafed to come down and accept our offerings. They may easily be hovering about somewhere on their cranes, and it would be a good plan to take advantage of their presence. I suggest that we should beg for some holy water and a little Elixir. We should get a lot of credit at Court if we could use them to the king's advantage.' 'A good idea,' said the Tiger Strength Immortal. And sending for some of his disciples, he bade them recite the scriptures, while he himself in full robes danced the dance of the Dipper Star, calling upon the Trinity to vouchsafe to its devout worshippers a little Elixir and holy water, that the king might live for ever.

'Brother,' whispered Pigsy to Monkey, 'there was no need to let ourselves in for this. Directly we finished eating we ought to have bolted. How are we going to answer their prayer?' Monkey pinched him, and then called out in a loud, impressive voice, 'My children,' he said, 'I must ask you to defer this request. My colleagues and I have come on straight from a peach banquet in Heaven, and we haven't got any holy water or elixir with us.' Hearing the deity condescend to address them, the Taoists trembled with religious awe. 'Father,' they said, 'you surely realize that for us this is too good an opportunity to be lost. Do not, we beseech you, go back to Heaven without leaving us some sort of magical receipt.' Sandy pinched Monkey. 'Brother,' he whispered, 'they are praying again. We're not going to get out of this so easily.' 'Nonsense,' whispered Monkey. 'All we've got to do is to answer their prayers and give them something.' 'That would be easier if we had anything to give,' whispered Pigsy. 'Watch me,' whispered Monkey, 'and you'll see that you are just as capable of satisfying them as I am.' 'Little ones,' he said, addressing the Taoists, 'I am naturally not keen on letting my congregation die out; so I'll see if we can manage to let you have a little holy water, to promote your longevity.' 'We implore you to do so,' they said, prostrating themselves. 'All our days shall be devoted to the propagation of the Way and its Power, to the service of our king and the credit of the Secret School.' 'Very well then,' said Monkey. 'But we shall each need something to put it into.' The Tiger Strength Immortal bustled off and soon re-appeared carrying, single-handed, an enormous earthenware jar. The Deer Strength Immortal brought a garden-vase and put it on the altar. The Ram Strength Immortal took the flowers out of a flower-pot and put it between the other two. 'Now go outside the building, close the shutters and stay there,' said Monkey. 'For no-one is permitted to witness our holy mysteries.' When all was ready, Monkey got up, lifted his tiger-skin and pissed into the flower-pot. 'Brother,' said Pigsy, highly delighted. 'We've had some rare games together since I joined you, but this beats all.' And that fool Pigsy, lifting his dress, let fall such a cascade as would have made the Lü Liang Falls seem a mere trickle. Left with the big jug, Sandy could do no more than half fill it. Then they adjusted their clothes, and sat down decorously as before. 'Little ones,' Monkey called out, 'you can come and fetch your holy water.' The Taoists returned, full of gratitude and awe. 'Bring a cup,' said the Tiger Strength Immortal to one of his disciples. 'I should like to taste it.' The moment he tasted the contents of the cup, the Immortal's lip curled wryly. 'Does it taste good?' asked the Deer Strength Immortal. 'It's rather too full-flavoured for my liking,' said the Tiger Strength Immortal. 'Let me taste it,' said the Ram Strength Immortal. 'It smells rather like pig's urine,' he said doubtfully, when the cup touched his lips. Monkey saw that the game was up. 'We've played our trick,' he said to the others, 'and now we'd better take the credit for it.' 'How could you be such fools,' he called out to the Taoists, 'as to believe that the Deities had come down to earth? We're no Blessed Trinity, but priests, from China. And what you have been drinking is not the Water of Life, but just our piss!'

No sooner did the Taoists hear these words than they rushed out, seized pitchforks, brooms, tiles, stones and whatever else they could lay hands on, and with one accord rushed at the impostors. In the nick of time Monkey grabbed Sandy with one hand and Pigsy with the other, and rushed them to the door. Riding with him on his shining cloud they were soon back at the temple where Tripitaka was lodged. Here they slipped back into bed, taking care not to wake the Master. 'Now we are all going to Court to get our passports put in order,' Tripitaka announced when he woke.

The king of the country, on hearing that three Buddhist pilgrims sought admittance to the palace, was in a tearing rage. 'If they must needs court death,' he said, 'why should they do it here, of all places? And what were the police doing, I should like to know. They ought never to have been let through.' At this, a minister stepped forward. 'The country of T'ang,' he said, 'is ten thousand leagues away and the road is as good as impassable. If they do indeed come from there, they must be possessed of some mysterious power. I am in favour of verifying the papers and letting them proceed. It would be wiser not to get on to bad terms with them.'

The king agreed, and ordered the passports to be sent in. . . .

7 The Manchu Empire and Western Imperialism

The Ch'ing Dynasty, A.D. 1644–1912

HISTORICAL OUTLINE

The Ch'ing dynasty was a foreign one. This fact was never forgotten by the Chinese, though there were significant differences in attitude to the new government adopted by the North and the South. Since the Manchus had been invited to enter the Great Wall, the experience of people living to the north of the Yangtze valley was a more or less peaceful takeover of power. The North acquiesced, too, because of the relative lack of friction in daily life, caused by the rapid cultural assimilation of the Manchus, which culminated in the disappearance of their own language. The situation in South China was entirely different: several Chinese leaders, including Wu San-kuei, remained almost undisturbed till 1673, when the young Ch'ing Emperor, K'ang Hsi, began reducing the whole Empire to obedience. Only in 1683 when the island of Taiwan was captured by the Manchus had the last Chinese stronghold fallen. That the Ch'ing dynasty sought assistance from Dutch ships for this campaign shows how far from respectability the idea of a navy had slipped in the mind of the Court. The Manchus were powerful on land but their disregard of the sea proved a fatal error of policy for China in the nineteenth century. This dislike of overseas adventure was connected with the hostility of the South to Manchu rule. Fearing that foreign contacts and trade abroad would only encourage further restiveness among the southern Chinese, successive Ch'ing Emperors barred the coast to Chinese and foreigner alike. From 1757 all foreign trade was confined to the one city of Canton.

The Celestial Empire

The Manchus were outnumbered by Chinese, probably as much as thirty to one. This disparity between rulers and ruled obliged the Ch'ing Emperors to make the system of bannermen a permanent element of imperial government. Bannermen, Manchu soldiers sworn by an oath of personal loyalty to the throne, were stationed in large garrisons around the main centres of population. In the wars of expansion conducted by the early Emperors these men proved their worth and maintained a high standard of military efficiency. Mongolia was conquered; Sinkiang was annexed—for the first time since the T'ang Empire; Tibet was brought under Chinese suzerainty; Burma, Annam, Korea and Siam became tributaries; and the Emperor Ch'ien Lung was the only monarch able to subdue the kingdom of Nepal (1792). Yet the very success of these campaigns undermined the Manchu Empire, for with no enemies to fight the army began to decay; failure to modernize gave Western forces an immense advantage when conflicts eventually came, and the inability to meet sea-borne attacks left the country exposed from Peking to Canton. But for the Ch'ing dynasty the main threat seemed the Chinese themselves. Bannermen were kept in idleness for reasons of internal security.

The administration of the Empire provided the Ch'ing Emperors with a headache too. Posts had to be reserved for Manchus, otherwise the *shih* would gain control of the government. Fifty per cent of the places were awarded to Manchus, North China and South China having twenty-five per cent each. As the intellectual centre of the country had shifted southwards during the Sung Empire, this meant that the intense competition for awards in the southern examinations at Nanking ensured that successful candidates from this centre were more learned than their peers. Paradoxically, the hostile South produced the leading Confucianists of the Ch'ing Empire.

From the outside the Ch'ing Empire appeared almost ideal. 'The Celestial Empire' was the name by which China was known to admirers in eighteenth-century Europe. The long reign of Ch'ien Lung (1735–95) was the showpiece of the Manchu Empire. The Empire enjoyed peace at home and victory abroad; the Court was a centre of culture, renowned for its splendid ceremonies. But the Ch'ing dynasty was becoming an elaborate façade, behind which Chinese civilization was undergoing a sweeping transformation. Decline came swiftly in the nineteenth century. Isolated and conservative, the Manchu Court lost contact with the mass of the population and its high officials misused their positions for the sake of personal gain through all kinds of corrupt practices. In desperation, a foreign dynasty

The Emperor Ch'ien Lung approaching his tent to meet the British Ambassador.

When in 1793 Lord Macartney tried to negotiate a trade agreement, he received this reply from the Ch'ing Emperor: 'The Celestial Empire possesses all things in great abundance and lacks no product within its borders. There is no need for the importation of any item manufactured by outside barbarians in exchange for our own goods.'

clung to a moribund tradition of thought, a kind of Confucianism that rejected any original idea out of hand as an unnecessary and dangerous innovation, while it exaggerated the 'turning inward' policy of the later Ming Empire into an absurd belief in isolationism. Ostrich-like the Ch'ing dynasty, supported by ultra-conservative officials, Manchu and Chinese, hoped that by not looking at all they would neither see nor encounter anything which might disturb them. The best of the *shih* were alienated from the Manchu Empire.

The Opium War (1840–2)
The 1757 imperial decree by which all foreign trade was restricted to Canton proved less workable every year. Since tea and silk, the main export commodities, were produced in the Yangtze

valley, Chinese merchants had to arrange a long overland haul of 800 kilometres to the official trading port, where facilities for the growing international commerce were quite inadequate. At such a vast distance from the capital, trade was out of sight and out of mind in Canton, but problems of regulation could not solve themselves. The Hoppo, always a Manchu of low rank, was in charge of the Canton trade, and during the three-year appointment he was expected to make as much money as he could for his Court patrons who had obtained the post for him. Extortion was normal. Those Chinese scholars in the imperial administration of South China, particularly Kwangtung and Kwangsi, were discouraged from thinking about the implications of commerce by the steady narrowing of Confucian orthodoxy in the Court and the examination system. It is not surprising, therefore, that pressure built up among the European trading nations for a freer approach to Chinese markets.

Financial difficulties caused a crisis. The East India Company found that having to pay in silver for tea and silk was a great strain, and attempts were made to reach a trade agreement whereby goods could be exchanged. Lord Macartney in 1793 and Lord Amherst in 1816 failed to accomplish anything when they visited Peking, while Lord Napier in 1834 was prevented from travelling beyond Canton. Manchu fears of outside influences on the Chinese population were reflected in the deliberately humiliating treatment accorded to these ambassadors, though the general bad impression of Europeans since the Ming period facilitated this propaganda exercise and helped to confirm Chinese suspicions of the Ocean Devils.

But there was an even stronger reason for the people of China to look upon our ancestors with distaste. To the lasting shame of Britain, India was used to grow opium for export to China after 1773. The British Empire became the world's largest grower, processor and exporter of the drug in order to reduce the outflow of silver in the trade with China. An imperial edict of 1800 sought to prohibit this dangerous import, but the British authorities replied that they were unable to prevent the trade as private vessels carried the opium. To the Manchu Court, the centre of all authority in the Empire, this answer seemed very hypocritical. What grated even more was the not-so-unjust British suggestion that the Manchu Empire was more concerned with the loss of the silver than the harm opium smoking might do to its people. In 1839 the Emperor sent an honest official, Lin Tse-hsu, to Canton to end the opium trade. British merchants were shut up

A woman drags her husband home; his friends urge him to enjoy his pipe. An illustration from a Chinese book on the evils of opium smoking.

in their factory and the opium stock destroyed—without compensation. Chinese junks clashed with two British warships at Hong Kong and in 1840 the British were formally excluded from Canton.

An American cartoonist's view of Europeans grabbing land in China. Russians and Germans carve large slices, while France waits vulture-like. Britain, lordliest bully of them all, demands 'the lion's share.'

The Opium War startled the world. A brigade of British troops from India and a small naval squadron were sufficient to humble the Manchus. The bannermen were annihilated by superior weaponry and no resistance at all could be offered to the British navy. Three imperial commissioners had to sue for peace on the deck of a British warship; the Treaty of Nanking, 1842, which legalized opium trade, ended the Canton monopoly, opened up other ports, made the island of Hong Kong a British base, freed British subjects from Chinese law and gave them concession areas to live in, was the first of what the Chinese call the 'Unequal Treaties.' It was something of a model for later

A sea-battle during the Opium Wars, when the Chinese learned that their slow-moving, cumbersome wooden junks were no match for European cannon.

agreements which Western nations imposed on China. With the seclusion policy of the Tokugawa Shoguns after 1640, which had reduced the sea power of Japan at the same time as China turned inwards, there was nothing to stop this 'gunboat policy.' Britain and France actually captured Peking in the Second Opium War (1858–60) and the Franco-Chinese War (1883–5) wrung suzerainty of Indo-China from a dynasty unwilling to face up to the desperate need for modernization. But, unlike China, under the Emperor Meiji (1868–1912) Japan became an industrial power soon capable of defending its sovereignty.

'If the Chinese must be poisoned by opium, I would rather they were poisoned for the benefit of our Indian subjects than any other exchequer,' Sir George Campbell said in the House of Commons in 1880.

The T'ai P'ing Rebellion (1851–64)

Taoism and Buddhism were losing their hold on the mass of the Chinese people at the very time that the Ch'ing Empire was in decline. Protestant Christianity, introduced to China by the British, Dutch and American missionaries, provided momentarily spiritual succour and political direction for a popular movement against the Manchus and their misgovernment of the country. Missionary activity by Protestants was directed at the Chinese man in the street, so from the very beginning the Christian inspired T'ai P'ing rebellion was opposed by both the Court and the *shih*. Hung Hsiu-ch'uan, the leader of the movement, was a southerner who had failed in the civil service examinations.

A portrait of Hung Hsiu-ch'uan, the leader of the Tai P'ings. The characters—t'ien teh—mean 'heavenly virtue.'

Visions and religious conviction followed his reading of a translation of the Bible during an illness. The T'ai P'ing rebellion, or the Great Peaceful Heavenly Kingdom, began in Kwangtung and its armies, reinforced by numerous oppressed *nung*, captured Nanking (1853).

240

Hung was an embarrassment. The European missionaries were split over his interpretation of the Gospels; the Catholics saw him as a dangerous heretic, while the Protestants felt he led an unorthodox crusade against a corrupt and pagan régime. The European imperialist governments used the civil conflict to increase the dependence of the Manchus on their support: a Chinese national revival was not in their interests. Military advisors, including the British general Gordon, were sent to help suppress the rebels. Again, the Ocean Devils had done little to endear themselves to the Chinese people. Eye-witness accounts of the T'ai P'ing rebels are entirely favourable. They mention the self-discipline of the soldiers and the honesty of the officials, a startling contrast to conditions prevailing in provinces still in the Manchu Empire. The social policy of the T'ai P'ings was liberal and modern—opium and foot binding were outlawed, the status of women was raised, and sensible encouragement was given to trade and industry. Because the North did not join the rebellion and the *shih*, bound to Confucian tradition, were obliged to raise Chinese armies for the defence of the throne against an alien system of thought, the T'ai P'ings were defeated. The long struggle left the Manchus weak and destroyed forever the chance that China might be converted to Christianity. For the T'ai P'ing movement was unusual in that it looked outside Chinese civilization for its inspiration. In this sense it pointed the way to future national renewal, in the twentieth century.

Reform—too little, too late

The unchecked encroachments of Western countries on the Empire forced the *shih* as a class to reconsider their belief in isolationism, which had been fostered so carefully by the Ch'ing dynasty. A reform movement gathered strength from the 1870s and K'ang Yu-wei, a Cantonese scholar whose family had raised loyal bands during the T'ai P'ing rebellion, emerged as its spokesman. The young Emperor Kuang Hsu gave his confidence to the southern reformer and in 1898 a programme of sweeping reforms was announced. China was to be modernized within the context of the Manchu Empire. The recent Sino-Japanese War of 1894–5, after which Korea, Taiwan and parts of Manchuria were ceded to Japan, had shown the advantage an oriental country could gain from Western technology. The modernized Japanese armies had inflicted a crushing defeat on China's forces.

241

But the Empress Dowager Tz'u Hsi, who had been the power behind the throne since the death of Emperor Hsien Feng (1861), feared that such changes would threaten her influence and she determined to stop the programme. Hearing of her plans, Emperor Kuang Hsu ordered Yuan Shih-k'ai, commander of a modernized unit in the imperial army, to arrest Tz'u Hsi. But Yuan betrayed the Emperor, who was imprisoned in the Palace at Peking. More fortunate, K'ang Yu-wei and other leading reformers of the Hundred Days escaped abroad.

The Boxer Rebellion and the Fall of the Chinese Empire
The Empress Dowager Tz'u Hsi, old but resolute, used her eunuchs to keep a check on any innovation, while the Manchu Empire fell apart. In 1900 'The Society of the Harmonious Fist,' or the Boxers, became active in Shantung. This violent agitation was directed against the growing power of Western nations in China and involved attacks on foreigners, foreign importations and Chinese converts to Christianity. Tz'u Hsi foolishly decided to back the Boxers and they were permitted to invest the legation quarter in Peking. The South remained undisturbed by the Boxers, and the war with the 'barbarians' was confined to the North. Peace meant, of course, more concessions and even foreign garrisons, not less interference with Chinese affairs.

When Tz'u Hsi died (1908), the captive Emperor Kuang Hsu was dispatched by her order, so that the Manchu Empire was left with a child Emperor. P'u-yi (Hsuan T'ung) was, in fact, the last Emperor of China, for in 1911 the accidental discovery of a republican plot in Hankow triggered a nation-wide revolution that swept away the Empire and established the Chinese Republic.

EXPANSION AND CONTRACTION UNDER THE CH'ING DYNASTY

By 1683 the Chinese rebels had been defeated or pacified and the rising prosperity of the new régime gained it tacit support from the *nung* who suffered greatly since the decay of the Ming Empire. The last outpost of rebellion was Taiwan, the fertile island 240 kilometres off the coast of Fukien province. The Chinese migrated there in large numbers in the seventeenth century to escape both population pressure and exploitation. After 1623 the Dutch had gained control of the island, defeating Japanese

P'u-yi, the last Emperor of China.

traders and Chinese pirates. In 1661 the Dutch were overthrown by the rebel general Cheng Ch'eng-kung who maintained an independent Chinese state for the next twenty years before the Ch'ing dynasty finally incorporated it as a prefecture.

The North-West

In the period of consolidation following the founding of the dynasty the Ch'ing sought to safeguard their frontiers. Even before they conquered China, they had brought Korea and Inner Mongolia under their control. Now they sought to strengthen the north-west. Mongol tribes were defeated, reducing Outer Mongolia to a vassal state. Further west, however, lay the Mongol kingdom of Dzungaria, occupying Turkestan and the Altai Mountains. It was not finally defeated until the mid-eighteenth century.

Tibet

After moving their capital from Mukden to Peking the Manchus invited the leaders of the Lamaist Church, which dominated Tibet, to send tribute. An opportunity arose to make their presence more concrete when the Dzungars invaded Tibet and captured Lhasa in 1717. The Ch'ing Emperor sent a relieving army which routed the invaders but stayed on first to install the Dalai Lama and then to offer him permanent protection, thus ensuring the maintenance of Chinese influence.

The south-west provinces of China proper were subjected to increasing government control in the early eighteenth century after Oh-erh-g'ai, the governor of Yunnan, successfully abolished indirect rule over the minority tribes, commonly known as the Miao. A large number of tribes in Yunnan, Kwangsi, Kweichow, Szechuan and Kwangtung had formerly ruled themselves. After 1720 the principle of direct rule by Chinese officials spread throughout the south-west.

Attempts to gain the allegiance of Burma had little success until the late eighteenth century. Successive armies were defeated in the heavily forested malaria-ridden valleys of the north-east frontier. Internal problems eventually forced the king to accept Ch'ing protection. The Vietnamese in Annam, on the other hand, readily accepted the payment of tribute to Peking and in so doing kept Chinese intervention to a minimum.

The Erosion of Chinese Authority

European trading activity was restricted to Canton from 1757. With the increase in British companies involved in the China

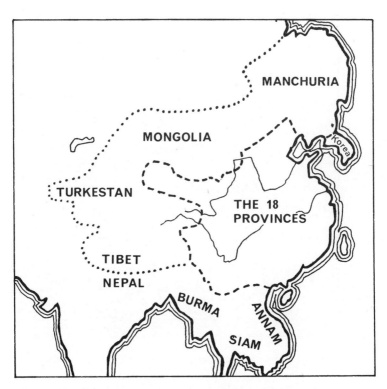

The Ch'ing Empire in 1800 showing 'China proper' and the outlying provinces and countries paying tribute.

trade after 1834, when the monopoly of the East India Company expired, pressure increased for more port facilities. The Opium War of 1839 allowed Britain to increase the number of 'treaty' ports to five (Canton, Foochow, Shanghai, Amoy and Ningpo). Hong Kong was ceded to Britain. 'Gun boat' diplomacy further extended the number of coastal and inland ports licensed for trade. While the British and French were sacking Peking and the T'ai P'ing rebels were ravaging the South, the Russians were advancing eastwards in the North. Early treaties in 1689 and 1727 attempted to control their expansion. In 1858 Count Nicholas Muravier, the governor-general of eastern Siberia presented a new set of territorial demands based on the exploration and gradual colonization of the region north of the Amur River which was nominally Chinese. Two years later the Russians offered to mediate with and influence the Europeans in their treatment of Peking, if the coastal territories west of the Ussuri River were given to them. Vladivostock was founded at the southern tip of this territory.

245

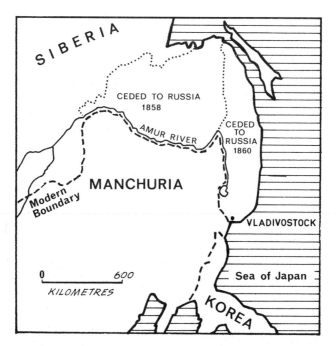

Territories ceded to Russia by China 1858 and 1860.

France was increasingly interested in Annam and obtained trading and navigation rights in 1862. It was recognized as an independent country by France in 1874 but it continued sending tribute missions to Peking until the 1880s, when the French dominated it. The Chinese sent troops to stop the French expansion but their surprising success on land was nullified by the French naval policy of bombarding China's harbours in retaliation. In 1885 Annam was recognized as a French protectorate. China had already recognized British control of Burma in 1866.

The Rise of Japan

From the sixteenth century onwards the Japanese were increasingly involved in piracy and trade in East Asia. Europeans were encouraged to establish factories there in the early seventeenth century. By 1640 the increasingly conservative and insular Tokugawa Shoguns, the family which ruled Japan in the Emperor's name for over two-hundred-and-fifty years, finally banned most foreigners and established a policy of isolation which lasted until 1850.

The earliest clashes with China came over control of the kingdom of Korea. Traditionally China was stronger and maintained its influence. After 1850 an increased desire for modernization gave Japan military and technological supremacy. The first show of strength came in 1874 when Japan invaded Taiwan to back its claim to the Ryukyu Islands, which the Chinese disputed. In 1876 two Korean ports were opened to Japanese ships after further hostilities. Korea was the gateway to the fertile Manchurian Plain, the homeland of the Ch'ing dynasty, and China reacted strongly to further Japanese attempts at extending its influence, by annexing Korea. In 1894 a civil war led to the invitation of both armies. Japan gained the support of the new Korean ruler who wanted the Chinese thrown out. Japanese troops penetrated South Manchuria and sank a Chinese fleet. Moving towards Peking they forced China to sue for peace. Under the Treaty of Shimonoseki, China:

- recognized the independence of Korea;
- ceded Taiwan, the Pescadores and Liaotung Peninsula to Japan;
- had to pay reparations of 200 m taels;
- had to open up her ports to Japan on the same terms as those offered to Europeans.

Taiwan was occupied immediately and remained a colony until 1945. Intervention by the European powers, lobbied by Russia, led to the return of the Liaotung Peninsula to China. (They did not wish to see Japan in an area on which they themselves had designs. The Russians were invited to build a railway linking the Trans-Siberian line, via Manchuria, to Vladivostock. Railway building was very limited in China because of the fears of disturbance of the natural elements. Having backed up China against Japan the Europeans now made their claims that:

- the Germans obtained Chiao-Chow Bay and the rights of mineral development in Shantung;
- Russia obtained the southern part of the Liaotung Peninsula including Dairen and Port Arthur;
- the French, having gained the rights of mineral development in the south-west, obtained a lease of Kwangchow Bay for 99 years and the right to build a railway from Tonkin to K'unming;
- Britain guaranteed the safety of her sphere of influence in the Yangtze valley and obtained a 99-year lease on Kowloon.

The Boxer rebellion conveniently gave each of these the opportunity to reinforce its position. Only disagreement among them prevented China from being carved up like Africa a decade before. The USA unexpectedly became an ally of China by suggesting an 'open-door' policy which would maintain trading

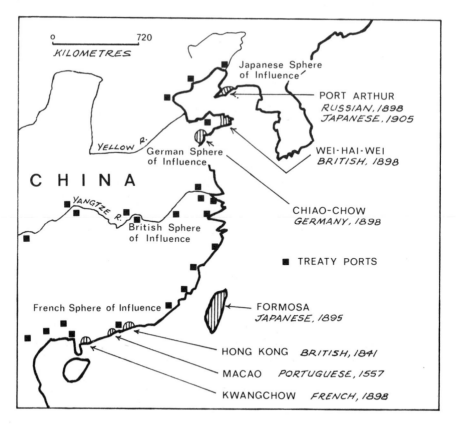

Foreign concessions in 1900.

opportunities for all without disturbing the spheres of influence, and thus kept China intact. In 1904–5 Japan soundly defeated Russia in a land war fought largely on Chinese territory and in a sea battle that revealed the true extent of Japan's modernization programme. The resulting treaty gave Japan the Liaotung territory of Russia and confirmed its influence in Korea.

ECONOMIC DEVELOPMENT

Population Growth and Distribution

The initial stability afforded by the Ch'ing dynasty, coupled with the increasing use of New World food crops, created a rapid rise in population from 1750 to 1850 to over 400 million. By 1910 this had fallen to under 350 million. The decline was partly due to natural catastrophes, and partly to civil war and occupation by foreign aggressors. In 1855 the Yellow River's course

248

An early view of foreign ships at anchor off Whampoa Island in the Pearl River, sixteen kilometres downstream from Canton.

changed, through lack of maintenance of the levées, with massive loss of life, through flood and ensuing famine and disease. A four-year drought in the northern provinces of Shensi, Shansi, Honan and Hopei led to over ten million deaths in the late 1870s. The T'ai P'ing Rebellion is estimated to have cost the lives of over 20 million in South and Central China.

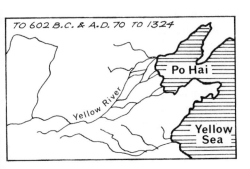

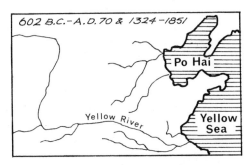

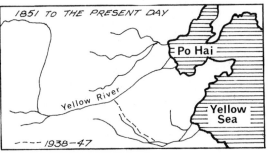

Some changes in the course of the Yellow River. Chinese history records 1500 inundations in the last 3000 years and 26 changes in course.

249

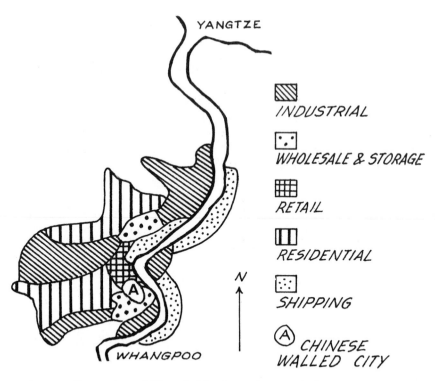

INDUSTRIAL

WHOLESALE & STORAGE

RETAIL

RESIDENTIAL

SHIPPING

CHINESE WALLED CITY

Expansion of Shanghai in the early twentieth century.

The frequent annihilation of population in the fertile lowlands stimulated great internal migration. As the population grew so did pressure on land. The peasants of the North China plain and Shantung peninsula increasingly moved into South Manchuria which had been officially 'closed' to migrants in 1668. The Manchus objected to the racial 'pollution' of their homeland but eventually came to depend entirely on the agricultural produce of the Chinese in the Liaotung Peninsula and the basins of the Liao and Sungari Rivers.

There was also increasing migration to the growing centres of trade and industry such as Shanghai. This was transformed from a fishing village into a commercial metropolis after the creation of the International Settlement in 1863. By 1895 it had a population of over 400000 and in 1900 this had exceeded 1 million. Today it is the largest city in the world. The nineteenth century saw urban growth increasingly divorced from the traditional administrative and protective function and steadily following the Western pattern where growth was based on industry, trade and communications.

Economic Growth

Agriculture In the nineteenth century agriculture inevitably maintained its role as the basis of the economy and the major employer. The economic history of China does not record an agrarian revolution at this time but it must be remembered that farming was already highly efficient in the use of fertilizer, if somewhat restricted by the pattern of land holding. The patchwork of small farms covering the country was increasing continually through sub-division at the death of the owner, among his heirs. Thus, they were almost entirely subsistence holdings subject to crises at the slightest climatic irregularity. Produce from the small farmers did enter the local market because they were forced to sell to pay taxes. In years of bad harvest the taxes had to come before the stomach. The large estates that existed did produce a surplus for the Court, for other non-agricultural inhabitants and for export.

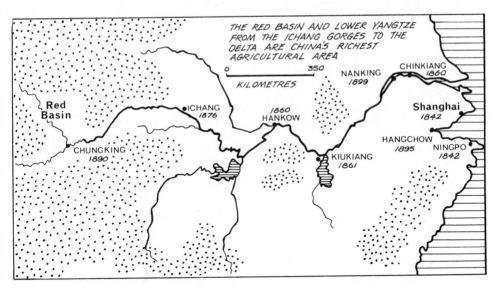

The hinterland of Shanghai showing European concessions and date of opening. The Red Basin and Lower Yangtze were China's richest agricultural areas.

Increasing demand from world markets for tea, cotton and silk stimulated a response often financed by merchants. In the South, beef was introduced to meet the demands of Europeans and dairy herds were maintained around the Treaty Ports. The

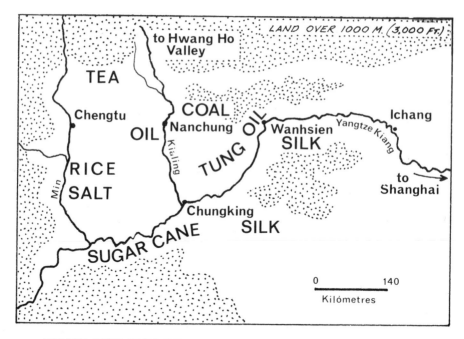

THE RED BASIN OF SZECHUAN, THE MOST DENSELY POPULATED PROVINCE

- Protective mountains create an equable climate, despite being 1 600 kilometres inland.
- Growing season of eleven months per annum.
- Virtually all crops grown in China can be grown here.
- Two-thirds of cultivated land is double-cropped.
- Rice output per hectare is up to twice as high as elsewhere.
- Important commercially for fruit, tea, sugar and silk.
- Chengtu Plain's long established irrigation helps make it the most densely populated agricultural area in the world.

Irish potato and American maize proved adaptable in the southern highlands which were increasingly encroached upon, resulting in destruction of their tree-cover and accelerated soil-erosion. The problem was recognized by the government who ordered a halt to such pioneering, and encouraged the growing of tree crops in plantations.

The pioneer frontiers of Tibet and Mongolia attracted relatively small numbers of migrants, who were forced either to adopt the survival pattern of the indigenous peoples or modify the environment to allow them to maintain traditional Chinese methods. In Tibet house and dress styles were copied, while in Mongolia irrigation was used to increase cropland at the expense of pasture. Chinese 'oases' emerged with whole villages seemingly lifted from the North China plain. The Manchus did not feel the need for protection of the northern frontiers to the same extent as former dynasties, because the nomadic tribesmen were increasingly being controlled by the eastern movement of the Russians, who

252

initially showed little interest in China. The main areas of expansion were Manchuria, where physical restrictions were much less intense, and Szechuan, where the population rapidly recovered from the massacres of the seventeenth century peasant rebellion. In 1786 its population was registered at around $8\frac{1}{2}$ million. By 1850 it was over 44 million.

Industry Industrial expansion in the nineteenth century was closely linked with the impact of the Europeans. Existing industry was small-scale and limited to water, wind and manpower, although the Chinese had devised so many of the techniques and principles on which industrial expansion had been made possible in the West. After the defeat of the Chinese forces by a small number of Europeans with advanced weapons in 1840 and 1856, some Chinese realized the need for modernization. Li Hung-chang, a Governor General of Kiangsu, advised the Emperor in 1864 to acquire the use of modern weapons and to install machinery to make them. By 1865 Shanghai was producing naval vessels, rifles, cannons, gunpowder and cartridges. Following this, many companies were established by the Ch'ing government including the following:

China Merchant Steam Navigation Company, 1872;
Kai Ping Coal Mines, 1877;
Shanghai Cotton Cloth Mill, 1878;
Imperial Telegraph Administration, 1881;
Hanyang Iron Works, 1896;
Imperial Bank of China, 1896.

The British financed the first railway linking the coal of Woosung with the arsenals of Shanghai. In 1876, just two years later, the government broke it up and sent it to Taiwan following agitated opposition from *nung* and *shih* on the grounds that it was disturbing the harmony of the land. Russia was later allowed to build an arm of the Trans-Siberia railway to Vladivostock, across Manchuria, and having entered Chinese territory, manoeuvred successfully to obtain a southward link to its Treaty Ports of Dairen and Port Arthur.

Li Hung-chang also criticized Chinese education as being 'divorced from utility.' Despite Court opposition 120 students were sent to study Western technology. In 1861 a Board of Foreign Affairs had been established to deal with the Western traders. The following year saw the establishment of a school of languages. Such 'modernization' was frowned on by the Court, which was increasingly influenced by the reactionary Dowager

MANCHURIA
KEY INDUSTRIAL AREA OF CHINA—EARLY TWENTIETH CENTURY
1896–1904 Russian Sphere of Influence
1904–45 Japanese Sphere of Influence. The region was developed as a reservoir for food and raw materials for Japan. Agricultural development in the North was limited by the extreme winter temperatures (as low as −40°C) and the short growing season (five months).

Tz'u Hsi. Industrial development was impeded by the imposition of a transit tax initially for goods carried on the Grand Canal. By the 1890s it had been extended to a production tax and a sales tax as the Ch'ing government's indemnity payments to the occupying forces soared.

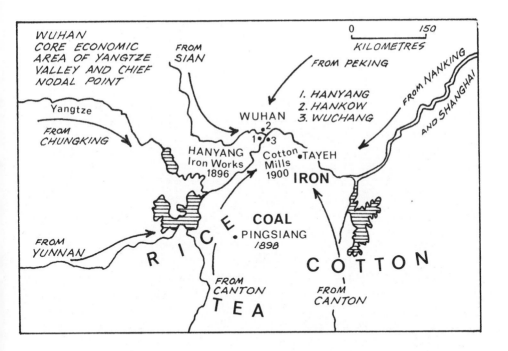

WUHAN
CORE ECONOMIC
AREA OF YANGTZE
VALLEY AND CHIEF
NODAL POINT

The Hanyang Iron Company, Pingsiang Coal Mines and Tayeh Iron Works amalgamated in 1908 to form the Hanyehping Iron Company.

Following the treaty of Shimonoseki in 1895, foreigners were allowed to develop industries in China and this, coupled with their exemption from the transit tax and other impositions, created China's first industrial boom. Between 1904 and 1908 227 joint-stock companies were registered. However, many of these were small in size. A survey of 'factories' in 1912 noted that only 363 out of 20 749 employed mechanical power. The increasing amount of foreign investment gave the outsiders even greater influence in China and increasingly the only government officials who could meet them on their own terms were those involved in similar industrial enterprises, such as the Hanyehping Iron Works founded in 1908. This was an amalgamation of the Hanyang Iron Works, Tayeh Iron Mines and Pingsiang Coal Mines, formed by Chang Chih-tung, governor general of Hupeh and Hunan. Only in the Yangtze valley and South Manchuria did heavy industry prosper. Elsewhere, the growth was confined largely to modernized and enlarged versions of traditional processing industries and textiles, and these were mainly located in the Treaty Ports.

Trade The Treaty of Nanking (1842) gave limitless opportunities for trade to the British, establishing five treaty ports (Canton, Amoy, Foochow, Ningpo and Shanghai) and ceding the island of Hong Kong to Britain. Chinese tariffs (taxes on imports) on British goods were made low and uniform. Yet the British failed to capitalize on these advantages at first. They flooded the market with useless goods such as Sheffield steel cutlery, though the infamous opium trade was maintained, providing an easy and vast source of income for the British. Even with the soaring exports of silk, and tea, the Chinese could never hope to obtain a favourable trade balance. The low tariffs and exemption from transit tax made imported British cotton goods cheaper than Chinese ones with a resulting decline in the domestic industry. Having revealed China's vulnerability, the Europeans pressed for more treaty ports and inland and coastal concessions, at every opportunity. The Peking Convention of 1860 opened up ten new ports to all and virtually carved up China among the European powers. The Chinese had little jurisdiction over the concessions. The 'most favoured nation' concept was introduced to extend any individually negotiated rights with the Chinese, to all other countries. In 1899 at a point in which China was about to be split politically between the European powers, the USA suggested the 'open-door' idea that was to form the basis of American relations with China until 1949. Under this idea all spheres of influence were to remain open to all other traders on the principle of 'equal and impartial trade with all parts of the Chinese Empire.' Thus China was preserved as a territorial and administrative entity.

THE GROWTH OF CHINESE SETTLEMENTS OVERSEAS

One of the earliest references to Chinese communities overseas derives from a thirteenth-century Mongol Embassy to Cambodia. The Chinese settlers were scathingly referred to as 'men of the sea,' implying that they originated as coastal traders or pirates. Another community was recorded at Tumasik in 1349 but this declined until the British revived the port as Singapore in 1819. The longest continual settlement may be that of Malacca which outlasted successive rules by Portugal, Holland and Britain. Among the earliest settlers intermarriage was frequently recorded.

The descendants known as 'Babar' Chinese maintained the culture if not the language of China. As the numbers of migrants increased in the seventeenth century intermarriage became less common.

Origins and Destinations

Migrants to the Nanyang (Southern Ocean) were almost entirely from Kwangtung and Fukien. The reasons for the movement can be summarized as follows:

- ever increasing population pressure on the south-east coastal lowlands;
- increasing alienation between the people of the south-east and successive harsh northern régimes under the Mongols, Ming and Manchu;
- inability of China to extend its southern boundaries overland;
- the availability of both sea-going sailing craft and knowledge of the Nanyang in south-east China.

The people of Kwangtung and Fukien spoke many dialects and when migrating they often chose to go to areas already peopled by those whose dialect they understood. Sibu in Sarawak became known as 'New Foochow' because of the large Chinese settlement from that area. Hokkien speakers from Amoy went to Java and Malaya. Teochin speakers from Swatow went to Siam, Sumatra and Malaya. The Hakka, a people who had fled to the south of China from the Mongol invaders, went in large numbers to Borneo. A major exception were the Cantonese traders who were found wherever commercial opportunities presented themselves.

The Role of the Migrants

It would be wrong to categorize all Chinese in South-East Asia as traders. Many of the wealthiest did originate as energetic middlemen who risked their lives collecting the produce of inland tribes for export to Europe and distributing European produce likewise. A growing number after the seventeenth century were poor peasants prepared to work in mines and on plantations as 'coolies.'

The Chinese were the only ethnic group common to all countries of the Nanyang including Siam, the only independent state by the nineteenth century. Although speaking different dialects they maintained a common written language and culture. Illiterate migrants who 'made good' endeavoured to obtain instruction for their children in traditional language and literature. As

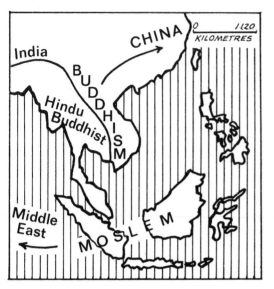

(Left) Major cultural division of Nanyang based on religion.
(Right) Major partition pattern by late nineteenth century showing spheres of influence of Britain, Holland, France and Spain. (Thailand remained independent.)

a result a vast intelligence network operated in the Nanyang via the Chinese newspapers which few others could understand. This was backed up by secret societies which acted to control and police the behaviour of the communities.

Generally the Chinese were eager to evade political confrontation with the governments of South-East Asia. This encouraged a general view that they were effete and cowardly. However, the Chinese by maintaining a policy of non-confrontation, so consistent with traditional philosophy, in particular Taoism, were to become one of the strongest and most permanent elements of the economy of the Nanyang.

Relations with the Countries of Settlement
The Portuguese and Spaniards feared the Chinese as rivals in trade. They resented also their unwillingness to be converted to Christianity. The Chinese community in the Philippines was periodically wiped out and on each occasion the economy of the islands collapsed. In 1603, 20 000 Chinese in Manila were killed. The Portuguese sphere of influence declined after the loss of Malacca to the Dutch in 1641. The Dutch were less evangelical,

258

being Protestants, but they attempted to restrict Chinese influence in trade in order to promote their own monopoly in Sumatra, Java, Borneo and the Malacca Straits. Some Chinese in the long established settlement at Palembang became wealthy through their appointment by the Dutch as tax collectors. By the nineteenth century the Chinese mining interests in Borneo had been severely restricted but at the same time the Dutch were encouraging migration into South Sumatra for work on the sugar and tobacco plantations.

The British considered a large Chinese community to be proof of the prosperity of a colony. They presented no apparent political danger and the Straits Settlements (including Penang founded 1785, Malacca in 1824 and Singapore in 1819) rapidly became major centres of Chinese occupation. The Moslem sultans of the western inland states of Malaya encouraged the Chinese to open up the rivers for trade and mining purposes and actually appointed Chinese 'River Lords' to control these developments. This system of indirect rule succeeded better than the British policy of direct intervention in Malaya, which failed to prevent outbreaks of fighting between rival secret societies, in which hundreds were killed. At a time when British administrators were mainly from the Indian civil service, speaking neither Malay nor Chinese, control of the Chinese community was only possible with the tacit consent of the leaders of the secret societies. Burma became a colony of Britain in 1886. Although sharing a border with China there was only a small settlement of emigrants and they were in Rangoon which represents the western limit of Chinese maritime migration in the Nanyang. There, they had to compete with Indians in trade and face the great hostility towards all foreigners from the Burmese.

Only in Malaya and Borneo were the Chinese of great numerical significance as a total proportion of the population. Elsewhere in the Nanyang they were relatively small minorities. In Siam they were assimilated to a much larger extent than in the colonial countries. Sanctions against migration had been in operation since the late Ming period and the zeal for ancestor worship is often considered as a stabilizing factor for the Chinese population, but economic factors were more important and acted to 'push' them as far away as San Francisco and Melbourne. (The latter two centres recruited Chinese labour for their respective gold rushes in the nineteenth century. Most of the miners were peasants from Si Yap which was a predominantly agricultural area in Canton.)

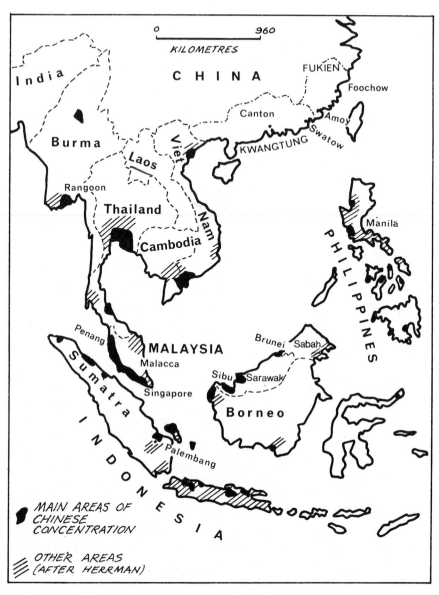

South-East Asia.

SOCIETY AND CULTURE

The Manchus were not destructive like the Mongols. They were semi-agriculturalists when general Wu San-kuei opened the gate at Shanhaikuan and invited them to enter the Great Wall. By the beginning of the eighteenth century the Ch'ing dynasty

LETTRE XVIII.

DE MONS. DE LEIBNIZ

SVR LA

PHILOSOPHIE CHINOISE

A

MONS. DE REMOND,

Confeiller du Duc Regent, et Introducteur des
Ambaffadeurs.

SECTION PREMIERE

DV SENTIMENT DES CHINOIS
DE DIEV.

1. *Les fentiments des anciens Chinois, font beaucoup preferables à ceux des nouveaux.* 2. *Les penfées des Chinois des fubftances fpirituelles.* 3. *Qu'il nous faut donner un bon fens aux dogmes des anciens Chinois.* 4. *Du premier principe des Chinois, qu'ils appellent Li.* 5. *Des attributs de ce premier principe.* 6. *De l'unite de ce principe.* 7. *Dans quel fens les Chinois appellent Dieu le grand Vuide ou Efpace, la capacité immenfe.* 8. *Des autres Noms, que les Chinois impofent au premier principe.* 9. *Le Pere Longobardi iuge, que ce Li n'eft autre chofe, que la matiere premiere.* 10. *Mr. de Leibniz refute cette opinion.* 11. *Des proprietes diuines, que les Chinois felon la recenfion du P. de S. Marie attribuent à leur premier principe.* 12. *Pourquoi le Li des Chinois ne foit pas la matiere premiere? la premiere raifon.* 13. *Vne autre raifon.* 14. *Les fentimens des Chinois de l'Efprit.* 15. *De la premiere raifon qu'apporte le P. Longobardi pourquoi le Li des Chinois ne foit que la matiere premiere.* 16. *La feconde raifon.* 17. *La troifieme raifon du même.* 18. *Toutes les expreffions des Chinois de leur Li, reçoivent un bon fens.* 19. *La quatrieme objection du P. Longobardi.* 20. *La 5me objection.* 21. *Dans quel fens les Chinois difent, que les chofes.*

The title-page of the Letter on Chinese Philosophy *by Gottfried Wilhelm Leibniz (1646–1716).*

In 1598 Father Matteo Ricci arrived in Peking. The *shih* were opposed to his arrival, which had been largely arranged by the eunuch party; the Board of Rites respectfully reminded the throne of Han Yu's memorial on the religious excesses of Buddhism. Ricci did have some impact among the officials of the Court, but Christianity made little headway after his death (1610). Yet Chinese philosophy, the ideas of which were reported back in Europe by Jesuit missionaries from the East, had an important influence on Western thinkers, particularly Leibniz. While the Jesuits were making available to China Western science, Neo-Confucianism seems to have made a significant contribution to Western thought.

What stirred the philosophers in the West was the organic basis of Neo-Confucianism, which had derived from the ancient Chinese concept of the Yin-Yang. Leibniz wanted an explanation of the universe that was realist, but not mechanical. He rejected the con-

porary view that the world was a vast machine, and proposed the alternative view of it as a vast living organism, every part of which was also an organism. He called these organisms 'monads.' They fitted into a pre-established harmony, like the *li* of Chu Hsi (A.D. 1130–1200). The organic view of the world, as first put forward by Leibniz, was to be most important in the nineteenth century, witness Hegel, Darwin, Pasteur and Marx. It has been suggested that Neo-Confucianism provided an initial stimulus. 'We may applaud the modern Chinese interpreters,' Leibniz wrote, 'when they reduce the government of Heaven to natural causes, and when they differ from popular ignorance, which looks on miracles and the supernatural as signs from God. And we shall be able to enlighten them further on these matters by informing them of the new discoveries of Europe, which have furnished almost mathematical reasons for many of the great marvels of Nature. . . .'

found that the process of cultural assimilation was becoming a serious threat to the survival of the Manchu tongue itself. Imperial insistence that all official documents should be written in both Manchu and Chinese, and the sponsorship of a huge programme of translation from Chinese, did ensure that Manchu lasted down till 1911, but long before that date it had changed into a 'dead language' which the Manchus themselves were forced to study in schools.

One of the chief reasons for the decline of Manchu was the intense admiration for Chinese culture that the conquerors felt. Emperor Ch'ien Lung (1735–95) was an enthusiastic patron of the arts and he gave a status to painters which they had not enjoyed since the days of the Sung Emperor Hui Tsung. The imperial collection acquired the greatest works of Chinese tradition, but, unfortunately, Ch'ien Lung could not resist the temptation to add his own poems to these paintings and stamp them with very large seals. Although such a practice was an old Chinese custom, Emperor Ch'ien Lung has embarrassed later admirers of Chinese painting by the sheer number of works he felt obliged to enhance. The Ch'ing Court was conservative in taste, so that architecture and painting tended to be rather pale imitations of previous dynasties, particularly the Ming. Not for nothing had the significant artists of the Ch'ing dynasty died before Ch'ien Lung mounted the throne. One of these painters, Wang Hui (1632–1720) was commissioned by Emperor K'ang Hsi to prepare illustrations for a book describing an imperial visit to the South, after the fall of Taiwan (1683). The great southern cities of Soochow and Hangchow produced all these painters, a monopoly of talent that clearly underlines the fact

A Chinese school in the nineteenth century. The teacher is listening to a pupil recite a classical text by heart. This test was called 'backing the book'; it had become the basis of the learning process during the Ch'ing dynasty, and reflected the uncritical and conservative attitudes prevailing among the shih.

that this early creative achievement was a legacy of the Ming Empire, not any fresh development. Indeed, the emphasis on tradition at the Ch'ing Court led to a vogue in making exact copies of old masters, which in turn took the painter and poet yet another step from the possibility of creative renewal, the right to experiment freely within a living tradition.

The narrowing of outlook in the Court at Peking, a rigorous censorship, and the reduction of places available for would-be officials in the Ch'ing civil service led to a growing disenchantment among the *shih* of the South. It seemed to many of them that the North was living off the wealth and toil of the South. Idle Bannermen were everywhere for people to see, and their military ineffectiveness became legend after the first Opium War. The *nung* were restive too. They bore the brunt of an agricultural economy annually proving itself more and more inadequate. Landless peasants formed the backbone of the T'ai P'ing armies, just as they had joined rebellions during the famine years preceding the fall of the Ming dynasty. Secret societies flourished everywhere.

K'ang Yu-wei (1858–1927)
To deal with the rising tide of confusion, reformers like K'ang Yu-wei tried to provide an intellectual basis for the changes in Chinese society that were necessary to save the Empire. The T'ai

263

P'ing rebellion had forced on the Ch'ing dynasty a moderate adoption of Western technology—arsenals, modern ships and improved communications—but peace took the urgency out of the need for reform. The Sino-Japanese War (1894–5) would have been the catalyst, but for the Empress Dowager Tz'u Hsi and the inherent conservatism of the *shih* themselves. K'ang's writings bear witness to the insoluble dilemma of the best of his class. The whole purpose of reform was to sustain the old order; thus, when innovation threatened that order, opposition was a natural response. K'ang had to work within a conception of reality that rested on a belief in the teachings of Confucius and Buddha.

In his book *Confucius as a Reformer* (1897), K'ang attempted to transform Confucianism into a viable system of thought that could hold its own in the modern world. The failure of Emperor Kuang Hsu's reform programme and his own exile forced K'ang to develop a radical line of argument that made Confucian tradition the framework for a single world civilization. *The Book of the Grand Unity* (1902) envisaged a world society of small democratically self-governing communities, each equally represented in a world parliament. Property and the family were to be abolished, because a false notion of Confucian righteousness had restricted affection to the enclosed circle of one's kin. K'ang was conscious of social injustice. He opposed the binding of women's feet and the restrictions placed on widows. The development of his thought reflects a profound discontent with existing conditions as well as a strong desire to change them. Moreover, the influence of Western ideas on K'ang pointed the way to the present intellectual renewal that has come through Communist theory. Unlike Confucianism, Taoism has proved to be most capable of modern political interpretation, possibly through its age-old subversive tendencies. Compare these two translations of a passage from the *Tao Teh Ching*:

Thirty spokes together make one wheel
And they fit into nothing at the centre;
Herein lies the usefulness of a carriage.
Clay is moulded to make a pot
And the clay fits round nothing;
Herein lies the usefulness of the pot.
Doors and windows are pierced in the walls of a house
And they fit round nothing;
Herein lies the usefulness of a house.
Thus whilst it must be taken as advantageous to have something there,
It must also be taken as useful to have nothing there.

(Modern Western Version)

Thirty spokes combine to make a wheel,
When there was no private property
Carts were made for use.
Clay is formed to make vessels,
When there was no private property
Pots were made for use.
Windows and doors go to make houses,
When there was no private property
Houses were made for use.
Thus having private property may lead to profit
But not having it leads to use.

(Modern Chinese Version)

The End of the Examination System

In 1905 the imperial examination system was abolished. At once the *shih* lost its privileged avenue of advancement to authority and influence, while the opening of modern schools caused a massive inflow of Western ideas. The Confucian Classics lost their eminence, which had been virtually undisputed since the Han Empire. Intelligent young men now looked outside China for an understanding of their lives and times. They realized that industrial products without the knowledge of the science and technology that lay behind them were valueless. They were prepared to take advantage of mission schools in order to acquire a Western language, which was a way into the modern world, not theology. China would be saved, not westernized, by their studies. However, the *nung*, who formed more than eighty per cent of the Chinese population, were hardly touched by this cultural change till the Communists came to power in 1949.

8 China in the Twentieth Century

From the foundation of the Republic in 1911 to the present day

HISTORICAL OUTLINE

From the moment that Emperor Kuang Hsu's programme of reforms failed and it became obvious that the Empress Dowager Tz'u Hsi would resist any fundamental change in Chinese society, serious revolutionary activity concentrated on the overthrow of both the Ch'ing dynasty and the Empire. Revolutionaries were convinced that the republican model of government would be the saving of China. Accordingly, Dr Sun Yat-sen, the leader of the revolutionary movement, the T'ung-meng hui, or Alliance Society, spent many years raising funds and support from the overseas Chinese. There were ten abortive revolts in the South before, on 9th October 1911, a bomb exploded accidentally in the office of the main revolutionary organization in Hankow, one of the three cities that comprise Wuhan, the great industrial and communications centre of the middle Yangtze valley, and precipitated an anti-Manchu revolution that captured fifteen of the eighteen provinces in the Empire by the end of November. In February 1912 the six-year-old Emperor Hsuan T'ung formally abdicated.

Sun Yat-sen and the Warlords
Sun Yat-sen (1866–1925) was the culmination of a tendency that had begun when the T'ai P'ings first looked outside China to Protestant Christianity for a solution of the problems that were besetting the Empire. For Dr Sun was an 'overseas Chinese'; though born in Kwantung, he had lived in Hawaii, receiving his education in Western schools there and at the Medical College in Hong Kong. In outlook Dr Sun was scientific and modern— his own answer to China's plight was the establishment of a democratic republic. He and his followers worked hard for this liberal goal, but it was too immense a change to introduce at

266

once. The revolutionaries had been able to form cells among the officers of the modernized regiments from 1905. This move proved decisive in the struggle against the Ch'ing dynasty, but it left military governors at the apex of the provincial administrations of the Republic. Many of these officers were warlords, men determined to exploit the uncertainty of the times and the power of their troops for the sake of personal ambition. The *shih* were in disarray with the end of the imperial examination system and the rise of modern schools. So the civil arm of government lost prestige as different generals asserted provincial independence.

Yuan Shih-k'ai.

Yuan Shih-k'ai, recalled by the Ch'ing dynasty as a last resort, was the best placed to take advantage of the confused situation. His military reputation was sound and he controlled the strong northern army. Disposing of the Manchus and intimidating the rebel forces, Yuan obliged Dr Sun, the provisional president, to retire in his favour. By 1914 President Yuan felt secure enough to dismiss not only the National Assembly but all the provincial assemblies as well. Supported by Western powers—they preferred a ruler who would keep the peace in China and protect trade—he made a bid to found a new dynasty, hoping to demonstrate clearly that he had received the Mandate of Heaven. But there were two factors he had overlooked, namely the historical sense of the Chinese people and the empire-building intentions of the Japanese.

Japan was alarmed at the rise of Yuan Shih-k'ai, since another dynasty might lead to the recovery of the Chinese Empire, so reducing its own ability to expand on the Asian continent. Joining the Allies in 1914, Japan had seized the German-leased territories in Shantung, claiming that this was done 'with a view to its eventual restoration to China.' In January 1915 the Japanese government presented Yuan Shih-k'ai with the Twenty-One Demands, whose purpose was the reduction of China to a virtual protectorate of Japan. With no more than moral support from the Western powers, now locked together in total war, Yuan was forced to accept the least offensive Demands. The news led to a nation-wide protest by the Chinese. It seemed that the would-be Emperor was about to betray the country, as he had the Emperor Kuang Hsu (1898), the boy Emperor P'u-yi (1911–12), and the Republic (1914). The Confucian virtues of loyalty and righteousness were singularly lacking in Yuan: he commanded neither respect nor confidence. His downfall came as one military governor after another declared for the Republic. Japanese agents and money found these warlords easy prey for the simple reason that Yuan himself had shown them the way to power. In 1916 Yuan was dead, after a nervous illness caused by disappointment.

The removal of Yuan Shih-k'ai from the political scene left a power vacuum, particularly in the North, where competing generals sought to control Peking. Yuan's personal eminence had permitted the almost peaceful transition from Empire to Republic in 1911–12; political revolution was contained within the continuity of the military establishment. The Warlord Period (1916–26) showed the real extent to which the Empire had disintegrated. In the South Dr Sun resumed as President of the Republic, but there was a complete breakdown of government at a national level. Since all foreign countries persisted in seeing the various régimes in Peking, not the South, as the legal government of China, the country remained divided till after the launching of the Northern Expedition in 1926. Financial motives were behind this diplomatic *impasse*, for foreign loans were financed by custom duties collected from Peking. It appeared that the 'barbarians' were only concerned to keep China weak, when, suddenly, the Russian Revolution (1917) provided the struggling Republic with a new friend, the USSR.

The Kuomintang and the Chinese Communist Party

In order to maintain its political base in the South the Republic had to depend on the protection of local warlords. So precarious was the position that Dr Sun barely escaped with his life in 1922, when the Kwantung warlord, supported by the British, moved against him. Against this background of continued imperialism in alliance with the warlords three events should be placed. They are:

● *The May Fourth Movement*, which marked the continued influence of *shih* in Chinese society. The scholars had gained control of the modern universities, colleges and schools; a new generation had appeared by the Treaty of Versailles (1919), when the Allies awarded the former German-leased territory to Japan. In Peking 3 000 students protested in T'ien An Men square and then burnt down the houses of the puppet ministers. Soon the country had followed the lead of the new young *shih*; cities and towns joined the protest; even *nung* in the remote countryside were stirred by the patriotic appeal. Pro-Japanese ministers fell, the Chinese delegation at Versailles was instructed not to sign the peace treaty, and modern Chinese nationalism emerged.

● *The Chinese Communist Party* had its First Congress in Shanghai (1921). Among the delegates was Mao Tse-tung, one of the leaders of the May Fourth Movement. Although the CCP joined Comintern (the Communist International), the Russians found Dr Sun's nationalist movement more promising at first.

● *The Kuomintang*, the Nationalist Party of Dr Sun, accepted Russian advice and aid. What prompted this alliance was the attitude of the new Communist government in Moscow. 'The Unequal Treaties' obtained by the Tsars were declared void and normal relations established. The *shih* were deeply impressed by this change in policy. It was so unlike the behaviour of other foreign powers, despite their talk about the defence of freedom and democracy. Throughout his life Dr Sun's government was never recognized by any other Western country—on the grounds that his was not the legal one. The Kuomintang, therefore, opened its membership to communist and non-communist members alike, though the differences between Left and Right rent the party asunder after Dr Sun's death (1925).

Chiang Kai-shek (born 1887) became Dr Sun's military adviser in 1917. He was the son of a well-to-do landowning family from Chekiang; his revolutionary beliefs were confirmed in Japan, when he was training as a military officer at the Tokyo Military Academy. But, unlike Mao Tse-tung (born 1893) and

Dr Sun Yat-sen and his wife photographed with officers trained at Whampoa Academy. In 1923 Chiang Kai-shek had been sent to Russia to study the organization of the Red Army. A year later Whampoa was opened with Russian aid; Chiang Kai-shek became its military commandant and developed his influence in the Kuomintang through his appointment.

other left-wing followers of Dr Sun, Chiang was less concerned with a thorough transformation of Chinese society than the creation of a strong national state. He had little sympathy with Mao's trust in the *nung*, for by both birth and training he felt called to command those below him in rank. His associates tended to be the military and the new Chinese business class in Shanghai and other commercial centres. Soon after Dr Sun died a struggle developed inside the Kuomintang between the leftist-political officials and the rightist-military group: Chiang emerged as the new leader, though his power within the party was still limited by the ever active Left. As Mao Tse-tung said: 'Political power grows out of the barrel of a gun.' What Dr Sun had striven to avoid most of all had happened—the Kuomintang military, like another set of the warlords, had become the dominant force in the Republic. The Northern Expedition gave the Kuomintang control of all the South: Nanking and Shanghai fell in 1927. But the victory brought Chiang and the Communists into open conflict, since the extent and violence of the agrarian revolt encouraged by Mao Tse-tung frightened many of Chiang's officers, themselves members of southern landlord families. Chiang ordered Kuomintang troops and underworld toughs to

*Dr Sun Yat-sen and
Chiang K'ai-shek.*

attack the rebellious workers in Shanghai. Chou En-lai, an
important organizer of the Communist movement there, just
escaped the massacre. From this moment the CCP and the
Kuomintang were bitter enemies, despite the Japanese invasion
of China, which produced a temporary united front.

Mao Tse-tung and the Long March

By 1927 Chiang had driven all the Communists out of the
Kuomintang. From Nanking, the Nationalist capital, he gradually
extended his influence northwards till few independent warlords
were left. But over the *nung*, particularly where Communist
guerillas were operating, Chiang had no effective control, for in
1928 Mao established a separate peasant state in the wilds of
Hunan, his native province. On the advice of Moscow, the CCP
had tried armed risings in cities, such as Canton, but they were
quickly crushed. Limited to a Western historical perspective,
Karl Marx, the German-Jewish revolutionary on whose writings

271

communism is based, had argued that the peasantry could never be a truly revolutionary force. Only the proletariat, the urban wage-earners, could be expected to seize power—as in 1917 the Russian experience seemed to confirm. Mao disagreed with this view of revolutionary change. For him the proper order of Chinese society was:

- *nung,* the peasant farmers;
- *kung,* the artisans;
- *shih,* the gentry and scholars;
- *shang,* the merchants.

Though the Comintern disavowed Mao, and Chiang's armies were thrown against him, the peasant movement spread. The Nationalists were allied to the Shanghai business world, representing

'The ruthless economic exploitation and political oppression of the peasants by the landlord class forced them into numerous uprisings against its rule. . . . It was the class struggles of the peasants, the peasant uprisings and peasant wars that constituted the real motive force of historical development in Chinese feudal society.'

Mao Tse-tung in 1939

international finance as well as the *shang,* while the Communists drew on the historical rebelliousness of the *nung.* Between these two opposing forces the *shih* found themselves with little choice but to wait and see.

'While we recognize that in the general development of history the material determines the mental, and social being determines social consciousness, we also—and indeed must—recognize the reaction of mental on material things, of social consciousness on social being and of the superstructure on the economic base. This does not go against materialism; on the contrary, it avoids mechanical materialism and firmly upholds dialectical materialism.'

Mao Tse-tung in 1937

'In many ways dialectical materialism is familiar to the Chinese mind. Neo-Confucianism subsumed a long tradition of organic thinking that stretched back through early Taoists to the ancient Yin-Yang theory.

So serious had the peasant movement become by 1934 that Chiang made an all-out attempt to crush Mao. The Communist base areas were encircled with blockhouses and other military barriers in order to deny them supplies. To escape and continue the revolution the Communists were forced to break out of the closing Nationalist vice; the trek to safety, the famous 'Long

Mao during the Long March. It was at this time that he wrote 'On Protracted War'.

'Weapons are an important factor in war, but not the decisive factor; it is people, not things, that are decisive. The contest of strength is not only a context of military and economic power, but also a contest of human power and morale. Military and economic power is necessarily wielded by people.'

Mao Tse-tung in 1934–5

March,' took them a distance of 9 600 kilometres, through eleven provinces and 200 million *nung*, before reaching the safety of Shensi. Only about a quarter survived the ordeals of the journey— the rugged terrain and the numerous battles—but Chairman Mao emerged as the respected leader of the CCP.

Japanese Aggression

Since the Sino-Japanese War of 1894–5, the military faction allied with the new business and industrial class had come to dominate the political life of Japan. The spectacular victories of the Russo-Japanese War of 1904–5—the majority of the Tsarist navy was sunk and an entire army surrendered in Port Arthur—gave the Japanese Empire immense confidence: this conflict was the first one in which an Asian power, albeit modernized through Western technology, had inflicted total defeat on any European nation for several hundred years.

As a result Japan extended her influence from Korea into Manchuria, which the Russians had been developing. At first Dr Sun had looked upon modern Japan as a friend of the Chinese Republic, but the Twenty-One Demands (1915) and the continued

Troops on the Long March. Of the 80 000 men that set out only 20 000 arrived in Yenan.

occupation of the German-leased territories permanently soured relations. Japanese infiltration of the North became open aggression in 1931, when an incident was faked at Mukden by Japanese officers in order to serve as an excuse for occupying all Manchuria. Despite opposition from the Japanese government itself, the military took over control of the province and installed the deposed Ch'ing Emperor P'u-yi as a puppet ruler of a new state, called Manchukuo.

The Kuomintang wavered. Nation-wide demonstrations, strikes, boycotts, and protests failed to induce Chiang to declare war on Japan. Chang Hsueh-liang, the Manchurian warlord, was in China with half his troops, and Chiang advised him to stay there. In the minds of Chinese patriots Nanking became associated with a policy of appeasement, for Chiang used his forces against the Communists, not the steadily encroaching Japanese. The assassination of the Japanese Prime Minister by a group of young officers freed the military establishment from all restrictions in its Chinese campaigns (1932). Atrocity and widespread destruction marked the Japanese advance.

But at Sian, near the ancient site of Chang-an, Chiang was obliged to reverse his policies by a mutiny (1936). The army there was supposed to be pressing a final attack on Mao's Yenan base area, but Chang Hsueh-liang and his men had come to the conclusion that a united front of Kuomintang and Communists was needed against the Japanese. 'Chinese should not fight

274

Chinese' propaganda by Communist agents had sapped the will of Chang's army, though for these troops a guerrilla war in Shensi made little sense when the Japanese armies were looting and raping their native provinces. Taken prisoner by the mutinous soldiers, Chiang was persuaded to end his harassment of the Communists. Chou En-lai came and agreement was reached.

In 1937 Japan captured Peking and hostilities became general. The North was soon overrun and, using the International Settlement at Shanghai as a base without regard to international law, the Japanese launched an offensive along the Yangtze valley. Nanking suffered dreadfully; there were several weeks of massacre, rape, looting and arson. Although the Japanese armies had complete technological superiority, they had not the measure of Chinese resistance, particularly in those areas where the *nung* had come under Communist influence. While they sought to destroy the Chinese field armies, those of the Kuomintang, they failed to check guerilla activities, even behind their own lines. In effect, the Japanese armies held only the major cities and towns besides the main lines of communications. Chiang retreated to Chungking, where from 1938 to 1944 he remained inactive, much to the embarrassment of his American advisers. Accumulating equipment and military supplies via the Burma Road and later airlifts from India, Chiang claimed he was awaiting the right moment to strike. But it soon became obvious that he still regarded Mao as his main opponent and was saving his strength for an anti-Communist campaign after the withdrawal of Japan, now involved in a global conflict in alliance with the Fascist powers and overstretched in South-East Asia and the Pacific.

What the Japanese invasion meant for Chinese history was the triumph of Communism. While Chiang's troops deteriorated in idleness at Chungking, Mao raised a militia force of two million *nung*, whose bravery and determination ensured that they were liberated not only from the Imperial Army of Japan but also the military domination of the Kuomintang landlord and business faction.

The People's Republic of China
When in 1945 the dropping of atomic bombs on Hiroshima and Nagasaki caused the surrender of Japan, the Kuomintang held the West and the CCP controlled the North, apart from cities with Japanese garrisons. To whom these Japanese should surrender proved an immediate point of dispute. As the legal government of China and an ally, the Kuomintang demanded

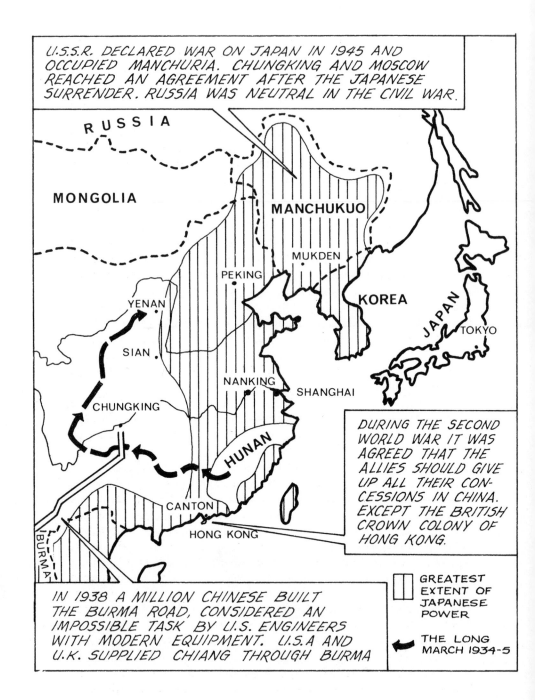

U.S.S.R. DECLARED WAR ON JAPAN IN 1945 AND OCCUPIED MANCHURIA. CHUNGKING AND MOSCOW REACHED AN AGREEMENT AFTER THE JAPANESE SURRENDER. RUSSIA WAS NEUTRAL IN THE CIVIL WAR.

RUSSIA

MONGOLIA

MANCHUKUO

MUKDEN

PEKING

KOREA

YENAN

JAPAN

TOKYO

SIAN

NANKING

SHANGHAI

CHUNGKING

HUNAN

DURING THE SECOND WORLD WAR IT WAS AGREED THAT THE ALLIES SHOULD GIVE UP ALL THEIR CONCESSIONS IN CHINA. EXCEPT THE BRITISH CROWN COLONY OF HONG KONG.

CANTON

HONG KONG

BURMA

GREATEST EXTENT OF JAPANESE POWER

THE LONG MARCH 1934-5

IN 1938 A MILLION CHINESE BUILT THE BURMA ROAD, CONSIDERED AN IMPOSSIBLE TASK BY U.S. ENGINEERS WITH MODERN EQUIPMENT. U.S.A AND U.K. SUPPLIED CHIANG THROUGH BURMA

The Sino-Japanese War.

air support from the United States and its troops were flown into occupied cities. Peace efforts by the Americans failed and in 1947 the CCP and Kuomintang were fighting earnestly. The low morale of Chiang's forces and their dismal wartime record inspired no one. The CCP seemed to offer a viable alternative to the corruption and weakness of the Kuomintang. Isolated and disliked the Nationalists lost ground before the poorly equipped but disciplined People's Liberation Army. On the surrender of Peking to the CCP in 1949, a massive victory parade in T'ien An Men Square included *nung, kung* and *shih*. This combination of classes signalized the defeat of the Kuomintang. During the Yenan years Chairman Mao had transformed the ideology of the CCP into something distinctly Chinese, a system of thought attractive to many of the *shih*. Mao, the Hunanese school teacher and peasant leader who had never been abroad nor learnt a foreign language, had achieved the successful combination of *nung* and *shih*, but, unlike the first Ming Emperor, he was not prepared to give the scholars a privileged position. From the outset he made it clear that their skills should be used for 'serving the People.' Meanwhile, Chiang, like the last Ming partisan, retired to Taiwan with 300 000 troops. More fortunate than his historical predecessor, the Kuomintang leader had a foreign ally whose navy could defend his refuge.

American opposition to the People's Republic of China (formally established on 1st October 1949) compelled the Chinese Communist leaders to seek aid exclusively from Russia. Technical assistance and loans were made—by 1965 China had repaid its debts through exports to the Soviet Union—but differences in ideology have caused friction between Peking and Moscow. It should not be forgotten that Mao, like Hung Hsiu-ch'uan, has translated foreign doctrines into a Chinese form. The Thought of Chairman Mao offers a radical interpretation of socialism, an unnecessary disturbance of communist theory from the point of view of the Russians, who abolished the Comintern in 1943.

Land reform and the nationalization of businesses prepared the way for a large-scale industrial revolution, which began in 1952. Membership of the CCP increased as more urban workers have joined and the initial violence of the civil war has altered to an emphasis on re-education for dissidents. 'Remoulding through labour' and political study has been the lot of reluctant *shih* and *shang*. The 'Hundred Flowers' episode in 1957, when Chairman Mao relaxed censorship and encouraged the educated classes to voice their views, was followed by a programme of

Troops of the People's Liberation Army on their arrival in Nanking in 1949. 'Without a people's army', Mao Tse-tung had written in 1945, 'the people have nothing'. In contrast with the Nationalist forces, these soldiers did not live by pillaging the land. They were expected to follow three commandments, 'Do not even take a needle or a thread. Consider the people as your family. All that you have borrowed you must return'.

re-education for those 'rightists' who did criticize the régime from mistaken viewpoints. The revolutionary *nung* and *kung* were their teachers.

The Great Proletarian Cultural Revolution (1966–68)

The Cultural Revolution was nothing less than an attack on the CCP by its leader, Chairman Mao. He is one of those rare individuals who seem to reverse the usual effects of growing old—that is, he has become more radical as the years have passed. Since the Great Leap Forward in 1958, when an ambitious drive to increase both agricultural and industrial production met with mixed success, Mao had less influence on the direction of policy than Liu Shao-ch'i, whose outlook was 'revisionist.' Two main issues between Mao and Liu were the education system and the People's Liberation Army. Under Liu's 'rightist'

278

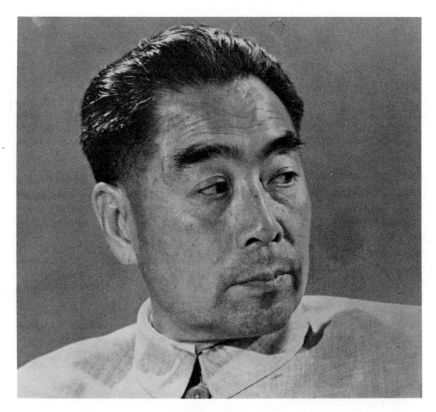

Chou En-lai a year after the Bandung Conference (1955). He was born in a family long-established as shih. *His encounter with communist theory occurred when he was a student in Paris (1921).*

philosophy both of these institutions were divisive, encouraging the re-emergence of the old class divisions of Chinese society. This was Mao's view. Liu claimed that China needed technicians and a strong army, so that Mao's insistence on truly proletarian organization was a mere day-dream inspired by nostalgia for Yenan. In 1962 Mao succeeded in introducing a programme of 'social education,' and in 1965 military ranks were abolished in the PLA. However, this proved to be the limits of his power in spite of the support of Lin Piao, then Minister of Defence.

On 5th August 1965 Mao wrote a wall poster entitled *Bombard the Headquarters!* It represented a call to the young to rout out the 'revisionists' and purify the revolution. Within months 13 000 000 Red Guards had travelled to Peking as the revolutionary fervour spread from universities and colleges into schools. The movement split the CCP and the country. Chiang Ch'ing,

Mao's wife, directed the activities of the Red Guards, who had denounced Liu Shao-ch'i as the 'top person in authority taking the capitalist road.' Conditions in China were chaotic but Mao removed his opponents.

Lin Piao used the PLA to good purpose and Chou En-lai, a consummate politician in any crisis, managed to arrange compromise governments in the provinces and save officials from unjust attack. 'The working class,' Mao said, 'must exercise leadership in everything.' Whether this will be the result of the Great Proletarian Cultural Revolution remains to be seen. The CCP has been weakened at the very time that the leadership had to rely on the PLA. Perhaps the disappearance of Lin Piao was Mao's reassertion of control over the military arm of government (1971), just as the more recent campaign against the philosophy of Confucius represents continued pressure on those who would 'take the capitalist road' (1974). Whatever is concluded about the Cultural Revolution in one respect it remains unique. For it was a movement of the young, a continuing revolution in a revolution. Sensing the frustrations of young people, Mao guided their revolt into an attack on the complacency of their parents. Grandfather and grandchildren opposed the 'rightist' tendencies of the middle-aged.

China and the World
Today, China is a world power again. Here are the events that have led to the international acceptance of the People's Republic:

● Recognition of the Communist government by Britain, but Peking resented the consulate which London maintained on Taiwan (1949). The United States continued to support Chiang Kai-shek.

● Mao went to Moscow and Sino-Soviet alliance was signed (February 1950). This was the first contact between Chinese Communists and Russian Communists since the Shanghai massacre of 1927. Mao had proved that peasants could be a truly revolutionary force.

● Korean War (1950–53). North Korea, a Russian ally, invaded South Korea, an American ally. Chinese 'volunteers' went to the aid of the North when United Nations forces under the command of General MacArthur approached their own borders. The PLA acquitted itself well and a ceasefire left Korea divided into two separate countries. This was the first time that Chinese arms had matched those of the West.

● Liberation movements, 'People's Wars,' were aided by

China in South-East Asia. Ho Chi-minh was helped to expel the French in Indo-China, where a decisive victory was gained at Dien Bien Phu (1954). The region had been a Chinese protectorate under the Ch'ing dynasty.

● At the Bandung Conference, Chou En-lai told Afro-Asian neutralist nations that China had no intention of interfering in their affairs (1955). However, the United States, France, Australia and Britain had set up the South-East Asian Treaty Organization in 1954 to contain China's growing power. In the event, only Pakistan, Thailand and the Philippines joined.

● Vietnam War (officially over in 1973) was a continuation of the struggle between the North and the Western powers, through their client rulers in the South. In the 1960s the United States became embroiled and fighting spread into Laos and Cambodia. The Vietcong, Communist guerrillas, had the edge in the war, despite the advanced technology of the Americans.

● Tibet (1959). The People's Republic had drawn Tibet back into the Chinese sphere of influence in 1950, though the Dalai Lama at first remained head of state. A revolt against Communist influence caused the intervention of the PLA in 1959.

● India (1962). The PLA invaded and occupied territories in the Himalayas claimed by India. Peking disclaimed the Simla Agreement and the MacMahon Line; these had been forced on a weakened Ch'ing dynasty by the British Empire in the nineteenth century. The Indian army was soundly beaten by the PLA, though after the fighting the Chinese only retained the Aksai Chin plateau, which lies between Sinkiang and Tibet.

● Differences arose between China and Russia, whose advisers were soon withdrawn (1960). Khruschev had offered arms to India and was attempting to improve relations with the United States, the antithesis of Communism in Mao's eyes. In 1963 Russia, Britain and France signed a treaty banning further nuclear tests. But there were border disputes too. Tsarist aggression had taken large areas of Sinkiang and Manchuria from the Ch'ing Empire. Armed clashes occurred in the late 1960s.

● China exploded its first atomic bomb (1964); three years later an H-bomb was set off. Hence, the People's Republic is the only non-Western country possessing nuclear weapons.

● The People's Republic replaced the Nationalists (Taiwan) as the representative for China at the United Nations (1971).

● President Nixon visited Peking (1971). The U.S.A. and China set up liaison offices in each other's capitals in 1972.

LITERATURE AND PAINTING

The outstanding modern writer of twentieth-century China was Lu Hsun (the pen name of Chou Shu-jen, 1881–1936). An opponent of the Empire, Lu Hsun's writings have a very strong element of social criticism in them. His short story, *A Madman's Diary*, was the first modern work of fiction; it appeared in 1918 and was written in the vernacular. But *The True Story of Ah Q* (1921) is justly regarded as his masterpiece. By choosing as his main character an illiterate, landless labourer, Lu Hsun struck on a brilliant device for ridiculing those who still believed in Confucian values. The 'polite' classes are shown up as hypocrites, using a system that depends on the misery of countless *nung*. Like a true fool, Ah Q always succeeds in winning a 'moral victory' over his tormentors. Here is an episode from the story:

THE TRAGEDY OF BEING IN LOVE

Ah Q felt so buoyant, it seemed as though he would fly away. His sense of elation came from pinching the cheek of the young novice who had passed him in the street. . . . So he floated for most of the day, till in the evening he found himself in the barn, where his sleeping quarters were situated. Normally, he would have turned in and gone to sleep, but tonight he was restless. He felt something smooth between his index finger and thumb. He wondered: was it something soft and smooth from the face of the novice, or had his fingers become smooth and soft through touching her face?

'May all the generations of Ah Q perish,' (rather strong language from such a young nun) the novice had cried out. Her curse still rang in his ears. He thought she had spoken correctly. But again, there certainly was a need for a woman. 'Perish.' . . . There was no-one to cook him a meal, he pondered; he did need a woman. Had not Mencius said: 'Among the three great sins of the unfilial, the greatest of all is the discontinuation of the family line.' His thoughts were perfectly attuned to the teaching of the sage. It is indeed a pity that later he should have run amok. 'Woman, woman!' he said to himself, 'the monk could touch . . . woman, woman, woman!'

It is not certain when Ah Q actually fell asleep that night. His fingers seemed very smooth, more so each day. 'Woman!' he used to think all the time. (Clearly, from this example, we can tell that women are harmful. Indeed, Chinese men, the vast majority of them that is, are the material from which saints are made, but, they are ruined by women. It's a shame! Shang kingdom was ruined by Ta Chi, Chou kingdom by Pao Ssu, Ch'in . . . though not clearly recorded, it could hardly have fallen otherwise. It must have been because of a woman. Tung Chok was definitely ruined by Chou Shan.)

Ah Q himself is a gentleman. We cannot be sure which illustrious teacher he followed, but he was precise in his behaviour towards men and women. Normally, he was very careful, particularly with novices and imitation 'ocean devils.' He had come to a number of philosophical conclusions, like all nuns have affairs with monks, a lone woman walking through the town is trying to catch a man, and a conversation between any man or woman must be underhand. Accordingly, Ah Q often glared, mumbled rude comments, and even threw stones.

Now, Ah Q, who would have thought that a novice should have so affected you? The feelings which oppressed him were outlawed by religion and society. (How disgusting is a woman! If only the novice had worn a veil. A little piece of cloth would have made so much difference. No sensation would be troubling Ah Q's fingers.) Once Ah Q did pinch the bottom of a woman in a crowd of people watching a street opera. However, there had been a layer of trousers between the woman's flesh and Ah Q's fingers, so nothing had happened. With the novice, the situation was entirely different.

'Woman!' Ah Q thought. He had guarded himself against women. They tried to entice him, though they did not smile. Indeed, he paid special attention to those women who spoke to him, though he had never encountered a hint at anything clandestine. 'Oh dear!' Ah Q reflected, 'how detestful are women, ever pretending to be respectable!'

One day Ah Q was pounding rice for his master, Chou. After dinner, he sat in the kitchen, smoking a pipe. . . . The Chou household had an early evening meal and went to bed. No light was allowed, unless young master Chou was preparing for his degree examination or, more likely, Ah Q had been given the job of pounding rice. . . .

Wu Ma, the only maidservant in the Chou household, came and sat in the kitchen, when the washing up was done.

'Our mistress,' she told Ah Q, 'has not eaten for two days, not since our master bought a young lady. . . .'

'Lady . . . woman . . . Wu Ma,' Ah Q thought.

'Our mistress,' the maidservant continued, 'is having a baby in August. . . .'

'Woman,' Ah Q thought, putting down his pipe. He stood up.

'Our mistress . . .' rattled on Wu Ma.

'Sleep with me,' Ah Q suddenly said, kneeling at Wu Ma's feet. Complete silence followed, then, with a scream, the maidservant fled, trembling, from the kitchen. Trembling himself, Ah Q got up and leant on the bench. He felt uncertain as he tucked his pipe in his belt. 'Better get back to work,' he thought, when 'pong'—a big bamboo descended on his head.

'You rebel, you!' shouted young master Chou, a first class *shih*, as he struck Ah Q on the skull again. Ah Q used his hands to shield himself but the bamboo stung his finger joints so badly that he was forced to quit the kitchen in haste.

'Turtle's egg!' shouted young master Chou, using an oath favoured by high officials.

Ah Q rushed to the shed for pounding rice. Despite the pains in his finger joints, he could not help recalling the oath. 'Turtle's egg!' was not a phrase belonging to the speech of rustic folk. No *nung* used it. Only the rich and noble classes, Ah Q was sure, understood what was meant. So impressed and frightened was he that the idea of women left his mind without trace. (In fact, a beating and a scolding usually seemed to solve his problems.)

He began pounding. Hard and hot work it was. Soon he had shed his shirt. Pounding away, Ah Q heard a commotion in the Chou house. Attracted by the noise—he loved to watch a scene—Ah Q made his way towards his master's rooms. In the dusk, he was able to discern many people, including the entire Chou household and their next door neighbour. . . .

Mistress Chou was dragging Wu Ma out of her room. She told the maidservant: 'Come out of your room and stop brooding over what has happened. Who doesn't know you are an honest girl? . : . Suicide is silly!'

While Wu Ma, crying and weeping, was being dealt with by the Chou family, Ah Q approached, full of curiosity. 'I wonder what it all means,' he thought, 'perhaps I had better find out.' Unexpectedly he saw young master Chou rush in his direction, brandishing a bamboo.

In a flash it all came back to him. Another beating seemed inevitable. . . . But he succeeded in making an exit through a side door and ran off to his sleeping quarters in the barn. There he sat for a time, shivering in the chilly evening air. Although he knew that he had left his shirt in the pounding shed, the bamboo deterred him from going back to collect it. . . .

As a punishment it was agreed that Ah Q should:

1. give the Chou household expensive candles and joss-sticks as well as apologize in person;

2. pay for a priest to drive the evil spirit of suicide from the Chou house;

3. no longer enter buildings belonging to the Chou family;

4. be blamed if Wu Ma died;

5. not ask Master Chou for any wages or the return of his shirt.

Fortunately for Ah Q, Spring had arrived. He was able to sell his cotton quilt in order to raise enough cash to carry out the conditions forced on him. What little money he had left afterwards, he spent on drink. . . .

Lu Hsun was no advocate of wholesale change. China, he maintained, had to adopt from the rest of the world only those things that suited its essential nature. By 1930 he had decided that the CCP offered the best hope for national renewal.

Two great artists have continued the tradition of painting this century. They are Ch'i Pai-shih (1863–1957) and Huang Pin-hung (1864–1955). The humble origins of Ch'i have impressed the officials of the People's Republic as much as his marvellous paintings. A man of the people, he has done much to revive and reinterpret the role of the painter.

Ch'i Pai-shih (1863–1957):
Mountains, pinetrees and sailing
boats; painted at the age of 89.
Hanging scroll; ink and slight
colour on paper.

Huang Pin-hung (1864–1955): Landscape; painted at the age of 89.
Hanging scroll; ink and slight colour on paper.

Shanghai in 1973. A cyclist delivering yarn casts a glance at an enormous revolutionary street poster, which exhorts him 'To be vigilant and protect China'. The people represented in it are all holding 'Quotations from Chairman Mao', the little red book. Such public art is a feature of the contemporary scene in China.

MODERN CHINA—THE ECONOMIC MIRACLE

In the past twenty-five years China has undergone a revolution which is still continuing. This revolution contains three inseparable elements:

- a change in the social system typified by public ownership of the means of production;
- a change in technology reflected by increased productivity and output which results from the substitution of small-scale handicrafts by large-scale mechanization;
- a revolution in philosophy by which China maintains its cultural identity but which inevitably forces it to participate in world affairs as a model for other underdeveloped countries.

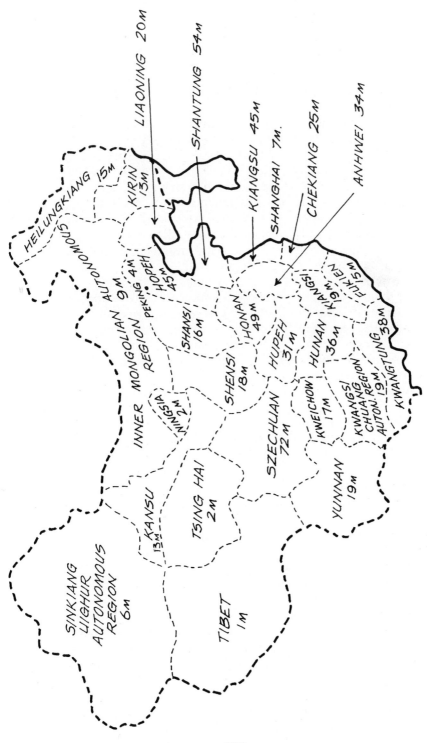

Provinces and autonomous regions of China with size of population to nearest million in 1957.

HEILUNGKIANG 15M

KIRIN 13M

LIAONING 20M

SHANTUNG 54M

KIANGSU 45M

SHANGHAI 7M.

CHEKIANG 25M

ANHWEI 34M

INNER MONGOLIAN AUTONOMOUS REGION 9M

PEKING 4M

HOPEH 45M

SHANSI 16M

HONAN 49M

SHENSI 18M

HUPEH 31M

KIANGSI 19M

FUKIEN 15M

NINGSIA 2M

HUNAN 36M

KWEICHOW 17M

KWANGSI CHUANG REGION AUTON. 19M

KWANGTUNG 38M

SINKIANG UIGHUR AUTONOMOUS REGION 6M

KANSU 13M

TSING HAI 2M

SZECHUAN 72M

YUNNAN 19M

TIBET 1M

287

Land Reform, or the Transformation of Agriculture

An English economist in 1932 considered much of the unrest reported in China was less a product of theoretical Marxism than one of irregularity of land holding and unemployment. The peasants were successively exploited by Manchus, Europeans, warlords, landlords, bandits, government troops and Japanese invaders; they were subject to the age-old irregularities of climate; they were increasingly forced to sell their land to pay taxes or buy grain in times of famine. It is not surprising that they were likened 'to a man standing permanently up to the neck in water, so that even a ripple is sufficient to drown him.' When the Communists not only proposed, but implemented land reform in their areas of influence, it was understandable that they received the support of the masses.

The *nung* are essentially conservative. The peasant's ambition would be to own land. While Communist doctrine implied state ownership of land, the leaders were generally pragmatic enough to recognize the need for gentle and informed change. The first reform known as *'land to the tiller'* involved total redistribution of land on the basis of family need. Since this broke up the estates it increased fragmentation of holdings, already an acute problem with the rapid population growth, and initially decreased productivity. This did not automatically lead to worsening conditions of life since, before this, great food surpluses had often been achieved. The main reasons for starvation had been the inability or unwillingness of those with reserves to transfer them to areas of need.

Between 1949 and 1952 *mutual aid teams* of 3–6 families were encouraged to form permanent production groups. Individual ownership of land was maintained but any reclaimed land became common property and was jointly cultivated. Thus socialism was gradually introduced. The next stage was the establishment of *independent producers co-operatives* with voluntary membership and the right of withdrawal. Land was amalgamated and decisions were formulated by a democratically elected management committee. In practice leadership increasingly fell into the hands of CCP members. By 1956 ninety per cent of the rural population was involved. Labour was organized to build roads, dams and ditches in the winter and increasingly the government was able to control and direct agricultural output.

Advanced co-operatives or *collective farms* comprised of up to 200 family units were introduced in 1956. Land under individual ownership, draught animals and implements were forfeited and

Major Cities.

289

some compensation paid. The increasing bureaucracy of these large units and the decrease in personal motivation led to discontent and a decline in productivity. They gave way in 1958 to the *commune*, which was an even larger unit but which in fact took over the administrative functions of the *hsiang* while remaining in the traditional *hsien* framework. A State Planning Organization passed targets to the Commune Management Committee, who in turn fed the information to brigade leaders. Each brigade was made up of several production teams and they alone made the decisions as to how to achieve the targets.

The reform of agricultural organization was consistently adopted more rapidly in the North than the South, where the numerous minority groups resented the seemingly perpetual intervention of Chinese governments into their affairs.

To increase the output of food during the gradual process of socialization, the Communist government opened its own large, modern and efficient farms. Because of the shortage of suitable land for expansion within the eighteen provinces, they have been

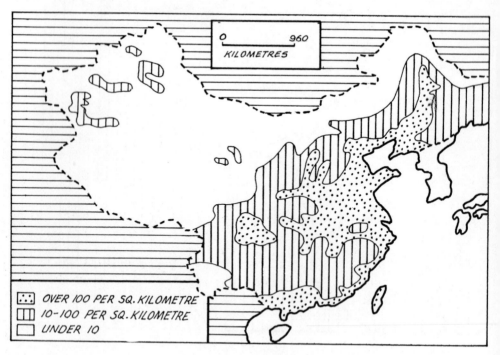

OVER 100 PER SQ. KILOMETRE
10-100 PER SQ. KILOMETRE
UNDER 10

Population.

increasingly concerned with reclamation of wastelands, particularly in frontier and coastal areas, and these schemes have served to stimulate migration to such areas. Some of the state farms in the South are used to train and resettle Chinese returning from overseas.

To back up agricultural improvements the State initiated three five-year plans from 1953–7, 1958–62 and 1966–70. Under these Mao Tse-tung hoped to completely transform production through mechanization and settlement of virgin lands in order to meet the escalating demands for foodstuffs and industrial raw materials. Industrial development was seen to be completely dependent on an efficient agricultural base. The success of agricultural policy was revealed from 1959–62 when China survived one of the worst droughts in history without the mass starvation typical of former times. This was partly due to increased production but also to better distribution of reserves and strict rationing.

'The Great Leap Forward,' or the Socialization of Industry

The 'Hundred Days Reform' of 1898 failed in its objectives of modernization of industry because of Tz'u Hsi's opposition and the conservative nature of most Chinese administrators. Even so, by 1913 there were nearly 700 firms involved in mining, smelting, textiles, food processing and public utilities.

	Foreign owned	*Chinese owned*
Number of firms	136	549
% of total	45%	55%
Capital (total £30 m)	(Main investors Britain 50% Japan 25%)	

From this point on industry increased to satisfy the demands of Japan and the West. The Chinese resented the role of foreign imperialists and many activities were taken over as the Kuomintang and CCP took control of the Yangtze valley, by 1930. This coincided with the annexation of Manchuria by Japan which the Chinese Nationalists were helpless to prevent. The Japanese played an important role in developing the industrial regions of the north-east for their own benefit, and maintained control over them until 1945. When the Chinese regained control, the Russians had already stripped Manchuria of much industrial equipment. The civil war between the CCP and Kuomintang created industrial stagnation and commercial chaos; the result was rapid inflation. The Communists, on taking power,

- took over entire wholesale trade;
- took control of banks;
- established a price index related to the basic commodities of rice, flour, oil, coal and cotton and successfully held down prices;
- began a take-over of industry which was completed by 1956.

Initially industrial development was made a priority receiving nearly sixty per cent of total capital investment, most of which went on new plant and modernization of heavy industry. Consumer industries were a low priority. Aid was given by the USSR in the building of 156 key productive units including integrated steel works at Anshan and Wuhan, electric power stations, tractor and lorry factories, cotton mills and coal mines. The increase in bureaucracy resulting from the first five-year plan (1952–7) led to Mao Tse-tung's 'Hundred Flowers' policy under which constructive criticism could be freely voiced. Some economists criticized the economic policy for being inefficient and over-centralized. The government had directed much new industry away from the coast and into the interior, but this in itself was restricting the efficiency and raising their costs. They also suggested more material incentives to production. For their pains they were demoted and criticism ended.

Mao, however, was too astute not to heed the rumblings from below and under the second five-year plan, starting in 1958, he allocated a greater proportion of capital to agriculture and set no detailed production targets. He rejected the Russian pattern of planned urban industrialization and put the onus on the people to expand production with the 'Great Leap Forward.' The commune movement which accompanied this 'spontaneous' and 'unplanned' surge facilitated the development of hundreds of small units of production such as 'back-yard iron-smelters.' While production increased rapidly, the main result was chaos.

In 1960 the Russians withdrew their experts and cancelled their policy of co-operation. A new policy of 'readjustment, consolidation, filling out and raising standards' was introduced with increased emphasis on agriculture and light industry, both of which suffered during the 'Great Leap.' The resulting successes in creating a more balanced and better integrated system still did not satisfy Mao Tse-tung who feared that stability would bring complacency. Thus one aspect of the Cultural Revolution of 1966 was to shake up the bureaucrats and intelligentsia to maintain their awareness of the grass root problems of industrial production.

Transport, Trade and Urbanization

Industrialization inevitably increased urbanization, and created landscapes similar to any other industrial society. The juxtaposition of allotments and fields with factories, warehouses and new housing projects stresses the overall shortage of land and interdependence of the two types of economy. At the 1953 Census, 163 settlements had over 100 000 people, with nine over a million strong. Today the number of 'million' cities is nearer twenty. The proportion of people living in urban settlements (i.e., over 2 000 inhabitants) has risen slowly from thirteen per cent in 1953 to a figure probably not exceeding twenty per cent.

To facilitate industrialization, transport and communications have been improved. Before 1949 the densest railway coverage was found in Manchuria where it had been financed by Russia, then Japan. The Civil War and Sino-Japanese war reduced the

One of the most important factors contributing to the vast material development is the rapidity with which the Chinese have acquired the skills and techniques of modern industry. This shows the State Northwest Printing and Dyeing Mill.

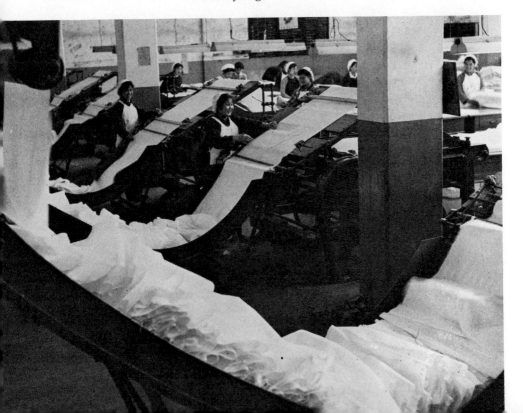

total distance covered by about 1 920 kilometres to 3 200 kilometres. Most of this has now been restored and most of current capital investment seems to go on improvement and maintenance of these predominantly industrial networks. New developments on both economic and military grounds have extended the network 1 120 kilometres to the oil fields of Sinkiang; they have linked the upper Yellow River valley with Szechuan, joining Paoki, Chengtu, and Chungking, going both through and over the Chin-Ling Shan: and Liuchow in Kwangsi was linked to Hanoi in 1951. The river is still a major means of transporting both goods and people, witness the lack of railways in the lower Yangtze valley. The road network was long limited by topography and until 1950 most was unfit for motor vehicles. Now, great arterial highways are being built by the government, leaving local road maintenance and extension in the hands of the communes.

China's ports have continued to develop. Greater Shanghai now has twelve million inhabitants. The Communist victory in 1949 heralded the end of semi-colonial trade bases (with the exception of Macao, Hong Kong and Taiwan). Initially the necessity for obtaining urgent credit facilities and supplies of capital equipment from sympathizers led to the reopening of the 'Jade Gate' as the main trade route. The embargo imposed by the UN during the Korean War, the continued cessation of trade

Between 1955 and 1960 the annual road construction leaped from 20 160 kilometres to 64 000. This picture shows the Changan Boulevard in Peking.

with the USA after this, and growing anti-imperialism in China, further restricted contact with the non-communist countries. In 1951 seventy-eight per cent of exports went to Russia and seventy per cent of imports came from there. With the withdrawal of Russian technicians and increasing hostility between the two countries in 1960, this figure has declined to be replaced by trade with Cuba and countries outside the Communist bloc. Since 1956 China has maintained a favourable balance of trade allowing it to repay its Russian loans in full by the mid 60s. The continual import of grain does not necessarily reflect constant shortage as China finds it profitable to sell rice abroad and buy cheaper wheat. Trade forms a very small percentage of GNP (about four per cent) and China's increasing self-sufficiency even in the most advanced goods, coupled with her increasing willingness to give no-interest aid to other developing countries such as Tanzania, may become an increasing embarrassment to those trying to foster Western-type 'democratic' solutions to their problems.

SOCIETY TODAY

The People are the sea: the government is the fish
—*Mao Tse-tung*

Social Change since 1949

The social revolution in China has largely been one revolving round the relationship between the masses and the leadership. Since Mao Tse-tung knew his Chinese history, he realized the importance of *nung* support in the maintenance of power. For him the 'Revolution' was neither theoretical nor geared to an urban proletariat, but practical and based on the countryside. To convert and maintain the confidence of a traditionally conservative peasantry he recognized the need for involvement and decision-making by them. This would give them proof of their role in changing the destiny of China and give them confidence to carry it through without falling prey to the 'revisionists' or 'progressives,' whether *shang* or *shih*.

Mao's doctrines on contradiction state that life is a struggle, but that this is a good thing. For any given situation with conflicting viewpoints there is always a right way which can be achieved, given discussion and experiment. So Mao accommo-

The Yangtze River bridge (1810 yards long) carries a lower double railway track and an upper six-stream vehicle and pedestrian highway. It is an engineering feat of which the Chinese are justly proud.

dates genuine mistakes as well as providing workers and peasants with the confidence required to take initiatives and make suggestions. In this manner the continuing revolution is carried through by the workers who are credited with seventy per cent of the contribution by Mao. Needless to say this has created problems with the communist intelligentsia and theoreticians who have frequently criticized the failure to follow the orthodox pattern of communist development.

THE FOOLISH OLD MAN WHO REMOVED THE MOUNTAINS

The Foolish Old Man's house faced south and beyond his doorway stood the two great peaks, Taihang and Wangwu, obstructing the way. He called his sons, and hoe in hand they began to dig up these mountains with great determination. Another greybeard, known as the Wise Old Man, saw them and said derisively, 'How silly of you to do this! It is quite impossible for you four to dig up these two

296

huge mountains.' The Foolish Old Man replied, 'When I die, my sons will carry on; when they die, there will be my grandsons, and then their sons and grandsons, and so on to infinity. High as they are, the mountains cannot grow any higher and every bit we dig they will be that much lower. Why can't we clear them away!' Having refuted the Wise Old Man's wrong view, he went on digging every day, unshaken in his conviction. God was moved by this, and he sent down two angels, who carried the mountains away on their backs.

The Role of the Commune

The total frenzy of the early commune days with their complete insistence on public ownership of virtually all private possessions has given way to a better balanced and more viable set-up. Initially, the commune was a combat unit with a high degree of infused motivation to get China out of its immediate problems. Collective living under the 'five-together' system (working, eating, living, studying, and drilling) has been replaced by a return to the normal family pattern. The commune's success lies in the width of its responsibilities—agriculture, rural industry, water conservancy, afforestation, communications, education, civil defence, health and public hygiene, and cultural and recreational activities. Some members of the commune management committee are paid officials but most are rewarded by a system of work points according to the jobs they do in the production teams.

The income of a production team of a commune is generally divided so that about half distributed goes to members and one-quarter to production expenses. But these figures vary according to region and year. All-out attempts are being made to increase the earnings of backward communes.

Here is the distribution of expenditure in 2nd Team of Paching Brigade 1964 Yangtan People's Commune—South Shansi (covering 11 000 people and 61 production teams):

	% of expenditure
Production expenses	38·6—heavy rain necessitated replanting
Agricultural Tax	6·5
Reserve Fund	5·0—used for capital expenditure
Welfare Fund	1·0
Reserve Grain	4·4
Members	44·5

The large state farms and collectives of the northern plains lend themselves to the use of machinery. This shows harvesting on the Eastern plains.

The Welfare fund caters for accidents, sickness and old age, as well as for those with no relatives. Senior citizens are entitled to the Five Guarantees—enough to eat, adequate housing, clothing, day-to-day needs, and a decent burial. The standard of living is undoubtedly rising; taxation is stable; there is no extortionate rent to meet; employment is constant. Furthermore, the relaxed rules allow cultivation of one's own allotment. Thus more can buy consumer goods such as bicycles, sewing machines and radios.

Population Growth

The first census of individuals as opposed to number of households was carried out in 1953. It revealed a population of nearly 600 million, over 100 million higher than a Post Office census of 1926. The distribution of the population was uneven. On the Chengtu Plain of Szechuan densities of up to 1200 people per square kilometre were found. Kiangsu, overall, had a density of 154 per square kilometre, while the Tibetan Plateau and the Taklamakan desert averaged less than 1 per square kilometre. Over 85 per cent of the population were under 50, giving a great percentage of productive labour. The reasons for the rapid growth in population since 1949 are obviously the comparative

A production team planting rice in the small terraced paddy-fields. Here mechanization is much more difficult.

Anshan Integrated Steel Works. Over 4 million tonnes of steel a year are produced by the Anshan Steel Works, which is the greatest integrated centre in the country. Other big centres are now at Paotow and Hankow.

peace and secure food supply, coupled with a vast improvement in public hygiene and personal cleanliness. Communism has brought a 'puritanism' which imposed much responsibility for street cleanliness and sewage disposal on the public; it also removed prostitutes and beggars from the streets overnight. Striking advances in preventative medicine have halved the infant mortality rate in the cities; Shanghai 1952 had an IMR of 8·12 per cent; by 1956 this was 3·11 per cent.

The Chinese thought themselves well able to feed any number of mouths, and actually encouraged an increase in the number of hands available to work for the revolution. However, since population growth began to exceed food output, this had to be revised so that in 1957 a birth control campaign was introduced. Mao's critics of the 'Hundred Flowers' period stressed the need for greater mechanization and automation, if living standards were to be raised, and pointed to a large population as a major impediment to development. The birth-control programme was lost in the confusion of the 'Great Leap Forward' until the three hungry years of 1959–61 re-emphasized the need. Today, the birth-rate has been reduced by the recommendation of late marriages and planned childbirth by the state. Not surprisingly this policy has achieved more success in the cities than in the country.

Since Communism aimed to abolish feudal exploitation, it was not unexpected that the Confucian family system came under heavy criticism in the early days. A law of 1950 banned bigamy, concubinage, child betrothal and arranged marriages. It gave opportunity for divorce proceedings by either party and encouraged, sometimes by coercion, self-criticism and public confession, which led to the break-up of many families. Now that women are fully emancipated and can live completely independent lives—thanks to crèches and nurseries—the family unit is more secure from party interference.

Chinese by Blood and Chinese by Birth
Chinese communities in the Nanyang. With the exception of Malaya and Singapore, the Chinese in South-East Asia were worse off after the Second World War than before. Because:

    ● during the Japanese occupation much of their property was expropriated by collaborators;
    ● the growth of anti-imperialist nationalism was directed at all who had become prosperous under the system;

● the Communist success in 1949 persuaded some of the indigenous peoples that the Chinese communities must be fifth-columnists working for a world communist movement;

● even Socialist governments have feared the sheer size and power of China.

Wherever the Chinese took the lead, the rest of the people have been reluctant to follow. Hence, they failed to win any ground in the 'Emergency,' in post-war Malaya. Before the war the Kuomintang had a conscious policy of encouraging strong nationalism in the Nanyang. It had traditionally supplied revolutionary leaders and funds for resistance to the Japanese and the CCP. The nationalism and wealth of the overseas community led to increasing migration control in the 1930s, so that they were not reinforced by new members and increasingly they were Chinese in blood, not by birth.

Enforced educational integration and sometimes restriction on their language has not in any way submerged the communities, which have remained the target for suspicion and sometimes violence. The Chinese government has consistently shown a lack of interest in using the communities overseas as staging posts for communist expansion. In the 1950s they were recommended to adopt the language and customs of the countries they were in, in a policy of 'survival.' Chinese communist parties in the Nanyang were seen as counter-productive. The Communist Party of Indonesia positively reacted against Chinese membership. The official Chinese attitude was attacked as being 'revisionist' by the Red Guards in 1966. As yet little change of policy has occurred. The reason for fifteen years of official 'revisionism' is basically the insecurity of the new Chinese State, which needed breathing space from foreign entanglements to develop economically. The major exception to the general political indolence of the Nanyang Chinese was Singapore, completely independent from Malaysia after 1965. Its population is eighty-five per cent Chinese and again, though its government leans to the left, the Communist Party is severely suppressed. Malaysia itself may prove to be an enduring democratic country in which people of Chinese origin can play their full part; the constituent states of Sarawak and Sabah, in Borneo, could well act as a balance to any conflict between Malays and Chinese in West Malaysia. These two states of East Malaysia possess more diverse populations and have long traditions of multi-cultural harmony.

Minority Communities within China. In 1953 the 'national minorities' within China numbered over thirty-five million, or

A contemporary painting of Bako, a village on the coast of Sarawak, by an overseas Chinese artist, Chin Khee. The work is in the Lin Nam style, which seeks to combine Western perspective with traditional Chinese brushstrokes. The painter is also a teacher in a Chinese language school, an institution concerned with the preservation of Chinese culture. It is customary among Chinese families living outside China to ensure that at least one boy in every generation receives a full Chinese education.

six per cent of the total population. These comprise over fifty different groups, ten of which have over one million each. In areas where they are concentrated they have been allowed some measure of autonomy and self government—in Kwangsi Chuang Autonomous Region, in Sinkiang Uighur Autonomous Region, in Ningsia Hui Autonomous Region and in Inner Mongolian Autonomous Region. The majority of smaller tribes are found in the highlands of the south-west provinces of Szechuan, Kweichow and Yunnan. The policy towards such groups who have frequently come into conflict with the Chinese in the past, is now one of preserving their unique cultures and languages, while gradually introducing the facilities for education and economic improvement which will bring these people more fully into the communist system. These tribal peoples will become Chinese by birth, if not by blood.

A Hokkien temple in Kuching. The photograph presents some interesting contrasts. The British roadsign is a survival from colonial days, whilst the Chinese villa on the hill behind has become a boarding house for local girls attending the Anglican Mission School. Meanwhile the daily life of the street continues around the temple entrance, as younger children buy tit-bits to eat in the late afternoon. Opposite the front entrance, on the other side of the road, stands a covered stage, which is used for dramatic perform-ances, particularly opera, during religious festivals.

Education, Science and Technology

China exploded its first nuclear bomb in 1964; it leads the world in the development of advanced steam dynamos; it has a satellite—'the man-made earth guiding star'—circling the earth; it has developed a high speed teleprinter capable of coding, decoding and printing out 1 500 Chinese characters per minute. It might be easy to dismiss these as prestigious copies of Western technology designed to impress the world. In actual fact, they merely pick up the threads of medieval and earlier Chinese technology, which we have shown to be the forerunners of many nineteenth-century Western developments. If these advances were produced while China starved and stagnated, we might be justified in our early dismissal, but on looking closely we can see that they are just one part of a whole range of developments stretching back to the grass roots. Southern communes have pioneered the extraction of creosote from coconut refuse. To transport it they have constructed their own narrow gauge railways *and* diesel locomotives.

The people who bring about such changes are not necessarily well educated specialists. The *nung* may work from childhood and receive only part-time education, but increasingly they are

The Fengman Hydroelectric Power Station in North-East China. It has an estimated generating capacity of 56 700 kilowatts.

being taught techniques of problem-solving stemming from Mao's view that all is possible, and that every problem has a solution. Another aspect of this is solving one's own personal contradictions, such as the desire for wealth and power which can conflict with the desire to see a classless society where each receives according to his need rather than according to his job. Whether this doctrine will be fostered long enough for it to succeed is uncertain. Because so many of the people in power were not educated under its principles, it may not survive Chairman Mao, though the future of China will be socialist. His recruitment of the Red Guards was to mobilize the young in order that they might be aware of the conservatism which comes with relative prosperity and middle age.

To help China develop, three distinct methods are now equally applied. *Yang Fa,* 'the foreign way of doing things,' recognizes that most modern science and much technology has been developed in the West and that there are no satisfactory alternatives to explain things such as nuclear fission or electricity. *Thu Fa,* 'earth methods,' are those long employed by local people who have subjected them to the test of time. Some of these have declined in the past and are now being revitalized. Even Western societies are acknowledging that there is more to folklore and tradition than was ever previously imagined. *Hsin Fa,* 'entirely new methods,' are those being pioneered by the Chinese 'three

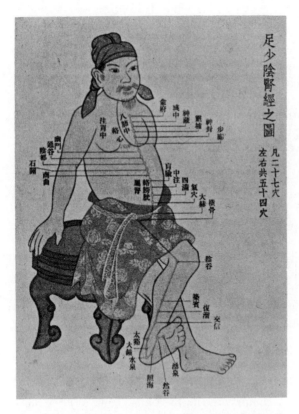

足少陰腎經之圖

凡二十七穴
左右共五十四穴

A Ming
acupuncture chart.

in one' groups of 'revolutionary workers, progressive administrators, and sympathetic scientific and technical personnel.' These three can be illustrated well in the development of modern medicine in China.

Chinese medicine evolved from alchemy, with an emphasis placed on healing drugs of plant and mineral origin. Ancestor worship restricted surgery and autopsies so that scientific knowledge of the body remained relatively primitive. The development of acupuncture and moxibustion 2000 years ago are recorded earlier. In the nineteenth century Chinese medicine began to be neglected in higher circles and a great effort was made to modernize the training of doctors. This trend continued throughout the twentieth century until in the 1940s when the number of Western-trained doctors was in the ratio of around 1 to 25000 of population. By 1957 the growth of medical schools reduced this ratio to 1 to 6000, but at the same time traditional medicine regained its respectability and half a million of its practitioners swelled the ranks of the medical profession. Now not only are the two branches well established with mutual co-operation between

305

them, but the Chinese are making the traditional methods more scientific and virtually creating '*Hsin Fa*,' or new methods. Complicated surgical parts such as artificial kidneys, cardiac pumps, artificial hands are produced and the Chinese have a reputation in the restoration of severed limbs and fingers and bone grafts. In acupuncture, which relies on subjective diagnosis, greater attempts are being made to understand and capitalize on a treatment that obviously works in specific cases in conjunction with other treatments. Electric currents can be passed through needles, and hollow needles can contain minute anaesthetic or biological solutions. Radio isotopes have been added to needles and the paths of the radioactive elements in the body have been traced with a geiger counter. In 1956–7 a group of Soviet doctors completed a course of traditional medicine at the Institute of Experimental Acupuncture and returned to practice in the USSR. Elsewhere in the West the use of traditional Chinese methods is generally limited, though one London hospital is investigating acupuncture techniques.

THE FUTURE

> The unification of our country, the unity of our people and the unity of our various nationalities—these are the basic guarantees of the sure triumph of our cause.
>
> *Chairman Mao in 1957*

Few Chinese would disagree about the need for unity. National cohesion, as we have seen, is a very old idea in China. When a petty king begged for independence in A.D. 960, the first Sung Emperor asked: 'What wrong have your people done to be excluded from the Empire?' Nor would many Chinese doubt that the Mandate of Heaven did pass to the CCP in 1949. But 'the sure triumph of our cause' might give reason for pause. For the two chief pillars of Chinese society, the *shih* and the *nung*, the experience of communism has been somewhat different. While the peasant has enjoyed a measure of freedom and peace unknown in human memory, the scholar has suffered from the loss of both these prized possessions. In the aftermath of the 'Hundred Flowers' episode constructive criticism was difficult to sustain. The Cultural Revolution, however, may represent an attempt to reopen discussion on important aspects of the revolution. How far the *shih* will be allowed to interpret and to criticize, remains

306

a mystery. As a class the educated are indispensable for the smooth running of government. The old saying: 'Confucianism is the doctrine of the *shih* when in office, and Taoism is the attitude of the *shih* out of office,' could well apply to Maoism. Patient opposition has been a constant Taoist virtue, for:

> As the soft yield of water cleaves obstinate stone,
> So to yield with life solves the insoluble:
> To yield, I have learned, is to come back again.

A humorous tale which has recently done the rounds in Kwantung makes the point exactly. Uncle Chang, tiring of nightly sessions of political study, asked to address his study group before the meeting one evening. Since he insisted that he had something of the greatest importance to say, the group leader was forced to agree. 'What I should like you to know,' Uncle Chang announced, 'is that I agree one hundred per cent with whatever you are going to explain to us about Chairman Mao, even before you say it.' With a shrug of despair, the group leader told Uncle Chang to go home.

A painting of Mao addressing a revolutionary meeting. Meetings were also called by the workers themselves, at which they criticized Liu Shao-ch'i's revisionist line.

307

But the Thought of Chairman Mao does relate powerfully to the conditions in China at present, as contemporary eye-witness reports testify; revolutionary excitement is not waning, though such dogma could prove stifling in time. While the success of the mass literacy campaigns among the *nung* will do much to help de-centralize the administration, the nerve centre of the country needs must stay alive in order to ensure national survival. What happened to Confucianism in the Manchu Court is a nightmare that probably haunts Mao. Could not Maoism become just as inflexible after his own death?

The young people of China are the future of China. Population growth ensures that they will remain the majority for many years to come. Between 1970 and 2000 the population is expected to rise from nearly 800 million to over 1 000 million. To them Chairman Mao has given the task of continuing the revolution. Their experiments may, or may not, advance Chinese civilization, but they will have an effect on the course of events in China and the world. For China today has become as fascinating a country as Cathay was to Marco Polo. It is a place to look on and be amazed. An ancient culture and a quarter of mankind are striving to meet the challenges and complexities of life in the twentieth century. Perhaps China will regain its early pre-eminence and have things to teach the world again, particularly the developing countries.

Specific predictions about the future are always difficult to make. However, a study of China does illustrate how history repeats itself, if nothing else. The CCP will survive as long as it retains the Mandate of Heaven. Although Chairman Mao has emerged as a new Emperor figure following the Cultural Revolution, everything has not been perfect since 1949. The PLA remains an unknown quantity, while the rising standard of living enjoyed by the mass of the Chinese people may bring the country eventually into the World Economy itself. China, which maintains an annual trade surplus, would be a huge market. Yet the Chinese could decide to isolate themselves, as they have chosen to do on previous occasions. What is certain is the survival of Chinese civilization as a powerful cultural and political force in the world. Because China is an ecosystem it has come through the enormous stresses and strains of the past hundred and fifty years intact. Modern China is a reality, which even the United States, reversing its entire post-war foreign policy, had to recognize in 1972.

OUTLINE CHRONOLOGY OF CHINESE HISTORY, WITH MAIN DYNASTIES

PREHISTORIC PERIOD	Old Stone Age New Stone Age (Hsia Kingdom?)	500 000–7 000 B.C. 7000–1500 B.C. (2000–1500 B.C.?)
HISTORICAL PERIOD BEGINS	Shang Kingdom Chou Dynasty Warring States period	1500–1027 B.C. 1027–256 B.C. 481–221 B.C.
IMPERIAL UNIFICATION	Ch'in Dynasty Han Dynasty Usurpation of Wang Mang	221–207 B.C. 202 B.C.–A.D.220 A.D.9–23
DARK AGES	Three Kingdoms T'sin Dynasty Northern and Southern Dynasties	A.D. 221–265 A.D. 265–316 A.D. 316–589
REUNIFICATION OF CHINA	Sui Dynasty T'ang Dynasty	A.D. 589–618 A.D. 618–907
DIVISION AGAIN	Five Dynasties period	A.D. 907–960
SECOND REUNIFICATION	Northern Sung Dynasty Southern Sung Dynasty	A.D. 960–1126 A.D. 1127–1279
MONGOL INVASION	Yuan Dynasty	A.D. 1279–1368
CHINESE RECOVERY	Ming Dynasty	A.D. 1368–1644
MANCHU INVASION	Ch'ing Dynasty	A.D. 1644–1912
END OF IMPERIAL ERA	Chinese Republic	A.D. 1912–1949
COMMUNISM TRIUMPHS	People's Republic	A.D. 1949 onwards

Chinese Index

310

Chinese index

Chinese index

Red Basin (Yunnan)	紅河	Tsin dynasty	晉朝
San Kuo, the Three Kingdoms	三國	Tu Fu, the T'ang poet	杜甫
Sian, the city of	西安	Tun-huang, the great Buddhist cave temple complex	敦煌
Sinkiang, the province of	新疆	Tung-meng hui, the Alliance Society	同盟會
Shang Dynasty	商朝		
Shanghai, the city of	上海	Tz'u Hsi, the Ch'ing Empress Dowager	慈禧
Shen Tsung, the Sung Emperor	神宗	Wang An-shih, the Sung reformer	王安石
Shantung, the province of	山東	Wang Mang, the usurper	王莽
Shansi, the province of	山西		
Shang, the merchants	商	Wang Shu Ho, author of the 'Pulse Classic'	王叔和
Shih, the scholars and gentry	士	Wang Wei, the T'ang poet and painter	王維
Shih Huang Ti, the Ch'in Emperor	始皇帝	Warring States	戰國
Shu, one of the Three Kingdoms	蜀	Wei, one of the Three Kingdoms	魏
Shun, legendary ruler	舜	Wei, the ancient state of	衞
Su Sung, the Sung scientist	蘇頌	Wei River	渭河
Sui Dynasty	隋朝	Wei-hai-wei, British leased territory	威海衞
Sun Yat-sen, the revolutionary	孫中山	Wen Ong, Han governor of Szechuan and educationalist	文翁
Ssu-ma Ch'ien, the Han historian	司馬遷	Wu Ti, the Han Emperor	武帝
Sung, the ancient state of	宋	Wu, one of the Three Kingdoms	吳
Szechuan, the province of	四川		
T'ai P'ing rebels	太平	Wu San-kuei, the Ming general	吳三桂
T'ai Tsung, the T'ang Emperor	太宗	Wuhan, the industrial centre	武漢
Taiwan	臺灣	Yang Chien, founder of the Sui Dynasty	楊堅
Tali, the Kingdom of	大理		
Tao Teh Ching	道德經	Yang Kuei Fei, the favourite of Ming Huang	楊貴妃
Tarim	塔里木盆地	Yang Shao (culture)	仰韶
T'ang dynasty	唐朝	Yang Ti, the Sui Emperor	煬帝
Tibet	西藏	Yangtse River	揚子江
Tientsin, the city of	天津	Yao, the legendary king	堯

Chinese index

Yellow River	黃河	Yü, the Great Engineer	禹
Yelu Ch'u-ts'ai, the Kitan statesman	耶律楚材	Yuan Dynasty	元朝
Yenan, the region of	延安	Yung Lo, the Ming Emperor	永樂
Yin-Yang	陰陽	Yunnan, the province of	雲南

Further Reading

Historical and General

JEROME CH'EN, *Mao and the Chinese Revolution*, Oxford University Press, 1965.

C. P. FITZGERALD, *The Birth of Communist China*, Penguin, 1964: 3rd ed. Praeger, 1966.

C. P. FITZGERALD, *China: A Short Cultural History*, Cresset, Praeger, 1961 edition.

C. P. FITZGERALD, *The Empress Wu,* Cresset, 1956.

C. P. FITZGERALD, *The Southern Expansion of the Chinese People,* Barrie and Jenkins, Praeger, 1972.

J. K. GALBRAITH, *A China Passage*, Houghton Mifflin, André Deutsch, 1973.

J. GERNET, *Daily Life in China on the Eve of the Mongol Invasion 1250–1276* (translated by H. M. Wright), George Allen and Unwin, 1962, Stanford University Press, 1970.

E. R. HUGHES, *The Invasion of China by the Western World*, 2nd ed., A. and C. Black, Barnes and Noble, 1968.

KEESING'S Publications, Ltd., *The Cultural Revolution in China: Its Origins and Course Up to August 1967*, Keesing, 1967, Charles Scribner's Sons, 1968.

M. LOEWE, *Everyday Life in Early Imperial China*, G. P. Putnam's Sons, Batsford, 1968.

JOSEPH NEEDHAM, *Within the Four Seas,* George Allen and Unwin, 1969.

JOAN ROBINSON, *The Cultural Revolution in China,* Penguin, 1969.

EDGAR SNOW, *Red Star over China*, rev. ed., Grove Press, 1968, Gollancz, 1969.

RICHARD WILHELM, *A Short History of Chinese Civilization* (translated by J. Joshua), Harrap, Kennikat Press, 1929.

Literature

CYRIL BIRCH, *Anthology of Chinese Literature,* Grove Press, 1965, Penguin, 1967.

WITTER BYNNER, *The Jade Mountain,* Random House, 1957.

CLARA CANDLIN, *The Herald Wind,* John Murray, 1955.

GARY SNYDER, *A Range of Poems* (includes his translations of Han Shan), Fulcrum, 1966.

ARTHUR WALEY, *The Life and Times of Po Chü-I,* George Allen and Unwin, 1949, Hillary House, 1951.

ARTHUR WALEY, *Monkey,* George Allen and Unwin, 1959.

ARTHUR WALEY, *One-Hundred-and-Seventy Chinese Poems,* Jonathan Cape, 1969.

ARTHUR WALEY, *The Poetry and Career of Li Po,* George Allen and Unwin, 1950.

Philosophy and Religion

C. F. BAYNES, *I Ching* or *Book of Changes* (translated by Richard Wilhelm), 3rd ed., Princeton University Press, 1967, Routledge and Kegan Paul, 1968.

WITTER BYNNER, *The Way of Life According to Laotzu*, G. P. Putnam's Sons, 1962.

H. A. GILES, *Chuang Tzu: Taost Philosopher and Chinese Mystic*, George Allen and Unwin, 1926, Hillary House, 1961.

L. GILES, *Taoist Teachings*, John Murray, 1947.

D. H. SMITH, *Confucius*, Temple Smith, 1973.

ARTHUR WALEY, *The Analects of Confucius*, George Allen and Unwin, 1938, Hillary House, 1964.

A. W. WATTS, *The Way of Zen*, Pantheon Books, 1957, Penguin, 1962.

A. F. WRIGHT and D. TWITCHETT, *Confucian Personalities*, Stanford University Press, 1962.

Science

JOSEPH NEEDHAM, *Clerks and Craftsmen in China and the West: Lectures and Addresses on the History of Science and Technology*, Cambridge University Press, 1970.

JOSEPH NEEDHAM, *The Grand Titration*, George Allen and Unwin, 1969.

JOSEPH NEEDHAM, *Science and Civilization in China*, Cambridge University Press, from 1954. The first volume is essential background reading, but all of this remarkable series should be looked at.

Art and Architecture

CHIANG YEE, *The Chinese Eye: An Interpretation of Chinese Painting*, Faber, 1935, Indiana University Press, 1964.

LIN YUTANG, *The Chinese Theory of Art*, Heinemann, 1967.

L. SICKMAN and A. SOPER, *The Art and Architecture of China*, Penguin, 1956.

ANIL DE SILVA, *Chinese Landscape Painting in the Caves of Tun-Huang*, Methuen, 1967.

MICHAEL SULLIVAN, *A Short History of Chinese Art*, rev. ed., University of California Press, 1970.

Geography and Economics

M. ELVIN, *The Pattern of the Chinese Past*, Eyre Methuen, Stanford University Press, 1973.

A. HERRMANN, *An Historical Atlas of China*, Aldine, Edinburgh, 1966.

THEODORE SHABAD, *China's Changing Map: National and Regional Developments, 1949–71*, rev. ed., Methuen, Praeger, 1972.

R. H. TAWNEY, *Land and Labour in China*, George Allen and Unwin, 1932, Octagon Books, 1964.

T. R. TREGEAR, *An Economic Geography of China*, Butterworth, American Elsevier, 1970.

T. R. TREGEAR, *A Geography of China*, Aldine, 1965, Butterworth, 1967.

YI FU TUAN, *The World's Landscapes: China*, Longmans, 1970.

Index

316

Index

Index

318

Index

Index